Microsoft® SharePoint® Foundation 2010 Inside Out

Errin O'Connor
Penelope Coventry
Troy Lanphier
Johnathan Lightfoot
Thomas Resing
Michael Doyle

Published with the authorization of Microsoft Corporation by:
O'Reilly Media, Inc.
1005 Gravenstein Highway North
Sebastopol, California 95472

ISBN: 978-0-7356-2724-6

1 2 3 4 5 6 7 8 9   QG   6 5 4 3 2 1

Printed and bound in the United States of America.

Microsoft Press books are available through booksellers and distributors worldwide. If you need support related to this book, email Microsoft Press Book Support at *mspinput@microsoft.com*. Please tell us what you think of this book at *http://www.microsoft.com/learning/booksurvey*.

Microsoft and the trademarks listed at *http://www.microsoft.com/about/legal/en/us/IntellectualProperty/ Trademarks/EN-US.aspx* are trademarks of the Microsoft group of companies. All other marks are property of their respective owners.

The example companies, organizations, products, domain names, email addresses, logos, people, places, and events depicted herein are fictitious. No association with any real company, organization, product, domain name, email address, logo, person, place, or event is intended or should be inferred.

Acquisitions and Developmental Editors: Juliana Aldous and Kenyon Brown
Production Editor: Adam Zaremba
Editorial Production: Octal Publishing, Inc.
Technical Reviewers: Marlene Lanphier and Troy Lanphier
Proofreader: Octal Publishing, Inc.
Indexer: Ginny Munroe
Cover Design: Twist Creative • Seattle
Cover Composition: Karen Montgomery
Illustrator: Robert Romano

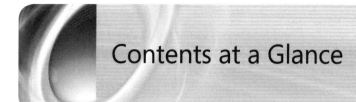

Contents at a Glance

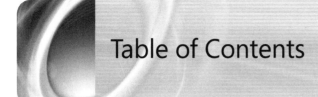

Table of Contents

What do you think of this book? We want to hear from you!

Microsoft is interested in hearing your feedback so we can continually improve our books and learning resources for you. To participate in a brief online survey, please visit:

microsoft.com/learning/booksurvey

What do you think of this book? We want to hear from you!

Microsoft is interested in hearing your feedback so we can continually improve our books and learning resources for you. To participate in a brief online survey, please visit:

microsoft.com/learning/booksurvey

Introduction

Welcome to *Microsoft SharePoint Foundation 2010 Inside Out*. Microsoft SharePoint Foundation 2010 is provided as a free download and provides a robust collection of services that can be used to build powerful web solutions. It forms the basis for a number of other SharePoint products such as SharePoint Server 2010 and Office 365, which incorporates Microsoft's SharePoint 2010 cloud-based solution, called SharePoint Online.

SharePoint Foundation helps teams stay connected and productive by utilizing an infrastructure with which they can easily access the people, documents, and information that they need. With SharePoint Foundation, teams can create websites to share information and foster collaboration with other users. You can access content stored within a SharePoint site from a web browser and through desktop applications, such as Microsoft Office.

Who Should Read This Book

This book offers a comprehensive look at the features most people will use in SharePoint Foundation 2010 and serves as an excellent reference for users who need to understand how to accomplish what they need to do. In addition, this book provides useful information to advanced users and IT professionals who need to understand the bigger picture.

Assumptions

This *Inside Out* book is designed for readers who have some experience with SharePoint Foundation 2010 and are fairly comfortable finding their way around the product. You will need access to an installation of SharePoint Foundation 2010 or have the ability to install it on a server or in a virtual environment.

This book touches only briefly on some of the basic topics that you'll find covered in more detail elsewhere (such as in *Microsoft SharePoint 2010 Plain & Simple*, *Microsoft SharePoint Foundation 2010 Step by Step*, and *Microsoft SharePoint Designer 2010 Step by Step*). We focus on techniques and topics that are likely to appeal to readers who have already mastered the many basics of this SharePoint 2010. Whether you are a business analyst, site owner, a server administrator, or a developer, there is something in this book for you.

Organization of This Book

This book gives you a comprehensive look at the various features you will use. It is structured in a logical approach to all aspects of using and managing SharePoint Foundation 2010, starting with an introduction of the features that are included. The early chapters concentrate on what you can achieve by using the browser; later chapters detail features from the perspective of the power-end user, administrator, and developer.

Chapter 1, "Introduction to Microsoft SharePoint Foundation 2010," introduce SharePoint Foundation 2010 as the entry-level component of the SharePoint family of technologies; this is the software that will get organizations started using SharePoint. The chapter examines the capabilities, features, and functions of SharePoint Foundation 2010.

Chapter 2, "Administration for Business Users," breaks down the administration of Share-Point into two categories: Business User Administration and Information Technology Professional Administration. The chapter provides you with the tools to set up your SharePoint sites that are serviced on the back-end, either by your organization's IT group or an external hosting company, or both.

Chapter 3, "End-User Features and Experience," explains how organizations can take advantage of the powerful, built-in features of Microsoft SharePoint Foundation 2010. The items discussed in this chapter are those that end-users will utilize on a daily basis. These items will increase collaboration with other SharePoint users and also increase productivity on day-to-day tasks and activities.

Chapter 4, "Creating Sites and Workspaces by Using the Browser," helps you to set up a site or workspace. There are several methods with which a user can accomplish this, but the most straightforward and intuitive method is via the browser. The browser is a tool with which all computer users are acquainted. With the familiarity of the browser and intentional ease-of-use design, the user can begin creating sites in no time at all.

Chapter 5, "Designing Lists and Libraries," shows you how to use a browser to create, modify, and display lists and libraries. Lists and libraries can be used as repositories for almost anything you want to store within the SharePoint environment. With the help of new form dialogs and the introduction of the ribbon, the experience of reading, editing, and creating content has been greatly enhanced in SharePoint Foundation 2010. Lists and libraries are a powerful solution for organizations that currently create content in many different types of applications, which is subsequently saved in many, varied locations.

Chapter 6, "Creating and Formatting Webpages," introduces you to the Team Site wiki page library, named Site Pages, where the web pages are stored and where new pages are stored when created. These pages have been enhanced and are easy to change. Web Part pages are still used in SharePoint Foundation and are the default page type on sites such as Group

Work Sites, Meeting Workspaces, and Blog Sites. Web Part pages can also be used on Team Sites, but on such sites, they are usually used for list views, list item edit forms and list item display forms.

Chapter 7, "Adding, Editing, Connecting, and Managing Web Parts on the Page," shows you how to add a Web Part to a SharePoint site. A Web Part is a key component of any Share-Point installation and is present in all versions, from SharePoint Foundation to SharePoint Server (Standard or Enterprise). Its core function is to represent customizable content on a webpage. It is only intended to receive input and display content.

Chapter 8, "Managing Site Content," provides tools and strategies for designing a great site. Using the strategies, you discover ways to present information that is up to date and relevant in your sites.

Chapter 9, "Working with External Content," shows you how to use the Data Source gallery and the Business Connectivity Services (BCS). It also presents the differences between the two methods. You examine the architecture of the BCS including the security options. You also look at managing the data connections and how to expose the data from the external systems on webpages and in lists and libraries. The chapter ends showing you how to use Microsoft Visual Studio 2010 with BCS.

Chapter 10, "Using and Creating Workflows," details how to use the out-of-the-box work-flows in the browser. It explores how to extend them by using SharePoint Designer 2010, and how Visual Studio can help your organization to integrate SharePoint Foundation 2010 into its business processes.

Chapter 11, "Integrating SharePoint with Microsoft Office 2010," examines the differences in Office 2010 versions as they relate to SharePoint Foundation 2010. The SharePoint 2010 platform has many strengths; one of the greatest is its integration with the Microsoft Office desktop client. Office applications installed on the client desktop interface directly with not only SharePoint sites and workspaces, but also the entities within these sites, such as document libraries, content, and workflows. The chapter also makes reference to other, non-Windows Office versions that provide a measure of interaction with the SharePoint 2010 platform.

Chapter 12, "Taking Lists and Libraries Offline," shows you several ways to take content offline in SharePoint 2010. The need for this is simple: some people only have to take a document or two offline, whereas others must interact with an entire list, folder, or library.

Chapter 13, "Managing Site Settings," explains how you can be both site owner and Site Collection administrator. You learn about site settings within a Microsoft SharePoint Foundation 2010 site/Site Collection.

Chapter 14, "Creating, Managing, and Designing Sites by Using SharePoint Designer 2010," details a number of techniques that are useful when working with Microsoft SharePoint Designer 2010 and SharePoint Foundation 2010 sites. You can now develop solutions in non-production environments and transfer them to the production environment. The focus of SharePoint Designer is not on adding static images and text to webpages, but instead on using it as an alternative tool for site administration. Site owners who administer and manage sites are able to go beyond what the browser provides.

Chapter 15, "Customizing the User Interface," shows you that building a SharePoint 2010 solution is more than a collection of lists, libraries, pages, and workflows. Each of these components should be combined to provide users with a holistic solution, where the components work together, not as discrete entities. SharePoint 2010 provides components that you can use to improve the users experience. In your solutions, you can extend many of these improvements, specifically by displaying links, relevant text, and commands.

Chapter 16, "Developing SharePoint Solutions by Using Visual Studio 2010," introduces you to the development of SharePoint artifacts and solution-development programming. The chapter assumes you already have some experience with .NET programming and with web-based programming, in general. Developing solutions for SharePoint helps you to become a valuable asset to your organization.

Conventions and Features in This Book

This book uses special text and design conventions to make it easier for you to find the information you need.

Text Conventions

Convention	Meaning
Abbreviated commands for navigating the ribbon and command menus	For your convenience, this book uses abbreviated commands. For example, "Click Home	Insert	Insert Cells" means that you should click the Home tab on the ribbon, click the Insert button, and then finally click the Insert Cells command.
Boldface type	**Boldface** indicates text that you type.
Initial Capital Letters	The first letters of the names of tabs, dialog boxes, dialog box elements, and commands are capitalized. Example: the Save As dialog box.
Italicized type	*Italicized* type indicates new terms.
Plus sign (+) in text	Keyboard shortcuts are indicated by a plus sign (+) separating key names. For example, Ctrl+Alt+Delete means that you press the Ctrl, Alt, and Delete keys at the same time.

Design Conventions

INSIDE OUT   This statement illustrates an example of an "Inside Out" heading

These are the book's signature tips. In these tips, you get the straight scoop on what's going on with the software—inside information about why a feature works the way it does. You'll also find handy workarounds to deal with software problems.

Sidebar

Sidebars provide helpful hints, timesaving tricks, or alternative procedures related to the task being discussed.

TROUBLESHOOTING

This statement illustrates an example of a "Troubleshooting" problem statement.

Look for these sidebars to find solutions to common problems you might encounter. Troubleshooting sidebars appear next to related information in the chapters. You can also use "Index to Troubleshooting Topics" at the back of the book to look up problems by topic.

Cross-references point you to locations in the book that offer additional information about the topic being discussed.

CAUTION

Cautions identify potential problems that you should look out for when you're completing a task or that you must address before you can complete a task.

Note

Notes offer additional information related to the task being discussed.

Acknowledgments

We'd like to include a special thanks to Kenyon Brown (O'Reilly Media Senior Editor), who nurtured us and kept us on track during the many months that it took to produce this book. Without his patience and excellent suggestions, this book would never have been produced.

It is never easy to write a book, especially one that covers such a vast subject area and in such detail. A number of us have authored and contributed to many books. For others, writing chapters for this book was a new experience, but we can all agree that it placed a considerable amount of strain on our personal and professional lives. However, now that it is finished, there is such a sense of accomplishment that is due to the phenomenal dedication to the project shown by everyone and the amount we have learned along the way. We are happy that we have been able to share this knowledge with you, our reader.

A huge thanks goes out to the following people for contributing to the production of this project: Teresa Elsey (Senior Production Editor at O'Reilly), Dianne Russell (Project Manager at Octal Publishing, Inc.), Troy Lanphier and Marlene Lanphier (Technical Reviewers), and all other people at O'Reilly who helped with the production of this book.

Last but not least, our greatest appreciation and admiration to our families for their continued support while writing this book. We thank them all for their love, support, and understanding.

The Authors
September, 2011

Errata & Book Support

We've made every effort to ensure the accuracy of this book and its companion content. Any errors that have been reported since this book was published are listed on our Microsoft Press site at *oreilly.com*:

http://go.microsoft.com/FWLink/?Linkid=227950

If you find an error that is not already listed, you can report it to us through the same page.

If you need additional support, email Microsoft Press Book Support at *mspinput@ microsoft.com*.

Please note that product support for Microsoft software is not offered through the addresses above.

We Want to Hear from You

At Microsoft Press, your satisfaction is our top priority, and your feedback our most valuable asset. Please tell us what you think of this book at:

http://www.microsoft.com/learning/booksurvey

The survey is short, and we read every one of your comments and ideas. Thanks in advance for your input!

Stay in Touch

Let's keep the conversation going! We're on Twitter: *http://twitter.com/MicrosoftPress.*

CHAPTER 1

Introduction to Microsoft SharePoint Foundation 2010

In today's world, organizations are looking for an advantage over their competition. These organizations have increasingly turned to technology to gain that edge. About 10 years ago, Microsoft introduced a suite of tools that have evolved to become known as Microsoft SharePoint. Using these tools, organizations can share, exchange, and distribute information to their employees, partners, shareholders, and customers. Microsoft's SharePoint technology has also given organizations throughout the world the means to implement information systems that increase productivity and enhance organizational collaboration, while giving users the tools they need to accomplish their jobs more quickly and efficiently.

SharePoint Foundation 2010 is the entry-level component of the SharePoint family of technologies; it's the starting point for organizations that want to begin using SharePoint. As time goes on, an organization might require additional tools and features. At that point, it might decide to go forward with a complete SharePoint Server 2010 configuration. Even though this book will look at the abilities, features, and functions of SharePoint Foundation 2010 specifically, Foundation is the baseline for SharePoint Server 2010; as such, the content of this book is still relevant to you, even if you are currently running (or foresee going to) SharePoint 2010 Server.

With SharePoint Foundation 2010, you will be able to store and access content while simultaneously linking your organization's departments and teams together in a way that offers users a familiar, web-based experience. The beauty of SharePoint Foundation is that it can be utilized as a hybrid solution to meet a number of needs within your organization. Whether you are new to Microsoft SharePoint or are a seasoned veteran to this technology, Microsoft has worked hard to introduce a solution that ensures your organization will benefit from its implementation.

When your organization deploys SharePoint Foundation 2010, it can take advantage of a set of robust tools to create solutions that will help people stay connected, regardless of size, geographic location, and (most important) the available IT budget. And whether the organization is a Fortune 500 company, a startup, or a home-based business, it can utilize the features and functions immediately and effectively.

SharePoint is designed around an easy-to-use web-based interface that is fully integrated with Microsoft Office. As such, users do not need to learn a new piece of software—they can use their existing knowledge and apply it to the SharePoint environment. Always remember, *SharePoint is designed to adapt to your organization, not the other way around*.

SharePoint Foundation 2010 is built on the Windows Server 2008 platform, meaning if you have a Windows Server 2008 server, you can run SharePoint. Also, as an added benefit, Microsoft offers SharePoint Foundation 2010 as a free product, which you can easily download from the Microsoft website. By doing so, Microsoft has truly engineered a software platform that is accessible to any organization.

If your organization requires functionality, such as enterprise-wide records management, Excel Services, InfoPath Form Services, Business Intelligence capabilities, and My Sites, then SharePoint Server 2010 is a platform that you should definitely consider. If your goals are less complex, then SharePoint Foundation 2010 is a robust and cost-effective platform that should be strongly considered; We encourage organizations that are new to SharePoint or that have an existing SharePoint 2007 (WSS 3.0 or MOSS) implementation to "get your feet wet" by implementing SharePoint Foundation 2010.

SharePoint Foundation 2010 is amazingly powerful, flexible, and easy to use. The remainder of this chapter provides a brief overview of SharePoint Foundation 2010, what is new in comparison to previous SharePoint versions, how to customize and enhance it, how it works with the Microsoft Office system, and how to develop entirely new SharePoint applications. Subsequent chapters will explain these topics in much greater detail.

> **Note**
> You can download SharePoint Foundation 2010 at *www.microsoft.com/downloads/en/ details.aspx?FamilyID=49c79a8a-4612-4e7d-a0b4-3bb429b46595&displaylang=en*.

Presenting SharePoint Foundation 2010

At a high level, SharePoint Foundation 2010 aims to assist organizations in the following six areas:

- **Sites**   These provide an infrastructure that your organization can use for all of your business websites. Through these sites, you can share documents with colleagues, shareholders, partners, and customers. You can also use these sites to manage projects and publish information to external entities.

- **Communities**   These are places within SharePoint that are used by teams and individuals for collaborating on ideas and work in ways that are familiar and useful to them. Communities also assist your colleagues to accomplish their task assignments more quickly than they could in the past.

- **Content**   Organizations produce a lot of content in the course of conducting business. In the past, this content was mostly utilized and then forgotten. Through content management practices, your organization has powerful tools in place for the production of content; more important, you can set up retention policies, automated records management tools, and compliance measures. All of these tasks can be done through the familiar interface of the Office platform.

- **Search**   No matter how well your content is produced or stored, it is meaningless if your organization cannot locate the correct content when it needs it. With SharePoint's uniquely powerful search tools, you can "cut through the clutter" and find content based on relevance, refinement, and social cues, thus providing the results that you want and need.

- **Insights**   Organizations have data and Business Intelligence (BI) stored away in numerous databases, reports, spreadsheets, and business applications. SharePoint 2010 provides a way for an organization to finally tap into these rich information resources to locate the information it needs to make better business decisions.

- **Composites**   Business solutions are always needed and are retooled based on business needs at the time. With SharePoint Composites, your organization can custom build both coded and no-code solutions to rapidly respond to business needs.

Together, each of these areas combine to be known as the SharePoint Circle, which is depicted in Figure 1-1.

Figure 1-1 The SharePoint Circle.

In the sections that follow, we'll take a look at each area individually.

Sites

SharePoint Foundation 2010 is designed to provide organizations with an infrastructure with which they can build either internal or external websites. Through the use of Internet Information Services (IIS), SharePoint Foundation comes out of the box with a very stable web platform, thereby offering a web environment that is easy to use and secure.

With sites you are able to design websites in a matter of minutes, which could be ideal for:

- Project team members who have many recurring meetings throughout the year, for which agendas, meeting minutes, and related project-specific documentation differ from meeting to meeting.

- When a specific document exists that requires feedback from a large audience but requires granular security so that only document owners can perform updates.

- When an ad hoc meeting is called to discuss a specific topic, and this information must be retained and allow for collaboration throughout a period of time.

- When a series of websites need to be created for different departments so that specific content can be disseminated throughout an organization but still remain secure, based on each member's role.

You might or might not initially know what types of sites that you need or what types of tools and functionality that might be required for each site that you create. Never fear: SharePoint Foundation 2010 comes with several built-in site templates that you can use to get started. Each of these templates come set up with lists, libraries, Web Parts, layouts, and (in some cases) workflows already activated for use. Also, each of these templates are fully functioning sites when you set them up by using the easy setup interface in SharePoint 2010. In a matter of minutes, you can have a new SharePoint site up and running, thus cutting down on the setup time that you would typically need if you had to design and build sites from scratch. At the same time, these sites are fully customizable, as well. If there are a few libraries that you do not need, you can easily delete these libraries. You can also add in any desired functionality.

Table 1-1 lists the templates that come with every copy of SharePoint Foundation 2010. With the new and improved functionality in SharePoint Foundation 2010, these collaboration and meeting templates continue to be ideal for information workers in corporate environments. People use these same templates more than ever to create sites for professional and charitable organizations, schools, social clubs, sports teams, churches, youth groups, and almost any other kind of group that you can think of. This same platform can also be utilized to develop custom applications of any kind.

Table 1-1 Collaboration and Meeting Templates Supplied with SharePoint Foundation 2010

Template	Purpose
<Select template later>	An empty site for which you can select a template later.
Basic Meeting Workspace	A site on which you can plan, organize, and capture the results of a meeting. This template provides lists for managing the agenda, meeting attendees, and documents.
Blank Meeting Workspace	A blank meeting site that you can customize, based on your requirements.
Blank Site	A blank site that you can customize, based on your requirements.
Blog	A site on which a person or team can post ideas, observations, and expertise about which site visitors can comment.
Decision Meeting Workspace	A site on which you can track status or make decisions at meetings. Decision Meeting Workspace provides lists to create tasks, store documents, and record decisions.
Document Workspace	A site on which colleagues can work together on a document. This template provides a document library for storing the primary document and supporting files, a tasks list for assigning to-do items, and a links list to point to resources that are related to the document.

Template	Purpose
Group Work Site	This template provides a groupware solution that teams can use to create, organize, and share information. It includes the Group Calendar, Circulation, Phone-Call Memo, the document library, and the other basic lists.
Multipage Meeting Workspace	A site on which you can plan a meeting and capture the meeting's decisions and other results. This template provides lists for managing the agenda and meeting attendees. It also provides two blank pages that you can customize based on your requirements.
Social Meeting Workspace	A site on which you can plan social occasions. It provides lists for tracking attendees, providing directions, and storing pictures of the event.
Team Site	A site on which a team can organize, author, and share information. It provides a document library and lists for managing announcements, calendar items, tasks, and discussions.

Table 1-1 demonstrates that SharePoint Foundation 2010 comes with several templates that can be used to fit practically every business scenario you might come across. Keep in mind that these are the templates that come with SharePoint Foundation 2010 out-of-the-box. And if you are using SharePoint Server 2010, there are even more templates available for you to use.

These collaboration and meeting templates give you the flexibility to accomplish fast-paced and effective collaboration on documents, meetings, events, projects, discussions, and ideas; they are ideal for maintaining version control on documents, conducting discussions, and tracking tasks, issues, and agendas.

In today's business environment, using file share drives is quickly becoming a thing of the past. While these were useful for storing files, today's organizations are finding that they need to have strong content management in place; as such, SharePoint sites are increasingly becoming the tool of choice to meet this demand. With site quotas, file exclusion lists, improved governance, and advanced administration features, SharePoint Foundation 2010 can easily accommodate tens of thousands of users, and thousands of sites within an organization.

With sites, you are able to share and publish content easily. Setting up SharePoint sites is easy (see Chapter 4, "Creating Sites and Workspaces by Using the Browser"), and by using the new features found within SharePoint Foundation 2010, anyone can build a site from start to finish in a matter of minutes. Several out-of-the-box features provide instant value to your organization by assisting the site owner with content changes, adding interaction, or applying different design themes.

SharePoint sites are as easy to use as they are to build. This is due in part to the integration of SharePoint 2010 with other technologies (such as Office) that you probably already use in the course of performing your job.

Connecting SharePoint to Office makes saving documents directly to a SharePoint site a breeze. The SharePoint site shows up as a directory location within the Save As dialog; you can select and save documents to the appropriate library, thus avoiding the need to go into a SharePoint site to upload a document once it is finished. You can also access sites and content offline via Microsoft SharePoint Workspace and then synchronize changes by simply reconnecting to the network. Also, with cross-browser support and mobile webpages, anyone can access and share content, in the office or on the go.

With features such as audience targeting, multilingual interface support, and user tagging, a highly customized and personal experience can be created for each person using SharePoint Foundation 2010.

Communities

Each organization works differently; the same can be said of the individuals that work within these organizations. There is no right or wrong way to work, as long as the tasks and goals are accomplished; Microsoft recognized this fact. It then incorporated this philosophy into the Communities portion of SharePoint Foundation by providing collaboration tools that anyone can use to share ideas, find people and expertise, and locate business information.

With SharePoint Foundation 2010, you can manage all of these tools from a single platform; thus, you can mix and match the tools in ways that work for you. With SharePoint 2010 Communities, you can be more creative and productive while at the same time knowing that you are working in a secure and well-managed environment.

With SharePoint 2010 Communities, you can work with your team in the manner that you want by using a full set of collaboration tools, from blogs to workflows, and team sites to tagging. SharePoint is a single, flexible platform that makes it easy to manage these tools and design the right collaborative experiences for different business needs.

SharePoint Foundation 2010 is secure, easy to manage, and can be scaled to the size that you need. With granular security and privacy features, your team will be able to work knowing that their content is safe.

Your team already uses several other technologies; SharePoint Foundation 2010 is not necessarily designed to supplant these. In fact, SharePoint is designed for you to be able to use your other technologies seamlessly through the SharePoint interface.

Nowhere is this more apparent than with Office 2010, which is the *de facto* productivity platform for much of the business world. SharePoint works seamlessly with the rest of the Microsoft Business Productivity infrastructure, including Office applications, Microsoft Exchange Server, Microsoft Office Communications Server, Microsoft SQL Server, and Microsoft Dynamics. Because SharePoint does adhere to open standards, you can also use third-party applications and systems.

Using Business Connectivity Services, you can easily reveal information located in other business applications through the SharePoint interface.

My Profile

Your colleagues can set up their own individual profile page in SharePoint Foundation 2010 called My Profile. These pages contain information about employees including biographies, job titles, location, contact information, interests and skills, and previous projects.

This information might sound unneeded at first glance, but think back to a time when you needed people to assist you with a project that required certain skills or experiences; you might have been hard pressed to locate the correct skills in a timely manner. With the My Profiles pages, you can now search for the expertise and skill set that you need within your organization's workforce.

Tags

By using tags, you can collect and manage content for your projects from the vast amount of information that your organization currently contains. Not only can you search for content, but through the use of tags and ratings, you can see rather quickly how useful the content will be for your requirement, based on the experiences of others.

Colleague Suggestions

Perhaps your organization is large and dispersed across many regions. With SharePoint Foundation 2010, in addition to the colleagues with whom you interact every day, you can also receive suggestions from SharePoint about colleagues whom you did not even know exist. Based on your reporting structure, communities memberships, email distribution lists, Office Communicator contact lists, and analysis of most common Office Outlook email recipients, you will be presented with colleague suggestions regarding individuals who might be of interest to you or vice versa. With this new functionality, you can finally locate talented people that are doing the same types of things that you're doing.

Organization Browser

Most organizations have large, confusing organization charts. With SharePoint, you can establish the colleagues, managers, and direct reports that your contacts have, thus saving you time when searching for resource connections within your organization.

Ratings

Content within your organization is growing exponentially by the day, but in some areas, it's not the amount of content that is produced but rather the quality of that content that assists users with accomplishing their tasks and goals. In the past, if you searched for information about a subject, you would receive results but you couldn't determine if the content was relevant to what you were working on. With ratings, your organization can rate Share-Point pages, lists, libraries, and individual documents by using a five-star rating system.

Wikis

You can create pages that provide information from multiple sources. In doing so, you can receive a more complete view of a topic or subject. With SharePoint 2010, you can combine the powerful ease of wikis with the functionality of Web Parts.

Blogs

Your organization has a lot of talented people working within it. Unfortunately, even with the vast amount of communications tools available today, a lot of their ideas, suggestions, and opinions remain unknown. This could be due to them not having a convenient place to express this information. SharePoint 2010 solves this issue with blogs, which give your organization a place where this valuable content can be captured and acted upon. Through the new SharePoint ribbon, formatting blog text and uploading images are easy.

My Content

SharePoint 2010 gives you a personal, private SharePoint site called My Site, on which you can store and manage documents, favorite links, a personal blog, and wiki pages. You can customize your pages and set access and permission levels for any content in the section.

Photos and Presence

A lot of people think visually; as such, SharePoint comes with the ability to help people recognize each other via profile photos. Users can also use presence information to email, instant message, or call someone with the click of a button. Imagine being able to read a white paper, and then clicking a button to talk with the author via telephone, instantly.

Recent Activities

You can post your status to let others know what projects you are working on. You can also locate people who worked on a similar project or task from whom you might need expertise.

Content

Organizations need the ability to manage the content that they currently have along with the new content being produced constantly. Enterprise Content Management (ECM) can help you to do just that. ECM controls the flow of information within an organization—this might be through how content is produced, approved, stored, or discarded.

In the past, other technologies have been too complex for the everyday business user to understand, much less utilize. SharePoint Foundation 2010 employs a suite of tools that make ECM available for everyone to use. Also, with its automated features, your ECM practices can be set to run on their own with minimal human intervention.

Although SharePoint 2010 does have traditional management tools, it combines those with social capabilities and a powerful search, and it is very natural to use. With simple administrative tools, you can set up compliance policies, and the familiar interface allows your staff to work just as they would in Office. The result is information management that is easy to find, share, and use.

Since SharePoint 2010 is closely aligned with the Office 2010 suite of tools, you are presented with a familiar user experience. Studies have revealed that when people are comfortable using a system, they tend to use it more. And in doing so, they can find the information they need easier, and their work is managed from start to finish.

Through SharePoint 2010 ECM, you are able to tag content, enforce retention schedules, declare records, and apply legal holds easily. With these measures in place, you can address the need for compliance and reduce the risk of mistakes when information is archived or discarded.

On a single platform, SharePoint Foundation 2010 manages documents, records, web content, and rich media, helping you to reduce your IT costs. SharePoint can also connect to legacy (older) ECM systems through its use of interoperability standards, such as Content Management Interoperability Services (CMIS), eXtensible Markup Language (XML), and REpresentational State Transfer (REST). SharePoint Foundation helps your organization gain more value from its current investments.

Chapter 1

Compliance Becomes Natural

With SharePoint Foundation 2010, you can manage versions, apply retention policies and schedules, declare records, and place legal holds on content. It does not matter whether you're dealing with traditional, web-based, or social content.

Document Sets

You can create document sets, with which you can manage related content as a single entity, thus saving you time and resources for common processes, such as RFP responses, procurement requests, and others.

Search

Even if your organization has produced millions of quality documents, this fact is useless if you are not able to accurately locate the information when it's needed. With SharePoint Foundation 2010, you can find just the right information to get your job done, quickly and conveniently.

Besides offering the traditional search capability for documents or other types of content, SharePoint also provides intranet search, people search, and a platform to build search-driven applications, all on a single, cost-effective infrastructure.

The biggest driver that sets SharePoint 2010 Search apart from other search technologies is its combination of relevance, refinement, and people. You can drill down through clutter to locate the specific content, individuals, or information that you need.

Chances are that your organization has a lot of information in several different formats located within several different systems and databases. If you were to look for a specific piece of information, you might become inundated with all of the possible choices. Share-Point Foundation 2010 brings order to this chaos via its interactive and visual search experience. You can use visual cues to find information quickly, while the refiners (a tool with which you can select the actual information that you want to view, be it by format, author, size, or date) let you drill down into the results to find even greater insights.

It is a well-known fact that an organization's greatest assets are its people. Each person is on staff to fill specific duties, but an individual does more than just fill a position. Each person brings with them education, expertise, and experiences that can be useful in other areas beyond the job description alone. By using SharePoint Foundation 2010, your organization can unlock these skills and talents. In turn, you can locate the human resources that you need so that you can share ideas and expertise to solve problems, improve processes, and foster innovation.

Not everyone searches for information using the same techniques; as such, previous search systems were not always useful to everyone. With SharePoint Foundation 2010, you can customize and personalize the search experience to meet the needs of those using it. On a single platform, you can add your own vocabulary, tune relevance, and use each person's specific information to deliver a great search experience.

Metadata-Driven Refinement

By using the new refinement panel in SharePoint 2010, you can narrow the results of your search and find the content that you are looking for even faster than before.

People and Expertise Search

Unlock the vast store of the human knowledge, expertise, and experiences by searching for people, either by name or by associated terms.

Contextual Search

Based on a individual's particular details, he can search for different items, even though he uses the same search terms. Perhaps someone in the sales department is looking for information related to product offerings in Fiscal Year 2010. Someone in the finance department might be looking for budget information for that same period. Using traditional search technologies, each user could enter a search term of "FY 2010" and receive results from both sets of information. For both individuals, that's probably more information than either one wanted.

Through the use of keywords and audience targeting, you can provide a search experience that delivers the relevant information each person needs, based on the profile of the user or audience. In this example, the sales person could see at the top of his results the product catalogs from 2010, whereas the finance person could see the budgets for Fiscal Year 2010 presented at the top of her search results.

Insights

You can use SharePoint 2010 Insights to allow everyone access to the business information needed to make sound business decisions. By employing interactive dashboards and score-cards, you can access and use information stored away in databases, reports, spreadsheets, and other business applications.

Additionally, accessing and using information is easy and natural due to Insights' utilization of well-known applications and interfaces such as Oracle databases. For example, a colleague can use Excel Services to publish Microsoft Excel workbooks. After these workbooks are available, your team can access the data, comfortable in the knowledge that they have the most current and up-to-date information with which to work.

Users can access the information they need to do their jobs because the reporting and analysis features are both powerful and easy to use. Due to the familiar interfaces, anyone can feel comfortable looking at the data in a three-dimensional form by slicing and dicing the available information to gain greater insight.

The ability to set up scorecards and dashboards can assist your team in defining and measuring success goals. These metrics can be matched to specific strategies and then shared, tracked, and discussed. By giving each user access to needed BI, you are empowering your team to be more efficient and effective.

You can deploy the powerful tools and features of SharePoint 2010 Insights under centralized system control. You can determine what information is available along with who can access the information. You can be even more efficient as you use the rich programming capabilities and development tools to deploy the solutions that you need when you need them.

Decomposition Tree

With the Decomposition Tree you are able to slice your data and drill down to the factors that affect your data. This powerful analytics tool can be used to examine the core data. You are finally able to answer the question "How did we get here?"

Dashboards

Combined with PerformancePoint Services, you can create dashboards that are accurate and reliable. You can combine data from either structured or unstructured sources to put forth correct data upon which your team can act to make the best decisions. Using the interactivity, you can analyze up-to-the-minute information and work with the data quickly and easily to identify key opportunities and trends.

Composites

SharePoint 2010 Composites gives you the capability to assemble, connect, and configure collaborative business solutions. From sites to more complex business applications, you can respond quickly to specific business needs with a custom solution.

You don't need to be a programmer (although it is helpful) to use the building blocks in SharePoint 2010. Even without using code, you can create highly customized business solutions in a matter of minutes. For example, you can share Microsoft Visio diagrams and Microsoft Access databases easily and quickly. You can also use Microsoft SharePoint Designer and Microsoft InfoPath to design solutions based on workflows and forms that you currently have in use at your organization.

Despite what you might think of developing coded solutions, you will be surprised by how many no-code solutions you can develop to solve your business challenges.

Many organizations have data stored away in sources and systems that are difficult to access. This data has value, but you might need to log on to each system individually to get at the information. This is not only time consuming but also inefficient. With SharePoint 2010 Composites, you are finally able to connect to these resources and work with the data as if the information resided within the SharePoint environment. You can enable full Create, Read, Update, and Delete (CRUD) capabilities on the data along with integrating it into Share-Point's powerful search engine. No matter where the data is located you can work with it to develop business solutions or to assist you in making the best decisions for your problems.

You also have the option to work with the data online or offline through Microsoft Share-Point Workspaces. Once you have a chance to reconnect to your network, your changes can be uploaded automatically.

In many organizations, there are several hundreds of Access databases and Excel spread-sheets that are in use for various reasons. Typically, there are several instances of databases and spreadsheets that are duplicates of others. Due to the nature of the software, these databases and worksheets tend to be decentralized, with each department or division maintaining the information in "silos." With SharePoint 2010 you are able to centralize these data sources and deploy them as a shared solution so that not only is the originating department able to use the information, but the rest of your organization is able to, as well.

Security is always an issue when it comes to an organization's information resources. Thanks to SharePoint's powerful security measures, you can secure your information down to the item level. This means that you can determine not only what information is available but also who can access the information.

With SharePoint 2010 Composites, just about anyone within your organization will be able to develop business solutions. But although this is a great benefit, it can also become a liability really fast. Suppose that someone decides to create a solution that will access hundreds of spreadsheets and databases and display them by using Visio Services. This solution, while helpful, can be a serious drain on resources. Also, while this solution is running the rest of your organization could suffer from slow response times from the SharePoint platform.

Sandboxed solutions give you the ability to create a controlled environment within SharePoint in which you can use to test out new solutions. You can control various factors such as resource throttling, time to execute, and code checking (to name a few). Through a sandboxed solution, you can avoid over burdening your resources. You are also able to encourage innovation without risking the health of the overall SharePoint environment.

With End-User solutions your IT department can now dedicate more of its time to higher priorities, while at the same time giving you the opportunity to come up with the solutions that you need for your specific scenario.

What's New?

With the release of SharePoint Foundation 2010, Microsoft introduced several new features and capabilities along with upgrading items from previous versions of SharePoint. In this section, you will read a brief description of each of these new and upgraded features, along with an example that demonstrates why you should care about them.

The Ribbon

One of the most obvious changes in SharePoint Foundation 2010 is that the ribbon from Microsoft Office 2007 has been incorporated in the platform. This change in the user interface is fundamental when it comes to interacting with Office products. As such, anyone who is familiar with Office 2007 will see this familiar feature in your sites now, as well.

For those of you who are not entirely comfortable with the ribbon, you can relax; it's easy to use; you just need to understand the layout. The ribbon is context driven, meaning that you see the options that you need when you need to use them.

For example, if you are using a library within SharePoint, the ribbon will display options for tasks that are typically done in a library, such as creating a new document, uploading a document, checking-in a document, and so on.

The ribbon is divided into tabs, which are further divided into groups. Typically, a library has a Documents tab, which is divided into groups, such as New, Open & Check Out, Manage,

Share & Track, Copies, Workflows, and Tags and Notes. Each of these groups contains specific actions that you can choose. For example, if you want to set up an Alert, on the Document tab, select the Share & Track group, and then click the button labeled Alert Me.

What's more, as you perform different functions within the platform, you will notice additional tabs appear on the ribbon that are related to the task you're currently performing. For example, you see the Edit tab when you are editing content properties, but you won't see it if you are simply browsing a list of items.

Alerts Enhancements

Alerts were available within Microsoft Office SharePoint Server (MOSS) 2007; they were great as long as you had access to your email account. At the same time, they were a bit annoying because they were email messages that were sent to your email account. As many business users discovered, some of the alerts they set up generated a lot of excess email traffic that they had to manage.

SharePoint Foundation 2010 has expanded the alerts framework so that you can have alerts sent as Short Message Services (SMS) to your mobile devices. You can now tailor a business solution that sends out an SMS Alert to mobile devices. You can even create a totally customized alert system if you want, such as in the following examples:

- You might want the initial assignment of a task to send an email message to the person to whom it was assigned.

- Next, you might want the project manager to be notified by an email message when the task is three days from its due date.

- You might want it to send an SMS Alert hourly to your team members when the task is in the last 12 hours before its due date and it does not show a completed status.

- And finally, you might want to know if someone is able to take up the task and work on it to completion.

Business Connectivity Services

The Business Data Catalog (BDC) from MOSS 2007 has undergone a facelift and a name change; its new name is the Business Connectivity Services (BCS). It is now included in SharePoint Foundation and is no longer exclusive to the SharePoint Server product.

The BCS is able to provide full CRUD capabilities to external data from Line-of-Business (LoB) systems, web services, databases, and other external systems. This information is then presented within SharePoint Foundation 2010. The features within the SharePoint platform are able to access external data sources directly, both online and offline. By using familiar tools such as SharePoint Designer 2010 and Microsoft Visual Studio 2010, you can build solutions that can exploit these external sources within the SharePoint platform.

With the BDC in previous releases of SharePoint, you could only view the data in external sources. With BCS, you can not only view the data, but you can fully interact with it, all through familiar interfaces such as Microsoft Outlook. You can, for example, begin the onboard process for a new employee by simply adding them as a contact to Outlook, which can be tied to a business solution that copies the information to an External list (an external legacy data source such as Oracle), which in turn starts a workflow to make this person an employee.

You can connect to a wide variety of data sources, such as:

- Databases

- Web and Windows Communication Foundation (WCF) services

- Microsoft .NET connectivity assemblies

- Custom data sources

In addition to connectors for existing data sources, BCS provides a pluggable framework for developers to use to create connectors for new external system types, thus enabling these new data source types to be accessed via BCS.

The BCS is more efficient than the older BDC model. In the past, the BDC could only perform single item operations such as search, and if you needed other operations to be performed, they had to be done in a separate call. You are now able to provide batch and bulk operation support, with which you can read multiple items in a single call; in doing so, the number of round trips to the data source is greatly reduced, resulting in better overall performance.

BCS now supports the reading of Binary Large Objects (BLOB) data, which is really useful when it comes to streaming BLOBs of data from external systems. You can also use dot notation in field names, which you can use to read and write complex types.

Client Object Model

SharePoint Foundation 2010 introduces three new client application programming interfaces (APIs) that you can use to interact with SharePoint sites from a .NET managed application (must be no earlier than Microsoft .NET Framework 3.5), a Microsoft Silverlight application (no earlier than Silverlight 2.0), or from ECMAScript (JavaScript, Jscript) that executes in the browser.

You are now able to design solutions that are fully interactive from within the browser. For example, you can use Silverlight to see different "what if" scenarios graphically, using real-time data.

Custom Field Rendering Enhancements

In Windows SharePoint Services 3.0, fields were rendered on list views by a *RenderPattern* element in a field definition file, fldtypes*.xml. In SharePoint Foundation 2010, fields are rendered on list view pages by XSLT stylesheets. This means that you now must define the rendering of your custom field types by creating a custom XSLT stylesheet rather than by adding a custom *RenderPattern* element to a field type definition.

Events Enhancements

SharePoint Foundation 2010 supports multiple new events, including *onCreate* events for lists and websites and support for synchronous after events. It also offers a more approachable events infrastructure that is easier to program against than earlier versions.

SharePoint Foundation 2010 new events include:

- Add and delete events on lists

- Add events on websites

- Synchronous or asynchronous after events.

Additionally, new event model capabilities include the following:

- Event registration at the Site Collection level

- XML event registration at the site receiver

- Improved semantics for retrieving event data

- Improved user interface for form-level events

Health Analyzer

The Health Analyzer is an extensible, rules-based infrastructure that not only monitors but also maintains the health of the entire SharePoint Foundation environment throughout a server farm. It is designed to automatically check for potential configuration, performance, and security issues and to identify these items to farm administrators.

SharePoint Health Analyzer monitors the farm by applying a set of health rules. A health rule is nothing more than executable code that is deployed at the farm level and is registered with the SharePoint Health Analyzer by a farm administrator. SharePoint Foundation 2010 ships with a number of health rules. You can create and deploy custom health rules by writing code that utilizes the SharePoint Foundation object model.

List Enhancements

SharePoint Foundation 2010 comes with several enhancements and features to the list infrastructure, which improve the user experience along with data integrity.

Large Lists

Microsoft Office SharePoint Server 2007 demonstrated that when deployed on an enterprise level, the contents of lists can grow to become so large that performance can be diminished substantially. SharePoint Foundation 2010 addresses this issue by incorporating a new List View Threshold feature that allows you to specify the maximum number of items that a database operation can retrieve. If a search query exceeds the threshold, the query is blocked to avoid adversely affecting site performance. The user is notified that the limit has been achieved and is given the opportunity to refine the search query to retrieve a more manageable set of results.

Alternatively, you can also schedule "happy hour" controls to avoid times when you expect heavier loads. By scheduling during these less active time periods, users can run queries or reports that will return a large number of items without affecting other users on the platform.

Referential Integrity for List Items with Lookup Columns

Previously, you could create a loosely defined relationship between lists though a lookup field, whereby a child list would look to a parent list. With SharePoint Foundation 2010, items in a parent list are "aware" of related items in the child list, and you can set referential integrity constraints on the child items by specifying delete behavior. These list relationships and delete behaviors can be set either through the user interface or through the object model.

Enforcing Unique Column Constraints

With SharePoint Foundation, you can set a primary key on column fields. This is done by using (or "enforcing") a new feature called Unique Column Constraints, which you can use to enforce unique values in a list or document library column.

For example, you might want to ensure that the same Customer ID number is not applied to multiple customers. By enforcing the uniqueness of the column, you prevent the same Customer ID number from being used more than one time.

Not all column types support this feature. Table 1-2 lists which column types are supported and which are not.

Table 1-2 **Column Type Support for Unique Column Constraints**

Column type	Supports unique column constraints
Boolean (yes/no)	No
Calculated field types	No
Checked out to	No
Choice field (but not multi-choice)	Yes
Content type ID	No
Created time	No
Currency	Yes
Custom field types	No
Date/Time	Yes
Hyperlink/Picture	No
Lookup (but not multi-value)	Yes
Modified by	No
Modified time	No
Multiple lines of text	No
Number	Yes
Person or Group (but not multi-value)	Yes
Single line of text	Yes
Title (but not in a document library)	Yes
UI version	No

External Lists

BCS has introduced a new kind of list called the *External list*, with which you can access external data residing in different systems, databases, and spreadsheets in the same way that you access SharePoint Foundation list data. You can interact with the External list in the same way that you interact with other SharePoint lists; moreover, you can write to these lists (if the external data source allows it) and synchronize these changes with the click of a button.

Microsoft Sync Framework

Within SharePoint Foundation, the Microsoft Sync Framework provides a comprehensive and unified synchronization architecture that provides data-agnostic and bi-directional capabilities to developers. Due to its design, other Microsoft and third-party applications can synchronize more easily with SharePoint 2010 deployments.

The Sync Framework provides three core building blocks:

- Sync Metadata Services

- Sync Provider

- Sync Runtime

Mobile Device Development Enhancements

The ability to use mobile devices to access SharePoint Foundation functionality, lists, and pages has been greatly expanded.

Mobile Web Part Adapters

You can now have a mobile page that corresponds in purpose, data, and functionality to a nonmobile Web Parts page. Any Web Part on a nonmobile page can be adapted to be duplicated on a mobile page by adding a control. Some of the major Web Parts that are built in to SharePoint already have these adapters. You can develop your own adapters for Web Parts that you want to make available on mobile pages, so when a mobile device accesses a Web Parts page, it is redirected to the corresponding mobile page.

Mobile Messaging

Your SharePoint Foundation solutions can now have SMS messages sent to mobile phones. If your solution uses the Outlook Messaging Service (OMS) protocol, most of your development work has been done for you.

SharePoint Foundation 2010 expands this mobile support, enhancing its Alerts feature. You can now choose to have Alerts sent via SMS messages to mobile devices. This is done by giving the SharePoint Foundation web application its own account (which can be changed programmatically) with a messaging service provider.

New Mobile Pages and Controls

You can do more within the SharePoint environment by using your mobile phone. SharePoint Foundation 2010 adds many new types of mobile pages and over 60 new public mobile controls. These improvements provide new or enhanced support in mobile devices; which include view filtering, contact selection, file uploading, images, wiki pages, Web Part pages, and other functionality. The visual appearance of mobile pages is more colorful, as well. You can now duplicate the mobile experience through the full range of appearance, functionality, and data access that your SharePoint Foundation solutions provide to nonmobile users.

Mobile Document Viewers

You can create mobile pages that host document viewers, with which mobile users can open documents located in SharePoint Foundation Document Libraries on their mobile device. This happens even if they have been formatted for a particular desktop application such as a spreadsheet or word processor.

Performance Monitoring and Request Throttling

Through the use of a programmable system of throttling HTTP requests, SharePoint Foundation 2010 can control the number of requests when the front-end web server handling the requests becomes too busy to accommodate them all.

Using your existing system, the server code can perform the following:

- Determine which Windows Server 2008 performance counters are used to establish whether a front-end web server is busy.

- Define what values of a counter are poor enough to cause the worker thread to begin throttling.

- Define which kinds of HTTP requests are throttled and whether they are throttled as soon as the server is busy or only when it has been busy continuously for at least 60 seconds.

- Exempt certain kinds of HTTP requests from throttling.

The system can also report the current health score of the front-end web server in the HTTP response object so that your client-side code can do its own request throttling.

Query Enhancements

SharePoint Foundation 2010 includes several new ways to query and filter data.

New Query Support for Server-Side Code

It is now significantly easier to query data by using server code in SharePoint Foundation 2010.

LINQ to SharePoint Provider

It is no longer necessary to compose a Collaborative Application Markup Language (CAML) query when your code needs to query a list. Instead, SharePoint Foundation 2010 comes with a Language-Integrated Query (LINQ) to SharePoint provider, with which you can query

SharePoint lists from server code by using LINQ syntax. The provider can translate your LINQ queries to CAML queries for submission to the content database. Furthermore, since SharePoint Foundation 2010 also adds a new *Join* element to its Query Schema, you can have both implicit and explicit joins in your LINQ queries by using the *join* keyword. You can also write to lists by using the LINQ to SharePoint provider.

> **Note**
>
> To use this functionality, remember that you must have classes that provide an object-oriented interface over the relational content databases. These classes are generated for you by the SPMetal tool that comes with SharePoint Foundation 2010.

You can use LINQ syntax in your code even if you are not using the LINQ to SharePoint provider. Any SharePoint Foundation object that implements *IEnumerable(Of T)* can be queried by using LINQ syntax.

List Joins Supported in CAML Queries

You can now join multiple lists in a single query utilizing the new *Join* element. Use the new *ProjectedFields* element to specify what list fields to include in the results; there are some details that will need to be considered when using these elements, such as the following:

- You cannot join just any two lists, regardless of type.

- If two lists are able to be joined, you cannot use just any primary or foreign field as the "join on" pair of fields

INSIDE OUT   Lookup type fields

The field in the primary list must be a Lookup type field and it must lookup to the field in the foreign list. It is due to this that all joins mirror existing lookup relations between lists.

Querying in Client-Side Code

Client applications can now access SharePoint Foundation data in entirely different ways.

Queries in the Client Object Model

You can query within the client model in two ways:

- Write CAML queries for use with the *SPQuery* class

- Query any SharePoint Foundation object that implements the *IEnumerable(Of T)* with *LINQ to Objects*

Support for ADO.NET Data Services Framework

You can query by using the ADO.NET Data Services Framework if the client application does not utilize the new SharePoint Foundation client object model and you only need to query list data.

Avoid Using SharePoint Data Providing Web Services

Unlike previous SharePoint releases, it is encouraged to use either the client object model or the ADO.NET Data Services Framework for the best performance and usability. You can use previous web services such as the List Data Retrieval web service (which is still supported) but they are in place primarily for providing backward compatibility and interoperability with web service clients.

Avoid Making Direct Calls to owssvr.dll

To maximize the new client application's compatibility with future versions of SharePoint Foundation, it is highly recommended that you make direct calls to the owssvr.dll file as a method of client access.

The SharePoint Foundation 2010 Software Development Kit (SDK) does include documentation about client-side access to the SharePoint Foundation deployments by using RPC calls, but this information is only included to provide troubleshooting assistance to client applications that already make such calls.

The Ribbon

The ribbon serves as the primary user interface that you use to interact with SharePoint Foundation 2010 sites. Earlier versions of SharePoint had commands that were accessed through multiple surfaces and located in various menus.

By contrast, the introduction of the ribbon presents an interface that is grouped in a logical manner through the use of tabs and groups, making them easier to find. Furthermore, the ribbon's functionality can be extended to include your own custom commands.

Sandboxed Solutions

Microsoft has introduced a new concept called *sandboxed solutions* with the SharePoint Foundation 2010 platform. A sandboxed solution gives Site Collection users a safe place where they can develop, deploy, and test custom code solutions. This is accomplished by using a subset of the *Microsoft.SharePoint* namespace. These solutions are stored within a solution gallery. Additionally, farm administrators can monitor and validate these solutions prior to deploying them into the production environment. Performance can be monitored by measuring CPU execution time, memory consumption, and database query time. You can also monitor other aspects of operation, including abnormal termination, critical exceptions, unhandled exceptions, and data marshalling size.

Security Enhancements

SharePoint Foundation 2010 continues Microsoft's tradition of building on and enhancing security.

Claims-Based Identity and Authentication

Claims-based identity is an identity model in SharePoint Foundation 2010 that includes features such as authentication across users of both Windows-based and non–Windows-based systems, multiple authentication types, stronger real-time authentication, a wider set of principal types, and delegation of user identity between applications.

When you sign in to SharePoint Foundation 2010, your token (issued by a Windows Server 2008 claims provider during your initial logon to a network) is validated and then used to sign in to SharePoint. SharePoint Foundation 2010 and SharePoint Server 2010 support five sign-in or access modes:

- Windows Classic-Mode Sign-In

- Windows Claims-Mode Sign-In

- SAML (Security Assertion Markup Language) Passive Sign-in Mode

- ASP.NET Membership and Role Passive Sign-In

- Anonymous Access

> **Note**
>
> SAML Passive is when a web application is configured to accept tokens from a trusted logon provider. A trusted logon provider is an external (resides outside of SharePoint) Security Token Service (STS) that SharePoint trusts.

When claims-aware applications are built and deployed, the user needs only to present an identity to the application as a set of claims. One claim might be a user name and another might be an email address. The idea here is that an external identity system can be configured to give the client application all the information that it needs to about the user with each request, along with cryptographic assurance that the identity data received by your application comes from a trusted source.

Under this model, single sign-on can be achieved much easier than before, and the client application is no longer burdened with:

- Authenticating users

- Storing user accounts and passwords

- Calling to enterprise-wide directories to lookup user identity details

- Integrating with identity systems from other platforms or companies.

Under this model, the client application makes identity-related decisions based on claims supplied the user.

ASP.NET Membership User Token Converted to Claims Security Token

The SharePoint Foundation STS creates the claims security token from the user name validated by the membership provider, and from the set of group memberships associated with the user name that are provided by the membership provider.

Automatic Password Change and Managed Accounts

A new feature within SharePoint Foundation 2010 is the automatic password change feature. With it, you can update and deploy passwords without the need to perform manual password update tasks across multiple accounts, services, and web applications. You can use the automatic password change feature to determine whether a password is about to expire and to reset the password utilizing a long, cryptographically-strong random string.

You use managed accounts to implement the automatic password change feature. Managed accounts in SharePoint Foundation improve on security and ensure application isolation.

Effective Permission API

With Windows SharePoint Service (WSS) 3.0, it was difficult to get a user's effective permissions on securable objects. There was simply no built-in way to see accurately all of the sites, lists, libraries and content to which a user had access. Over time, it became even more difficult if a site had complex permission settings, especially if inheritance was broken and unique permissions were applied to items. Not only was it difficult to see what permissions a user had, but you could not determine how a particular user gained permission to a particular object. SharePoint Foundation 2010 introduces a new command on the ribbon called Check Permissions. With this new command you now have a quick way to enumerate all of the role assignments for a specific user within a specific scope.

The *SPSecurableObject* class exposes a new *GetUserEffectivePermissionInfo* method. This method retrieves an object with detailed information about the effective permissions that a specified user has in the current scope and the role assignments related to this user at this scope. This method does not include web application security policy information in the permission mask if the provided user belongs to a policy that is marked "Account Operate as System." This method is available for users who have the *EnumeratePermissions* permission granted.

Secure Store Service

The Secure Store Service replaces the SharePoint Server 2007 single sign-on feature. Secure Store Service is a service that provides storage and mapping of credentials such as account names and passwords. With it, you can securely store data that contains credentials that are required for connecting to external systems and for associating those credentials to a specific identity or group of identities.

It is common for solutions to try to authenticate to an external system in which the current user is known differently or has a different account for authentication. In such cases, Secure Store Service can be used to store and map user credentials that are required by the external system. You can configure Secure Store Service so that multiple users can access an external system by using a single set of credentials on that external system.

Service Application Framework

The Service Application Framework replaces the Shared Services Provider in SharePoint Server 2007. The Service Application Framework model is much more flexible than the Shared Services Provider model. Service applications can be consumed by a single server farm or shared across farms, allowing for centralized sharing of your IT investments. Service Application Framework applications are easily scaled out for load balancing high-demand service applications.

Improved Development Experience

Service developers are now able to focus on the business logic of their applications through the use of the Service Application Framework. The Framework also makes it easy to implement details such as writing code to configure a server that is running IIS, installing a Secure Sockets Layer (SSL) certificate, creating a virtual directory, managing credentials for a pool of application users, managing and caching distributed settings, tracking and load balancing endpoints, and also performing many back-up and restore tasks.

Improved Integration with SharePoint

Services can now plug their management user interface (UI) in to the SharePoint Service Management page to provide a common experience for administrators. All services can now benefit from common SharePoint administration tools, such as Upgrade, Backup/ Restore, and Account management. Administrators can also use this common UI to manage, start, stop, group, associate, federate, and back up services.

In addition, not only can service developers create their own administrative pages to manage their service, but they can also host these pages by using SharePoint Central Administration. Services can also be configured to have their own additional specialized administrative roles.

Management of Service Application Framework applications can be performed through either the Central Administration UI or Windows PowerShell.

WCF Integration

The WCF service model deals with communication between client and service. The Share-Point service model deals with deployment, management, and discovery of services in a server farm. The Service Application Framework is ideal for deploying, managing, and discovering WCF service clients and applications.

Round-Robin Load Balancing

SharePoint Service Applications are typically hosted on multiple servers and are invoked from a service client application that is running on a front-end web server. Service Application proxy method invocations must be routed from the front end web server to the appropriate application server by using a load balancing tool.

Normally, SharePoint Foundation administrators tend to configure load balancing solutions for the front-end web servers; it is not normally expected that there will be calls between the front-end web servers and application server to require an additional external load balancer. SharePoint provides a simple round-robin load balancer implementation that is handled in the *SPRoundRobinServiceLoadBalancer* class, which can be either replaced or enhanced by third-party developers as needed. Service application proxies can use the built-in round-robin load balancer to route requests to the appropriate back-end service application.

Claims-Based Identity

The claims-based identity model for SharePoint Foundation is built upon the Windows Identity Foundation (WIF). This new identity model includes features, such as authentication of users across both Windows-based and non–Windows-based systems, multiple authentication types, stronger real-time authentication, a wider set of principal types, and delegation of user identity between applications.

When claims-aware applications are built, the user presents an identity to the application as a set of claims. One claim could be a user's name and another claim could be the user's email address; the idea being that an external identity system is set up to give the application all of the information it needs to know about the user.

Backup and Restore

The Service Application Framework allows for easy integration with SharePoint's built-in backup and restore tool.

Silverlight Integration and Cross-Domain Data Access

Within the WSS 3.0 platform, you can host a Microsoft Silverlight application in a Web Part (which required some modifications to the Web.Config). SharePoint Foundation 2010 has gone beyond this capability by providing a built-in, extensible Silverlight Web Part designed specifically to host Silverlight applications. Also, a closely related object to this new Web Part is Cross-Domain Data Access (Silverlight CDA) which enables secure cross-domain integration between Silverlight applications and SharePoint Foundation deployments. Silverlight CDA can be also used by non-Silverlight external applications, as well.

Silverlight Web Part

SharePoint Foundation development efforts are not necessarily needed to add a Silverlight application to your SharePoint Foundation solution. In the simplest of scenarios, users would install your Silverlight application within the same domain as their SharePoint Foundation web application and add the hosting Silverlight Web Part through the UI; they would only need to supply the URL of the application. In the case where the Silverlight application would access SharePoint Foundation data and the application is also hosted on a server located outside of the domain of the web application, you need to create an External Application XML that the user would use to register the hosting Silverlight Web Part. An added benefit is that the Silverlight Tool Part comes built in to SharePoint Foundation 2010.

Silverlight Cross-Domain Data Access

You could have a scenario in which you need to have host applications located in a different domain from the SharePoint Foundation Web application. This might be due to a need to host many applications on an application server so that the applications can be made available to all web applications in the farm. SharePoint Foundation 2010 ushers in the Silverlight CDA, which makes this scenario available in a secure manner. Silverlight CDA gives administrators the ability to control the permissions on external applications without the need to implement overly restrictive security processes that could hinder users.

In the Silverlight CDA scenario, the application would log on to the SharePoint Foundation web application as a distinct type of user known as an *application principal*. The application's permissions would be an intersection of the permissions that the administrator has granted this special user and the permissions of the actual user who opened the webpage (that contains the hosted applications Web Part).

UI Enhancements

One of the more significant upgrades to come with SharePoint Foundation 2010 is the UI. Included with this upgrade is the Server ribbon, master page, and cascading style sheets (CSS). With these changes, SharePoint Foundation has a more consistent user experience across pages and makes working with objects inside of SharePoint Foundation a lot easier.

UI Improvements

These elements have been specifically upgraded in SharePoint Foundation 2010:

- **The Server ribbon**   The Server ribbon was introduced to better display commonly used commands for ease of use; this follows Microsoft's inclusion of the ribbon in all of the Office 2010 applications. The ribbon works on the basis of combining commands logically, grouped into tabs and groups that make finding commands easier than was the case with the old Item Menu User Interface. The ribbon can also be customized with your own tabs, groups, and commands.

  For more information on how to customize the ribbon, see Chapter 3, "End-User Features and Experience."

- **Cascading Style Sheets**   Cascading Style Sheets with SharePoint have been divided into multiple files to make more targeted customization scenarios possible as well as providing a means to improve page loading performance.

Unified Logging Systems

There are some new logging features available within SharePoint Foundation 2010 for developers, along with improvements to existing logging mechanisms.

SPMonitoredScope

The *SPMonitoredScope* is a code attribute that, when applied to a class or method, allows a developer to write logging information to the SharePoint Foundation usage database with complete application information and custom strings.

Request Usage Database

Every SharePoint Foundation resource request can be captured utilizing the request usage database; this capture is done in real time when a page is rendered.

Developer Dashboard

The Developer Dashboard utility can be enabled to assist with debugging a SharePoint Foundation webpage. This is similar to ASP.NET tracing in which this dashboard displays all of the details of the user request, which are then relayed to the developer.

API Improvements

In Windows SharePoint Services 3.0, to write to the SharePoint Trace and Unified Logging Systems (ULS) Logs, you had to implement the *IDiagnosticsManager* interface (requiring additional code). In SharePoint Foundation, the preferred method is to use the *SPDiagnostics ServiceBase* class, which contains a much simpler and more efficient way to interact with ULS Logs; specifically, the *WriteEvent* and *WriteTrace* methods are simpler to implement.

Windows PowerShell for SharePoint

In previous versions of the SharePoint platform, you would use the STSADM.exe administration tool to perform command line scripting. While STSADM.exe is still available for use within the SharePoint Foundation tool, the preferred tool for command-line scripting is Windows PowerShell, which is a new tool from Microsoft that complements Cmd.exe in Windows administration context. Going forward, you should use PowerShell scripting when developing any new command-line scripts in SharePoint Foundation 2010.

INSIDE OUT   Phasing out STSADM

Although STSADM is still available within SharePoint Foundation, it is deprecated and will not be available in the next version of SharePoint.

Workflow Enhancements

SharePoint Foundation 2010 continues to build upon functionality available in WSS 3.0 through the Windows Workflow Foundation; it also improves and widens your options so that you can build even richer workflows that can support even more business scenarios.

New Workflow Activities

SharePoint Foundation's core installation now comes with new workflow actions. Workflow activities (also known as *actions*) are the basic building blocks for all workflows. With the addition of these new actions, you have even greater flexibility with your workflow designs.

Pluggable Workflow Services

You can now create workflows that are able to interact and receive data from external sources through pluggable workflow services.

Workflow Events

The workflows in WSS 3.0 could only respond to a limited number of events. You can now create workflows that are able to respond to even more events. You can even create your own custom events and event receivers with SharePoint Foundation 2010.

Site Workflows

The new site workflows break away from the previous dependency of being tied to list items. With site workflows, you can create workflows that can be associated with specified events and other workflow activities.

Reusable Declarative Workflows

In the past, workflows had to be associated with either a list or library. You could not package and deploy these workflows to other lists or libraries. In SharePoint Foundation, you now have the ability to develop declarative workflows that can be reused. This means that you can now apply workflows that you developed for one list or library to multiple lists or libraries.

Summary

SharePoint Foundation 2010 comes with a considerable number of additions and improvements over past incarnations of the platform. This chapter discussed the SharePoint Foundation 2010 platform and briefly described the capabilities of the platform. In the following chapters, we will go over these improvements in greater detail and show you how you can activate and use the features described in this book.

Administration for Business Users

ADMINISTRATION of Microsoft SharePoint can be broken down into two categories: Business User Administration, and Information Technology Professional Administration.

Business User Administration

If you are a typical person who works in this category:

- Your main job doesn't revolve around computers.

- You create and modify sites, libraries, and lists.

- You might also be responsible for the site content. For example, you might upload documents to libraries for others to download.

The majority of this book includes information targeted to the advanced business user who might perform some of this type of administration. This chapter will give you the tools to set up your SharePoint sites that are serviced on the back end either by your organization's IT group or an external hosting company, or both.

Information Technology Professional Administration

If you are a typical person who works in this category:

- You work in a room surrounded by the server's network hardware.

- You install and configure SharePoint on a server.

- You create web applications and Site Collections for business users to administer.

The IT professional at an organization with SharePoint is often an advanced user of Share-Point, as well. Although this chapter is not intended to describe the step-by-step processes to implement back-end changes for SharePoint Foundation, an IT professional can benefit from this chapter by learning the business perspective of the same changes.

Why Administration Matters: One Search Example

Have you ever searched a website and been disappointed by the results? Maybe your search for chocolate chip cookies on your favorite recipes website returned no results. What would you do next? With the amount of websites available to choose from today, you're probably heading over to your second favorite recipe website or a search of the Internet. You're less likely to continue on that website when your search comes up with no results. And, you are less likely to return to it in the future.

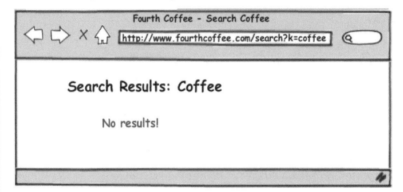

Now, think about the sites for which you have some responsibility in your organization's world of SharePoint. Do you want visitors to your sites staying for more and returning the next time they want to find something you've got there? Of course you do, or you wouldn't have created the site or accepted some responsibility for it in the first place. With your name on the site, you want to make every visit to it rewarding and enjoyable. Understanding administration will help avoid bad experiences like this search example. Ownership of a site in SharePoint doesn't make you an IT professional. You might not be the one pushing the buttons on the computers that host the site, but what that person does affects how your site is perceived. You need every visitor to come away with the information they came for (especially if that visitor is you).

Installation and Configuration Decisions

You might not be the one installing and configuring SharePoint. In fact, based on current common usage over the past few years, 99 percent of SharePoint users will never install it. However, if you expect SharePoint to become an important tool in your work life, you will want to be a part of the planning process that should come before the installation and configuration.

During installation and configuration of SharePoint, important choices are being made that in part determine your user experience. For the health and performance of your Share-Point sites, it's always better that the installation and configuration follows a preset plan that takes into account your needs and those of others in the business community at your organization. Depending on who is responsible for the back-end administrative tasks, you might have the opportunity to tailor the installation and configuration to your exact needs or choose a hosting provider whose terms match your needs.

To get the most out of your effort—both for you and for those with whom you plan to share web content via SharePoint—read this chapter and perform the planning steps before installation. If SharePoint is already installed and configured, many of the decisions have been made. Understanding the effect of this configuration on the pieces you care about will help you decide if you need to make a change.

INSIDE OUT   I've successfully installed Microsoft Word before, and even installed Windows, so why wouldn't I install SharePoint?

SharePoint is a different kind of software from traditional titles that you might be used to. Unlike Word or Windows, which are installed once per computer, one SharePoint install provides services to many computers. SharePoint is installed in one place and then accessed from web browsers like Internet Explorer, Safari, or Firefox by 1 to 100 million people.

For very active installations used by hundreds of people at the same time, SharePoint is installed on more than one server and it might be supported by other servers, such as directory servers to handle all the logons and database servers to hold all the content. When deployed on multiple servers, there will likely be a dedicated IT support staff with specialized skills to maintain this environment.

A List of All Supported Web Browsers

The TechNet article "Plan browser support (SharePoint Server 2010)," located at *http://technet.microsoft.com/en-us/library/cc263526.aspx*, contains the latest support information for all browsers. As of this writing, 32-bit versions of Internet Explorer 7 and Internet Explorer 8 have full support for all collaboration actions in SharePoint 2010. Versions of Safari and Firefox (and 64-bit versions of Internet Explorer) have limited support; these limitations are listed in the TechNet article. The Service Pack 1 for SharePoint Foundation 2010 adds support for Internet Explorer 9 in Standards Mode and Google's Chrome browser. For more details on the features included in this recommended update, read the Service Pack 1 for SharePoint Foundation 2010 White Paper, which you can find at *http://technet.microsoft.com/en-us/library/hh301732.aspx*.

Internet Explorer 6 was not tested with SharePoint 2010 and is not supported. Users viewing SharePoint 2010 sites with Internet Explorer 6 might experience some issues. For the broadest reader base, sites hosted on SharePoint 2010 should be customized and tested for increased support of Internet Explorer 6. In fact, SharePoint 2010 can support any browser for readers at the discretion of the site's designer and the HTML markup used to layout the publishing site.

Hosted SharePoint or On-Premises SharePoint?

Knowing who is responsible for your installation is important so that you know who to go to when you need a change. This responsible party is called your service provider. The location of your installation is called your host. Since your host might not be physically close to you, you depend on your service provider to keep the installation running and make changes.

SharePoint installations normally fall into one of two models: on-premises or hosted.

On-Premises

If the IT staff in your company is comfortable installing, configuring, and maintaining a computer server, you might decide on an *on-premises* installation. In such a situation, the computers running SharePoint 2010 are located within your business or maintained at an off-site data center.

On-premises installation are typically how the majority of SharePoint sites have been implemented. When set up with great in-house IT support and dedicated resources, SharePoint has proven to be a reliable and worthwhile addition to the server rooms of many organizations.

CAUTION

Watch out for the "Under-the-Desk" effect. SharePoint is so easy to download and install that an entire subset of on-premises installations are on desktop workstations. The term "Under-the-Desk" refers to the fact that a careless kick of a foot can turn the power off on the computer hosting the SharePoint site.

These types of installations can quickly prove the value of SharePoint within your organization; watch out for the negative feelings that can quickly occur when a kick of the foot disrupts the work of many others. You might find that one extended outage can quickly cause the loss a lot of user goodwill. A site that regularly experiences outages will not be used by nearly as many people as a reliable site.

If you are using an on-premises installation, Active Directory can be configured to require approval for SharePoint installations on the corporate network. This type of configuration is appropriate when there is a strong desire for centralization of resources or to prevent loss of data resulting from a lack of IT professional support.

Hosted SharePoint

Hosted SharePoint is an opportunity to both get started quickly and have a website that is always available for those who depend on it. If SharePoint isn't running on computers at your business location, you can take advantage of a growing number of online service offerings.

Microsoft has recently introduced the Office 365 service. For as little as $6 per user, per month, you can use servers at a Microsoft data center to host your collaboration site on a SharePoint installation that Microsoft engineers will maintain for you. This is one example of a service made possible by improvements in SharePoint 2010 to support multitenancy.

To learn more about Office 365, go to *http://office365.microsoft.com*.

Previous versions of SharePoint were not as well suited for hosting offsite. The designers of SharePoint 2010 specifically had this "hosted SharePoint" design in mind to allow more people access to SharePoint without the need for dedicated in-house IT support staff and the specialized skills required to install and configure SharePoint.

Offshore and Heavy Customization

If you know that some of your organization's data cannot be stored outside your company facilities or at the physical location of the hosting provider, hosted SharePoint might not be a good fit. At the very least, you and others at your organization are responsible for the information that you post to sites on the Internet, and you must keep this in mind when selecting a provider and deciding what kind of projects to host with the provider. For example, you might come across laws or regulations that prevent you from hosting your data in another country.

Similarly, you might not want to host your site if you plan to apply many customizations to the out-of-the-box features SharePoint provides. If your project requires customizations beyond what can be done from the browser, SharePoint Designer, or sandboxed solutions, hosted SharePoint might not be a good fit. For example, if you would like to install third-party products or give developers full access to customize SharePoint, hosted SharePoint might not provide the flexibility you need.

Sandboxed solutions are a subset of the custom code deployment solution types that are available with SharePoint. They come with restrictions that allow hosting providers to accept their use when resources for your site are shared with others.

Chapter 2

Figure 2-1 summarizes the key strategic points of the on-premises versus hosted SharePoint decision.

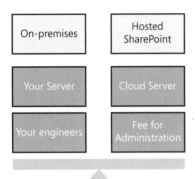

Figure 2-1 SharePoint installation models: on-premises versus hosted installation.

INSIDE OUT   SharePoint moves into the cloud

If you've been following technology news, you've probably read something about the *cloud*. What the cloud really refers to depends on who's saying it, but it can be described as a metaphor for the Internet; simply put, SharePoint in the cloud means running SharePoint as an Internet-based service. If you've ever used web-based email, you understand the benefit of using software running on a server in the cloud.

Cloud-based SharePoint is just another step in the direction away from relying on in-house IT for installation and configuration of every server-based application you use. Sometimes, moving toward a service provider allows a business to benefit from huge economies of scale most businesses can't achieve with their own in-house IT staff.

The SharePoint Structure

Have you ever thought about the way a SharePoint site is built? In the following section, key structural pieces of a SharePoint installation are explained. SharePoint sites often grow organically—the section, "Comparing a SharePoint Web Application to a Tree," later in the chapter, introduces you to the basic building blocks of a SharePoint installation's structure. Table 2-1 lists the nine main SharePoint structural elements of interest.

Table 2-1 **The Definition of Nine Main SharePoint Structural Elements**

Structure element	Definition
Farm	The term farm is used in two main ways. The farm can be considered to be the physical computers and the software required to be running on them to host SharePoint. In addition, each farm's settings are held in a unique Configuration Database stored inside SQL Server.
Service application	A service application runs within a farm to provide capability to the sites hosted on it or another farm.
Content database	The majority of the information added to a SharePoint Site is stored in a content database.
Web application	A SharePoint site is accessed through a web application that provides the address and authentication configuration among other configuration properties. A web application must have a corresponding website in Microsoft's web server, Internet Information Services (IIS).
Site collection	One or more sites that are grouped together into a Site Collection. Sites are organized hierarchically in Site Collections, and some configuration settings and administrative actions applied to Site Collections effect every site in the group.
Site	A site is a logical grouping of content within SharePoint. Each Site Collection has a root site, the main point of entry.
Document library	Document libraries are historically the most used element of a SharePoint site. Library settings control visibility and content types among other critical configuration.
List	The majority of all content in a SharePoint Site is held in a list. Sites have many lists of many types. Even a document library is a list, but a very specialized kind of list with tools designed to work best with documents.
Webpage	In SharePoint 2010, webpages take on new importance for SharePoint sites. Every webpage in SharePoint 2010 is a wiki page with rich text editing capability. Each web page you create from the browser is stored in a document library.

Chapter 2

Comparing a SharePoint Web Application to a Tree

Think of a Web Application as a tree. Each trunk is a Site Collection, with the first site in the collection coming from the same set of roots as the other trunks. The branches are like sites branching off the first site and the leaves are list items and documents.

Some web applications are like a pomegranate tree, which can have more than one trunk in the same tree; SharePoint Server 2010 (a product built on SharePoint Foundation 2010) has a good example of this type of tree, the web application configured to be the My Site Host. Each individual's My Site is itself a Site Collection; in an organization with 80,000 users you would end up with 80,000 Site Collections sprouting out of the same web application root base.

The base address of the application, *my.litware.com*, for example, redirects to the current authenticated user's personal Site Collection, which is located at *http://my.litware.com/personal/<username>*. In this example, you could browse to any other My Site public profile by entering **my.litware.com/personal/** followed by the other user's name (if you know it).

It might help to picture the SharePoint components of a public website like a tree with many trunks and even more main branches. Figure 2-2 illustrates how the web addresses of such a site might map to the tree picture.

Leaves: Pages, Documents and List Items
  Leaves are the content sprouting from the smaller limbs

Smaller Limbs: Lists and Libraries
  Each site has it's own lists and libraries branching off

Main Branches: Sites
  For example, www.litware.com/ from trunk one and
  www.litware.com/sites/Asia from trunk two

Trunk: Site Collection
  This tree has many trunks from the same root base
  For example, www.litware.com and
  www.litware.com/sites/Europe and
  www.litware.com/sites/Asia

Roots: Web Application
For example www.litware.com

Figure 2-2 The SharePoint pomegranate tree.

Many web applications look more like a pecan tree. The pecan tree has one trunk; the Site Collection, has a few thick, strong branches off it, supporting other branches and lots of leaves (not to mention tasty nuts in the fall...). Figure 2-3 illustrates how the web addresses of this type of site might map to a single-trunk tree.

A classic intranet publishing portal matches this version of the metaphor: *http://portal.contoso.com* is the address of the web application and the first site of the Site Collection. The entry page for this web application is at the address *http://portal.contoso.com/pages/welcome.aspx*. Human Resources might have a main trunk site at *http://portal.constoso.com/hr*. Benefits information might be stored in a leaf document library at *http://portal.contoso.com/Locations/Lists/Benefits*. The webpage about medical benefits might be at *http://portal.contoso.com/Locations/Lists/Benefits/Medical.aspx*, with a link to the provider's benefit statement at *http://portal.contoso.com/Locations/Lists/Benefits/ProviderStatement.pdf*.

Leaves: Pages, Documents and List Items
For example, http://portal.contoso.com/Pages/welcome.aspx,
http://portal.contoso.com/Lists/info/benefits.pdf and
http://portal.contoso.com/Locations/Lists/Benefits/ProviderStatement.pdf

Smaller Limbs: Lists and Libraries
For example, http://portal.contoso.com/Pages and
http://portal.contoso.com/Locations/Lists/Benefits

Main Branches: Sites
For example, http://portal.contoso.com/ and http://portal.contoso.com/HR/

Trunk: Site Collection
This tree has one trunk site collection, all the sites belong to it

Roots: Web Application
For example http://portal.contoso.com

Chapter 2

Figure 2-3 The SharePoint pecan tree.

The SharePoint Farm Supports the Web Applications

The SharePoint farm is the set of servers hosting all of the sites and support they need. A farm can have as few as one server, which would host the entire infrastructure needed for a small organization.

SharePoint is very scalable. A farm supporting higher user demand would benefit from a large amount of server resources. Such a farm could be much more like an industrial nut orchard that provides the benefits of its fruit to large amounts of people.

Some service applications provided to the farm are analogous to the water and fertilizer that are applied to an entire orchard. Other service applications are applied with more discretion, similar to spraying insecticide at the site of an infestation. Business Data Connectivity (BDC) is a service that can be applied across all the web applications and the content in their Site Collections. You can configure a connection to a business data source (such as Microsoft CRM) once and provide that data to all the web applications in a farm. In the preceding examples, a workflow that begins when a new client is added in CRM might add a task list item. Because BDC is a shared service, you can make use of the data it provides on a user's My Site or in a department's Team Site from the same BDC source.

The database is important in planning large implementations of SharePoint. You might or might not know about the relationship between SharePoint and the database. The designers of SharePoint chose to leverage the power of the entire Microsoft platform stack. One place mature technology was exploited is the storage of items added to or created in

SharePoint. By taking advantage of the efficient, secure, and reliable platform provided by Microsoft SQL Server, all of those benefits are passed on to the users and administrators of SharePoint sites.

All of the content in a SharePoint 2010 farm is stored in one or more databases on one or more servers running SQL Server. When SharePoint use really takes off in a large organization, it becomes very important to understand the relationship between the items discussed above and a content database.

The relationship of the content database to the web application and Site Collection is explained as follows: one content database holds content from one or more Site Collections of one web application. In the example web applications presented earlier, at least two content databases would be required to hold the two web applications for the My Sites and the intranet. Further, the contents of a single Site Collection must be stored together in the same database; however, one content database can hold the content of multiple Site Collections. A web application can spread out the storage of multiple Site Collections across multiple content databases.

The tree metaphor is helpful to get across many important administrative concepts of SharePoint. Visualizing the structure of your SharePoint environment can be helpful in decisions about content upload, creation of webpages, and new site creation. You will be well on your way toward understanding the structure if you can keep in mind the relationship between the first five main structural elements described previously. The farm, web application, service application, web application, content database, and Site Collection are critical concepts for the intermediate to advanced user of SharePoint who wants to speak to IT professionals about the supporting structures of her SharePoint site or sites.

The Content Database as a Unit of Storage

Of all the SharePoint structural concepts introduced so far, the content database might be the most important point to understand toward achieving a very successful SharePoint implementation. If the users in your organization begin to depend on SharePoint for hosting all of their critical files, lists, and webpages, the amount of storage used can grow dramatically. You can take your understanding of the tree metaphor, add your understanding of content databases, and apply it to an example where quick storage growth becomes a challenge for performance and stability of the SharePoint implementation. You will also be able to see how the same elements can explain the solution.

Let's go back to the intranet portal example and assume that the entire organizational structure was represented in the site structure such as the Human Resources department. A common business structure might have sites for Sales, Marketing, and Operations. Teams under those groups might also receive sites below their parent group site. As more and more sites are created with more and more members of the organization creating and uploading documents, pictures, list items, and webpages, the one content database for this one tree in the orchard is storing all the content.

This implementation is a classic example of three issues common in successful SharePoint implementations: 1) disorganization of information; 2) delays backing up and restoring the content; and 3) deteriorating performance of the entire web application. All of these issues occur gradually over time, so a great approach is to be aware and monitor growth and change and plan for reorganization or new hardware purchases ahead of time.

Using a Content Database as a Unit of Backup and Restoration

First, consider the case of backing up and restoring the content of your intranet in this example. A successful SharePoint implementation with a SharePoint structure like this can result in a database measured in terabytes of storage space. If you've ever tried to back up a 200 GB hard disk, you understand the amount of time it requires to save your important information.

The amount of time it takes to back up data is affected by two critical restore parameters. The first is how often data can be backed up; if it takes eight hours to back up the content database and you only run one backup at a time, your SharePoint content will only be safely backed up once during a business day. For certain tasks at some organizations, it is acceptable to lose a day's worth of information; for others, losing even a minute of information could be trouble.

The second restore parameter affected by large content databases is the amount of time it takes to restore. Again, it is up to the task and the organization to determine how long is too long. However, in some situations, waiting a day for SharePoint to be restored after a disaster or an unexpected failure is just too long.

INSIDE OUT   Your backups might be interrupting SharePoint operations

You might not care for the full detail of the backup operation, but as a site user and business influencer, some backup details are important to pay attention to. Certain types of backup operations can diminish your SharePoint experience. For example, the method called the Site Collection Backup requires that the Site Collection is placed in a Read-Only mode for the duration of the backup. Other types of backups are resource intensive and might cause competition with user operations. Both issues can be mitigated by scheduling backup tasks during off hours if you do not run a 24-hour operation. Awareness of how and when your backups are running can help you to understand the performance implications for your users.

Managing Content Database Size for Performance

Next, consider the case of deteriorating performance in your web application. In a really large content database, there are probably a few ways performance can be affected. One of the biggest performance issues in large SharePoint 2007 implementations is that of the large list. SharePoint 2010 has been improved in many ways in how it deals with large lists. The effect of a large list on the performance of a web application has been reduced, but there is still a chance that you might be affected by it.

The detail of why large lists impact performance is mostly uninteresting to the average SharePoint user. The highlight is that a database can be locked in certain situations and one of these can occur with large lists. A lock occurs on the database level when more than 5,000 items in a list are queried at one time. During this lock, all other reads and writes for all lists in all Site Collections are queued until the previous transaction is complete and the lock is released. When a database is locked, everyone accessing the database experiences a delay in receiving results. If this lock situation happens in the one database holding all the content for your one Site Collection holding all the sites for every group in your organization, many people will be unhappy.

If you or someone in your organization is interested in the full technical details of database locking in SharePoint, read the White Paper, "Working with large lists in Office SharePoint Server 2007," which you can download at *http://technet.microsoft.com/en-us/library/cc262813(office.12).aspx*. **Although written for 2007, the database and list fundamentals still apply in the 2010 version of the product. Many of the SharePoint Customization issues detailed in the White Paper have been addressed, but the underlying principle of locking is still possible (and well explained by the paper).**

Organizing for Content Database Growth

Finally, consider the case of disorganization of information. This one is probably not hard to imagine if you've been using a computer for many years and you've ever lost a file on your hard disk or a file share. Over time, file storage tends to become filled with documents that are rarely accessed and out of date. The same can happen to any kind of content in a SharePoint site. Remember that a SharePoint site is intended to be dynamic; therefore, you need to plan accordingly. Identify the areas that are important to the users of your site. Plan to repeatedly highlight timely, relevant information. Collect feedback from your users on organization and usefulness to ensure that your growing site meets not just your needs, but the needs of your collaborators, as well.

The best case scenario for your organization is to plan ahead of time and accommodate growth where anticipated. SharePoint sites intended for team collaboration and document sharing tend to grow in database size over time. Document sharing sites are popular, but they can often be isolated into Site Collections by audience. Site collections are natural security and audience boundaries. Interaction within a legal team, for example, deserves this type of isolation for the sensitivity of the information alone. However, other teams can also follow the model, whereby internally important information is contributed on one Site Collection and more generally interesting information is uploaded to a shared portal. Again, if we look to the SharePoint Product Team's example of building out My Sites in SharePoint Server, we see this model in its extreme. A My Site gives a user a place to upload content and control access in his own Site Collection. If the team designing SharePoint puts that architecture forward as a model, you can feel safe in assigning small to medium sized project teams similar workspaces that they can control.

Creating Site Collections for unique audiences reduces the amount of content in each Site Collection. The added benefit beyond security is added mobility of the content within the content database. Individual Site Collections can be moved between content databases with more flexibility than sites or lists. Also, storage size quotas can be placed on Site Collections but not sites or lists. If the size of a content database becomes an operational issue, the ability to move content to reduce the size of existing databases becomes a big benefit.

If you find yourself in the situation where too much content has been added too quickly, there is good news. Others have been through this before and strategies have been developed to overcome all three of these issues related to the inevitable growth in a successful SharePoint implementation. For example, if you find that you want to reduce your backup or restore period time, there are two possible paths. Relying on IT professional analysis if necessary, identify if the current read or write speed for your content database storage, your backup storage, or the network in between can be increased by the purchase of new hardware or optimization of the current hardware.

At the same time, use your understanding of the SharePoint structure to look at how you might reorganize your sites to meet your goals. If all of your sites are currently held in one Site Collection and subsequently, one content database, you have an opportunity to create a new Site Collection in a new content database where existing sites can be moved. However, moving is always stressful and sometimes items become lost in the move. Professional tools and consultants will help you move more quickly with less loss, but there is always a cost associated with that kind of help. The best strategy is to be proactive and move early. If you identify the level of service you need from SharePoint and you can estimate when potential support milestones will be hit, you can build a roadmap for potential changes ahead.

The time to backup or restore is a common service level requirement for electronic information. When you leverage the Site Collection as a mobile unit of SharePoint Content, you can arrange your Content Databases to accomplish your service level requirements. In a common method of backup, the Content Database is the container that is backed up or restored. Moving your most critical Site Collections to a new content database will allow your IT professionals to backup and restore those sites more quickly. If you consider this type of reorganization, keep in mind that you can host multiple Site Collections under one web application. In that way, you can maintain one base web address for multiple Site Collections and reduce the backup and restore time of your most critical information.

Search Administration

Search is one of the most powerful pieces of functionality Microsoft has provided with the SharePoint product. Think about how often you use search on the Internet. Is a web search engine one of the most frequently accessed websites in your browser? If you are taking advantage of the large amount of information available on the web through search, you probably don't have to stretch your imagination too much to see how search can benefit you in SharePoint, as well. A great SharePoint search experience can help you tap into the information you and your colleagues create on computers about and for your organization.

For a public search versus SharePoint search example, consider a scenario similar to one you might have already experienced if you've worked in a business that sells directly to consumers: a search on the topic of customer service on the general Internet. Using an ad-sponsored, public web search engine, you might find links to the mostly highly-rated books on customer service, online articles on the subject, and opinions about customer service experiences at lots of other businesses.

Using a well-configured SharePoint search against your own webpages and files, your results will be more refined and specific to the needs of your organization. If the material is there, you should expect to find customer service guidelines, training materials, or experiences that relate specifically to your product and customer. Understanding SharePoint search better will help you maximize the benefit of search against the information your organization has captured electronically.

Search Products

The search products deployed and configured in your SharePoint farm can have a big effect on the search experience in your SharePoint sites. Microsoft provides three different search products that integrate well with SharePoint Foundation 2010. Beyond SharePoint Foundation 2010 Search, you might consider integrating Search Server 2010 Express or the full Search Server 2010 with your SharePoint installation.

In addition to these three products, you have two options for upgrading search when you move to SharePoint Server. Table 2-2 lists all of the available search features by product in the SharePoint family with which they are installed. For example, the table shows that SharePoint Server adds a number of social search options around people. If People search is important to your organization, the improved search features of SharePoint Server 2010 might be enough of a reason for you to consider upgrading from SharePoint Foundation 2010. FAST Search Server 2010 for SharePoint is an add-on to SharePoint Server. FAST goes beyond even the search features of SharePoint Server and provides yet another upgrade option for organizations that need to go beyond the search options available in SharePoint Foundation installations. Learning more about these five search products will help you to take advantage of which product you currently have available and understand how you might benefit from one the other options.

Table 2-2 **Search Product Comparison**

Feature	SharePoint Foundation 2010	Search Server 2010 Express	Search Server 2010	SharePoint Server 2010	FAST Search Server 2010 for SharePoint
Basic site search	Y	Y	Y	Y	Y
Best Bets		Y	Y	Y	Y
Visual Best Bets					Y
Similar results					Y
Duplicate results	Y	Y	Y	Y	Y
Search scopes		Y	Y	Y	Y
RSS feeds for search results	Y	Y	Y	Y	Y
Alerts for search results	Y*	Y*	Y*	Y*	
Advanced search page		Y	Y	Y	Y
Search enhancement based on user contexts					Y
Crawled and managed properties		Y	Y	Y	Y**
Entity extraction					Y
Query federation		Y	Y	Y	Y
Query suggestions		Y	Y	Y	Y
Sort results on managed properties or rank profiles					Y
Relevancy tuning by document or site promotions		Y	Y	Y	Y**
Shallow results refinement		Y	Y	Y	Y
Deep results refinement					Y
Document preview					Y
Windows 7 federation		Y	Y	Y	Y
People search				Y	Y

Chapter 2

Feature	SharePoint Foundation 2010	Search Server 2010 Express	Search Server 2010	SharePoint Server 2010	FAST Search Server 2010 for SharePoint
Phonetic name search***				Y	Y
Nickname search***				Y	Y
Self search				Y	Y

*For NT LAN Manager (NTLM) environments
**FAST Search Server 2010 for SharePoint provides enhanced capabilities in these areas.
***For a subset of the supported languages

SharePoint Foundation 2010 Search

Search Server Express will be introduced in the next section. Search Server Express is another free product that extends SharePoint Foundation. Many organizations will take advantage of the benefits of this free product and will not rely on the search features of SharePoint Foundation alone. However, you might not have Search Server Express installed on your server, so this first search section is a baseline on the out-of-the-box functionality inherent to SharePoint Foundation 2010.

Table 2-2 is excerpted from the book *Getting Started with Enterprise Search in SharePoint 2010 Products*, which you can download free of charge from Microsoft TechNet. You can see from the table that Microsoft's premier search platform, FAST Search Server 2010 for SharePoint, provides eight times the features of SharePoint Foundation 2010 Search. However, basic site search and the other three features included with SharePoint Foundation provide a solid base to start working with SharePoint Search.

To download *Getting Started with Enterprise Search in SharePoint 2010 Products*, **go to** *http://technet.microsoft.com/en-us/library/ff631149.aspx.*

When configured correctly, SharePoint Foundation 2010 Search will crawl all of the pages, list items, and documents in your SharePoint sites. It will index the titles and content of those search items. It will provide a basic search interface for you to query the index and retrieve results. And it will do all of this in an intuitive, easy-to-use and manage manner with excellent relevancy in the results. No matter the amount of features added through the upgraded search products, this base crawl, index, and query functionality remains relatively similar.

Adding functionality to SharePoint Foundation 2010 Search by adding another search product is the first search upgrade consideration you might plan for. However, the number of items that can be accessed from search is an important limitation. There are item limits for all five search products including FAST, which is a dedicated search product engineered for maximum scalability. The number of items that you can use effectively with SharePoint Foundation 2010 search can be limited by the version of SQL Server installed and licensed for your

SharePoint farm. If you are using SharePoint Foundation 2010 with the freely available SQL Server Express product, expect to hit a search bottleneck around 300,000 searchable items; this number is a rough estimate by the Microsoft SharePoint Product Team (refer to the figure in the Inside Out that follows), but it gives you an idea of the level at which a problem might start. If your organization uses a license for SQL Server beyond the free license, the search item limit for your SharePoint Farm is around 10 million items per search server.

The item limits related to the SQL Server license apply to Search Server 2010 Express in the same way that they apply to SharePoint Foundation. In theory, SharePoint Foundation search has one benefit over Search Server 2010 Express: with SharePoint Foundation, you can scale to more than one search server. However, given the limited feature set of Share-Point Foundation 2010 Search, it is more likely that you will benefit from one of the other search products at the point you need to scale out to additional servers.

INSIDE OUT   Scalability in Enterprise Search

The figure that follows illustrates how much scale factors into the product decision for SharePoint Search for the Enterprise. The graphic is excerpted from Microsoft's excellent technical diagrams for SharePoint Foundation 2010 (specifically the Search Technologies for SharePoint 2010 Products, located at *http://technet.microsoft.com/en-us/library/ee806874.aspx*).

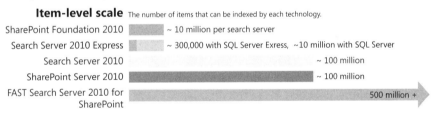

Item-level scale The number of items that can be indexed by each technology.

SharePoint Foundation 2010	~ 10 million per search server
Search Server 2010 Express	~ 300,000 with SQL Server Exress, ~10 million with SQL Server
Search Server 2010	~ 100 million
SharePoint Server 2010	~ 100 million
FAST Search Server 2010 for SharePoint	500 million +

The numbers are based on assumptions about the limits of acceptable delay to your users on recommended server hardware. You can see that entry level products start you at a capacity of around 300,000 items available from your SharePoint search. The items included in the limit will include all the webpages from SharePoint or other websites, documents stored on SharePoint Sites, or Networked File Shares and other sources that SharePoint is configured to make available to search or keep in the search index.

For many organizations, this might be adequate to get started. However, you can see from the diagram, that the number of searchable items alone might determine your base search product requirement. Keep in mind that the higher numbers come from the ability of the products to distribute work to additional servers. If you need to search more than 10 million items, you will need Search Server 2010 or greater as well as more servers.

Chapter 2

Search Server 2010 and Search Server 2010 Express

In parallel to the SharePoint 2010 products release, Microsoft released a related product, Microsoft Search Server 2010. Search Server 2010 is a standalone product that can be used to provide a web-based search experience for any website, but it works very well in combination with SharePoint Foundation 2010. The free version of Search Server, named Search Server 2010 Express, includes all of the features of the licensed product—the one important difference between the two is scale. Search Server 2010 Express is limited to one search server and around 10 million searchable items. When you need to search more items in one farm, you will need to license the full product.

Both versions add great capabilities over the out-of-the-box search included with SharePoint Foundation 2010. And either version of Search Server 2010 can be used to replace the base search functionality of SharePoint Foundation 2010.

If you refer again to Table 2-2, you can see a number of features listed out that are added when compared to SharePoint Foundation 2010 Search. Figure 2-4 highlights the links added in your Site Settings page when Search Server has been installed.

Figure 2-4 Search Server Express adds three new menu items in your Site Collection site settings menu. The image on the left shows the items on the list without Search Server Express installed.

Figure 2-5 shows the Search Scope drop-down menu available with the addition of Search Server. Search Scopes are especially useful as the number and complexity of SharePoint sites grow. By selecting a scope with your query, you can limit search results to a particular Site Collection, site, document library, or list, allowing quick retrieval from large document libraries or lists in particular. If you'd like to set up search scopes as shown in Figure 2-5, you must add a new site based on the Search Center site template that will be installed with Search Server Express. The search settings link shown in Figure 2-4 opens a page on which you can set the address of the new Search Center site to enable the All Sites feature of the Search Scope drop-down list.

Figure 2-5 Search Scope can be set to add a drop-down menu to your search box on every page.

Crawled and managed properties are also added with Search Server. These properties will be set up in cooperation with an IT professional with access to the Central Administration of the SharePoint farm. When used effectively, these additional search properties give the opportunity to present search results effectively, sometimes even without a user initiated search query.

Figure 2-6 shows an example of an advanced search results page with refinement options on the left menu. The advanced search page allows more control over the search query and allows more exact results. Results refinement adds a panel to the search results page with which you can toggle whole sets of results on or off. For example, if your search results return a large number of documents, but you know you are looking for a certain type—for example, a Microsoft PowerPoint presentation—you can easily remove the other document types from the results.

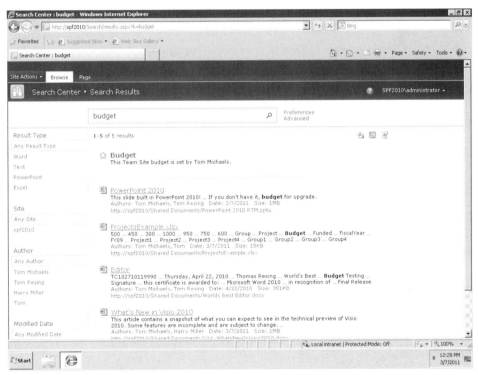

Figure 2-6 SharePoint Foundation with Search Server Express displays the results of a search using the keyword "budget." Notice the refinement pane on the left.

In addition to the above features provided by Search Server 2010, you gain the ability to extend your search index beyond SharePoint sites. When Search Server 2010 is configured correctly to replace the out-of-the-box search, SharePoint search can return results from

Windows file shares, Exchange public folders, Lotus Notes, and non-SharePoint websites. Adding even more functionality, Search Server extends Business Connectivity Services (BCS) so you can search structured content from databases and other external sources. Search Server 2010 even accommodates custom plug-ins for non-SharePoint content to be searched from SharePoint.

Overall, Search Server Express is a very good addition to your SharePoint farm with no additional license cost. Besides the business user improvements included in this section, there are benefits for your IT staff, as well. In Central Administration they will find an improved administration user interface that allows for easier operation of search.

For a full description of all of the features in Search Server and the free Express version, read *Professional Microsoft Search: FAST Search, SharePoint Search, and Search Server* by Mark Bennett, Jeff Fried, Miles Kehoe, and Natalya Voskresenskaya (Wrox).

SharePoint Server 2010 Search

The capabilities of Search Server 2010 are included in SharePoint Server 2010. If you choose to move from SharePoint Foundation 2010 to SharePoint Server 2010, you will get the added features and scalability discussed in the preceding section. In addition, search in SharePoint Server 2010 can take advantage of My Sites. My Sites, combined with Search, provide a user directory capability called people search (neither people search nor My Sites are available in SharePoint Foundation 2010). People search was a popular feature with previous versions of SharePoint Server, and it was enhanced with the 2010 version of the product. Because of its ability to connect you to a relevant colleague, people search can be a critical decision point in licensing SharePoint Server 2010.

FAST Search Server for SharePoint 2010

The Enterprise Search Platform named FAST was acquired by Microsoft during the SharePoint 2010 development cycle. Microsoft was able to release a new server product based on the technology acquired with FAST in parallel with the SharePoint 2010 product release. FAST Search Server for SharePoint 2010 adds a number of features beyond the other search products. It also allows nearly unlimited scalability, so you can search very large collections of information. In limited scenarios, FAST Search Server for SharePoint 2010 might be used to index SharePoint Foundation 2010 sites, though it is likely the search interface would be provided by SharePoint Server 2010.

Search Results Freshness

Do you want your search results to represent the most up to date information from your SharePoint site? Most users of search engines do, and SharePoint search users are not much different. Any search engine will take some time to consume and process the information you add to your sites. After all, when you search against a properly configured SharePoint site, your results come from the contents of every document, list item, and page on the site.

The delay you see between when a document is added and when it shows in search results can be reduced by proper planning. From the most basic search engine included with SharePoint Foundation through the enterprise class FAST Search Server, configuration decisions and the amount of information to be searched and your hardware resources combine to determine how fresh the search results are.

The search crawl is an automated exploration of the content in your SharePoint sites. The crawler is given a starting address or SharePoint Site and it explores every link or list item found from the start. It crawls until it finds every page and item on the site. At each location, the crawler marks changes for inclusion in the search index. When you search from a SharePoint site, your query goes to the index, which determines the results you see. Freshness comes into play when you search for a newly added document or page and it is not returned in the results. If this happens frequently or all your results seem to be from older content, you might want to investigate how often, if at all, your search crawls are scheduled.

The search engine included in SharePoint Foundation only allows one schedule for all SharePoint content. This might be a decision point for upgrading to one of the other search products that are compatible and integrated. Search Server Express is free and provides more control over crawl schedules; it can also crawl file shares and websites that are not hosted on SharePoint.

When you have some content sources for which it is more important to keep fresh search results and you've hit the limits of the out-of-the-box search engine, you can improve search freshness by upgrading and then scheduling separate crawls of some content sources. A member of your farm administration team will be configuring your SharePoint Search crawl schedule. You and your users will be seeing the effects of the configuration. If search results aren't fresh, you must communicate this to your operations team to be diagnosed and addressed. Ensuring that search results are fresh is one of the great benefits of having your own in-house search engine and results.

TROUBLESHOOTING

When you think your search results are out of date and you'd like to be sure.
You already know that you don't want inconsistent or out-of-date search results—it's disappointing for you and your users. But how can you tell when Search isn't configured properly? One way is to search for a keyword contained in a recently uploaded document. Figure 2-7 shows an example of search results the day after uploading a document. If you can't find documents with recent dates in your search results, it might be a sign that your search engine could use some tuning or repair.

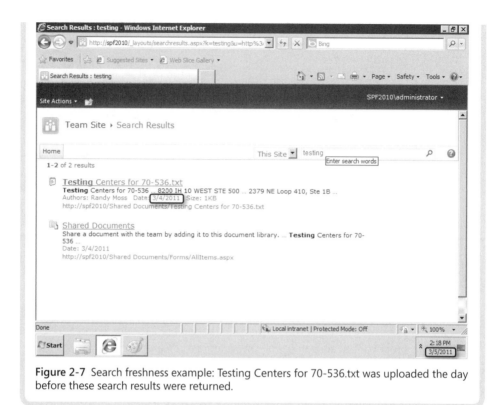

Figure 2-7 Search freshness example: Testing Centers for 70-536.txt was uploaded the day before these search results were returned.

Security

SharePoint offers secure, web-based collaboration that is easy to set up. Security options are pervasive throughout the product. You'll find information about security's role in different contexts in various chapters of this book. The focus of this section, as well as the rest of the chapter, is on security options in the product that are often hidden from you as an advanced business user. Whether you are preparing for a new SharePoint installation, making configuration changes, or you just want to learn more about security, pay close attention to the rest of this section.

> **Note**
> Most of what applies to security at this level for SharePoint Foundation 2010 also applies for SharePoint Server 2010.

Authentication and Authorization

Regardless of the secure application, two important security principles to understand are authentication and authorization. Authentication is the method of identifying the current user of the application. Authorization is the access the user has within the application. Together, these two concepts provide a means for securing your SharePoint Sites.

Most important authentication settings are configured by IT at the web application level. An example of the effect of these settings is when and how you are prompted for logon information to a SharePoint site. Your business needs determine how the web application should be configured for authentication.

On the other hand, authorization settings are pervasive throughout the product. In fact, the number of places and ways SharePoint can be configured for access has increased over previous versions of the product. For example, Microsoft responded to customers' needs to limit the access IT professionals have to content and settings that only business users need to see or set. A properly configured SharePoint Foundation 2010 web application allows content to be secured so that you, as the site owner, have the final say as to who sees what on your site. However, if you desire this level of security to your site, be sure to discuss this with your site host to guarantee the proper safeguards are in place. For example, SharePoint Foundation provides auditing of item and page views, updates, and deletes, but it is not configured by default.

INSIDE OUT   Authentication isn't just for the Internet browser

Authentication settings configured by IT can be critical to your SharePoint solution's ultimate level of success or failure. Also, these settings often determine your ease of use. For example, the Office Integration Features depend on the proper authentication settings for the web application and your client environment.

The Connect To Outlook button, visible on a SharePoint Calendar, is one place that an incorrect configuration for your environment can have an effect. If your web application is set to use forms-based authentication and your Outlook client does not have the latest update that works with this setting, clicking the button will have no effect. This type of error is one of the quickest ways to lose the trust of your visitors because it gives no indication of what is wrong. If you were the visitor who clicked a button that doesn't do what you expected, would you get the feeling the site is not working? Some visitors might lose confidence in the entire solution after a few experiences like that because they are not sure what will work and what is broken or why.

Types of Authentication

The five most common authentication types are outlined in this section. Each of these authentication types play a part in the secure web scenarios presented in the next section. Of the five, the classic Windows authentication has been most common in past SharePoint deployments and it is the type that SharePoint has supported most completely over the course of the product's history. In contrast, claims-based authentication is newly introduced in the 2010 versions of the product to broaden the scope of authentication approaches used for SharePoint sites. For example, you can use claims-based authentication to allow Windows Live ID accounts to authenticate against your SharePoint site.

Classic Windows Integrated

Classic Windows integrated authentication is the default option when creating a new web application, so it might be very commonly in use. It is also the option most similar to the Windows integrated authentication in the previous versions of SharePoint.

Claims-Based Windows Integrated

Claims authentication is new for SharePoint 2010, but it is also the recommended setting for new web applications. Upgrades from SharePoint 2007 can also use this setting, but if customizations are being upgraded, they might need code changes to work with the new security model. You will know claims-based Windows integrated authentication is in use when you see an account name with a short prefix before a pipe symbol (|). Compare the account name in Figure 2-8 to the account name displayed in Figure 2-9. The latter is an example of the User Information Display with a classic Windows integrated authentication web application. The prefix distinguishes user accounts with the same name in more than one identity provider. For example, if your user name was the same on *www.live.com* and in Windows, the prefix is the way you can keep track of two SharePoint accounts for the same user name.

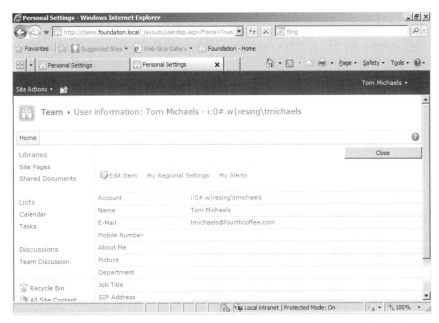

Figure 2-8 An example of a User Information Page with claims-based Windows integrated authentication.

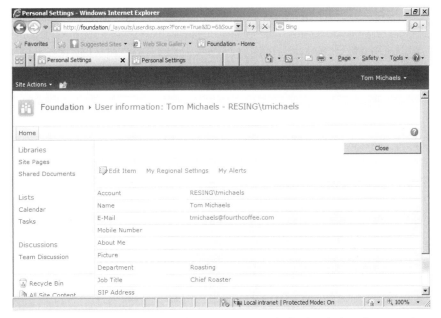

Figure 2-9 An example of a User Information Page with classic Windows integrated authentication.

Forms-Based (with Claims)

In a change from the previous version, forms-based authentication can only be enabled with claims in SharePoint 2010. This type of authentication is popular in extranet scenarios because it doesn't require an Active Directory account for each authenticated user. However, you might find that certain features don't work as well with this setup. Particularly challenging is Office integration without the latest versions of the Office clients.

Claims-Based Without Windows

Claims-based without Windows authentication is where SharePoint 2010 really starts to differentiate itself from the previous version of the product. This authentication method allows some advanced scenarios but also requires more complexity on the back end. If you require claims-based authentication without Windows integration, keep in mind that this is a new technology, and it might take some time for the administration best practices to be established. If you need to integrate with some external types of identification systems, like Windows Live authentication, this can be a good option.

Anonymous Access

Anonymous access is most commonly used with publishing sites that are public facing, but might also make sense within a very large organization where many readers access the site, but only a few content authors publish information. Anonymous access can be used in combination with the previous four authentication types on one web application. Be sure to provide your content publishers with a way to log on through a link published on your intranet or on the page in the public site. In addition to the IT settings for the web application, ensure that you enable your site for anonymous access in the permissions settings of your Site Collection settings.

> **Note**
> You can read more about authentication methods and modes on Microsoft's TechNet website in the section Plan Authentication Methods, at *http://technet.microsoft.com/ en-us/library/cc262350.aspx*.

Securing Web Applications

There are three common scenarios for web application security needs:

1. Public websites available for anyone on the Internet to read

2. Secured intranets for use only by users of one organization

3. Secured extranets for access by visitors across more than one organization

Public Websites

For the first scenario, your web application might be configured by IT for both anonymous access, for readers, and authenticated access of any type, for content authors. If your business needs demand extra security through separation of authoring from reading environments, you would need two separate web applications, possibly in different SharePoint farms and you would need a method to copy the content between the two.

> ### Note
>
> For public websites with complex workflows, you might consider upgrading to SharePoint Server. SharePoint Server provides the publishing site templates and authoring process designed for sites with many more readers than writers.
>
> If you are unable to move to SharePoint Server, but your organization requires the security of a read-only public Internet presence, you have at least one out-of-the-box option, though it is manual. One method for moving the information is by copying the content database backup from an authoring farm to a production farm. When the backup is restored for reading, all the authored content will be moved over without the need for anyone to have access to change it.

Secured Intranets

Secured intranets are probably the most common use of SharePoint technologies over all versions of the product. Windows integrated authentication is a great choice for this scenario because it provides a great user experience. When all of the users of a SharePoint installation are members of the Active Directory domain, you can avoid logon prompts in many scenarios. Also, a secured intranet environment is most likely to benefit from the maturity of the Office client integration with SharePoint when combined with Windows integrated authentication. The other types of authentication will also work in this scenario, but they do increase the complexity of the configuration for the SharePoint farm's host IT staff.

Secured Extranets

Secured extranets are a special case because they often involve collaboration between members of more than one organization. This scenario in particular is a great example for the use of claims-based authentication and how it might be of the most use to you.

The implementation of claims in SharePoint 2010 uses open standards. The use of open standards for authentication allows integration with a wide and growing amount of identification systems. So, when you use claims to authenticate your SharePoint web application, you might be able to allow more users from outside organizations with greater ease.

Chapter 2

As mentioned earlier, forms-based authentication has historically been a popular option for extranets because it provides the option to use an account database to store user account information (instead of Active Directory). Whether you use forms-based authentication with Active Directory or another user directory, you might want to invest in a firewall such as Microsoft Forefront Threat Management Gateway (TMG). TMG integrates well with SharePoint and provides an extra layer of protection beyond the security provided through SharePoint and Windows Server.

INSIDE OUT   For new implementations, start with what you know

Does your organization use some version of Microsoft Office and Windows on most computers? Are you familiar with logging on to a network driven by a Windows Server? If you are like a large amount of SharePoint users, those pieces are probably true. If that is the case, you're lucky because it's also the sweet spot of SharePoint.

Historically, SharePoint adoption has been high when people need a place to share Office documents on a Windows-based network. That is why such a focus had been placed on classic Windows authentication in past versions and why it was the default option for many SharePoint 2007 implementations. If you are starting from a clean slate in 2010, claims-based windows integration is the suggested starting point. Claims-based Windows integration offers the benefits of classic Windows authentication with the flexibility of claims management for future enhancements. On the other hand, if you're a communications professional, and you want a way to get your organization's message out to a large number of people—internally or externally—you will probably be comfortable with anonymous access to your SharePoint sites. SharePoint offers lots of authentication options, but you don't have to use them all. Simple plans can yield powerful results.

More Security Settings at the Web Application Level

SharePoint Foundation 2010 includes other security features that are configured outside the Site Collection that you might want to take advantage of. Each of the following features has settings that must be configured by the farm administrator at the web application level. Configuring each can have a significant effect on all of the Site Collections in a web application.

Extended Web Applications for Your Site Collection

In some cases, you might need more than one method of authentication for your Share-Point sites. The previous section described the authentication options that are available for your web application. Public websites can allow anonymous authentication and another method, but other combinations require some additional changes.

For example, you might want multiple forms of authentication for an extranet. You might use forms-based authentication for extranet users outside your organization so that you don't need to add them to your internal directory. You also might use your existing Active Directory Domain Services to provide identification for your internal users so that they don't have to learn a new password.

In this case, you would like your IT staff to extend the web application to include an additional authentication method at a new web address. In this way, you effectively have two doors into your SharePoint house. One is locked with Active Directory, the other with a database of external user names and passwords.

User Policy on a Web Application

In the previous section, authentication is described as the way of identifying the person who has logged on to your SharePoint site; authorization defines what SharePoint resources the identified person is allowed to access. You can read about controlling permissions for Site Collections, sites, lists, libraries, and individual content items later in this book.

The User Policy setting is an important authorization setting that affects authorization on your sites; configuration of this setting is left up to the IT staff supporting your SharePoint web application. The User Policy setting defines global authorization rights to a user for all the Site Collections in a web application.

CAUTION

Ask for your IT staff to communicate changes made to this setting. Changes aren't visible to site or Site Collection administrators. And, the user policy changes override the authorization set by sites and Site Collections administrators. There are some valid reasons for user policy changes, but understanding SharePoint security is crucial to getting the best value out of your SharePoint sites. You can put yourself in the driver's seat of your Site Collection by requesting information such as this from your operational staff, if it is not already clearly documented in the support policy or service level agreements.

Self-Service Site Collection Creation

An IT professional can enable Self-Service Site Creation on each web application individually. This will give the specified users permission to create new Site Collections in a web application. Did you notice the disconnect between the last two sentences? The former uses the word site and the latter the words Site Collection. The former is the wording used in Central Administration, but it would be clearer if it used the words Site Collection in the place of the word site.

There is a big difference between creating a Site Collection and a site. As a site administrator, you control the permission of users to create sites below your site; however, those sites are all contained within one collection of sites. On the other hand, allowing creation of Site Collections can be useful, as well. Each Site Collection provides a unique security boundary, a storage quota, and a context boundary. Often, Self-Service Site Collection Creation is extended with customizations. For example, it might be useful to track the reasons the Site Collection is needed and the length of time it will be needed for. My Sites are an example of this type of customization that has been added to SharePoint Foundation in SharePoint Server. To start, each My Site is provisioned through Self-Service Site Creation when first accessed by the owner of the site. SharePoint Server includes a workflow for decommissioning the site when the user is deactivated in Active Directory. While it is not necessary to upgrade from Foundation to Server to use Self-Service Site Creation, the SharePoint Product team provides a model of this feature's use in the prime example of extending SharePoint Foundation, SharePoint Server.

Enabling Client Integration

Forms-based authentication can be useful, as described in the authentication section earlier. However, it doesn't work well in some situations such as SharePoint integration with older versions of Office. If your site uses forms-based authentication and the visitors to your site encounter problems with older versions of Office, you can ask to have this setting disabled at the web application level. Disabling client integration can prevent errors that otherwise are confusing. However, some features, such as the Edit In Datasheet option for lists in the browser will also be disabled for all users when client integration is disabled.

Encryption

You're probably familiar with encryption for purposes such as securing online banking. Banks add this layer of security because without it, all information passed over the Internet is sent in clear text that can be captured and read by anyone between you and your bank. If your SharePoint site contains information that is sensitive, you will want encryption configured for your web application. Ask your IT staff to purchase and install a Secure Sockets Layer (SSL) certificate on the web servers and configure your web application for encryption. You will know when you are accessing an encrypted site when the web address begins with HTTPS instead of the normal HTTP prefix.

Another situation for which encryption is important is when your site's authentication doesn't encrypt user names and passwords. For example, forms-based authentication should always be used in combination with encryption to ensure the security of your Share-Point sites.

> **Note**
> Windows authentication, either with claims or classic mode, securely authenticates users without the additional need for encryption to secure user names and passwords. However, it is still a good practice to encrypt your site if other personal or sensitive information might be sent to or from your website besides user names and passwords.

Chapter 2

Upgrades and Migration

If you've been managing a website previously and would like to move it to a SharePoint Foundation 2010 environment, you have two choices for bringing over the content: upgrade and migration. Upgrade and migration are often confused because they both cover moving content into SharePoint; however, there are distinct differences between the two. Understanding the choices available to you will help make the decision easier when you do choose to plan and execute a move.

For more details, download the Microsoft TechNet Guide "Upgrading to Microsoft SharePoint Foundation 2010," which is tailored to administrators and IT professionals who are upgrading to SharePoint Foundation 2010. You can download the guide at *http://go.microsoft.com/ FWLink/?Linkid=196159*.

Upgrading from Windows SharePoint Services Version 3

Microsoft supports upgrades from Windows SharePoint Services Version 3 to SharePoint Foundation 2010.

Upgrade Approaches

If your current site or sites are running on Windows SharePoint Services Version 3 with at least Service Pack 2 installed, you and your IT staff might have two approaches to choose from when directly upgrading to SharePoint Foundation: in-place upgrade and content database upgrade.

In-Place Upgrade

If you are directly responsible for all of the sites in one Windows SharePoint Services farm, you might work directly with IT to execute an in-place upgrade. The entire farm will be upgraded at one time with this approach—for better or worse. A coordinated effort is necessary if the farm to be upgraded supports multiple groups within an organization.

An in-place upgrade is a lot like upgrading your personal computer's operating system from one major version to another. In some cases, it can seem like the simplest option, but (as with a personal computer upgrade) you are using the same computer before, during, and after the upgrade.

There are good reasons to think twice before taking what might seem like the easy upgrade path. If the upgrade fails, the entire SharePoint environment will be unavailable until either, a) the failure is corrected, or b) the environment is restored to its previous state from backups.

Before using this approach there are some important steps you and your IT staff must take to safeguard your content. These steps are outlined in the Caution elements that follow.

> **CAUTION**
>
> If something goes wrong during the upgrade, you risk being left without a working system in Windows SharePoint Services or SharePoint Foundation. You must have a *tested* backup and restore process before you attempt an in-place upgrade. Ask the IT staff to show you the restored SharePoint sites from a test restore before executing an in-place upgrade on your production data. If the restored sites match your existing sites to your satisfaction, you can be sure that an in-place upgrade can be repeated if it fails. Regardless of your upgrade approach, verifying the completeness of your restore process is a great way to ensure that you have working backups of your important information contained in your SharePoint sites.

INSIDE OUT   **Old hardware and software can negate the simplicity of the in-place upgrade approach**

Your existing SharePoint farm must meet hardware and software requirements that were not common in 2007 when many systems were built with the previous version of SharePoint. The requirements might make it impossible to run an in-place upgrade on many existing Windows SharePoint Services installations without upgrading both hardware and dependent software such as the Windows Server Operating System and SQL Server.

If this is the case for your environment, you might choose to use the second approach (described in the next subsection). When upgrading hardware or other software in combination with a SharePoint upgrade, the complexity has already increased and a content database upgrade might help decrease complexity in some cases.

CAUTION

An in-place upgrade can take a long time to run, and the content in the farm will be unavailable to users while it is running. For the most accurate time estimate, ask your IT staff to test the in-place upgrade process on similar hardware prior to executing an in-place upgrade on your production data; this upgrade test can be combined with the restore test previously mentioned. As part of the upgrade preparation, your IT staff has tested the restore to a new farm. A test of the upgrade on the second farm should produce similar upgrade result and timing if using similar hardware to the production farm.

Content Database Upgrade

If you've read the section on SharePoint structure, you've seen one explanation of the connection between the content database and SharePoint sites:

- All of the information you see when you use your SharePoint site is held in a content database.

- Each content database can hold more than one collection of sites.

- Each Site Collection is stored in one, and only one, content database.

This second approach is called a content database upgrade because each content database can be upgraded individually by using this approach.

When IT executes a direct upgrade from Windows SharePoint Services Version 3, you can choose not to upgrade every content database in a farm at the same time. If you have more than one content database, this offers some flexibility for a phased upgrade.

For example, you might choose to move the database containing your most important sites first. Or, you might choose a less important database as a first upgrade to refine your process and become more familiar with the steps involved.

A benefit of the content database upgrade approach is the option to leave the existing content available for viewing only while the upgrade is being performed. Because the content database can be copied to the new server, the original copy is still available for read-only use while the new copy is being converted to the SharePoint Foundation format. This is especially helpful for large content databases that require a long time to upgrade.

This approach requires that the customizations applied to your Windows SharePoint Services installation are well documented and ready to move to the new environment. It also requires a strong understanding of the configuration settings on the farm and web application level. In many organizations, this might not be a problem, because configuration and customization documentation are also both required for disaster recovery.

The content database upgrade occurs on a new SharePoint Foundation 2010 farm. This means additional hardware is required besides the hardware currently running Windows SharePoint Services farm. Besides being a requirement, it is also a benefit to have two environments available because the upgrade can be tested and repeated on the new hardware before committing to the final move from the old hardware.

Visual Upgrade for That SharePoint 2007 "Look"

Visual Upgrade is a new feature of the SharePoint 2010 products that can keep your upgraded site looking a lot like your old site.

While the back-end and some menus will be changed after upgrade, the default state for all upgraded sites is a look and feel that is very close to SharePoint 2007. The reason for this old look in your new upgrade is to allow time to update your old sites to the new visual features of SharePoint 2010.

SharePoint 2010 makes some important and wide-ranging changes to the visual layout of pages on a site. It will take some work to create new master pages, page layouts, and style sheets for your old site. You can test your upgraded sites in the 2010 style with the Visual Upgrade menu options in your site settings.

While you are testing the new "look," only you will be able to see it. Once you are happy with the new look of your upgraded site, you can commit the change for everyone to see.

INSIDE OUT
Be prepared to execute a Visual Upgrade plan before your SharePoint 2010 Upgrade on the back-end

While Visual Upgrade is a great feature that gives you some time to get up to speed with some of the new layout and style changes in SharePoint Foundation 2010, it is only meant to be a temporary fix. You will find that some features are not supported until you've used the Visual Upgrade menu options to move to the new style. Being prepared to move out of the SharePoint 2007 mode as soon as possible after the back-end upgrade of your systems will give you the full advantage of your upgrade.

Migrating Content to SharePoint Foundation 2010

If you have content on websites that are not running Windows SharePoint Services Version 3, you have two options for moving that content to SharePoint Foundation 2010. You can migrate the content manually to a SharePoint Foundation 2010 farm or you can do it with a third-party tool.

Note

For the purposes of this chapter, an upgrade is moving from Windows SharePoint Services Version 3 to SharePoint Foundation 2010. Any other move is considered a migration. In either case, customizations, including installed third-party add-ons and branding, must be considered separately from the content. The migration steps that follow discuss moving content.

You can find more help for branding and customizing SharePoint Foundation in Chapter 14, "Creating, Managing, and Designing Sites by Using SharePoint Designer 2010," which covers branding with respect to master pages and cascading style sheets. Chapters 15, "Customizing the User Interface," and 16, "Developing SharePoint Solutions by Using Visual Studio 2010," cover authoring customizations.

Manual Migration

For sites that have a small amount of content, manual migration can be a good option. You might choose to replicate the previous sites as closely as possible through the creation of lists and libraries first and adding content second. Or, you can take the chance to redesign the information architecture of your site. If you take the time to review the site to be upgraded, you might find that you only need to move over a small amount of information that is still relevant and useful to you and your users now.

Chapter 2

Manual migration is often a team effort. You might want to involve site designers to work on a new look that matches or builds on the previous look. You want to plan for some testing, even if it's just to get a second set of eyes on the work you do yourself. Breaking up the repetitive parts like copying and pasting documents or text from old to new can help make this go faster.

INSIDE OUT
Manual migration might sound hard, but it can be a great option

It could be easy to dismiss manual migration as an unacceptable option for moving your content. After all, it can be hard enough to motivate yourself to do repetitive manual work for any period of time—motivating a team can be harder, still.

If your team is excited about the new capabilities of the platform, as many are, this one time division of labor can pay off with big dividends. Often, the time saved in the future with modern tools provided by SharePoint 2010 can be a great reward when you've become frustrated with the technology you've been using for a long time to update your old site. Keep in mind that even with automated migration tools, you will want to do extensive testing to ensure that your content has moved over correctly. When you move over content manually, you can be confident that everything you've moved over went to the right place.

Migration Tools

There are more than half a dozen migration tools specifically built and sold by third-party software companies to move content into new SharePoint 2010 sites. The basic premise of tool-assisted migration is no different than that of the manual migration. You can still choose to try to replicate the site that you are migrating from or you can take the opportunity to re-assess your site and build into a new design that fits SharePoint 2010 better.

The big difference is that these tools help do some of the repetitive manual work that is involved in migrating to SharePoint Foundation. In fact, you might find yourself appreciating one of these tools so much that you keep it around to help you reorganize your content in SharePoint Foundation long after the initial migration is complete.

There are two kinds of third-party migration tools available. The simplest kind treats the source website as a collection of HTML webpages. Using this kind of tool, you move each page over, one by one, into a document library in SharePoint Foundation. That method really only works if all you have is content in pages, as opposed to items in lists or documents in libraries.

On the other hand, many of the third-party tools have specific features that target particular sources of information from which to migrate. You can find tools that help you pull data from older versions of SharePoint, competing products like Lotus Notes, and other technologies used to share information like Networked File Shares and Exchange Public Folders.

Each tool available works a little differently than the other, so it's best to go to the vendor for information on how to use the tool you choose. They are all happy to provide product demonstrations and many provide trial versions so that you can test them out on your actual content.

The websites *www.EndUserSharePoint.com* and *www.SharePointReviews.com* both have great collections of information on third-party migration tools. Look in both the Migration and Content Organization categories.

Summary

A successful SharePoint environment is the result of a close interaction between the site users, site owners, and supporting technical staff. This chapter introduced you to some of the concepts that you need to understand for advanced business uses of SharePoint.

The SharePoint list items that you add and the documents that you upload all reside in a SharePoint site. Every SharePoint site is part of a Site Collection, which is a hierarchy that starts with one top-level site at the root of a tree, and sites which can grow from it. Site collections are accessed through web applications and contained in content databases. Web applications and content databases run on the servers that make up the SharePoint farm that hosts it all. Service Applications provide supporting resources to the farm.

Your day-to-day work is done on the site and Site Collection level. Understanding the full structure can inform your design decisions when you would like to improve your SharePoint installation.

Search is a very powerful tool provided by SharePoint Technologies. While SharePoint Foundation 2010 provides search out of the box, you have a range of possibilities for enhancing the search by adding other products in the family. Search Server Express 2010 is a free download that provides enhancements in the number of items that can be searched and the ways you can search them. Upgrading from the Express version and licensing the full version of Search Server 2010 will provide capabilities closer to the search features provided by SharePoint Server 2010. One popular search feature you get in SharePoint Server but not in SharePoint Foundation is People Search.

The last search product that is covered in this chapter is FAST Search for SharePoint 2010. It is the top-of-the-line Enterprise Search product from Microsoft and it can be used to provide search results from SharePoint Foundation 2010 websites.

Regardless of the search product that you choose, it is important to pay attention to how well your searches perform and follow up on issues such as stale results.

Chapter 2

It's also important that SharePoint identify your site's users and understand the options for securing your site content. SharePoint Foundation 2010 adds a few authentication options for your web applications. Choosing authentication methods for your web applications requires identifying who your users are and what level of access they need. The authentication methods you may choose from include classic Windows integrated, claims-based with Windows or without, and anonymous authentication. Authorizing the users to perform actions in SharePoint is mostly controlled in the Site Collection. However, User Policies can effect permissions globally and are not visible outside the web application settings. Working closely with IT, you can ensure a secure experience for the visitors to your site and the content you host in SharePoint.

You probably have been using some tool to share files and other information with others before moving to SharePoint Foundation 2010. Any sites that you have running in Windows SharePoint Services Version 3 can be upgraded in place or by copying the content databases to SharePoint Foundation. If you'd like to migrate data from other sources, you might choose to manually move the most important pieces over yourself. If you have a lot of data, you might consider purchasing a third-party tool to help you move into SharePoint Foundation 2010.

This chapter has been an introduction to administration settings made beyond the Site Collection. In the chapters that follow, you will find other ways with which you will interact with SharePoint Administration outside site settings available to an advanced business user. For example, you will find information on importing BDC models in Chapter 9, "Working with External Content." Chapters 15 and 16 both cover creating customizations for SharePoint that can be added to the Farm by an administrator. Chapter 15 focuses on SharePoint Designer, and covers some settings exposed only to technical staff.

T HIS chapter explains how organizations can take advantage of the powerful, built-in features of Microsoft SharePoint Foundation 2010. The items presented here are those that end-users will utilize on a daily basis. These factors will increase collaboration with other SharePoint users and also increase productivity on day-to-day tasks and activities.

This chapter addresses SharePoint site functionality from the perspective of managing content in document libraries and lists as well as how to use discussion boards to increase knowledge management and collaboration. Issues and task tracking help team members stay on track with their current projects and initiatives, and team members can be alerted whenever items are updated or changed within their site.

We will also go into some planning details that you will need to consider to ensure that your end-users can take full advantage of the features and functionality.

Whether you're new to SharePoint or a seasoned SharePoint user or administrator, this overview of built-in features will help you gain a better understanding of SharePoint Foundation 2010, which in turn will help you get the most out of the platform.

Recommended Computer Environment

The optimum computer environment for using SharePoint Foundation 2010 includes:

- Level 1 Internet browser options for Windows:

    — Windows Internet Explorer 7, 32-bit

    — Windows Internet Explorer 8, 32-bit

    — Firefox 3.x, 32-bit

- Level 2 Internet browser options:

    — Windows Internet Explorer 7, 64-bit

    — Windows Internet Explorer 8, 64-bit

    — Firefox 3.*x*, on non-Windows operating system

    — Safari 3.*x*

- A complete installation of Microsoft Office 2010. (Microsoft Office 2007 and 2003 users will have a similar but not identical experience.)

- Windows 7, Windows Vista, or Windows XP operating system.

Once you have the proper environment set up, you are ready to begin using SharePoint Foundation 2010.

Browser Support

SharePoint Foundation 2010 runs in the browser. Because of enhancements to the platform, it supports many different browsers; however, not all browsers are created equal. Some browsers might cause the functionality of SharePoint Foundation 2010 to be downgraded, limited, or available only through alternative means. In some cases, functionality might simply be unavailable for noncritical administrative tasks. As such, you will need to carefully plan your browser strategy to effectively implement SharePoint Foundation within your organization.

It is highly recommended that you audit the browsers in use within your organization as a part of the planning process for your deployment. It is very important that you know which browsers SharePoint Foundation 2010 supports. The following sections go into the different browser support levels and the peculiarities between the various, commonly used browsers.

Browser Support Levels

There are three different levels used when describing the compatibility of browsers with SharePoint Foundation 2010. Those levels are as follows:

- Level 1—Supported

    A supported browser is a web browser that is known to work with SharePoint Foundation 2010, and all features and functionality will work. If you should encounter an issue, support can help you resolve the issue.

- Level 2—Supported with known issues

  A supported web browser with known limitations is one that works with SharePoint Foundation 2010, but there are identified limitations with it. The majority of features and functionality do work; however, if there is a feature or functionality that does not work or has been disabled by design, documentation on how to resolve these issues is available.

- Not Tested

  This is a browser for which the compatibility with SharePoint Foundation 2010 has not been tested and is therefore unknown. As such, you might experience issues when using that particular web browser. Always remember that SharePoint Foundation 2010 works best with up-to-date, standards-based web browsers.

Browser Support Table

Table 3-1 presents a summary of the support levels of the most commonly used browsers.

Table 3-1 **Support Levels for Commonly Used Browsers**

Browser	Supported	Supported, with limitations	Not tested
Internet Explorer 8 (32-bit)	X		
Internet Explorer 7 (32-bit)	X		
Internet Explorer 8 (64-bit)		X	
Internet Explorer 7 (64-bit)		X	
Internet Explorer 6 (32-bit)			X
Mozilla Firefox 3.6 (running on a Windows based system)		X	
Mozilla Firefox 3.6 (running on a non-Windows based system)		X	
Safari 4.04 (running on a non-Windows operating system)		X	

Chapter 3

Sites and Workspaces Features

SharePoint Foundation 2010 improves upon previous editions of the platform by providing a rich set of features and functionality. Once employed, these powerful features are easily accessible and can be used by anyone within your organization who has the access and security permissions to the site. The following are just some of the features to which you'll be introduced:

- Blogs

- Discussion Forums

- Photos and Presence

- Wikis

The following section covers site navigation. As you might recall from Chapter 2, "Administration for Business Users," there are numerous built-in templates that can be used when setting up a SharePoint site. The Team Site template has a little bit of everything when it comes to objects and functionality (along with being the most widely used site template for setting up a SharePoint site within organizations).

The Team Site template provides a basis for the parts of a typical SharePoint Site. Although the other site templates offer different functionality, we believe that the Team Site template is a good reference point. We will also go into some of the peculiarities of using some of the other site templates later in the book.

Creating Sites and Subsites

The chances are that you will have a SharePoint Administrator who will implement the initial set up of the SharePoint farm. This individual will be responsible for establishing the Central Administration site and might build out some individual Site Collections and related top-level sites.

A common point of confusion is deciding whether to create a Site Collection or a Subsite. This is because a Site Collection and a Subsite look and act the same (at first glance). SharePoint is flexible, so you could create a top-level site for Site Collection and deploy it to the organization to use as a regular SharePoint site. Table 3-2 provides guidance for choosing when to use a Site Collection versus a Subsite.

Table 3-2 **When to Use Site Collections and Subsites**

Use a Site Collection when:	Use a Subsite when:
You need to delegate the administration of sites to someone other than the administrator of existing sites.	Permissions need to be inherited from the parent site. (Parent sites are higher-level sites from which Subsites are created).
Search features or workflows need to be scoped differently than existing Site Collections.	Design elements (styles or themes) need to be shared between sites.
You need to establish a security border between your sites or other sites.	Lists need to be shared between sites.
A different size quota for the existing Site Collection needs to be set.	You would like to use only a small amount of your allotted SharePoint space.
Site collection Features are needed that are not readily available within other Site Collections (for example, the Publishing Infrastructure Feature).	Shared navigation between sites is needed.

> **Note**
> Central Administration is used to perform administration tasks for SharePoint products and technologies from a central location.

Once the top-level site has been created, the SharePoint Administrator will assign the site to either a Site Collection administrator or a site administrator (depending on the governance policy that is in force for the organization).

At this point, a new site can be set up for use. To learn more about creating a new site, read Chapter 4, "Creating Sites and Workspaces by Using the Browser," and Chapter 8, "Managing Site Content."

Using Team Sites and Related Subsites

Figure 3-1 shows a typical SharePoint Foundation 2010 Team Site, which includes features for collaboration, such as Shared Documents, Calendars, Tasks, and Team Discussions.

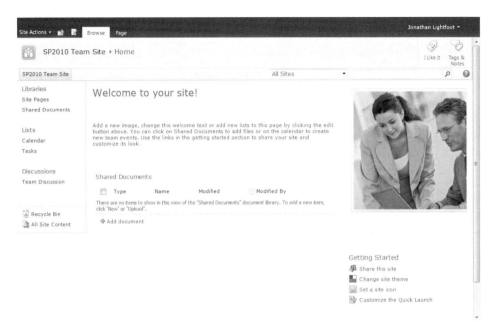

Figure 3-1 A typical SharePoint Foundation 2010 Team Site.

The out-of-the-box template for a Team Site provides the following elements:

- **The ribbon**   This serves as the primary command interface that you use to interact with objects within SharePoint Foundation.

- **Site Actions**   A user with the appropriate permissions will have the Site Actions link displayed, which contains a drop-down list with which the user can access the Create, Edit Page, or Site Settings pages.

- **Search box**   Users can use this box (located at the right side of the screen) to search for content. The default setting is to search within the current site and any Subsites.

- **Navigate Up**   Used for navigating up to the parent site of the current site.

- **Edit page**   Users with Edit Page permissions can use this icon to toggle the current page into the Edit Mode, in which the page can be customized.

- **Browse tab**   Provides resources for *Liking* the page or tagging and typing notes about the page.

- **Page tab**   Use this to edit the page (either within the browser or in SharePoint Designer). You can also check out the page, edit properties; rename the page; view the version history for the page; view and set permissions for the page; delete the page; email a link to the page; set up and manage alerts on the page; assign the page as the Homepage; view incoming links to the page; alter the settings, library permissions, and view all pages for the page's library.

- **Quick Launch**   The Navigation pane on the left provides links that you can customize; by default, it contains the following links:

  — **Documents**   Links to a list of all the document libraries within the site, including the out-of-the-box libraries for Shared Documents and Site Pages.

  — **Lists**   Links to a list of all of the SharePoint lists within the site, including the out-of-the-box lists for Calendars and Tasks.

  — **Discussions**   Links to a list of all of the SharePoint discussion libraries within the site, including the out-of-the-box discussions for Team Discussion.

  — **Recycle Bin**   Links to the site's Recycle Bin.

  — **All Site Content**   Links to a page that shows you all of the content to which you have access within the site.

By default, Team Sites are created with a page layout that includes areas for Web Parts, site images, and text boxes to display information to users of the site such as a title and description of the site and its purpose.

> **Note**
> SharePoint Foundation 2010 pages are security trimmed, which means that users only see the items and actions for which they have the proper permissions to access.

Using SharePoint Libraries and Lists

SharePoint Foundation 2010 lists represent editable, web-based tables that facilitate concurrent, multi-user interactions against a common, centralized, extensible set of columns and rows. You can use lists to provision your own repositories of structured information in which list items behave like rows consisting of self-labeled columns.

Each of these lists starts out with a different assortment of columns, but you can add, remove, and modify the columns in any list by using nothing more than a browser.

Chapter 3

New List Functionality in SharePoint Foundation 2010

SharePoint Foundation 2010 adds features to the list infrastructure that improve user experience when manipulating large lists. Other new features enhance data integrity:

- **Large Lists**   Lists in Share Point Foundation can contain up to 30 million items. As you can imagine, displaying 30 million items at one time would be an enormous drain on your SharePoint farm resources, and performance would be adversely affected. Scale limits on lists prevent useful modeling, limiting user experience with respect to organization, exploration, and retrieval of list data. The Large List feature addresses these limitations by optimizing large lists for deployments in cases where, for example, getting a flat view of all the items is not a valid scenario for end users.

- **List relationships**   In SharePoint Foundation 2010, a list relationship provides additional functionality so that list items in the parent list are inherently "aware" of related items in the child list and data integrity constraints are enforced on the child items. You can use this to ensure that objects in the child list are not deleted if they are attached to an object in a parent list.

- **Enforcing unique column constraints**   SharePoint Foundation 2010 makes it possible to provide a primary key on column fields by using (or "enforcing") a new feature called *unique column constraints*. You can use this feature to ensure that a column cannot contain duplicate entries.

- **External lists**   SharePoint Foundation 2010 has the ability to access and interact with list information located outside of SharePoint. Now you can access a spreadsheet located on another server and display its contents and interact with the data as if it were in SharePoint.

Viewing Lists and List Contents

Clicking the Lists link within the Quick Launch of any page displays the All Site Content page with the Lists view applied, as displayed in Figure 3-2. This page not only presents all of the lists that are currently available to the signed-in user but also provides authorized users with the ability to create new lists and display site workflows. Each list contains a different combination of fields, serving different purposes, and also providing different views.

Figure 3-2 The All Site Content page in SharePoint Foundation 2010.

SharePoint Foundation 2010 comes with a number of list templates. You will use different lists for different purposes on your site.

The out-of-the-box list templates available in SharePoint Foundation 2010 are:

- **Announcements**   Use an announcements list to share news, status updates, and to provide reminders. Announcements support enhanced formatting with images, hyperlinks, and formatted text.

- **Calendar**   Calendar lists are used to display the events relevant to a team (such as meetings, holidays, milestones, social events, and so on). Think of the calendar as the group calendar that you might already be using in your email client. If you are using a calendar program that is compatible with SharePoint 2010 (such as Microsoft Outlook 2010), you can view and update calendar items on your SharePoint 2010 site while working in the other program. In addition, you can view your SharePoint calendar either side-by-side or overlaid on your personal calendar.

- **Contacts**   Contact lists hold people, teams, and organizations that you work with, your associates, and your customers. If you are using an email or contact management program such as Outlook 2010, you can create and modify your Outlook contacts from within SharePoint. A contacts list does not manage who the members are on your site, but it can be used to store and share contacts for your organization, such as a list of external vendors.

- **Discussion boards**   When you need a central location to record and store team discussions, a discussion board is your solution. Your SharePoint administrator can also set up your list to accept incoming email messages, as well. For example, you can send an email message with either a question or answer to another question from your email client. Discussion boards can accept and store a message like this as if it were typed directly in the list.

- **Tasks**   Use a tasks list to track information about projects and other to-do events for your team. You can assign tasks to people as well as track the status and percentage complete of tasks as they progress. If you are using an email or task management program that is compatible with SharePoint 2010, you can view and update the tasks in your SharePoint site from your other program. For example, you can create a task list for office moves within your organization and then view and update it in Outlook 2010, along with your other tasks.

- **Issue tracking**   At first glance, issue tracking lists appear to be tasks lists, but they are not. Unlike a tasks list, an issue tracking list is designed to store very specific information on issues such as Help Desk support problems. Issues can be assigned, categorized, and related to other issues. For example, you can create an issue tracking list to monitor Help Desk support calls. You can also comment on the issues (each time you edit them) without altering the original description of the issue, thus creating a history of all of the comments. A Help Desk specialist can record the progress of an issue as it progresses toward resolution. Furthermore, the Three-State workflow can be run on an issue tracking list to help your team with tracking management.

- **Links**   These lists contain all of the hyperlinks commonly accessed by your team. For example, you might create a links list for your supplier's websites.

- **Project tasks**   These lists are similar to tasks lists, except they provide a visual (or Gantt) view with progress bars. You can track the status and percentage complete for a task as it progresses toward completion. If you are using an email or task management program that is compatible with SharePoint 2010 (such as Microsoft Office Project 2010), you can also view and update your project tasks from the other program. For example, your events team can create a project tasks list on your SharePoint site to set up for a conference, and then your project management team can track the progress of the tasks from within Project 2010.

- **Survey**   You can use survey lists to collect and compile feedback. For example, you can survey a group of software engineers on the feasibility of adding a new programming language to the list that they support. There are many design choices for your questions and answers. You can also see an overview of the feedback received. If you have a database or spreadsheet program that is compatible with SharePoint 2010 (for example Microsoft Access 2010 and Microsoft Excel 2010), you can export your results to that program for detailed analysis of the feedback.

- **Custom**   If you want to build a list without any preconfigured columns, you can use a custom list. You can also create a custom list that is based on a spreadsheet or table. For example, you can import a spreadsheet from Excel 2010 or a table from Access 2010 that you created to store customer information.

- **External lists**   If you need to work with data that is stored outside of SharePoint, you can use an External list. With External lists, not only can you read the data, you can also update, write, create, and delete items from the data source from within SharePoint Foundation 2010. Unlike a native SharePoint list, an External list uses Business Connectivity Services (BCS) to access data directly from an external system (such as SAP, Siebel, and Microsoft SQL Server), whether that system is a database, web service, or Line-of-Business (LoB) system.

- **Custom list in Datasheet**   This template is very similar to a custom list with the primary difference being that is created to display the list in datasheet view by default. In doing so, you can show the data in a grid for viewing and editing data as rows and columns. You can edit and add rows and columns. In addition, you can apply filters and adjust the sort orders, and display calculated values and totals. Datasheet view requires that Office 2010 be installed on a 32-bit client computer, and the browser must support ActiveX controls.

- **Status list**   This is used to display and track the goals of your project. This list comes with a set of colored icons that are used to graphically display the degree to which goals are being met.

Think of these preconfigured lists as a good starting point for a list that you might need to create. You can always add, delete, and alter the details and properties of lists as your needs change.

Updating List Content

SharePoint Foundation 2010 has built-in features for adding list items, viewing, editing, or deleting them, managing their permissions, and attaching alerts to them. To perform any of these actions, first display the list, and then choose from among the following, as needed:

Chapter 3

- To add a new item, in the list main view, click the Add New Item link. Additionally, on the ribbon, on the List Tools tab, you can use the Items tab. Click the New Item tab, and then select the list item that you want to add.

- To view existing content in a list, hover over the list title, open the drop-down menu that appears, and then choose View Item.

- To edit an existing item in a list, hover over the list title, open the drop-down menu that appears, and then choose Edit Item.

- To edit permissions for an existing item in a list, hover over the list title, open the drop-down menu that appears, and then choose Manage Permissions.

- To delete an existing item in a list, hover over the list title, open the drop-down menu that appears, and then choose Delete Item.

- To add an alert to an existing item in a list, hover over the list title, open the drop-down menu that appears, and then choose Alert Me.

  If Outgoing message settings have not been configured, Alert Me will not appear in the drop-down menu.

Choosing either New or Edit Item opens a page similar to the one shown in Figure 3-3. For a new item, all of the input fields will be blank or have default values. For an existing item, each input field will contain that item's current value. There will also be time and date information as well as information about the creation and last-modified times and the identity of the user that performed these actions. If a file is attached to the list item, the name of the attachment with an embedded link will appear along with a delete link next to the attachment.

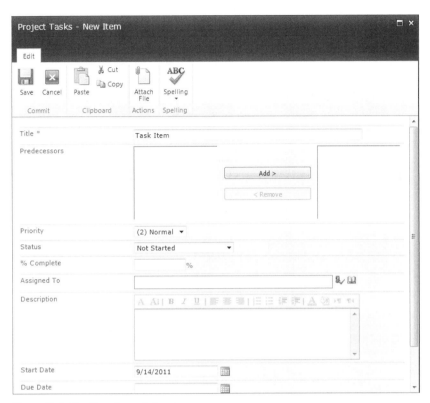

Figure 3-3 The New Item dialog box.

Versioning in Lists

With SharePoint Foundation 2010, you can track versions of list items. Each item's version is numbered and saved as part of the version history. Versioning is not enabled by default; to enable and configure versioning in a list, on the ribbon, on List Tools tab, select the List menu, and then select Settings. In the drop-down list that opens, select List Settings and then under the General Settings section, select Versioning Settings.

The resulting configuration page (see Figure 3-4) contains the following options:

- **Content Approval** The list administrator selects either Yes or No to require (or not require) content approval for submitted items. Selecting Yes causes new items or changes to existing items to remain in a draft state until they have been approved. When an item is added to the list, it is displayed with a Pending status. During this status, the item is visible only to the user who created it and members with approval permissions.

- **Item Version History** The list administrator selects either Yes or No to determine whether a version is created each time you edit an item in the list. The administrator can choose to limit the number of versions to retain as well as the number of approved version drafts to retain.

- **Draft Item Security** The list administrator selects who can see draft items in the list. The administrator can choose from the following options:

  — Any User Who Can Read Items

  — Only Users Who Can Edit Items

  — Only Users Who Can Approve Items (And The Author Of The Item)

Figure 3-4 The Versioning Settings page.

Using Document Libraries

A document library is a file repository that can store many different types of files. Document libraries provide a central location where users can manage, store, and organize documents across their organization. Document libraries are similar to the lists that you find within SharePoint Foundation 2010; however, they are specifically optimized to hold documents as their items. The document library is designed to be a user-friendly, intuitive tool that can be easily customized to meet the changing needs of the user.

In previous sections, you learned that lists are an effective way to work with all types of data; libraries function similarly for documents and forms, such as Microsoft Office Word documents, Excel workbooks and Microsoft InfoPath forms. Using SharePoint Document Libraries, you can filter and group documents as well as view metadata for documents stored in the library.

Creating Document Libraries

When you create a new SharePoint site, a generic document library called Shared Documents is created for you. Because this library lacks a descriptive name, you might prefer to create new libraries for your particular business category or subject, instead. Document libraries also display key information about each file and provide many powerful features, including version control, item-level permissions for libraries, documents, folders, and built-in workflows.

If you have the appropriate permissions, you will see the Site Actions tab in the upper-left corner of your site. Click the Site Actions tab, and then in the drop-down menu that opens, click New Document Library, as shown in Figure 3-5.

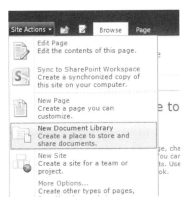

Figure 3-5 Click New Document Library on the Site Actions Tab to create your new library.

Chapter 3

The Create New Document Library dialog box opens, in which you provide information to set up your library. The options to create a new document library include:

- **Name**   This is the name that you want to appear in the headings and links throughout the site.

- **Description**   Although this is not required to set up a document library, the description field can be very beneficial by describing the intended purpose of the library.

- **Navigation**   You can specify whether the document library is listed in the Quick Launch bar of the site to make navigation easier. The default selection for this field is Yes.

- **Document Version History**   Use this option to specify if you want a new version created each time a file is edited in the library. The default selection for this field is No.

- **Document Template**   Use this option to specify which template is opened when the New button is clicked in the library. This is tied to a default content type that the document library uses to create new files.

Viewing Document Libraries

To view a document stored in a library, you can enter the specific library by either clicking the link to the library on the Quick Launch menu or by going into View All Content and selecting the library from the site contents. Navigating to the selected document library by clicking its name produces a display similar to Figure 3-6.

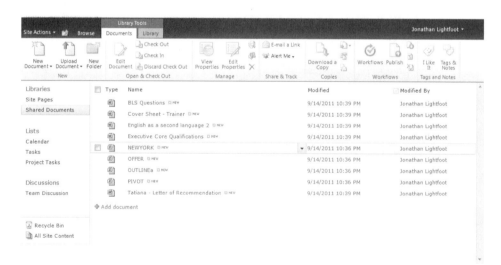

Figure 3-6 The Library view.

The following four columns are set up when a document library is created:

- **Type**   The classification by document's file type (for example, .docx, .xlsx, and so on)

- **Name**   The name of the file

- **Modified**   The date and time when the document was either last uploaded or last modified

- **Modified By**   The name of the user who last modified the document

Here's how the document library works:

All of the SharePoint Foundation 2010 menu items are located on the ribbon. When you are in the document library, the ribbon consist of three tabs: Browse, Document, and Library. Note that the Document and Library tabs are located within the Library Tools contextual menu group, which contains tools that are related to specific commands with the library in SharePoint Foundation 2010. The following is a description of each of the tabs and the menu items within them:

- **Browse**   Select this tab to browse, search, filter, and sort through the document library.

- **Documents**   Use the following tools on this tab to manage content in the library:

  - **New Document**   Creates a new document with the default content type or one that you can select from the drop-down menu by clicking the down-arrow on the button.

  - **Upload Document**   Uploads a single document into the document library from your computer or other directory.

  - **Upload Multiple Documents**   Uploads multiple documents all at once into the document library from your computer or other directory.

  - **New Folder**   Creates container folders to separate and organize content within your library.

  - **Edit Document**   Opens the document for editing.

  - **Check Out**   Checks out a document for editing. While the document is checked out, only the person who checked out the document can make changes that are saved back to the library. Other users are able to view the copy of the document that is saved on the server, but cannot make changes and save them back to the library.

— **Check In**   Checks a document back in so that changes can be updated and other users can edit the document. Only the user who has the document checked out or someone with Override Checkin permissions can use this option.

— **View Properties**   Displays the SharePoint properties of the selected document.

— **Edit Properties**   Use this to edit the SharePoint properties of the selected document.

— **Version History**   Displays the version history for the selected document.

— **Document Permissions**   Displays the permissions for the selected document.

— **Delete Document**   Moves the selected documents to the site's Recycle Bin.

— **E-mail A Link**   Use this to email a link to the selected document to others. Outgoing email must be configured on the list and Site Collection before you can do this.

— **Alert Me**   Users can set up a notification for changes that have occurred within the library. Clicking this command displays a New Alert page, in which users can specify the title of the alert. If the user has Manage Alerts permission assigned, he can also create an alert for other users of the website. Otherwise, a user can only create alerts for himself. Users can also specify when to receive the alerts (immediately, daily, or weekly summary).

— **Download A Copy**   Downloads a local copy of the selected document. The local copy will not remain synchronized to the original file located on the server.

— **Send To**   Sends a copy of the selected file to another document library located on the same server, or you can create a new Document Workspace to which to send the file. You can also send a hyperlink of the file to someone else via email.

— **Manage Copies**   If the document has been copied to another location by using the Send To command, you can use this command to see locations that contain copies of the document. You can also synchronize all of the copies of the document with the parent document by using this command. Additionally, you can send a new copy of the document to another library located on the same server.

— **Go To Source**   If the document is a copy of an original document, this command displays the properties of the document as they appear in the source library.

— **Workflows**   Use this to run workflows for content contained within a document library.

— **Publish**   This command will be active if the library is set to require documents to be published before others on the site can see it.

— **Unpublish**   This command is available in case there is a document that you do not want to check out or delete, but you need to set it so that no one can view that document's existence. If selected, only the person who published the document and library administrators can see the document listed.

— **Approve/Reject**   When Content Approval is activated on the document library, this command is used by those with Approve Item permissions to open the Approve/Reject page to either approve or reject a submission.

— **Unapprove**   Reverses a prior approval of a document, changing its status in the library to "pending." When you click Unapprove, the selected item will not be available for everyone to see. Only the item creator and those members who are on the approvers list will be able to see the item.

— **I Like It**   Marks the selected item with an *I Like It* tag. Post the item to the user's newsfeed which lets them keep track of content in which they have expressed an interest.

— **Tags & Notes**   Tags help you to remember links and selected items. Notes are comments that other users can view; thus, you can share your comments and thoughts on the selected item.

- **Library** This tab focuses on the format and structure of the library itself:

    — **Standard View**   Shows the document library in the default view.

    — **Datasheet View**   Shows the document library in Datasheet view.

    — **New Row**   Within SharePoint 2010, libraries and lists share the same ribbon; as such, you cannot use this command within a library. This command is enabled in Datasheet view only; use this command to create a new row for adding list items.

    — **Show Task Pane**   This command is enabled in Datasheet view only. Use this to open a task pane in which you can cut, copy, sort, and work with library items in Access and Excel.

    — **Displays Totals**   This command is enabled in Datasheet view only. Use this to display totals columns underneath each column.

Chapter 3

— **Refresh Data**   This command is enabled in Datasheet view only. Use this to update the library listing with any changes to the library carried out by other users.

— **Create View**   Creates a custom view of the library contents. You can select which columns are displayed, along with setting up filters and other display settings in the document library.

— **Modify View**   Modifies a user's personal view of the library, either within the browser or in SharePoint Designer 2010.

— **Create Column**   Create columns to store additional information about items. You must have Manage Lists permission to use this command.

— **Current View**   Displays which view is currently being used. Users can select alternate views from the drop-down menu.

— **Current Page**   Navigates to other pages when working with large libraries.

— **E-mail A Link**   Sends an email containing a document hyperlink to a mail recipient.

— **Alert Me**   Displays a New Alert page for which you can specify the alert's title as well as the list of users to whom the alert's email notification should be sent when there are changes to a specific item, document, list, or library.

— **RSS Feed**   Use this command to keep track of the information via a Really Simple Syndication (RSS) feed. You can use RSS feeds to receive view updates about libraries by using an authenticated RSS feed viewer (for instance, Internet Explorer 9).

— **Sync To SharePoint Workspace**   Creates a synchronized copy of the library on a user's computer. SharePoint Workspace must be installed on the local computer for this to work.

— **Connect & Export**   Provides options for connecting to Outlook. This adds a shortcut (under SharePoint Sites) to a user's computer with which she can connect to the library when creating, opening, and saving documents in Microsoft Office applications such as Word, Excel, and PowerPoint. Users can select Export To Excel, which creates an .iqy file that can be opened in Excel for analysis. Selecting Open With Windows Explorer opens the document library in a Windows Explorer window, thus allowing files to be dragged into the library, along with creating folders, and deleting multiple files at once.

- **Customize Library**   This drop-down menu allows user-defined changes for the library structure:

  — **Form Web Parts**   Use this to modify either the Display or Edit Form dialog boxes by adding or deleting additional Web Parts.

  — **Edit Library**   Use this command to edit library settings, add or remove columns, and create new views, workflows, and custom actions with SharePoint Designer 2010.

  — **New Quick Step**   Use this command to create a new button on the Items tab, which executes a custom action on library items.

- **Settings**   Controls library and workflow configurations within the library:

  — **Library Settings**   Opens a page that contains options to manage document library settings such as version settings, permissions, columns, views, workflow, and policies.

  — **Library Permissions**   Opens a page with which you can add, remove, or modify the permissions for the library.

  — **Workflow Settings**   Opens a page with which you can modify the settings of workflows associated with the library.

Creating a New Document and Adding It to a Library

When you click the New Document button on the ribbon, SharePoint Foundation 2010 displays either the default document template or the list of content types that have been associated with the document library. Content types allow for the document library to have multiple item types or document types, of which each can have unique metadata, policies, or behaviors.

After content has been added to the library, SharePoint automatically records your name, the date and time, and the type of document in the item's properties. If you select a New Item that was associated with a content type, the metadata associated with that document will also be saved into SharePoint.

Adding an Existing Document to a Library

To add a document that already exists on your computer, network share, CD, or other location to a document library, click the Add New Document link in the Standard View, or on the ribbon, click Document Library Tools, and then select the Upload Document menu item. This displays two options: Upload Document or Upload Multiple Documents.

Chapter 3

When uploading a single document, you must browse to your local directories for the target file, as shown in Figure 3-7.

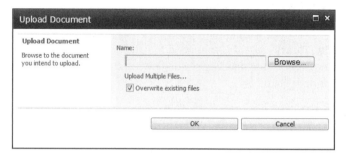

Figure 3-7 The Upload Document single document dialog box.

When uploading multiple files, you have the option to either browse for files or—new to SharePoint Foundation 2010—drag files and folders directly into the upload dialog box, as shown in Figure 3-8.

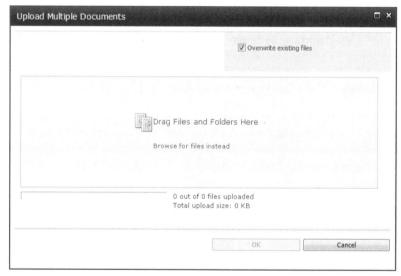

Figure 3-8 New in SharePoint Foundation 2010, you can now drag files and folders into the Upload Multiple Documents Dialog box for uploading.

After you locate the correct document and select OK, a dialog box appears, asking you for any additional data (metadata) about the document. It is important to note that when additional content types or custom columns are created or applied to the document library, you will be prompted to provide data regarding those additional fields.

Deleting Content from a Document Libraries

To delete a library document, perform the following steps:

1. Hover over the document name of the item that you want to delete, and then click the down-arrow to the right of the document name to open a drop-down list.

2. Select Delete, and then click OK to confirm the deletion.

Once an item is deleted, it is moved to the First-Stage Recycle Bin, which is located on the site itself. Items that are deleted from the First-Stage Recycle Bin are moved once more into the Site Collection Recycle Bin, which is controlled by the Site Collection Administrator.

Items stored in the First-Stage Recycle Bin are permanently deleted after a fixed period of time (the default is 30 days). Items contained in the Second-Stage Recycle Bin are automatically deleted after a preset period of time (the default is 30 days) or until the allotted Recycle Bin size is exceeded, at which point the oldest items are deleted first.

> **Note**
>
> It is a common misconception that the Recycle Bin retention time is given per stage (for example, 30 days for the First-Stage Recycle Bin and 30 more days for the Second-Stage Recycle Bin). The retention period is applied to the cumulative time that has passed since the file was originally deleted. See "Plan to protect content by using recycle bins and versioning (SharePoint Server 2010)" at *http://technet.microsoft.com/en-us/library/cc263011.aspx* for detailed information on Recycle Bin configuration.

Versioning in Document Libraries

When versioning is enabled, SharePoint Foundation 2010 creates a separate copy of the document each time it is edited. Although this takes up extra space on the server, it also makes it easy to revert to an older version of the document, if necessary.

Versioning is not enabled by default. To activate it, an administrator or site owner/manager must select Settings | Document Library Settings, and then under the heading General Settings, click Versioning Settings.

Versioning is the method by which SharePoint stores successive iterations of a document in a numbered format. SharePoint Foundation 2010 has three versioning options:

- **No Versioning** Turns off versioning. All previous versions of documents can no longer be retrieved and are discarded.

Chapter 3

- **Create Major Versions** This versioning option employs a sequential numbered schema (1, 2, 3, 4, and so on). It is possible to specify the number of major versions that SharePoint will store. Once a document is classified as a major version, all users who have access to the document will be able to view it.

- **Create Major And Minor (Draft) Versions** This versioning option uses numbered versions similar to Create Major Versions, but employs a major/minor numbering schema (1.0, 1.1, 1.2, 2.0, 2.1, 3.0, 3.1, and so on). Versions ending with zero (.0) are major versions; versions ending with non-zero extensions are minor versions. Similar to major versions, it is possible to specify the number of major and minor versions that SharePoint will store. In this versioning scenario, all users with read permissions can view major versions of the documents, and you can specify which users are permitted to view the minor versions.

When you view a document's version history, you see a list of the occasions when this document was edited and saved as well as the author's comments on those changes, as illustrated in Figure 3-9.

Figure 3-9 The Version History dialog box.

The following information and options are displayed:

- **No.** The current version number.

- **Modified** The date and time at which each version of the document was last modified. You can hover over the Modified field of a version to access a drop-down list that contains the following items:

  — **View** Specifies whether to allow the selected version to be viewed.

  — **Restore** Restores a previous version as the latest version. This does not delete the replaced version, it only saves the selected view as the latest version with the next sequential version number.

- **Modified By** Identifies the user who last modified the document.

- **Size** Shows the file size of the version.

> **Note**
>
> Keep in mind that versioning saves a complete copy of the document. For example, if a document is 10 MB in size and has 10 versions attached to it, storing that single document (and its versions) could potentially consume 100 MB of space on the server. This space would be counted against your Site Collection storage quota.

Advanced List and Library Features

In the following sections, you learn about advanced list and library features in SharePoint Foundation 2010. Working closely with Office 2010, using workflows, and taking advantage of the Recycle Bin offer significant improvements over previous versions of SharePoint.

Connect, Open, Sync, and Export with Office 2010

SharePoint Foundation 2010 was designed to work closely with the Office 2010 suite of applications. This means that you can work with content seamlessly between the applications. One example of this is the connection between Outlook 2010 and SharePoint.

Incoming Email Settings

Lists and libraries in SharePoint Foundation 2010 can receive and store email messages and attachments, just as they can in SharePoint 2007. This feature can assist team members within the organization when archiving email or uploading the contents of a specific email to a SharePoint list or library. Additionally, external team member can email to the list so that entire teams can review a specific discussion without retrieving the messages from their mailboxes.

Based on your organization's policies, you might not be able to use this feature, which must be enabled by the SharePoint administrator at the Central Administration site.

RSS Settings

RSS feeds deliver new content to you on the topics in which you are interested. RSS provides a convenient way to syndicate information from a variety of sources, including news stories, updates to a website, or important bulletins. Most people take advantage of some form of feed-reader software to monitor updates to RSS feeds.

Chapter 3

SharePoint Foundation 2010 can offer RSS feeds from any SharePoint list, including announcements, discussion boards, picture libraries, blogs, document libraries, form libraries, calendars, and surveys; these must be viewed by using an "authenticated" RSS browser (such as Outlook 2010).

SharePoint administrators can enable RSS support within the Central Administration site at the web application level so that RSS feeds can automatically be enabled throughout your SharePoint enterprise.

Workflow in SharePoint Foundation 2010

Workflows in SharePoint Foundation 2010 were introduced and discussed in Chapter 1, "Introduction to Microsoft SharePoint Foundation 2010," and Chapter 2 (and will be further examined in detail in several more chapters, as well). Workflows are basically automated business processes. Workflows in SharePoint Designer 2010 can be made available within lists or libraries.

SharePoint 2010 Foundation comes with several out-of-the-box workflows that can be used as-is or modified to fit your business process. New workflows can also be developed by users without development knowledge (using a "no-code" solution such as SharePoint Designer 2010 or Microsoft Visio Premium) or by .NET architects and developers (Utilizing Windows Workflow Designer in Microsoft Visual Studio 2010). Unlike Windows SharePoint Services 3.0, the architecture of SharePoint Foundation 2010 now allows for an organization to develop the custom workflow solution that is tailored to meet its exact needs.

The Recycle Bin

The Recycle Bin in SharePoint Foundation 2010 gives you an opportunity to easily recover deleted documents without the need to send a request to the SharePoint administrator to have an entire site, list, or library restored. When a document is deleted, it is sent to the site Recycle Bin, similar to how a file is deleted in Windows 7.

Summary

SharePoint Foundation 2010 is a web-based platform that can be used in most modern standard browsers. While the platform has been designed and optimized for Internet Explorer 8 and above, other browsers can be used, as well, with known limitations.

The optimum desktop environment in which to use SharePoint Foundation 2010 consists of a Level 1 browser, a complete installation of Microsoft Office 2010, and the Windows 7 operating system. While this is the optimum setup, you are can also use older versions of Microsoft Office (2007 & 2003) and Windows (XP or Vista), but you might experience some issues when trying to use some of the platform's newer features.

While the platform has undergone significant upgrades from previous versions, the majority of functionality and features have been preserved in SharePoint Foundation 2010. As such, if you are familiar with Windows SharePoint Services 3.0, you will be able to perform the same operations that you did in that version on this new platform. The biggest change you will encounter, however, will be the new location of commands. But experience has shown that the new user interface (the ribbon) is quite intuitive; therefore, the learning curve is relatively small.

SharePoint Foundation 2010 provides a wealth of features and functionality in the area of end-user experience for working in lists and libraries. Improvements to the platform can assist organizations with gaining user buy-in, negating concerns expressed about earlier SharePoint versions by users and consultants.

Chapter 3

Creating Sites and Workspaces by Using the Browser

B EFORE you can begin to add content and collaborate with others in Microsoft Share-Point Foundation 2010, you need a site or workspace. There are several methods by which a user can accomplish this, but the most straightforward and intuitive way is via the browser. The browser is a tool with which all computer users are acquainted. With the familiarity of the browser and intentional ease-of-use design, you can begin creating sites in no time at all.

INSIDE OUT   Choosing a template

Choosing the appropriate template is an important step. Once you have selected it, you cannot change it. So, be sure that you have determined how the site will be used before you decide upon the template. It will save you a lot of time down the road.

SharePoint Foundation 2010 comes with ten site and workspace templates. Each of these templates is designed to get you started with a basic layout and some predefined libraries and lists. A description of these templates follows:

- **<Select Template later>**   Not truly a template, but a placeholder. This is an empty site to which a template can be applied later.

- **Basic Meeting Workspace**   A site that has libraries and lists created that can be used to plan, manage, and document a meeting.

- **Blank Meeting Workspace**   Similar to the Basic Meeting Workspace but without the libraries and lists. This template is intended for users who want to do their own customization of the site.

- **Blank Site**   Similar to the Team Site template but without the libraries and lists.

- **Decision Meeting Workspace**   A meeting workspace designed to track decisions as well as provide the functionality in a normal meeting workspace.

- **Document Workspace**   A site designed to focus on a single primary document with supporting documents, links, and tasks.

- **Group Work Site**   Similar to a Team Site template but with a Group Calendar and other lists and libraries focused on a groupware solution.

- **Multipage Meeting Workspace**   Similar to Basic Meeting Workspace but with the addition of paging capabilities. Two additional blank pages are added by default.

- **Social Meeting Workspace**   Used for social events, it comes with a photo library, space for providing directions, and a list to show attendees.

- **Team Site**   A collaboration site intended for teams within your organization. It comes with several libraries and lists intended to support collaboration, such as the Calendar, Task, and Team Discussion.

Each site or workspace has a distinct URL. The URL can be changed but you should put some thought into choosing an appropriate one. People still tend to bookmark URLs and changing them can result in lost time searching for the new location of a site or workspace.

The template only provides a starting point for the site. New libraries and lists can be added; existing ones can be deleted or changed. The look and feel of the site can be changed as well as the home page. Pretty much everything within the site can be modified. The templates are intended as a starting point, giving users a head start on creating and sharing content with others. As needs change, so can the site and that is the true objective of the site. With that in mind, you still want to choose a template that is as close to your needs as possible. It will save a considerable amount of time that could be more productively spent creating and collaborating on content. The purpose of SharePoint 2010 Foundation is to help users be more productive, not less so.

Creating a Basic Team Site by Using the Browser

Let's begin by using the browser to create a basic Team Site. The Team Site is the most common site created in SharePoint 2010 Foundation. The Team Site comes by default with two libraries and three lists already created. The Site Pages library is normally used for storing webpages (such as the Home page you land on when you create the site). The Shared Documents library is intended as a common repository for all sorts of documents that are to be shared among the users of the Team Site. Documents that you will normally find there include Microsoft Word, Microsoft Excel, and Microsoft PowerPoint files. The first two lists are Calendar and Tasks. A Calendar list is used to place events that are relevant to the primary users of the Team Site. For example, if you create a Team Site for the Human Resources team, then the Calendar list could be used to show vacation days of all the Human Resources employees. This would help them to ensure proper coverage when employees take time off. The Tasks list can be used to assign and keep track of tasks related to the Team Site. A task can be assigned to anyone in your organization but the location of this task list would indicate that tasks be related to usage of the Team site. The third list, Team Discussion, is a specialized type of list referred to as a Discussion Board. It is designed to accommodate the discussion of any topics of concern to the users of the Team Site. It is a threaded discussion, and anyone with rights can post a topic or reply to a topic.

To create a site with Team Site template, perform the following steps:

1. Browse to the URL where you want the site to be located.

   For example, if you wanted a site named Engineering under the top-level Site Collection, then you would type the URL of the top-level Site Collection in your browser (for example **http://contoso**).

2. Click Site Actions | New Site, as demonstrated in the following:

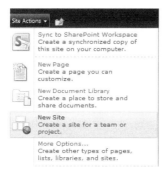

   If you don't see New Site, then you probably don't have proper permissions. You will need to obtain authorization before continuing.

3. Click Team Site.

   This is usually the default, but just in case, go ahead and click it.

4. Provide a Title and a URL name.

For this example, enter **Engineering** for both. You can change both of these in the future, but for actual sites, you want to try to pick a URL that remains consistent to avoid bookmarking issues.

5. Click Create. We will worry about the More Option button in the next section.

You should see a green spinning wheel with the text "Processing." Shortly thereafter, you will see your brand new site.

You have now created a site based on the Team Site template. It has document libraries and lists ready to use. You can start adding documents, tasks, calendar events, and discussions without doing anything to customize this site. This is the quickest and easiest way to start using SharePoint 2010 Foundation sites and begin your journey to more collaborative experience. Next, you will look at what's available under the More Options section.

Using More Options with a Team Site

Now that you have created a basic site with the Team Site template, you will create a new site and explore some of the other options that are provided via the browser. The additional options are centered on navigation and permissions as well as giving you an option for adding a description. All of these options can be changed later, but if you know what you want, then it makes sense to choose them when you make the site. Let's take a look at each of these options.

Title and Description

The Title is available without using the additional options. The Description allows for a short description to appear under the Title. The description text can actually be quite long, but it is plain text and not HTML. You can press the Enter key while in the text box (for line breaks), so you can type in a few sentences and still have it appear in a readable fashion. If you wanted to add a description for the Engineering site under the More Options section, it would appear as shown in Figure 4-1.

Title and Description

Type a title and description for your new site. The title will be displayed on each page in the site.	**Title:** Engineering **Description:** Team Site for the Engineering Team

Figure 4-1 Adding a title and description to your site.

Once you have created the site, the description displays right below the title. Since the text in the box is word wrapped and no line breaks were entered (pressing the Enter key), the text should appear in a single line, as shown in Figure 4-2.

Engineering ▸ Home
Team Site for the Engineering Team

Figure 4-2 The site description appears directly below the site title.

The description will only show up on the home page, which will be at *http://<site>/ SitePages/Home.aspx* by default, with *<site>* being the complete URL of the site.

Chapter 4

Web Site Address

The Web Site Address is the same as the spot for the URL name that you entered earlier when you created the new site. The key in determining the URL to put in this section is to come up with something that is short (to make it easy for users who type it manually) and that makes sense. For example, you could shorten Engineering to Eng.

INSIDE OUT   Forbidden characters

Website addresses cannot contain any of the following characters:

% & . * : < > ? / { | } -->

If you enter a space in the URL, it will be converted to %20, which is rather difficult for most users to type on a regular basis (errors are bound to occur). With the use of breadcrumbs and menu navigation, it isn't as important as it used to be, but it is still considered good form to keep the URL easy to read and type.

Permissions

Permissions determine who has access to your site, whether it is just the ability to read (and see search results), contribute, or have complete control over your site. The default is to use the same permissions as the parent site. This is referred to as *permissions inheritance*. It is the easiest way to handle permissions for the site, but also the least flexible. You can always break permissions inheritance on individual libraries or lists without using unique permissions for the site. You can even break inheritance for individual items. To change this setting, click More Options, and then go to the Permissions section, as shown in Figure 4-3.

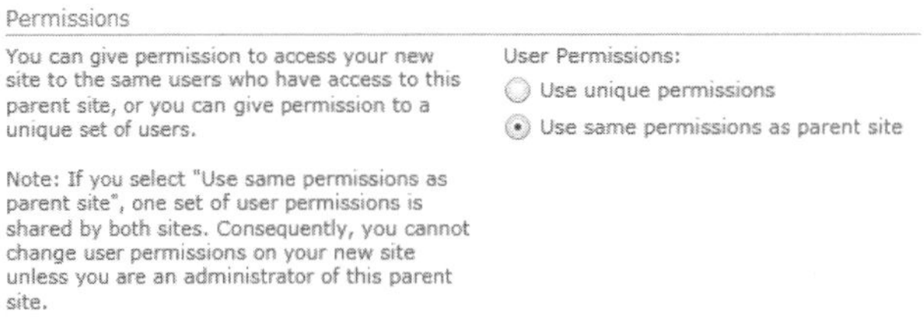

Permissions

You can give permission to access your new site to the same users who have access to this parent site, or you can give permission to a unique set of users.

User Permissions:

○ Use unique permissions

● Use same permissions as parent site

Note: If you select "Use same permissions as parent site", one set of user permissions is shared by both sites. Consequently, you cannot change user permissions on your new site unless you are an administrator of this parent site.

Figure 4-3 Changing the permissions setting in More Options.

The two choices are Use Unique Permissions and Use Same Permissions As Parent Site. Both of these options are reversible, but care should be taken in choosing Use Unique Permissions. When you choose this option, a dialog box opens, (see Figure 4-4), in which you create three new security groups.

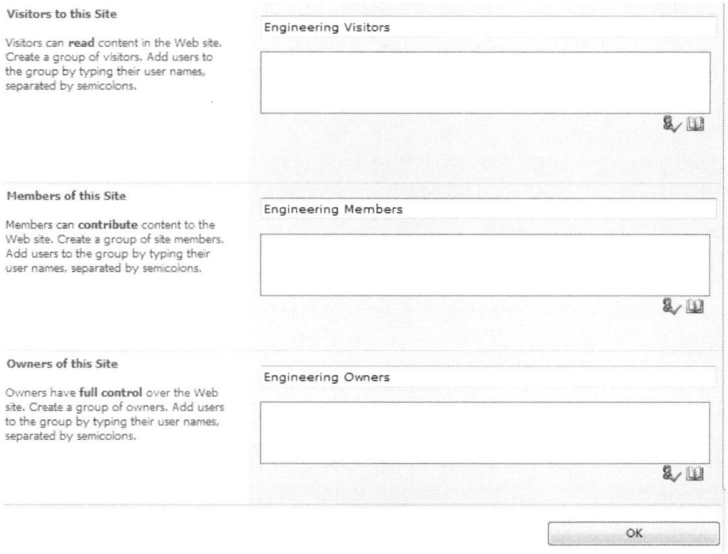

Visitors to this Site

Visitors can **read** content in the Web site.
Create a group of visitors. Add users to
the group by typing their user names,
separated by semicolons.

Engineering Visitors

Members of this Site

Members can **contribute** content to the
Web site. Create a group of site members.
Add users to the group by typing their
user names, separated by semicolons.

Engineering Members

Owners of this Site

Owners have **full control** over the Web
site. Create a group of owners. Add users
to the group by typing their user names,
separated by semicolons.

Engineering Owners

OK

Figure 4-4 Setting up the unique permissions groups.

INSIDE OUT   Security group considerations

Although SharePoint 2010 Foundation supports up to 10,000 security groups, there is
an inherent supportability issue if you have too many security groups. The more security groups you define, the more resources that are needed to support them.

The three new security groups are arranged into the following sets of users, each with their
own distinct needs.

- **Visitors**   Individuals of this group have read-only access by default. If you want to
  give everyone in your organization permissions to read the content in this site then
  you can add the special security group NT AUTHORITY\Authenticated Users. This will
  only work for any users that are authenticated by using Windows, but not with other
  methods of authentication such as Forms-Based Authentication (FBA).

- **Members**   This is for people who will be contributing and using this site on a regular basis. They can add, modify, and delete documents and list items. You will want to
  add the day-to-day users to this group.

- **Owners**   These users have complete control over the site. Owners can perform such tasks as add users, change the home page, and even delete the site. Use caution with this group; "accidents" are not uncommon when too many people have Owner permissions.

SharePoint provides some default names for the security groups. For example, if your site is named Engineering, then the three groups would be named Engineering Visitors, Engineering Members, and Engineering Owners, respectively. You can change the names of these groups at any time.

> **Note**
> Every group created exists at the Site Collection level. This means that they are available in any site within the Site Collection. It also means that creating many sites with this option will fill up the security groups, rendering them harder to maintain.

Navigation

The navigation section contains a pair of options, as shown in Figure 4-5. The first option determines whether to display this site on the Quick Launch of the parent. The default setting is No. Choosing Yes places a link to the site on the parent under the heading of Sites. The second option determines if a tab is added to the Top Link Bar that links to the site being created. If you are going to have a large number of sites, you might want to rethink adding a tab every time because they will begin to wrap such that you end up with two lines of tabs (and then three, and so on). It is not a very user-friendly interface after a certain point.

Figure 4-5 The options for displaying navigation links.

If you choose Yes on either of these, you will need to go to the parent site and manually remove the entries if you change your mind. It will also be necessary to go to the parent site to change the wording if it needs to be changed. Changing the Title of the site will not change it on the Top Link Bar or the Quick Launch.

Navigation Inheritance

The last option available in the More Options dialog box determines whether the Top Link Bar is inherited. The default is No (see Figure 4-6), which means that the Top Link Bar will be unique for this site. It means that clicking the Home tab takes you to the current site and not to the top-level Site Collection. This can be confusing to some users because there is no obvious way to navigate to the top-level Site Collection. You can navigate using the Navigate Up button to any site directly above the current one.

Navigation Inheritance

Specify whether this site will have its own top link bar or use the one from its parent.

Use the top link bar from the parent site?

○ Yes   ⦿ No

Figure 4-6 Setting navigation inheritance in the More Options dialog box.

Navigation inheritance can be turned on and off by navigating to the Top Link Bar page under Look And Feel in Site Actions. You will lose any links that have been manually entered if you click Use Links From Parent, as shown in Figure 4-7.

New Navigation Link   Use Links from Parent

Home

Figure 4-7 Clicking Use Links From Parent removes any manually entered links.

> ## INSIDE OUT   Consistent navigation
>
> Choosing to use links from the parent site is a personal choice, but having a consistent navigation has some benefits. Users who are presented with familiar navigation will find it easier to get around a Site Collection. The down side of using links from the parent site is that it limits flexibility.

Creating and Using a Basic Meeting Workspace

The Basic Meeting Workspace template provides a site for collaboration that is specifically designed for meetings. There is a place for the agenda, a list of attendees, a place to list objectives, and a document library for the storage of documents relating to the meeting. You can, of course, add, delete, or modify the items in the site, but this template provides a platform from which you can get started. Meeting Workspaces are different from normal sites in that they can be directly tied to a meeting (or series of meetings) within Microsoft Outlook. When you create a meeting, you can choose to create a Meeting Workspace or link to an existing one. The Meeting Workspace can be also be used for multiple meetings, which creates a series of related meetings. Each of the document libraries and lists can show items just for an individual meeting or they can be made to show items that cross all meetings (series). Before you get into the options and how to use the workspace, you will create one with your browser.

Creating a Basic Meeting Workspace by Using the Browser

Creating a Basic Meeting Workspace is similar to creating a regular a site with the Team Site template. But even though the process is similar, you will want to take more care in creating the Basic Meeting Workspace, especially if you are going to be using it for a series of meetings. The location of the meetings shouldn't change and you won't be able to create Subsites, so carefully choose where you want to locate the site. For this scenario, you will be creating a site for the weekly Engineering meeting; you will want to place it under the Engineering Team Site that you created earlier. You can do this by performing these steps:

1.   Navigate to the Engineering site.

2.   Click Site Actions, and then click Create Site (you must have permissions to create sites for this option to show up).

     The Create dialog box opens.

3.   Click the Basic Meeting Workspace template, as shown in the following illustration.

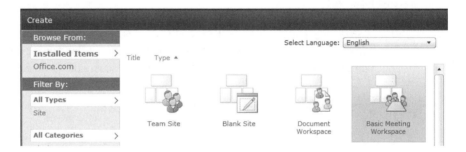

4.   In the Title text box, type **Weekly Meeting**.

5.   In the URL text box, enter **weekly**.

6. Click Create.

    You now have a new site that should contain the document libraries and lists.

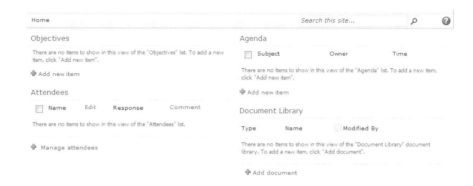

The Basic Meeting Workspace is now ready to use. The simplest way to use the new site is to send a link to the site in the meeting email, but you don't truly realize the full power of the Meeting Workspace unless you connect to it via Outlook when you create a meeting. In the next section, you will learn how to link to an existing workspace.

Connecting to an Existing Meeting Workspace

When you create a meeting by using Outlook (2007 or 2010), you have the option to connect to an existing Meeting Workspace, or you can create a new one. In this scenario, you will connect to an Existing Workspace. Not only will the link show up in the meeting, but once you have connected more than one meeting to the workspace, you will see dates appear where the Quick Launch normally appears (for example, in Team Sites). But before you get to that, you will need to connect your first meeting. Connecting the workspace might not be straightforward the first time you do it, so let's make sure that the Meeting Workspace icon is easily accessible by customizing the Quick Access Toolbar. To do this, perform the following steps:

1. Start Outlook 2010.

2. Open a new meeting by clicking New Items, and then click Meeting, as shown in the illustration that follows.

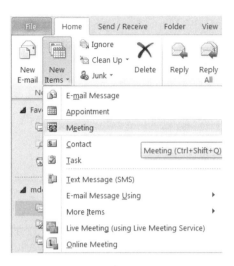

3. Right-click the ribbon, and then from the context menu that appears, click Customize Quick Access Toolbar.

4. Click Meeting Workspace from the list on the left.

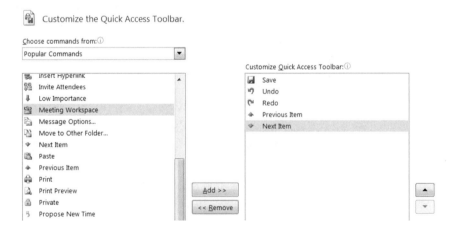

5. Click the Add button.

The Meeting Workspace item moves to the right column.

6. Click the OK button at the bottom of the dialog box.

The Meeting Workspace icon should appear in the top level navigation bar of the Meeting item.

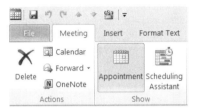

The Meeting Workspace icon will appear every time a meeting is created.

With the Meeting Workspace icon in place, it's easy to connect any meeting workspace to a meeting. Although Meeting Workspaces can be reused multiple times, it makes sense to put a reasonable limit on the number of times that you want to use them. It becomes confusing and hard to navigate if there are too many meetings (especially different types of meetings) using the same workspace. Now you can use the newly-displayed icon to connect the meeting to the meeting workspace by performing the following steps:

1. On the meeting item, click the Meeting Workspace icon

The Meeting Workspace dialog box opens on the far right.

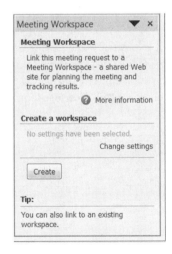

2. Click Create (or click You Can Also Link To An Existing Workspace).

The dialog box that follows replaces the previous one.

> **Note**
> If a workspace has been linked or created in the past, then the link You Can Also Link To An Existing Workspace must be used to link to a workspace.

3. Choosing a location is the next step, but if this is the first time you have used this location, it will be empty. To add a new location click the drop-down list, and then click Other.

To access the Meeting Workspace, it is necessary to enter the URL of the site above the meeting workspace. For example, if the Site Collection is named Contoso and the Meeting Workspace is located in the Engineering Team Site name (with a URL name of eng), then the URL you want to enter is **http://contoso/eng**.

4. Click OK.

You can now select Link To An Existing Workspace and choose the workspace that was created earlier (Weekly Meeting).

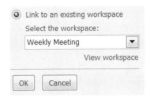

5. Click OK, and then click Link to finish linking the meeting to the Meeting Workspace.

    When you finish adding attendees and filling in the information for the meeting, it is ready to send. The link to the Meeting Workspace will appear in the body of the message, as shown in the following:

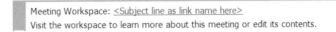

INSIDE OUT   Creating workspaces from Outlook

It is perfectly acceptable to create the workspace directly from Outlook. You can even reuse it just the same as a Meeting Workspace created with the browser. Use caution with this method though. Although the template can be chosen, that is the only option available through this interface.

Navigating a Meeting Workspace

Once you have linked to a Meeting Workspace more than once, a new navigational element will appear on the left of the main content area (in a Team Site, this is where the Quick Launch section is located). For every meeting there will be a date shown, as shown in Figure 4-8.

Figure 4-8 You can select from a list a meeting dates.

If there is more than one meeting on a given day, then there will be multiple instances of the same date and you might need to click on each one of them to find the meeting space you're looking for. The Meeting Workspace should default to the next meeting that appears in the future. If you have many meetings that use a particular Meeting Workspace, you can use the previous and next links to go back to older meetings or forward to future meetings. When you click an item, the page will show the meeting time and location at the top, as illustrated in Figure 4-9.

Weekly Meeting ▸ Home
Subject: Week 2 meeting
Date: 8/10/2011 **Time:** 12:00 PM - 12:30 PM >>
Location: Conference room

Figure 4-9 Clicking a meeting date displays the weekly meeting description.

The meeting description includes the subject, date, time, and location. With this information, it should be an easy task to identify any individual meeting. Clicking the >> (right angle bracket characters) displays the time zone in which the meeting occurs. This is important if you are meeting with people in different time zones.

Changing a Library or List to a Series

Any document library or list can be converted to a series. A series is a document library or list that crosses all meetings. A good example of when to use a series is for a set of meetings about a particular project. Documents that pertain to the project such as blue prints or project plans could go in a series document library. From a user's perspective, a series looks the same as any other document library or list. The only difference is that the items stay the same from one meeting to the next. While you can change a document library or list to be a series, it is a one-way street; you cannot change a series into a document library or list. The only way to go back would be to save off the items, delete the list or library, and then re-create it. After re-creating the list or library, it will still need the items added back to it. After the decision to turn a library or list into a series has been made, the browser can be used to make this happen. For example, if you want to convert the Objectives list to a series, perform the following steps:

1. On the home page of the Meeting Workspace, click the word Objectives to go to the Objectives list.

2. On the List Tools tab, click List, as shown here:

3. In the Settings group section on the far right of the ribbon, click List Settings.

4. In the General Settings section, click Advanced Settings.

5. Click the Yes option under Change Items Into Series Items.

6. Click OK to convert the list into a series

Once the decision to create a series has been made, all the items from the list that were separated by meeting times will be consolidated. These items will show up in every single meeting.

INSIDE OUT   Consider converting the Attendees list into a series

If you are going to use the Meeting Workspace for a specific set of meetings that always involve the same people, you can make the Attendees list into a series. A series saves space and makes the site more responsive.

Chapter 4

Creating and Using a Multipage Meeting Workspace

Multipage Meeting Workspaces are very similar to Basic Meeting Workspaces, with the exception that there are additional pages. The default is three pages (including the Home page), but it is possible to add and/or remove pages as needed. The pages can be named to match their purpose or remain with their default names (Home, Page 1 and Page 2). A Multipage Meeting Workspace is usually reserved for a more involved meeting with lots of supporting documents. An example of possible usage would be to put an agile burn down chart on one of the pages. There are lots of other uses for this type of workspace, but if you aren't going to use at least one of the additional pages, then it will just serve to confuse end users because of the left hand navigation. Before you learn how to customize the Multipage Meeting Workspace, you need to create one, first:

1. Open up the site above where you want to create the Multipage Meeting Workspace with the browser.

2. In the Site Actions menu, click New Site.

3. From the template page, select the Multipage Meeting Workspace, as shown in the following:

4. Provide a Title and URL name for the site.

5. Click OK to create the site.

    The site is created with two default pages, an Objectives list, Attendees list, and an Agenda list.

Now that the site has been created, the pages can be customized. The preceding screen-shot shows the Home page. The other pages, Page 1 and Page 2, have links in the navigation pane and are blank by default. They are meant to be customized as needed. The navigation pane is somewhat confusing. Clicking Pages does not go to a place to manage the pages; it goes to the same place as All Site Content. Managing the pages can be done through the Site Actions menu. For example, if you want to add a new page, perform the following:

1. Click Site Actions, and then click Add Pages, as shown in the following figure:

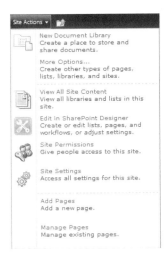

The Pages dialog box appears on the far right of the page.

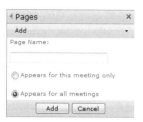

2. Enter a name in the Page Name text box.

3. Select either the Appears For This Meeting Only or the Appears For All Meetings option.

4. Click Add.

This adds a blank page to the site and places a navigation element in the Pages section on the left side of the page. Depending on the choice made, the new page will appear just for this one meeting or for all meetings. The new page is a normal Web Part page with three Web Parts (left, center, and right), as shown in Figure 4-10.

Figure 4-10 The new blank page containing Web Part sections.

This view is obtained by clicking Site Actions | Edit Page. There are a few items to notice when editing the page on the ribbon (see Figure 4-11). The Workflow and Approval sections are grayed-out. Normally, workflows are not associated with Meeting Workspaces because they are considered temporary. Publishing features are not normally used either because Meeting Workspaces are not intended to be viewed by people outside of the attendee list.

Figure 4-11 The Edit Page ribbon.

Another item to note is Delete Page, which, not surprisingly, is used to delete individual pages. Be aware though, that if you created a page that crosses all meetings, it will be deleted across all the meetings. Normally this is used for pages that were created for just one meeting and a decision was made to make a similar page that crosses all meetings.

Now that you have learned how to add pages, you are going to learn how to manage pages. There are only a few items that can be modified. The order of the pages can be changed, but the pages that appear in all the meetings must be on top of those pages that show up for individual meetings. You can manage the order of pages by performing the following steps:

1. In the Site Actions menu, click Manage Pages, as shown in the following:

The Pages dialog box appears on the right side of the page. It should default to Order, but if it doesn't, you can select it from the drop-down at the top of the window.

2. To move Page 1 down, click the words Page 1, click the down arrow, and then click Apply.

The order can be changed as often as needed. From this same dialog box, it's also possible to add a new page, delete a page, or change the settings. The only setting that is available is the one that changes a page from just being on a particular meeting or one that crosses all meetings and the title of the page, as shown in Figure 4-12.

Figure 4-12 Additional settings that you can change in the Pages dialog box.

INSIDE OUT   Customizing a workspace

When you use the browser, you are limited to adding only Web Parts to the workspace pages in a Multipage Meeting Workspace. For more advanced customization, you can use SharePoint Designer 2010. Workspaces are designed to be more utilitarian than attractive (hence, the "work" in the name), but there is nothing to stop you from making workspaces just as attractive as the rest of your sites.

Creating and Using the Document Workspaces

Document workspaces are perfect for complicated documents that have input from multiple users and supporting documents. It also comes with an announcements list, tasks list, a discussion board, calendar, a links list, and a list of members. The only document library is the Shared Documents library. If you are going to have one large document and many supporting documents, I recommend creating a new document library to store just the main document. There are many kinds of documents that fit this description, but one that is particularly representative is the Disaster Recovery document or set of documents. This document should cover what to do in case of potential disasters. It involves input from a large number of stakeholders, is revised often (if it is kept up to date), and potentially has dozens of supporting files. Of course, once a publishable version of this document is finished, it should be copied to several other locations just in case SharePoint is the system that is suffering from the disaster. This type of document fits perfectly as a Subsite of the Engineering Team Site. Before, you can start using a Document Workspace site, you need to create one. Carry out the follow instructions to create a site for your disaster recovery document based on the Document Workspace template:

1. In your browser, open the location where the site is to be created (for example, *http://contoso/eng*).

2. Click Site Actions | New Site.

3. Select the Document Workspace template from the list of available templates, as shown in the following:

4. Provide a Title and URL name for the new site (for example, **Disaster Recovery Document** and **disaster**).

5. Click Create.

A site should now be created below the Engineering Team Site. It is ready for tasks to be assigned, important dates put on the calendar, and members to be added. Documents can be added to the Shared Documents library, which is perfectly adequate for smaller documents, but for more involved documents, it makes sense to create an additional document library. Because the Disaster Recovery Document is a complicated document, it deserves its own document library as well as having versioning enabled. The first step is to create a new document library. This can be done in one of two ways. The first is to choose More Options from Site Actions:

1. In the browser, navigate to the Document Workspace (*http://contoso/eng/disaster*).

2. Click Site Actions, and then click More Options, as illustrated in the following:

3. Select the Document Library template. Notice that the Document Workspace template is located next to it.

4. Provide a name for the document library in the Name section, and then click Create.

The document library is now created, but it doesn't have any versioning, and there should be a link to the document library in the Quick Launch. While these can be changed in the List Settings, choosing New Document Library allows for setting options at the time of creation. To use this option, follow these instructions:

1. In the browser, navigate to the Document Workspace.

2. Click Site Actions, and then click New Document Library.

   A dialog box opens, presenting several options. First, enter the Name and Description to identify this as the location of the master disaster recovery document.

3. Select whether to display the document library in the Quick Launch.

   Because this is the main document, it should be located on the Home page, so either option is acceptable.

Navigation

Specify whether a link to this document library
appears in the Quick Launch.

Display this document library on the
Quick Launch?

○ Yes   ○ No

4. Select whether to have versioning turned on.

Because this is the main document, enabling versioning on is recommended.

Document Version History

Specify whether a version is created each time
you edit a file in this document library.

Create a version each time you edit a
file in this document library?

○ Yes   ○ No

5. The final option to consider is which document template to use. For this scenario, you will stick with the default Microsoft Word Document.

Because this document library houses only one document and it will probably be uploaded, it doesn't make much difference which template you choose.

Document Template

Select a document template to determine the
default for all new files created in this
document library.

Document Template:

Microsoft Word document   ▼

6. Click Create to generate the document library.

A document library has now been created to host the disaster recovery master document. It has versioning turned on, but it only has major versioning turned on and it is not limited in the number of versions. There is also no requirement that the document be checked out before it is edited. This will increase the likelihood that changes are overwritten. So, to make your document library more sophisticated and facilitate better collaboration (by keeping users from overwriting each other and notifying users if a document is checked out), you will need to look at some of the more advanced settings.

INSIDE OUT   Versioning

Each version of the document is stored as a complete document within the database. Unlimited versions of very large documents can cause bloating of the database, increasing the amount of time to backup and restore. The recommend practice is to limit the number of versions on documents that are large and are changed frequently, and to take advantage of draft versions because they are deleted when a major version is published.

Chapter 4

To modify these options, you will need to go to the version settings page for the document library. This can be done by following these steps:

1. Click the disaster recovery document library from the Quick Launch to go to home page of the document library.

2. On the Library Tools tab, click Library, as shown in the following:

3. In the Settings section, click Library Settings.

4. In the General Settings section, click Version Settings.

The version settings page should now appear in the browser.

The first choice to consider is Content Approval. If you choose Yes, then changes to the document will need to be approved before members of the site (who do not have full control) can see them. For now, leave this set to No.

5. Select the Document Version History settings.

This section presents several options.

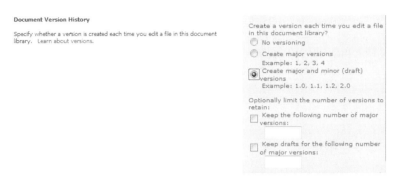

There are three main choices: No Versioning, Create Major Versions, and Create Major And Minor (Draft) Versions. This example uses the major and minor version but leaves the number of versions blank. That means they are unlimited.

Because we're using Create Major And Minor (Draft) Versions for this example, the Draft Item Security option is available. This gives you the option to control who sees the drafts. There are three options but as this example didn't choose to require content approval, that option is grayed-out.

6.   The final option to configure is Require Check Out.

This is recommended if there are going to be several different people editing the same document. This prevents collaborators from overwriting each other (as long as they get the latest copy). To require check out, choose the Yes option.

7.   Click OK to apply the changes.

The document library is ready to use with versioning (major and minor), and it requires check out to edit.

Chapter 4

The disaster recovery document library is ready to be used. There is a link to the document library in the Quick Launch, but it would be even better to have the document accessible on the Home page. Then, users can open up the document with one click and it would be intuitively obvious which one was the primary document. To carry this out, you need to add the document library as a Web Part. To do so, perform the following steps:

1. Browse to the Document Workspace Home page.

2. Click Site Actions, and then click Edit Page, as shown in the following:

3. Click Add a Web Part in the Top web zone.

   This places the document library in the same zone as Announcements by default.

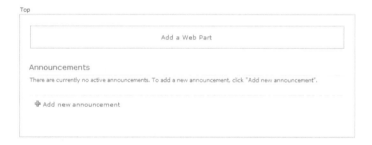

4. In the Categories section that appears in the upper-left corner, click Lists And Libraries, and then in the Web Parts section, click Disaster Recovery Document.

5. Click Add on the far right side of the page.

   This adds the document library.

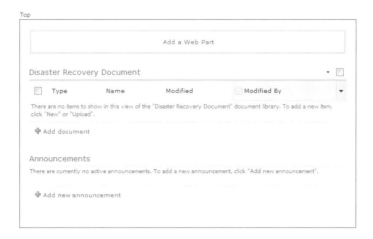

The Disaster Recovery Document library is now above Announcements, but you can place it farther down by dragging it below Announcements.

The Document Workspace is now ready to use and even has some built-in disaster recovery of its own with the addition of versioning and edit control. If this Document Workspace is used to create a completed document (rather than a living document that changes continually), it's best to save the document to another site or location and then delete the Document Workspace, freeing up valuable resources and keeping your SharePoint Foundation installation clean. This will help to keep your crawl times shorter, the content databases smaller, and improve the time it takes to restore.

Creating and Using a Group Work Site

The Group Work Site template is great for groups that come together to work on projects. It is similar to a basic Team Site template but with some additional items that focus on a larger task. One example that ties into the Engineering theme is designing a new widget. Designing a new widget can involve members from a variety of teams or a subset of engineering. Either way, the site would work. One of the most notable additions that facilitate this collaboration is the Group Calendar. This can be used to keep track of resources and show availability in a similar fashion to Microsoft Project (but on a much smaller scale). The template doesn't have a list for members because the members of the site will be normally listed as resources. Before you look at the site in more detail, let's go through the steps for creating one:

1. Browse to the location where the site is to be located (for example, *http://contoso/eng*).

2. Click Site Actions, and then click New Site.

Chapter 4

3. Select the Group Work Site template, as shown in the screenshot that follows:

4. Type **Widget Group** in the Title text box and **widget** as the URL name.

5. Click Create.

Now that a site has been created, you should notice the Group Calendar at the top of the site, as shown in Figure 4-13.

Figure 4-13 The Group Calendar in your new site.

It looks like a normal calendar is some ways with a navigation element that moves through the calendar a week at a time. What stands out is the Add Resources link and the Add Person input box. The group calendar can be used to keep track of people as well as resources. This helps utilize people effectively without overbooking them and helps to prevent resources from being double booked (as well as alerting people about what resources are available). At the moment your calendar has neither resources nor people, so you need to add them before you can assign them to the calendar. People are added by typing their name in the Add Person dialog box and then clicking the check person icon, as illustrated in Figure 4-14.

Figure 4-14 To add a person, type a name in the Add Person text box.

It is also possible to use the directory by clicking the Browse icon (the one that looks like a book). Adding resources is a little more complicated. Clicking the Add Resources link opens an empty dialog box along with an error indicating that there are no resources, as demonstrated in Figure 4-15.

Find

No resources exist in the Resource list.

Figure 4-15 Because there are no links in the Resources list, you see an error when you click Add Resources.

The error occurs because there are no links to the Resources list. There are a couple of ways to populate the list of resources: click either the Lists link or the All Site Content link. Each brings you to a page that shows the Resources list, as shown in Figure 4-16.

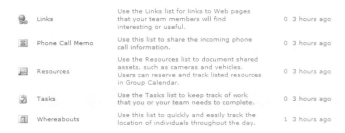

Links	Use the Links list for links to Web pages that your team members will find interesting or useful.	0	3 hours ago
Phone Call Memo	Use this list to share the incoming phone call information.	0	3 hours ago
Resources	Use the Resources list to document shared assets, such as cameras and vehicles. Users can reserve and track listed resources in Group Calendar.	0	3 hours ago
Tasks	Use the Tasks list to keep track of work that you or your team needs to complete.	0	3 hours ago
Whereabouts	Use this list to quickly and easily track the location of individuals throughout the day.	1	3 hours ago

Figure 4-16 Click Resources in the Resources list.

Clicking the Resources link will take you to the list where any sort of resource can be added. A resource is generally defined as something that has to be shared and/or reserved. It could be a room, a vehicle, a computer, or any sort of equipment with limited quantities. For this example, you will add a round table video camera that can be checked out by performing the following steps:

1. Click the Resources link.

2. Click Add new item, as shown in the following illustration:

Name   Description

There are no items to show in this view of the "Resources" list. To add a new item, click "New".

➕ Add new item

Chapter 4

3. Add Round Table Video Camera #1 for the name, and then type a description of the item such as **Used for panorama view**.

4. Click Save to add the resource.

There is now a resource to choose when you click Add Resources on the Group Calendar. It is important to use resource names that distinguish them in a manner that is clearly discernable by the end user. This will help to avoid confusion and ensure maximum usage.

INSIDE OUT   Adding resources

If you need resources that are used by more than the people in this group you can use workflows to either notify the person responsible for scheduling the resources or actually put it on other lists to let other users know that it is in use.

Now that a resource has been added, you need to add it to the calendar by following these instructions:

1. Browse to the Home page of the Widgets Group site.

2. Click the Add Resources link in the group calendar.

3. When the Select Resources And Resource Groups dialog box opens, select Round Table Video Camera #1 (or whatever the resource was named), and then click the Add button, as shown in the following screenshot:

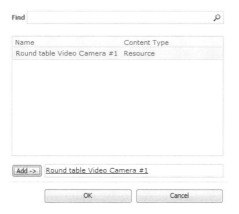

4. Click OK to add the resource.

   The resource should now appear on the calendar where it can be assigned dates and times

Notice that the name of the resource is cut off. The width of the title field is fixed, and you would need a tool like SharePoint Designer 2010 to modify it. Keep that in mind when naming the resources. You don't want users to be forced to guess which resources are in use. And changing the view will not change the width of the Title field. Now that a resource has been added, it can be scheduled via the Add Person input box. A resource can be scheduled by following these steps:

1. Browse to the Home page of the Widgets Group site.

2. Hover over the bottom area in the column of the day for which you want to schedule the resource. It must be on the last resource or person in the Title column, as shown in the illustration that follows.

3. Click the Add link.

   The New Item dialog box opens.

4. Type in a Title (for example, **Kickoff Meeting**), and then select a Start Time and End Time. You must also add at least one person in Attendees.

   For this example, you will add the round table video camera, which is in the resources column. It will show up in the left column unless the Add link was clicked in a resource row, in which case it will appear in the right column by default

5. Click Add after the resource has been selected.

6. Click Save.

   The people and the resources will be booked on the calendar. As shown in the following screenshot, the meeting appears in both the row for Michael Doyle and the row for the resource.

There are some options that we did not address when creating the meeting. There is the Free/Busy section that checks to see if the resources and/or people are already busy during the time that the meeting is to occur (or other activity). The Free/Busy might not update until you click the Check button in the Check Double Booking section. Once you click the Check button, it should update. For example, if a meeting is scheduled on top of the one that was scheduled above and the Check button is clicked, it would appear as in Figure 4-17.

Figure 4-17 Free/Busy checks whether resources are available for the designated time of the meeting.

Notice that it shows that Michael Doyle and the round table video camera are marked as booked during the hours of 9 a.m. and 11 a.m. This will help prevent double booking, but remember that this calendar is not tied to any other calendar. End user training and education will be required to properly use the group calendar effectively.

The Category field can be used, but it will only show up if you open the item or if you create a new view of the calendar. New fields can be added, but if a new drop-down item is desired, then the calendar itself will need to be modified. This is done by going to the List Settings of the calendar and then clicking the Category field link. A list of categories appears in the Additional Column Settings section, as illustrated in Figure 4-18.

Chapter 4

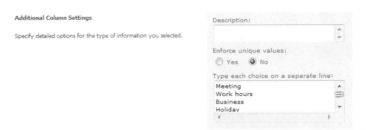

Figure 4-18 Modifying the calendar by using options in Additional Column Settings.

The reason that categories might be important becomes apparent if they are used for reporting. Specific time codes could be used to keep track of people and resources time. A good example would be if this was a contract job and the account manager needed to keep track of specific hours spent in meetings and on projects.

The next two options available are All Day Event and Recurrence. The All Day Event option will block off all resources and people for the entire day, for each day that the item covers. This can be a real time saver if the item covers a large period of time. Instead of creating several eight-hour events, you can use just one event that uses the Add Day Event. Of course, if time needs to be specified exactly, then this option will not work. The Recurrence option is used to create meetings that occur on a regular basis, such as every day, week, or month. Again, if you are keeping track of specific hours for accounting purposes, creating an individual meeting or item will be more accurate.

The final option is the Workspace option. This creates a workspace for the meeting. If this option is checked, then it will bring up a new page in which options can be selected. Unlike using the New Site option, there are very few options that can be chosen. The options you can select are Title, Description, URL name, User Permissions, and Language. There is no option to select a template until a user clicks OK. Then the user can choose from the available templates, as shown in Figure 4-19.

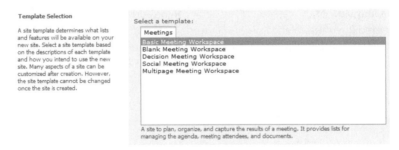

Figure 4-19 Selecting a template for the meeting workspace.

Once you select a template and click OK, a workspace will be created for the meeting under the group site. There is no option to place the workspace in a different location.

INSIDE OUT   Using customized templates

You can select a customized site template if it is uploaded to the solution gallery and then activated. Usually, this is only an option in larger organizations, but it does allow for a large degree of customization.

Now that the calendar has been set up, the group work site is ready to use. There are some other options to explore. These are mainly the Whereabouts, Circulations, and Phone Call Memo. These options can help round out the functionality of the site. The Whereabouts option can help you find where people are located; Circulations can help ensure that notifications are received by specified individuals; and the Phone Call Memo can be used to share information about phone calls that have been received. Other lists and documents can be added as needed but the Group Work Site template should provide a great start to any group that needs a SharePoint Foundations website for any group-related project.

Creating and Using a Blog Site

It seems like everyone has a blog these days, and with the Blog template in SharePoint Foundation 2010, you can create one, too. Creating a blog with the browser is similar to creating other websites and workspaces. The first decision to make is where to create the blog. In this example, you will create a blog for the Engineering Team Site created earlier in this chapter. A blog located here should contain posts related to the Engineering team. This could be anything that the team comes up with. The more blog posts the better. They can always be trimmed down later. Most blogs start off with lots of enthusiasm and contributions, but that enthusiasm eventually dwindles and the contributions become few and far between if there is not a champion for the blog. This doesn't mean that a single individual has to be the person that contributes all the posts, but having a person that contributes and reminds others to also contribute will help to make the blog worthwhile for years to come. But before you worry about that, you need to accomplish the first step, which is to create the blog:

1.   Browse to the site where the blog is to be located (for example, *http://contoso/eng*)

2.   Click Site Actions, and then click New Site.

3. From the list of templates, select the Blog template, as shown in the following screenshot:

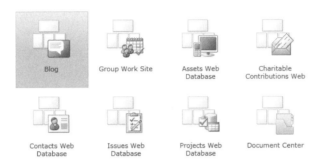

4. Enter a Title and URL name. For this example, type **Engineering Blog** and **Blog**, respectively.

5. Click Create to generate the new blog.

   Once you create a blog, a sample blog post will be created.

The blog site comes with lots of features built in. Notice the Really Simple Syndication (RSS) Feed and the Alert Me at the bottom of the preceding screenshot. These two options provide update methods when a person enters a new blog post. You can leave comments on the blog post, email it, and make it a permanent link in the Favorites list of your browser. Now that the blog site has been created, new blog posts can be created. It is probably a good idea to go ahead and delete the default entry, but you will focus on creating a new one. Before you do that, you should create some proper categories (instead of Category 1, Category 2, and Category 3). Follow these instructions to add a new category:

1. Browse to the Home page of the blog.

2. Click Add new category.

    The New Item dialog box opens

3. Categories are just a list of titles. Add a Title to the New Item dialog box, and then click Save.

A new category has just been added. Having proper categories can greatly speed up the time it takes for a person to find a particular blog post. If the content of the blog is technical in nature, then categories are a necessary part of creating blog posts. People will come to rely on blog posts for answers to difficult decisions. The Blog Tools appear for people who can contribute to the blog. The tools available are shown in Figure 4-20.

Blog Tools
- Create a post
- Manage posts
- Manage comments
- Launch blog program to post

Figure 4-20 Use the links in Blog Tools to start contributing.

From the Blog Tools, you can create posts, manage posts, manage comments, and click the launch blog program link to post a new blog post. If you don't specify a blog program (via the browser) it will default to Word. When you open Word and post, you will be asked to enter credentials but other than that it's easy to use Word to publish your blog posts. You are now ready to start creating blog posts and sharing information with your fellow workers. Just remember, the more people share on blogs, the quicker other users will find the information needed to solve their problems.

Summary

This chapter explained the basics of how to create sites and workspaces with the browser in SharePoint Foundation. It started off with the basic Team Site and worked through several workspaces and other site templates, while exploring some of the options available. It also showed how to customize some of the main elements of each type of site as well as how to hook into Meeting Workspaces with Outlook. After finishing this chapter, you should have a firm understanding of the sites and workspaces available as well as how to create them. Finally, you touched on creating a blog site. With blog sites, end users are empowered to create and share information that helps them on a day-to-day basis. The more people who contribute to internal blogs, the quicker difficult problems will be solved for others in your organization. Hopefully, you have also gained some insight into when to use which template to get the most out of your site. Consequently, by following the process, you will be able to minimize the amount of additional customization work that might be required to meet your business needs.

Designing Lists and Libraries

L ISTS and libraries can be used as repositories for almost anything that you want to store within the Microsoft SharePoint environment. With the help of new form dialogs and the introduction of the ribbon, the experience of reading, editing, and creating content has been greatly enhanced in SharePoint Foundation 2010.

Lists and libraries are a powerful solution for organizations that currently create content in many different types of applications that are then saved in various locations. If you have a collection of spreadsheets that you store and track on your desktop, it is very easy to import them directly into a SharePoint list so that they are available to a larger audience, but in a more secure manner. Why create a large number of Microsoft Excel spreadsheets or Microsoft Word documents on your desktop that are hard to keep track of or have many different mechanisms for collecting and presenting data when you can accomplish this quickly and store the content in lists and libraries? Once you have stored the data, you can configure Web Part pages to display the lists and libraries in your SharePoint site.

You will soon discover this is much easier than handcrafting a never-ending series of Excel spreadsheets, and it is certainly easier than developing custom code. This chapter explains how to create lists and libraries, including not only the standard types that come with SharePoint Foundation 2010, but also custom types that you design yourself to meet your specific needs. It goes on to explain how you can then utilize the powerful features of SharePoint Designer 2010 to display data via Really Simple Syndication (RSS) feeds or use workflows to automate specific tasks and receive content approval and feedback. The chapter also goes into detail about how you can use content types to standardize your organization's procedures for capturing metadata and managing information.

This chapter concentrates exclusively on using a browser to create, modify, and display lists and libraries. SharePoint Designer 2010 can also perform these tasks, and Chapter 14, "Creating, Managing, and Designing Sites by Using SharePoint Designer 2010," will explain that approach.

Creating Lists

Whenever you want to add data to a SharePoint site, or whenever you want others to do so, you should first locate the proper list (or library). If an appropriate list or library does not exist, a new one needs to be created.

Tip

When deciding whether to create a new list or library or use one that already exists, it is important that you not duplicate efforts in SharePoint. A little investigation about what is currently available can go a long way toward upholding the "one version of the truth" philosophy.

If a list or library exists that meets your needs, store your content there. But what if your SharePoint site doesn't contain a list or library that seems right for the type of information that you need to store? SharePoint Foundation 2010 list and library functionality is flexible in that if you need new ones, you can create them with ease and without expert knowledge of the product. The next two sections provide guidance for new list and library creation.

Creating Built-In Lists

To begin creating a SharePoint list of any kind, open the site where you want the list to reside, click the All Site Content link at the bottom of the Quick Launch, and then click Create. This displays the Create page, as shown in Figure 5-1.

Note

It is also possible to access the Create page by clicking Site Actions, and then clicking New Document Library or More Options.

Figure 5-1 The Create page displays options for creating all available types of SharePoint lists, libraries, and pages.

The simplest lists to create are the built-in types that appear under the Communications and Tracking headings. Table 5-1 lists these types.

Table 5-1 Built-In SharePoint Foundation 2010 List Types

Type	Description	Interface to Microsoft Office Outlook?
Announcements	Stores news, status, and other short bits of information.	No
Contacts	Stores information about people your team members work with, such as customers, vendors, or partners.	Yes
Discussion Board	Stores information regarding team discussions on any given subject. Information can be captured here such as a team's best practices and lessons learned. It is also great for knowledge management. Furthermore, it can be set to allow for email traffic.	Yes
Issue Tracking	Stores issues or problems associated with a project or item. This list allows you to assign, prioritize, and track issue status.	No
Links	Stores links to webpages or other resources to which your team needs access.	No

Chapter 5

Type	Description	Interface to Microsoft Office Outlook?
Calendar	Stores information about upcoming meetings, deadlines, and other important team events.	Yes
Tasks	Stores work items that you or your individual team members need to complete.	Yes
Project Tasks	Stores work items that your team needs to conclude to complete assigned projects. Additionally, it also offers a Gantt chart view with progress bars overlaid on a timescale.	Yes
Survey	Stores feedback from users within the organization. This list is a great tool for collecting and compiling feedback such as an employee-of-the-month survey. You can also design custom questions for your audience.	No
External lists	Stores list items that are made available from an external content type via the Business Connectivity Service (BCS). Using this, you can quickly and easily connect to external databases, web services, Microsoft .NET connectivity assemblies, or other custom applications.	Yes

Although many aspects of working with these and other list types are the same, each built-in list type has properties that you cannot change; for example:

- You can't change the icon assigned to a built-in list.

- Each type of list has certain required fields that you can't delete. For example, you can't delete the Title and Start Time fields in a Calendar list.

Creating a New List from the Built-In Lists

Site administrators or those with the appropriate permissions can easily create a new list from the built-in lists available in SharePoint Foundation 2010 by performing the following steps:

1. At the bottom of the Quick Launch, click All Site Content, and then click Create on the All Site Content page.

2. Either scroll through your options or under the Filter By heading, click List, and then select the type of list that you want to create, such as Issue Tracking or Project Tasks, as shown previously in Figure 5-1.

3. In the Name box, type in a name for the new list (this is a required field; see Figure 5-2).

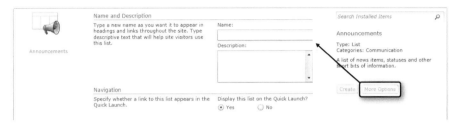

Figure 5-2 Use the New page to name, describe, and set navigation details for a new SharePoint list.

The name you type here will appear at the top of the list's page and will become part of the URL for the page and any related navigational elements.

4. To type in a Description and/or select if this list should appear in the Quick Launch, click More Options.

The Description field is optional, but it will appear at the top of the list in most views.

5. If you would like the new list to display in the site's Quick Launch bar, select Yes in the Navigation section.

6. Click Create to complete the process.

The new list is created, but it will not contain any items, as shown in Figure 5-3.

Figure 5-3 The new list contains no items yet.

Once the list exists, you can enter data, create new views, display views in web pages, or even modify the list's data fields and features. You'll learn how to do all of this later in this chapter.

Creating Custom Lists

For maximum flexibility when creating a new list, choose any one of the custom links under the Lists heading: Custom List, Custom List In Datasheet View, or Import Spreadsheet. Here's how these links work:

- **Custom List**   This option displays the New page (see Figure 5-4) and then creates and displays a list with only the Title column displayed. Two columns, Created By and Modified By, are created behind the scenes to store information about the users who work with the content of the list.

Figure 5-4 The Custom List dialog box.

  In almost every case, you would use the instructions in the next section—"Modifying Lists"—to modify this starting point with additional fields and features.

- **Custom List In Datasheet View**   Like Custom List, this option displays the New page and creates a list with Title as the only column that is displayed. This option, however, opens the new list in the Datasheet view so that you can view and modify list items in a tabular interface.

- **Import Spreadsheet**   Creates a list from data contained in a spreadsheet.

Creating a List from a Template

With SharePoint Foundation 2010, you can create lists from templates so that lists that are already proven to work within the organization—or those that contain customizations—can be easily reused. List templates can be imported and exported to different Site Collections and can be made available to a larger audience.

If desired, a list template can contain the actual content that existed within the list when it was saved as a template. It can also retain any of its views. You create lists from list templates via the same process that you use when creating lists from built-in templates, as detailed earlier in this chapter. The list templates will display as available links on the Create page, as shown in Figure 5-5.

Figure 5-5 Several list templates are now available on the Create page.

Creating a Library

As discussed in earlier chapters, the main area for storing content in SharePoint Foundation 2010 is a library. Using a library, you can store, create, and manage files within your organization. If a library does not already exist within your organization that satisfies your needs, you can create a new one.

Creating a New Library

Site administrators or those with the appropriate permissions can easily create a new library from the available built-in libraries offered in SharePoint Foundation 2010 by performing the following steps:

1. Click All Site Content, and then on the All Site Content page, click Create.

2. Under Library heading, click the type of library that you want (such as Document Library).

3. In the Name text box, type a name for the library, as shown in Figure 5-6.

Chapter 5

Figure 5-6 Use the New page to name and describe a new document library.

The library name is required and displays at the top of the library page. It becomes part of the library's URL and navigational elements.

4. If you want to add additional details, click More Options.

5. In the Description box, you can optionally type a description of the purpose of the library.

The description appears at the top of the library page.

6. To add a link to this library on the Quick Launch bar, verify that Yes is selected in the Navigation section.

7. To create a new version each time a file is checked into the library, select Yes in the Document Version History or Picture Version History section.

8. Depending on the type of library you are creating, a Document Template section might be available. It lists the compatible programs that are available as the default for creating new files. If content types are enabled, the default template is specified through the content type. In the Document Template section, in the drop-down list, select the type of file that you want to be used as a template for files that are created in the library.

9. Click Create.

> **Note**
> It's likely that you will have several lists and libraries in use on your site. Because of this, it is highly recommended that you opt to type a description for each list or library that is created. By doing so, you can help alleviate confusion among team members as to what information should be stored in the list or library. The range of descriptions can be as simple as an explanation of what the library is, up to posting information regarding governance and usage policies for the list or library.

Defining Site Columns

Site columns are metadata or columns that are defined at the Site Collection level and then allowed to be available through the Site Collection. Site columns can be created to ensure that relevant information on the content entered is made readily available to assist in locating information, through filtering or sorting as well as being used as triggers for workflows. Managing site columns is still very similar in SharePoint Foundation 2010 as it was in Windows SharePoint Services 3.0.

To manage site columns, perform the following steps:

1. Navigate to the top level of the Site Collection.

2. Click Site Actions, and then select Site Settings.

3. Under the Galleries heading, click Site Columns.

4. As in Windows SharePoint Services 3.0, you can manage site columns from the Site Column Page. To edit a particular site column, click its Name.

To create a new site column, follow steps 1 through 3, and then perform the following:

1. Click the Create button.

   The New Site Column Page opens.

2. In the Name And Type section, type the name that you want in the Column Name text box.

3. Under The Type Of Information In This Column Is, select the type of data that should be entered into the new column.

4. In the Additional Column Settings section, type a description in the Description box to help users within the organization understand the purpose of the column and what data it should contain. This description is optional but recommended.

5. Depending on the type of column that you selected, more options might appear in the Additional Column Settings section. Select the additional settings that you want.

6. To require that the column contain information, click Yes. Also, if you would like to enforce unique values click Yes.

7. Click OK to create your new Site Column.

Chapter 5

Modifying Lists and Libraries

You might find an existing list or library within your organization that would meet your requirements if it only contained a few additional fields (that is, content types or columns). The topics in this section explain how to modify an existing list or library to better suit your needs.

Numerous organizations have similar data that is being captured on the same topic, but the data is in multiple lists or libraries on separate sites. The challenge is working with different users and groups to see if these lists or libraries can either be combined into a centralized one that contains all of the content types and columns; if not, then how one or more of the lists or libraries can be modified to meet the organization's needs. Performing a quick proof-of-concept with a new list or library that contains all of the fields is sometimes a great way to show users that one centralized repository can work for everyone.

Modifying List and Library Settings

SharePoint lists and libraries are extremely flexible and customizable right out of the box. You can change their properties, behavior, security, appearance, workflow settings, and fields at will. To begin, display the list or library that you want to modify, and then under the List or Library Tools Heading, click List or Library. Select List Settings or Library Settings to display the customization page, which is illustrated in Figure 5-7. This layout should look very familiar to users of previous versions of SharePoint.

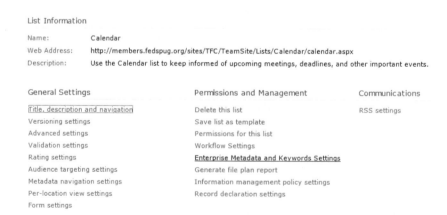

Figure 5-7 The Customize page displays and changes the configuration of a SharePoint list.

The next few sections explain how to use the commands on the customization page.

Updating General Settings

In SharePoint Foundation 2010, four links are available under the General Settings header with which you can change the general settings for the list or library. These links are Title, Description, and Navigation; Versioning Settings; Advanced Settings; and Validation Settings. To change any of these items, click the corresponding link.

Updating Title, Description, and Navigation

To change the title, description, or navigation, click the corresponding link to display the List General Settings page, as shown in Figure 5-8.

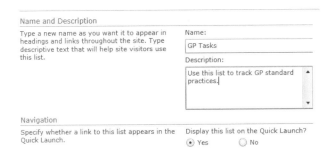

Figure 5-8 The List General Settings page, in which you can change the title, description, or navigational settings of a SharePoint site list or library.

With the List General Settings page open, make any desired changes to the following fields:

- **Name**   Type a name that will identify the list or library throughout the site.

- **Description**   Briefly describe the list or library's content or purpose.

- **Display This List (or Library) On The Quick Launch?**   Select Yes if you want the Quick Launch bar to display a link to this list or library.

Versioning Settings in a List

To change the versioning settings in a list, navigate to the list, and then click its link. Under the List Tools heading, click List, select List Settings, and then click the Versioning Settings link to display the List Versioning Settings page, as illustrated in Figure 5-9.

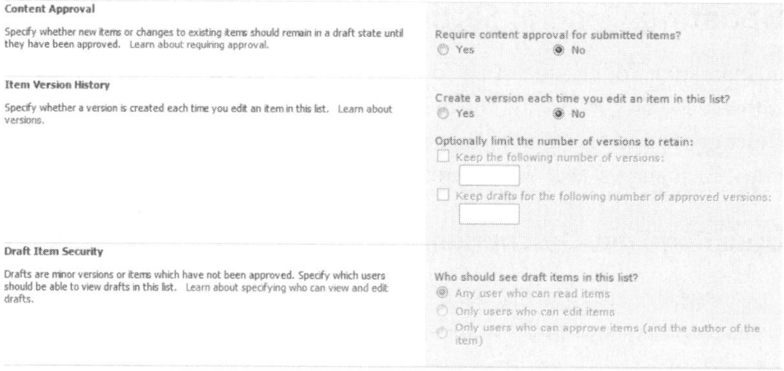

Figure 5-9 In the List Versioning Settings page, you can configure the versioning settings of a SharePoint list.

With the List Versioning Settings page open, make any desired changes to the following fields:

- **Content Approval**   Select Yes if you want to require approval for items submitted to the list; or No if you do not require approval.

- **Item Version History**   Select Yes if you want to create a new version each time you edit an item in the list. If you select Yes, you have the option to then limit the number of drafts to be retained.

  Select the number of versions and the number of drafts for each version to retain. Due to SharePoint saving complete copies of a document for each version created, a considerable amount of storage space can be consumed rather quickly. As such, it is a good idea to limit the number of versions. It is generally recommended to keep three to five versions unless there is a business need to retain more. Refer to your organizations Governance Plan for specific requirements.

- **Draft Item Security**   Specify which users can see draft items in the list. The available options are Any User Who Can Read Items, Only Users Who Can Edit Items, and Only Users Who Can Approve Items (And The Author Of The Item).

Versioning Settings in a Library

To change the versioning settings in a library, browse to the library, and then click its link. Under the Library Tools heading, click Library, select Library Settings, and then click the Versioning Settings link to display the Document Library Versioning Settings page, as depicted in Figure 5-10.

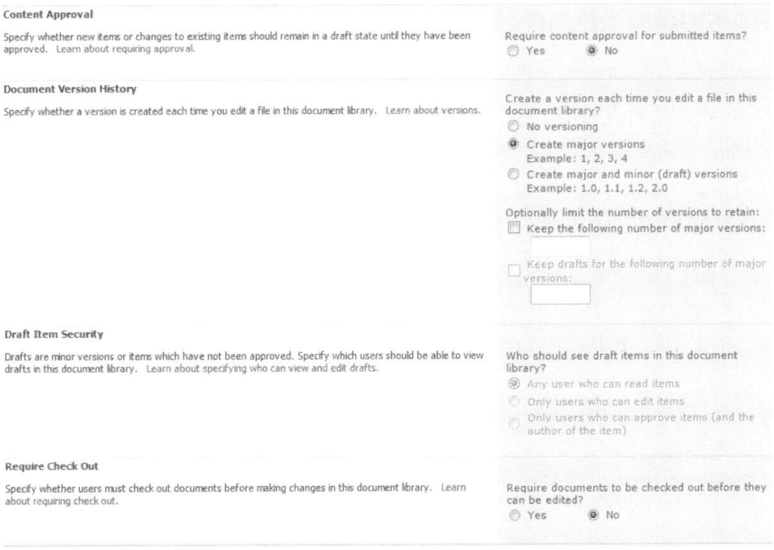

Content Approval

Specify whether new items or changes to existing items should remain in a draft state until they have been approved.   Learn about requiring approval.

Require content approval for submitted items?
○ Yes   ◉ No

Document Version History

Specify whether a version is created each time you edit a file in this document library.   Learn about versions.

Create a version each time you edit a file in this document library?
○ No versioning
◉ Create major versions
   Example: 1, 2, 3, 4
○ Create major and minor (draft) versions
   Example: 1.0, 1.1, 1.2, 2.0

Optionally limit the number of versions to retain:
☐ Keep the following number of major versions:

☐ Keep drafts for the following number of major versions:

Draft Item Security

Drafts are minor versions or items which have not been approved. Specify which users should be able to view drafts in this document library.   Learn about specifying who can view and edit drafts.

Who should see draft items in this document library?
◉ Any user who can read items
○ Only users who can edit items
○ Only users who can approve items (and the author of the item)

Require Check Out

Specify whether users must check out documents before making changes in this document library.   Learn about requiring check out.

Require documents to be checked out before they can be edited?
○ Yes   ◉ No

Figure 5-10 Use the Document Library Versioning Settings page to configure the versioning settings of a SharePoint library.

With the Document Library Versioning Settings page open, make any desired changes to the following fields:

- **Content Approval**   Select Yes if you want to require approval for items submitted to the library; No if you do not require approval.

- **Document Version History**   Select from No Versioning, Create Major Versions, or Create Major And Minor (Draft) Versions. If you select Yes, you have the option to then limit the number of versions that are retained.

   Select the number of versions you want to retain and the numbers of drafts for each version to retain. It is a good recommendation to limit the number of versions to reduce unnecessary storage allocation. There might be business needs for a larger number of versions to be kept, but generally between three and five versions are plenty.

- **Draft Item Security**   Specify which users can see draft items in the library. The available options are Any User Who Can Read Items, Only Users Who Can Edit Items, and Only Users Who Can Approve Items (And The Author Of The Item).

- **Require Check Out**   Specify whether users will be required to check out the documents before they can be edited.

Advanced Settings in a List

To change the advanced settings for a list, on the list's Settings page, click the Advanced Settings link to display the List Advanced Settings page, as shown in Figure 5-11.

Figure 5-11 In the List Advanced Settings page, you can configure the advanced settings options for a SharePoint list.

With the advanced settings page open, make any desired changes to the following fields:

- **Content Types**   Select Yes if you want to allow management of content types on the list, or select No if you do not wish to allow it. If you will be adding other content types for use on the list, you will need to select the Yes option.

- **Item Level Permissions**   Specify for which items users have either read or edit access. In the Read Access section, you can specify either All Items or Only Their Own. There is also a section for Edit Access. You can specify either All Items, Only Their Own, or None.

- **E-Mail Notification**   Select Yes if you want to have the list send an email when ownership is assigned to an item or when an item has been changed. Select No if you do not want the email notifications to be sent.

> **Note**
> Some available options might vary, depending on your overall environmental settings.

- **Attachments**   Specify if users are allowed to attach files to items in the list. Select Enabled if you would like to allow attachments in the list or Disabled if you do not wish to allow attachments.

- **Folders**   Specify whether you would like to display the New Folder command on the New menu within the list. Select Yes if you want to have New Folder displayed or No if you do not wish to show this command. Changing this setting does not affect existing folders in the list.

> **Note**
> The use of folders within the SharePoint environment has both pros and cons. Before deciding to use this option, you should investigate these issues and discuss them with your team. You might also want to consult with your organization's Governance Plan for guidance.

- **Search**   Specify whether the list should be visible within SharePoint's search results. Select Yes to allow the items to appear in the search results; select No if you do not wish them to appear. Regardless what setting you choose, users who do not have permissions to view the list items will not see them within search results.

- **Offline Client Availability**   Specify whether the list should be available for offline clients. Select Yes to allow items from the list to be downloaded to offline clients (for example Microsoft Outlook 2010); No if you do not wish them to be downloaded offline.

- **Datasheet**   Specify whether the datasheet can be used to bulk edit data on this list. Select Yes to allow items in the list to be edited by using the datasheet; No if you do not want your users to be able to edit in Datasheet.

- **Dialogs**   You can launch New, Edit, and Display Forms either in a dialog box (select the Yes option) or in a full webpage (select the No option).

Advanced Settings in a Library

To change the advanced settings for a document library, on the library's Settings page, click the Advanced Settings link to display the Document Library Advanced Settings page, as illustrated in Figure 5-12.

Chapter 5

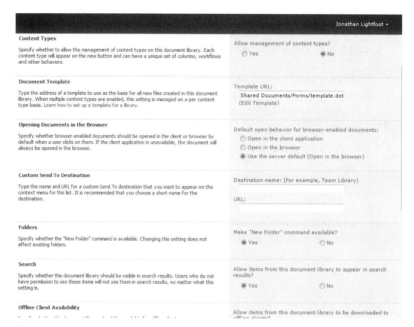

Figure 5-12 Use the Document Library Advanced Settings page to configure the advanced settings of a SharePoint document library.

With the Document Library Advanced Settings page open, make any desired changes to the following fields:

- **Content Types**   Select Yes if you want to allow management of content types in the library; No if you do not wish to manage them. If you will be adding other content types for use on the list, you will need to select the Yes option.

- **Document Template**   Specify the URL of the template to use as the basis for all new files created in this library. If multiple content types are enabled, this setting is managed on a per-content–type basis.

- **Opening Documents in the Browser**   Specify how to display documents that can be opened in either a browser or in a client application. Select from Open In The Client Application, Open In The Browser, or Use The Server Default.

- **Custom Send To Destination**   Specify the destination name and URL of a custom Send To destination that you would like to appear on the context menu for this library. This can be used for moving files to other locations within your site.

- **Folders** Specify whether you would like to display the New Folder command on the New menu within the library. Select Yes if you want to have New Folder displayed; No if you do not wish to show this command. Changing this setting does not affect existing folders in the library.

- **Search** Specify whether the library should be visible within SharePoint's search results. Select Yes to allow the items to appear in the search results; No if you do not wish them to appear. Users who do not have permissions to view the library items cannot see them within the search results, regardless of this setting.

- **Offline Client Availability** Specify whether the library should be available for offline clients. Select Yes to allow items from the library to be downloaded to offline clients; No if you do wish to allow them be downloaded offline.

- **Site Assets Library** Specify whether the library should be presented as the default location for storing images or other files that users upload to their wiki pages. Select Yes to make this library appear as the default library for users to upload wiki-related images and files; No if you do not wish this to be the default library presented to users for loading wiki-related materials.

- **Datasheet** Specify whether the datasheet can be used to bulk edit data on this library. Select Yes to allow items in the library to be edited by using the datasheet; No if you do not want your users to be able to edit in Datasheet.

- **Dialogs** You can launch New, Edit, and Display Forms either in a dialog box (select the Yes option) or in a full webpage (select the No option).

Updating Validation Settings in a List or Library

To change the validation settings for a list, on the list's Settings page, click the Validation Settings link to display the List Validation Settings page, as presented in Figure 5-13.

Figure 5-13 The List Validation Settings page, in which you can configure the validation settings of a SharePoint list or library.

Chapter 5

With the List Validation Settings page open, make any desired changes to the following fields:

- **Formula**   Specify the formula that you want to use to validate the data in this column when new items are saved to this list. To pass validation, the formula must evaluate to True.

- **User Message**   Type descriptive text to help site visitors understand what is needed for a valid list item. This description is shown if the validation expression fails.

Updating Permissions and Management

In SharePoint Foundation 2010, five links are available under the Permissions and Management header in a library, which you can use to change the permissions and management settings for the library. These links are: Delete This Document Library; Save Document Library As Template; Permissions For This Document Library; Manage Files Which Have No Checked In Version; and Workflow Settings. To change any of these items, click the corresponding link.

For lists, there are four links available under Permissions And Management, which you can use to change the permissions and management settings for the list. These links are as follows: Delete This List, Save List As Template, Permissions For This List, and Workflow Settings.

Deleting a List or Library

To delete a list or library, browse to its Settings page, and then under the Permissions And Management category, click Delete This List or Delete This (*Library Type*) Library on the customization page of the list or library.

For the list, a dialog box appears, asking Are You Sure You Want To Send This List To The Site Recycle Bin or Are You Sure You Want To Delete This List.

For the library, a dialog box opens, asking either, This Document Library Will Be Removed and All Its Files Will Be Deleted; Are You Sure You Want To Send This Document Library To The Recycle Bin, or This (*Library Type*) Will Be Removed And All Its Files Will Be Deleted; Are You Sure You Want To Delete This (*Library Type*) Library.

On sites that have the Recycle Bin enabled, you see the message about sending the list or library to the Recycle Bin; for those sites with a disabled Recycle Bin, you see the dialog box that does not mention the Recycle Bin.

> **Note**
> The Recycle Bin is enabled within a Site Collection by default and can be configured in Central Administration at the Site Collection web application level. Recycle Bin functionality is covered in Chapter 3, "End-User Features and Experience."

Saving a List or Library as a Template

With SharePoint Foundation 2010, you can save an existing list or library as a template so that new lists can be created from ones that are already proven to work within the organization or contain customizations that it requires. List or library templates can also be imported and exported to different Site Collections. When you save a list or library as a template, you can specify whether to include the existing content in the template. Lists saved as templates are then made available in the List Template Gallery.

Saving an Existing List or Library as a Template

You can easily save a list or library as a template by performing the following steps:

1. Click All Site Content, and then click the link for the list or library that you would like to save as a new template.

2. From the List or Library Tools Header within the list or library, click List or Library, and then click List Settings or (*Library Type*) Library Settings to display the Customize page for the list or library.

3. Click Save List As Template for a list or Save (*Library Type*) Library As Template for a library.

4. In the File Name box, type in a file name for the new list or library template, as shown in Figure 5-14. This file name will be displayed in the appropriate Template Gallery.

5. In the Template Name box, type a name for the new template. The template name field will be displayed on the site's Create page.

6. In the Description box, type a description for the new template. This description of the template will be displayed on the site's Create page.

7. If you would like the content of the list or library to be saved in the template so that new lists and libraries will automatically have the content available to them when they are created, select the Include Content check box. If you would like the template to be created without including the content, leave this check box clear.

Chapter 5

Note

You can save up to 10 MB of data in a list or library template.

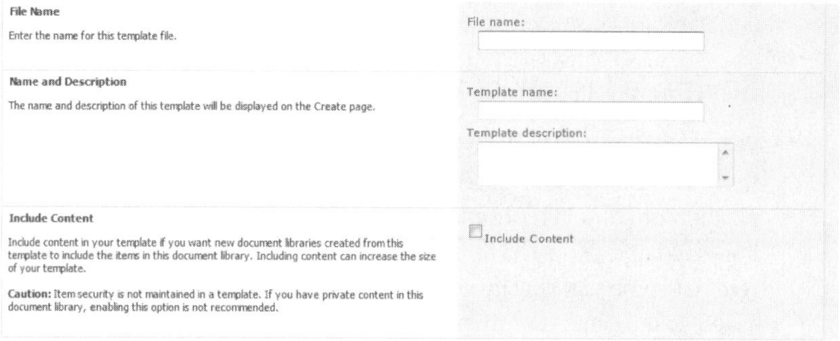

File Name

Enter the name for this template file.

File name:

Name and Description

The name and description of this template will be displayed on the Create page.

Template name:

Template description:

Include Content

Include content in your template if you want new document libraries created from this template to include the items in this document library. Including content can increase the size of your template.

Caution: Item security is not maintained in a template. If you have private content in this document library, enabling this option is not recommended.

☐ Include Content

Figure 5-14 Use the Save As Template page to save a list or library as a template.

CAUTION

Templates neither save security settings nor apply them to new lists or libraries. Take this into account before including confidential content in a template.

Adding a Template to a List Gallery

If you have a list template file available to you and would like to add it to the Template List gallery, perform the following steps:

1. On the Site Actions menu, click Site Settings.

2. On the Site Settings page, in the Galleries section, click List Templates.

   It is possible that you might need to click Go To Top Level Site Settings in the Site Collection Administration column to see this link.

Note

Some available options might vary, depending on your overall environmental settings.

3. On the List Template Gallery page, under the Library Tools heading, click Documents, and then select Upload Document.

4. In the Name box, type the path to the template. Alternatively, click Browse.

5. Click OK to add an existing list template file to the List Template gallery.

Deleting a Template in the List Template Gallery

Users with the appropriate permissions can delete a template within the List Template gallery. To delete an existing list template, perform the following steps:

1. On the Site Actions menu, click Site Settings.

2. In the Galleries column, click List Templates.

   The List Template Gallery page appears.

3. In the Edit column, click the Edit Document Properties icon for the list template that you want to delete.

> **Note**
> It is also possible to edit the properties of an existing list template on this page without having to delete the template.

4. Click Delete Item, and then click OK to confirm the list template deletion.

Changing Permissions for a List or Library

SharePoint Foundation 2010 offers robust and granular management of the permissions for list and libraries. List and libraries can either inherit permissions from a parent site or object, or have their inheritance broken so that they can have unique SharePoint groups or permissions levels assigned to them.

> **Note**
> If a list or library's permissions are customized so that they no longer inherit permissions from a parent site or object, you can still reinherit permissions from the parent site or object at a later time.

Chapter 5

It is a best practice to use Active Directory Security Groups or SharePoint groups to manage list permissions whenever possible. In some cases, you might need to break the parent's inheritance to manage a list. Within the SharePoint environment, it is good practice to track all lists, libraries, or items that have been assigned unique permissions so that future permission updates to SharePoint can be appropriately applied.

Editing the Permissions for a List or Library

To change the permissions for a list or library, perform the following:

> **Note**
> You must have the appropriate permissions to carry out this procedure.

1. Open the list or library.

2. On the List Tools heading, click List, and then click List Settings or (*Library Type*) Settings.

3. On the Customize page, in the Permissions And Management column, click Permissions For This List/(*Library Type*) Library.

   The Permissions page displays all of the users and SharePoint groups associated with this list or library, along with their assigned permission levels.

4. If the list or library is inheriting permissions, you must first break the inheritance of the permissions before you edit permission levels on this list. To do this, on the Permission Tools menu, click Stop Inheriting Permissions, and then click OK, as shown in Figure 5-15.

   If you would like to edit the permissions of the parent, on the Permission Tool menu, click Manage Parent, and then click Manage Permissions Of Parent, which will take you to the parent's permission area.

Figure 5-15 Editing permissions breaks the inheritance of permissions from the parent.

5. Select the check boxes for the users and SharePoint groups whose permissions you want to edit.

6. On the Permission Tools menu, select Edit User Permissions.

7. In the Choose Permissions section, select the permission levels that you would like to apply, and then click OK.

> **Note**
> If you decide to reinherit permissions after having created custom permissions, the parent objects will be applied, and any customizations you might have made to the list or library will be overwritten.

Adding Users to a List or Library

To add users to a list or library, perform the following steps:

> **Note**
> You must have the appropriate permissions to carry out this procedure.

1. Open the list or library.

2. On the List or Library Tools menu, click List or Library, and then select List Settings or (*Library Type*) Settings.

3. In the Permissions And Management column, click Permissions For This List/(*Library Type*) Library.

    The Permissions page displays all of the users and SharePoint groups associated with this list, along with their assigned permission levels. If the list or library is inheriting permissions, you must first break the inheritance of the permissions before you can edit permission levels for this list or library. To do this, on the Permission Tools menu, click Stop Inheriting Permissions, and then click OK. If you would like to edit the permissions from the parent, on the Permission Tools menu, click Manage Parent, and then Manage Permissions Of Parent, which will take you to the parent's permission area to edit permissions.

4. On the New menu, click Grant Permissions, as shown in Figure 5-16.

Figure 5-16 Choose Add Users to add users or groups to a list or library.

5. In the Select Users section, specify the users and SharePoint groups that you want to add to the list or library.

It is best to add users into a SharePoint Group, but note that SharePoint Groups can't be added into other SharePoint Groups. Their permissions must be assigned directly.

> **Tip**
>
> **If you know the username of the person who you want to add, you can type that name into the Select User text box, and then press the Enter key.**

6. In the Grant Permission section, you can add users to an existing SharePoint group or give them permissions directly, as shown in Figure 5-17. Select one or more of the check boxes to give these users the permissions that you want to apply. SharePoint Groups will need their permissions assigned directly.

7. Choose the permissions you want for the selected team members or groups.

8. In the Send E-Mail section, select the check box if you want an email notification to go out to the users to whom you are granting permissions, or clear it if you do not want an alert email to be sent, and then click OK.

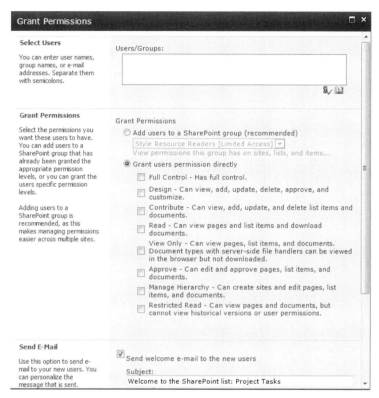

Figure 5-17 With the Give Users Permission Directly option, you can add users to the list or library without adding them to an existing SharePoint group.

Removing Users from a List or Library

To remove users from a list or library, perform the following steps:

> **Note**
>
> You must have the appropriate permissions to carry out this procedure.

1. Open the list or library.

2. On the List or Library Tools menu, click List or Library, and then select List Settings or (Library Type) Settings.

3. On the Settings page, in the Permissions And Management column, click Permissions For This List/(Library Type) Library.

   The Permissions page displays all users and SharePoint groups associated with this list or library and their assigned permission levels.

   If the list or library is inheriting permissions, you must first break the inheritance of the permissions before you can edit permission levels. To do this, on the Permission Tools menu, click Stop Inheriting Permissions, and then click OK. If you would like to edit the permissions from the parent, on the Permission Tools menu, click Manage Parent, and then Manage Permissions Of Parent, which will take you to the parent's permission area to perform permission editing.

4. Select the check boxes for the users and SharePoint groups that you want to remove from this list or library.

5. On the Permission Tools menu, click Remove User Permissions, and then click OK to remove the selected users and groups.

Manage Files That Have No Checked-In Version

This option is in place to assist the site administrator with cleaning up files that might not have a checked-in version. This scenario applies in cases where a document might have been created and uploaded to a library that requires documents to be checked out prior to editing. In this scenario, someone could upload a document but forget to check it in. As such, this newly uploaded document is not visible to other members of the team. This option is used to manage these types of documents.

To manage files that have never been checked in, perform the following steps:

> **Note**
> You must have the appropriate permissions to carry out this procedure.

1. Open the list or library.

2. On the List or Library Tools menu, click List or Library, and then select List Settings or (Library Type) Settings.

3. On the Settings page, in the Permissions And Management column, click Manage Files Which Have No Checked In Version.

4. Select the check box of any files that you want to manage, and then click Take Ownership Of Selection.

Workflow Settings

Workflows can be applied to lists and libraries similar to how you apply templates or permissions. SharePoint Foundation 2010 includes one predefined workflow by default. The Three-State workflow, which is designed for the Issue Tracking list, can be applied to a list or library. Additional workflows that are developed or purchased by an organization in the future can be made available and applied by using the methods described in the following section.

Adding a New Workflow or Change the Settings of an Existing Workflow

To add a new workflow to a list or library, perform the following steps:

> **Note**
>
> You must have the appropriate permissions to carry out this procedure.

1. Open the list or library.

2. On the List or Library Tools menu, click List or Library, and then select List Settings or (*Library Type*) Settings.

3. On the Settings page, in the Permissions And Management column, click Workflow Settings:

    — If an existing workflow has been applied, you will go directly to the Workflow Settings page, and you must click Add A Workflow to go to the Add A Workflow page.

    — If no workflows have been added, you will go directly to the Add A Workflow page.

4. On the Change Workflow Settings page, click Add A Workflow or click the name of a workflow to change the settings.

5. If you are adding a workflow, on the Add A Workflow page, in the Workflow section, click the name of the workflow template that you want to use.

Chapter 5

If you are changing the settings for a workflow, on the Change A Workflow page, change the settings according to the following steps:

1. In the Name section, in the text box, type in a unique name for the workflow you're adding, as shown in Figure 5-18.

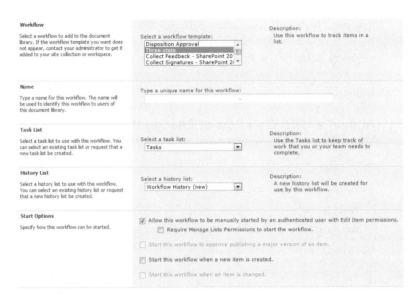

Figure 5-18 You can use the Add A Workflow page to add a workflow to a list or library.

2. In the Task List section, specify a task list to use with this workflow.

    You can use the out-of-the-box tasks list or create a new one.

3. In the History List section, select a history list to use for this workflow.

    This history list contains and displays all of the workflow events that occur during each instance of the workflow.

4. In the Start Options section, specify how, when, or by whom the workflow can be started, and then click next.

    This might be limited if the workflow template does not support certain options. Major and minor versioning must be enabled to support some features.

5. The Customize The Workflow page opens, in which you can specify and configure the additional options that are available to that particular workflow.

6. Fill in the fields to customize the workflow as needed, and then click OK.

> **Tip**
>
> If you have a task list for a workflow that possibly contains any of the organization's confidential content, it is a best practice to create a new task list for that workflow rather that utilizing the out-of-the-box task list.

Information Management Policy Settings

You can use Information Rights Management (IRM) in SharePoint Foundation 2010 to protect and control content within a list or library. IRM can limit how list and library content is distributed and block specific content from being shared with others. IRM can restrict access to list content for a specific interval and can require users to confirm their logon credentials to access or download specific content.

IRM is applied at a list or library level and uses an application called a *protector,* which is installed on the front-end web servers to encrypt and decrypt content within the list or library. You can restrict the use of a file based on a user's security credentials.

Applying IRM to a List or Library

To apply IRM to a list or library, perform the following steps:

> **Note**
>
> You must have the appropriate permissions to carry out this procedure.

1. Open a list or library.

2. On the List or Library Tools Menu, select List or Library, and then click List Settings or (Library Type) Settings.

3. Under Permissions And Management, click Information Rights Management.

   Note that if you do not have this link available, it is possible that IRM is not enabled. IRM can be enabled in Operation page in Windows Central Administration.

4. On the Information Rights Management Settings page, select the check box adjacent to Restrict Permission To Documents In This Library On Download to apply restricted permission to documents that are downloaded from the list.

5. Under Permission Policy Title, enter a unique descriptive name for the policy.

6. Under Permission Policy Description, type a description that people who use this list or library will see. This description should help explain how they are to handle the documents or items.

    You can now apply any additional restrictions to the documents in this list or library by specifying available IRM restriction criteria.

7. After you finish specifying the criteria and specific IRM options for the list or library, click OK.

RSS Settings on Lists or Libraries

As discussed in Chapter 3, RSS feeds can enable users to receive periodic updates about specific lists in the organization without having to browse to a specific list to find this content. To change RSS settings for a list or library, browse to its Settings page and click the RSS Settings link. Once the RSS Settings page is on display, make any desired changes to the following fields:

- **List RSS**   Select Yes if you want to enable RSS for the list or library; No if you do not wish to enable it.

- **RSS Channel Information**   Specify the channel elements that define the RSS feed. You have the options to truncate multiple line fields to 256 characters as well as to specify a title, description, and image URL.

- **Document Options**   Configure Link and Enclosure settings for RSS Items. Specify whether or not to include file enclosures for items in the feed. Select Yes to include file enclosures for items in the feed. Also, specify whether to link RSS items directly to their files. Select Yes to Link RSS Items directly to their files.

- **Columns**   Specify which columns to display in the RSS description.

- **Item Limit**   Specify an item limit for the most recent changes for the RSS feed as well as the maximum number of days to include an item in the RSS feed.

Subscribe to an RSS Feed in a List or Library

To subscribe to an RSS Feed for a specific list or library, perform the following steps:

1. Open the list or library.

2. On the List Tools or Library Tools menu, select List or Library, and then click RSS Feed The feed will load in your browser window.

3. On the page that appears, follow the instructions for how to subscribe to the feed. You might see a link called Subscribe To This Feed, which you can click to subscribe.

4. Closely follow any instructions you receive in the RSS reader, browser, or email program that you plan to use to view the list's RSS feed.

Adding Columns to Lists or Libraries

With SharePoint Foundation 2010, you can easily add columns to lists or libraries to capture additional information about content. Doing so speeds up the information retrieval process. Out-of-the-box list templates contain certain default columns, but adding organizationally tailored columns can greatly improve the user experience in both browsing and searching.

You can add a custom column at almost any time, allowing users to choose from several column types, such as a single line of text, a calculated column, a drop-down list, or even a column that acts as a lookup for displaying data from other lists.

Creating a Custom Column

To create a custom column, perform the following steps:

> **Note**
> **You must have the appropriate permissions to carry out this procedure.**

1. Open the list or library

2. On the Library Tools menu, click Library, and then click Create Column.

3. In the Name And Type section, type the name that you want in the Column Name text box, as shown in Figure 5-19.

4. Under The Type Of Information In This Column Is, select the type of information that you want to appear in the column.

5. In the Additional Column Settings section, type a description in the Description box to help users within the organization to understand the purpose of the column and what data it should contain. This description is optional but recommended.

6. Depending on the type of column that you selected, more options might appear in the Additional Column Settings section. Select any additional settings that you want.

Chapter 5

7. To add the column to the default view that visitors to your site automatically see
    when they access the default view of the list or library, select Add To Default View,
    and then click OK.

Figure 5-19 Use this page to create a new column.

Creating a Site Column

To create a site column for your organization that you can use later within a list or library,
perform the following steps:

> **Note**
> You must have the appropriate permissions to carry out this procedure.

1. On the Site Actions menu, click Site Settings.

2. On the Site Settings page, under Galleries, click Site Columns.

3. On the Site Column Gallery page, click Create.

4. In the Name And Type section, type the name that you want in the Column Name text box.

5. Select one of the choices under the heading The Type Of Information In This Column Is.

   Table 5-2 lists the available choices and the type of control each choice will display on input forms.

Table 5-2 **SharePoint List Column Types**

Select this	To display this
Single Line Of Text	Columns that collect and display small amounts of text in a single line, including text only, combinations of text and numbers, and numbers that are not used in calculations (such as phone numbers).
Multiple Lines Of Text	Columns that collect and display one or more sentences of text or formatted text.
Choice (Menu To Choose From)	Columns that display a list of options.
Number (1, 1.0, 100)	Columns that provide a box in which you can type a numerical value.
Currency ($, ¥, £)	Columns that provide a box in which you can type a monetary value.
Date And Time	Columns that store calendar or time-of-day information.
Lookup (Information Already On This Site)	Columns that make it easy for you to select information that's already stored on a site. These columns utilize information located in other lists or libraries in the site.
Yes/No (Check Box)	Columns that store true/false information.
Person Or Group	Columns that display the name of Active Directory users or SharePoint groups.
Hyperlink Or Picture	Columns that display a hyperlink to a webpage or display an image from the Web.
Calculated (Calculation Based On Other Columns)	Columns that display information that is based on the result of a formula. The formula can use information from other lists and columns, dates, or numbers. You can use standard mathematical operators.

Chapter 5

6. In the Group section, select the existing group in which to store the new site column, or create a new group.

7. In the Additional Column Settings section, select any additional column settings that you want. The options available in this section can differ depending on the type of column that you selected in the name and type sections. When you've completed the configuration, click OK.

Calculating Column Values

SharePoint Foundation 2010 can perform calculations to determine the value of a column in a given row. You can invoke such calculations in two situations:

- When initializing New Item Form that will add a new list item.

- Each time you retrieve the list item. SharePoint Foundation 2010 calculates the value every time you request data from the column.

Calculations use formulas very much like those in Excel. The input for calculations generally comes from system functions or from the columns in the list.

If there's any ambiguity as to the name of a function or column, or if the name contains any special characters, enclose the column name in square brackets. For example, the expressions FirstName and [FirstName] both refer to a column named FirstName because there's no function named FirstName. Most of the functions and operators from Excel are available to SharePoint. Thus, to add the Number Present and Number Absent columns, you would code:

```
=[Number Present] + [Number Absent]
```

To combine text from two columns, use the ampersand operator, as in the following example:

```
=[Last Name] & ", " & [First Name]
```

You can also use functions in formulas. The following example returns the weekday for the date in the Date Due column:

```
=TEXT(WEEKDAY([Date Due]), "dddd")
```

Changing and Deleting List Columns

To change or delete a column, click its name in the Columns section of the Settings page. This displays the Change Column page.

To change any other aspect of the column, correct the setting, and then click OK. To delete the column and the data it contains, click the Delete button at the bottom of the page.

Reordering List Columns

It's easy to reorder list columns in SharePoint Foundation 2010. To change the order of columns within a list or library, go to the list's Settings page, and then under Columns, click Column Ordering. After you have reordered the columns, click OK.

> **Note**
>
> When you reorder a column, you are actually changing the order in which the column will appear in the New Items Form. If you want to reorder the way the column displays in a List view you will need to modify the view instead.

Working with Site Columns in a List or Library

The content-type functionality of SharePoint Foundation 2010 provides organizations with a powerful content-management feature for capturing metadata and categorizing content in a way that is both configurable and reusable.

You might have a list, for example, that contains items that contain multiple types of items (for example, contacts and inventory items); in which case, depending on the type of information that is entered, you might need to handle it differently. You might need your contact information to contain certain required information as opposed to inventory items that will require different required information. In a situation such as this, you can employ the use of content types to the list, thereby ensuring that the appropriate required information is captured for the item.

The New command in a list displays all the content types that were added to the list, which means that users can create new items of those types.

Adding a Content Type to a List or Library

To add a content type to a list or library, it must first be configured to allow multiple content types. To ensure that the list or library you are configuring is configured properly, browse to the Settings page for the list or library, in the General Settings section, click Advanced Settings, and then in the Content Types section, select Yes for Allow Management Of Content Types.

Once this setting is properly configured, you can add a content type by performing the following steps:

Chapter 5

> **Note**
> You must have the appropriate permissions to carry out this procedure.

1. Open the list or library

2. On the Library Tools menu, click List or Library, and then select List Settings or (*Library Type*) Settings.

3. Under Content Types, click Add From Existing Site Content Types.

4. In the Select Content Types section, open the Select Site Content Types from the drop-down list to select the group of site content types from which you want choose a type, as illustrated in Figure 5-20.

5. In the Available Site Content Types list, click the content type that you want, and then click Add to move the selected content type to the Content Types To Add List.

6. To add additional content types, you can repeat steps 4 and 5.

7. When you finish selecting all of the content types, click OK.

Figure 5-20 Use the Add Content Types page to add a content type to a list or library.

Modifying the New Button Order or the Default Content Type

In SharePoint Foundation 2010, it is possible to change the order in which content types are displayed on the New button for a list or library. When a list or library is first created, the first content type that is displayed on the New button will become the default content type. To change the default content type, you must simply change the content type that is displayed first on the New button. There is also the option to either show or hide the content types that have been added on the New button.

To modify these settings, perform the following steps:

> **Note**
>
> **You must have the appropriate permissions to carry out this procedure.**

1. Open the list or library that you want to modify.

2. On the Settings menu, click List Settings or (*Library Type*) Settings.

3. Under Content Types, click Change New Button Order And Default Content Type.

4. In the Content Type Order section (see Figure 5-21), perform either of the following:

   — To remove a content type from the New button for the list, clear the Visible check box.

   — To change the order in which a content type appears on the New button, click the arrow next to that content type in the Position From Top column, and then select the ranking that you want.

5. When you are finished modifying these settings, click OK.

Figure 5-21 Use the Change New Button Order And Default Content Type page to set the default content type on a list or library and to specify the ranking of other content-type menu options.

Creating and Modifying List and Library Views

You'll often want to modify an existing view of a list or library or create a new custom list to meet your organization's exact needs. This is a straightforward process in SharePoint Foundation 2010, and you can create a view on the fly easily with SharePoint Designer.

Chapter 5

Creating List and Library Views

If a task list is created to manage tasks for an initiative going on within an organization, a project manager will want to be able to easily view which tasks are assigned to specific teams or individuals without having to browse through every single task in the list. This is where a new list view could be created for each of the different teams or individuals.

Tip

A view is actually a webpage, and as such, when you create a new view, it will be assigned a unique URL. By having views with unique URLs, a link can then be added to the Links List Web Part of a group's or team's SharePoint site to provide easy access to the customized view of the list.

Keep in mind that the default view for a list or library displays all of the columns available. Depending on what you are trying to accomplish, you might only need to see specific columns appropriate in a specific order for what you are doing. Views allow you to temporarily sort and filter the items in the list by choosing the names of the columns with which you want to work.

Creating a New List View

To create a new view in a list, perform the following steps:

Note

You must have the appropriate permissions to carry out this procedure.

---

1. Open the list or library.

2. On the List Tools or Library Tools menu, click List or Library, and then click Create View, as demonstrated in Figure 5-22.

Figure 5-22 To define a new view, on the Library Tools tab, click Library, and then in the Manage Views group, click Create View.

3. Under Choose A View Format, click the type of view that you want to create, as shown in Figure 5-23.

Figure 5-23 Choose a format for your new view on the Create View page.

4. In the View Name text box, type a name for your view, as illustrated in Figure 5-24.

Figure 5-24 Configure the new view to meet your individual needs.

5. If you want to make this the default view, select the Make This The Default View check box.

   A list view can only be made the default view if it is a public view and if you have permission to change the design of a list.

6. In the Audience section, under View Audience, select whether you want to create a personal view that only you can use or a public view that others can use.

   Remember that only a person with the appropriate permissions can create a public view. All other users can only create personal views.

7. In the Columns section, you can show or hide columns by selecting the appropriate check boxes. Next to the column name, enter the number for the order of your column in the view.

8. In the Sort section, choose whether and how you want the information to be sorted.

   You can use two columns for the sort, such as first by author, and then by file name for each author for example.

9. In the Filter section, choose whether and how you want to filter the files.

   A filtered view shows you a smaller selection, such as items created by a specific department or with an approved status.

10. In the Group By section, you can group items with the same value in their own section, such as an expandable section for documents by a specific author.

11. In the Totals section, you can count the number of items in a column, such as the total number of issues.

    In some cases, you can summarize or distill additional information, such as averages.

12. In the Style section, select the style that you want for the view, such as a list in which every other row is shaded.

13. In the Folders section, for lists with folders, you can create a view that doesn't include the folders.

    To view all of your items at the same level (without folders), click Show All Items Without Folders.

14. In the Item Limit section, you can limit how many files can be viewed or how many files can be viewed on the same page.

    This is really helpful if your list contains a lot of items. By default the view will show 100 items at a time.

15. In the Mobile section, set the view for a list or library that will be delivered to users of mobile devices.

16. When you are finished, click OK.

Table 5-3 illustrates that the sections that appear on the Create View page will vary depending on the type of view you selected on the View Type page.

Table 5-3 SharePoint List View Settings

Section	Standard view	Datasheet view	Calendar view	Gantt view
Name	✓	✓	✓	✓
Audience	✓	✓	✓	✓
Columns	✓	✓		
Gantt Columns				✓
Sort	✓	✓		✓
Filter	✓	✓	✓	✓
Group By	✓			✓
Totals	✓	✓		✓
Style	✓			✓
Folders	✓	✓		✓
Item Limit	✓	✓		✓
Mobile	✓			
Time Interval			✓	
Calendar Columns			✓	
Default Scope			✓	

> **Note**
> Users who have Microsoft Access 2007 or newer loaded on their computers can create an additional view called an Access view, which is discussed in the following sections.

Modifying and Deleting List views

Several views come right out of the box with a newly created list or library. You might want to modify these views or even delete those that you know you will never use or others that have served their purpose. The process of modifying or deleting a list view is similar to that of creating a new view (described in the preceding section). After opening the view that you want to modify or delete, just click the View menu, and then click Modify This View. A screen will load with all the same options as the Add View page: you can modify settings, and then click OK, or to delete the view, click Delete.

Creating an Access View of a SharePoint List or Library

Users who have Access 2007 or newer loaded on their computers can create an additional view called an Access view. This view will open the Access software on your computer and display the items within a table that can be modified.

To create a new Access view, perform the following steps:

> **Note**
> You must have the appropriate permissions to carry out this procedure.

1. Open a list or library.

2. On the View menu, click Create View.

3. On the Create View page, click Access View.

   Access will load, and you'll be prompted to save a local copy of the database that will contain your new view.

4. In the Save A Local Copy dialog box, browse to the location on your computer where you want to save the copy, type a name for the local copy in the File Name box, and then click Save.

   Access saves and opens the local copy and the Create Access View dialog box opens.

5. In the Create Access View dialog box, double-click the type of view that you want to create.

   Access creates your new view and opens it.

6. You can customize your new view in Layout view, or you can switch to Design view.

   In Layout view, you can resize and rearrange the controls in your view, but you can-not add controls. In Design view, you can resize and rearrange controls, and you can add additional controls. However, Design view does not provide a data preview.

7. After you are finished with your customizations, on the Message Bar, click Save To SharePoint Site to finish the operation.

Working with List Content

SharePoint Foundation 2010 provides a variety of ways to work with lists and views, all of which require little effort or programming to set up. This includes displaying attractive input forms and reports. This section explains how these features work.

Working with List Content in Standard View

After a list contains all the fields you want, team members can view it or update it by:

- Clicking its link in the Quick Launch (provided, of course, that you chose to display this list on the Quick Launch when you created or later modified the list).

- Clicking the All Site Content link and then, under Lists, clicking the list name.

- Adding the list to a Web Part page.

Adding Items to a List

To add an item to a list, proceed as follows:

1. Open the list view by using any of the methods previously provided.

2. Click Add New Item at the bottom of the page. Or click Items under the List Tools Menu, and then click New.

3. When the New Item page appears (see Figure 5-25), enter data into the list.

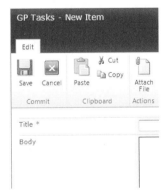

Figure 5-25 A SharePoint site automatically creates a data entry page like this for each list.

4. To save the data you entered, click OK.

5. To enter more data into the list, click New again, as in step 2.

Changing or Deleting the Content of a List Item

To change or delete the content of a List item, perform the following steps:

> **Note**
> You must have the appropriate permissions to carry out this procedure.

1. Click the item's title (which should be a hyperlink).

2. When the item appears on its own page, click the Edit Item or Delete Item button. Alternatively, you can move the mouse pointer over the item's title, click the drop-down arrow, and then choose Edit Item or Delete Item from the shortcut menu, as shown in Figure 5-26.

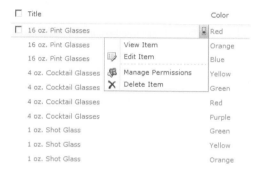

Figure 5-26 Using the drop-down menu to edit or view a list item.

Working with Lists and Libraries in Datasheet View

If you have Excel 2007 or 2010 installed, you can create, modify, and delete content by using the Datasheet view. To invoke this view, navigate to the list or library page. On the List Tools menu, click List, and then click Datasheet View. Alternatively, if you have created a Datasheet view for the list or library, you can open that view, as well.

The Datasheet view presents an editing format similar to that of Excel so that you can edit large numbers of items at once. The view can also be useful for exporting data into an external application such as Excel.

Exporting Content to Spreadsheets

With SharePoint Foundation 2010, you can export your list or library data to an external spreadsheet. If you have data that you would like to share with a user who does not have access to your list, or possibly with a user outside of your organization, you can use this functionality to quickly export your data into a spreadsheet in the exact or very similar format.

> ## Tip
> Many users ask why all of their fields do not export properly when they click Export To Spreadsheet. This is because the user did not select a view that contains all of the columns. Remember, when you export to a spreadsheet, you are actually exporting items that are in the current view. To preclude the possibility that some items are not exported, make sure that the view you are on contains all of the fields that you want to export.

Exporting a SharePoint List or Library to a Spreadsheet

To export a list or library to a spreadsheet, perform the following steps:

> ## Note
> You must have the appropriate permissions to carry out this procedure.

1. Open a list or library.

2. On the List Tools menu, click List and then click Export To Excel.

    Follow the prompts from your spreadsheet program to open and activate the file. If you are using Excel 2007 or Excel 2010, you might receive a security query asking whether you want to enable a data connection. You might also receive a query from your spreadsheet program asking how you would like to view the data.

3. After you have selected the criteria about the export, click OK.

Chapter 5

INSIDE OUT Saving the Excel Query (.iqy) file

It's possible that you follow the steps outlined above and the list still does not export to Excel. Keep in mind that SharePoint exports an OWSSVR.iqy file. If you are unable to open it directly, try saving the file to a location on your computer. You should then able to open your spreadsheet program and import the saved file.

Connect, Open, Sync, and Export with Microsoft Office 2010

Some of the new and improved functionality associated with SharePoint Foundation 2010 and lists will be covered in this section. Enhanced list interaction functionality in this version of SharePoint includes:

- Connecting list information to Outlook 2010

- Synchronizing list information using SharePoint Workspaces

- Automatically generating a Microsoft Visio Diagram from a list

- Exporting a list to Excel

- Opening a schedule with Microsoft Project 2010

Connecting a SharePoint List to Outlook

Improved integration of SharePoint Foundation 2010 with the new Outlook 2010 client allows for better management of SharePoint List items.

To connect a SharePoint list with Outlook, perform the following steps:

1. Open a list.

2. On the List Tools menu, click List, and then select Connect To Outlook.

3. Click Allow to permit this website to open a program on your computer. Outlook should open on your desktop.

4. Click Yes to Connect This SharePoint List to Outlook.

5. The list is added to the appropriate heading and opens automatically for you in Outlook.

Synchronizing with SharePoint Workspace

Formerly known as Microsoft Groove, SharePoint Workspace 2010 is a great new addition to the range of SharePoint functionality. Your SharePoint Sites and lists can be synchronized to make this content available offline. You can set up your workspace to synchronize automatically or do it manually.

The following list types cannot be synchronized; however, a link is available that you can use to access the information, provided that you have a connection to the network in which your SharePoint site resides:

- Calendar
- Phone Call Memo
- Resources
- Survey
- Site Pages

To synchronize a SharePoint list with your SharePoint Workspace, perform the following steps:

1. Browse to the list that you that want to synchronize.

2. On the List Tools menu, click List, and then select Sync To SharePoint Workspace.

   A dialog box opens, asking if you want to synchronize the list to your computer.

3. Click OK.

   Another dialog box opens, showing the status of your synchronization.

4. Click Open Workspace or Close when the synchronization is complete.

Exporting SharePoint Lists to Office 2010 Applications

Microsoft continues to improve the export functionality from SharePoint into Office 2010 products. The new and improved version offers three new commands: Export To Excel, Create A Visio Drawing, and Open Schedule (in Microsoft Project).

To perform an export of data to either Excel or Visio, complete the following steps:

1. Browse to the list that you want to export.

2. On the List Tools menu, click List, and then in the Connect & Export Section, select Export To Excel or Create Visio Diagram.

Chapter 5

3. Click Yes to launch the client application.

The client application should open and display your data automatically for you.

> **Note**
>
> Not all lists support all of these menu selections—if one or more items are grayed-out on your ribbon, it's likely that either you do not have the correct client application loaded on your computer to support the chosen functionality or the list itself does not support this export type.

Viewing RSS Feeds

To view RSS feeds to which you have subscribed within SharePoint Foundation 2010, you can use an RSS reader such as Microsoft Internet Explorer or Outlook.

Creating Discussions

A SharePoint discussion board is a list that supports newsgroup-style dialog. Discussion boards can be as open as you like, but there are also features for managing discussion threads and ensuring that only approved posts appear.

Email-enabling discussion boards can be a great way to handle a large amount of email on a particular subject or project. Project managers who receive a large volume of email on a particular project can set up a discussion board to manage and share these communications.

Discussion boards are also a great place to capture knowledge-management information within your organization. Capturing best practices, lessons learned, and other similar types of information can be quickly and easily accomplished in a SharePoint discussion board.

Creating a New Discussion Board

To create a new discussion board, perform the following steps:

> **Note**
>
> You must have the appropriate permissions to carry out this procedure.

1. On the site for which you would like to create the new discussion board, click All Site Content, and then on the All Site Content page, click Create.

2. Under List, click Discussion Board.

3. In the Name text box, type a name for the discussion board, as shown in Figure 5-27.

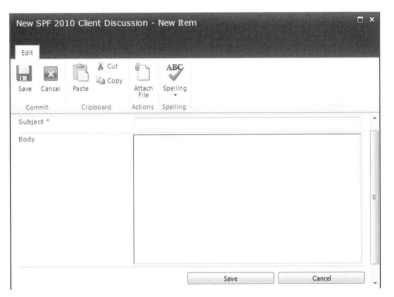

Figure 5-27 This is the New page used to name and describe a new discussion board.

The name is required and will be displayed on the discussion board page. It will become part of the page's URL.

4. To enter a Description, click More Options, and then in the Description text box, type a description of the discussion board.

5. In the Navigation section, specify whether you want the discussion board to appear on the Quick Launch bar.

6. To enable the discussion board to receive email, under Allow This List To Receive E-Mail, select Yes.

> **Note**
> This option is not be available if your server is not set up to receive email.

7. In the E-Mail Address text box, type a unique name to use as part of the email address for the discussion board, and then click Create.

Creating a New Discussion

You can begin creating new discussions as soon as the discussion board has been created, or you can even use the out-of-the-box Team Discussions board that is created by the default Team Site template. To create a new discussion, do the following:

1. Open the discussion board for which you would like to create a new discussion.

2. In the content area, click Add New Discussion. Or, click List Tools, select Items, and then on New Item, click Discussion.

   The rich-text editor opens, as shown in Figure 5-28.

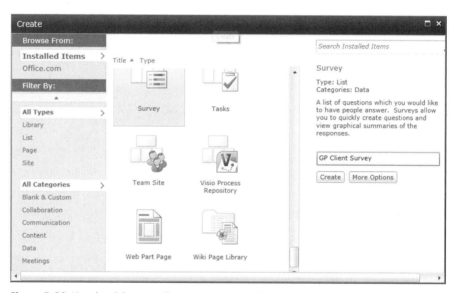

Figure 5-28 Use the rich-text editor to create new discussion items.

3. Type the text that you want for the subject and body of the message, apply any formatting that you want, and then click Save.

Creating Surveys

A SharePoint survey list is a great way to capture feedback and information within your organization. A survey can capture employee feedback or even pose questions to the user base regarding how they like a new SharePoint site or how it could be improved.

Surveys can be configured so that a user can only see responses to the surveys he has taken. And the user who created and owns the survey can use the out-of-the-box reporting that comes with all surveys.

Also, you can export the results to another program, such as Excel 2010, to analyze the responses. However, keep in mind that when Survey results are exported, all fields will be exported, with the exception of the Rating Type field.

Creating a New Survey

To create a survey, perform the following steps:

> **Note**
> You must have the appropriate permissions to carry out this procedure.

1. On the site for which you want to create the new survey, click All Site Content.

2. On the All Site Content Page, click Create.

3. Under List, click Survey, as shown in Figure 5-29. In the Name text box, type a name for the survey.

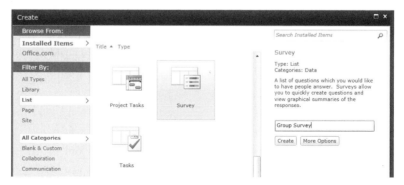

Figure 5-29 Start creating your survey.

This name will appear at the top of the survey page and will become part of the page's URL.

4.   To enter a Description, click More Options, and then type a description of the survey.

5.   To add a link to this list survey on the Quick Launch bar, in the Navigation section, click Yes.

6.   In the Survey Options section, specify whether you want an individual's name to appear with her responses and whether users can respond more than once to the survey.

7.   Click Create.

8.   On the New Question page, in the Question And Type section, enter your question text, and then select the type of answer that you would like for your first question.

9.   In the Additional Question Settings section, specify additional settings for your question, such as whether an answer to the question is required.

Depending on the question type, you might also display possible answers for the question. Then do one of the following:

— To create additional questions, click Next Question, and then enter the information for the next question.

Continue the process until you add all the questions that you want.

— If you are finished adding questions, click Finish.

INSIDE OUT   Branching surveys in SharePoint Foundation 2010

With SharePoint 2010, you are also able to use branching logic with your surveys. You can use branching to determine what the next question should be based on the response from the current question. As such, when branching logic is employed, you could have a survey that consists of 100 questions. However, based on the answers to the questions, survey participants might only need to answer 10 questions. Remember, for this to be effective, you must ensure that you have the questions listed in the order that you would like for them to appear. Otherwise, you could end up with a survey that jumps around with no real logic.

Once your survey questions are finished, you can then select how you would like to use branching.

To use branching on your survey, perform the following:

1. Access the survey to which you want to add branching.

2. Click Settings, and then select Survey Settings.

3. Select the survey question to which you would like to apply branching.

4. For each of the possible responses, select the question that you would like to be the next question that appears for the participant, and then click OK.

5. Repeat steps 3 and 4 for each question to which you want branching applied.

> **Note**
> If you leave the default choice of No Branching selected, the next question in order will be displayed if that response is chosen by the participants.

Summary

This chapter explained how to create, modify, display, and delete lists and libraries. This includes the standard lists and libraries that come with SharePoint Foundation 2010 as well as custom lists and libraries that you can design yourself. Chapter 14 explains how to use SharePoint Designer 2010 to create and modify all aspects of SharePoint. Using SharePoint Designer 2010 involves some extra complexity, but it also provides much more power and flexibility than you can possibly obtain with a browser interface.

Creating and Formatting Webpages

In Microsoft SharePoint Foundation 2010, there is a change of emphasis: a SharePoint site is now seen as a collection of webpages. In Microsoft Windows SharePoint Services 3.0, a site was seen as a container for list and library data, and webpages were used to display data held in the lists and libraries. The webpage most commonly used, was the Web Part page where the addition of static text and images was possible only by adding the Content Editor Web Part (CEWP) or the Image Web Part. Such pages can be changed by using the browser, but many users did not find the mechanism for changing these pages to be easy. Wiki sites in Windows SharePoint Services 3.0 used *wiki pages* stored in a wiki page library. On other sites you could create a wiki page library and use wiki pages.

In SharePoint Foundation, when you create a new Team Site, SharePoint creates a wiki page library, named Site Pages, in which the webpages are stored and new pages are stored when created. These pages have been enhanced and are easy to change. Web Part pages are still used in SharePoint Foundation and are the default type of page on sites such as Group Work sites, Meeting Workspaces, and Blog sites. Web Part pages can also be used on Team Sites, but on such sites, they are usually used for list views, list item edit forms, and list item display forms.

> ## Note
> Wiki pages and Web Part pages are known as content pages or site pages because they contain the content that is unique to a site.

Another type of page that you will see on SharePoint Foundation sites are *application pages*, which are also known as system pages. You can identify these pages by the word "_layouts" in their URL. Application pages cannot be changed by using the browser or SharePoint Designer 2010. They contain the same information or type of links no matter which site you are on and can be shared across all sites on the server. The site settings page is an example of an application page. Application pages are stored on the SharePoint server file system and are never stored in a SharePoint SQL Server content database.

This chapter introduces the basic concepts of content pages and application pages. Using the browser, you will learn how to view content pages in different ways as well as how to change the appearance of these pages by adding and removing static text and images. You will learn how to use SharePoint Designer to create and customize your pages, and then you will learn how to use Microsoft Visual Studio to create application pages.

Creating and Modifying Content Pages by Using a Browser

The first page you see on a Team Site is known as the home page, because as with any website, this is the page on which all site visitors start. As you click the links on the Quick Launch, you are directed to other pages that display the site's content, such as when you click the Shared Documents link and are taken to the All Documents view. This page dynamically changes as you upload, modify, and delete files in the Shared Document library. You might also have pages that contain static text and images that describe, for example, the company's expenses policy and contains links to other pages that are related to that information. Your site can comprise pages that contain both static text and dynamic content. This approach of thinking of your site as a number of pages is more natural and in line with websites that are not based on SharePoint, where each site is a collection of webpages, and those webpages are interconnected.

In SharePoint Foundation, you use two types of content pages: wiki pages and Web Part pages. When you display these pages in the browser, it's hard to differentiate between the two page types. However, when you place the pages in edit mode, then you can tell the difference. You might also be able to differentiate between them, if you know the type of site you are working with. Wiki pages are the default pages when a site is created from the Team Site template. Wiki pages consist of a mix of free-format static text and images as well as Web Parts, whereas you can only add Web Parts to Web Part pages by using the browser. Web Parts are reusable components that can contain any type of web-based information, including analytical, collaborative, and database information.

You can find more details about Web Parts in Chapter 7, "Adding, Editing, Connecting, and Managing Web Parts on the Page."

Both wiki pages and Web Part pages are flexible and highly customizable by using three types of tools:

- A browser

- A SharePoint Foundation–compatible webpage editing tool, such as Microsoft Share-Point Designer 2010

- A professional development tool such as Visual Studio 2010

No one tool can do everything, and therefore, it is likely that in any deployment of Share-Point Foundation, all three tools will be used at some point.

Whatever type of content page you display in the browser, the ribbon will display at least the following two tabs:

- **Browse**   One of the biggest advances of SharePoint Foundation over previous versions is the incorporation of the ribbon into the user's browser experience. However, there can be occasions when you prefer that it not be displayed. This is when you should use the Browse tab. To make the ribbon visible again, click one of the other tabs.

- **Page**   Use the Page tab to manage the wiki pages on your site. More information on this tab is detailed later in this chapter.

The Composition of a SharePoint Page

When you enter the URL of a SharePoint site into a browser's address box, the browser contacts the SharePoint server, which duly responds with a number of components that the browser then uses to present the information to you. These components can include an HTML file that contains content and instructions on the data structure, cascade style sheet (CSS) files that contain format and layout instructions, and JavaScript files that contain client-side code that the browser uses to respond to the interaction you have with the page. On the SharePoint server, the HTML file is created from the combination of two Microsoft ASP.NET pages: a master page and a content page, as well as the wiki page content that you might have entered, such as text and images, Web Part details, and list and library content that you might have included on your page, as shown in Figure 6-1.

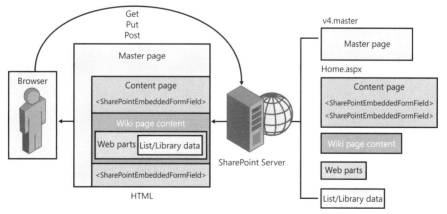

Figure 6-1 The composition of a SharePoint wiki page.

A master page is a special ASP.NET 2.0 page that is used to provide a consistent appearance and navigation for each page within one or more sites. A master page cannot be viewed by a browser, but you can view and customize a master page by using SharePoint Designer.

For more information about master pages, see Chapter 14, "Creating, Managing, and Designing Sites by Using SharePoint Designer 2010."

On a wiki page, the content that you enter in the browser is placed in an *Embedded FormField* SharePoint control. A Web Part page is composed using similar components, except that it has no wiki page content; therefore, it has no *EmbeddedFormField* SharePoint control. When you use the browser and add, delete, or modify Web Parts, those Web Parts are placed in the *WebPartPages WebPartZone* control. Using SharePoint Designer, you can modify the content within both of these controls, and when you are in Advanced Edit mode, you can also modify content that resides elsewhere on the page (more on this later in the chapter).

Sites are grouped into a Site Collection, and the content for all sites in a Site Collection are stored in one Microsoft SQL Server content database. A content database can contain content from one or more Site Collections. The content database contains a number of tables. For example, the AllDocs table is the main table that contains the information about files, such as webpages and documents that you might attach to list items or upload into libraries. This table contains the contents of the file as well as the file's properties, such as file size, the person who created the file, and whether the file is checked out, and if so, the name of the person who checked it out. The Sites table stores information about sites, and when you add a Web Part to a page, then that information is stored in another SQL table, AllWebParts. The information for lists and libraries is stored across a number of tables.

When you request a content page, such as the home.aspx page for a Team Site, the following events occur:

- The home.aspx page is retrieved as well as any files that the home.aspx page references, such as the master page.

- The business logic for controls that the home.aspx and the master page contain is executed, which can produce additional HTML and links to files such as CSS, JavaScript, and image files.

- The site properties are retrieved. The properties include the site title, permissions, and the links that should be shown on the Quick Launch bar.

- The home.aspx page properties are retrieved, including its title, the information of the data stored in the *EmbeddeFormField* control, and whether it contains any Web Parts.

- If the page contains any Web Part zones, information of the Web Parts they contain is retrieved.

- The Web Parts' properties and any data they contain are retrieved. If the data to be presented in the Web Part is stored in lists and libraries, that data and associated properties, such as permissions is then also retrieved.

- The master page, the home.aspx page and all the data retrieved (taking into account the security settings of the user) are merged to form one HTML page.

- The merged HTML page together with any other files, such as CSS and JavaScript files, is sent to the browser.

- The browser parses and interprets the content of the files it has received, executes any client-side code that might produce additional HTML and page content, and then renders the page.

The logic that is executed on the SharePoint server is called server-side code, and the logic that the browser interprets and executes is called client-side code.

Modifying Wiki Pages

On a Team Site, the default webpages are wiki pages, and the home page of such sites is a wiki page. Wiki pages are stored in a SharePoint Foundation–based wiki library, named Site Pages, which by default inherits its permissions from the site. Therefore, anyone who is mapped to the Contribute permission level at the site level—that is, anyone who is a member of the site's Members SharePoint group—is allowed to change any wiki page or create new pages. If a page is found to be incomplete or poorly organized, any member of the site can edit it as necessary. Therefore, as users share their information, knowledge, experience, ideas, and views, the content evolves. Site members can work together to change or update information without the need to send emails or attend meetings or conference calls. This is known as *open editing*. All users are allowed to control and check the content because open editing relies on the assumption that most members of a collaboration site have good intentions.

INSIDE OUT   What happened to the Wiki Site template?

In Windows SharePoint Services 3.0, it was possible to create a site from the Wiki Site template. The default webpages on this site were also wiki pages that were stored in a wiki library, named Wiki Pages. In SharePoint Foundation you can no longer create new sites based on the Wiki Site template. However, you can create new wiki libraries on any site. SharePoint Server 2010 provides a new type of wiki page that is created when you create a site based on the Enterprise Wiki site template, which is built on the SharePoint Server publishing infrastructure Site Collection feature. You can find more information about Enterprise Wikis at *http://technet.microsoft.com/en-us/library/ee721055.aspx*.

You can edit a wiki page by using one of the three methods described here and shown in Figure 6-2:

- Click the Edit icon that is displayed to the left of the Browse tab. The Edit icon only appears on wiki pages.

- On the ribbon, on the Page tab, click Edit in the Edit group.

- Click Site Actions, and then click Edit Page.

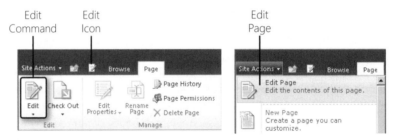

Figure 6-2 The three methods by which you can edit a wiki page.

When a wiki page is in Edit mode, the Editing Tool contextual tab set appears, which contains two tabs: Format Text and Insert (see Figure 6-3). These tabs appear when you enter content in a CEWP, and just like with the CEWP, you are provided with a What You See Is What You Get (WYSIWYG) environment for adding content to your page. Using these tabs, you can format the text, control the layout of the page, as well as insert tables, images, and hyperlinks.

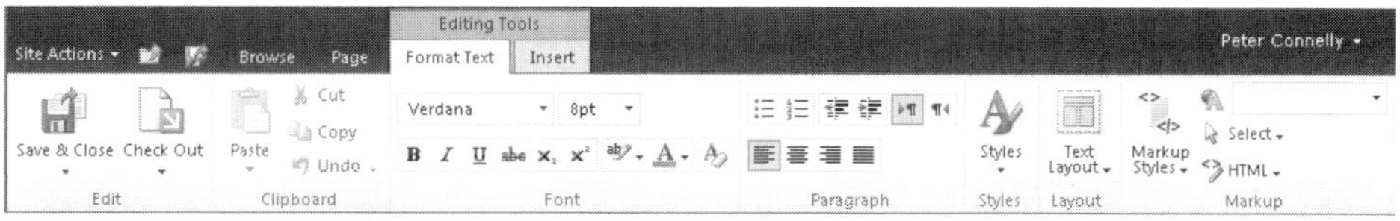

Figure 6-3 The Editing Tools contextual tab set: the Format Text tab.

Using the Format Text tab

To format your text, use the Format Text tab. Select the text that you wish to format, and then click the appropriate command in the ribbon. To include new static text on your page, place the insertion point in the area of the page where you want the text to appear and then begin typing. The Format Text tab contains seven ribbon groups: Edit, Clipboard, Font, Paragraph, Styles, Layout, and Markup. Each group is described in the sections that follow.

Edit

Use the commands in this group to save and close the page, save and keep editing the page, and stop editing the page, which means any changes you make to the page will be lost. The other two commands in the Save & Close drop-down list—Edit and Edit In Share-Point Designer—are inactive. These commands are available on the Page tab, when the page is not in Edit mode.

The other set of commands in this group can be used to check out the page. Any team member mapped to the contribute permission level, which on most Team Sites is most users, can amend the wiki pages of the site. When you edit a page, you should always check it out before you modify the content. This prevents other users in your team from editing the page at the same time. Once the page is checked out, the Check In, Discard Check Out, and Override Check Out commands are available.

Check Out locks the page so other contributors cannot edit the page; however, while the page is checked out to you and in Edit mode, you will be the only person to see the changes that you're making to the page.

Clipboard

Use the commands in this group to cut, copy, paste, undo, and redo your modifications. These commands are placed in a group named Clipboard because they use your computers clipboard feature; therefore, you are able to copy and paste content from other applications and websites. The paste command, by default, maintains the formatting from the copy or cut source. To paste the unformatted text, click the down-arrow on the Paste command button, and then click Paste Plaintext. When pasting content from other programs, such as Microsoft Word, the formatting instructions can be verbose and might not generate the most efficient HTML code; therefore, use the *Paste Text* command, unless you specifically created the text in Word to generate the formatting you required, such as a table.

As with other Microsoft applications, you can use the standard shortcut key combinations to complete these commands; for example, press Ctrl+C to copy selected text, and Ctrl+V to paste the copied text. Use Ctrl+Z (undo an action) and Ctrl+Y (redo an action) to cycle through the history of changes. If you do inadvertently paste content with the format and later decide that you want to remove that format, use the Clear Format (Ctrl+Space) command in the Font group.

Font

Use the set of commands in this group as you would in other Microsoft Office applications to change the font face, font size, font color, as well as formatting text to a specific style—bold, italics, underline, strikethrough, subscript or superscript—just as you would in Word, for example.

Paragraph

Use the commands in this group, which again are similar to those you would find in Word, to arrange the text on the page as bulleted lists, numbered lists, to increase or decrease the indent level, and align a paragraph Left, Center, Right or Justify. You can also choose to display the paragraph for the selected text so that it displays in left to right or right to left reading order. This is primarily used for languages that read right to left.

Styles

Use this method of formatting text in preference to the commands in the Font group to consistently apply styles across all wiki pages in your site. Select the text that you wish to format, and then use the Styles drop-down list to select a style. Similar to any Office 2010 application, a preview of the styling is provided when you hover over the style command, as shown in Figure 6-4.

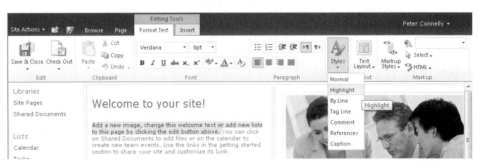

Figure 6-4 You can apply a style to text by using the Styles command. Hovering over an item in the list displays a preview of the text formatting.

The drop-down options for both the Styles command and the Markup Styles command in the Markup group are populated dynamically by client-side code using Microsoft ASP.NET Ajax and the CSS classes that are available for the wiki page when you place it in Edit mode. For each style that appears in the Styles drop-down list, there is a matching CSS class in the corev4.css with a name .ms-rteStyle-*SSSS*, where *SSSS* is the style name in the drop-down list; for example, .ms-rteStyle-Highlight. The CSS for this style is shown in the following code sample:

```
.ms-rteStyle-Highlight
{
  -ms-name:"Highlight";
  /* [ReplaceColor(themeColor:"Dark1-Darker")] */
  color:#312a26;
  /* [ReplaceColor(themeColor:"Accent6")] */
  background-color:#fae032;
}
```

INSIDE OUT   So what is Ajax?

Ajax is not a programming language. It was originally an acronym for *Asynchronous JavaScript and XML*. Today, the term used to represent a combination of related web development methods that allows the browser to send and retrieve data asynchronously from the server without the need to reload the webpage. When a user interface (UI) object is selected by a user and the logic for that object is implemented by using Ajax technologies, the user does not have to wait for the page to refresh to see changes on the page. As a result, users experience a more responsive application. An overview of user experience approaches can be found at *http://msdn.microsoft.com/en-us/library/ff798414.aspx*. The World Wide Web Consortium (W3C) schools site contains a tutorial for Ajax that you can find at *www.w3schools.com/ajax/default.asp*.

Layout

When you create a Team Site, the home page, with the Rich Content area, has two rich text editing areas (also known as divisions) structured as two columns. Use the Text Layout command in the Layout group to create additional editing areas and to change the structure of your page. You can reformat the page by using any of the eight options shown in Figure 6-5. A thumbnail to the left of each option provides a view of the editing areas and structure that will be applied to the Rich Content area when selected.

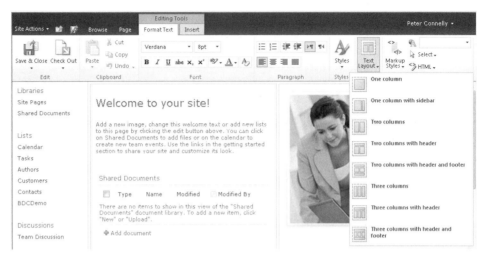

Figure 6-5 Text Layout options.

The Layout group and the Text Layout command are not available when you add content to a CEWP. The Rich Content area of a wiki page is created by using a SharePoint control named *EmbeddedFormField*, with which you can modify the layout of the wiki page by using the Text Layout command. This command creates the rich text editing areas and the layout you choose by using HTML <TABLE> and <DIV> tags. The rich text editing areas are not Web Part zones.

When you select a layout that has fewer rich text editing areas than the current layout, then the content from the area not included in the layout is combined into an area that is included in the layout.

> **Note**
> If you are using SharePoint Server 2010 and working on a publishing or enterprise wiki page, then the Format Text tab you see in the ribbon is very similar to the Format Text tab on wiki pages. However, on publishing and enterprise wiki pages, there is no Text Layouts command but a Page Layout button.

Markup

This ribbon group provides four commands:

- **Markup Styles**   Use this command to format text by using a markup style, such as Heading 1, Colored Heading 1, or Paragraph. For each style that appears in the Markup Styles drop-down list, there is a matching CSS class with a name

.ms-rteElement-*SS*, where *SS*, and the –ms-name property of the class is the style name in the drop-down list; for example, the class *.H1.ms-rteElement-H1* has a –ms-name property of "Heading 1". These styles are defined in the corev4.css file.

- **Languages**   When a SharePoint site is created, it is defined with a default language. A *lang* attribute appears in the <HTML> tag for each page of the site—this is the webpage's primary language. When you incorporate text in your page that is of a different language, select the text, and then use this command to identify the language of the text. This surrounds your text with an HTML <SPAN> tag with the *lang* attribute. The *lang* attribute, whether it is applied to a webpage or a portion of a page, is used by search engines to identify pages that include text in specific languages. Therefore, when a user specifies in a search engine to return only pages of a specific language your page would appear in the search results if it meets the search criteria. The *lang* attribute is also used by some screen reader applications, such as JAWS, so that they can pronounce words correctly when they read them out loud.

- **Select**   Use this command to select all the text of the parent tag; for example, you might have created a table and want to select a specific row in that table. Place the insertion point in a cell in the row, use the Select command to highlight the row, and then format or style the row. A red dotted line surrounds the area related to the HTML tag when you hover over the each tag, as shown in Figure 6-6.

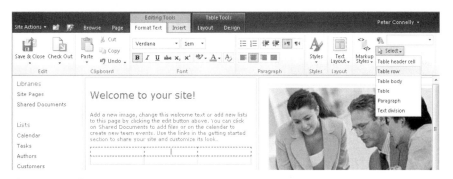

Figure 6-6 Select a parent HTML tag.

The inner tags are listed at the top of the drop-down list, and the most outer parental HTML tag—Text Division—is listed as the last item on the drop-down list. The Text Division tag represents the column in which the select text appears.

- **HTML**   This command provides two options: Edit HTML, and Convert To XHTML. The Edit HTML option opens a plain-text dialog box that displays the HTML code in a fixed-width font. The HTML for the whole wiki page is not displayed, only the HTML that is displayed in the division of the *EmbeddedFormField* SharePoint control, where you had placed the cursor. For example, if you have a two-column layout and you place the cursor in the left column, only the HTML for the left column is displayed in

Chapter 6

the dialog. The commands available on the ribbon support only a limited number of features; for example, you cannot format the line type of a table. Unfortunately, no IntelliSense is provided, so it might be easier to use SharePoint Designer to modify the contents of the *EmbeddedFormField* control if you have limited knowledge of HTML or you have a considerable amount of HTML code to write. The section, "Writing Standards-Based Code," later in this chapter, details the code that you can enter in this text box and the validation process that occurs when you save the page.

> You can learn more about how to extend the server use experience, including modifying and the addition of tab sets, groups, and the ribbon commands, in Chapter 15, "Customizing the User Interface."

Using the Insert tab

When the wiki page is in Edit mode, a second Editing Tools tab labeled Insert displays, as shown in Figure 6-7. This presents a number of objects that you can now add to a wiki page that you could not in Windows SharePoint Services 3.0. You can mingle these objects with text anywhere within a wiki page.

Figure 6-7 Use the Insert tab to add other objects to your wiki page.

The Insert tab contains four ribbon groups: Tables, Media, Links, and Web Parts, which are described in the sections that follow.

Tables

Click the down-arrow on the Table command to add an HTML table. You can use the grid provided to quickly create a table by dragging the mouse across the grid to select the number of columns, and then drag the mouse down the grid to select the number of rows. On the Table drop-down menu, you can also click Insert Table, which displays a dialog in which you can type the number of columns and rows that you need.

> **Note**
> The maximum number of cells that a table can contain—that is, the number of rows multiplied by the number of columns—is limited to 625.

Once the table is created, an additional tab set, Table Tools, is added to the ribbon. This contains two tabs, Layout and Design, as shown in Figures 6-8 and 6-9.

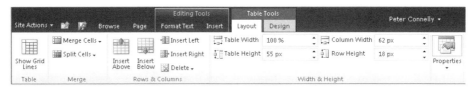

Figure 6-8 The Layout tab in Table Tools.

The Layout tab consists of four groups:

- **Table** The Show Grid Lines command can be used to display the cell boundaries of the table, when the table is not configured with borders.

- **Merge** Use the commands in this group to combine or split cells. You can only merge two cells to a single cell.

- **Rows & Columns** Use this group to add and remove rows and columns. You can also use the Delete drop-down menu to delete the table.

- **Width & Height** Use the commands in this group to resize your table as well as resize a column or row. You can select a size by using up or down-arrow on the controls, or you can type a specific number followed by % or px to specify the unit of measurement.

- **Properties** This group contains a Summary text box. You can use this to type summary information that will display to site visitors and screen reader applications when the table is not visible.

Figure 6-9 The Design tab in Table Tools.

The Design tab contains two groups:

- **Table Style Options** Use the four check boxes to select the table components for which the special formatting selected in the Table Styles group should be applied. For example, select Header Row and Footer Row to apply the special formatting to the first and last rows of your table.

- **Table Styles** Use this command to format the entire table by using one of four preformatted table styles. As you hover your mouse over each style, the style is applied to the table in preview mode. Each preformatted table style is a collection of CSS classes. When you click the style in the Table Styles menu, the CSS classes from the style sheet linked to the page are dynamically applied to the table. The naming standard for these styles are ms-rteTable*XXX-NNN*, where *XXX* is the table section, such as, HeaderRow, HeaderFirstCol, OddCol, EvenRow and FooterLastCol, and *NNN* is the name to identify the table styling. These styles are defined in the corev4.css file. An example of one of the default styles is shown in the following example:

```
.ms-rteTable-0 {
  -ms-name: "Table Style 1 - Clear";
  border-width:0px;
  border-style:none;
  border-collapse:collapse;
}
```

Media

Click the Picture command down-arrow to insert a picture from your computer or to reference a web address where a picture is currently stored. No longer do you need to upload your images prior to editing the page. Using the first option, the Select Picture dialog opens in which you can now both upload and add an image to the page with one click of the mouse. Use the Select Picture dialog box to browse to the location on your computer where the picture is stored. You can then select a library on your site where you want to upload the picture. By default the Site Assets library is chosen. The Site Assets library is the location where site supporting files, such as images displayed on pages, CSS files, or JavaScript files should be stored. Do not combine team documentation with files that are needed to brand a site.

If the image is already uploaded into a library, then the Picture, From Address drop-down menu option opens the Select Picture dialog, where you need to manually type or paste the URL of the image. The dialog does not provide any browse button with which to navigate to the library where the picture is stored. To guard against you typing the incorrect URL of the image, which would result in a broken link, it is easier to open another browser window, navigate to the picture and copy the URL, and then paste the URL into the Select Picture, Address text box.

Once an image is added to a page and that image is selected, the Picture Tools contextual tab set appears, as shown in Figure 6-10. When a picture is selected, you can press the Delete key to remove it from the page.

Figure 6-10 The Design tab in Picture Tools.

This Picture Tools tab set contains one tab, the Design tab, which contains five ribbon groups:

- **Select**   This group contains the Change Picture drop-down menu, with which you can change the image that is displayed on the page. This menu provides you with the same options as the Picture command on the Insert tab.

- **Properties**   Use the commands in this group to replace the image on the page and set the alternative text for the image. You can replace an image by typing the URL in the Address text box. Use the Alt Text text box to type text that displays in place of an image if that image does not load. This also provides text for screen reader applications. Append a period to the end of the words you enter so that users listening to screen readers are able to understand your content more easily, especially when two alternate text tags are next to each other.

- **Styles**   Use this command to format the borders of the image by using one of five preformatted image styles. As with other style commands described in this chapter, these border image styles are controlled by CSS rules in the corev4.css file. The standard used for these styles are ms-rteImage-*x*, where *x* is a number, such as:

  ```
  .ms-rteImage-0 { -ms-name:"No border";}
  ```

- **Arrange**   Use the Position command drop-down menu to arrange the image on the page. The drop-down provides two Float styles (Left and Right) and three Inline Styles (Top, Middle, and Bottom) that are defined in the corev4.css file, such as:

  ```
  .ms-rtePosition-1 { -ms-name:"Left";float:left;}
  ```

- **Size**   Use the commands in this group to reduce the size of the image on the page. These commands do not alter the image file, but place *width* and *height* attributes on the <IMG> tag. The browser uses these attributes to display the image file differently than the physical size of the image, as stored in the image file. For prototyping purposes this might be adequate. However, the image file still must be stored on the server and requires network bandwidth when it is downloaded from the server to the client computer, even if the browser then displays the picture smaller than its original size. So if users to your site complain that a page takes more time to load than other pages, you might need to look at the size of the image files.

It is good practice to create image files to the correct size before loading them into the Site Assets library. You can use SharePoint Designer, Microsoft Office Picture Manager, Microsoft PowerPoint, or a third-party image editing tool to resize the image as saved in the file. You can find Picture Manager by clicking the Start Menu, and then clicking Microsoft Office Tools. Resizing the image file can affect the picture quality; therefore, if the same file is needed as different sizes on a number of pages you might find using one picture file does not meet your needs. You might need to provide a number of files at different sizes for the same picture. This process of resizing an image to find the right balance between file size and picture quality is called *image optimization*.

Optimizing Images for Websites

Two common formats used for images displayed on webpages are GIF and JPEG. To resize your pictures by using Picture Manager, perform the following steps:

1. Using My Computer, browse to the picture file. Right-click the picture file to open the shortcut menu. Click Open With, and then select Microsoft Office Picture Manager.

2. Right click the picture, and then select Properties to open the Properties task pane.

3. On the Toolbar, click Picture, and then click Resize to open the Resize task pane.

   Use this task pane to resize the picture. You can also use the Crop task pane to select a portion of the original picture to display on the webpage.

4. On the Toolbar, click Picture, and then click Compress Pictures to open the Compress Pictures task pane.

5. Under Compress For, select Web pages, and then at the bottom of the Compress Pictures task pane, click OK.

6. Save the file.

To resize your pictures by using PowerPoint, carry out the following steps:

1. Open PowerPoint.

   A blank slide is displayed.

2. On the Insert tab, in the Images group, click Picture to open the Insert Picture dialog box. Browse to where you have stored your picture, and then click Open.

3. Click the Format tab. In the Size group, type the height and size of the picture. Click the down-arrow in the lower-right corner of the Size group to open the Format Picture dialog box to display more options.

4. Right-click the picture, and then click Save As Picture to open the Save As Picture dialog box.

5. In the Save As Type drop-down list, select the picture type, and then in the File Name text box, type the name of the file. Click Save.

When you save a picture file, use a naming standard that identifies the subject of the picture and the dimensions of the picture, especially if you have a number of files that contain the same picture but at different resolutions. If your site contains a large number of picture files, then in the Site Assets library or the library where the picture files are stored, create a column that you can use to categorize your pictures. This will make it easy for your contributors to find the pictures.

Links

On the Insert tab, in the Links group, two commands are provided: the Link command and the Upload File command.

You use the Link command to associate a hyperlink with text on the page so that when you click the text you are directed to the page associated with the hyperlink.

The Insert Hyperlink dialog does not provide you with any options to configure the hyperlink to open in a new browser window; therefore, when the user clicks the hyperlink, he is redirected from the wiki page and will need to use the browser's back button to return to it. However, once you add a link to the wiki page, the Format tab within the Link Tools tab set is displayed, which you can use to remove the link, edit the URL, display an icon to the left of the hyperlink and configure the hyperlink so that when a user clicks it, the page that the hyperlink is pointing to is displayed in a new tab, and the user is not redirected from the wiki page. You can also associate a description with the hyperlink which displays when a user hovers over the hyperlink. This is sometimes known as a *ScreenTip*; you should configure this for accessibility reasons.

Chapter 6

INSIDE OUT
Opening a new browser window

If you want a new browser window to open when the user clicks a link, you can use the Edit HTML Source command in the Markup group on the Format Text tab to add a `target="_blank"` attribute to the <A> tag. However, before you make any changes, verify that this is permissible; your organization might have a stated policy with regard to opening a new browser window. Generally, you should only open a new browser window in scenarios such as displaying a printable version of a webpage and large images. You can find expert usability references on this topic at *www.sitepoint.com/article/beware-opening-links-new-window*, and by using the search keywords, opening, new, browser, window, usability.

You can use the second command in the Links group, the Upload File command, to upload a file and store that file by default into the Site Assets library, in one action, and then create a hyperlink pointing to the file that you have just uploaded. An icon appears to the left of the hyperlink, indicating the type of file the hyperlink points to.

If you want to create a link to an existing wiki page, it is easier to use a method known as wiki links or forward links than it is to use either of the two commands on the Links tab. You'll read more about wiki links in the section "Creating Wiki Links," later in this chapter.

Web Parts

This group provides commands to insert Web Parts into your wiki page. When you click the Web Part or Existing List commands, the Web Parts pane is displayed at the top of the page, below the ribbon, as shown in Figure 6-11.

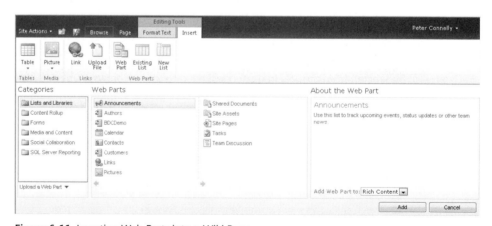

Figure 6-11 Inserting Web Parts into a Wiki Page.

Web Parts, if not fully tested, can cause a page to not display in the browser. If this occurs, append *?contents=1* to the page's URL to navigate to the page's Web Part Page Maintenance page, where you can close, reset, or delete the offending Web Part. You can use this page to delete all Web Parts from the page.

The two most commonly used types of Web Parts via the browser are:

- **XSLT List View (XLV) Web Parts**   These are Web Parts that display the contents of lists and libraries. These Web Parts are displayed in the lists and libraries and lists category. Each time that data in the list or library changes, the changes are reflected in the XLV Web Part. SharePoint Foundation introduced this new version of the List View Web Part (LVWP), which uses Extensible Stylesheet Language Transformation (XSLT) to define how to display the data from lists or libraries.

- **Built-in Web Parts**   These are Web Parts that display other content. In SharePoint Foundation, there are 13 built-in Web Parts displayed in five categories.

You can use the third command in the Web Parts group, New List, to create a list or library and then insert a Web Part that displays the contents of that list or library, all in one action.

For more information about Web Parts, read Chapter 7.

Writing Standards-Based Code

Out of the box, SharePoint Foundation complies with the Web Content Accessibility Guidelines (WCAG) 2.0 AA and targets standards-based browsers, such as Internet Explorer (IE) 7.0, IE 8.0, and Firefox 3.x, but not IE 6.0. Although SharePoint 2010 sites use master pages that are based on the XHTML Strict Doc Type, SharePoint sites are not XHTML compliant. If you test a sample SharePoint 2010 site against any of the XHTML validators such as Total Validator (*www.totalvalidator.com*), XHTML errors will occur, but it should pass US Section 508, WCAG v1 A and WCAG v1 AA standards. Of course, if you create your own pages, including your own master pages, then you could create SharePoint sites that comply with W3C XHTML recommendations. This is not a trivial task, and typically, it includes raising a business case to acquire resources such as a developer and web designer. In addition, such a development would involve strict control of the pages and code, and the introduction of a standards base test of the pages and code in your release management process, from the development environment into the production environment. Such an expenditure might only be approved for your organization's Internet website.

You can find information about application lifecycle management (ALM) and SharePoint 2010 at *http://msdn.microsoft.com/en-us/sharepoint/dd552992.aspx*.

XHTML is a stricter and cleaner version of HTML and attempts to reduce the need for browsers to correct invalid client-side code. Without standards, a page can look radically different when rendered by different browsers or even different versions of the same browser. You have also seen earlier in this chapter that the functionality of the WYSIWYG editing environment and the commands provided on the ribbon are dynamically created by using HTML, CSS, and JavaScript, known as client-side code. Therefore, new with this version, to prevent the entry of malicious code, SharePoint Foundation now sanitizes user-entered HTML content that is entered in the wiki page content control when you use the browser or SharePoint Designer 2010.

SharePoint validates and changes the code, and if you click the Convert To XHTML in the Markup group on the Format Text tab, it will make the code XHTML compliant. If the user enters JavaScript as well as HTML, then the JavaScript is removed. If you have used a CEWP on your wiki page and entered HTML and JavaScript in the CEWP, SharePoint will sanitize the code in the CEWP, but it will not remove the JavaScript code. However, by sanitizing the HTML code, the JavaScript might not continue to work. This can cause problems, especially with end-users who might not understand the difference between HTML and XHTML, and copy HTML and JavaScript code from samples that they find on the Internet. A workaround is to tell users to copy the JavaScript into a file, which they load into a library such as the Site Assets library, and then within the CEWP, link to the file. Figure 6-12 shows how to reference a file that is stored in the Site Assets library. SharePoint does not follow the link and therefore will not validate the code within the file.

Figure 6-12 Linking client-side code into a wiki page by using the CEWP.

If you do want to incorporate the client-side code within the page, then use the HTML Form Web Part, which you can find in the Forms category of the Web Parts pane. The client-side code you enter into the Text Editor dialog box is not sanitized by SharePoint.

> **Note**
> As SharePoint sanitizes the code, extra spaces might appear, this usually occurs when an HTML object is inserted in the middle of <P> and </P> tags, for example, when a table is inserted on the same line as some text. SharePoint tries to modify the code so that the paragraph is added below or above the enclosed HTML object. In the HTML source window, you see the inclusion of <p> </p> where the spaces are included.

For users who want to learn more about HTML and XHTML, the w3schools website has free tutorials. To check your code against the formal standards, you can use validation services such as those that can be found at *www.htmlhelp.com/tools/validator/* or *www.w3schools.com/xhtml/xhtml_validate.asp* or *http://validator.w3.org*. You can read details about common errors that are found in HTML code at *www.htmlhelp.com/tools/validator/problems.html.en*.

Creating Wiki Pages

There are four methods available for creating a new page by using the browser:

- Use wiki links, also known as linking or a forward link.

  This is the recommended method for creating new wiki pages because it creates a hyperlink to the new page on an existing wiki page, and users find it easier to find a page when another page is linked to it.

- Click Site Actions, and then click New Page.

- Click Site Actions, and then click More Options. In the Create dialog box, under Filter By, click Page, and then in the middle pane, click Page (see Figure 6-13).

Figure 6-13 Creating a wiki page.

- In the All Pages view of the Site Pages library, click New Document on the Documents tab, or below the list of pages, click Add new page, as shown in Figure 6-14.

  You might be thinking that you can add a new wiki page template by adding a new content type to the Site Pages library, and then the New Document menu would list two types of pages. Although you cannot do this by using the browser, you can enable the management of content types by using SharePoint Designer, and then associate a content type with the Site Pages library.

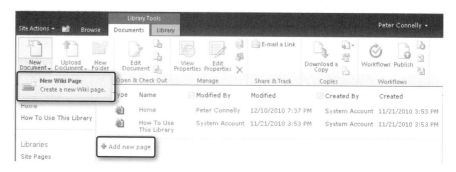

Figure 6-14 Creating a new wiki page by using the Documents tab on the ribbon.

INSIDE OUT Using the Wiki Page Home Page site feature

If you have created a blank site or a site other than a Team Site, and later you decide that you want to have wiki pages as your default pages, you can use a new site feature in SharePoint Foundation called Wiki Page Home Page to enable wiki page functionality. When this feature is activated, it creates a document library with a URL of SitePages that has a name of Site Pages, and then adds a wiki page named *default.aspx*, which is then set as the home page for your site. You can now create, modify, and delete wiki pages just as you could if the site were created from the Team Site template.

Creating Wiki Links

You can create hyperlinks that point to wiki pages by using wiki links. This is a quicker and easier method than using the Links command on the Insert tab. The first wiki site, WikiWikiWeb, was created for the Portland Pattern Repository in 1995 by Ward Cunningham, who devised a system that created webpages quickly—and this method is what is now called wiki links. You can create a wiki link to an existing page or you can create a wiki link to a wiki page that is not created. You can then click on the wiki link to create a new wiki page.

INSIDE OUT The origins of wiki links

Wiki is the Hawaiian word for quick. To add emphasis in Hawaiian, words are doubled; thus, wiki wiki means very quick. Ward Cunningham used double characters as formatting clues. These formatting clues are standard to many wiki applications. To create a wiki link, you type the name of the page within two set of double square brackets. To display double open or closed square brackets without making a link, type a backslash before the two brackets, such as \[[or \]].

To create a wiki link to an existing page, perform the following:

1. Open a wiki page in Edit mode and place the insertion point where you would like a hyperlink to the new page to appear.

2. Type **[[** to display a list of pages that exist in the Site Pages wiki library.

If the Site Pages library contains a large number of pages, you can filter the list by typing the first few characters of the page name. You can then use your mouse or press the Up and Down keys to select the desired wiki page. You can also type the first characters for the name of the wiki page until only one page remains in the list, and then press Tab. You do not need to type the page name in full; you only need sufficient characters to uniquely identify the page.

3. Press Enter to close the brackets.

To create a new wiki page by using the forward link method, use the following procedure:

1. Open a wiki page in Edit mode and place the insertion point where you would like a hyperlink to the new page to appear.

2. Type **[[**, and then type the name of the new page. The page name needs to be unique within the Site Pages library, and it will form part of a URL. When you have typed sufficient characters of the page name to make it unique, a message appears stating that the item does not exist.

    Webpage names are usually short and terse, yet the text on the wiki page that represents the hyperlink are descriptive so that a user who reads the page can make a decision whether to click the link or not. To create descriptive text that is displayed as the text for the link, type **|** followed by the descriptive text, and then type **]]**, such as [[TrainingMaterial|training material]].

3. On the Format Text tab, in the Edit group, click Save & Close. The descriptive text, such as, training material, is underlined with dashes. This indicates that the wiki link points to a nonexistent page.

Add a new image, change this welcome text or add new lists to this page by clicking the edit button above. You can click on Shared Documents to ⬛ HideNavBar.cssor on the calendar to create new team events. Use the links in the getting started section to share your site and customize its look.

training material

4. Click the wiki link.

   A New Page dialog appears, stating that the page TrainingMaterial does not exist and asks whether you want to create a new page. Click Create to generate the page in the Site Pages library. In the left navigation pane, above the Quick Launch, a Recently Modified section appears, displaying in modified date order the wiki pages recently modified.

> **Note**
>
> The naming convention for Wiki pages, known as WikiWords or WikiNames, is to con-catenate two or more words, where each word is composed of two or more letters, with no spaces between words and where the first letter of each word is capitalized and the remaining letters are in lowercase. This formatting is known as *camel case*. However you might have your own naming standard for URLs.

Managing Wiki Pages

Once you have created your pages, to ensure the accuracy of your content, you need to manage them. This is where the Page tab becomes useful. This tab consists of five groups:

- **Edit** When the wiki page is in Edit mode, the two drop-down menus provide the same options that the Format Text tab provides. When the page is not in Edit mode, then you can use the Edit drop-down menu to open the page in SharePoint Designer.

- **Manage** Use the commands in this group to edit the properties of the page, rename the page, view the page history, manage the page's permission, and delete the page. You cannot rename a site's home page. The Edit Properties command will be inactive if you have not created any additional columns in the Site Pages library.

  A wiki page is just a file in the Site Pages library, and therefore, it can be deleted and have item level permissions, as can any file in any library. Also similar to other files, once a wiki page is deleted, it moves to the site's recycle bin.

- **Share & Track** This group contains two commands: the E-Mail A Link command, and a split button labeled Alert Me:

— The E-Mail A Link command opens a new Mail message, and creates a hyper-link to the wiki page in the body of the email message.

— The Alert Me split button allows you to either set an alert on the page or man-age your alerts. By setting an alert on a wiki page, you can receive an email or a text message (Short Message Services [SMS]), when the page changes, and you can choose when to receive that message: immediately, daily, or weekly. If at the farm level your SharePoint Foundation installation does not have the outgoing email settings configured, the Alert Me split button is not displayed. If the mobile account settings are not configured, the SMS option cannot be used. Use the SharePoint 2010 Central Administration website to configure outgoing email settings and mobile accounts, which can be found on the System Settings page.

- **Page Actions**   This group consists of two commands: Make Homepage and Incom-ing Links. If a user types the URL of a site and does not specify a webpage, then the home page of the site is displayed. Use this command to replace the site's current home page with the current wiki page. When you click Incoming Links, you are redi-rected to a page that displays all pages that link to the current page.

- **Page Library**   This group consist of three commands:

— **Library Settings**   This redirects you to the list settings page for the Site Pages library. You can use the list settings page as you can other libraries, for example you can use content approval and workflow with the Site Pages library.

— **Library Permissions**   This command redirects you to the library permissions page for the Site Pages library, which you can use to restrict the rights with respect to who can create and edit wiki pages.

— **View All Pages**   This redirects you to the All Pages view for the Site Pages library.

Lists and libraries are described in Chapter 5, "Designing Lists and Libraries."

Working with Page History

A SharePoint Foundation–based wiki library has all the features of a document library, such as history and version management. Therefore, no changes or modifications are lost. Major versioning is enabled by default when you create a wiki page library.

On the Page tab, in the Manage group, click Page History to display the History page. In the left pane, there is a list of all the versions for the page, together with the date and time that the versions were created. Figure 6-15 illustrates how you have the option to choose which two versions of the wiki page to compare. In the content area, content that is deleted from the older of the two versions appears on the page but is displayed with a strikethrough red font. Content that is added after the creation of the older of the two versions appears with a green background. The History Page does not show changes in Web Parts, images, or client-side code, such as changes to HTML tags or their attributes.

Figure 6-15 Viewing and comparing Wiki Page versions on the Page History page.

The Page History page provides links to edit the properties of the wiki page, delete the wiki page and all its versions, manage its permissions, check out the page, and create an Alert Me for the page. In addition, in the left pane, a link to each version of the wiki page is displayed.

Managing Versions

The Versions Saved page is displayed when you click Version History on the Page History page. This page displays as a dialog if you have Silverlight installed and when you use the Version History command in the Manage group on the Documents tab for the All Pages view of the Site Pages library. Similarly the Saved Versions dialog is displayed when you use the Version History command on the list item menu.

You can use the Versions Saved page to replace the current version of a wiki page with the selected version. When the previous version of the page is restored as the current version of the page, a yellow status bar appears, stating that the current page has been customized from its template, as shown in Figure 6-16. This occurs when you restore a previous version of a page by using the browser or when using a program such as SharePoint Designer 2010. Click Revert To Template, and then click OK to revert the page to its template.

Figure 6-16 Restoring a wiki page version customizes the page.

For more information about customizing pages, see the section "Site Template Pages," later in this chapter.

Using Web Part pages

On sites such as the Group Work site, Meeting Workspaces, and Blog sites, Web Part pages are the default type of page. Lists and libraries also use this page type to display their content. Web Part pages consist only of Web Part zones and do not contain the *Embedded FormField* SharePoint control, as shown in Figure 6-17. Therefore, they cannot use wiki links to quickly and easily create new pages. You cannot mix text and Web Parts anywhere on the page; they can contain only Web Parts. To add static text or images to a Web Part page, you must first add either the CEWP or the Image Web Part, and then use the Web Part tool pane to alter the properties of the Web Part and to add text or images.

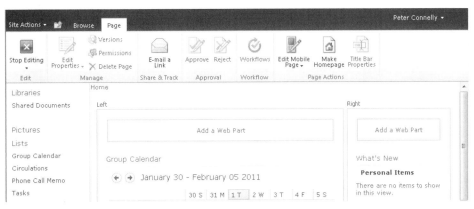

Figure 6-17 A Web Part page containing two Web Part zones: Left and Right.

INSIDE OUT   Beware—SharePoint Foundation validates the code within a CEWP

Similar to the *EmbeddedFormField*, when client-side code is added to the CEWP, SharePoint Foundation sanitizes the code. However, unlike with the *EmbeddedFormField*, SharePoint Foundation does not remove client-side code, such as JavaScript. But be aware that the modifications that SharePoint made to the HTML code could make the JavaScript not work correctly. If you are upgrading from Windows SharePoint Services 3.0, and you have entered non-compliant HTML and JavaScript into a CEWP, when you migrate your SharePoint site to SharePoint Foundation, the HTML and JavaScript will continue to work on the upgraded page as it did in the Windows SharePoint Services environment. However, when you edit the CEWP and save, SharePoint 2010 validates the code and the JavaScript could then fail.

Chapter 6

Using the browser, you can only add Web Parts to Web Part zones. Using SharePoint Designer, you can add Web Parts outside of Web Part zones on a Web Part page when the page is opened in Advanced Edit mode. Web Parts added outside Web Part zones and outside the *EmbeddedFormField* control on wiki pages are called static Web Parts, whereas Web Parts added to Web Part zones or the *EmbeddedFormField* control are called dynamic Web Parts. The properties of a static Web Part are stored in the page and not in the Web Parts SQL server table. By inserting a static Web Part in a page, users can view the content of the Web Part, but prevent them from using the browser to modify the Web Part or the way that it is displayed on the page.

You can read more about Web Parts in Chapter 7.

There are two types of a Web Part pages: shared and personal versions. All Web Part pages have a shared version, but not all Web Part pages have a personal view. Wiki pages only have a shared version.

Shared Version

The shared version of a Web Part page is displayed for all users who have at least the view permission. To modify the shared version, you must have the following rights, all of which are included in the Design and Full Control permission levels by default:

- Manage Lists

- Add and Customize Pages

- Apply Themes and Borders

- Apply Style Sheets

A member of a website's Site Owners group has Full Control permissions and therefore is able to customize the Shared Version of all Web Part pages. To edit the Shared version of a Web Part page, use the Edit Page option on the Site Actions menu, or on the Page tab, click Edit page. If the Edit Page command is not active, then you do not have permissions to edit the page.

Personal Version

The personal version of a Web Part page is displayed for the person who created the page and cannot be viewed by others. To create a personal version of any Web Part page, the Web Part page must be designed to be personalized. In addition, you must have the following rights, all of which are included in the Contribute, Design, and Full Control permission levels by default:

- Manage Personal Views

- Add/Remove Personal Web Parts

- Update Personal Web Parts

The site's Members group is mapped to the Contribute permission levels; therefore, any member of that group is able to customize the personal version of a Web Part page if the pages are designed to be personalized.

To edit your Personal version of a Web Part page, click the down-arrow to the right of your name in the upper-right corner of the page, and then click Personalize This Page, as shown in Figure 6-18.

Figure 6-18 Edit your Personal version of a Web Part page.

A yellow status bar below the ribbon displays, stating that you are editing the Personal Version of this page. This will always display when you are editing the Personal Version of a Web Part page.

Once you have personalized a page, the menu in the upper-right corner will contain two other options: Show Shared View and Reset Page Content. To remove the Personal Version of a Web Part page, use the Reset Page Content option.

When you have a personal view of a Web Part page, it is displayed by default when you first visit the page. This can be confusing to some users, who then do not see the same components on the page as other users. In Windows SharePoint Service 3.0, it was easier for a user to accidently edit their personal view as the edit options for both versions of the page were placed closed together. This is no longer the case.

INSIDE OUT   Controlling Web Part personalization

When a Web Part page is designed to be personalized, editors of the shared version of the page can disable the personalization of Web Parts on an individual basis by configuring the Web Part properties in the Web Part tool pane.

How to Control Page Personalization

You can control page personalization by using the following methods:

- **Permissions** By default, the Manage Personal Views, Add/Remove Personal Web Parts, and Update Personal Web Parts permissions can be enabled or disabled in permission levels at the site and Site Collection level. However, at a web application level, you can configure whether sites and Site Collections within the web application can use these permissions in permission levels. To configure whether to allow the use of these permissions, browse to the Web Application page within the SharePoint 2010 Central Administration website. Select the web application, and then on the Web Application table, click User Permissions in the Security group. Then, clear the check boxes of the permissions that you do not want to be enabled within permission levels.

- **Web Part property** There are two supported types of Web Parts in SharePoint Foundation. They are referred to as SharePoint and ASP.NET Web Parts. ASP.NET Web Parts use the *System.Web.UI.WebControls.WebParts.WebPart* base class, whereas SharePoint Web Parts use the *Microsoft.SharePoint.WebPartPages.WebPart* base class. Both types are supported, but the ASP.NET Web Part is recommended for all Web Parts. When a developer creates a SharePoint Web Part, the Web Part property definitions use the *WebPartStorageAttribute* and *Personalizable Attribute* attributes to decide whether a value for a Web Part property is stored the same for all users or is stored on a per-user basis. When a developer creates an ASP.NET Web Part, the *Pesonalizable* property attribute should be used. You can find information about Web Part personalization at *http://msdn.microsoft.com/ en-us/library/ms178182.aspx*. To learn more about the *WebPartStorageAttribute* go to *http://msdn.microsoft.com/en-us/library/microsoft.sharepoint.webpart- pages.webpartstorageattribute.aspx*, and for *PersonalizableAttribute*, go to *http://msdn.microsoft.com/en-us/library/system.web.ui.webcontrols.webparts. personalizableattribute.aspx*.

- **Web Part zones** By default most Web Part zones placed on Web Part pages allow users to change personal settings for any Web Part within the Web Part zone, if the Web Part is designed to be personalized and the user has the permission to personalize Web Parts. However, a developer can create a Web Part page and disable Web Part personalization on a per-Web Part zone–basis. You can also use SharePoint Designer in Advanced Edit mode to modify the settings of Web Part zones to disable personalization of Web Parts. Therefore, by configuring Web Part zones differently, you can allow users to personalize some parts of a Web Part page and prevent them from personalizing or modifying other parts of a page. To disable personalization on a Web Part zone in SharePoint Designer, click the Web Part zone label, and then on the Format tab, in the Web Part Zone group, click Properties. The Web Part Zones Properties dialog box opens, in which you can select or clear the check box to the right of Allow Users To Change Personal Web Part Settings. This adds the attribute, `allowpersonalization="false"` to the *WebPartPages:WebPartZone* control.

- **Pages** Web Parts personalization is enabled by default on Web Part pages. On websites for which you do not want users to personalize or modify pages, you can disable personalization for the entire page by using the `personalization-enabled:"false"` attribute on the ASP.NET *control: WebPartPages:SPWebPartManager*. This control is present in all the out-of-the-box master pages; therefore, when the personalization-enabled attribute is set to false on the master page, all pages associated with that master page cannot be personalized.

Editing Web Part Pages

You can edit a Web Part page, by either using the Edit Page option on the Site Actions menu or by using the Edit Page command in the Edit group on the Page tab. When the Web Part page is in Edit mode, the Format Text and Insert tabs do not display. These only appear when you are typing content into the CEWP. The commands on the Page tab for Web Part pages contain some different groups and commands than the Page tab on wiki pages. It does not contain a Page Library group. The Web Part page Page tab consists of six groups:

- **Edit** Only one drop-down menu is provided, which contains the options Edit Page, Stop Editing, and Edit In SharePoint Designer. In Edit mode, only the Stop Editing command is active. When the page is not in Edit mode, then the other two commands are active. Changes to Web Parts are saved immediately; therefore, the Edit group does not contain commands to Save & Close or Save & Stop Editing, nor can you discard changes. Web Part changes are versioned, so you can restore a previous versions of the page, which will restore all the Web Part changes. You cannot restore the state of only one Web Part on the page.

- **Manage** Use the commands in this group to edit the properties of the page, view versions, manage the page's permission, and delete the page. Initially, when you create a site, the home Web Part page is stored in the root of the site and not in a library; therefore, these options are not active. When a Web Part page is stored in a document library and versioning is enabled at the library level, all the commands in this group are active.

- **Share & Track** The E-Mail A Link command and the Alert Me split button behave as do the same commands on wiki pages.

Chapter 6

- **Approval**   The commands Approve and Reject are active if content approval is enabled at the library level.

- **Workflow**   The Workflows command is enabled if the Web Part page is stored in a library and a Workflow template has been associated with the library.

- **Page Actions**   This group consists of three commands, Make Homepage, which is the same command as on wiki pages, and two other commands, Edit Mobile Page and Title Bar Properties. There is no Incoming Links command.

Creating Web Part Pages

Using the browser, there are a number of methods available for you to create Web Part pages:

- Use the Site Actions and More Options action. In the Create dialog box, under Filter By, click Page. In the middle pane, click Create.

- Create a document library and specify Web Part page as the library's document template. You might need to click More Options to be able to choose a document template for the library. Then, to create a new Web Part page, click New Document on the Documents tab.

- On Meeting Workspaces, from the Site Actions menu, click Add Pages. The current page is open in Edit mode and a Pages task pane displays, as shown in Figure 6-19. In the Page Name text box, type the name of the new page, and then click Add. The three-column Web Part page is created in a hidden library named Workspace Pages, with a URL of pages.

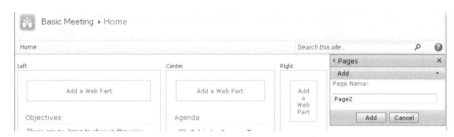

Figure 6-19 Creating a Web Part page on a Meeting Workspace.

- Create a view for any list or library. The page created is a Web Part page.

When you use one of the first two methods, the New Web Part Page window displays, in which you type the name of the new Web Part page, choose a Layout Template and a document library in which to store the new Web Part page, as shown in Figure 6-20.

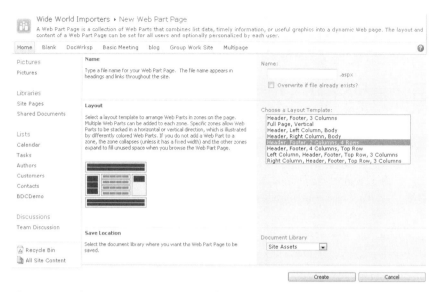

Figure 6-20 Choosing a Layout Template for a new Web Part page.

To the left of the Choose A Layout Template list box, when you select a layout template, a thumbnail preview displays, showing the Web Part zones and the organization of the Web Parts within the zones for the layout. For example, the Header, Footer, two Columns, four Rows layout, consists of eight Web Part zones. The four rows of Web Part zones show the Web Parts side by side; therefore, if you insert Web Parts in one of those Web Part zone rows, the Web Parts will not be displayed above and below each other, which is the usual configuration, but to the right or left of each other. These Web Part templates do not provide a left navigation area for the Quick Launch links.

Once you have created a Web Part page from a layout template, you cannot change the layout of Web Part zones on the page by using the browser; to do that you need to use a tool such as SharePoint Designer. You can also use SharePoint Designer on a page-by-page basis to re-establish the Quick Launch in the left pane.

The implementation of the Web Part layout templates has not changed from Windows SharePoint Services 3.0. The eight Web Part page templates are located in the SharePoint root directory (%PROGRAMFILES%\ \Common files\Microsoft Shared\Web Server Extensions\14) in the subfolder \TEMPLATE\1033\STS\DOCTEMP\SMARTPGS. These files, named spstd1.aspx through spstd8.aspx, cannot be renamed because SharePoint Foundation still uses a page called spcf.aspx to list the Web Part layout templates and owssvr.dll to initiate the page. Therefore, you can use the same technique to change and add your own layout templates to SharePoint Foundation as you might have done when using Windows SharePoint Services 3.0. A good starting point to add your own custom Web Part page templates can be found at *www.dontpapanic.com/blog/?p=58* and *http://msdn.microsoft. com/en-us/library/ms916835.aspx*. However, it does entail updating files provided by

Chapter 6

Microsoft in the SharePoint root directory for each server in your SharePoint farm, so this method has some severe limitations, such as the possibility that future Service Packs could overwrite the changes.

INSIDE OUT   Using the New Page Site Actions option

The New Page option on the Site Action menu is used to create wiki pages only. It is available on some sites other than a Team Site, such as a site created from the Document Workspace site template. If you use the New Page option on such sites, a dialog box might open stating that in order to create wiki pages on this site, there must be a default wiki page library and a site assets library. It also gives you the option to create them at that time.

Mobile Pages

Windows SharePoint Services 3.0 supported a number of mobile pages that you could navigate to in your desktop browser by appending /m to the end of the website's URL. This displayed links to the site's lists and libraries. SharePoint Foundation includes support for mobile devices by appending *?mobile=1* to the end of the URL of any page. When a mobile device navigates to a page on a SharePoint site, it is automatically redirected to these mobile pages, which restructures the requested page for mobile devices and inserts links at the bottom of every mobile page to View All Pages, All Site Content, and the home page of the site. The pages used to redirect the browser are stored in the _layouts/mobile virtual directory and are listed in Table 6-1.

Table 6-1 **The Default Mobile Pages Used for Viewing Specific Types of Pages**

Page type	Redirection mobile page
List and library views	View.aspx
Wiki pages	Mblwiki.aspx
Web Part pages	Mbllists.aspx
Application pages	Mblerror.aspx
Page used to display a list items properties	Dispform.aspx
Page used to edit a list items properties	Editform.aspx

For more information about creating mobile pages, go to *http://msdn.microsoft.com/en-us/library/ms462572.aspx*. You can read more about mobile view pages at *http://msdn.microsoft.com/en-us/library/ms414170.aspx*. And finally, to learn how to create a mobile adapter, which should be created for each Web Part that needs to be accessed by mobile devices, go to *http://msdn.microsoft.com/en-us/library/ee539079.aspx*.

Accessibility

SharePoint Foundation has a prime focus on meeting accessibility guidelines which makes it much easier than with previous SharePoint versions for you to meet WCAG version 2.0 A, AA, and even AAA guidelines. Some of the improvements include:

- A W3C XHTML DOCTYPE reference.

- Use of <DIV> tags for page construction, rather than tables.

- Correct heading hierarchy; that is, H1, H2, H3.

- The *UseSimpleRendering* property for the <SharePoint:AspMenu> control. When *UseSimpleRendering* is set to true, the SharePoint navigation menu is rendered by using a cleaner, unordered XHTML list.

You can find information about accessibility and SharePoint 2010 on the Microsoft SharePoint team blog site at *http://sharepoint.microsoft.com/blog/Pages/BlogPost.aspx?pID=431*.

You should always try to create content so that it conforms to accessibility guidelines. The additional benefit is that it helps to ensure that your website is compatible and interoperable with any assistive technologies that visitors to your site might use. However, do not rely on testing your pages against accessibility guidelines; when possible, enlist the assistance of disabled users to test your pages.

Site Template Pages

When you create a site from one of the built-in site templates, the pages on the newly created site refer to pages stored in the TEMPLATE subfolder of the SharePoint root directory. No files or pages are created. Instead, table entries are created in a SQL Server content database in the ALLDocs tables, and those table entries point to files in the TEMPLATE folder. Each site appears to have its own pages, but in reality, they all share the same files. The files in the TEMPLATE folder are known as site definitions. Site definition files are cached in memory on the server at process startup. As a result, when a user requests a page, such as home.aspx (which is one of the site definitions files), it is retrieved from the server's memory. SharePoint retrieves from the SQL server content database the content entered in the *EmbeddedFormField* control on wiki pages or Web Parts inserted in Web Part zones, because this content is stored separately from the site definition files, as shown in Figure 6-21. Therefore, a relatively small set of files can support a large number of SharePoint sites with many pages, resulting in improved performance.

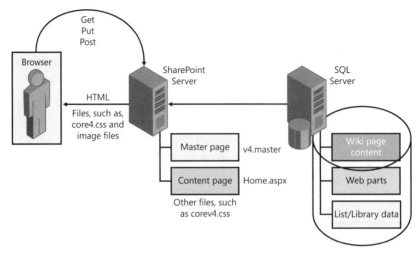

Figure 6-21 The location of files when a site is first created.

Similar to the browser, when you use SharePoint Designer to modify the contents of the *EmbeddedFormField* control and Web Parts in Web Part zones, only the data in the content databases is being modified. This is SharePoint Designer's default Edit mode. However, with SharePoint Designer, when you open a page in Advance Edit mode, you can modify content that is defined outside the *EmbeddedFormField* and Web Part zone. You are then modifying content that is defined in the site definition files; therefore, SharePoint Foundation saves a copy of the site definition files from the SharePoint root to the SQL Server, as shown in Figure 6-22. This copy of the site definition file, is specific to the site you are modifying, all other sites continue to use the site definition files stored in the SharePoint root.

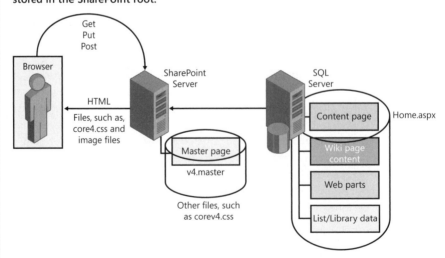

Figure 6-22 Customized pages are stored in the SQL Server content databases.

Site definition files that are modified by SharePoint Designer in Advanced Edit mode are known as customized or *unghosted* pages. Site definition files that have not been customized are known as uncustomized or *ghosted* files. The master page, v4.master, CSS files (such as corev4.css), JavaScript files, and the Web Part layout template files are all site definition files. Thus, when you edit these files in Advanced Edit mode, you are creating customized pages that are unique to your site.

For a site that is frequently visited and where SharePoint page cache is enabled and available, the customized page introduces little significant overhead when the page is requested. However, if page cache is not available, and if a large number of users request the customized page, the performance level of the customized page could be significantly affected. So, as you plan your solutions, you should take this into account. A common decision is not to customize an organization's master pages or a site's home page.

Customizing pages can also make global changes to all your sites difficult. For example, if your organization has deployed its own site definition files, including its own master page, which you customized in SharePoint Designer, and then it subsequently redeploys a new version of that master page, you will not see the changes to the organization's master page. Using the browser or SharePoint Designer, you can reset your customized page back to the site definition pages.

You can prototype your master page modifications to a specific site by using SharePoint Designer. Once the modifications have been signed off, you can export your customized master page and either store the master page into the site master page gallery that is located at the top level site of a Site Collection, or use Visual Studio 2010, package the master page in a solutions file, and deploy it as a site definition file into the SharePoint root directory. Using the browser to upload the master page into the master page gallery is storing the master page into the SQL Server content database. Any file that is stored in the content database is considered to be customized.

When you deploy files to SharePoint, you deploy them as features. The feature specifies what to do with the file. If the file is to be stored in the SharePoint root directory as an uncustomized file and cached in memory, then you can use the *Ghostable* or *GhostableInLibrary* type attribute. If you want to deploy a file, such as a master page, as an uncustomized file, but you want the file to appear as if it is stored in a library (for example, _catalog/masterpage), then use *GhostableInLibrary*. The user can then see the file in any of the list views and work with the file as she would with any other file. For example, she can check it in, approve, or reject it. If you deploy a file without the type attribute *Ghostable* or *GhostableInLibrary*, then the file is customized—Unghostable—and is stored in the content database.

Chapter 6

Using SharePoint Designer to Create and Modify Webpages

The browser is still SharePoint's main web content editing tool for most users; however, SharePoint Designer 2010 is now "the preferred" tool for designing powerful, no-code solutions and applications in SharePoint 2010. SharePoint Designer 2010 has undergone major improvements over its predecessor, SharePoint Designer 2007. When you open a site in SharePoint Designer 2010, you'll notice that it uses the Microsoft Office Fluent user interface, which was designed to make it easier for users to use and find features within a product. It incorporates the ribbon and the companion feature—the Backstage view—which can be accessed from the File tab.

As you build your solutions by using SharePoint Designer, it is important to know how to use it to create and modify webpages. Before you can modify any pages, you must open a SharePoint site with SharePoint Designer. Then you can open individual files, whether they are stored within the SharePoint site or outside the site, such as files on your computer's hard disk. You should never use SharePoint Designer to make changes to files on the SharePoint server's file system, especially on your production computers. Modifications or the creation of files on SharePoint servers should be tightly managed and deployed with SharePoint solutions files, which you create by using Visual Studio 2010.

For more details about using SharePoint Designer, see Chapter 14.

When you open a SharePoint site with SharePoint Designer, the Navigation pane is displayed. This replaces the Folder List task pane in SharePoint Designer 2007 and focuses on SharePoint objects and not where the objects are stored. Previously in this chapter, you worked with webpages stored in the site objects: Site Pages, Site Assets and Master Pages, which are listed on the Navigation pane.

When you click the first site object in the Navigation pane, the site's information is displayed in SharePoint Designer's workspace, as shown in Figure 6-23.

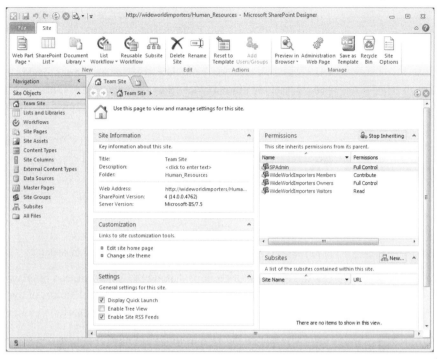

Figure 6-23 The ribbon, Navigation page, and workspace in SharePoint Designer.

You can then navigate to the Home page of the site by clicking Edit Site Home Page in the Customization area. A new tab opens, displaying the Editor page for the site's home page (which for a Team Site is the wiki page), Home.aspx, and in the Navigation pane, below the site objects, a mini gallery displays the contents of the Site Pages library. You can also navigate to the Home page by clicking Site Pages in the Navigation pane.

As with the previous version, you can complete similar activities to the browser by using SharePoint Designer in a WYSIWYG environment—the Design view. SharePoint Designer provides two other views of a page:

- **Code view** This displays the HTML tags, client-side code (such as JavaScript), and controls (such as the SharePoint control for the ribbon), SPRibbon, if you had opened a master page, or content controls on webpages, where the content for the page is positioned. The Code view provides you with a number of features that help you to write code, for example:

  — The Code view uses colors to identify different code elements so that you can quickly identify coding errors.

Chapter 6

— IntelliSense is also included in Code view. As you type, it detects what you are writing and provides suggestions. The IntelliSense in Code view is not limited to HTML tags but is also provided when writing CSS or selecting parameters.

— The Code view also offers snippets of code. These snippets are predefined and you can include them in your code, by pressing Ctrl+Enter, which displays a drop-down list of the available code snippets, as shown in Figure 6-24.

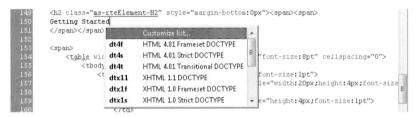

Figure 6-24 Use code snippets for frequently typed in code.

Use the Page Editor Options dialog box, which you can open via the Backstage view of SharePoint Designer, to change the default colors of the code elements, disable IntelliSense, or to add your own code snippets.

- **Split view** Use this to divide the workspace horizontally. When set, the Code view displays at the top of the workspace, and the Design view appears at the bottom.

You will use all three views as you edit webpages. When you first open the home.aspx page, you are in Design view, and when you move the pointer over the page, in some areas of the page, the pointer changes to a no-entry icon. This identifies that the area of the page as not within the *EmbeddedFormField* control.

If you click Split or Code, you will see that some of the code in the home.aspx page is colored yellow (a light-gray shade, as depicted in Figure 6-25). This is the code that resides outside the *EmbeddedFormField* control, which you cannot modify either in Code view or Design view. This behavior mimics the behavior when editing a page in the browser.

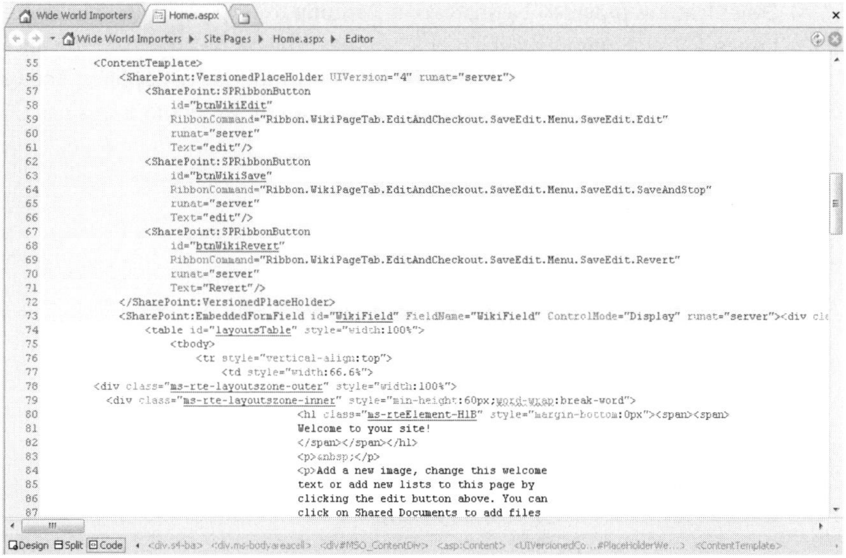

Figure 6-25 The Code view of a wiki page.

By looking at the code view for home.aspx, you can see that the code that is used to present content on a wiki page is as follows:

```
<SharePoint:EmbeddedFormField ID="WikiField" FieldName="WikiField"
   ControlMode="Display" runat="server" />
```

Also note that just above the *EmbeddedFormField* control, there is reference to UIVersion="4". When you upgrade from Windows SharePoint Server 3.0 to SharePoint Foundation, you can separate the upgrade of the content of your sites from the visual changes. Therefore, although the servers are now running SharePoint Foundation, it still looks to the user as if he is using Windows SharePoint Services. By setting the *UIVersion* attribute to 4, the code is specifying that if the site has visually upgraded, then the contained markup should be used. A *UIVersion* attribute of 3 represents Windows SharePoint Services 3.0, and any contained markup would only be used if a site was not visually upgraded. This does add a lot of text to pages, including master pages, so if you plan to redesign your pages and you either never upgraded from Windows SharePoint Services 3.0 or all your sites are visually upgraded, you can remove all the UIVersion="3" tags.

Other features provided by SharePoint Designer to help you with your page modifications are Visual Aids, with which you can see some of the aspects of the underlying code in Design view, and the ability to set Design view to specific dimensions. The current dimensions used to display the page in Design view are shown in the status bar. Click the dimension in the status bar to change the page size, as shown in Figure 6-26. If the dimension that you want to use for your page is not shown, you can create your own dimension by clicking Modify Page Sizes.

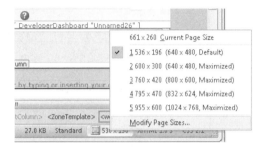

Figure 6-26 Use the Status bar to change the size at which the page is displayed in the workspace.

> **Note**
> You should not rely on how the page looks in SharePoint Designer; you should frequently test your page in the browsers used by visitors to your site. When you have your page in Edit mode, on the Home tab you can use the Preview In Browser command in the Preview group to open the page using one of the browsers installed on your computer as well as the size of the page to match the screen sizes your visitors might have. You can edit the browser list used in the Preview In Browser command to meet your needs. You should never design a page that causes a visitor to your site to scroll to the right to see all the content of the page.

Adding and Formatting Content

SharePoint Designer includes many of the same commands on its ribbon as you used in the browser when using the SharePoint server ribbon. You can add static text, links, tables, images, and Web Parts by using the Home and Insert tabs, as shown in Figures 6-27 and 6-29.

Figure 6-27 Use the Home tab to format static text and add hyperlinks.

Other tabs will appear as you click different page objects. For example, if the cursor is within a table object, then the Table Tools tab set will appear and display the Layouts tab. These are known as contextual tabs. The server ribbon for SharePoint sites in the browser behave in a similar manner.

The Home Tab

The Home tab provides some additional commands beyond those offered on the server ribbon Format Text tab that you see in the browser, including quick access to editing tools and a spelling checker. You can also quickly open the page that you're editing in the browser. You use this command to frequently check your modifications, because although the Design view tries to mimic how a page would look in the browser, it does not fully implement all the features of the browser. For example, it does not execute client-side code and posts back to the server to simulate user interaction with the page. Therefore, the hyperlinks on the page do not respond as they would in the browser. Also the process of using wiki links to create new wiki pages or link to existing pages in the Site Pages library does not work.

In the Editing group, there are a number of commands that are not available in the browser: the Advance Mode command, which is discussed in the next section, as well as the Skewer Click and Quick Tag Editor. To use the Skewer Click command to simplify the editing of the page, perform the following steps:

1. On the Home tab, in the Editing group, click Skewer Click.

   The cursor changes to display three overlapping rectangles.

2. Click an object on the page such as an image.

   A drop-down menu displays the HTML that immediately surrounds the object and then lists other parent tags relevant to this object.

3. Click the tag to select an area of the page.

To use the Quick Tag Editor, click the object whose tag you want to modify, and then on the Home tab, in the Editing group, click Quick Tag Editor. The Quick Tag Editor dialog box opens (see Figure 6-28). You can use this dialog box to edit, insert, or wrap the tag selected, without switching to Code view. It also shows you only a portion of the code, making it easier to concentrate on the section of code that you want to edit. Because SharePoint pages contain many objects, some of which are hidden in Design view, to correctly change the correct tag, you might need to use the Skewer Click command or the Quick Tag Select in the status bar below the workspace.

Figure 6-28 Use the Quick Tag Editor to edit tags without the need to switch to Code view.

The Insert Tab

The Insert tab illustrated in Figure 6-29 is similar to the Home tab in that it is always visible when you have a file open for editing. It is also similar to the Insert tab on the server ribbon that you see in the browser, and it allows you to insert tables, images, links, and Web Parts. The addition in the Web Parts group is Web Part zone. You can only add a Web Part zone when the page is in Advanced Edit Mode.

Figure 6-29 Use the Insert tab to place tables, images, links, data views and forms, controls, Web Parts, and symbols.

The Insert tab also contains the ribbon groups, with which you can insert:

- **The Data View Web Part (DVWP) (also known as the Data Form Web Part [DFWP])**   This Web Part can only be created with SharePoint Designer. You cannot create it by using the browser.

- **Controls**   SharePoint Designer has a number of task panes, and the Toolbox task pane can be used to insert controls; however, by using the Controls group, you can quickly add HTML, ASP.NET, and SharePoint controls to your page.

- **Symbols**   Use this to insert special characters into your page.

INSIDE OUT   Web Part Zones on wiki pages

As you look at the controls on the home.aspx page in Code view, you might also discover that the page contains a Web Part zone named Bottom, and although the Web Part zone's properties are set to allow users with a browser to interact with Web Parts place in the zone, as shown in Figure 6-30, you cannot add Web Parts to this Web Part zone by using the browser. On wiki pages, only content within the *EmbeddedFormField* can be modified with a browser. With SharePoint Designer, you can add Web Parts to the Bottom Web Part zone. You can add other Web Part zones to a wiki page; however, these and any Web Parts that they contain, like the Bottom Web Part zone, will not be visible when the page is in Edit mode while using the browser.

Figure 6-30 Web Part zone properties of the Bottom Web Part zone.

Saving Modifications

When you save your webpage, if your page contains an *EmbeddedFormField*, then a SharePoint Designer dialog box is displays, stating that the content might be changed by the server to remove unsafe content. This is the same sanitization process that occurs when you save a wiki page by using the browser. When you click Yes in the dialog box, the page is reloaded so that you can see the result of the save.

Managing Pages

To manage pages by using SharePoint Designer, in the Navigation pane, click Site Pages to display the pages gallery and to display the Pages tab, as shown in Figure 6-31. The Pages tab contains an Edit group, with which you can delete and rename a page, navigate to the page settings, and edit the page in Safe Mode or Advanced Mode. With the Actions group, you can reset a page to its site definition or set a page as the home page for the site.

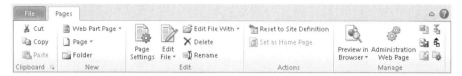

Figure 6-31 Use the Pages tab to manage files in the Site Pages library.

Use the Manage group to:

- Preview the page in the browser.

- Open a browser window to display the administration webpage for a page.

- Check out, check in, or undo check out.

- Import or export files from the Site Pages library.

- Open the Site Pages settings page in SharePoint Designer.

Creating Pages

With SharePoint Designer, you can create a number of types of different files, includ-ing ASPX and Web Part pages. You cannot create a wiki page or site definition files. The browser is the best method for creating wiki pages, and you should use Visual Studio to create and deploy site definition pages. However, if you create new wiki pages in the browser and do not enter any content, the *EmbeddedFormField* control in SharePoint Designer is displayed as a thin line, and you will need to go into Code view initially to enter content. If you do not do this, then you will accidently enter content into the Bottom Web Part zone.

To create a Web Part page, perform the following steps:

1. In the Navigation pane, click Site Pages to display the Site Pages gallery.

2. On the Pages tab, click Web Part Page, and then select the Web Part zone layout for the page.

   These are the sample template layouts that you used in the browser when you cre-ated a Web Part page.

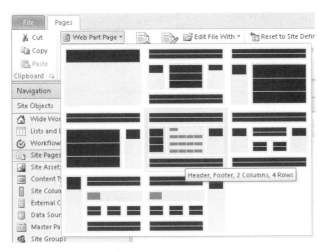

A file, Untitled-1.aspx is created and displayed in the Site Pages gallery, with Untitled_1.aspx selected.

3. Type the name that you want to use for the page, and then press Enter to rename it.

4. To edit the page, on the Pages tab, in the Edit group, click Edit File.

To create an ASPX or HTML file, perform the following:

1. In the Navigation pane, click Site Pages to display the Site Pages gallery.

2. On the Pages tab, click Page, and then select either ASPX or HTML. The file, Untitled-*x*.aspx, is created, where *x* is a number that makes the page name unique.

By using this method, the newly created ASPX or HTML files do not contain any controls; specifically, they do not contain the *EmbeddedFormField* control or Web Part zones, so they do not contain any regions that are editable in Safe Mode. You will need to edit the pages in Advanced Edit mode; that is, these pages are not associated with a site definition file, and the entire contents of the page is stored in the content database.

To create a file from a master page, perform the following procedure:

1. In the Navigation pane, click Master Pages to display the Master Pages gallery.

2. On the Master Pages tab, in the New group, click Page From Master.

The Select A Master Page dialog box opens, in which you can select to create a page from the master page designated as the site's master page or a specific master page. Custom master pages are used on publishing sites, which is a SharePoint Server feature.

Chapter 6

3. Alternatively, in the Master Page gallery, right-click the appropriate master page, and then in the shortcut menu, click New From Master Page.

Another way to create webpages as well as other file types is as follows:

1. Click the File tab, and then click Add Item.

2. In the middle pane, you can create a Web Part Page or a New Page From Master. For other file types, click More Pages.

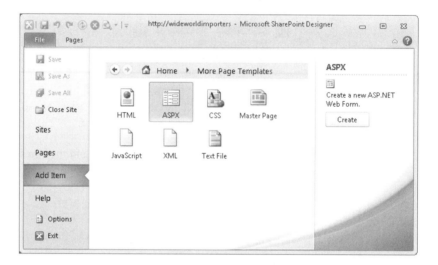

3. Select the page type that you want to create, and then click Create.

INSIDE OUT   Site definition pages and SharePoint Designer

Using SharePoint Designer, you cannot create a site definition page, but you can create a page from a site definition by copying an existing site definition page. This allows you to have the same performance benefits as the original file. Another benefit is that you can maintain the same look and feel across a set of pages. For example, if you added a completely new page to your original site—for example, if you replaced default.aspx with a different file rather than making changes to the existing default.aspx file—the new page has no site definition association. If for any reason the site definition file changes, such as when your company upgrades to the next version of SharePoint, then the new page might not look like the other pages in the upgraded site, nor can it be reset to look like them.

Chapter 6

Advanced Edit Mode

Up to this point in the chapter, you have opened the webpage in Safe Mode, where you are unable to modify specific areas of the page. In Safe Mode, you can only edit the content in the *EmbeddedFormField* control or modify and insert Web Parts in Web Part zones. Both of these components are placed into an area of the page called *PlaceHolderMain*. On the Home tab, in the Editing group, there is a new command for SharePoint Designer 2010 called Advanced Edit Mode, which was not part of SharePoint Designer 2007. In SharePoint Designer 2007, you could only edit files in Advanced Edit Mode.

In Safe Mode, you are changing content that is not stored within the page, but instead is stored in tables in the content databases. In Advanced Edit Mode, you can modify content that is stored in other areas of the page. Therefore, if the page is a site definition page, SharePoint will take a copy of that file from the SharePoint server's file system—usually the subfolder in the SharePoint root directory—apply your changes, and then store the file in the content database. This process, known as customizing a page, was described earlier in this chapter, in the section "Site Template Pages."

If you edit a site template page in Advanced Edit Mode and modify content outside the *EmbeddedFormField* or Web Part zones, then the Site Definition Page Warning dialog box is displayed, as shown in Figure 6-32.

Figure 6-32 Customizing Site Definition files.

In the Site Pages gallery, a blue circle surrounding a white "i" character is displayed to the left of the page. This indicates that the page is a site definition file that has been customized. To reset the page back to the site definition file, right-click the file, and then in the shortcut menu that appears, click Reset To Site Definition, as shown in Figure 6-33.

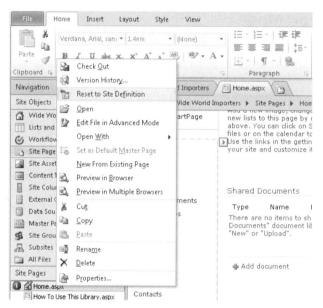

Figure 6-33 Resetting a page to its Site Definition file.

When you reset a page back to its site definition page, the contents of the page is replaced with the original contents of the site definition file and a backup copy of the current page is created. However, remember that content in areas of the page, for example, in the *Embedded FormField* control and Web Part zones, are not stored in the page; therefore, when the page is reset to the site definition file, if the site definition file contains those areas of the page, then the content for those areas is still retrieved from the content database.

If a Web Part zone exists in a customized (unghosted) page but not in the site definition, upon the reset to site definition, the Web Parts from that Web Part zone might have been moved into the bottom zone on the page.

In Advanced Edit Mode, you have the full range of tools to modify the page; for example, tabs are available that normally are not when the page is in Safe Mode, such as the Style and Layout tabs. Unfortunately, there is no ribbon command to switch the editing mode from Advanced to Safe. If you have the page in Advanced Edit Mode, you will need to close the page and then open it again to edit the page in Safe Mode.

SharePoint Designer also provides a number of task panes that help you to create solutions and customize your pages. Some task panes are displayed automatically when you complete a task. To display a task pane, on the View tab, in the Workspace group, click the down-arrow for the Task Panes command. However, most of these task panes can only be used when a page is in Advanced Edit Mode, and then only if you are working with certain components. For example, the Behaviors task pane can only be used to enter small predefined scripts or CSS attribute sections in the page when you are editing the page in Advanced Edit Mode. In Safe Mode, the Insert button in the Behaviors task pane is inactive.

Creating Application Pages for SharePoint Sites

SharePoint Foundation 2010 provides some flexibility when developing pages for your SharePoint environment. One of the nice features about SharePoint is having the ability to create application pages. You can identify an application page by the text _layouts in its URL, such as the site settings page. Application pages are deployed once per SharePoint server and have the ability to be shared across all sites and Site Collections in the farm. They also have the ability to contain code that runs behind the page that is compiled into a single dynamic link library (DLL), which improves performance.

Most of the typical pages are content pages. Content pages can be customized with an application such as SharePoint Designer, whereas application pages cannot be customized. Also, application pages can include inline code and page markup, whereas content pages cannot because this could be accidentally manipulated by users with SharePoint Designer so that it does not work correctly, or manipulated with malicious intent.

Therefore, if you want to create a page that will contain some heavy custom code, and you want that capability across all sites, application pages are the way to go.

SharePoint Foundation incorporates a Modal Dialog framework that allows users to stay in context of the page to see additional information that is related to the page without navigating away from the page, for example, displaying the properties of a list item. To read more about how to use the Modal Dialog framework with application pages, go to *http://blog.mastykarz.nl/sharepoint-2010-application-pages-modal-dialogs*.

Visual Studio 2010 provides out-of-the-box templates with which developers can quickly create an application page in Visual Studio. The following steps outline how to create a SharePoint application page:

For more information about using Visual Studio to create SharePoint Foundation solutions and how to set up your development environment, see Chapter 16, "Developing SharePoint Solutions by Using Visual Studio 2010."

1. Open Visual Studio with administrative privileges. On the Start Page tab, click New, Project, or on the toolbar, click File, select New, and then click Project to open the New Project dialog box.

2. Under Installed Templates, under the appropriate language (such as Visual C#), expand SharePoint, if it is not already expanded, and then click 2010.

3.   In the middle pane, select Empty SharePoint Project.

This is the most basic SharePoint project type; it must be used for application pages because they are only available as project items.

4.   In the Name textbox, type **SharePointApplicationPage1** for the Project Name, and then click OK.

The SharePoint Customization Wizard opens.

5.   Specify the site on which you want to deploy and test the application page, and then select Deploy As A Farm Solution for the trust level.

Application pages are deployed on the server and are available to all sites; therefore, they are deployed at the farm level. Sandboxed solutions are scoped at a Site Collection level and can be deployed without administration privileges. Click Finish to close the SharePoint Configuration Wizard.

6.   In Solution Explorer, right-click the SharePointApplicationPage1 project, select Add, and then click New item.

7.   In the Add New Item dialog box, in the middle pane, select Application Page. In the Name textbox, type **CustomApplicationPage1**, and then click Add.

Visual Studio automatically creates the required files to create a basic application page and opens the source view for the ASPX file. Visual Studio does not provide any WYSIWYG editing environment for applications pages. If you add other application pages to this project they will be stored in the SharePointApplicationPage1 folder, in the Layouts folder.

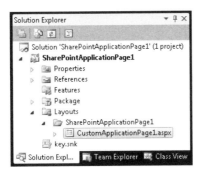

> **Note**
>
> The Project now contains a Layouts folder. This folder maps to the _Layouts virtual directory created by the SharePoint server, which on the file system is the SharePoint root \TEMPLATE\LAYOUTS subfolder. You will also notice that it has created a subfolder called SharePointApplicationPage1. This will contain the application pages for this project. When the pages are deployed, they will automatically be placed under the _layouts directory in the same folder directory that they are listed under in Solution Explorer.

The initial markup for the application page is shown in the following code block:

```
<%@ Assembly Name="$SharePoint.Project.AssemblyFullName$" %>
<%@ Import Namespace="Microsoft.SharePoint.ApplicationPages" %>
<%@ Register Tagprefix="SharePoint" Namespace="Microsoft.SharePoint.WebControls"
    Assembly="Microsoft.SharePoint, Version=14.0.0.0, Culture=neutral,
    PublicKeyToken=71e9bce111e9429c" %>
<%@ Register Tagprefix="Utilities" Namespace="Microsoft.SharePoint.Utilities"
    Assembly="Microsoft.SharePoint, Version=14.0.0.0, Culture=neutral,
    PublicKeyToken=71e9bce111e9429c" %>
<%@ Register Tagprefix="asp" Namespace="System.Web.UI"
    Assembly="System.Web.Extensions,
    Version=3.5.0.0, Culture=neutral, PublicKeyToken=31bf3856ad364e35" %>
<%@ Import Namespace="Microsoft.SharePoint" %>
<%@ Assembly Name="Microsoft.Web.CommandUI, Version=14.0.0.0, Culture=neutral,
    PublicKeyToken=71e9bce111e9429c" %>
```

Chapter 6

```
<%@ Page Language="C#" AutoEventWireup="true"
   CodeBehind="CustomApplicationPage1.aspx.cs"
   Inherits="SharePointApplicationPage1.Layouts.SharePointApplicationPage1.
   CustomApplicationPage1" DynamicMasterPageFile="~masterurl/default.master" %>

<asp:Content ID="PageHead" ContentPlaceHolderID="PlaceHolderAdditionalPageHead"
   runat="server">
</asp:Content>

<asp:Content ID="Main" ContentPlaceHolderID="PlaceHolderMain" runat="server">

</asp:Content>

<asp:Content ID="PageTitle" ContentPlaceHolderID="PlaceHolderPageTitle"
   runat="server">
Application Page
</asp:Content>

<asp:Content ID="PageTitleInTitleArea"
   ContentPlaceHolderID="PlaceHolderPageTitleInTitleArea"
   runat="server" >
My Application Page
</asp:Content>
```

When the assembly is built, it will be deployed to the Global Assembly Cache (GAC). The assembly parameter *$SharePoint.Project.AssemblyFullName$*, will be replaced with the full assembly reference—the full assembly name, version number, culture and Pubic Key Token.

The @Page directive points to the code-behind file and links the application page with a master page by using the *DynamicMasterPageFile* attribute. This attribute is set to the token ~masterurl/default.master, which when the user requests the application page is replaced on the server with the site's default master page. Unless you have customized the default master page, the token will be replaced with v4.master.

The sample application page contains four content placeholders:

- **PlaceHolderAdditionalPageHead**   Content added to this placeholder appears in the page's <HEAD> tag.

- **PlaceHolderMain**   This is the main content area of the page.

- **PlaceHolderPageTitle**   Content added in this placeholder appears in the browser's title bar.

- **PlaceHolderPageTitleInTitleArea**   Content added in this placeholder appears in the title area of the page.

Once you have entered content in the content placeholders and code in the code behind file, set the application page as the Startup item for the project by right-clicking the page, and then clicking Set As Startup Item. When you press F5 to start debugging the page, Visual Studio will browse to the application page.

INSIDE OUT   Application master page files in SharePoint 2010

A major change in SharePoint Foundation is that application pages now use a dynamic master page that can be set on a per-site basis. A code behind file was added to the SharePoint Foundation application pages to determine which site master page to use. Now application pages can take on the same look and feel as the site, whereas in Windows SharePoint Services 3.0, unless you used themes, the look and feel of application pages were defined once for the whole farm by using the file application.master. Changing this file was not supported by Microsoft. The content of the application page was also changed so that areas—content placeholders—on the application page are similar to content placeholders on content pages. Now, if an error is made to the master pages used by application pages, then SharePoint Foundation will use the v4.master page with application pages so that they can still be viewed. You can find more information at *http://msdn.microsoft.com/en-us/library/ee537530.aspx*.

Summary

This chapter explained the basics of webpages used by SharePoint Foundation. The two main types of webpages that can be created by using the browser are wiki pages and Web Part pages. Each wiki page or Web Part page contains unique content; each type is created from a template stored in a specific location on the SharePoint server file system, known as the SharePoint root directory.

The chapter then explained how to create and format these pages by using SharePoint Designer, where you saw that you can modify the same content area that you can by using the browser. But with SharePoint Designer, when you use Advanced Edit Mode, you can edit content outside the main content area. However, this results in a customized page that might cause performance problems. Finally, you saw how to create application pages; that is, those pages with _layouts in their URL.

The next chapter will provide details on how to add, edit, and connect Web Parts on pages.

Chapter 6

Adding, Editing, Connecting, and Managing Web Parts on the Page

Web portals gained immense popularity in the late 1990s, giving companies an easy way to relate information to both internal and external users. Up until that point in time, content had been largely static and was maintained by a one or more webmasters on a series of HTML webpages. Any content that was generated had to be converted to a webpage by someone with technical skills in HTML, JavaScript, and so on.

One of the key concepts introduced by web portals was the notion of interactivity. Content pages could be assigned to a designated author who could modify content directly. In addition, content could be added, deleted, or moved on a web page by an end user.

In this new model, the webmaster was still responsible for the core site structure as well as the initial layout of content on the page. Zones could be designated by the webmaster to contain customizable areas of content, and then modular components could be added by content authors to display content.

Finally, these modular components could be customized by users on a per-user basis. A good example of this would be a module that displayed a weather report. If the user wanted to customize a weather report for their city, region, or ZIP code, these changes would not affect other users visiting the site.

Over time, these modular components have had different names and varied slightly in format. Whether you call them Web Widgets, Portlets, Gadgets, or Web Parts (in the case of Microsoft SharePoint), they all have the same core function—to represent customizable content on a webpage.

A Brief Introduction to Web Parts

Web Parts are a key component of any SharePoint installation. They are present in all versions, from SharePoint Foundation to SharePoint Server (Standard or Enterprise). They can be purchased from third-party providers or created by developers (perhaps within your own company) to accomplish a specific task.

A variety of Web Parts exist, but there really are only two things a Web Part is intended to do:

- Receive Input

- Display Content

Sometimes a Web Part accomplishes both of these tasks. Consider the weather component. If we reimagined this as a custom Web Part, it could both receive input (the city or ZIP code) and display content (the weather report for the appropriate area).

Web Parts can also be connected to each another. One Web Part might receive input and then provide this input to filter the content displayed by a second Web Part. You will see more of this behavior in the section "Connecting SharePoint Web Parts," later in this chapter.

Adding Web Parts to a SharePoint Site

So, now that you've learned a little something about Web Parts, let's put a few on a site. You will actually do this twice in this section: once to put a Web Part on a wiki page, and again to put a Web Part on a Web Part page. We will run through both scenarios so that you can see the subtle differences between them.

INSIDE OUT   Different site templates default to different page types

The template you choose when creating a site determines the default page type it will use. Sites built using the Team Site template create wiki pages in the Site Pages library, whereas sites built using any other site template create a Web Part page at the root of the site; any additional Web Part pages are created within a document library.

To begin, let's open up a Team Site (see Figure 7-1). This site template is a true step forward from the Team Site template present in Windows SharePoint Services 3.0; it includes the Site Pages library, which is where all pages are stored.

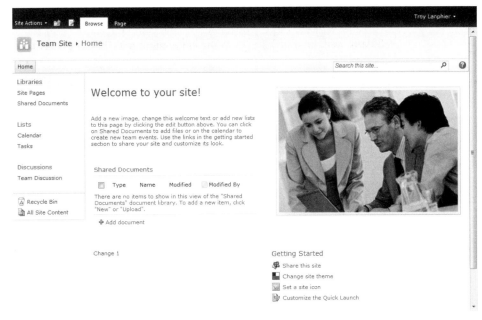

Figure 7-1 The Team Site home page.

Text, graphics, and other content can be added freely without the need for Content Editor Web Parts. Changes to a wiki page are also tracked, which gives you the ability to compare with previous versions.

Next, we will begin editing the page by selecting the Page tab and then clicking the Edit button, as shown in Figure 7-2.

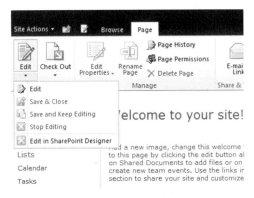

Figure 7-2 Placing the page in Edit mode.

As this is a wiki page, edits are freeform; changes can be made by simply clicking in a content area (as indicated by the boxes around the content in Figure 7-3) and adding text, Web Parts, and other items. Click in the left content area, below the existing content.

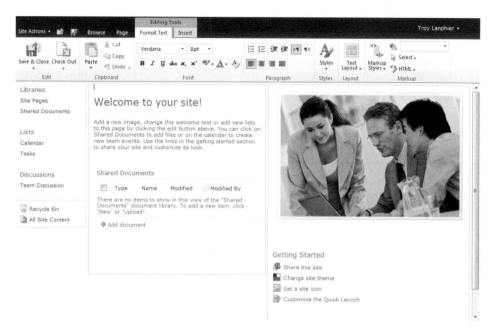

Figure 7-3 Our wiki page, showing the two content areas (columns).

To begin making changes to the page, in the Editing Tools tab group, select the Insert tab (see Figure 7-4). In the Web Parts section, you see three choices: Web Part, Existing List, or New List.

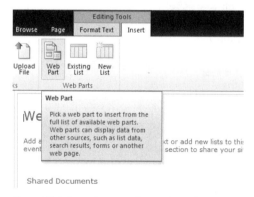

Figure 7-4 Inserting a Web Part into the page.

Essentially, the Existing List and New List buttons are simply shortcuts; you can use them to insert a Web Part, and at the same time, save some extra steps. Using Existing List, you can insert a Web Part that is based off of an existing list. If you do not already have a list and instead need to create one for use in a Web Part, you can choose New List, which creates a new list and then represents it on the page, saving you an extra step.

For this example, you will be adding a Web Part that does not represent a list or a library, so click Web Part.

The Web Categories pane appears below the ribbon, displaying a series of Categories and Web Parts, as shown in Figure 7-5.

Figure 7-5 The Web Parts Categories pane.

The core set of SharePoint Foundation Web Parts are broken up into categories, based on function. There are five main groupings that appear in any SharePoint Foundation 2010 installation. Table 7-1 presents these categories along with a brief description of their function.

Table 7-1 **Web Part Categories**

Category	Function
Lists And Libraries	Shows all Web Parts that represent lists or libraries within the SharePoint site.
Content Rollup	Shows the Web Parts that are responsible for "rolling up" or aggregating data from different sources.
Forms	Contains Web Parts specifically built to consume input and relay it to other, connected Web Parts.
Media And Content	These Web Parts are heavily used, displaying text, graphics, and other content (such as Microsoft Silverlight applications).
Social Collaboration	Contains Web Parts that are responsible for showing content targeted toward specific users.

For the sample site, select the Social Collaboration category, and then choose Site Users, as illustrated in Figure 7-6. This Web Part will be beneficial to our site because it displays users who belong to this site along with their online status (if available). Click the Add button to add this Web Part to the wiki page.

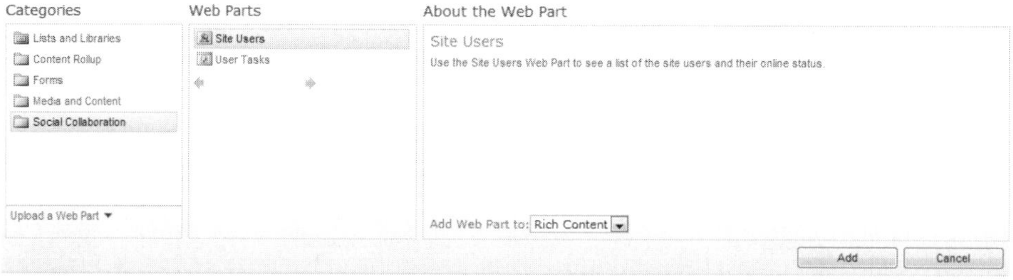

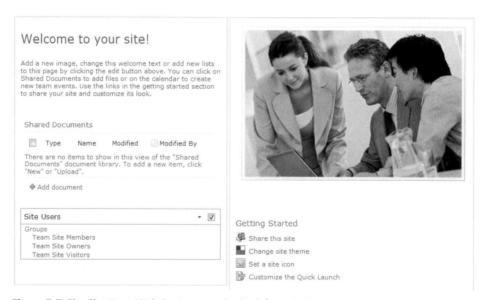

Figure 7-6 Selecting the Site Users Web Part.

The Site Users Web Part appears in Figure 7-7. Because the left content area had been selected when the Web Part was added, that is where it appeared by default.

Figure 7-7 The Site Users Web Part appears in the left content area.

Let's move the Site Users Web Part over to the right pane, under the photo but above the Getting Started Web Part. Drag the "Site Users" title bar from the left to the right content area (Figure 7-8).

Notice that the page is still in Edit mode (as indicated by the large squares around the content). Also notice that the existing Getting Started Web Part moved down when the new Site Users Web Part was inserted.

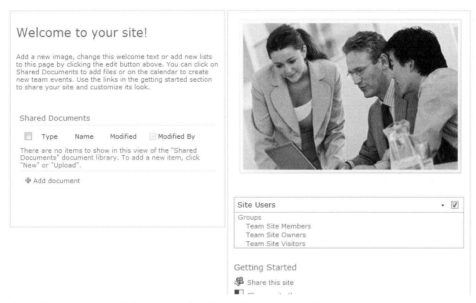

Figure 7-8 To move a Web Part, just drag it to where you want it to go.

Here, the Site Users Web Part has been moved to the right content area, below the photo.

Next, you will add in a Web Part that represents an existing list. Click again at the bottom of the left content area; this is where the next action will take place.

In the Editing Tools tab group, select the Insert tab, and then click Existing List (see Figure 7-9). Each SharePoint list in a site has a corresponding Web Part by default; this Web Part is created alongside the list it represents.

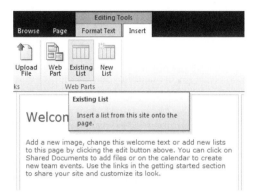

Figure 7-9 Inserting an Existing List Web Part.

From the Web Parts section, select the Announcements Web Part (see Figure 7-10), and then click the Add button.

Figure 7-10 Selecting the Announcements Web Part for insertion onto the site.

When the Web Part appears, note that it is in the content area and location that you selected earlier, as illustrated in Figure 7-11. If this is not the case, simply drag its title bar to where you want it located.

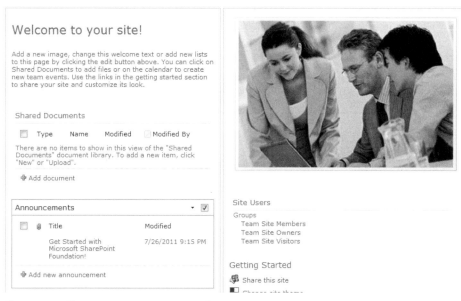

Figure 7-11 The new Announcements Web Part.

Now let's build a new list and insert its Web Part at the same time. Click in the left content area below the Announcements Web Part that you just added, as shown in Figure 7-12.

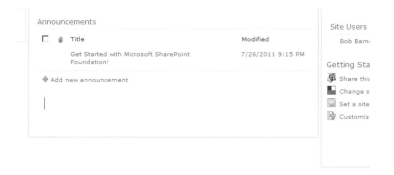

Figure 7-12 Selecting the content area below the Announcements Web Part.

The Navigation ribbon in SharePoint Foundation 2010 not only aids in grouping similar items together, but it also acts as a (sort of) macro functionality in certain instances; this is one of those instances. When you click New List from the Web Parts section (see Figure 7-13), you not only add a Web Part, but you generate the underlying SharePoint list.

Figure 7-13 Click the New List button to create new list in the content area of the site.

Add in the Contacts list title. In the Communications section, select the Contacts list type, and then click the OK button, as depicted in Figure 7-14.

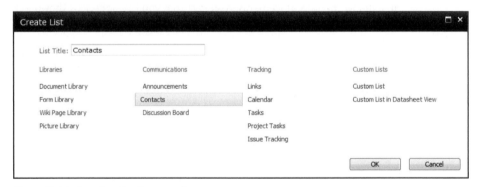

Figure 7-14 Creating the Contacts list.

The completed page appears, with the Announcements and Contacts Web Parts in the left content area and the Site Users Web Part in the right content area, as shown in Figure 7-15.

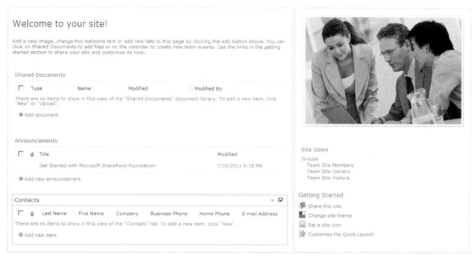

Figure 7-15 The new Home page layout after adding a Contacts list.

Editing and Maintaining Web Parts on a SharePoint Site

Now that you have some Web Parts on the page, let's examine how they are configured. The Site Users Web Part that you inserted in the preceding section currently shows only SharePoint permission groups. You will be changing its configuration so that it shows only individual users on this site.

There are two ways to configure the Site Users Web Part: Web Part Properties or Edit Web Part. The page from the last section is still in Edit mode.

Configuring a Web Part via Web Part Properties

To configure the Web Part by using Web Part Properties, perform the following:

1. Click the Site Users Web Part (to select it)

2. On Web Part Tools tab, click Options.

3. Click the Web Part Properties button, as demonstrated in Figure 7-16.

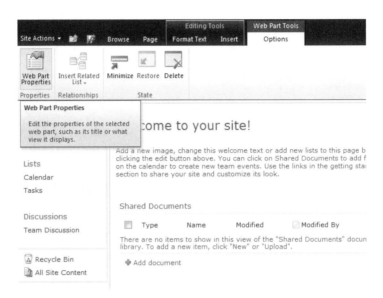

Figure 7-16 Configuring a Web Part by using Web Part Properties.

On the Web Part Properties sidebar that appears, there are several groupings of configurations with which you can work.

Default Items

There is always a default section near the top of the item with configuration items that are specific to the Web Part that you're editing.

For this Web Part to display users rather than groups, you need to change the Display Type section from Show People And Groups With Direct Permissions On This Site to Show People In This Site's Member Group (see Figure 7-17). You can also choose to display only certain people on this Web Part. For this example, this is the only change that you will make to this Web Part's configuration.

Figure 7-17 Setting the default properties for the Site Users Web Part.

The Toolbar Type drop-down list contains two selections: Summary Toolbar and No Toolbar. Some Web Parts (including Site Users) have no Toolbar.

Don't click the OK button just yet, there are three other sections to look at: Appearance, Layout, and Advanced.

Appearance

The Appearance section (see Figure 7-18), controls the overall look of the Web Part on the page. Note that changes made to this section might not appear until the Web Part/Page is no longer in Edit Mode (change the Web Part, and then save it to see the result).

Figure 7-18 The Appearance section in Web Part Properties.

In the Title text box, type the name that you want to appear on the title bar of the Web Part.

You can use the Height and Width fields to specify the height and width of the Web Part in pixels, or to allow the Web Part to automatically scale to fit the height and width of the Web Part zone in which it resides.

INSIDE OUT Web Parts and Chrome: and no, we don't mean the browser

Before going on to the next section, you need to know what Chrome means with respect to a Web Part. On any given Web Part, there are two major components that comprise its appearance: a title bar and a graphics box that surrounds the contents of the web part. Chrome is the name that is used to describe this appearance.

In the Chrome State section, you can specify whether the Web Part content is displayed (Normal) or not (Minimized).

Next, the Chrome Type drop-down list contains five distinct states:

- **Default**   Shows the Web Part in its default configuration, which is usually a title with no border

- **None**   Shows no Chrome (title or border)

- **Title And Border**   Shows both title and border

- **Title Only**   Shows only the title

- **Border Only**   Shows only the border

Layout

The Layout section controls the location and layout of the Web Part, as shown in Figure 7-19.

Figure 7-19 The Layout section in Web Part Properties.

Select the Hidden check box if you want to make the Web Part invisible to users. Note that this is different than closing a Web Part; the Web Part is still visible in Edit Mode.

Use the Direction drop-down list for languages that display content which reads from right to left (such as Arabic). You can choose from one of three choices:

- **None**   You are not specifying any particular direction, merely accepting the default orientation (right to left or left to right).

- **Right To Left**   Aligns the content starting at the leftmost side of the page.

- **Left To Right**   Aligns the content starting at the rightmost side of the page.

Use the Zone drop-down list to specify in which Web Part Zone the Web Part will appear. This is used on a Web Part page, and has no effect on a wiki page.

The Zone Index indicates the order in which the item appears in the Web Part Zone. In Figure 7-19, it is the second Web Part (in order from top to bottom or left to right).

Advanced

The Advanced section has several properties, which are shown in Figure 7-20.

Figure 7-20 The Advanced section in Web Part Properties.

This section presents several check boxes with which you can control the following:

- Whether the Web Part can be minimized

- Whether the Web Part can be closed

- Whether the Web Part can be Hidden

- Whether the Web Part's zone can be changed (Web Part pages only)

- Whether the Web Part can be connected to another Web Part

- Whether the Web Part can be edited in Personal view

INSIDE OUT   What's a Personal view?

A Web Part has two faces—one Public, and the other, Personal. The Public view is created by the site owner and shows the default view for everyone visiting the site. A Private view can be configured on a per-user basis to suit the user's individual needs. Both Public and Personal views of a Web Part can be reset (as you will see shortly in the section about Maintenance Mode).

You use the Export Mode drop-down list to choose whether or not sensitive data can be exported along with a Web Part. Some Web Parts can be configured, downloaded, and then saved only to be uploaded onto a different page or site.

In the Title URL text box, you can enter a URL to link to a site that contains more information about the Web Part. Clicking on the Web Part title opens this link in another Web Browser window.

Use the Description text box to provide descriptive information that will appear when you hover the mouse over the Web Part's title or icon.

With the Help URL, you can designate a help file for use when the user clicks the Help icon on the Web Part.

The Help Mode offers three choices, but only two of these modes function within SharePoint:

- **Modal**   Opens Help in a new browser window. You must close the Help window to return to the Web Part.

- **Modeless**   Opens Help in a new browser window. You can return to the Web Part without closing the Help window.

- **Navigate**   This option is available in ASP.NET Web Parts and indicates that the Help window will open in the current browser window. Although SharePoint is built on top of ASP.NET, it cannot use this mode.

In the Catalog Icon Image URL text box, you can specify a URL that links the Web Part to a 16×16-pixel icon that will appear in the Web Part listing.

Use the Title Icon Image URL text box to specify a URL that links the Web Part to a 16×16-pixel icon that will appear in the Web Part title bar.

You can enter a message into the Import Error Message text box to describe issues that might arise when importing a previously exported Web Part into your site. Usually you will have no need to change this field. If you need, you can change it from the default message, "Cannot import this Web Part".

INSIDE OUT   How about two good pieces of information within a single URL?

The article "Use the HTML Form Web Part to filter and display data in another Web Part," on *http://office.microsoft.com*, gives a good primer for the HTML Form Web Part (you will see this in the Connecting Web Parts section, later in this chapter). The bonus comes near the end of the article, in the section called "Configure the Common Properties of a Web Part." This section details all of the Web Part configuration items (including those we just covered) in an easy to print table. You can find this article at *http://office.microsoft.com/en-us/sharepoint-foundation-help/use-the-html-form-web-part-to-filter-and-display-data-in-another-web-part-HA101791813.aspx*.

At this point, you're done configuring this Web Part, so click the OK button, which is located beneath the Advanced section of the Web Part configuration sidebar. The reconfigured Web Part appears on the page, as shown in Figure 7-21.

Figure 7-21 The newly-configured Site Users Web Part.

Configuring the Web Part via Edit Web Part

To configure the Web Part by using Edit Web Part (see Figure 7-22), perform the following:

1. Click the Site Users Web Part (to select it).

2. Click the drop-down arrow in the upper-right corner of the Web Part.

3. Selecte Edit Web Part.

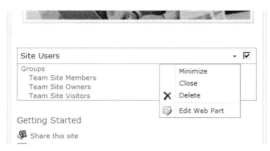

Figure 7-22 Editing the Site Users Web Part by using Edit Web Part.

The Web Part configuration menu opens, as when you configure the Web Part by using Web Part Properties, but there are other menu items.

When you click the drop-down arrow, there are three additional menu items for a Web Part: Minimize, Close, and Delete; let's have a look at each.

Minimize

Minimize causes the Web Part to hide all but its top menu bar (which in Figure 7-23 is Site Users). Depending on the Web Part's configuration, the user can click the drop-down menu again and then select Restore to revert the Web Part to its original appearance.

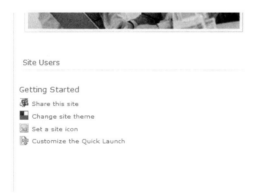

Figure 7-23 Site Users Web Part with the Minimized option enabled.

Close

Easily the most misunderstood choice, Close causes the Web Part to be removed from view without altering its configuration. A closed Web Part does not even remain visible on the page in Edit mode; more important, the SharePoint server renders the Web Part with the page whether the user sees it or not. Web Parts that are closed on a webpage do incur a performance penalty, which depends on the complexity of items rendered in the Web Part.

In a site managed by inexperienced owners, you might find several copies of the same closed Web Part. This causes the site to load slowly as a result of each of the multiple versions being rendered by the server. If you have a page that is rendering slowly, consider looking for closed Web Parts as one of your first troubleshooting actions.

So, why have the ability to close a Web Part? Why not just delete it? Here's why: you will want to use Close when you have a Web Part that you want to temporarily remove from the page, but you haven't yet decided to delete it.

Maintenance Mode

Once a Web Part has been closed, there are two ways to interact with it. The first is to add **?contents=1** to the end of your page's URL; this places the page into maintenance mode, wherein you can delete the Web Part, as illustrated in Figure 7-24.

Figure 7-24 Web Part page in Maintenance mode.

Categories

The second way to interact with a closed Web Part is to click Closed Web Parts in the Categories section of the Insert A Web Part menu, as shown in Figure 7-25.

Figure 7-25 You can click Closed Web Parts to interact with a closed Web Part.

Delete

Delete simply removes the Web Part from the page. This is a permanent action; you will have no opportunity to recover a Web Part once it has been deleted. If you have a doubt about deleting a Web Part that perhaps you have spent a good deal time configuring, consider temporarily closing it for a period of time before deleting it permanently.

Saving the Webpage

It is *not* necessary to edit a webpage in order to begin editing a Web Part (a major improvement in efficiency from the previous version of SharePoint). In this example, however, you had placed the page in Edit mode before starting the Web Part configuration. Therefore, it is good practice to remember to save the webpage before proceeding (Figure 7-26).

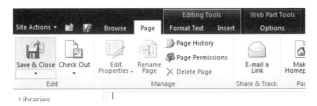

Figure 7-26 Remember to click Save & Close to ensure that you don't lose any changes made to the webpage.

The completed page should appear in your web browser; Figure 7-27 demonstrates that it is no longer in Edit mode.

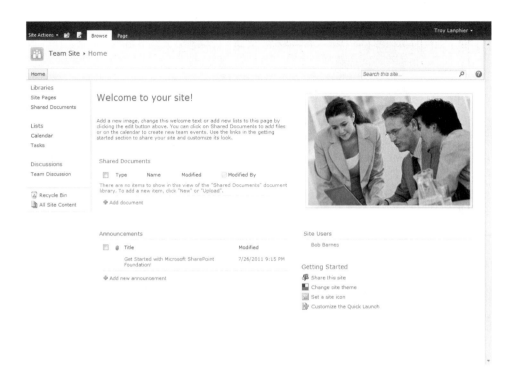

Figure 7-27 The completed webpage.

Connecting Web Parts in a SharePoint Site

So far, you have seen individual Web Parts in action on a SharePoint Site. Configuring these Web Parts can be as simple as placing one on the page and then making minor changes in the configuration, or as complex as specifying behaviors for appearance and function.

What you haven't seen yet is the interaction between two distinct Web Parts. SharePoint Web Parts can be interconnected, with one Web Part providing values that can be consumed by another. Not all Web Parts have this functionality, and as you have seen, the configuration of a Web Part can be restricted such that connectivity is not allowed.

This section begins with the creation and mild alteration of a wiki page (this activity is covered in Chapter 6, "Creating and Formatting Webpages"). Web Parts will then be added and connected to demonstrate this defined Web Part relationship.

Creating the New Wiki Page in the SharePoint Site

To begin creating a new page, click Site Actions | New Page, as shown in Figure 7-28.

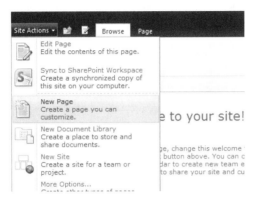

Figure 7-28 Creating a new page.

When the new page appears, on the Editing Tools tab, click Format Text. Next, click the Text Layout button. You can use this tool to dynamically change the layout of the page. The page only had one content area when it was created; change this to Two Columns With Header, as depicted in Figure 7-29. Note the tip that appears, describing each layout.

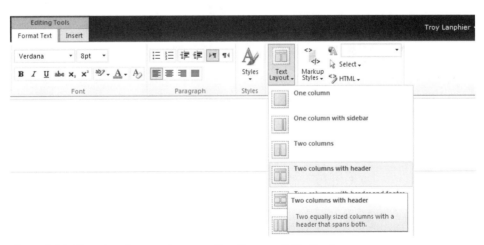

Figure 7-29 Changing the page layout to Two Columns With Header.

The new page layout appears with the three content areas. Click the header (the top content area), and then type **Inventory List** for the page title. Format the text by using the ribbon, just as you would in Microsoft Word (see Figure 7-30).

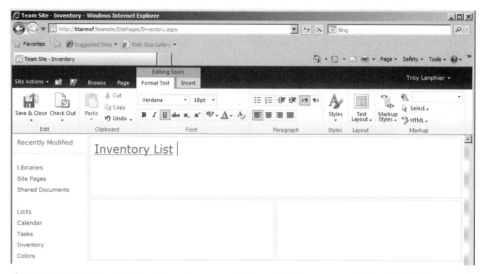

Figure 7-30 Type in a title for the webpage, and then style it as you would in a Word document.

Adding Web Parts to the New Wiki Page

It's time to add the first of two Web Parts. First, click inside the lower-left content area to select it. On the Editing Tools tab, click Insert (see Figure 7-31), and then click the Web Part button to display the Web Part Categories selector.

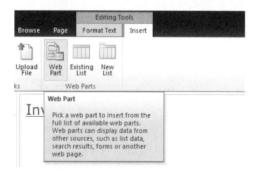

Figure 7-31 Inserting a new Web Part into a content area.

Select Forms in the Web Parts section, and then click the HTML Form Web Part. This Web Part accepts input and can pass it to another, connected Web Part.

Click the Add Web Part To drop-down list. Notice that there is only one choice: Rich Content. This is because you are adding this Web Part to a wiki page. If this were a Web Part page, there would be Web Part Zones specified in this drop-down and you could choose to which Zone to add the Web Part.

Click the Add button to complete the addition of the Web Part to the site, as shown in Figure 7-32.

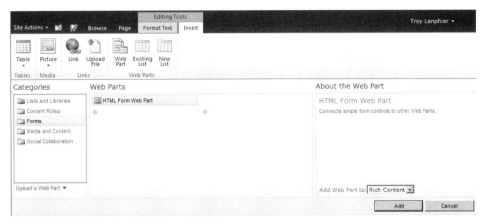

Figure 7-32 Adding the HTML Form Web Part.

Figure 7-33 shows that the HTML Form Web Part appears in the lower-left content area that you selected previously. At this point, the Web Part is not configured and is of little to no use; it has one text form input box and a button that can execute whatever code has been placed in the Web Part.

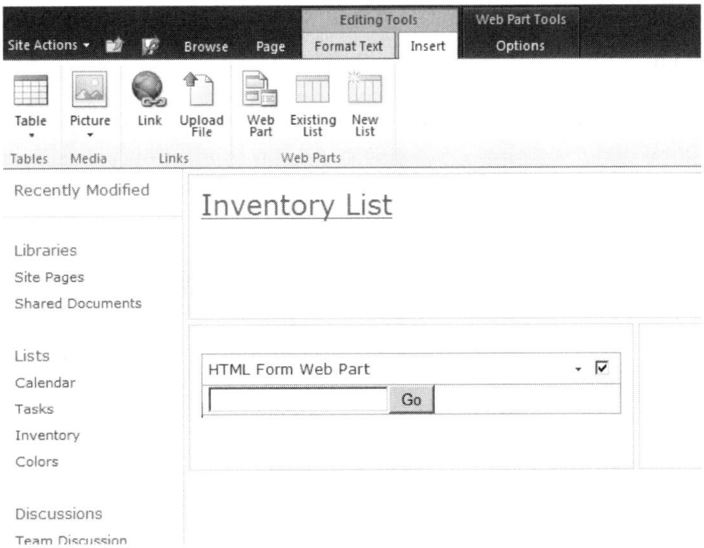

Figure 7-33 A basic HTML Form Web Part.

You will edit the HTML Form Web Part shortly; in the meantime, place the other Web Part on the page. As before, click in the lower-right content area to select it.

This time, you will be inserting a Web Part from an existing list (see Figure 7-34). On the Editing Tools tab, select Insert, and then click Existing List.

Figure 7-34 Inserting a Web Part from an existing list into the content area.

A list was created for this example called Inventory. It has three columns:

- **Title**   The title of the item

- **Color**   A choice field (Red, Orange, Yellow, Green, Blue, Purple)

- **Quantity**   A number field with no decimals

If you have difficulty building this list, for a refresher, refer to Chapter 5, "Designing Lists and Libraries." There were also views created for this library, which look at the Title field:

- Pint Glasses

- Cocktail Glasses

- Shot Glasses

- Wine Glasses

These views will be used in the next section.

In the Web Parts selection screen, click Inventory, and then click the Add button, as shown in Figure 7-35.

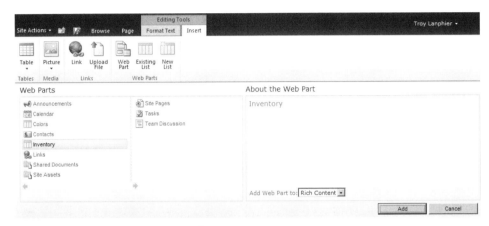

Figure 7-35 Adding the Inventory Web Part.

The page should now appear similar to Figure 7-36, which includes:

- A Text title in the top "header" content area

- The new HTML Form Web Part in the left content area

- The Inventory List Web Part in the right content area

Next, you can begin editing the HTML Form Web Part. Select its drop-down arrow, and then click Edit Web Part.

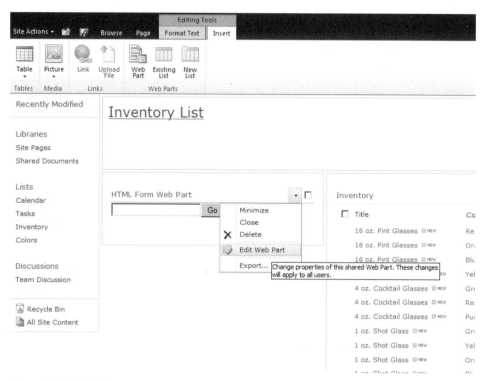

Figure 7-36 Click the HTML Form Web Part drop-down arrow, and then select Edit Web Part.

In the HTML Form Web Part dialog box, you can specify HTML/Javascript to alter its appearance as well as how it handles information that will be passed to another Web Part. Click the Source Editor button (see Figure 7-37) to begin the process of altering the Web Part's content.

Figure 7-37 Select the Source Editor to modify the content of the Web Part.

Next, you define the Web Part's actions. The intended goal is to have the HTML Form Web Part specify a color and pass this as a filter to the Inventory Web Part. This will result in the Inventory Web Part being filtered according to input from the HTML Form Web Part (using the Color column of the Inventory list).

The Text Editor box opens, presenting the basic text that creates the form you see in the Web Part's default configuration (see Figure 7-38).

This code contains the following JavaScript and HTML components:

- A Text Box

- A "Go" Button

- An Action (in the <DIV> field) that submits the form

One thing is important to remember here—this Web Part is capable of passing only one value to a particular Web Part at a time. If you have multiple values, you can connect them to multiple Web Parts, again one at a time. You cannot, however, connect multiple fields from the HTML Form Web Part to a single Web Part; it's just not that fancy of a tool.

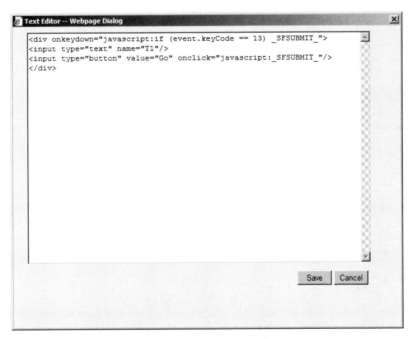

Figure 7-38 The default code in the HTML Form Web Part.

The code in this Web Part will need to be replaced for this Web Part to meet your needs.

INSIDE OUT   Working with the HTML Form Web Part

In the aforementioned article on *http://office.microsoft.com*, titled "Use the HTML Form Web Part to filter and display data in another Web Part," there are several examples of how to interact with this Web Part as well as some code snippets that teach you a little bit about creating an HTML form with JavaScript components. In case you misplaced the link from the last section, you'll find this article at *http://office.microsoft.com/en-us/ sharepoint-foundation-help/use-the-html-form-web-part-to-filter-and-display-data-in-another-web-part-HA101791813.aspx*.

The code you will see momentarily is derived from that contained on the website that you were just referred to. It has been modified to accomplish a bit more than was required in the article, however.

Let's have a walk through the following code, which you will use to add the required functionality to the Web Part:

```
<div onkeydown="javascript:if (event.keyCode == 13) _SFSUBMIT_">
<p>Please select a color to sort your inventory by</p>
<input type="Radio" name="color" value="Red"/> Red<br/>
<input type="Radio" name="color" value="Orange"/> Orange<br/>
<input type="Radio" name="color" value="Yellow"/> Yellow<br/>
<input type="Radio" name="color" value="Green"/> Green<br/>
<input type="Radio" name="color" value="Blue"/> Blue<br/>
<input type="Radio" name="color" value="Purple"/> Purple<br/>
<p align="right">
<input type="button" value="Select Color" onclick="javascript:_SFSUBMIT_"/>
<input type="button" value="Reset Filter" onclick="location.href='../SitePages/
Inventory.aspx'"/>
</p>
</div>
```

The JavaScript code within the default HTML Form Web Part performs the following actions:

- It creates a "Submit" action for the "Select Color" button.

- It prompts the user for a color selection.

- It creates six radio buttons, one for each color in the library (note that the name of the radio button is "color"—this will be important later).

- It moves both buttons to the right side of the Web Part.

- It creates a button to select the color—this one will be linked to the Inventory Web Part.

- It creates another button that resets the filter on the Inventory Web Part by simply reloading the page (admittedly, this is not elegant, but it works for this example).

Copy the code and then replace the original code in the HTML Form Web Part (see Figure 7-39). Click the Save button to close the text editor.

INSIDE OUT   Writing your code outside of the built-in text editor

One thing you will learn very quickly when experimenting with these Web Parts is that the text interface can be challenging to use because of its small work area; it also does not validate your code. If you plan on adding code of any complexity, you could use something as basic as the Notepad editor (built in to Windows) or something nicer such as NotePad++ (*http://notepad-plus-plus.org*) or Microsoft Visual Studio (*http://msdn.microsoft.com/en-us/vstudio*), and then paste your results into the Web Part.

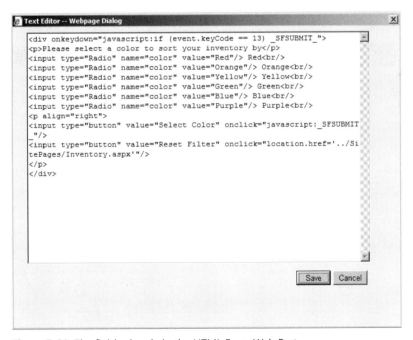

Figure 7-39 The finished code in the HTML Form Web Part.

Before you save the completed Web Part, change its title on the page. In the Appearance section of the Web Part Configuration pane (right side of your screen), select the HTML Form Web Part text, as shown in Figure 7-40.

Figure 7-40 Changing the Web Part title.

Connecting the Web Parts

Now it's time to connect the Web Parts to each other; let's begin with the Color Selector. To connect Web Parts, they must be in Edit mode. You can check if you are by clicking the drop-down arrow. If the ensuing list doesn't show the Connections menu item, your Web Part is not currently in Edit mode (although the page itself is). Select the Edit Web Part menu item, as illustrated in Figure 7-41.

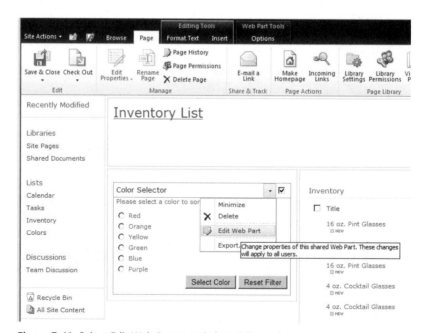

Figure 7-41 Select Edit Web Part to switch to Edit mode.

If you click the drop-down arrow again, you should see the Connections menu; if this is not the case, one of two things is most likely happening:

- Your Web Part has been prevented from making connections to others.

- The particular Web Part you chose does not have connection capability.

Click Connections | Provide Form Values To | Inventory to set the connection to the Inventory Web Part, as shown in Figure 7-42.

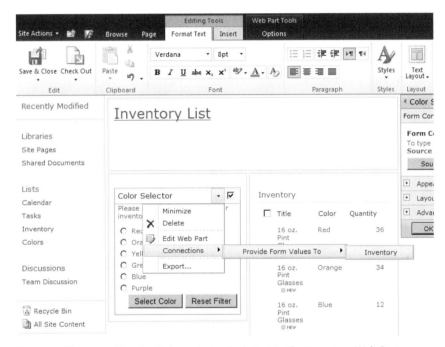

Figure 7-42 Connecting the Color Selector Web Part to the Inventory Web Part.

The Choose Connections dialog box opens, in which you are presented with two tabs: 1. Choose Connection, and 2. Configure Connection (see Figure 7-43).

Both of these steps are required to secure the connection between Web Parts. For step 1 (Choose Connection), select Get Filter Values From, and then click the Configure button, which will move you on to step 2.

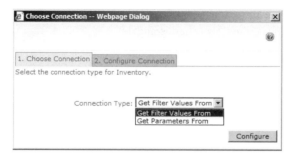

Figure 7-43 Select the Get Filter Values From in step 1.

In the second step, choose the Provider Field Name (color) from the Color Selector Web Part. This was intentionally left in all lowercase (in step 3 of the HTML Form Web Part code) to distinguish it from the Consumer Field Name (Color). Click the Finish button to complete the connection, as demonstrated in Figure 7-44.

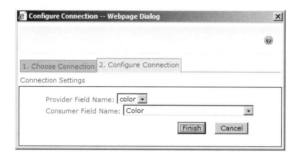

Figure 7-44 Configure the connection, and then click Finish.

All that remains is to save the page. On the ribbon, on the Editing Tools tab, click the Save & Close button (see Figure 7-45).

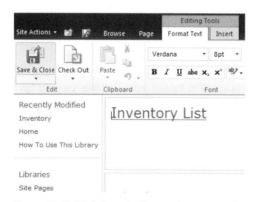

Figure 7-45 Click Save & Close to keep your changes.

The completed page appears, as shown in Figure 7-46. If you see no values in the Inventory Web Part, click the Reset Filter button in the Color Selector Web Part.

Inventory List

Color Selector		Inventory		
Please select a color to sort your inventory by		☐ Title	Color	Quantity
○ Red		16 oz. Pint Glasses	Red	36
○ Orange		16 oz. Pint Glasses	Orange	34
○ Yellow		16 oz. Pint Glasses	Blue	12
○ Green		4 oz. Cocktail Glasses	Yellow	89
○ Blue		4 oz. Cocktail Glasses	Green	45
○ Purple		4 oz. Cocktail Glasses	Red	11
	[Select Color] [Reset Filter]	4 oz. Cocktail Glasses	Purple	65
		1 oz. Shot Glass	Green	47
		1 oz. Shot Glass	Yellow	58
		1 oz. Shot Glass	Orange	25
		1 oz. Shot Glass	Blue	55
		5 oz. Wine Glass	Orange	55
		5 oz. Wine Glass	Yellow	66
		5 oz. Wine Glass	Green	33

✦ Add new item

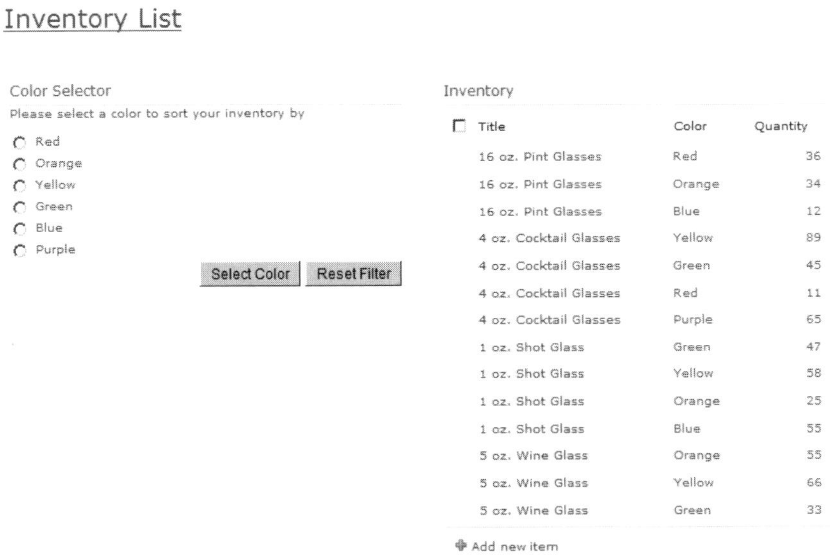

Figure 7-46 The completed page, with connected Web Parts.

Select any color in the Color Selector Web Part, and then click the Select Color button. This passes the value to the Inventory Web Part to filter the result. For example, if you select Red, only red items are presented in the inventory list, as shown in Figure 7-47.

Notice the small, triangular icon adjacent to the Color field on the Inventory Web Part—we'll talk about that next.

Inventory List

Color Selector

Please select a color to sort your inventory by

- ⦿ Red
- ○ Orange
- ○ Yellow
- ○ Green
- ○ Blue
- ○ Purple

[Select Color] [Reset Filter]

Inventory

☐ Title	Color ▽	Quantity
16 oz. Pint Glasses	Red	36
4 oz. Cocktail Glasses	Red	11

✦ Add new item

Figure 7-47 A filtered Inventory list, showing only red glasses.

In case you missed it earlier, clicking the Reset Filter button removes the applied filter by reloading the page—don't do this yet; let's first have a look at how filtering a Web Part works.

Filtering itself does not require a connected Web Part; in fact, you can filter within a single Web Part. On the Inventory Web Part, you could simply click the Color field to accomplish the same action. A drop-down menu appears (see Figure 7-48) with options to accomplish several tasks:

- Choose a sort order (Ascending or Descending).

- Choose to clear an applied filter from the field.

- Choose a particular field value by which to filter the web part.

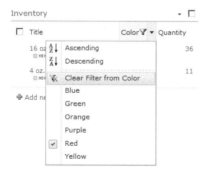

Figure 7-48 The filtering control.

Disconnecting the Web Parts

Occasionally, you will want to reverse this process and disconnect Web Parts on your page. This is a fairly straightforward process, but just in case you change your mind at a later date, you should document the existing Web Part connections.

To begin, select the drop-down list for the Color Selector Web Part, and then click Edit Web Part, as shown in Figure 7-49.

Inventory List

Color Selector

Please select a color to sort your in[
- Red
- Orange
- Yellow
- Green
- Blue
- Purple

Minimize

Edit Web Part

Export...

Select Color   Reset Filter

Figure 7-49 To disconnect Web Parts, begin by selecting Edit Web Part from the drop-down list.

Click Connections | Provide Forms Values To | Inventory to indicate which connection you want to remove (see Figure 7-50).

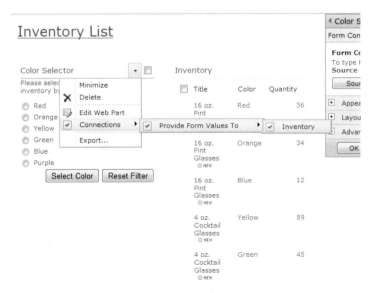

Figure 7-50 Selecting a connection to delete.

The Configure Connections dialog box opens, as it did when you initially made this connection. Verify that the field you want to disconnect is selected, and then click the Remove Connection button, as shown in Figure 7-51.

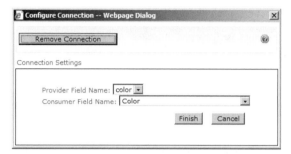

Figure 7-51 Removing the connection to the Color Selector Web Part.

This is your last chance—clicking OK at this point removes the connection for good, so a dialog box appears (see Figure 7-52), asking if you're sure that you want to remove the connection. Click the OK button to remove the connection.

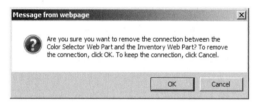

Figure 7-52 Before you disconnect the Web Part, a message appears, asking you to verify that the connection should be removed.

If you have no other changes that you want to make to this Web Part, click the OK button to close the Web Part Configuration pane (on the right side of your page), as shown in Figure 7-53.

Figure 7-53 When you're done, click OK to close the Web Part Configuration Pane.

Web Parts on a Web Part Page

While there is little behavior difference between Web Parts on a wiki page and Web Parts on a Web Part page, let's build a Web Part page to illustrate what the differences are.

Wiki pages are most often stored in the site pages library of a Microsoft SharePoint Foundation site, Web Part pages can be built in a document library, regardless of the library name.

Web Part pages are found in all but the Team Site template as the *de facto* page type and have a few interesting characteristics that make them different in behavior from their wiki page counterparts, such as:

- No version control

- No area for freeform content (graphics, images, and so on)

- A very rigid structure that cannot be changed quickly—once a page layout is chosen, it cannot be altered by the site owner

We will pass quickly through the process of creating first a document library for the Web Part Pages, and then the Web Part Page itself. These topics have been covered previously in both Chapter 5 and Chapter 6.

To begin, click the Site Actions menu, and then select New Document Library, as shown in Figure 7-54.

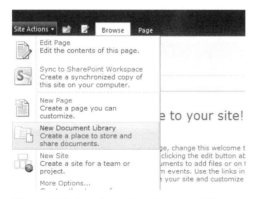

Figure 7-54 Creating a New Document Library.

Name your new library **Catalogs**, and use the Document Template. When your new library appears (see Figure 7-55), do not click the Add Document link because it will merely prompt you for a file to upload to the library.

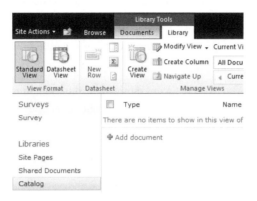

Figure 7-55 Don't Choose the Add Document link.

On the ribbon, click Library Tools | Documents | New Document to begin the creation of a new Web Part page, as depicted in Figure 7-56.

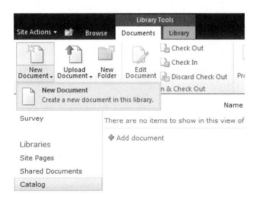

Figure 7-56 Creating a New Document.

Next, choose the name and layout. For this example, use the title **Barware** and select the Header, Footer, 2 Columns, 4 Rows template (see Figure 7-57). Click the Create button.

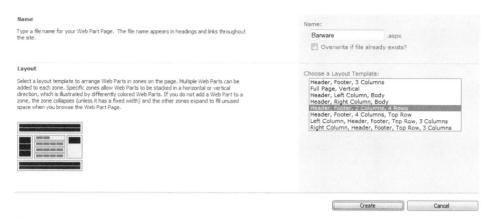

Figure 7-57 Enter a name in the Name text box and select a Layout Template.

When the new page appears, select the Header Web Part zone, click the Add A Web Part section inside it, as shown in Figure 7-58.

Figure 7-58 Adding a Web Part to the new document.

Add the first Web Part. The Page Tools menu provides four options:

- **Text**   Adds a Content Editor Web Part to display rich text

- **Image**   Adds an Image Web Part to display an image

- **Web Part**   Adds a Web Part of any type

- **Existing List**   Adds a Web Part derived from an existing list

Because it's not possible to add freeform text to a Web Part zone, you need to add a Content Editor Web Part to start. On the Page Tools tab, click Insert, and then click the Text button, as shown in Figure 7-59, to add this Web Part to the Left Column Web Part zone.

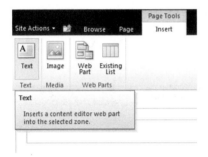

Figure 7-59 Insert a Content Editor Web Part into the Web Part zone.

Once the Web Part has been inserted, change its title to **Barware Title**, and then add content to it, as illustrated in Figure 7-60.

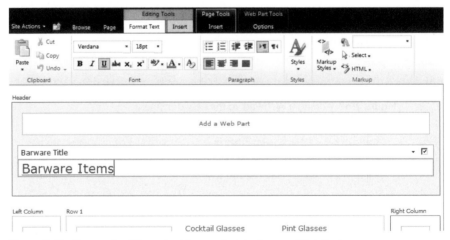

Figure 7-60 Change the title and add some text to the new Web Part.

In case you forgot how to change the Title, here's a hint—look to the right of the screen at the Web Part Properties (shown in Figure 7-61).

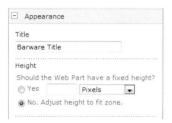

Figure 7-61 Changing the Web Part's Title.

A couple of things are different in the Layout section of this Web Part, which you can see in Figure 7-62:

- The Zone control allows you to choose between the available Web Part zones for the location of the Web Part.

- The Zone Index indicates the order in which the Web Part appears.

Figure 7-62 Adjusting the Web Part's settings in the Layout dialog box.

INSIDE OUT   Working with Web Part zone indexes

You can have several Web Parts in a particular zone. If you want the one you added to appear at the top of the Web Part zone, set its Zone Index number to 0. The other Web Parts will automatically change their index number and move down the page.

Next, you will insert an existing list. More important, you will insert this list four times. From earlier in this chapter, four library views were created that refer to the Title field:

- Pint Glasses

- Cocktail Glasses

- Shot Glasses

- Wine Glasses

The Row Web Part zones (Rows 1–4) in the middle of this page layout distribute Web Parts horizontally instead of vertically. Thus, when you set the Zone Index of a Web Part to 0, it becomes the leftmost Web Part).

The same Web Part on a page can display a particular list view. You will use this to your advantage by adding a Web Part for each view:

1. Select Row 1, and then click Insert | Existing List, as shown in Figure 7-63.

Figure 7-63 Add an Existing List Web Part.

2. Choose the Inventory List, and then add the Web Part to Row 1 (see Figure 7-64) by clicking the Add button.

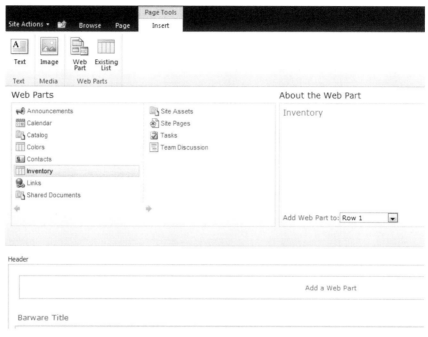

Figure 7-64 Adding the Inventory Web Part.

3. Repeat step 2 one more time.

You should now have two Inventory Web Parts in Row 1, as illustrated in Figure 7-65.

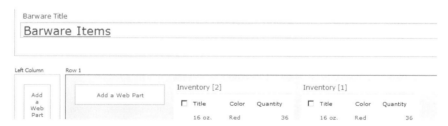

Figure 7-65 Two of the same Web Parts in one Web Part Row.

4. Choose the Inventory List, and then add the Web Part to Row 2 (not shown) by clicking the Add button.

5. Repeat step 4 one more time.

You should now have two Inventory Web Parts in Row 2 (not shown).

6. Select and edit one of the Web Parts. Then, change its view, as demonstrated in Figure 7-66.

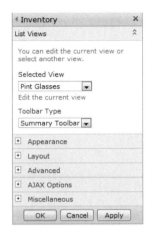

Figure 7-66 Changing the Web Part view.

A warning appears, notifying you that changing the view of a Web Part will break any existing Web Part connections (see Figure 7-67). Build your Web Parts and decide on a view before making Web Part connections.

Figure 7-67 Altering Views Breaks Web Part Connections.

7. Alter the Title of the Web Part to match its view, as shown in Figure 7-68.

Figure 7-68 One completed Inventory Web Part.

8. Repeat steps 6 and 7 for all four Web Parts. The finished page (still in Edit mode) should look something like Figure 7-69.

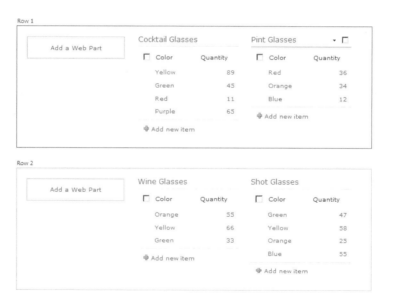

Figure 7-69 All four completed Inventory Web Parts.

9. At this point, stop editing the page. On the Page tab, click the Stop Editing button, as depicted in Figure 7-70.

Figure 7-70 Click Stop Editing to save the page and Web Part configuration.

10. Click the Browse tab to show the completed page, as shown in Figure 7-71.

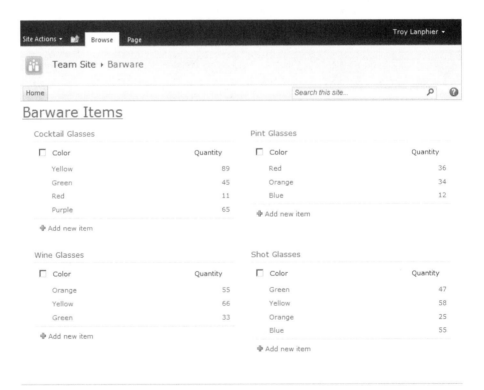

Figure 7-71 The completed Barware Items page.

Summary

In this chapter, you were introduced to the concept of Web Parts, which are used to display both static and interactive content. The combination of Web Parts on a page allows for the creation of an interactive portal with a default configuration; this configuration can be further customized on an individual basis to accommodate the needs of a subset of users.

Web Parts can be combined with views to relate a particular piece of information in multiple views, based on metadata. They can also be connected to each other so that users can interactively query a subset of information from a Web Parts library.

Finally, you were able to see the differences in the application of Web Parts on both wiki and Web Part pages. It is through these differences that you can better define the type of page that you utilize to relate information to your SharePoint Users.

Managing Site Content

C ONTENT is the heart of a Microsoft SharePoint site. Organizing content and using the Web Parts available to you in a way that is accepted by those you work with on the site is the best way to provide value to your organization through SharePoint. This chapter provides the tools and strategies for designing a great site. Using the strategies here, you will find effective ways to present information that is up to date and relevant.

How do you manage site content? Understanding why this question is important is a little bit of a conundrum. Until you have enough content in your sites to make managing it an issue, you really can't have a full appreciation for the full breadth of the concerns involved in getting that content under control. On the other hand, planning site structure and strategy is more efficiently applied at the beginning of any site content undertaking.

Where is the middle ground? The practical approach to managing site content requires both ongoing content creation and ongoing planning around the existing content and for the future content. It is only through the experience of creating the content that you can truly appreciate why planning is a benefit. Some amount of planning must be done upfront, but it also must be revisited throughout the creation process to fine tune the architecture and rules of the road to match what you've put in place and can envision as you progress.

The earlier chapters of this book have provided the tools you need to create and publish content into SharePoint sites effectively. In fact, you started as an intermediate to advanced business user of SharePoint in the first place; you already have a good view of the breadth of features and functionality of the product. You understand the effects of proper administration of the SharePoint farm. You understand how to navigate and manipulate the views and interactions of web applications, Site Collections, sites, lists, libraries, and pages. Creating sites and workspaces, designing lists and libraries, creating and formatting webpages are all content creation processes. Adding, editing, connecting, and managing Web Parts adds more content to your sites.

SharePoint has no lack of options for getting content on the site. With a great SharePoint infrastructure in place, you and your colleagues in your organization are doing just that; you're creating content, and lots of it. However, like any great endeavor undertaken by a group of people, all that content—and you and your colleagues as the content consumers—will benefit from structure, strategy, and some basic rules of the road. You don't just want to create and consume content. You want to do it effectively.

Information Architecture (IA) is not a new field. Thinking about IA began around 10 thousand years ago when recording information started taking the form of the written word. Similarly, governance is an ages old field. These two areas of study can be applied to web content creation and management and used well with the SharePoint tools you're familiar with. What is presented in this chapter is only a brief overview of some of the tools from these fields with practical approaches to their application in SharePoint. If what you see interests you, there are entire books written on the subjects. In fact, Microsoft publishes quite a lot of practical planning information specific to this version of SharePoint that is referenced in the following sections.

Toward the end of this chapter, there are two sections on more techniques for content management that complement the other tools you already have for content creation. Identifying a content manager for a site is a great first step in taming what might be out-of-control sites in your SharePoint deployment. When you know who is responsible for a site, you can hold that person accountable for applying the plans and rules you've developed as an organization. Managing content for Internet sites requires special consideration because of the size of the audience that can find and view the published information publicly.

An Introduction to Information Architecture

The following quote from the Wikipedia article about Richard Saul Wurman is a good introduction to IA:

In 1976, Wurman coined the phrase "information architect" in response to the large amount of information generated in contemporary society, which is often presented with little care or order. Wurman said, "I thought the explosion of data needed an architecture, needed a series of systems, needed systemic design, a series of performance criteria to measure it."

You might have experienced an "explosion of data" in your organization. SharePoint can play a role in helping to increase the amount of content publishing; therefore, it must also be a part of this needed architecture to help control it. If you have ever seen file shares that seem unmanageable or hundreds of abandoned SharePoint sites that are out of date, you have a great reference point for understanding the architecture tools and strategies that are introduced in the following sections.

Start with Purpose

Starting from a blank site, your potential to create is mostly limited by your imagination. But before you create your first list or add your first Web Part, you have the opportunity to design your solution to fit your end purpose for the site. If you don't have a purpose in mind for your site, this would be a good time to reconsider what you hope to gain from your use of SharePoint.

The simplest purpose for a SharePoint Foundation site might be sharing documents with others in your organization. In fact, document sharing is a valid and well-received feature of SharePoint and many organizations start there. If this is the case with your organization, the simplest IA is one site with one document library. The only page needed to start the site and possibly the clearest view to a new user of such a site is to present the document library front and center. It might be that in your organization this is the case for departmental sites—for example, Human Resources. If so, state the purpose clearly on the page. A description of roles and responsibilities for the site help to reinforce the IA and introduce documentation of governance, as explained later in this chapter. An example of the simple site is depicted in Figure 8-1.

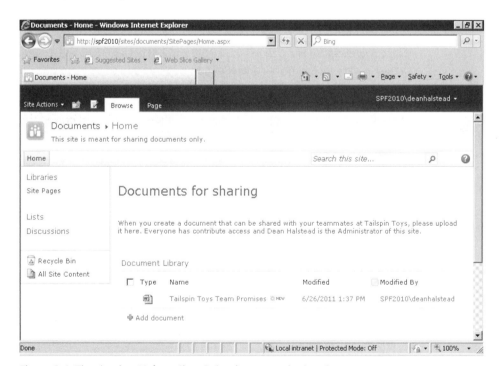

Figure 8-1 The simplest IA for a SharePoint document sharing site.

INSIDE OUT   Give the Team Site template a rest sometimes

The example above shows the simplest IA for a SharePoint site. Note that Figure 8-1 shows a site set up for document sharing. This is one of the most popular uses of SharePoint, without using the Team Site template, which is the most popular site template in previous versions of the product. When creating a new site, it pays to stop and think about the various lists that are created with your template. If you don't intend to use the Calendar, Tasks list and Team Discussion list that are created with the Team Site template, your IA will be better without them. Limiting choices for the end user to those that are the most important is an improvement in usability of your site.

At any given time, your purpose might simply be to play or experiment with some new piece of the tool. Even in this case, you could take a little extra time to exercise your IA process in your sandboxed environment. Like everything else, practice makes perfect, and you can't expect to design the perfect solution on your first try.

Use a Sandbox

Since SharePoint sites are so easy to create and just as easy to delete, you can really feel free to experiment with your SharePoint sites before you share them with others. Once you populate your site with content and share it with others, it becomes much more important to plan structural changes ahead of time and communicate them to the site's audience early. However, before you find yourself with others who depend on your site, it is important to try out the various tools that are at your disposal.

Figure 8-2 shows the picker for adding content to a blank site. The Team Site template is the most commonly used site template in the table, but the Blank Site template is just as valid in many cases, as discussed in the previous section. Using each template and Web Part at least once will give you a basis for architectural decisions. Before you create your next SharePoint site for use with others, try a little play in a sandbox to inform your decisions and make you more confident in your choices. How long do you think it would take to create one site of each of the template types available to you? On the other hand, if you don't create one of each type and explore it, how sure will you be that you are choosing the right template?

Figure 8-2 The SharePoint Foundation 2010 Blank Site template includes 30 options for lists, Libraries, Pages, and Sites.

INSIDE OUT   Silverlight not required

Does your list of SharePoint Templates look like Figure 8-3? It serves the same function, but you'll notice it's a plain list without the icons from Figure 8-2. This version also lacks the filtering and searching available in the richer selection dialog from which Figure 8-3 is taken. SharePoint Foundation 2010 uses Microsoft Silverlight for a richer in-browser experience, but falls back to plain HTML when you don't have the Silverlight plug-in installed. These content templates are crucial to SharePoint, and the fact that Microsoft provides these two versions serves to highlight their importance.

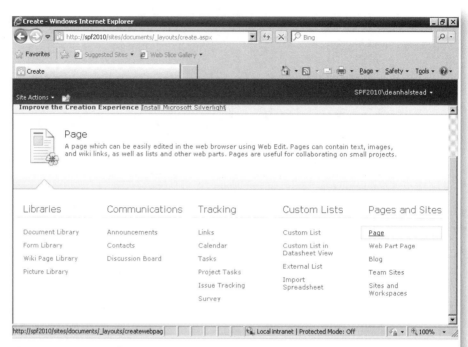

Figure 8-3 This view of list, library, page, and site template choices lacks search and filtering, but is still functional when Silverlight is not available.

It might sound less interesting than the other site templates, but try creating a blank site and adding all the various types of lists, pages, and Web Parts to it. Even the most advanced SharePoint user can benefit from occasional review. And again, if you start here with the purpose to discover, the experience you gain will help you design your next site or manage an existing site with confidence. Keep in mind that you can create a site template from any site that you originally create as a sandbox. If you accidentally happen upon the perfect site structure while playing, you can capture that structure and make it available so that others can benefit.

Figure 8-4 shows a custom view of the Web Part Gallery of a site created with the Blank Site template. Notice that there are ten Web Parts installed, but the List View Web Part is not one of them. You will see one instance of the List View Web Part in the Add New Web Part dialog for every instance of a list or library that exists on your site. The List View Web Part itself is not one that you can add without the connection to a list or library.

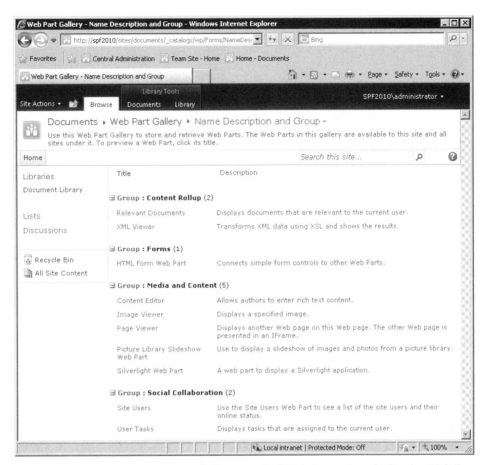

Figure 8-4 The Title and Description of all ten standard Web Parts, minus the list view Web Part.

The types of SharePoint content that you can experiment with doesn't stop with sites, lists, pages, and Web Parts. List columns, content types, list views, and workflows are just as simple to create and delete. Don't be afraid to create what you can easily remove later. Without the ability to create these types of content, SharePoint would be no different than any other website. When mastered, creating the right type of content for your needs allows you to reach the full potential of SharePoint management. Experience leads to mastery, and a sandbox is a great place to gain that experience.

INSIDE OUT   Using security trimming to hide your sandbox

You can standardize on creating one sandbox in every Site Collection when you use this method.

SharePoint's security trimming will hide your sandbox site from search results and features like the View All Site Content Page if you use unique permissions to remove most security groups. However, in most cases, the links will not be trimmed if you add them to the top navigation bar or the Quick Launch, so it's best not to list a sandbox in navigation. Each Site Collection and web application can be configured with different features activated, so it's often helpful to create one sandbox per Site Collection or at least per base Site Collection template. If you use a common address, such as /sandbox, you won't need to guess where it is when it's not in the navigation bars.

For more information about managing site navigation settings, refer to Chapter 4, "Creating Sites and Workspaces by Using the Browser."

Prototypes or Wireframes

While not strictly an IA tool, drawings or sketches of page prototypes can help solidify the vision for a site's content. Sometimes these prototypes are called *wireframes* or *storyboards*. This is in reference to the processes used in engineering and movie making to envision a project. When starting your drawing, you might find it helpful to start as simple as possible. Sit down with pencil and paper to quickly create a black and white rough sketch just to capture some ideas. Don't worry about making it pretty or adding color. The benefit in this process is in committing the ideas in your head to a rough visualization that can be perfected with time and effort later. If you're not comfortable with your artistic skills with a pencil, or you simply prefer an electronic method, products such as Microsoft Visio, Microsoft SketchFlow, or even Microsoft PowerPoint can help you to create visuals of your site content visions.

If you're not familiar with SketchFlow, which is a part of Microsoft Expression, you can read more about it and download an evaluation version at *http://www.microsoft.com/expression/products/sketchflow_overview.aspx*.

INSIDE OUT   A software tool for that hand-drawn look

There is a middle ground between hand-drawn sketches and professional looking mock ups. The benefit of a hand-drawn look is that it suggests change is as easy as an eraser and pencil. Mock ups that too closely resemble an end product might confuse the design process with actual implementation and move the viewer too far, too fast. Remember, the goal here is planning and refinement, not an exact blueprint for building. As an example, refer to Figure 8-5 for a typical first draft of an intranet portal that was drawn by using the rapid wireframing tool, Balsamiq Mockups.

Read more about Balsamiq Mockups and use the free, web-based version of the drawing software at *http://balsamiq.com*.

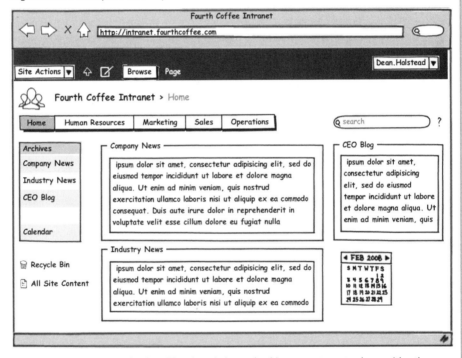

Figure 8-5 Create a professional but hand-drawn looking prototype to share with others when planning content to help solidify your shared vision of the site.

Chapter 8

Card Sorting

Often, when starting a site, you have many ideas for the types of things that should go on the site, but no concrete way to arrange it. Card sorting is a technique that will help you to organize your content. For example, if you want to determine the navigation headings for your site, card sorting can help start the process along.

The most common way to perform card sorting is to use stacks of 3 × 5 inch index cards. Think through every type of content that you have in mind for your site. Write these out on the cards, with one type of content per card. You can use a short title and add a sentence or two of description to clarify.

If you can get a group of people together to plan a site, everyone can contribute cards and participate in the sorting. Multiple minds contributing ideas and multiple eyes on the cards for sorting can yield stronger results than performing a card sort alone. However, even if you don't have a group, taking the time to commit each concept to paper requires thinking about each concept's uniqueness and importance. That thinking alone can often be one of the more important outcomes of this process.

After you have collected all the unique, important types of content on the cards, you can begin the sorting. Group the cards by common concepts. For example, if you see many items that represent events to happen in the future, they might fit nicely in a calendar group. Add a card for the group name if it isn't already captured on one of your cards. If you have 20 to 30 cards that you can fit into 4 to 6 groups, you have likely found your site's top navigation structure. If you have more total cards or you can't find commonalities between them, you might be planning a multi-site structure, or at least a top navigation structure and a side navigation structure. Card sorting is an exercise that commits site plans to a first informal structure. You can use these concepts and groups to plan your navigation, lists, and pages.

For more information about IA and user design for the Web, read *Head First Web Design* by Ethan Watrall and Jeff Siarto (O'Reilly) and *Information architecture for the World Wide Web* by Peter Morville and Louis Rosenfeld (O'Reilly).

Governance

Organizations can use SharePoint as a tool to empower individuals in new ways through the creation and sharing of web content. Sharing information within an organization is not new, but the publishing mechanism is. Whenever there is change that fosters growth, there is a corresponding challenge to the organization to respond to the change in positive ways. Governance is directly related to managing site content because it is the agreements, written or understood, between the participants in the websites.

How you decide on and document the governance of the SharePoint sites and content in your organization depends on many factors. Microsoft has built many capabilities into SharePoint that can help build strong communities. Understanding the tools at hand will help you better highlight the positive aspects of the SharePoint content for which you are responsible.

The Wild West of SharePoint

Governance comes up as a topic in many SharePoint implementations because the freedoms SharePoint gives to create can result in chaos and unmet expectations when not properly managed. In some ways, a new SharePoint installation can be compared with a wide open frontier. There is freedom and potential, but there is also the potential for lawlessness and failure due to the unknown. In theory, the tools SharePoint gives you are like any other tools you are given to use within your organization. Their use falls under the expectations of professionalism. However, there is potential for abuse and unintentional harm caused by misunderstanding.

Your SharePoint installation is not the Wild West, but it might benefit from some documented agreements on use and operation. As you begin to rely more and more on the servers hosting your content, your dependency on those same servers' consistent responsiveness and reliability grows. It is in your best interest to look out for the maintenance and upkeep of this resource. It is a given that SharePoint will be used by you and others because of the nature of web collaboration. Governance will help to ensure the shared resources that deliver your information will meet the demand.

What Is SharePoint Governance?

Microsoft's TechNet Library provides guidance on many aspects of SharePoint planning and operations management, including resources on governance. In the article, Governance Overview (SharePoint Server 2010), the following definition is given:

Governance is the set of policies, roles, responsibilities, and processes that guide, direct, and control how an organization's business divisions and IT teams cooperate to achieve business goals. A comprehensive governance plan can benefit your organization by:

- *Streamlining the deployment of products and technologies, such as SharePoint Server 2010.*

- *Helping protect your enterprise from security threats or noncompliance liability.*

- *Helping ensure the best return on your investment in technologies, for example, by enforcing best practices in content management or information architecture.*

You might find other definitions that suggest governance is generally applied at a higher level than most management and operations. However, for the purposes of this book, the broader definition given above is sufficient. Including the management and operational implications of a proper governance strategy is important. Not only must the strategy for governance be in place, but the strategy must be implemented effectively and followed up.

The full TechNet overview of SharePoint governance can be found at *http://technet.microsoft.com/en-us/library/cc263356.aspx.*

How to Govern SharePoint

If you don't personally govern your organization, you probably also won't be solely responsible for setting the strategy and implementation of governance for SharePoint. Organization-wide governance of any resource is usually an executive-level task, incorporating the concerns of all affected parties. However, that isn't to say that you cannot influence the direction of SharePoint use, management, and operations. As a business user, you have a stake in the outcome of governance decisions. As an advanced user of SharePoint, you might be looked upon as a thought leader in what is sure to be a new initiative within your organization.

TechNet provides some valuable resources for governance planning. The sections that follow contain a review of the highlights of the online material from the advanced user's perspective. Also included is analysis of the content and suggestions for their use in your work.

Governance by Site Audience

SharePoint sites can serve many purposes. You might find it helpful to tailor your governance to the use of the site. In general, the broader the target audience of a site, the more tightly controlled is the content publishing process.

Audience Size Growth

As a modern business professional, you share information electronically as part of your workday. You write emails, author documents, build spreadsheets, and produce slides. When you think about the process of writing a Microsoft Word document, do you feel that you approach the work a little differently than when you are writing an email? Traditional documents stored on your hard disk are hidden from others unless they have access to your computer. SharePoint provides a new opportunity to share and along with that should come a different approach. The opportunity is to securely share information with a broader network of people who you think might benefit from your hard work. And, unlike the network file shares that might be available to you, SharePoint can provide information securely to others beyond your work location without special secure connections like a Virtual Private Network (VPN). When the audience is broadened, your approach to authoring and sharing should and will change.

Consider Figure 8-6. It shows the amount of effort or rigor around the editorial process growing as the audience size grows. This is a visualization of one aspect of a good governance strategy, and it really represents something you do naturally and might consider common sense. You focus your effort where it will have the greatest effect. The width of the pyramid represents the total content at each level of a typical SharePoint installation. Your organization might have some or all of these levels of sites. Generally, the more people in the target audience of one site, the more effort you should consider putting in to the production of the content.

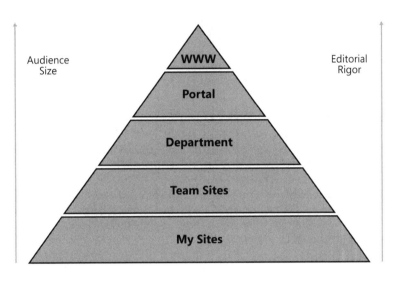

Figure 8-6 Editorial rigor increases as audience size grows. Sometimes, a large amount of content will have a small audience. For example, My Sites overall represent a large amount of content. But each My Site is viewed by only the individual My Site owner. Small audiences like that require and should receive less editorial control.

Large Audience Governance

Audience size and site type are strongly related. Figure 8-7 shows the typical amount of governance in a selection of site types. This isn't a hard-and-fast rule, but it does closely follow the editorial rigor pyramid of Figure 8-6. A central published site will have more eyeballs on it than a My Site and therefore warrants closer scrutiny.

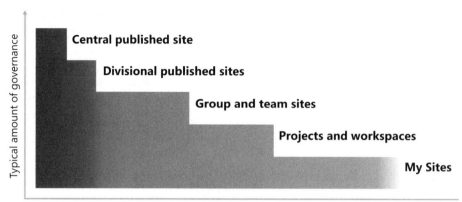

Figure 8-7 Some site types typically receive more governance effort than others.

Microsoft TechNet includes a number of nice wall poster graphics. You can download the governance model for SharePoint Server 2010 that's shown in Figure 8-7, along with supporting visualizations and text (for Visio or PDF version) from *www.microsoft.com/download/en/details.aspx?id=13594*.

There is also a zoomable version of the poster at *http://zoom.it/Zb4B*. Zoom.it is a free service from Microsoft for viewing and sharing high-resolution imagery. The combination of Microsoft's DeepZoom, Silverlight, and Azure technologies provide a great in-browser experience for viewing this normally wall-sized poster.

When web content is expected to be read by a large audience, the effect of the content's quality and compliance with guidelines are magnified. The payoff for care in creating and publishing the content is bigger when the audience is large. Intrinsically, there is an agreement between the publisher and the reader. By broadcasting your message wide and far, you are implying that your material is relevant and appropriate for everyone that the broadcast reaches.

SharePoint supplies a few tools that support a more thorough content creation process. Check-in and check-out help allow edits to be submitted with less conflict between versions. Similarly, revision history provides traceability regarding who added what, and when. And lastly, you can take advantage of minor versions for drafting content before publishing a major version that can be seen by the wider audience.

Personal Site Governance

Going to the other extreme, a personal site might defer all content addition decisions to the individual's discretion. When the permissions match the use, these types of guidelines can apply to good effect. For example, on a personal site where only one user has access, the same guidelines that apply to personal computer use might apply with slight adjustments, based on storage or network bandwidth needs. When you save a document to your computer's local storage, only you are affected by the reduction in available space for other new documents. On a SharePoint site, storage is most likely shared. One benefit in a shared space such as this is that storage space can be added without taking apart your personal computer. Another is that if your hard disk fails, your important documents stored online are safe.

INSIDE OUT   Behavior within your organization is governed by written and unwritten agreements with others; behavior on the web is no different in that respect

Many organizations new to SharePoint lack agreements on proper use. If web publishing is a new medium for communication within your organization, managing web content will involve many new experiences. Before you accept responsibility for a SharePoint site, take a minute to assess the agreements—formal or informal—that you've made about the site's use. If you don't have them already, can you find some agreements with others with little effort? For example, if you have permissions in SharePoint, you could create a new site of any type, including the blog site. A blog can be a great platform for sharing unique, individual viewpoints, including opinion. However, are all others in your organization willing and eager participants in the broad publication of your individual viewpoint? In many organizations, a brief discussion with a manager can help inform these types of governance decisions. Will your manager support, or even better, praise your content publishing efforts? A really good sign could be a performance goal around the type, quality, or quantity of your content creation efforts. Governance takes many forms, but agreed upon performance goals are one example of a method of encouraging content management agreement and compliance.

Search

Search presents opportunities to measure governance and highlight achievements of the shared community of electronic content. If you've agreed to present relevant, timely, and appropriate content to others, Search will help reveal how well you've delivered on those goals. Some website visitors find information through browsing the site, but many find what they need through Search. In addition to the standard search box and results page, SharePoint Search results can be exposed through Search Web Parts and in custom solutions. SharePoint sites that are shared publicly will also be crawled by public search engines such as Bing and Google. Your document, page, or list item title will be the most prominent wording displayed in search. If you have input on documented governance, you can include tips on creating good titles to help in the discovery of all the valuable web content in your organization's SharePoint sites.

Search can also expose items that previously were thought hidden from others. New discoveries in old content are common in initial implementations of SharePoint. Out of the box, SharePoint Foundation Search will provide search into the full contents of Office documents stored within a Site Collection. Extending SharePoint Foundation Search to the freely available Search Server Express extends the reach across all Site Collections, into network file shares and to non-SharePoint Foundation websites. While the results are trimmed according to SharePoint Security, incorrect application of security can result in exposing information that might not be appropriate for the full organization. For example, if your Social Security number is contained in documents uploaded to a SharePoint site, you want to ensure that those documents have the proper security settings. While document permissions are important beyond Search, probably no other tool within your organization will provide such broad discovery capability. To comply with corporate governance that likely includes privacy and other compliance required outside of your organization, review of content added to your sites is important. If you make it available to browse, it can be made available to search. And if it's available to search, all of the text within the content and even some graphics can be exposed to those with permissions to view the content.

INSIDE OUT   Use Search to validate your personal documents before sharing

To use Search to measure compliance of content that hasn't been exposed by it before, you can set up a test. Would you like to be able to search your files but you can't guarantee that the information is safe for everyone? You can create a site and break permission inheritance temporarily. After the documents in question are uploaded and the search engine has incorporated them into its index, you can safely search the documents without exposing the contents to everyone else. If over time you become comfortable sharing the whole site with more people, or if searching turns up documents that you would like to share before you become comfortable sharing the entire site, you can upload the individual documents that you're comfortable sharing to a site with broader permissions.

Search Alerts

Any account associated with an email address can be notified of new or changed keyword results through search alerts. To create a new alert, type your keywords into the search box and look for the link "create a search alert." Search alerts are a great tool for monitoring compliance when your governance agreements contain items that match a specific pattern.

For example, if you work for a company that develops and sells Windows Phone 7 Apps, you might add an alert for the keyword iPhone. When reviewing the information shared with that keyword, you might find content that's not appropriate for general consumption in your company. With the alert, you have access to the item's location and creator information. You could have the item removed or contact the creator of the item to discuss it.

Choosing a Content Manager

When you look at a freshly created, out-of-the-box webpage in SharePoint, can you tell who is responsible for updating the content? Knowing who authored the content gives you more security in the accuracy of the information. It also gives you someone to contact if you'd like to follow up on something you see that interests you. Identification could be grouped with governance, but it is worthwhile to identify the content manager of any given SharePoint site, regardless of the rules, policies, and organization-wide strategy in place. You care who the content manager is because you want quality information. Your audience cares for the same reason.

Identifying the Content Manager on the Page

On an internal website, you are more likely to know the owners of site content. To take advantage of your in-person social relationships, it can be very helpful to identify the site owner on most sites by name. This way, when you have a question about the site, not only can you look up the name and contact information easily if you are not close by, if you are close by, you can just walk over and talk to your colleague about an item that strikes you as interesting.

Here's one way to easily identify the content manager of a page by using a SharePoint Security Group and the Site Users Web Part:

1. Ensure that your content manager is in the group with Full Control of the Site.

   Often this is a group with the word "Owners" in it. For example, the Documents Owners group in the following example was created when a Site Collection called Documents was generated.

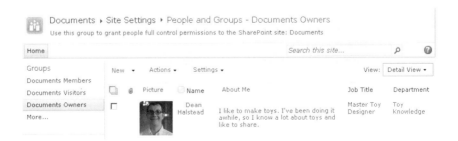

2. Modify the Security Group Settings to allow Everyone to see the membership of this group, as shown in the following illustration.

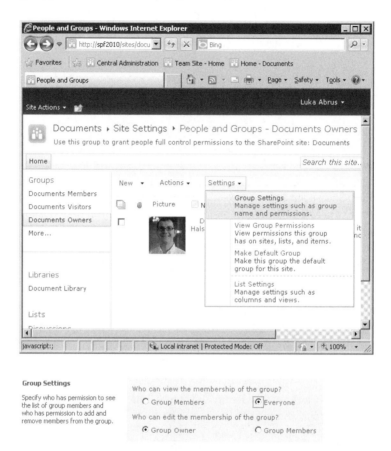

3. The Site Collection Administrators setting is a list of users that is not part of the standard SharePoint Security Groups. For this method, don't consider a user in the Site Collection Administrators list a content manger unless the user is also in a standard Security Group that also has full control. Occasionally, there might be a need for a user to belong to the Site Collection Administrators group, serving a support or auditing role that is not related to directly managing the content.

Chapter 13, "Managing Site Settings," includes more information on site permissions and Site Collection administration.

4.   Insert a Site Users Web Part on the Home page for the site.

Look in Chapter 6 "Creating and Formatting Webpages" for more detail about editing a wiki page to make it the Home page of the site.

5.   Edit the Site Users Web Part. Select the Show People In The Group option, and then browse for the SharePoint Security Group With Full Control that contains your content manager or managers. Modify the Web Part title to something appropriate such as **Site Owners** or **Content Managers**.

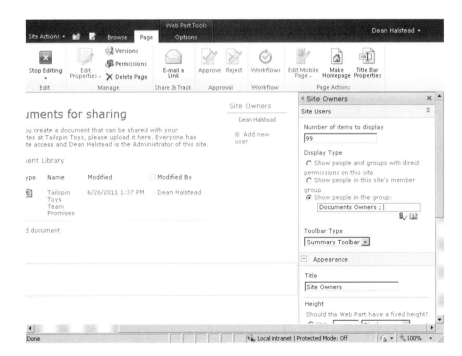

6. The site owner's name links through to the User Information display page, shown in the following screen shot, with contact and biographical information. When the membership of the SharePoint Security Group With Full Control is modified, the name and link will change on the page, keeping all the viewers of the page up to date on the content manager for this site.

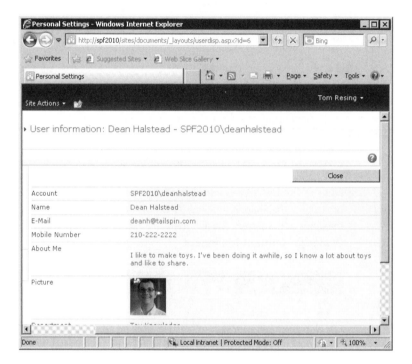

TROUBLESHOOTING

Standard users can't see the members of the Site Owners group.

If a user viewing a site you control sees the message in the Site Users Web Part shown in the following screen shot, review step 2 to ensure that it was completed successfully.

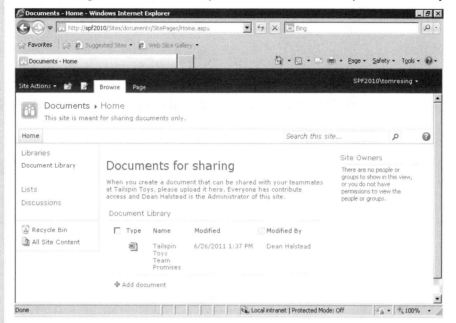

When logged in as a user in the same SharePoint Security Group that has Full Control, you will not see the message shown in the preceding screen shot, so this is something that is good to check with a less-privileged test user account.

Managing Content for Internet Sites

Special consideration must be taken when managing site content to be shared with the general public. The techniques you've learned for editing lists, pages, and Web Parts in previous chapters apply equally well to public and internal sites. However, if you are managing content with SharePoint Foundation for Internet sites, take into consideration the information presented in the sections that follow.

Tight Governance for Public Messaging

Generally speaking, the governance for this type of website will be tightly controlled because of the potential impact on the organization. In smaller organizations, content publishing might be handled directly by the person who is responsible for the public image of the organization. In many large organizations, an entire group is dedicated to publishing any content published for public consumption. As an example of tighter governance on content management, a public website is one case for which you most likely will not be putting the All Authenticated Users Active Directory group in the Contributors SharePoint Security Group. While contributions might be more limited than on an internal site, a public site uniquely grants broad viewing permissions to another set of users—unauthenticated, or anonymous users. A discussion of managing site content for anonymous users follows later in this chapter.

Separate Content by Audience

Separation of public site content from internal sites is common. The level of separation is dependent mostly on your tolerance for risk of intrusion or mixing of content. To start with, consider restricting the different types of content to separate Site Collections and web applications. Both Site Collections and web applications can provide unique administrative permissions and control, and two web applications require two content databases. However, it is not uncommon for security requirements to push organizations to keep some content types isolated at the SharePoint farm level. At the furthest extreme is separating the content out to farms both on both physically and logically separated networks.

Review Chapter 2, "Administration for Business Users," for more details on SharePoint farms, servers, content databases, and security.

At whatever level you choose to separate your content, keep in mind that it is important to treat the site that allows anonymous access as inherently more risky for intrusion by unwanted visitors. More risky than internal anonymous sites are those that allow anonymous, public access. One example of public website intrusion is automated spambots. A vigilant website manager will quickly detect and remove spam content. An even more proactive approach can keep the likelihood of unwanted content low, and one such approach is detailed in the next section.

Prevent Comment Spam

An unwelcome addition to a public site that doesn't necessarily require compromising server security is comment spam. If your public website includes a blog, you might start to find spam in your comments list when your site becomes popular. To reduce spam, you can add a field to your list to trip up the automated spam techniques. An effective field is one that is easy for your blog readers to understand but hard for an automated spambot to interpret. One example is asking for the name of the site. Just the addition of the field, which will prompt the user for the correct entry when entering a comment, can defeat some spam attacks. On top of adding a field, a standard manual method for preventing spam messages from view by the public is to turn on content approval for the list.

INSIDE OUT   Adding one extra column to your list can prevent spam

Sometimes, even the smallest change can make a big difference in managing site content. In the case of a public blog site, an open comments list invites spam. Enabling content approval in the list settings is a great first step. However, adding even one required field to the comment list can reduce the amount of spam comments you have to remove or disapprove. Figure 8-8 shows the additional field on the comments section of a blog post page. In this example, the blog author asks for the commenter to repeat the author's name as proof that the commenter is a real person and not an automated attempt to take advantage of your site.

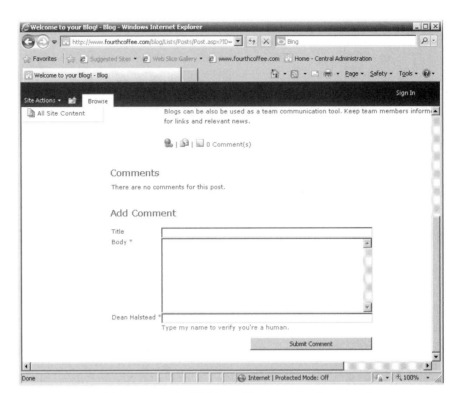

Figure 8-8 Just adding one required field to a blog comment form can deter spammers.

You Can License SharePoint Foundation for Public Use

While lacking the Publishing Features of SharePoint Server, SharePoint Foundation is a valid choice for Internet sites. The proper licensing of SharePoint Foundation depends on the proper licensing of Windows Server. Windows Web Server 2008 R2 is designed to be used as an Internet-facing server and is a low cost option for hosting a public site on SharePoint Foundation. Another good option is adding an External Connector License for Windows Server Standard. An External Connector License allows unlimited external users.

Microsoft TechNet has large sections on logical architecture planning for both SharePoint Foundation and SharePoint Server. However, only the SharePoint Server section includes the chapter "Design sample: Corporate deployment," which is located at *http://technet.microsoft. com/en-us/library/cc261995.aspx*. This chapter includes many helpful tips on public Internet site design. Many of the suggestions, like the uses of the Publishing Features, only apply to SharePoint Server and might help inform your decision regarding whether you would like to license SharePoint Server for Internet sites.

Anonymous Permissions on Four Levels

For a public site, you generally don't want to require all visitors to log on to view the content. If you don't want an authentication prompt to appear, you want to enable anonymous access. Enabling anonymous access is at the least a two part process that requires one change at the Web Application Zone level and one change at the site level. Additionally, there are options to set anonymous access for lists, libraries, and individual items.

Enabling Anonymous Access in Central Administration

You might be asking an IT professional to make this change for you, but the check box that needs to be selected is shown in Figure 8-9. This check box is found on the Edit Authentication Providers dialog box for the Web Application Settings in Central Administration. Selecting the Enable Anonymous Access option in Central Administration is a required preliminary step toward enabling anonymous access on each individual Site Collection in the web application. If you don't see the anonymous settings described in the sections that follow, it is likely this check box has not been selected for the Web Application Zone with which you are working.

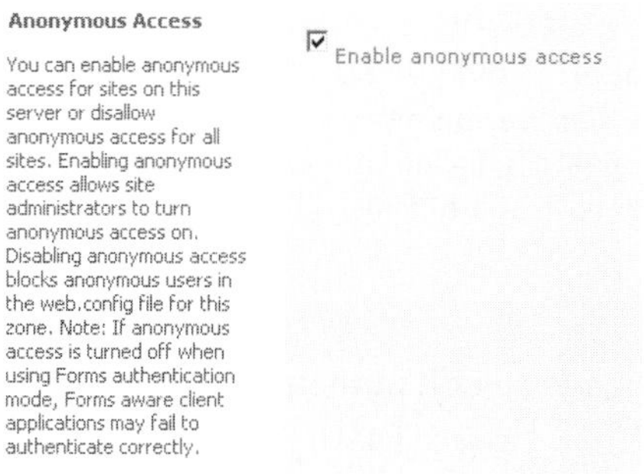

Anonymous Access

You can enable anonymous access for sites on this server or disallow anonymous access for all sites. Enabling anonymous access allows site administrators to turn anonymous access on. Disabling anonymous access blocks anonymous users in the web.config file for this zone. Note: If anonymous access is turned off when using Forms authentication mode, Forms aware client applications may fail to authenticate correctly.

☑ Enable anonymous access

Figure 8-9 The Enable Anonymous Access check box must be selected before Site Collection administrators can enable anonymous access for Site Collections in this web application zone.

Tip

For your IT professional administrators: the name of the zone is the link to the Edit Dialog. Figure 8-10 shows the zone selection dialog for Authentication Providers from the Central Administration Site. You might never view Central Administration, but when your IT staff accesses the dialog the first time, it can be easy to miss the link. The administrator must know to click the hyperlink over the name of the zone to open the Edit dialog for that zone.

Figure 8-10 In this example, Default is the name of the zone and the link to the Edit dialog.

If you want a refresher, Chapter 2 covers SharePoint architecture naming conventions, such as what a farm is, what a web application is, and how sites fit in Site Collections. Also, you can visit Microsoft TechNet's "Plan authentication methods" at *http://technet.microsoft.com/ en-us/library/cc262350.aspx* for more details, including planning web application zones and an explanation of web application zones in SharePoint.

INSIDE OUT   An alternate route to edit authentication providers

In some cases, your IT staff might find that the Authentication Providers button on the Web Applications ribbon is disabled for some user accounts in the Farm Administrators Group (see Figure 8-11). If this is the case in your farm, the Edit Authentication screen can be accessed through an alternate route. The Security Page in Central Administration has a link titled Specify Authentication Providers in the General Security section. Clicking Specify Authentication Providers, a user in the Farm Administrators Group will see a page similar to the zone selection dialog in Figure 8-10.

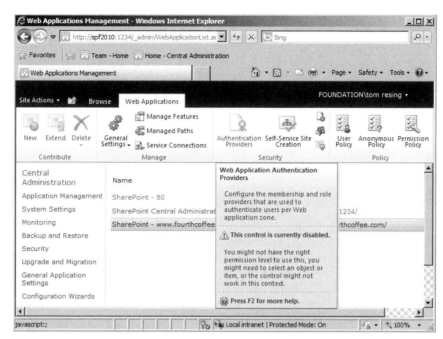

Figure 8-11 The Authentication Providers button might be disabled for some farm administrators.

Enabling Anonymous Access in Site Settings

After Anonymous Access has been enabled for the web application, site administrators will see a new option on the Site Permissions page ribbon, as shown in Figure 8-12. The quickest way to access the Site Permissions page is via the Site Actions menu, as shown in Figure 8-13. Site Permissions is also easily accessible from the Users And Permissions section of the Site Settings page for any site by a user with Full Control of the site.

Figure 8-12 The Anonymous Access button is highlighted in this example from a Site Permissions page.

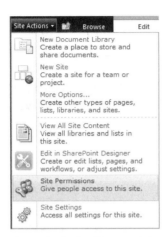

Figure 8-13 The Site Permissions page provides a link to the Anonymous Access Settings.

From the Anonymous Access dialog (see Figure 8-14), you can choose to expose the entire website or individual pieces of the site. Selecting the Entire Web Site option is the best option for publishing a public website if you want it to be available without specifying a list or library path. The next section explains the difference in more detail.

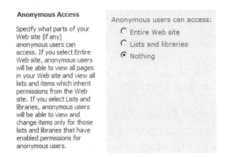

Figure 8-14 You have two anonymous access options at the site level: Entire Web Site and Lists And Libraries.

> **Note**
>
> If you select the Lists And Libraries option, all users viewing your site will be prompted for authentication unless navigating directly to a list, library, or individual item that has been configured for anonymous access. Follow the steps in the section "Enabling Anonymous Access in List or Library Settings," later in this chapter, to allow anonymous visitors to view a list or library.

How Anonymous Access Level Affects the Home Page Redirect

When Anonymous User Can Access Lists And libraries is selected at the site level, anony-mous users cannot access the root of the site directly. Figure 8-15 illustrates the steps that happen when an anonymous user does attempt to reach the root of the site. The user might start by typing **http://www.fourthcoffee.com** in the address bar of a browser. Brows-ing to the site by that root address will result in a redirect to the home page of the site. Without the Wiki home page feature enabled, the home page is default.aspx, so the anony-mous user's end location would be *http://www.fourthcoffee.com/default.aspx*, if allowed. When anonymous access for the entire web site is enabled, the redirect to the default.aspx home page will occur without issue. However, when you choose the Lists And Libraries option (see Figure 8-14), the redirection becomes an issue. Without access to the entire website, an authentication prompt will appear on the redirection. The user will receive an access denied message unless valid credentials are entered in the prompt (Figure 8-15).

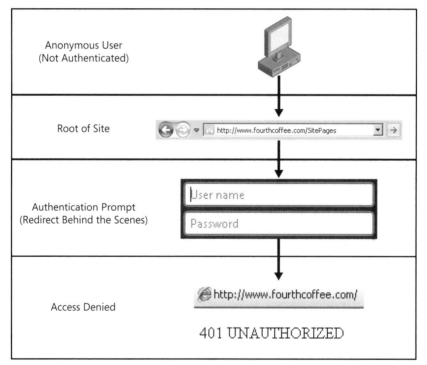

Figure 8-15 A user is denied at the site root when Anonymous Access is not set to Entire Web Site.

Figure 8-16 illustrates the alternative situation, wherein anonymous users do success-fully view a page when Anonymous User Can Access Lists And Libraries is selected at the site level. Anonymous access can be granted to the library named SitePages. When it is, a public user could successfully browse to *http://www.fourthcoffee.com/SitePages* without a prompt. In this case, the document library allows anonymous viewing and the redirection to the Wiki home page is allowed. Granting anonymous access to lists and libraries is demonstrated in the next section of this chapter.

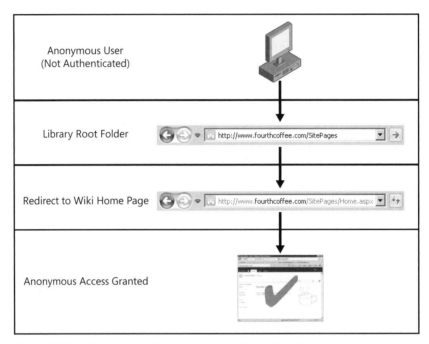

Figure 8-16 An Anonymous User can access a library directly.

Chapter 6 includes more information about wiki pages and the Wiki Pages library.

Enabling Anonymous Access in List or Library Settings

Figure 8-17 shows the ribbon for the Library Permissions page for the document library named Site Pages on an example site at the address *www.fourthcoffee.com*. To allow anonymous access to the library, on the ribbon, you must first click the Stop Inheriting Permissions button.

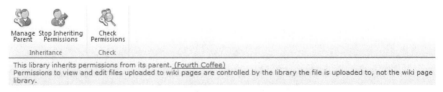

Figure 8-17 By default, all lists and libraries inherit permissions from the site level, including anonymous access.

After the inheritance chain has been broken for a list or library, an Anonymous Access button appears on the Library Settings page ribbon that is almost identical to the button in Figure 8-13 from the Site Permissions page. In a document library, your only option is to allow viewing of items, as shown in Figure 8-18.

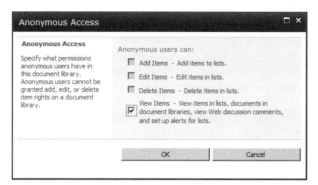

Figure 8-18 The Anonymous Access dialog box for a document library has one check box selected for View Items.

After you allow anonymous users the View Items Access level, items in the library (in this example, pages in a Wiki Page library) will be accessible to the public when accessed directly. Individual items might also be visible through the list or library root address, which redirects to the default view. The behavior in this base level of the product is in contrast to that of SharePoint Server with Publishing. For SharePoint Server with Publishing, the default view would not be publicly accessible. Anonymous access will be blocked by the Lockdown Feature described in the Inside Out Sidebar "A missing feature you might not miss."

> **Note**
> The steps are similar if you are enabling anonymous access on a list rather than a library. However, in the case of a list, you would be going to the List Permissions page rather than the Library Permissions page.

INSIDE OUT   A missing feature you might not miss

One difference between SharePoint Foundation 2010 and SharePoint Server 2010 is the Lockdown feature that affects anonymous use. The Lockdown feature is activated by default on Publishing sites in SharePoint Server. When this feature is activated, anonymous viewers of a site are prompted for authentication when they attempt to access pages like the All Items view of a list. You might not even miss this feature. For example, it's often deactivated on sites that use the Blog Site template because it prevents anonymous users from adding comments to blog posts.

On SharePoint Foundation sites, you can be secure on public sites despite missing the Lockdown feature by keeping one concept in mind: anonymous users do have Read access to all lists and items, which inherit permissions from the website when you choose the Entire Web Site option displayed in Figure 8-14. If you would like to hide a list or item from anonymous viewers in SharePoint Foundation, you have an option without the Lockdown feature. When you break inheritance on permissions, you can choose to remove the View Items permission for anonymous users as described in the next section.

Breaking Inheritance on a List Item to Prevent Anonymous Access

Unlike for sites and lists, the settings for List Item Permissions do not contain an Anonymous Access. Instead, when you break inheritance at the list item level for a list that has anonymous access allowed, the item you broke inheritance for does not allow anonymous access. Figures 8-19 and 8-20 show an example of the same list, named Contacts, first viewed by an authenticated user and then by an anonymous user. Because inheritance is broken on the item for Tom Resing, both items show in the first screen shot but not the second.

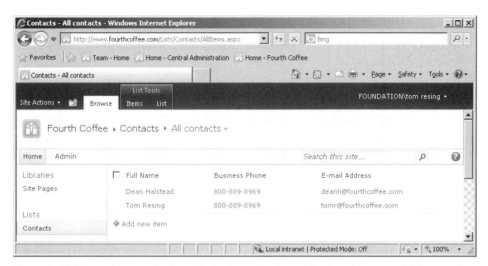

Figure 8-19 When the user viewing this site is authenticated, both contacts are visible.

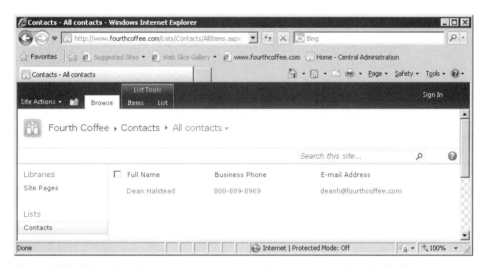

Figure 8-20 When viewed as an anonymous user, only one contact shows in the list.

INSIDE OUT
Enabling Themes for anonymous users with SharePoint Designer

By default, Themes will only be visible to authenticated visitors to your site. If you'd like anonymous users to see a theme you've selected, you can add the cascading style sheet (CSS) links to your default master page through SharePoint Designer. Viewing the source generated for an authenticated user, search for the tags with .css in them. Copy those link tags to the source code of your default master page by using SharePoint Designer. Be sure to remove the CSS Tag that already exists in the master page.

Review Chapter 6 for more details on applying and customizing Themes and working with master pages.

Summary

From one perspective, almost any act of creation, deletion, or editing on a SharePoint site can be seen as a part of managing site content. The area of management covered specifically by this chapter is the more strategic, higher-level approach to all of those other pieces of site interaction you learn about in detail in the other chapters of this book.

In this chapter, you learned how identifying the purpose of your site is critical to effectively planning its architecture. You learned how to safely experiment with all the SharePoint tools that you've learned about already and will continue to learn about throughout the rest of the book. Visualizations of site content are useful not just at the beginning of a new site content project. You can revisit and refactor your site's layout and organization at any point in time. When the users of your site could benefit from better organization, look to prototypes, wireframe diagrams, storyboards, and card sorting to help put the pieces in place.

Governance is a hot topic these days in many organizations using or planning to use SharePoint. SharePoint has fulfilled Microsoft's vision and empowered the members of the organizations who have implemented it. In many organizations—maybe in yours—SharePoint users have been creating and filling SharePoint sites for years. With so much content sprawl, the shared principles of fellow users must now be considered if they weren't at the initial implementation of the product. Thus, you learned what governance is and how you and your organization can benefit from it. You learned some governance strategies for different types of site audiences and taking advantage of search for governance.

By all means, use the wealth of references presented in this chapter to follow up on the topic of governance. Take advantage of the excellent free electronic books and posters that Microsoft has published on the Internet on the topics of planning and governance. Microsoft has learned from its customers, partners, and its internal implementations of SharePoint. If you've looked for information on governance published for previous versions of SharePoint, you wouldn't have found the breadth of resources available now. Microsoft has produced quality information that will help any organization to more effectively harness the spread of information across SharePoint sites.

Managing content for Internet sites is a practical example of IA and governance. SharePoint is an effective tool for creating a public Internet presence for your organization. However, when you open the doors of your site to the general public, make sure that the proper controls are in place. Like any public space, proper manners are common, but vandalism can happen. Use the anonymous permissions settings to open your site at the right level. Consider the availability of SharePoint Server which has specific features for publishing information to broad audiences. As you'll find throughout this book, SharePoint Foundation often is a starting point. Once your needs go beyond the basics for Internet sites available in this edition of the product, you might find your sites benefitting from the additional features of the next step up in the product, SharePoint Server.

As you read the remaining chapters of this book, you will pick up even more advanced ways you can interact with the content of your sites. Using what you learn, you will extend sites and customize them to meet your needs and the needs of the consumers of your sites. Whether you are adding content from external data sources or adding automated workflows to content creation, keep in mind the content management strategies and tools introduced in this chapter. Plan, create, and seek agreement for your site content's use with your fellow participants in your organization's SharePoint implementation.

T RADITIONALLY, Microsoft SharePoint stores data in lists and libraries; however, most organizations do not want to move all their data into SharePoint—nor should they. Most organizations have spent time and money to build or purchase specialized systems, such as Siebel, CRM, and SAP to assist with key business processes. Understandably, it makes sense to integrate the data from those external systems into SharePoint sites and applications, such as Microsoft Outlook 2010, Microsoft Access 2010 and Microsoft Workspace 2010 with an easy-to-use interface.

Using SharePoint Designer 2007 and Windows SharePoint Services 3.0, it was possible to connect to external content by using the Data Source Library task pane. This method is still available with SharePoint Designer 2010 and SharePoint Foundation 2010, but it is now known as the Data Sources gallery. However, in addition to this method of connecting to external content, in SharePoint Foundation, you can now use an enhanced version of functionality that was originally available only with the Enterprise Edition of Microsoft Office SharePoint Server 2007. It was then called the Business Data Catalog; now it is exposed as a service application called the Business Connectivity Service (BCS).

The BCS centrally stores the definition of the external content—both its location, the type of data it is, and the behavior of the data when it is integrated into SharePoint and Microsoft Office client applications—in the Business Data Connectivity (BDC) metadata store. The definition of the external content is known as the external content type (ECT). The definition of the location of the external system together with the ECT is known as the BDC model. Once an ECT is defined, then by using the browser or SharePoint Designer, you can manipulate the data from the external system similarly to other SharePoint objects, such as lists and Web Parts via a new list type to SharePoint Foundation, called the External list.

In this chapter, you will learn how to use the Data Source gallery and the BCS. You will also look at the differences between the two methods. You will look at the architecture of the BCS, including the security options. Then, you will look at managing the data connections and how to expose the data from the external systems on webpages and in lists and libraries. Finally, you will learn how use Microsoft Visual Studio 2010 with BCS.

Using SharePoint Designer with External Content

Using Microsoft FrontPage 2003, and then later SharePoint Designer, it has always been possible to connect and present data from several types of external data sources. For each site, you can specify the location and connection query to external data sources. For example, in SharePoint Designer, open the site in which you want to present the data, and then in the Navigation pane, click Data Sources. The Data Sources gallery appears in the SharePoint Designer workspace, as shown in Figure 9-1, where each data source is grouped by data source type.

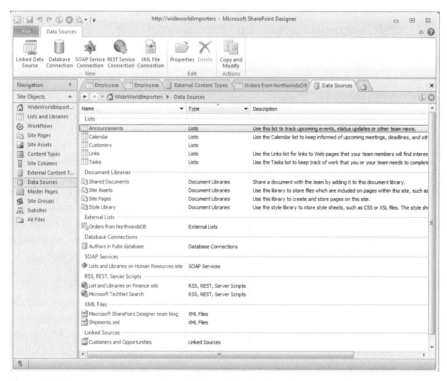

Figure 9-1 Data source connections displayed in the Data Sources gallery.

Table 9-1 describes the variety of data sources that can be used by SharePoint Designer to connect to external content.

Table 9-1 **Data Source Types**

Data source types	Description
SharePoint lists and libraries	Every list and library is automatically listed in the Data Source gallery. Those lists and libraries that have the hidden property enabled are not shown. Therefore, libraries, such as the Master Page gallery, List Template gallery, the Theme gallery, and the Web Part gallery are not displayed in the Data Sources gallery.
External lists	Although you cannot create External lists from the Data Sources gallery, External lists are displayed in the gallery. More information on External lists and ECTs is provided later in this chapter.
Database connections	When you first open the Data Source gallery, there are no connections to any databases. You can create connections to a variety of databases that reside on Microsoft SQL Server 2000 or later version, or to any data source that uses the OLE DB protocols, such as MySQL. You can create multiple data sources to the same database, each using a different table, view, or query.
SOAP services	A SOAP service is a special site that can return XML in response to a procedural query. SharePoint itself exposes its data as a SOAP service, with which you can create, for example, a list of announcements from the current site and its child sites, known as a rollup of announcements.
REST services	Similar to SOAP services, where data can be retrieved from a data source as XML data.
RSS and server-side scripts	You can connect to server-side scripts that return XML data; for example, a Really Simple Syndication (RSS) feed might use a server-side script. Such RSS feeds have a URL ending in .aspx or .php. When an RSS feed has a URL ending in .xml or .ashx, use the XML file data connection method. You can connect to server-side scripts written in a variety of languages, including Microsoft ASP, Microsoft ASP.NET, PHP, and Asynchronous JavaScript and XML (Ajax).
XML files	SharePoint Designer interrogates the root of your current site and the Site Assets library for any XML files it might contain. You can also import an XML file into your site or refer to an XML file in another library or on another site by using the XML File Connection command.
Linked sources	Many data sources contain related data. You can use this data source group to combine two or more data sources into one source.

Chapter 9

To create a new data source definition, either click in the Data Source gallery or click the icon to the left of an existing data source to activate the commands on the Data Sources ribbon tab. Then click the appropriate data source type in the New group to display the Data Source Properties dialog box, as shown in Figure 9-2.

Figure 9-2 Use the Data Source Properties dialog box to define the location and data that you want to be returned from the external system.

This dialog box can contain up to three tabs:

- **General**   Use this tab to give the data source definition a meaningful name. Share-Point Designer creates a name for the data source definition if you do not provide one.

- **Source**   This tab contains different options, depending on the data source type. For the database connections data source type, the Source tab contains one button, the Configure Database Connection, which when clicked opens the Configure Database Connection Wizard, in which you specify the server where the database is located, the provider name, and credentials that will be used to access the database. Alternatively, you can provide your own custom connection string. If you are not connecting to an SQL server, then the second page of the wizard allows you to select the table or view or specify custom Select, Update, Insert, and Delete commands using SQL or stored procedures.

- **Login** Use this tab to define the authentication method by which you connect to the external system. The Login tab on the Data Source Properties dialog box for the Database Connection data source is not displayed; however, you are asked which authentication method you want to use once you click the Configure Database Connection button. You need to consider carefully the authentication method used to connect to the external systems, because this has security and infrastructure implications. The three methods that you can use with most data source definitions are:

  — **Don't Attempt To Authenticate** This is equivalent to anonymous access.

  — **Save This Username And Password In The Data Connection** The user name and password is transmitted over the network in clear text. An attacker can possibly compromise this authentication option. You should ensure that your infrastructure is configured appropriately for the sensitivity of the external content, for example, by using Kerberos, Secure Sockets Layer (SSL), or Internet Protocol Security (IPsec).

  — **Use Windows Authentication** The user's authentication information is passed by SharePoint to the external system. This mode always incurs a double hop unless SharePoint Foundation 2010 and the external system are installed on the same server, which usually only occurs in small organizations or in larger organizations in a development, prototyping, or demonstration environment. Then, the user's identity has to make only the one hop from the user's computer to the SharePoint server. In most installations, when the external system and SharePoint Foundation are installed on different servers, SharePoint cannot pass the user's identity to the external system (the second hop). The workaround is to use Kerberos or SSL with this authentication method.

For more information about the double-hop issue, go to *http://blogs.msdn.com/b/ knowledgecast/archive/2007/01/31/the-double-hop-problem.aspx.*

Chapter 9

INSIDE OUT   Where are the data source definitions stored?

The details of the data source definitions that you create are stored in Universal Data Connection (UDC) version 1 file format in XML files in a hidden library, fpdatasources, in the _catalog folder. Users who can see the hidden URL site structure when using SharePoint Designer can view this library and the _catalog folder. SharePoint Designer creates the fpdatasources library when the first data source definition for a site is created. For the data source definitions that are dynamically created for lists, libraries, and XML files that are in the root of the site or in the Site Assets library, no XML file will exist. However, if you copy one of these automatic data source definitions, then an XML file will be created. You can copy a data source definition by using the Copy And Modify command in the Actions group of the Data Sources ribbon tab.

Once the external content connection is defined in the Data Source gallery, then these definitions can be used with the Data Form Web Parts to display the content. When a Data Form Web Part is used to display the external data, a copy of the data source definitions are placed into the Data Form Web Part's XSLT code. If you update the definition in the Data Source gallery, the definition stored in the Data Form Web Part is not updated.

For more information about the Data Form Web Part, see Chapter 7, "Adding, Editing, Connecting, and Managing Web Parts on the Page." You can find more information about how to use the Data Source gallery in the book, *Microsoft SharePoint Designer 2010 Step by Step*, by Penelope Coventry (Microsoft Press).

Using the BCS

The BCS is implemented as a service application. This allows you to create external system definitions once, and not only share those definitions to many sites within the same Site Collection or SharePoint web application, but to share those definitions with more than one web application. In addition, a SharePoint farm—a SharePoint installation that is installed on one or more servers that share the same SharePoint configuration database—can host more than one BCS; each one can be configured independently by different sets of administrators. Also, a BCS on one SharePoint farm, and therefore the external system definitions stored in that farm, can be referenced from another SharePoint farm so that access to external systems can be managed centrally but are consumed from SharePoint installations hosted in other locations. A BCS can also be partitioned in a multi-tenancy configuration, which is the term commonly used to describe the isolation of websites in a hosting environment.

INSIDE OUT   Service applications

In SharePoint Foundation, you can create only one type of service application. In SharePoint Server 2010, many service applications are provided such as the Managed Metadata Service (MMS), Access Services, Visio Graphics Service, and Secure Store Service (SSS).

The BCS can be divided into four areas:

- **The External System**   This is where the external content resides. It can be maintained by one of your organization's business critical applications often known as Line-of-Business (LOB) applications. They might have a custom user interface or a programmable interface, such as a Windows Communication Framework (WCF) service, web 2.0 source or as a database. Before using BCS, you should explore the external system to which you want to connect and evaluate the best method of connecting to that system. Check with creators of the external system as to the methods available to access the content. If there is more than one method, then ask which is the best option for you. In many cases, the web services method is the best; for example, if you can obtain the external content from the external system by either directly interrogating the database or by using web services, choose web services. If you have an external system that does not have a compatible interface, then you could develop your own BCS connectors or expose the content as a web service. The Microsoft BCS team has a two-part blog called "Making Web Services BCS Friendly." The first part of the series can be found at *http://blogs.msdn.com/b/bcs/ archive/2009/11/18/making-web-services-bcs-friendly-part-1.aspx.*

- **Connectivity**   Before SharePoint can access the content from an external system, the definition on how to connect to it and the authentication method used must be created. This is the BDC model. The BDC model consists of declaration XML that describes the external system that you want to access as well as the operations you might like to perform on this external content; for example, read a list of data, or read one item (row) of data, or update one item (row) of data. The BDC model can be created on a development or test SharePoint installation, from which it can be downloaded and imported into the SharePoint production farm where it resides in the BDC metadata store, or it can be used by Microsoft Office applications. The BDC model can be used in a SharePoint installation to create ECTs, also known as *entities*. However, in a SharePoint 2010 installation, before you can create or upload a BDC model, you must first create the BDC service application. Office 2010 applications only contain the components that allow you to upload a BDC model, and thus, there is no management or configuration interface provided.

- **Presentation**   This is the client-side consumer of the external content, such as an Office 2010 application, or if you are using SharePoint, it could be an External list created from the ECT.

- **Tools**   Microsoft provides two tools to create the BDC model, to interact with the BCS program interfaces, and manipulate the BDC objects. These are Microsoft Share-Point Designer 2010 and Visual Studio 2010. There are other third-party tools that can help ECT designers such as BCS Meta Man, which you can find at *http://lightning-tools.com.* You can also use an XML editor such as XML Notepad 2007 or Notepad to create a BDC Model.

Figure 9-3 shows the high-level interaction between these four areas. Notice the symmetry; the BCS architect is the same for Office 2010 applications as it is in a SharePoint installation. However, the Office 2010 applications do not have a BDC metadata store. In its place they have a BDC client-side cache so that when content in an External list is taken offline, the BDC model is taken from the BDC metadata store on the server and stored in the BDC client-side cache. The offline content from the External list is also stored in the client-side cache, which uses a SQL Compact Edition client database so that the offline external content and the BDC model is persisted when the user's computer is shutdown.

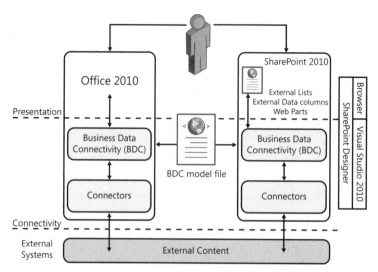

Figure 9-3 The components of the BCS.

Also, note in Figure 9-3 that the Office 2010 applications also have their own connectors; therefore, when a user switches to online mode, the Office application connects directly to the external content without connecting through SharePoint. Other Office 2010 applications such as Access 2010 can import a client-side version of the BDC model, and therefore in this scenario, Access 2010 does not need to connect to SharePoint at all; it would connect directly to the external system.

INSIDE OUT   Taking external data offline

To take the external data offline, additional logic is required. This logic is provided by a Visual Studio Tools for Office (VSTO) ClickOnce deployment package, which is only provided with the Enterprise Edition of SharePoint Server 2010. Therefore, with SharePoint Foundation you cannot take External list data offline in Outlook 2010 or SharePoint Workspace 2010. You can find more information about deploying Office solutions at *http://msdn.microsoft.com/en-us/library/bb386179.aspx*.

The advantage of using BCS as opposed to the Data Source gallery in SharePoint Designer is that you only need to define the external system and ECT once; you can then use that ECT on many sites across all web applications that are associated with the BDC service application. The disadvantage is that ECT designers must be given edit permissions to the metadata store, which is a high level of security, whereas with the Data Source gallery you only need to be, for example, a site owner. In addition, other BCS security settings are needed to allow users to access the external content that can only be set by using the SharePoint 2010 Central Administration website or Windows PowerShell. This results in a level of collaboration between the ECT designers and the SharePoint farm administrators, which in large organizations is typically two different people.

To connect and retrieve data from an external system with SharePoint Foundation, complete the following tasks:

1. Create a BDC service application and set permissions on the BDC metadata store to allow for the creation of the BDC model, external system definitions, and ECTs.

2. Define the external system connection.

3. Define the operations to create, read, update, and delete (CRUD) content stored in that external system as appropriate to your business requirements.

4. Create an ECT based on an external system definition.

5. Configure the permissions on the ECT so that users can see content from the external system.

6. Use the ECT to present the data from the external data source as External lists, an external data column, Web Parts, or from within an Office application.

Creating a BDC Service Application

You can use the SharePoint 2010 Farm Configuration Wizard, the SharePoint 2010 Central Administration website, or Windows PowerShell to create a BDC service application. Using the SharePoint 2010 Central Administration website or Windows PowerShell, you can specify the SQL server database name or use a preconfigured database name. When you use the configuration wizard an automatically generated BDC database name is created.

When using the SharePoint 2010 Central Administration website or Windows PowerShell, first check that at least one BDC machine service instance is started on one of the servers in your SharePoint farm. The machine service instance—also known as the SharePoint service—uses the service binaries to manage components such as any related timer jobs to make the service application function correctly. If you have more than one server in your SharePoint farm, then the machine instance can be started on one or more of your servers; SharePoint then provides its own round-robin load-balancing mechanism to evenly distribute user requests for data from the external systems.

Once a machine service instance is started, you can then create the BDC service application. This allows you to manage and create the definitions for the external systems. When the BDC service machine instance is started and its associated service application is created, an Internet Information Service (IIS) Virtual Application is created that runs in the context of an

IIS application pool within the SharePoint Web Services IIS website. It exposes a WCF web service, also known as the service application endpoint, as shown in Figure 9-4. This is used by SharePoint itself and can be used by your organization to develop new solutions. Such an endpoint is created by SharePoint on each server on which the machine service instance is started.

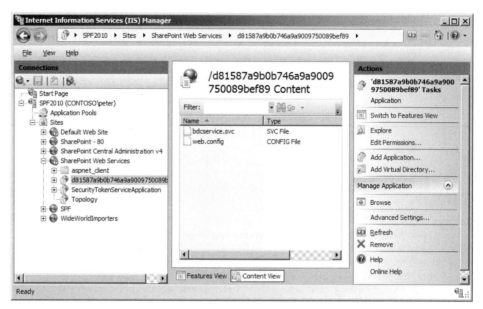

Figure 9-4 The BDC service application endpoint created within the SharePoint Web Services IIS website.

Once the BDC service application is started, in the Central Administration website on the Service Applications page, below the BDC service application, you see a BDC service application proxy, also known as the service connection (see Figure 9-5). This provides the connection between the components, such as webpages that want to access the data from the external systems and the BDC service application. The service application proxy also understands the load-balancing mechanism that SharePoint uses, and if you publish a BDC service application for use on other farms, then the service application proxy will be used for managing those connections, as well.

Figure 9-5 The BDC service application and the BDC service application proxy.

The BDC service application contains two interfaces:

- **BDC Administration**   This is used to manage the metadata store; therefore, this is the interface that is used when you use the SharePoint 2010 Central Administration website to upload the BDC model or when you use SharePoint Designer to create the definitions for the external system and the ECT. BDC Administration is also used by the External Data Picker when you create an external data column on a list or library.

- **BDC Server Runtime**   This is used to create, update, display, or edit the external content. External content is not saved in the BCS database. Instead, it is retrieved by the BDC server runtime by using bulk load routines when the content is needed. For example, if a user clicks a link to an External list, then this interface is used to populate the default view of the External list. Before the BDC runtime can populate the default view, it must first call the BDC Administration interface to find the location and format of the data from the BDC model so that it can call the appropriate connector, which is the component that obtains the external data. Calls to the BDC runtime result in network traffic between the SharePoint server that is servicing the user's request and the external system. The data is then passed from the SharePoint Server over the network to the user's computer. The BDC runtime, whether it is a component in an Office 2010 application or SharePoint 2010, uses the same connectors, and therefore, the Office 2010 applications do not need a connection with SharePoint to access the external data.

Chapter 9

When using the SharePoint 2010 Central Administration website, use the following steps to create a BDC service application:

1. Open a browser, and then go to the SharePoint 2010 Central Administration website.

2. Under System Settings, click Manage Services On Server.

3. Ensure that the server on which you want to start the service is selected in the Server drop-down list, and then in the Action column, click Start for the Business Data Connectivity Service, if it is not already started, as shown here.

4. In the left navigation pane, click Application Management, and then under Service Applications, click Manage Service Application.

5. On the Service Applications tab, click New in the Create group, and then click Business Data Connective Service.

6. On the Create New Business Data Connectivity Service Application page, type the name of the service application, the database server, the database name, the authentication method, and user name and password if appropriate, as shown in the illustration that follows.

   You can also specify a failover server if you are using SQL Server database mirroring as well as creating or using an existing application pool. Application pools created for service applications can only be used by other service applications; they cannot be used as application pools for web applications.

Web applications are linked to service applications through an application proxy group. When you create a new application, proxy it is placed in the default application proxy group. When you create a new web application, you can choose to use the default application proxy group or choose your own custom set of service applications. To change the set of service applications to which a web application is connected, use the Configure Service Application Associations under Service Applications on the Application Management page of the Central Administration website.

Configuring BDC Metadata Store Permissions

Once you have created the BDC service application, the next task you should complete is to set the permissions on the metadata store and the actions that the user or group or claim has, as shown in Table 9-2.

Table 9-2 **BDC Metadata Store Permissions**

Permission	Description
Edit	Use to allow users to create and modify BDC models, external system definitions, and ECTs. Only allow highly trusted users with this permission, especially in a production environment. Users with this permission can see external system definitions created by other users, and therefore, this can be a security risk, whereby a malicious user can exploit the security information in the external system definition to access and corrupt external content and adversely affect the running of the SharePoint installation. When you upload a BDC model from a development environment into a production environment with its security settings, remove the edit permissions from the BDC model for those users who created it in the development environment. If you do not have a development or prototype environment, you will need to give edit permission on the BDC model to users who create external system definitions and ECTs via either SharePoint Designer or Visual Studio.
Execute	There is no execute or selectable in Clients permission on the metadata store; however, you can choose to propagate these settings to child objects in the BDC model, external systems, ECTs, methods, and method instances, and their child objects.
Selectable in Clients	
Set Permissions	Users with this permission can manage BCS permissions on the BDC metadata store, and by propagating a user's settings, the user can set permission on any object in the metadata store. This permission is usually only given to BCS service application administrators.

You can find more information about BCS security on TechNet at *http://technet.microsoft.com/en-us/library/ee661734.aspx#Section4* and on the Microsoft Business Connectivity Services Team Blog at *http://blogs.msdn.com/b/bcs/archive/2009/11/24/permissions-in-business-connectivityservices.aspx*.

Perform the following steps to set permissions on the BDC metadata store:

1. Open a browser, and then go to the SharePoint Central Administration website.

2. Under Application Management, click Manage Service Applications.

3. On the Service Applications page, click the name of the Business Data Connectivity Service for which you want to manage permissions.

4. On the Service Application Information page, on the Edit tab on the ribbon, click Set Metadata Store Permissions.

5. On the Set Metadata Store Permissions page, enter the appropriate users or groups, and then select the appropriate permissions.

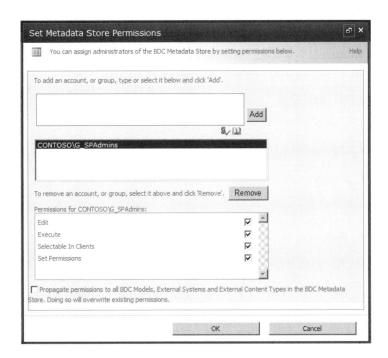

6. Select the Propagate permissions check box if you want the permissions settings to be copied to all child objects.

Before you select this option, you need to be aware that by propagating permissions, you are overwriting existing permissions on the child objects. Therefore, generally you should only propagate when you first create a BDC service application.

7. Click OK.

INSIDE OUT   BDC server application security

Farm administrators, SharePoint PowerShell users, and application pool accounts have full permissions to a BDC service application. Farm administrators can then maintain or repair the BDC service, if necessary, and allow the deployment of solutions packages that use BCS. However, these accounts do not have execute permissions on any metadata store objects. Therefore, such accounts could create a BDC model with its associated external system definition and ECT, and could even create an External list from those ECTs. These accounts would not be able to execute any of the operations on the external content, and therefore, when the External list is displayed in the browser, an authentication error would be displayed.

Defining External Systems Connections

To create an external system definition, you need to know which protocol to use to connect to the external content (known as the data source type) and the authentication method to use as well as the operations that you want to perform on the data. The following data source types can be used (these define the connector that the BDC server runtime uses to connect to the external system):

- Databases

- Cloud-based services

- WCF endpoints

- Web services

- .NET assemblies that can gather data from multiple sources

- Custom external systems that have non-static interfaces that change dynamically

The authentication methods that BDC server runtime uses to retrieve, modify, and delete, if appropriate, the data from the external systems are:

- **User's Identity (also known as *PassThrough*)**   When a user requests a SharePoint page that displays data from an external system, SharePoint sends the user's credentials to the external system, which uses that identity to decide whether the user is allowed access or not. If you use Windows authentication and have a single server SharePoint farm and the external system is installed on that server, then using the user's identity will work well. However, to use Windows authentication in any other configuration to mitigate the double-hop issue (explained earlier in this chapter), you will need to configure Kerberos on your servers or configure your SharePoint web applications to use SSL. The other disadvantage of using the user's identity is that if the external system is an SQL database, it causes a new SQL connection pool to be created for each user who is using the ECT to access the external content, which can cause performance issues. Connection pooling can be disabled, which can also affect performance.

- **Impersonate Windows Identity**   Specific Windows identities are used to authenticate with the external system. This Windows identity could be the same for all users or there could be some mapping mechanism so that the user requesting the content from SharePoint is matched to a different Windows identity that is passed on to the external system. To use this and the next authentication method, an application that does this mapping is required. If you are using SharePoint Server 2010, you could use the SSS application; if you are using SharePoint Foundation, you will need to write your own equivalent system.

- **Impersonate Custom Identity**   These could be credentials mapped in a database, or they could be claims-aware identities, which are sent to the external system.

- **BDC Identity (also known as *RevertToSelf*)**   SharePoint reverts to the web application's application pool identity to authenticate with the external system. This user name has a high level of privileges on a SharePoint installation. Any user who can create or edit a BDC Identity model can make themselves an administrator of Share-Point. Therefore, Microsoft does not recommend the use of this authentication mode, and it is disabled by default. When a user tries to import or change the authentication mode to RevertToSelf, an error message displays. The error message that displays when using SharePoint Designer is shown in Figure 9-6.

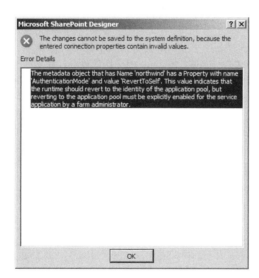

Figure 9-6 The BDC Identity (RevertToSelf) Import error dialog box.

INSIDE OUT When to use RevertToSelf authentication mode

Microsoft recommends that you should only use the RevertToSelf authentication mode in a production environment, when all of the following conditions are true:

- You are using SharePoint Foundation 2010.

- You do not have resources to create a custom SSS.

- You trust all of the people who use SharePoint Designer as completely as if they were SharePoint administrators.

- The application pool account is locked down so that the attack surface exposed to a malicious user of SharePoint Designer is limited.

RevertToSelf can be turned on by code or by using PowerShell, as shown in the following example, in which the variable *BCSName* is the name of your BCS application:

```
$bcs = Get-SPServiceApplication | where {$_.displayname -eq $BCSname};
$bcs.RevertToSelfAllowed = $True;
```

Although the BDC server runtime would use the application pool ID to retrieve data from the external system no matter which user wants to display the external content, remember that permission settings on the BDC service application can be used to restrict access to the external content.

The easiest way of defining an external system is to use SharePoint Designer 2010; however, by using this tool, you can only define external systems that use the data source types: SQL Server, .NET, and WCF Service.

Once defined, you can modify the external system definitions by using the SharePoint 2010 Central Administration website. To do so, go to the System Application Information page, click the external system, and then on the External System Information page, select the external system and click Settings to display the Property Settings page. The Property Setting page is not displayed if you select Settings on the System Application Information page.

Perform the following steps to create a BDC Model for an SQL Server database:

1. Open SharePoint Designer 2010, and then open a SharePoint site in the web application that is associated with the BDC service application where you have edit permissions on the BDC metadata store.

2. In the Navigation pane, click External Content Types to open the External Content Types gallery, which lists the ECTs to which you have permission.

The gallery might be empty if no ECTs are created or you do not have permission to see any.

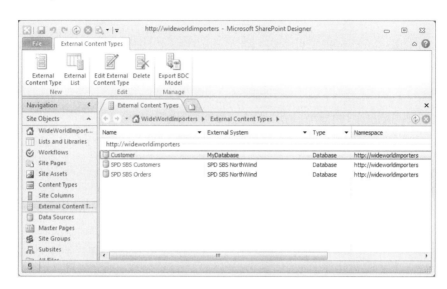

3. On the External Content Types tab, click External Content Type in the New group. The summary view of the ECT is displayed.

4. In the External Content Type Information area, to the right of Name, click New External Content, and then type the name of the ECT and enter a display name.

Once you have saved the ECT, you cannot change the ECT name in SharePoint Designer; however, you can change the ECT display name. You can export the ECT as part of a BDC model, alter the XML in the file (perhaps in Visual Studio), and then reimport the BDC model into the BDC metadata store. This creates a new ECT. You can then remove the misspelled ECT; however, this will impact any External lists that you have created from the misspelled ECT, because ECTs are based on the name of the ECT and the namespace. The namespace of a SharePoint Designer-created ECT is the URL of the web application. Therefore, it is important to think about the name that you want to give an ECT when you create one. Exporting and importing the BDC model is described later in this chapter.

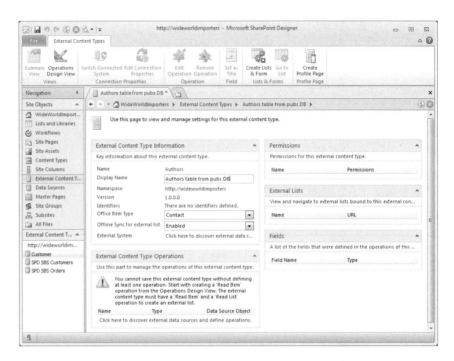

5. To the right of External System, select Click Here To Discover External Data Sources And Define Operations to display the operations design view of the ECT.

   You can toggle between the Summary view and the Operations Design view by using the two commands in the View group on the External Content Types ribbon tab.

6. Click Add Connection.

7. In the External Data Source Type Selection dialog box, select the appropriate data source type, such as SQL Server, and then click OK to display the source type connection dialog box.

8. Enter the connection details.

   For example, for a SQL Server source type, enter the database server name, the database name, and the authentication type: User's Identity, Impersonated Windows Identity, or Custom Identity. For the two impersonated identities, you need to use the SSS and provide the secure store application ID. The authentication details you enter here are used to authenticate with the external system when you use SharePoint Designer. You can specify different authentication methods for both SharePoint and Office application that you want to store in the BDC model by clicking Edit Connection Properties in the Connection Properties group.

9. Click OK.

The database is now registered in the BDC metadata store as an external system named SharePointDesigner-<databasename>-<userid >-<guid>, where <database> is the name of the SQL database,<userid> is the user name of the person who created the external system definition, and <guid> is a randomly generated number. For example, SharePointDesigner-pubs-Peter-581fd994-5891-49a5-8842-73b806483a04. These are placeholders to store the definitions you have created. It is not until you create an ECT for this external system that a valid external system definition is created that can be used by other ECT designers in other sites.

INSIDE OUT   Taking external data offline and the use of profile pages

The Offline Sync For External List refers to the use of External lists with SharePoint Workspace 2010. Taking external content offline using SharePoint Workspace is only available if you are using the Enterprise Edition of SharePoint Server 2010. Also on the External Content Type tab, you will see a command, Create Profile Page in the Profile Page group. This automatically creates a page to display all the fields returned for a specific ECT instance. This automatically created profile page uses the Business Data Web Parts, which again are only available with the Enterprise Edition of SharePoint Server 2010. You can manually create a profile page for an ECT by using the Data Form Web Part and BDC actions. If you click the Create Profile Page ribbon command, a Microsoft SharePoint Designer dialog box opens, stating that the server could not complete your request, but it does not provide any details as to why the request could not be completed. A second dialog box opens, stating that the expected changes to the ECT could not happen and that you should create the profile page again! Ignore these messages. The ribbon on the Central Administration website is trimmed not to display this option on a SharePoint Foundation installation.

Chapter 9

Working with External Content Types

Once the external system definition is defined, you can now create an ECT and specify the CRUD operations that you want to execute on that external system. Many organizations use ECTs in preference to using the Data Sources gallery for security and logistic reasons. The ECT can be defined once and stored centrally in the BDC metadata store but used many times for all sites and Site Collections, depending on the permission settings of the ECT. The schema and authentication methods need only be explained to a small number of ECT designers. Unlike the Data Sources gallery, where the data source definition would need to be created for each site on which you want to use the external content.

Creating ECTs

Use the following steps to create an ECT by using SharePoint Designer:

1. On the ECT summary page, give the ECT a name, and if the external content is to be displayed in Outlook 2010, then configure the Office item type as Appointment, Contact, Task, or Post. Switch to the operations view of the ECT.

2. In the External Data Source Type Selection dialog box, select the appropriate data source type, such as SQL Server, and then click OK to display the source type connection dialog box.

3. In the Data Source Explorer, expand the database node by clicking the plus sign (+) to the right of the database name, and then expand Tables or Views or Routines.

4. Right-click the table for which you want to create a BDC Model, and then click the operation for the methods that you want to create.

   Depending on the operations exposed by the external system, you can create all operations or add the individual operations: read item, read list, create, update and delete.

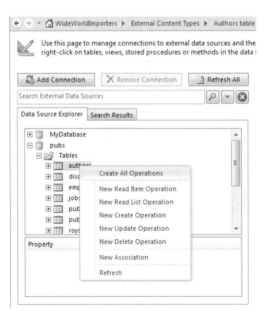

The Operations wizard opens; each page also contains a section that displays issues, warnings, and errors as you configure the operations. The three pages are:

— **Operation Properties**   Use this page to set the operation name, operation display name, and operation type. For a database external system, you can create all operations if you choose this option; the operation properties are automatically generated and the operation names will be Create, Read Item, Update, Delete and Read List.

— **Parameters**   Use this page to select those fields, known as elements, that you want to use in your SharePoint solution. You can modify each data source element, including, the identifier name, field name, and the name of the field when it is displayed in the browser. By default, all fields will be shown in the external item picker when adding an external data column to a list or library. If the table, view, or routine returns a large number of fields, displaying them all in the external item picker might confuse users. Therefore, it is best practice to select a small set of elements that best describes an item. If you select an Office item type on the summary view, you will use this page to map the external content data fields to Office properties. The Office mapping form is part of the Read Item operation, and therefore, if you wish to modify these settings once an ECT is created, modify the return parameter properties of the Read Item operation. You also change the Office item type on the summary page once an ECT is created.

— **Filter Parameters**   Use this page to add your own throttling conditions to your solution, this will optimize the time it takes to return the data from the external system. Remember, external content is not saved in the BCS database but retrieved by the BDC server runtime, when needed. The filter types available are: Comparison, Limit, Page Number, Timestamp, and Wildcard. For string data types, use the Wildcard filter type because this will internally translate to a like clause in queries to get the data. BCS throttling is enabled by default to prevent Denial of Service attacks. You are most likely to see the effect of this feature if no limit filter was created; thus, when the BCS runtime attempted to retrieve data from the external system it timed out due to the large amount of data it was trying to retrieve. For more information on BCS throttling, see the sidebar later in this chapter.

5. Click Finish, and then click Save.

   This will create an external system named *<databasename>* in the BDC metadata store if this is the first ECT created for the external system, and an ECT with the name you typed in step 1.

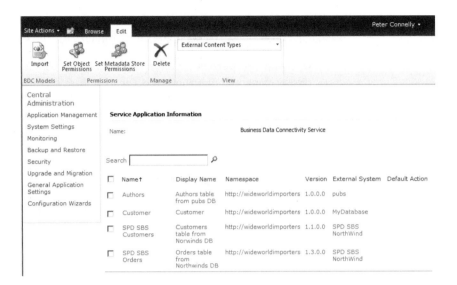

Managing Permission on ECTs

The ECT is just one of the BDC metadata store objects for which you can set permissions, and these permissions affect the interface between the SharePoint server and the presentation layer; that is, they do not define the authentication and security settings between the SharePoint server and the external system—those security settings are defined in the external system definition. The other objects present in the BDC metadata store that have their own access control list (ACL) are the BDC model and external system definitions, as described in Table 9-3. The information in this section is also relevant to those objects.

Table 9-3 **BDC Model Object Permission Settings**

Permission	Applies to	Description
Edit	Access-controlled metadata objects	Users with this permission can perform the following actions: • Update • Delete • Create child objects • Add property • Remove property • Clear property • Add localized display names • Remove localized display names • Clear localized display names • Give edit rights to administrators and users who use SharePoint Designer

Permission	Applies to	Description
Execute	ECT, Method Instance	Users with this permission can execute operations via various runtime API calls; that is, they can view the data of an ECT returned from a finder method. In most scenarios, you would assign this right to all users who have access to SharePoint.
Selectable in Clients	ECT	Users with this permission can use the external data picker to configure Web Parts and lists and create External lists. This permission should be available to administrators and users who design solutions via the browser or SharePoint Designer.
Set Permissions	Individually securable metadata objects	Users with this permission can manage BCS permissions on the object. This permission is usually given only to BCS service application administrators.

To set permissions on one or more models, external systems, or ECTs, complete the following steps:

1. Open a browser and go to the SharePoint Central Administration website. Under Application Management, click Manage Service Applications.

2. On the Service Applications page, click the name of the Business Data Connectivity Service for which you want to manage permissions.

3. On the Service Application Information page, in the View group on the Edit tab, select BDC Models, External Systems, or External Content Types from the drop-down menu.

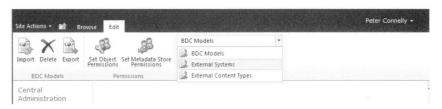

The page displays only objects of the type that you have chosen.

4. Select the objects that you want to modify, and then click Set Object Permissions in the Permissions group on the Edit tab.

5. On the Set Object Permissions page, enter the appropriate users or groups and assign the appropriate permissions.

If you choose to propagate the permission to any child objects, remember that you will overwrite the existing permissions for those objects.

Using External System Throttling

Each BDC application service can have a number of throttle configurations, and each configuration can be tuned by throttle type and/or scope. The five throttle types are:

- **None**   No throttle type specified

- **Items**   The number of ECT items returned, such as the number of authors

- **Size**   The amount of data retrieved by the BDC server runtime, in bytes

- **Connections**   The number of open connections to a database, web service, or .NET assembly

- **Timeout**   The time until an open connection is terminated, in milliseconds

Throttle scopes refer to the external system connection type, which can be a specific connection type, such as Database or WebService or a Global scope that includes all connector types, except for custom connectors. When a BDC service application is first created, all combinations of throttle types and scopes do not exist. The throttling rules that exist are:

- Global scope, Throttle type Connections

- Database scope, Throttle type Items, and Timeout

- WebService scope, Throttle type Size

- WCF scope, Throttle type Size, and Timeout

You can retrieve and modify the throttling rules by using the BDC PowerShell *cmdlets*, for example, obtain the BDC service application proxy in the variable *BDCName*, and then display the throttling rules for a BDC service application:

```
$bdcproxy = Get-SPServiceApplicationProxy |
   where {$_.displayname -eq $BDCname};
Get-SPBusinessDataCatalogThrottleConfig -ServiceApplication $bdcproxy '
   -Scope Global -ThrottleType Connections;
Scope        : Global
ThrottleType : Connections
Enforced     : True
Default      : 200
Max          : 500
```

The output displays five properties. The three properties that can be modified are:

- **Enforced**   Defines if the rule is enabled

- **Default**   Effects External lists and custom Web Parts, although custom Web Parts can override this value and therefore present more data than External lists

- **Max**   The limit used when custom Web Parts override the value in the Default property

To disable a throttling rule, use the following command:

```
Get-SPBusinessDataCatalogThrottleConfig -ServiceApplication $bdcproxy '
   -Scope Global -ThrottleType Connections |
        Set-SPBusinessDataCatalogThrottleConfig '
   -Enforced:$False;
```

To modify a throttling rule, use the following command:

```
$dbrule = Get-SPBusinessDataCatalogThrottleConfig '
   -ServiceApplication $bdcproxy '
   -Scope Database -ThrottleType Items;
$dbrule | Set-SPBusinessDataCatalogThrottleConfig '
   -Maximum 2000000 -Default 5000;
```

Exporting and Importing BDC Models and Resource Files

If you are fortunate to have a development environment, then you might have created your external system definition and ECTs in that environment. If the testing was successful, you must now deploy these BDC definitions to the production farm by first exporting the appropriate BDC model from the BDC service application in the development environment and importing the BDC model into the correct BDC service application in the production farm. You can use the SharePoint 2010 Central Administration website, a PowerShell cmdlet, or SharePoint Designer to export the BDC model.

You can find information about **Windows PowerShell Business Connectivity Services cmdlets** at *http://technet.microsoft.com/en-us/library/ff793356.aspx*.

If you created the External System definition and ECT by using SharePoint Designer, then you should use that tool to export them. The BDC model, SharePointDesigner-<databasename>-<userid >-<guid>, created by SharePoint Designer does not appear to link to the ECTs that are created by SharePoint Designer. Therefore, you cannot use the SharePoint 2010 Central Administration website to export ECTs developed with SharePoint Designer.

If the BDC model is to be used by Office 2010 applications, then you can only export them in the correct format by using SharePoint Designer. The permissions that you have configured on the BDC Model, the external system, and ECT can also be included in the exported BDC model.

You can use the SharePoint 2010 Central Administration website or a Windows PowerShell cmdlet to import a BDC model. You cannot use SharePoint Designer to import BDC models.

When you export a BDC model, make changes, and then import it into a BCS application, you should update the version number for the ECT. By default, the version number is set to 1.0.0.0. Changing the third or fourth digit of the version number indicates a small change, such as adding a new method or changing connection information. Changing the first or second digit signals a "breaking change" to the BCS, such as adding a new field to the *Read Item* operation (*SpecificFinder* method) or changing the identifier field. Breaking changes usually cause External lists that were defined using the previous version of the BDC model to fail. Therefore, before making an ECT widely available, ensure that your ECT meets all your business needs and is tested thoroughly.

You can find more information about **migrating the BDC Model and ECT from a development environment to testing environments and production environments** at *http://msdn.microsoft.com/en-us/library/gg650431.aspx*.

INSIDE OUT   Deploying BDC solutions with Visual Studio

With Visual Studio, you can create resource files and custom BCS Web Parts as well as a BDC Model. In this scenario, you would not use the export functionality; instead, you would commonly deploy the files as a solution package (.wsp). You can read more about packaging and deploying solutions in Chapter 16, "Developing SharePoint Solutions by Using Visual Studio 2010."

To export a BDC model by using SharePoint Designer, follow these steps:

1. Open SharePoint Designer 2010, and then open a SharePoint site in the web application that is associated with the BDC service application where you have created the external system definition and ECT.

2. In the Navigation pane, click External Content Types to open the External Content Types gallery.

3. Click the icon to the left of the ECT that you want to export, and then on the External Content Types tab, click Export BDC Model in the Manage group.

4. In the Export BDC Model dialog box, type the BDC model name; in the Settings list, select Default if the BDC Model is to be imported into another SharePoint farm, or select Client if you are going to use the BDC model with Office 2010 applications.

5. Click OK to save the BDC model as an XML file.

   The file will have an extension of .bdcm. If you are importing the file into an Office 2010 application, change the extension to .xml.

To export a BDC model or the resource information in a separate file by using the Central Administration website, follow this procedure:

1. Under Application Management, click Manage Service Applications, and then on the Service Applications page, click the name of the BDC service application that contains the BDC model that you want to export.

2. In the View drop-down list, select BDC Models, if it is not already selected, and then under Service Application Information, select the BDC model that you want to export.

3. On the Edit tab, click Export in the BDC Models group.

4. On the Export BDC Model page, select the Model or Resource file type option and the resource components that you want to export.

   If you select the resource file type option, a separate resource XML file will be created, which usually has an extension of .bdcr. When you export a BDC model in SharePoint Designer, you cannot export the resources separately, nor can you choose which resources to export. With SharePoint Designer, all resource information is exported.

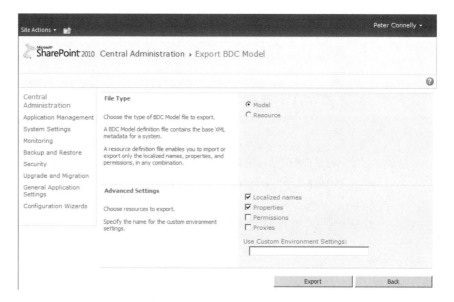

5. Click Export, and then save the file.

You can find information about the BDC model and resource files at *http://msdn.microsoft.com/en-us/library/aa674515.aspx*.

To import a BDC model by using the Central Administration website, perform the following steps:

1. Under Application Management, click Manage Service Applications, and then on the Service Applications page, click the name of the BDC service application that contains the BDC model you want to export.

2. On the Edit tab, in the BDC Models group, click Import.

3. On the Import BDC Model page, in the BDC Model section, use either the Browse button to navigate to the model file or type the location of the model file in the text box.

4. In the Advanced Settings section, select the Resource option if you are importing a file that only contains localized names, properties, or permissions.

5. Click Import.

   The Import BDC Model page then displays information on the progress of the import, and then when the model is imported, the page displays further information depending on whether the import was successful or not.

CAUTION

When you choose to import permissions that are defined in your BDC model and an entry for an ECT already exists in the ACL, the permission information from the imported file overwrites its value.

TROUBLESHOOTING

The import process parses the file and validates it; however, you should not rely on the import process to identity all errors in the BDC Model. If errors or warnings occur during the import process, the webpage will display additional information. You can find more information in the Windows event logs and in the SharePoint 2010 log file, located at %ProgramFiles%\Common Files\Microsoft Shared\web server extensions\14\ LOGS, where the relevant messages will be in the Business Data category. The software development kit (SDK) contains more information on troubleshooting metadata exceptions and interpreting the log files.

Once the BDC model is imported, SharePoint 2010 separates the external system and the ECT information. You should review both of these objects and set permissions according to your requirements. You should then check that an External list can be created from the ECT, and external content can be included in an external data column in a list or library.

You can also use the Delete command on the Edit tab to delete BCD models, external systems, or ECTs.

Chapter 9

Presenting External Content

Once an ECT is created, you can create solutions that use the external content. You can use the browser or SharePoint Designer to create these solutions. You can also create custom Web Parts or Windows Forms applications with Visual Studio that can access the data defined in the BDC metadata store.

Creating and Managing External Lists

The External list type is new to SharePoint Foundation 2010, and it is the preferred method of displaying external content. External list types can be created by using the browser, SharePoint Designer or PowerShell. Once created, they are similar to other lists that you use. Depending on the operations that you defined on the ECT, this could include creating, reading, updating, and deleting individual external content data, such as a specific customer, order, or employee from the external system. You can also add an XLV Web Part or Data Form Web Part (DFWP) to a page that displays data from an External list.

However, you cannot use the datasheet view, associate RSS feeds or workflows to an External list, or set item-level permissions. Remember, the external content is not stored in SharePoint content databases, so SharePoint does not have native control over the external content and does not know when data in the external system changes, and therefore, cannot trigger SharePoint workflow events when the external content changes. However, you can use content from an External list in a site workflow or a list workflow associated with a different list type.

To create an External list by using the browser, perform the following steps:

1. Open the site on which you want to create the External list. Click Site Actions, and then select More Options.

2. On the Create page, click External list, and then click Create.

    If you have a large number of list types, it's easier to find the External list option by using a Data category filter.

3. On the New page, enter the name and description for the External list, and then select whether you want a link to this External list on the Quick Launch bar.

4. To the right of the External Content Type text box, click the Select External Content Type icon.

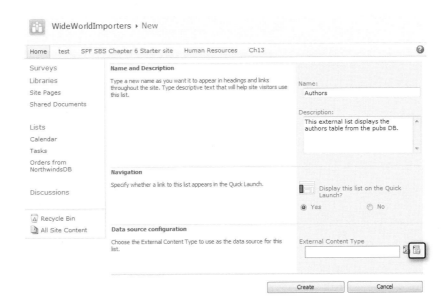

5. In the External Content Type Picker dialog box that appears, select the ECT that defines the external content that you want to display in your External list, and then click OK.

The dialog box displays the name of the external system and the display name of the ECT; therefore, it is important that your ECT designers have created a meaningful display name for the ECT so that your end users can quickly identify the desired external content. If you choose the incorrect ECT, you cannot choose a different one once the External list is created. You will need to delete the list and recreate it, choosing the correct ECT. The External list acts as a virtual container, displaying the contents from the external system. Therefore, when you delete an External list or ECT, you are not deleting any content from the external system, just the virtual container and the definition of external content.

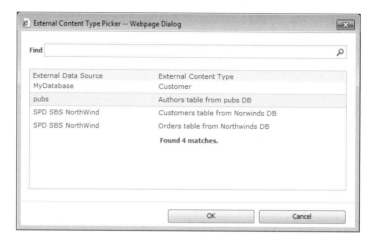

The External Content Type Picker dialog box closes and the ECT that you chose is specified in the External Content Type text box.

6. Click Create.

The External list is displayed using the Real List view, and the content from the external system is displayed.

TROUBLESHOOTING

Once you have created an External list, you might find that no data from the external system is displayed. If the Read List view of the External list displays the error message, "Login failed for user 'NT AUTHORITY\ANONYMOUS LOGON'," this could be an indication of the double-hop issue if you are using the user's identity to authenticate with the external system. Or, it can also mean that you do not have BDC permissions for the ECT or the external system, or that your user ID does not have the correct access permissions in the external system.

Working with Office Application ECTs

To create an Office application ECT in SharePoint Designer, you must select an Office item type on the summary view when you first create the ECT. Then, using the Operations wizard you can map the field properties of the external content to Office properties. The office item types are mostly aimed at Outlook. When you connect the External list to Outlook, the external content can be shown in the contacts, calendar, or task pane, as well as in the SharePoint External lists folder. If one of the external content fields is mapped to the Office email property, you can then send an email to a person, whose details are stored in the external system.

Using External Data Columns

External data columns allow you to add external content to a standard SharePoint list or library. You create an external data column as you would any other column; that is, on the List tab, click the Create Column command. Then, on the Create page, enter a column name, and then select External Data as the column type. In the Additional Column Settings section, to the right of the External Content Type text box are two icons, the Check ECT icon, which you use when you type the name of the ECT in the text box, and the Select ECT icon, which when clicked opens the External Content Type Picker dialog box.

Once an ECT is selected, the Additional Column Settings section contains a list of properties associated with the ECT, as shown in Figure 9-7. In the Select The Field To Be Shown On This Column drop-down list, select the column that your users will usually associate with the external content. If the external content is a CRM system, then this might be the customer name. You can then choose to add one or more fields from the external content to become columns in the list or library, such as the customers email address or phone number. You can then choose to add the fields to all content types as well as add them to the default view.

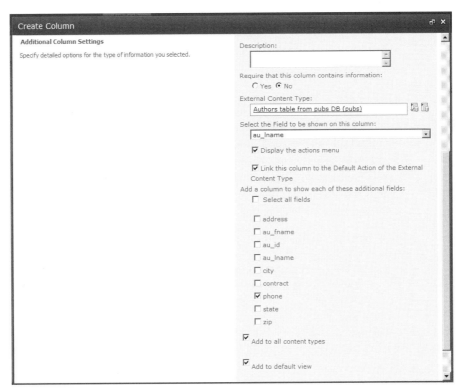

Figure 9-7 Creating an External Data Column.

It is only when you add a new list item and click the Select External Item(s) icon that the BDC server runtime connects to the external system to retrieve data to populate the Choose dialog box. The dialog box only shows those fields that had the external item picker check box selected when you configured the ECT operations. When the external item picker check box is not selected for any field, all fields are displayed in the Choose dialog box. When the new list item is saved, the external content is stored in the list in the SharePoint SQL content database, unlike the External list that only contains a link to the ECT definition. To update the data in the list, you can click the Refresh icon to the right of the external data column name, as shown in Figure 9-8. A webpage appears warning you that this operation could take a long time. If you click OK, the BDC server runtime connects to the external system to return the necessary data. By copying the external content in the list, it has inherited all list type operations, such as views, filters, and the ability to be used to trigger list workflows.

Figure 9-8 Refresh the external content stored in external data columns.

When an external data column is added to a library, the values in the external column can be made available as content controls in Microsoft Word 2010.

Creating External Data Actions

When an external data column is created in a list or library, there is an icon on each list item to the left of the external content. This icon provides a drop-down list of links to pages that display information relevant to the ECT item, such as displaying all the values for all the properties of the ECT item, or by using the postal code property of the ECT item, displaying a map of that location. These links are called Actions, and they can be created by using the Central Administration website, following these steps:

1. Navigate to the Business Data Connectivity Service where the ECT is defined.

2. On the Edit tab of the Service Application Information page, in the View group, select External Content Types from the drop-down menu.

3. Click the ECT to display the External Content Type Information page.

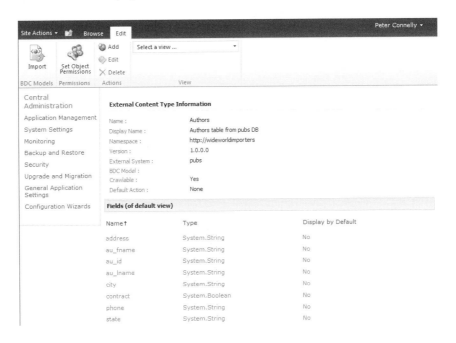

4. On the Edit tab, click Add in the Actions group.

5. On the Add Action page that appears, type a name for the action, type the URL, specify whether to launch the action in a new browser window or not (default), add parameters to the URL if required, and then add the icon to display next to the action. You can choose from the Delete, Edit, or New icons, or you can choose your own image.

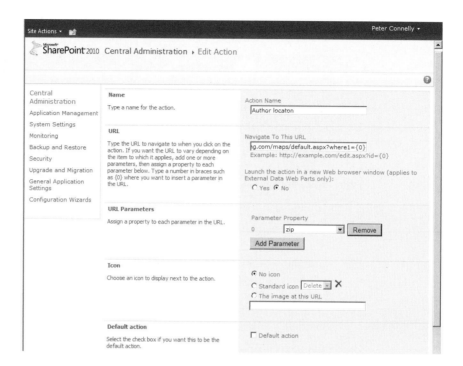

Using Visual Studio 2010 with the BCS

BCS is all about bringing data that lives outside SharePoint into SharePoint. The BCS provides connectivity to your external LoB systems by using connectors. Earlier in this chapter, SharePoint Designer was used as a no-code method to define the BDC model and use ECT as External lists and external data columns. This method has some limitations:

- You can only create CRUD operations. BCS supports other operations that cannot be created by using SharePoint Designer, such as the stream operation that allows you to access a file that is stored as a Binary Large Object (BLOB) in an SQL database.

- The declarative XML created in the BDC model can only be changed if you export the BDC model and then open the file created by the export activity in SharePoint Designer. You would then need to know the BCS model schema to amend the XML. SharePoint Designer does not provide any no-code assistance in editing the BDC model XML file.

- External lists cannot be used to represent any hierarchy or relationship between the content stored in the external systems. The data is presented as a flat, table-like structure; there is no built-in tree or folder structure that you can configure to match the relationship between the content.

- SharePoint Designer only allows the use of SQL Server, .Net Assembly, and WCF connectors, and typically no-code solutions use the SQL Server or the WCF connectors.

- SharePoint Designer does not allow you to create the VSTO add-ins that could provide extract functionality to work with the external content.

Understanding the BDC Model

The BDC model contains a hierarchy of XML elements that specify the external system settings and structure. The model must be a well-formed XML file and conform to the schema described in the file Bdcmetadata.xsd. When you have a separate resource file, the schema definition file is BDCMetadataResource.xsd. Both files are stored in the TEMPLATE\XML folder in the SharePoint installation root folder, which by default is C:\Program Files\Common Files\Microsoft Shared\Web Server Extensions\14.

You can see the metadata object hierarchy by reviewing the XML tags of the BDC model, which defines the data structures, such as Model, LobSystem, (the external system) LobSystemInstance, Entity (the ECT), Method, Parameter, and TypeDescriptor objects. These are presented in the following XML sample:

```xml
<?xml version="1.0" encoding="utf-16" standalone="yes"?>
<Model xmlns:xsi="http://www.w3.org/2001/XMLSchema-instance"
xsi:schemaLocation="http://schemas.microsoft.com/windows/2007/
BusinessDataCatalog BDCMetadata.xsd" Name="BdcModel1" IsCached="false"
xmlns="http://schemas.microsoft.com/windows/2007/BusinessDataCatalog">
 <LobSystemInstance Name="pubs">
  <Properties>
   <Property Name="AuthenticationMode" Type="System.String">
      PassThrough</Property>
   <Property Name="DatabaseAccessProvider" Type="System.String">
      SqlServer</Property>
   <Property Name="RdbConnection Data Source" Type="System.String">
      sql.wideworldimporters.com</Property>
   <Property Name="RdbConnection Initial Catalog" Type="System.String">
      pubs</Property>
   <Property Name="RdbConnection Integrated Security" Type="System.String">
      SSPI</Property>
   <Property Name="RdbConnection Pooling" Type="System.String">True</Property>
   <Property Name="ShowInSearchUI" Type="System.String"></Property>
  </Properties>
 </LobSystemInstance>
</LobSystemInstances>
<Entities>
 <Entity Namespace="http://wideworldimporters" Version="1.0.0.0"
   EstimatedInstanceCount="10000" Name="Authors"
   DefaultDisplayName="Authors Table in Pubs DB">
  <Properties>
   <Property Name="OutlookItemType" Type="System.String">Contact</Property>
  </Properties>
```

```
<Identifiers>
 <Identifier TypeName="System.String" Name="au_id" />
</Identifiers>
<Methods>
 <Method Name="Read Item" DefaultDisplayName="Authors Read Item">
 <Properties>
  <Property Name="BackEndObject" Type="System.String">authors</Property>
  <Property Name="BackEndObjectType" Type="System.String">
    SqlServerTable</Property>
  <Property Name="RdbCommandText" Type="System.String">SELECT [au_id] ,
    [au_lname] , [au_fname] , [phone] , [address] , [city] , [state] ,
    [zip] , [contract] FROM [dbo].[authors]
    WHERE [au_id] = @au_id</Property>
  <Property Name="RdbCommandType" Type="System.Data.CommandType,
    System.Data, Version=2.0.0.0, Culture=neutral,
    PublicKeyToken=b77a5c561934e089">Text</Property>
  <Property Name="Schema" Type="System.String">dbo</Property>
 </Properties>
 <Parameters>
  <Parameter Direction="In" Name="@au_id">
  <TypeDescriptor TypeName="System.String" IdentifierName="au_id"
    Name="au_id">
   <Properties>
     <Property Name="Size" Type="System.Int32">11</Property>
   </Properties>
   <Interpretation>
    <NormalizeString FromLOB="NormalizeToNull"
      ToLOB="NormalizeToEmptyString" />
   </Interpretation>
  </TypeDescriptor>
 </Parameter>
```

You can find more BCS sample XML and code examples at *http://msdn.microsoft.com/ en-us/library/ee559369.aspx*.

The BDC model includes the following XML tags (for a list of all metadata objects, refer to *http://msdn.microsoft.com/en-us/library/ee556378.aspx*):

- **LobSystem** This object represents the external system.

- **LOBSystemInstance** This object provides authentication and the connection string information.

- **Entity**   This is the key object and refers to the ECT. An entity belongs to a single LoB system and must have a unique name. Entity contains XML element tags (identifiers, methods, filters, and actions). Each entity should define two properties: an identifier (which uniquely identify a particular instance of an entity and in database terms; this is the primary key), and a default column.

- **Methods**   These are operations related to an ECT, such as Create, Read Item, Update, Delete, and Read List. If the data source is a database, the method is a stored procedure or an SQL statement; if the data source is a web service, the method is a *Web* method. The XML data must detail all that SharePoint needs to call that method, and therefore, it can be likened to an interface description. For each ECT, there should be a method defined as a *Finder* method, which returns one or more instances of an entity, such as Read List, a *SpecificFinder* method, or Read Item, which will return a specific instance of an entity.

- **Access Control List**   Defines permissions for the model objects.

- **Associations**   Used in conjunction with the business data Web Parts provided as part of the Enterprise Edition of SharePoint Server 2010.

You can find information on how to use stored procedures in BCS at *www.shillier.com/ archive/2010/10/18/how-to-use-a-stored-procedures-in-business-connectivity-services. aspx.*

Creating a BDC Model by Using Visual Studio

To create a new BDC model, start Visual Studio 2010 and create a new project based on the "Business Data Connectivity Model" project template, as shown in Figure 9-9. Give the project a meaningful name and connect to a SharePoint website that you want to use for debugging. Notice that you can only create BDC model projects as farm solutions. When you build a BDC model by using Visual Studio, you create a .bdcm file and an assembly. The assembly is deployed to the BDC service application database, which requires full trust and hence, why the project must be configured as a farm solution.

For information on how to set up your Visual Studio environment for SharePoint and more information on SharePoint solutions, see Chapter 16.

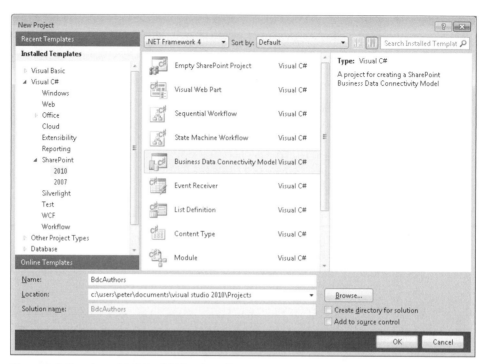

Figure 9-9 Creating a BDC Model Visual Studio project.

The project opens and displays a graphical representation of an entity (ECT) with one identity (property) and two methods (operations), the *ReadItem*—a specific finder method,
and *ReadList*—a finder method. This is the minimum needed to create an External list. The
External list displays one or more entity items that are returned by the *ReadList* method,
and if you select one of those items and choose to view properties, the *ReadItem* method is
called.

The other task panes open and might include the Solution Explorer, which displays the project structure that includes the BDC model, BdcModel1.bdcm, the Properties, BDC Method
Details, and the BDC Explorer, which abstracts the underlying XML and displays it in a
tree view (see Figure 9-10). To display the BDC Explorer, you can click the link in the BDC
Method Details task pane or on the View menu. Next, click Other Windows, and then click
BDC Explorer. It will then appear in the upper-right corner, in front of the Solution Explorer
task pane. If the Properties task pane is not open, press F4.

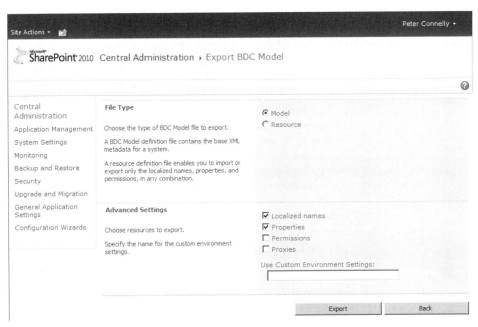

Figure 9-10 The Visual Studio workspace includes BDC-related task panes.

The task panes are related to one another. When you click the BdcModel1.bdcm file in Solution Explorer, the Properties task pane displays file properties. When you click the *ReadItem* method in the BDC Explorer, the Properties and BDC Method Details task panes are populated with related information. For example, you can see that the *ReadItem* method has two parameters: id with an *in* direction and *returnParameter* with a direction of *Return*. The *ReadItem* method passes the id parameter, the primary key, to the external system, and the item that is identified by the ID will be returned by the *ReadItem* method in the *Return* parameter.

When you make changes in any of these task panes—the graphical representation of the entity (known as the ECT designer), the BDC Method Details, the BDC Explorer of the Properties task pane—you are writing XML to BdcModel1.bdcm; you do not need to manually edit the XML in the file. Sometimes it is easier to see what is incorrect in your BDC model and correct the XML yourself. To quickly open the .bdcm file and write XML, in the Solution Explorer, right-click the file to open the shortcut menu, and then click Open With. In the Open With dialog box, select XML (text) Editor.

INSIDE OUT Importing a BDC solutions file

SharePoint Foundation does not allow importing a SharePoint solutions file (.wsp) that contains BDC models. There are three workarounds:

- To publish the BDC Model to SharePoint Foundation with Visual Studio, you need a Feature Event receiver. SharePoint Server 2010 already has the Feature Event receiver. Microsoft has provided the code for the receiver, which you can download from the MSDN code gallery at *http://code.msdn.microsoft.com/BDCSPFoundation*. Detailed instructions on how to use the code can be found in the blog post, "Deploy a BDC Model project to SharePoint Foundation 2010 using Visual Studio 2010," which you can find at *http://blogs.msdn.com/b/vssharepointtoolsblog/ archive/2010/04/02/deploy-a-bdc-model-project-to-sharepoint-foundation-2010- using-visual-studio-2010.aspx*. You only need to deploy the event receiver once because it will automatically be called when any BDC model is deployed.

- Use PowerShell to upload the BDC model and the compiled assembly to the BDC metadata store. Using this second method, you would also need to manually deploy the assembly to the Global Assembly Cache (GAC).

- Install Microsoft SharePoint Search Express (SSE), which, like SharePoint Foundation, is free and supports the importing of .wsp files that contain BDC models.

The project created from the "Business Data Connectivity Model" project template is a fully working example of a BDC model. After you add the Feature Event receiver to enable the deployment of BDC models from within Visual Studio, press F5 to compile, package, and deploy it. This will also check that you have coded the Feature Event receiver correctly.

There are two types of BCS connectors that you will use when creating BDC models with Visual Studio:

- **.Net Assembly connector** Use this to connect to a particular instance of an external system such as your own Exchange system that has all your organization's configurations and settings. This type of connector is typically developed internally to an organization. The .Net Assembly connector gives you complete control over the operations with the external system with the code you write.

- **Custom connector** Use this to connect to any external system; for example, any Exchange system. Custom connectors are typically developed by third-party companies so that the purchases of the third-party solution can integrate the solution with their SharePoint installation.

You can learn more about the differences between using the .NET Assembly connector and writing a custom connector at *http://msdn.microsoft.com/en-us/library/ee554911.aspx*.

A BCS solution is a combination of declarative and programmatic elements. This fact is hidden when you create a no-code solution with SharePoint Designer. When you display the External Content Types galley in SharePoint Designer, you can see that the BDC model is a .NET Assembly connector. The BDC model is therefore telling SharePoint that you are using a custom .NET Assembly implementation of the BDC model, thereby tying together the declarative XML with the custom code. Therefore, the "Business Data Connectivity Model" project template should really be named the "BDC .NET Assembly" project template.

When you create an External list from the BDC model that you create with Visual Studio, it contains two columns named Identifier1 and Message, which is defined in Entity1.cs and are called *Type Descriptors*. Use this file to define the entity and its fields. This file maps to the ECT:

```
Public partial class Entity1
{
    //TODO: Implement additional properties here.
    public string Identifier1 { get; set; }
    public string Message { get; set; }
}
```

The External list would display one external content item: *0,Hello World*. This is the result of the *ReadList* method that is defined in the Entity1Service.cs file. Use this file to define how to implement the operations, such as the CRUD operations. When you create methods in the task panes, stubs are created in this file, for which you will need to provide the code. You can therefore develop operations that SharePoint Designer cannot provide:

```
public static IEnumerable<Entity1> ReadList()
{
    // TODO: This is just a sample. Replace this simple sample with valid code.
    Entity1[] entityList = newEntity1[1];
    Entity1 entity1 = newEntity1();
    entity1.Identifier1 = "0";
    entity1.Message = "Hello World";
    entityList[0] = entity1;
    return entityList;
}
```

To create an ECT by using Visual Studio, perform the following steps:

1. In the designer, right-click the entity name to display the shortcut menu, and then click Rename. Type the name of the data type; for example, enter **Author**.

2. Repeat the previous step to rename the identifier1, and the two methods, *ReadList* and *ReadItem*, to meaningful names, such as **Au_id**, **GetAllAuthors**, and **GetAuthor**. You can also use the Properties task pane to rename these methods.

3. Add new methods by using the Method Details task pane because this will create the correct code stub in the services code file. To create a non-CRUD method, select Create Blank Method.

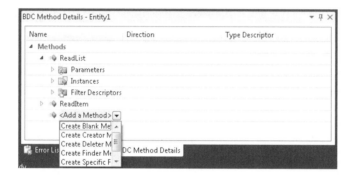

4. Using the Properties task pane, change the Type Name to match the data type of your entity's identifier.

5. Create the type descriptors for the returnParameter, and set the type name to match the data content in your external systems, using steps similar to the following:

    a. Using the BDC Explorer, navigate to the returnParameter below GetAllAuthors, click Entity1List, and then using the Properties task pane, rename it, for example, **AuthorList**.

    b. Expand AuthorList, and then using the Properties task pane, rename Entity1 to **Author**.

    c. Expand Author, and then using the Properties pane, rename Identifier1 to **Au_id** and the rename Message to **au_lname**. Use the Properties task pane to amend other properties as needed, such as the Type Name and the Default Display Name.

    d. Add any other type descriptors that your entity requires. Right-click Author to display the shortcut menu, click Add Type Descriptor, and then click TypeDescriptor and rename it using the Properties task pane.

6. Create type descriptors for the other methods.

   If other methods use the same type descriptor, you can copy them from one method and paste them to other methods. For example, right-click Author, and then click

Copy. Next, expand GetAuthor, right click returnParameter, and then click Paste. Click Yes to the Replacing Type Descriptor dialog box. The *GetAuthor* method, also has an ID parameter, its type descriptor needs to be renamed to the appropriate identifier, **au_id**.

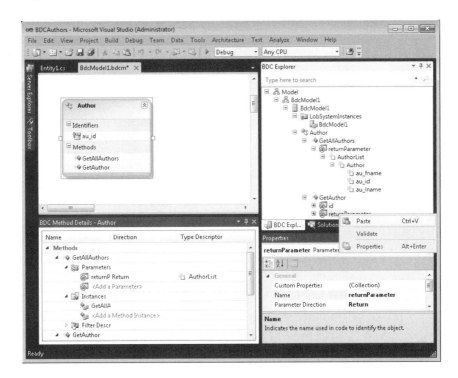

7. In Solution Explorer, rename Entity1.cs to **Author.cs**, and then click Yes to rename all references to the code element "Entity1". Entity1Service.cs was renamed to AuthorService.cs as the result of step 1.

8. Provide details in the Author.cs that represents the data structure that you described in the preceding steps. Replace the code in the body of the *Author* class to add properties to map to the type descriptors that you added in the BDC definition.

    Your code will look similar to the following example:

```
Public partial class Author
{
    public string au_id { get; set; }
    public string au_lname { get; set; }
    public string au_fname { get; set; }
    //TODO: Map all your type descriptors
}
```

9. Provide details in the AuthorService.cs for the methods that you have defined.

   For example, if you were using the pubs database to return content from the authors table, you will need to provide code for the two methods, *GetAllAuthors* and *GetAuthor*, for example, by returning the content of the table by using ADO.NET.

10. Once you have completed all the definitions and code, press F5 and test your solution by creating an External list.

You can see how to programmatically create a SharePoint 2010 ECT at *www.toddbaginski. com/blog/how-to-programmatically-create-a-sharepoint-2010-external-content-type*.

Importing BDC Models into Visual Studio

If you want to extend a BDC model created in SharePoint Designer, or you wish to deploy the BDC model as part of you BCS solution, you will first need to import the BDC model into Visual Studio. To import the BDC model, perform the following steps:

1. In your Visual Studio project, create a folder for your model.

2. Right-click the folder, and then select Add Existing Item. From the Add Existing Item dialog box, navigate to where you exported the .bdcm file from SharePoint Designer, and then click Add.

   The Add .NET Assembly LobSystem dialog box displays.

   The Visual Studio ECT designer only supports .NET Assembly BDC models. The BDC model that you created from SPD is likely to use the SQL server or WCF services connector. If you select the No option in the dialog box, the ECT designer is disabled and you will need to modify the .bdcm file by using the XML editor.

You can find the Microsoft Business Connectivity Services resource center at *http:// technet.microsoft.com/en-us/sharepoint/ee518675.aspx*.

Summary

This chapter detailed how you can incorporate external content by basic SharePoint Foundation no-code solutions with SharePoint Designer, using the Data Source gallery and BCS components: ECTs, External lists, and external data columns. The external content can be presented by using either the Data Source gallery or BCS with the Data Form Web Part. External content in External lists can also be presented by using the XLV Web Part. More advanced solutions can be built with Visual Studio 2010.

BCS is a new, massive addition to SharePoint Foundation 2010. It was first introduced in the Enterprise Edition of Microsoft Office SharePoint Server 2007, and the full capability of BCS, both on the client and server side, can only be achieved out-of-the-box with the Enterprise Edition of SharePoint Server 2010.

External content can be used with your users' computers by using Office 2010 applications, although with SharePoint Foundation, you might need to develop VSTO packages to fully exploit client-side solutions.

The BCS provides a method of providing access to external content without the need to redefine how to connect the external systems for each site that must use that external content. However, as an ECT designer, you do need higher permissions than is required with the Data Source gallery, and you will need to collaborate closely with the SharePoint administrator to implement BCS solutions. Also, as changes to BCS solutions can affect many sites over many web applications, a release management process should be implemented. Changes to Data Source gallery solutions only affect one site.

Chapter 9

Using and Creating Workflows

MICROSOFT SharePoint Foundation 2010 introduced a considerable array of new functionality concerning the creation, maintainability, reusability, and deployment of workflows. One of the first improvements to note is that the out-of-the-box workflows can be modified in SharePoint Designer 2010. Another improvement, again related to SharePoint Designer 2010, is the ability to create reusable workflows. In previous versions of SharePoint Designer and SharePoint, a workflow created in SharePoint Designer could only be associated with one list. Now, you can create a reusable workflow that can be associated with multiple lists. Once the workflow has been published to a SharePoint Site, you can then save the workflow as a workflow template in the form of a Windows SharePoint solution file (.wsp). This workflow template can then be imported to another site to be used to create the same workflow on the new site or imported into Microsoft Visual Studio 2010 where it can be further enhanced.

In the previous version of SharePoint, you could use the browser and SharePoint Designer to attach workflows to a list or library, and although SharePoint 2010 has introduced site workflows, attaching workflows to lists or libraries will probably still be the most popular type of SharePoint workflow.

This chapter details how to use the out-of-the-box workflows in the browser. It will then look at extending them by using SharePoint Designer, and then it will detail how Visual Studio can help your organization to use SharePoint Foundation 2010 with its business processes. Also in this chapter, you will use a holiday request business process to explore the use of the out-of-the-box Three-State workflow, Microsoft Visio Premium and SharePoint Designer.

SharePoint Workflow Basics

For several years now, there has been a push across both government and commercial sectors to do more work in less time, to minimize the number of files attached to emails, and to reduce the amount of information that needs to be printed. Many large organizations, especially in the civilian government, finance, and healthcare industries have been clogging their email systems with duplicate data and choking on paperwork and processes. Of course, forms and processes are required, and SharePoint Foundation can address many of these issues by using the Microsoft Windows Workflow Foundation (WF) components of Microsoft .NET 3.5 to provide user-driven process automation. WF offers all the functionality required for building enterprise-level workflows, such as built-in support for transactions, tracking, and notifications. WF does not act as a standalone application but always works with a program, which in this instance is SharePoint Foundation. And because SharePoint Server 2010 is built on top of Windows Foundation, it too has workflow capabilities.

Process Automation Methods

Using the browser, SharePoint can help with business processes by using one of the following methods:

- Really Simple Syndication (RSS) feeds, for finding information from a variety of sources on an ad hoc basis. Use this method when the information is not needed on a day-to-day basis. RSS feeds use a pull mechanism to find information; that is, you only find information exposed by RSS feeds when you open an RSS reader, such as Internet Explorer or Microsoft Outlook 2007 or 2010.

- Alerts, for regular notifications of new, modified, or deleted content. Use this method to send you an email when information is found. Alerts can be configured to send emails immediately when SharePoint finds information in which you have registered an interest, or a daily or weekly digest of that information.

- You can use content approval, which along with versioning to manage content and control who can see content that is classified as draft. When you enable content approval on a list or library, a column named Approved Status is added to the library, together with a number of views. In addition, enabling content approval activates the Approval/Reject command on the list item menu and on the ribbon. The Approval Status column can contain the choices Approved, Rejected, or Pending. Users who are assigned the Manage Lists permission can approve or reject items. No email is sent to the user with the Manage List permissions. They would need to visit the list to see if any items are in a pending state.

However, with none of these three methods can you automate business processes beyond a one-step method. You can combine these methods together with other SharePoint functionality, such as using content approval with alerts to provide a lightweight workflow that sends you emails when your team members publish documents as a major version so that you can approve documents according to a specific timescale. However, such a solution can help solve only a small number of your business processes. You might want to route a document or a webpage to a number of people before publishing it.

Microsoft's TechNet website contains an article on versioning, content approval, and check out planning. You can view this at *http://technet.microsoft.com/en-us/library/ff607917.aspx*.

SharePoint provides two other methods to help automate processes:

● **Workflows**   This is used to automate and track processes that require human intervention such as notifying users when their action is required to move the process forward. Such processes can take days, weeks, or months to complete and might need to wait for an event or another process to complete. Workflows can be created by using the browser, SharePoint Designer, and Visual Studio.

● **Event receivers**   Used to automate processes that require no human intervention such as moving job applications from one document library to a series of other document libraries for some purpose. Event receivers can only be created by using Visual Studio.

Planning for Process Automation

Workflows and event receivers cannot automate a task unless time is taken to understand it at a very detailed level. A workflow cannot track the status of information stored on paper documents; nor can you force users to perform a particular task by using the workflow you created. You must have a clear understanding of how the business process operates. If you do not understand how to complete a business process manually, you will not be able to describe the business process in sufficient detail to automate it. You also need the reassurance of the business process owners that upon the introduction of this workflow, it will be used by the process users. Using workflows to automate parts of a business process in reality means that you are involved in business process re-engineering. Managing the change of the new process and understanding the people, their fears, and worries is the most important part of automating process into the business workspace.

Therefore, there is more to creating a successful workflow than using the browser or SharePoint Designer to configure one. You need to plan how you intend to automate a process, taking into account people, processes, and technology. You need to choose the process that you are going to automate carefully—do not automate every little process in your organization. Look for processes that are predictable and for which the startup cost of creating a workflow and ensuring that your team is happy with the new process will be offset by the productivity improvement that the automated process will provide. Understand the technology that you are going to use to automate the processes, which in this case is SharePoint Foundation and the Windows Workflow Foundation.

Microsoft's TechNet website contains an article on planning SharePoint Foundation 2010 workflows. You can view this at *http://technet.microsoft.com/en-us/library/cc288553.aspx*.

Introducing Workflow Terminology

In the same way that you base a new site, list, or library on a template, you base a new workflow process on a workflow template. These templates are implemented as features that can be activated or deactivated at the site or Site Collection level by using the browser or by using a custom program or Windows PowerShell. A workflow template is available only when a workflow feature is activated.

Workflows are a series of tasks that produce an outcome. To create a workflow you configure and add (also known as *associating*) the workflow template to a list, library, or site. An instance of the workflow can then be initiated by using the configured workflow template, which defines the conditions that should be tested to decide what tasks to complete to produce the outcome. You can also associate a workflow template with a content type, and then associate the content type with a list or library to define a workflow.

At the top-level site of a Site Collection, you can use the Workflows page to see which workflow templates are available and active, the number of SharePoint objects (lists, libraries, content types, and sites) with which the workflow template is associated, and the number of workflow instances that are running in those workflows. Use the following steps to navigate to the Workflows page:

1. Click Site Actions, and then click Site Settings.

2. Under Site Administration, click Workflows.

    If you do not see the Workflows link under Site Administration, you are probably at a child site within the Site Collection, in which case, under Site Collection Administration, click Go To Top Level Site Settings to navigate to the top of the Site Collections.

Unfortunately, this Workflow page does not provide any links that you can use to identify which SharePoint objects the workflow template is associated with or which sites, list items, or documents are progressing through the workflow.

The workflow always has a start and an end. An instance of the workflow is created when a workflow event is triggered for a specific list item or file; the workflow instance then enters the workflow at its start point and progresses through the workflow process as defined by the configured workflow template until it reaches the end point, at which time the workflow instance is set to *Completed*, as shown in Figure 10-1. The workflow does no other work until a new workflow instance is created. A workflow can contain one or more workflow instances. A list item or file can be related to more than one workflow instance, as long as each workflow instance is related to different workflows.

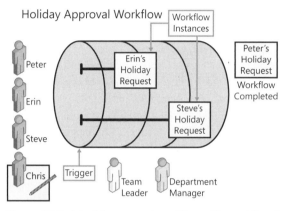

Figure 10-1 A holiday request workflow with workflow instances progressing through the workflow. One workflow instance is completed.

Depending on the workflow template and its configuration, the start of a workflow instance can be triggered by using one of the following options:

- Manually, when you want to test a newly added workflow or when the list or library to which you have added a workflow has a list item or document that needs to progress through the workflow. This option can be limited so that only users who have the Manage List permission can manually start a workflow instance.

- Automatically, when you create a list item or document.

- Automatically, when you change a list item or document.

Chapter 10

INSIDE OUT   Workflow start methods

Custom workflow templates might support other workflow start methods not listed previously. For example, when using SharePoint Server 2010, a fourth option is available for initiating a workflow instance by using information management policies on content types at the site, list, or library levels.

Although it is not strictly required, most workflows use the following two lists:

- **Task list**   Use this to create task items to remind users of the work that needs to be completed or to collect information for the next step of the workflow. Workflows can also send emails to a user with a link to the task item that is assigned to them.

- **Workflow History list**   This keeps track of the workflow instances that are running or have been completed for a given list item or document. The workflow writes key information to this list, such as the date, status, participant, and description. Based on the contents of the history list, you can create Activity Duration reports that you can use to analyze the duration of workflow instances and the activities within the workflow process. You can also create Cancellation and Error reports that show which workflow processes are being cancelled, or which workflow instances have encountered errors during execution. The default workflow history list is a hidden library and is not shown on the All Site Content webpage. The default workflow inherits permissions from the site; therefore, any user who is mapped to the contribute permission level can update items in this list. You can display this list in the browser by appending /lists/workflow%20history/ to your site's URL; for example, `http://wideworldimporters/lists/workflow%20history/`. By default workflows cannot write to the description field of a workflow history item larger than 255 characters.

If you use the same Tasks list and Workflow History list for all workflows in a site, they can become large and compromise site performance. As a result, Microsoft has created a daily Workflow Auto Cleanup timer job to purge items in the task list that exist 60 days after the related workflow instance completes or is cancelled and removes the links to those workflow instances on the workflow status pages. The workflow history items are not deleted. Because of the default security settings on these lists and the 60-day purge of list items, you should not use these lists as an audit of what the workflow is doing.

You can use an existing Task and Workflow History list when you first create a workflow. By default, these lists are indexed, but as they grow, performance will always decrease. If you believe you will have many workflow instances, then create a Task and Workflow History list for your specific workflow. Microsoft states that you should periodically change these lists in the workflow association settings as the number of list items within a list becomes large.

INSIDE OUT   Tracking workflows information for auditing purposes

When you create your own custom workflows—that is, those that are not provided by default with SharePoint Foundation—and you want to keep audit information concerning the workflow, then you should write such information to another list and apply appropriate permissions for the list to secure the items written to it, or use Visual Studio to create a custom audit report by using the *SPAuditEntry* class. You can find more information at *http://msdn.microsoft.com/en-us/library/microsoft.sharepoint.spauditentry.aspx*.

Working with List and Library Workflows

SharePoint lists and libraries allow content managers to provide users with a web-based user interface (UI) for linking to, downloading, and uploading information and files, and to provide workflows when information or documents are added to the list or library, or changed.

The person who has Manage List permissions on a list or library can use the Workflow Settings page to associate a workflow template with that list or library, and thereby create a workflow for that list or library. List and library workflow templates can be specific to one content type or they can be used for any content type. From the Workflow Settings page, you pick where the workflow tasks and history information are stored, and set the conditions that trigger a workflow instance for a list item or file. You can also modify and remove an existing workflow process on this page.

> **Note**
>
> To use the Three-State workflow template, you need a choice column on the list or library where you are associating it. The choice column is used to store the three statuses of the workflow; for example, Holiday Request Submitted, Holiday Request Approved, and Holiday Taken. The default value for the column should be set as the first status in the workflow, in this case, Holiday Request Submitted.

Adding a Workflow Template to a List or Library

To add a workflow template to a list or library, you need to provide a workflow name, choose how you want workflow instances to start, and complete an association form to provide values that are needed by the workflow, especially if the workflow is configured to start automatically. Perform the following steps to add a workflow template to a list or library:

1. On the Quick Launch, click the document library or list with which you want to associate a workflow template.

2. On the ribbon, click the List or Library tab.

    This tab could also be named Calendar if the list was created from a Calendar list template.

3. In the Settings group, click the arrow to the right of Workflow Settings, and then click Add A Workflow.

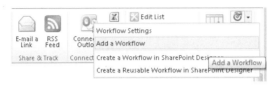

The Add A Workflow page opens.

4. In the Content Type section, select Any or click the name of the content type for which the workflow template will be created.

Ensure that you have associated that content type with this list or library before configuring the workflow.

5. In the Workflow section, select a workflow template.

> **Note**
> **The remaining steps in this procedure assume that you have selected the Three-State workflow.**

6. In the Name section, type a new name for this workflow, such as **Holiday Request Approval**.

This name will be used to create a column in the list or library, and therefore, it must be unique in the list or library. You must not use the name of an existing column or any of the reserved column names, such as Title, Created By, Modified By, Checked Out To, or Approval Status.

7. In the Task List section, select an existing tasks list or New Task List.

If you select New Task List, the name of the new task list will take the format of <workflow name> Tasks, such as Holiday Request Approval Tasks.

8. In the History List section, select an existing workflow history list or New History List.

The name of a new workflow history list will take the format of <workflow name> History.

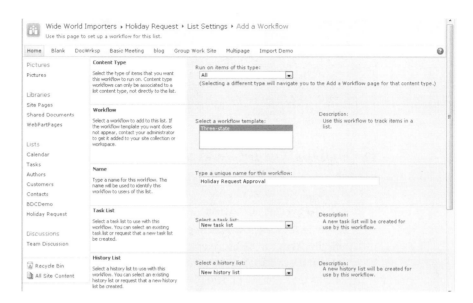

9. In the Start Options section, select one of the options that will initiate a workflow instance.

   When you first create a workflow, to quickly test it, select the Allow This Workflow To Be Manually Started By An Authenticated User With Edit Item Permissions check box.

10. Click Next to go to the association page named Customize The Three-State Workflow.

    The Workflow States section displays a choice column of the list or library if one exists, for example, if you are adding the workflow template to a list created from the Calendar list template, the Select A 'Choice' Field drop-down list will display *Category*.

11. In the Select A 'Choice' Field drop-down list, select the choice column you created for this workflow, such as Holiday Status and it's three states: Holiday Request Submitted, Holiday Request Approved, and Holiday Taken.

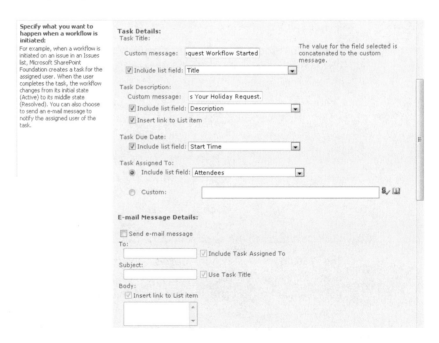

Workflow states:

Select a 'Choice' field, and then select a value for the initial, middle, and final states. For an Issues list, the states for an item are specified by the Status field, where:
Initial State = Active
Middle State = Resolved
Final State = Closed
As the item moves through the various stages of the workflow, the item is updated automatically.

Select a 'Choice' field:
Holiday Status
Initial state
Holiday Request Submitted
Middle state
Holiday Request Approved
Final state
Holiday Taken

12. In the Specify What You Want To Happen When A Workflow Is Initiated section, in the Tasks Details area, make changes as needed.

For example, under Task Title, in the Custom Message text box, type **Holiday Request Workflow Started**, and under Task Description, in the Custom Message text box, type **A Workflow Has Been Started To Process Your Holiday Request**. The new task item can be assigned to the person specified in the Assigned To column, or you can specify another person in the Custom text box. You also have the choice to send an email to the person you selected in the Task Assigned To section or to a different person, or to not send an email.

13. Repeat step 11 for the Specify What You Want To Happen When A Workflow Changes To Its Middle State section.

14. Click OK to be returned to the default view for the list or library.

Modifying a Workflow

Once a workflow template is added to a list or library, you might need to make changes to its configuration. To modify a workflow, complete the following procedure:

1. On the Quick Launch, click the document library or list to which you added the workflow template.

2. On the ribbon, click the List or Library tab. In the Settings group, click the Workflow Settings command to display the Workflow Settings page.

    This page displays all workflows that were added to the list or library, together with the number of workflow instances that are progressing through each workflow.

3. Under Workflow Name, click the workflow that you want to modify (such as Holiday Request Approval) to display the Change A Workflow page.

    Use this page to change the content type, Task list, and Workflow History list with which this workflow is associated, the name of the workflow, and the start options.

4. Click Next to open the Customize The Three-State Workflow page, in which you can select a different choice field and modify what you want to happen when a workflow instance is initiated or when a workflow instance changes to its middle state.

5. Click OK to confirm your changes.

Removing a Workflow

When a workflow is no longer needed, you should remove it from the list or library to prevent confusing users who use that list or library. To remove a workflow from a list or library, perform the following steps:

1. On the Quick Launch, click the document library or list to which you added the workflow template.

2. On the ribbon, click the List or Library tab. In the Settings group, click the Workflow Settings command to display the Workflow Settings page.

Chapter 10

3. Click Remove A Workflow to display the Remove Workflow page.

This page displays each workflow that was added to this list or library, together with the number of workflow instances that are currently progressing through the workflow. The three options allow workflow instances to start in the workflow, prevent any workflow instances from starting, or remove the workflow from the list or library. If you feel that you might need the workflow in the future, select the No New Instances option.

When you remove a workflow from a list, it removes the column that the workflow uses to indicate the status of a workflow instance in the workflow process. This column was created when a workflow template is associated with a list or library and contains such values as In Progress, Cancelled, and Completed. Removing columns on lists and libraries causes a database operation proportional to the number of items or files in the list or library. When the list or library contains more than a million items, do not remove the workflow from the list or library; instead, set the workflow to No New Instances.

INSIDE OUT   The implications of removing workflows

When you remove a workflow, all the task items and workflow history items that were created for that workflow are also removed.

Using a Workflow

Once a workflow is added to a list or library, a list item or file can progress through that workflow. The trigger that SharePoint uses to initiate a workflow instance for a list item or file is dependent on the following:

- The content type with which the workflow is linked and whether the list item or file is of the same type.

- The Start options that you configured on the association forms. You can start a workflow instance by manually starting the workflow, uploading or creating a new file, or modifying an existing list item or file.

To manually start a workflow instance for a list item or file, complete the procedure that follows. You might be provided with an initiation form that allows you to define values that the workflow requires. These might be similar to the values provided on the association form. When a workflow instance is automatically started, the initiation form is not displayed and the default values or the values provided on the association form are used:

1. Hover your mouse over the list item or file for which you want to start a workflow, and then select the check box that appears to the left of the list item or file.

2. On the Items tab (if this is a list) or the Document tab (if this is a library), click Workflows in the Workflows group.

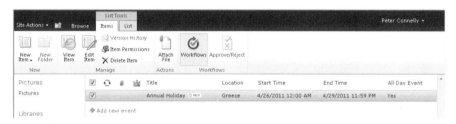

The <list or library name>: Workflows: <file or item name> page is displayed.

3. Under Start A New Workflow, click the name of the workflow that you want to start; for example, Holiday Request Approval.

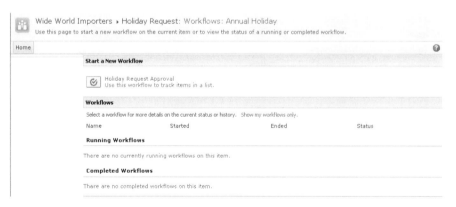

You are returned to the default view of the list and library, where a new column might appear. This new column is named with the workflow name and has a status of In Progress. This new column is not added to the default view when the default view is a Calendar view.

To review the workflow progress of the list item or file, perform the following steps:

1. Browse to the list or library where the item or file is stored.

2. In the workflow column, click In Progress. If the workflow column is not shown, select the check box to the left of the item, and then on the items tab, click Workflows. Under Running Workflows, click In Progress for the workflow that you want to review.

   The Workflow Status page displays.

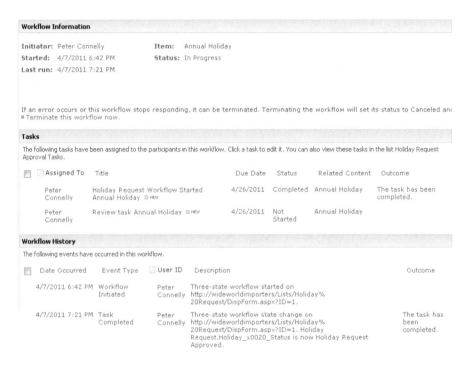

The workflow status page summarizes workflow instance information in three sections:

- **Workflow Information** This section details workflow instance information, such as who initiated the workflow instance, the start time, the name of the item that the workflow instance is linked to, and the status. You can also use the line at the bottom of this section to terminate the workflow for the list item or file. When you terminate a workflow instance, the status of the workflow changes from In Progress to Cancelled, and any task items created by the workflow are deleted.

- **Tasks**   This section displays task items that are associated with this workflow instance. It provides a link to the list item or file and a link to the Task list associated with the workflow. When you click on the title of a task item, if you have Silverlight installed, a modal dialog opens and displays the details of the task item.

- **Workflow History**   This section details messages that the workflow instance wrote to the Workflow History list.

To complete tasks assigned to you as a list item or file progresses through a workflow, complete the following procedure:

1. Browse to the Workflow Status page as described in the previous procedure, or alternatively, display the workflow task list by using the All Site Contents page if a link to the workflow task list is not displayed on the Quick Launch.

2. Hover over the title of the task item assigned to you, and then click Edit Item to display the task input form.

3. From the Status list, select Completed, and then on the Edit tab, in the Commit group, click Save.

   If the workflow instance has completed all tasks, then the status of the workflow will change from In Progress to Completed.

TROUBLESHOOTING

If the two tasks do not appear in the Tasks section and in the Workflow Information section, a message in red text states that due to heavy loads, the latest workflow operation has been queued. Refresh the page, and then click OK in the message box that appears.

INSIDE OUT   Permissions and the use of workflows

By default, when you first create a list or library, it inherits its permissions from the site. This is also true for the workflow task and history lists. By specifying a person to assign a task to, you have not modified the permissions of the task list. You have only configured the workflow to store the user name in the Assign To column of the task list. Any user in the site's members SharePoint Group can edit and therefore complete the workflow task item.

Chapter 10

Using Site Workflows

New with SharePoint Foundation is the introduction of site workflows, which are not associated with a list or library. However, site workflows can work with any SharePoint object within the site. By default, SharePoint Foundation 2010 does not provide any site templates to use with any sites; therefore, you would need to develop a site workflow template by using Visual Studio or you can publish a workflow to a site by using SharePoint Designer.

To manually start a site workflow instance or to monitor a site workflow by using the browser, perform the following steps:

1. On the Quick Launch, click All Site Content, or on the Site Actions menu, click View All Site Content to display the All Site Content page. To the right of Create, click Site Workflows.

2. Under Start A New Workflow, click the site workflow that you want to start, or under My Running Workflows or under My Completed Workflows, click the workflow that you want to monitor.

   If you cannot see the workflow that you want to monitor, under Workflows, click Show All Workflows.

To manage the site workflows associated with a site, complete the following procedure:

1. Browse to the Site Settings page.

2. Under Site Administration, click Workflow Settings.

   If the site workflow was developed by using Visual Studio, you might be able to change association parameters by clicking the workflow name. If the site workflow was created by using SharePoint Designer, you can only change the site workflow via SharePoint Designer, and therefore, clicking the workflow name displays a message box, stating that you need to use a SharePoint-compatible workflow editing tool.

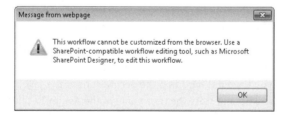

3. Click Remove A Workflow to display the Remove Workflow page. This page displays each workflow that was added to the site, together with the number of workflow instances that are currently progressing through the workflow. You can use this page to prevent the start of any new workflow instances or to remove site workflows.

To create a site workflow by using SharePoint Designer, perform the following steps:

1. Open the site in SharePoint Designer, and then in the Navigation pane, click Workflows.

2. On the Workflows tab, in the New group, click Site Workflow to display the Create Site Workflow dialog box.

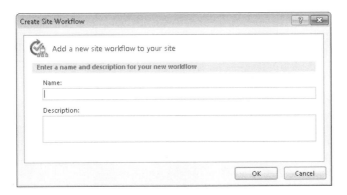

3. Type the name and description, and then click OK to open the Workflow Editor.

You can then create an initiation form, use actions and conditions, and publish the workflow, as described later in this chapter.

INSIDE OUT   Site workflow templates and SharePoint Designer

You cannot create a site workflow template by using SharePoint Designer; therefore, within SharePoint Designer, you cannot create association forms or association form variables for site workflows.

Gathering Requirements by Using Visio Premium

The ability for a Business Analyst to communicate effectively with developers is greatly improved through the implementation of Office Visio Premium 2010, SharePoint Designer 2010, and SharePoint Foundation 2010. In the past if business analysts needed to coordinate some new business process, they would create a Visio document or other graphical drawing that depicted the new process. When the process was handed to the developer, the developer would need to recreate each step in the development application to match the diagram.

With Visio Premium 2010, you can now create a Visio diagram from a new template called the Microsoft SharePoint Workflow. You can design your workflow diagram just like you can with any other Visio diagram by using the drag-and-drop functionality to create a nice layout. Once the diagram is complete, you can run the validation provided by Visio to ensure that no branches or paths have been missed.

Next, you export the Visio diagram as a Visio Workflow Interchange (.vwi) file, which can be imported into SharePoint Designer, where the conditions and actions, together with any additional rules that need to be added, can be configured. You cannot import the .vwi file into Visual Studio; however, once you configure the workflow in SharePoint Designer, you can then save the workflow as a workflow template solutions file (.wsp), which can then be imported into Visual Studio.

More information on using SharePoint Designer and Visual Studio to create workflows is detailed later in this chapter.

To create a SharePoint 2010 workflow by using Visio 2010, perform the following steps:

1. Open Visio 2010 to display the Backstage view.

2. On the New tab, under Template Categories, click Flowchart, and then click Microsoft SharePoint Workflow.

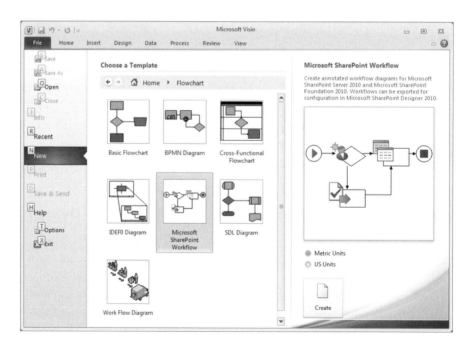

3. In the right pane, click Create to open a blank template.

In the Shapes pane (on the left), three stencils are displayed: SharePoint Workflow Actions, SharePoint Workflow Conditions, and SharePoint Workflow Terminators.

4. In the Shapes pane, under SharePoint Workflow Terminators, click Start.

5. Drag the Start shape to the left side of the template drawing area.

6. Repeat the steps 4 and 5 to add the Terminate shape to the right of the drawing area.

7. On the Home tab, in the Tools group, click Connector, and then drag a line from the Start shape to the Terminate shape so that a red square appears on the left-most edge of the Terminate circle.

The connecting line automatically connects the Start shape to the Terminate shape.

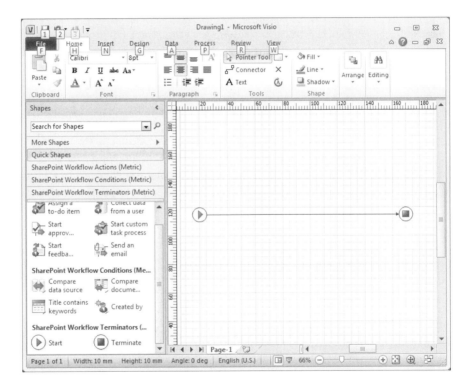

8. On the Home tab, click Pointer.

If you leave your cursor as a connector, you might inadvertently draw lines on your diagram. When you return the cursor to a pointer, you can drag other shapes to your diagram or move shapes around without accidently drawing lines.

You can now add conditions and actions that represent the tasks of your business process that you wish to automate. For example, you can add a condition to check whether a calendar item is set to a category of holiday and then creates a task item for the team leader.

1. In the Shapes pane, under SharePoint Workflow Conditions, click Compare Document Field. Drag it to the drawing area to the right of the Start shape and place it on the line connecting the Start shape to the Terminate shape.

2. In the Shapes pane, under SharePoint Workflow Actions, drag Send An Email to the drawing area to the right of the Compare Document Field, and then place it on the line connecting the Compare Document Field shape to the Terminate shape.

3. Right-click the line connecting the Compare Document Field shape and the Send An Email shape, and then click Yes.

4. On the Home tab, in the Tools group, click Connector, click the bottom corner of the Compare document field shape, and then drag a line to the Terminate shape. Right-click the connecting line, and then click No.

5. On the Home tab, in the Tools group, click Pointer Tool. Double-click Compare Document Field, and then type **Is Calendar Category = Holiday?**. Double-click Send An Email, and then type **Send email to employee's Team Leader to approve holiday**.

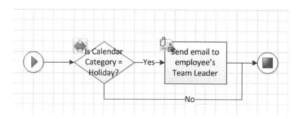

INSIDE OUT   Visio workflow actions and conditions limitations

The SharePoint Designer workflow conditions and actions that are displayed in Visio are coded into Visio. Visio does not connect to a SharePoint installation to find which SharePoint Designer conditions and actions are installed. So, if you use Visual Studio to develop any custom conditions and actions, they will not be visible in Visio, and more important, there are some action shapes displayed in the Shapes pane that are only installed if you have SharePoint Server 2010. The action shapes that you cannot use with SharePoint Foundation are:

- Start approval process

- Start custom task process

- Start feedback process

- Send approval for document set

- Send document set to repository

- Set content approval status for document set

- Look up manager of a user

If you do add one of these actions to your Visio diagram, when you import the .vwi file into SharePoint Designer, it will throw the error message, *Could not deserialize object. The <object name> could not be resolved*, where *<object type>* varies depending on the shape you added in Visio. For example, when you add the Look Up Manager Of A User action, the type is *Microsoft.Office.Workflow.Actions.LookUpManagerOfActivity*.

Once you have created a diagram of your workflow and modified the text for each shape to document the details of the process, you need to validate the drawing before you can export the diagram and give it to the person who will create the workflow as either a SharePoint Designer or Visual Studio workflow. To validate and export a Visio SharePoint Workflow, complete the following procedure:

1. On the Process tab, in the Diagram Validation group, click Check Diagram.

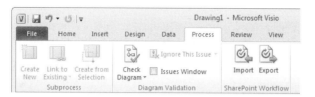

A Microsoft Visio dialog box opens, stating No Issues Were Found In The Current Document. If your workflow has issues, an Issues task pane opens at the bottom of the Visio window. The erroneous component is highlighted. The Issues pane can be opened or closed by selecting the Issues Window check box in the Diagram Validation group on the Process tab.

2. Click OK to close the Microsoft Visio dialog box.

3. On the Process tab, in the SharePoint Workflow group, click Export.

The Export Workflow dialog box opens so that you can browse to where you want to save the .vwi file. In the File Name text box, type the name of the file, and then click Save to save the .vwi file and close the dialog box.

4. Close Visio. You can choose to save the .vsd file of your workflow for documentation purposes, if needed.

To import a .vwi file into SharePoint Designer, perform the following steps:

1. Using SharePoint Designer, open a SharePoint site for which you want to develop a SharePoint Designer workflow.

If you want to create a globally reusable workflow from the file, the site must be a top-level site of a Site Collection.

2. In the Navigation pane, click Workflows. On the Workflows tab, in the Manage group, click Import From Visio to open the Import Workflow From Visio Drawing dialog box.

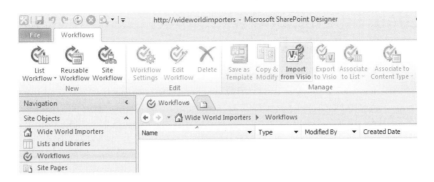

3. Click Browse, navigate to the location where you stored the .vwi file, click Open, and then click Next.

4. In the Workflow Name text box, type the name of the workflow as it will be seen by users on a SharePoint site, and then select either List Workflow or Reusable workflow.

    If you select List Workflow, you need to select a list with which to associate the work-flow defined in the .vwi file. If you select the Reusable workflow, associate a workflow with a content type.

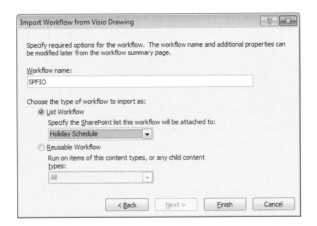

5. Click Finish.

    If this is the first time you've created a workflow, a dialog box opens asking you to wait while SharePoint Designer downloads the necessary information from the Share-Point site you have open. The information is related to the SharePoint Designer work-flow conditions and actions that are installed.

    You can find more information about SharePoint Designer in the next section and in Chapter 14, "Creating, Managing, and Designing Sites with SharePoint Designer 2010."

Creating, Editing, and Managing Custom Workflows by Using SharePoint Designer

The Three-State workflow is a simple workflow template that you can use with lists and libraries. However, this workflow will not be sufficient for many of the business-process–related tasks that you want to automate. This is when you will use SharePoint Designer to create workflows. SharePoint Designer provides a Workflow Editor with which you can create no-code, rules-based declarative workflows. There are three types of workflows that you can create with SharePoint Designer:

- **List workflows**   Also known as content workflows, these workflows are created to automate tasks associated with content stored in lists and libraries.

- **Site workflows**   These workflows are not associated with specific SharePoint objects and are started manually at the site level.

- **Reusable workflows**   These are workflow templates that can subsequently be added (associated) with a list or library on the site for which the reusable workflow is created. You create reusable workflows by binding them with content types. Reusable workflows can be published to the global workflows catalog, which makes it reusable on every site in the Site Collection, and visible to all users. Only reusable workflows at the top-level site of a Site Collection can be published as globally reusable workflows.

INSIDE OUT   Creating workflows by using SharePoint Designer on a client operating system

To create workflows by using SharePoint Designer, you must have the .NET Framework 3.5 installed on your computer. It is likely that unless you are a developer with your own copy of a SharePoint Foundation installation, you will be running SharePoint Designer on a computer that does not have SharePoint Foundation installed on it. If that is the case, you will be running a client operating system such as Windows 7, Windows Vista, or Windows XP. Windows 7 includes the .Net Framework 3.5; however, if you are using Windows Vista or Windows XP, you might need to install the .NET Framework 3.5 before you can work with workflows in SharePoint Designer. The .NET Framework is available from the Microsoft Download Center at *www.microsoft.com/downloads*.

When you create a workflow with SharePoint Designer, you are provided with two pages:

- **Workflow Settings**   Use this page to view and manage settings for the workflow. It consists of a contextual ribbon tab, as shown in Figure 10-2, and five areas, as shown in Figure 10-3.

Figure 10-2 On the Workflow Settings tab, you can save, edit, manage workflows, and create and manage variables.

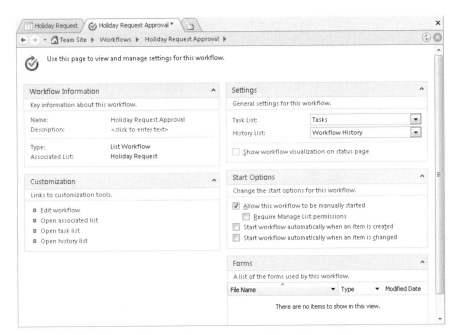

Figure 10-3 Use the Workflow Settings page to configure the workflow.

- — **Workflow Information**   This area displays basic workflow information, such as the workflow name, description and type (list, site, or reusable). When the type of workflow is a list workflow, then this area displays the name of the list or library with which the workflow is associated. When the workflow type is reusable, this area displays the name of the content type with which it is associated.

Chapter 10

— **Customization**   The links provided in this area will differ depending on the type of workflow. For example, for a list workflow, this area contains links to the Workflow Editor page and links to open the associated list, Task list, and Workflow History list.

— **Settings**   Use this area to select the Task and Workflow History list that the workflow is to use. For list and site workflows, this area contains a check box which is associated with workflow visualization within the browser. This option is only applicable when you have SharePoint Server 2010 Enterprise Edition installed. Leave this check box clear for workflows that are to be published to SharePoint Foundation sites.

— **Start Options**   Use this area to select the start options for the workflow.

— **Forms**   This area displays the pages that SharePoint Designer automatically creates during the publish process. Depending on the type of workflow and the start option selected, a number of pages will be created. Whenever a workflow can be started manually, an initiation page is created. When you use the task action to collect data from a user, then task pages are created.

- **Workflow Editor**   Use this page and the Workflow tab to create and change the workflow. Each workflow consists of conditions and actions, which can be grouped into steps. SharePoint Designer workflows can become large; you can use steps to document the major set of activities that need to be completed as part of your workflow. Use the content area of the workspace and Workflow tab to add, delete, and modify conditions, actions, and steps. The Workflow tab consists of five tab groups, as shown in Figure 10-4.

Figure 10-4 Use the Workflow tab to create and modify the logic of your workflow.

— **Save**   Use this group to check your workflow for errors, save your workflow, and publish your workflow. The Save and Publish commands are the same commands that you find in the Save group on the Workflow Settings tab. Use the Save command when you want to save your changes but have not completed the workflow, and therefore you do not wish other users on the site to use the workflow. When you click the publish command, it also saves the workflow.

— **Modify**   Use the commands in this group to move and delete conditions, actions, and steps, as well as to modify the advanced properties of conditions and actions. Actions can be moved between steps and within steps, whereas conditions can only be moved up or down within their respective condition block. A condition block starts with an *If* statement, subsequent conditions start with an *and* or an *or*. You cannot copy and paste steps, conditions, or actions within a workflow or between workflows—which at times can be very frustrating.

— **Insert**   Use the commands in this group to insert conditions, actions, and steps. Use the Else-If Branch commands to add another condition block so that you can define actions to be performed if the conditions of the first condition block are not true. Use the Parallel Block command when you want a set of actions to execute at the same time and not in sequence. Parallel actions might not be performed absolutely simultaneous. The exact order cannot be specified and can vary each time a workflow instance runs. You can use the Impersonate Step command to add a special step to your workflow that allows the conditions and actions within that step to execute by using the security credentials of the workflow author.

— **Manage**   This group contains three commands that are the same as those in the Manage group on the Workflow Settings tab. The commands available on the Workflow tab allow you to publish a reusable workflow as a globally reusable workflow, export the workflow as a .vwi Visio file, and switch to the Workflow Settings page. You can also switch to the Workflow Settings page by using the workspace breadcrumb and clicking the name of the workflow, which appears in the workspace breadcrumb to the right of Workflows.

— **Variables**   This tab group contains three commands that are the same as those in the Variables group on the Workflow Settings tab. Variables are temporary storage that persist for the lifetime of the workflow. Use the Initiation Form Parameters command when a workflow instance is manually started; thus, the initiator of the workflow can provide values stored in initiation variables, which can then be used in the workflow. The values entered by the workflow initiator are only available for the lifetime of the workflow instance. Use the Local Variables command to pass values from one condition or action to another condition or action; for example, to save the Task ID created from the Collect Data From A User action so that a subsequent action can use the values a person entered into the task. Use the Association Columns command to have the list or reusable workflow add site columns to the list or library with which the workflow is associated. Review existing site columns before you create new site columns within the Association Columns dialog box.

Using Conditions and Actions

Each workflow is created for a combination of conditions and actions. Conditions are used to create rules that portray the logic of the workflow. Actions are the basic unit of work performed by the workflow. When a condition is true, then all the actions associated with that condition are performed. To help you visually see which actions are associated with which conditions, the Workflow Editor surrounds conditions and their associated actions with a gray rectangle. A condition and its Else-If Branch conditions must be completed in a single step; that is, they cannot extend from one step to another.

Using a combination of conditions and actions, you can define which actions should be performed under which conditions. A workflow does not need to contain any conditions, but should contain at least one action such as writing to the history log or sending the creator of a list item an email. If a workflow does not contain any conditions, then all the actions defined in the workflow will be performed.

> **Note**
>
> When the set of built-in conditions and actions does not meet your business needs, a developer can create new conditions or actions, which are known as custom activities, by using Visual Studio 2010 or a third-party tool. Creating a custom activity by using Visual Studio is detailed later in this chapter.

SharePoint Designer divides the built-in conditions into two categories:

- **Common Condition**   This category contains two conditions:
    - If Any Value Equals Value
    - If Current Item Field Equals Value

- **Other Conditions**   This category contains eight conditions:
    - Check List Item Permission Levels (only available within an Impersonation Step)
    - Check List Item Permissions (only available within an Impersonation Step)
    - Created By A Specific Person
    - Created In A Specific Date Span
    - Modified By A Specific Person
    - Modified in A Specific Date Span

— Person Is A Valid SharePoint User

— Title Field Contains Keywords

You can find a quick reference guide to workflow conditions in SharePoint Designer 2010 at *http://office.microsoft.com/en-us/sharepoint-designer-help/workflow-conditions-in-sharepoint-designer-2010-a-quick-reference-guide-HA010376962.aspx*. For information about creating compact and powerful conditions, go to *http://blogs.msdn.com/b/sharepointdesigner/ archive/2008/05/14/create-compact-and-powerful-conditions-in-your-workflows.aspx*.

A SharePoint 2010 workflow action is a task that needs to be completed. You can choose to run actions in serial—that is, an action starts only if the preceding one is complete—or you can choose to run actions in parallel, known as a parallel block, where all actions start at the same time. SharePoint Designer divides built-in actions into four categories:

- **Core Actions**   This category contains the common actions that you will use in many of your workflows. It consists of twelve actions:

    — Add A Comment

    — Add Time To Date

    — Do Calculation

    — Log To History List

    — Pause For Duration

    — Pause Until Date

    — Send An Email

    — Send Document To Repository (only available on workflows associated with libraries)

    — Set Time Portion Of Date/Time Field

    — Set Workflow Status

    — Set Workflow Variable

    — Stop Workflow

- **List Actions**   This category contains actions with which you can manipulate list items in a list and files within a library. This category contains fifteen actions:

    — Add List Item Permissions (only available within an Impersonation Step and should be used with care.)

— Check In Item

— Check Out Item

— Copy List Item

— Create List Item

— Delete Item

— Discard Check Out Item

— Inherit List Item Parent Permissions (only available within an Impersonation Step)

— Remove List Item Permissions (only available within an Impersonation Step)

— Replace List Item Permissions (only available within an Impersonation Step)

— Set Content Approval Status

— Set Field In Current Item

— Update List Item

— Wait For Change In Document Check-Out Status (only available on workflows associated with libraries)

— Wait For Field Change In Current Item

- **Task Actions**   This category contains actions with which you can assign a task to a specific user or group. This category contains three actions:

    — Assign A Form To A Group

    — Assign A To-Do Item

    — Collect Data From A User

- **Utility Actions**   This is a new category in SharePoint 2010. It contains five actions that can be used to manipulate strings:

    — Extract Substring From End Of String

    — Extract Substring From Index Of String

    — Extract Substring From Start Of String

    — Extract Substring Of String From Index With Length

    — Find Interval Between Dates

> **Note**
> SharePoint Server 2010 provides two other categories: Document Set Actions and Relational Actions. The Relational Actions category contains only one built-in action, which you can use to look up a user's profile imported from Active Directory. The action then returns the user's manager from that profile. SharePoint Foundation does not support document sets or importing user's information from Active Directory; hence, this is why you will not see those categories when you work with workflows in SharePoint Designer on a SharePoint Foundation site.

For additional information, read the quick reference guide to workflow actions in SharePoint Designer 2010, which is available at *http://office.microsoft.com/en-us/sharepoint-designer-help/workflow-actions-in-sharepoint-designer-2010-a-quick-reference-guide-HA010376961. aspx*.

The best way to understand the options of building a workflow by using SharePoint Designer is to build a workflow. In the following section, you will use a number of conditions and actions as you build a workflow for a holiday request scenario, which will use a list workflow that is triggered to start a workflow instance when an employee creates a new calendar item in the Holiday Schedule list. During the course of developing the workflow, it's likely that you will use the option to manually start the workflow. The information needed for this workflow is stored in three related lists, as shown in Figure 10-5.

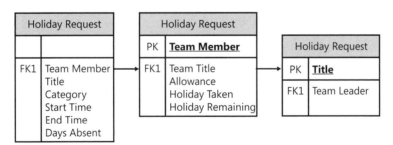

Figure 10-5 The relationship between the Holiday Request, Holiday Allowance, and Teams lists.

The three lists are:

- **Teams**   This list is based on the Custom list template and contains all the teams a department might have, such as IT, Help Desk, User Adoption, and Training. The Title column is used for the name of team. A People Or Group column is added, which is named Team Leader.

Chapter 10

- **Holiday Allowance** A list created from the Custom list template, which has a list item for each employee in a team and consists of four columns. Because you will not be using the Title column, this field should be set as not required. All other columns should be configured as required:

  — **Team Member** A People Or Group field.

  — **Team** This column is a lookup column to the Teams list and displays the Title field. Optionally, you can enforce restricted delete relationship behavior.

  — **Allowance** A number field with a default value of 20, a minimum value of 0, and a maximum value of 50.

  — **Holiday Taken** A number field with a default value of 0, a minimum value of 0, and a maximum value of 50.

  — **Holiday Remaining** A calculated column with a formula, [Allowance]–[Holiday Taken].

- **Holiday Request** This list is based on a Calendar list template with content approval enabled and two additional columns:

  — **Days Absent** This column is a number column with a default value of 1 and a minimum value of 1.

Prior to creating and testing the workflow, using either the browser or SharePoint Designer, you should create three lists and populate the Teams and Holiday Allowance lists with data similar to that in Tables 10-1 and 10-2 so that you can test your workflow.

Table 10-1 **Test Content for the Teams List**

Title	Team leader
IT	Peter Connelly
Human Resources	Erin Hagens
Marketing & Sales	Jack Creasey

Table 10-2 **Test Content for the Holiday Allowance list**

Team member	Team	Allowance	Holiday taken
Bruce	IT	25	3
Chris	Human Resources	20	0
Steve	IT	30	5

When a team member wants to submit a holiday request, he enters the following data:

- Set the category of the request to Holiday

- Holiday start date

- Holiday end date

- The number of days from their holiday allowance that they are requesting

You can enhance the solution by using list validation for the Holiday Request list to enforce that the [End Time] > [Start Time].

Creating a List Workflow

Perform the following steps to create a list workflow for a list or library:

1. In SharePoint Designer, using the Navigation pane, click Workflows.

2. On the Workflows tab, in the New group, click List Workflow, and then click the name of the list or library (such as Holiday Request) to display the Create List Workflow dialog box.

   You can also display the Create List Workflow dialog box by using the List Workflow command in the New group on the Site tab and the List Settings tab.

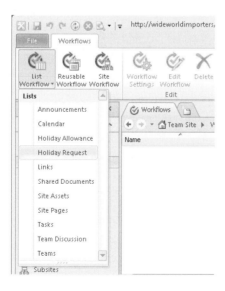

Chapter 10

3. In the Name text box, type Holiday Request Approval, and then click OK.

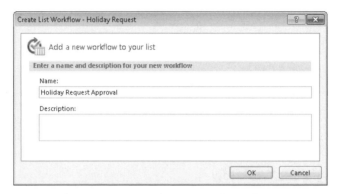

If the Downloading Data dialog box opens, wait for it to close.

A new tab, named Holiday Request Approval opens with an asterisk, indicating that the workflow is not saved. The Workflow Editor contains one step, Step 1, and a flashing orange horizontal line where the first condition or action can be inserted.

4. On the workspace breadcrumb, click Holiday Request Approval to navigate to the workflow settings page.

5. On the Workflow Settings tab, click Save.

The Microsoft SharePoint Designer dialog box temporarily opens as the workflow is saved back to the SQL content database.

Using Common Conditions

The two most commonly used conditions in a SharePoint Designer workflow are If Any Value Equals Value and If Current Item Field Equals Value. The first of these conditions is a generic condition that you can use to compare two values, where a value can be:

- A metadata value from the list item or file on which the workflow instance was initiated, known as the current item.

- A metadata value for a list item or file in list or library, where the workflow instance was not initiated.

- Workflow variables or parameters, such as initiation form parameters and local variables.

- Workflow context, such as the name of the workflow template, the current site URL, or the current user.

- A value from items stored in the workflow's associated tasks or history list.

When the value that you want to compare is not in the current item, you need to provide logic to specify from which item the workflow can obtain the value. You do this by using the Define Workflow Lookup dialog box. When the value to be compared in the condition is from the current item, then use the second common condition format, as described in the following steps:

1. In the Navigate pane, click the workflow that you want to modify to display the workflow settings page, and then in the Customization area, click Edit Workflow to display the Workflow Editor in the workspace.

2. Within the Workflow Editor, click where you would like the condition to appear (for example, within Step 1).

3. On the Workflow tab, click Condition in the Insert group, and then click If Current Item Field Equals Value.

A two-row gray rectangle is added to Step 1, with the text, "If Field Equals Value," added to the top row of the rectangle. The words Field, Equals, and Value are hyperlinks.

4. Click Field, and then click Category. Click Value, and then click Holiday.

The Equals link offers you with a number of comparison operators that differ depending on the data types of the comparison values.

INSIDE OUT   If Current Item Field Equals Value versus If Any Value Equals Value

When the value that you want to compare is a metadata value stored in one of the columns of the current item, then for performance reasons, you should use the If Current Item Field Equals Value condition. Obtaining metadata values for other list items, whether you are using the If Any Value Equals Value condition or actions such as Update List Item, can cause additional database operations, and when a list has many list items and many active workflow instances, each resulting in many database operations, this can cause performance issues for the workflow associated with the list and other lists as well as how quickly a SharePoint server responds to requests for webpages.

Therefore, when there are two similar conditions or actions, and the value you wish to reference is stored in a column of the current item, use the condition or action for the current item. Similarly, within your workflow, when you reference the same value again and again, such as Holiday Taken in the Holiday Allowance list, which is a value you might refer to in a condition, a calculation, the body of emails, and as values in the workflow history log, then you should store the value at the start of the workflow in a variable and use that variable throughout the workflow when you need to know the number of days that a person has taken as holiday. The use of variables is described later in this chapter.

Using the Workflow History Log to Monitor the Progress of a Workflow

SharePoint Designer does not provide any diagnostic or debug facilities. When your workflow fails to run to completion, the only way to track which branch of a condition or which actions completed successfully is to write many items to the History list by using steps similar to the following procedure:

1. Click where you would like the action to appear, for example, within Step 1, click Start Typing Or Use The Insert Group In The Ribbon. On the Workflow tab, in the Insert group, click Action, and then under Core Actions, click Log To History List.

The message "Log This Message To The Workflow History List" appears, with the words "This Message" being a hyperlink.

2. Click This Message to display a text box, the Ellipse button (also known as the *Display Builder* button), and the Define Workflow Lookup button.

This action creates a list item in the Workflow History list chosen on the workflow settings page. You can choose any of these three input methods to define the contents of the Description column for the History list item. You can use the text box to add static text; the Define Workflow Lookup button allows you to add content that is specified in one of the columns of the current item or from a column for a list item from another list. Choose the Display Builder button to use a combination of static text and content from list items in lists and libraries or workflow variables.

3. Click the Display Builder button to display the String Builder dialog box, and then type, **Holiday Request submitted by**.

4. Click Add Or Change Lookup to display the Lookup For String dialog box.

Chapter 10

5. In the Data Source list, leave Current Item selected.

This will allow you to retrieve values from the Holiday Schedule from the list item the team member created.

6. In the Field From Source list, select Created By and in the Return Field As list, select Display Name.

7. Click OK twice to close the Lookup For String and String Builder dialog boxes.

Creating Workflow Variables and Calculating Values

There will be circumstance in which you find yourself in need of information, but it is not saved in the list where the workflow is associated nor in other lists or libraries in your site. However, the information can be calculated from the information in your site. SharePoint Designer does not provide any looping facility, but it does allow you to specify a condition, so you are able to match retrieved data from a list item within another list or library; however, it will only return the first item that matches your condition. In the following steps, you will find the list item in the Holiday Allowance list that matches the team member who submitted the holiday request. You will then calculate the number of days a team member plans to take when adding the new holiday request to the number of days the team member has taken as holiday previous to this request:

1. Click where you would like the calculation action to appear (for example, within Step 1, in the same rectangle as the log action).

2. On the Workflow tab, in the Insert group, click Actions, and then under Core Actions, click Do Calculation. The words "Then Calculate Value Plus Value (Output To Variable: Calc)" appear.

3. Click Variable: Calc, and then click Create A New Variable to open the Edit Variable dialog box.

    You can also create new variables by using the Local Variables command on the Workflow tab in the Variables group. It is good practice to not use the variables that SharePoint Designer creates because it might not be of the correct data type for your calculation, and the name will not indicate the information stored in the variable. You should use the variable name as a mechanism to document your workflow, and in large workflows where there are many variables using an appropriate name, this can save you time when you need to change your workflows. When you create a new workflow variable, create it first before completing any links within an action or condition. When you create a variable after completing the links then the links will clear and you will need to complete them again.

4. In the Name text box, type **TotalHolilday**, and then in the Type list, select integer. Click OK to close the Edit Variable dialog box.

    Some actions, such as the Start Approval Process or the Start Feedback Process available in SharePoint Server 2010, when incorporated into your workflow will create their own variables; therefore, when you create a variable, it is advisable to devise a naming standard so that you can quickly identify the variables that you generated.

5. Click the first occurrence of Value, and then click the Define Workflow Lookup button to open the Lookup For Integer dialog box.

6. Leave Current Item as the selected item in the Data Source list, and then in the Field From Source list, select Days Absent. Click OK to close the Lookup For Integer dialog box.

7. Click the remaining Value link, and then click the Define Workflow Lookup button to open the Lookup For Integer dialog box.

8. In the Data Source list, scroll down and click Holiday Allowance.

   The Lookup For Integer dialog box expands to include a second section called Find The List Item.

9. In the Field Data To Retrieve section, click Field From Source, and then select Holiday Remaining.

10. In the Find The List Item section, click the down-arrow to the right of Field, select Team Member, and then in the Value, click the Ellipse button to open the Select Users dialog box.

11. Under Or Select From Existing Users And Groups, select User Who Created Current Item, and then click Add. Click OK to close the Select Users dialog box.

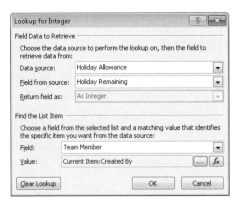

12. Click OK to close the Lookup For Integer dialog boxes.

    A Microsoft SharePoint Designer dialog box opens, stating that the lookup you defined does not guarantee to return a single value, and that if more than one value is returned, only the first value will be used. Therefore, when you use SharePoint Designer to join two lists or libraries, you should verify that your workflow design ensures that only one value is returned. In this scenario, there should only be one list item in the Holiday Allowance list for each Team Member. Unfortunately, you cannot use the Enforce Unique Value option when you create a column of type People Or Group.

13. Click Yes to close the Microsoft SharePoint Designer dialog box.

Using Workflow Variables and Comparing Data from Different Lists

In the following steps, you will check if the number of days that a team member requests, together with the number of holidays already taken exceeds the holiday allowance for the team member:

1. Click where you would like the condition to appear (for example, within Step 1, under the Calculation action).

2. On the Workflow tab, click Conditions on the Insert tab, and then under Common Condition, click If Any Value Equals Value.

   The words "If Value Equals Value" appears.

3. Click the first Value link, and then click the Define Workflow Lookup button to open the Define Workflow Lookup dialog box.

4. In the Data Source list, select Workflow Variables And Parameters, and then in the Field From Source list, select Variable: TotalHoliday. Click OK to close the Define Workflow Lookup dialog box.

5. Click Equals, and then select Is Less Than Or Equal To.

6. Click the remaining Value link, and then click the Define Workflow Lookup. In the Data Source list, select Holiday Allowance, and then in the Field From Source list, select Allowance.

7. In the Find The List Item section, in the Field list, select Team Member, and then to the right of Value, click the Ellipse button to open the Select Users dialog box. Select User Who Created Current Item, click Add, and then click OK twice to close the open dialog boxes. Click Yes to the SharePoint Designer dialog box.

If Current Item:Category equals Holiday

    Log Holiday Request submitted by [%Curren... to the workflow history list

    then Calculate Current Item:Days Absent plus Holiday Allowance:Holiday Remaining (Output to Variable: TotalHoliday)

    If Variable: TotalHoliday is less than or equal to Holiday Allowance:Allowance

        (Start typing or use the Insert group in the Ribbon.)

Chapter 10

Assigning Task Items to Users or Groups

Workflows developed by using SharePoint Designer are human centric, and therefore, as the workflow progresses, you will need to communicate with users of the site, either to complete a task or to obtain additional information. This is where you can use the three task actions: Assign A Form To A Group, Assign A To-Do Item, and Collect Data From A User. When you include one of these actions in the workflow, the workflow pauses until the task is completed. These actions are the same as they were with Windows SharePoint Services 3.0 and SharePoint Designer 2007; they are the only ones available in SharePoint Foundation 2010. Three new task actions are introduced with SharePoint Server 2010: Start Approval Process, Start Feedback Process, and Custom Task Process.

You can view a comparison of the three task actions at *http://office.microsoft.com/en-us/ sharepoint-designer-help/assign-a-to-do-item-in-a-workflow-HA010233623.aspx*. Although this write-up pertains to SharePoint Designer 2007, it is still relevant to SharePoint Designer 2010.

To assign a task item to a user, perform steps similar to those that follow. In this example, you will create a task item for the team leader of the user who created the holiday request. This will require a three-way lookup, because the team leader is in the Teams list and the team which the user is in can only be found from the Holiday Allowance list:

1. In the Workflow Editor, under the second If condition, place the insertion point, type **to**, and then press Enter. From the list of actions with "to" in their names, select Assign A To-Do Item.

   The words "Assign A To-Do Item To These Users" appear.

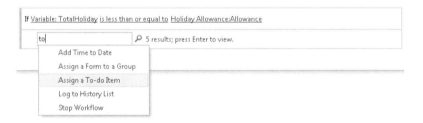

2. Click a To-Do Item to open the Custom Task Wizard dialog box, and then click Next to display the second page of the task wizard.

3. In the Name text box, type **Holiday Approval**, and in the Description text box, type **Please review the holiday request for one of your team members**. Click Finish to close the dialog box.

4. Click These Users to open the Select Users dialog box.

5. Under Or Select From Existing Users And Groups, select Workflow LookUp For A User, and then click Add to open the Lookup For Person Or Group dialog box.

6. In the Data Source list, select Teams. In the Field From Source list, select Team Leader In the Return Field As list, and then select Email Address.

7. In the Find The List Item section, in the Field list, select ID, and then in the Value list, click the Define Workflow Lookup button to open the Lookup For Integer dialog box.

8. In the Data Source list, click Holiday Allowance, and then in the Field From Source list click Team. In the Return Field As list, select Lookup Id (As Integer).

9. In the Find The List Item section, in the Field list, select Team Member, and then to the right of Value, click the Ellipse button to open the Select Users dialog box.

10. Under Or Select From Existing Users And Groups, select User Who Created Current Item, and then click Add. Click OK or Yes as appropriate to close all open dialog boxes.

   The words Assign Holiday Approval to Teams:Team Leader appear in the workflow.

INSIDE OUT Scenario alternatives when using SharePoint Server 2010

When using SharePoint Server 2010, and when Active Directory is populated to contain a user's manager, then in place of the Teams list, you could use the Lookup Manager Of A User action, which stores the user name of the manager in a variable. In step 6 of the previous procedure, in the Data Source list, select Workflow Variables And Parameters, and then in the Field From Source list, select the variable. Steps 7 through 10 would then not be necessary. This results in the SharePoint Server sending a query across the network to a domain controller. Alternatively, if the SharePoint Server 2010 User Profile Synchronization service is configured so that Active Directory Manager property has been imported into a user's profile, then in step 6, in the Data Source list, select User Profiles, and then in the Field From Source list, select Manager, matching the Account Name to Field in the Find The List Item section and User Who Created Current Item to Value. This second method results in a database operation.

Adding an Else - If Branch to Your Workflow

To create an Else block to an existing condition, perform the following steps:

1. Place the insertion point in the appropriate position, for example, under the Assign action and in line with the second If condition.

2. Type **Else**, and then press Enter. Alternatively, on the Workflow tab, in the Insert group, click Else-If Branch.

Using Workflows to Send Emails

To encourage the participants of the workflow to complete tasks or to keep them informed, use the Send An Email action, as described in the following steps:

1. Place the insertion point in the appropriate position, for example, under the Else branch, type **email**, and then press Enter.

   The words "Email These Users" appear.

2. Click These Users to open the Define E-mail Message dialog box.

3. Click the Book icon to the right of the To text box to open the Select Users dialog box. Under Or Select From Existing Users And Groups, select User Who Created Current Item, click Add, and then click OK.

4. Click the Ellipse button to the right of the Subject text box to open the String Builder dialog box. In the Name text box, type **Holiday Request Denied**, and then click OK.

5. In the body text box of the Define E-mail Message dialog box, type **Dear**, and then click Add Or Change Lookup to open the Lookup For String dialog box.

6. In the Field From Source list, select Created By, and in the Return Field As list, click Display Name. Click OK to close the Lookup For String dialog box.

7. In the body text box, on a new line, under Dear, type **Your Holiday Request for**, and then click Add Or Change Lookup to open the Lookup For String dialog box. In the Field From Source list, select Days Absent. Click OK to close the Lookup For String dialog box.

8. In the body text box, type **has been denied. You have exceeded your holiday allowance**.

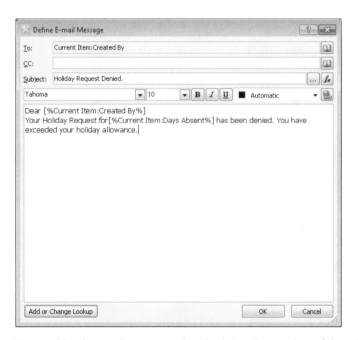

You could enhance the message by obtaining the number of days the team member is allowed as holiday from the Holliday Allowance list, or more efficiently, if you want to display the holiday allowance in the email, you should save this value in a workflow variable, when you retrieved the holiday allowance in the calculation action earlier in the workflow.

Chapter 10

9. Click OK to close the Define E-Mail Message dialog box.

If <u>Current Item:Category</u> <u>equals</u> <u>Holiday</u>

    Log <u>Holiday Request submitted by [%Curren...</u> to the workflow history list

    then Calculate <u>Current Item:Days Absent</u> <u>plus</u> <u>Holiday Allowance:Holiday Remaining</u> (Output to <u>Variable: TotalHoliday</u>)

    If <u>Variable: TotalHoliday</u> <u>is less than or equal to</u> <u>Holiday Allowance:Allowance</u>

        Assign <u>Holiday Approval</u> to <u>Teams:Team Leader</u>

    Else

        Email <u>Current Item:Created By</u>

Checking and Publishing Workflows

Once you have created or modified a workflow you should use the commands in the Save group of the Workflow tab to check for errors, save, and then publish the workflow. The Publish command also checks for errors and saves the workflow. Use the following steps to publish your workflow:

1. On the Workflow tab, click Save, and then click Check For Errors in the Save group.

A Microsoft SharePoint Designer dialog box opens, stating that the workflow contains no errors. Click OK. If errors are reported, then this is usually because you have failed to complete link values in conditions or actions. Review and correct any errors, and then recheck your workflow.

2. On the Workflow tab, click Publish in the Save group.

A Microsoft SharePoint Designer dialog box displays as the workflow files are saved to the server.

You can now test your solution by creating a holiday request in the Holiday Schedule list. You might need to manually initiate a workflow instance on your list item, depending on the workflow start options you set on the workflow settings page.

INSIDE OUT Where are SharePoint Designer workflows saved?

SharePoint Designer workflows are saved in a hidden document library named Workflows that contains a folder for each workflow you create. This folder contains the declarative workflow files as well as the workflow initiation page and any task pages. The Workflows library has version enabled, and therefore, theoretically you could revert a workflow to a previous state.

Using the Impersonation Step

When a workflow instance starts, it runs under the identity of the user who starts the workflow instance—the initiator; therefore, the actions that the workflow can execute is limited by the actions that the workflow initiator can perform. If you want to move an item from a list (source) to another list (destination), then the workflow initiator must have contribute rights on the destination list. However, in many scenarios, you do not want to give the workflow initiator access to the destination list. SharePoint Foundation contains a new workflow function—Impersonation Step—that allows the workflow instance to execute actions and conditions under the security permissions of the user who authored the workflow.

There are four additional actions that are available within the Impersonation Step. These are:

- Add List Item Permissions

- Inherit List Items Parent Permissions

- Remove List Item Permissions

- Replace List Item Permissions

> **Note**
> When you use the Add List Item Permissions action, you are breaking the inheritance of the item from the security settings of the list. This is known as using unique permissions within a list or library. This can result in performance implications, such as long page load times across the farm, cause high load on the SQL servers, and timeouts. Microsoft recommends that lists and libraries have no more than 50,000 unique permissions, which can be easily reached with a list that contains a couple of thousand items and accessed by a large number of users. Information on unique item permission limitations can be found at *http://msdn.microsoft.com/en-us/library/cc262787.aspx*.

The Impersonation Step comes with its own set of limitations that you must be aware of before you use it. Unlike the default step, the Impersonation Step cannot be nested within an existing step; therefore, the Impersonation Step command in the Insert group on the Workflow tab is only active when the insertion point is outside all steps in the workflow editor workspace. When the workflow author leaves the company and her user account is removed from the system, the workflow terminates when the Impersonation Step is executed. Similarly if the Impersonation Step moves an item from one list to another and the workflow author does not have contribute permissions on the destination list, then the Impersonation Step will fail. This is most likely to happen when using the Impersonation

Step within reusable and globally reusable workflows. It is important to document the permissions the workflow author must have to ensure that the Impersonation Step will work as designed. You can use the Add A Comment action to include documentation within your workflow.

To add an Impersonation Step to your workflow, perform the following steps:

1. Place the insertion point in the appropriate position (for example, outside and under Step 1).

2. On the Workflow tab, in the Insert group, click Impersonation Step.

> **Impersonation Step**
>
> The contents of this step will run as the workflow author:

Using Reusable and Globally Reusable Workflows

This is one of the greatest improvements incorporated by SharePoint Designer 2010. No-code, reusable workflows can be developed in non-production environments and then moved to the live environment. No-code, reusable workflows developed in the live environment can be used on other lists and libraries, within the same site, within all sites in a Site Collection, or on sites within other Site Collections. In fact, there is little reason to build list workflows.

When you create a reusable workflow you must associate it with a content type—either a specific content type, such as Event, or with All content types. The advantage of associating a reusable workflow with a specific content type, if you choose your content type carefully, is that the columns you need to retrieve values for the current item will be present. The disadvantage is that you will only be able to use that reusable workflow with lists or libraries where that specific content type is added.

When you create a reusable workflow associated with All content types, you need to create site columns and use the Association Column command to make columns that you want to work with available to your workflow. This entails more planning and forethought when you create your workflows.

INSIDE OUT   Association column naming considerations

When you add a reusable workflow to a list or library that already has a column with the same name as an association column, the association column is added, but the association column name is made unique by adding a number to the end of the name. The workflow is dynamically modified to refer to the new association column name.

Also, when you create a workflow to be used by other users, with slight variations to your business scenario, you need to create a more robust workflow, more error messages in the history log, and probably additional tests that will cater to values you had not envisioned. It is usual when such reusable workflows are created that the support and maintenance might be handed over to the central team that supports the SharePoint Foundation implementation, thereby allowing you, the business user, to continue with your day job.

If you create a reusable workflow not in the top-level site of a Site Collection, which you then need to use on all sites within a Site Collection, you will need to export the workflow as a solutions file (.wsp) and then import the .wsp into the Site Collection's Solution gallery.

Exporting a Reusable Workflow

Before you can export a reusable workflow, first publish the workflow, and then save the reusable workflow as a .wsp file by performing the following steps:

1. Open a site that contains the reusable workflow that you have created in SharePoint Designer.

2. In the Navigation pane, click Workflows.

3. Click the appropriate reusable workflow to display the Workflow Settings page.

4. On the Workflow Settings tab, in the Manage group, click Save as Template.

    A dialog box appears, stating that the template has been saved to the Site Assets library. The workflow template is saved with a filename that is the same as the name of the reusable workflow.

5. In the Navigation pane, click Site Assets to display the gallery page that displays all the files stored in the Site Assets library.

6. Click the icon to the left of the appropriate .wsp file, and then on the Assets tab, in the Manage group, click Export File to display the Export Selected As dialog box.

7. Choose a directory in which to save the file, and then click Save. A Microsoft SharePoint Designer dialog box opens, stating that the .wsp has been successfully exported.

Chapter 10

Importing a Reusable Workflow

To use a reusable workflow in a site where it was not created, execute the steps that follow. You can also use these steps if you create a reusable workflow in a Subsite of a Site Collection; therefore, you cannot publish it as a globally reusable workflow:

1. Using the browser, navigate to the top-level site of the Site Collection where you want to make the reusable workflow available.

2. Click Site Actions, and then click Site Settings.

3. Under Galleries, click Solutions.

4. On the Solutions tab, in the New group, click Upload Solution.

5. Click Browse to open the Choose File To Upload dialog box, navigate to where you saved the .wsp workflow template file. Click Open, and then click OK.

   The Solution Gallery – Activate Solution dialog box opens.

6. On the View tab, click Activate.

7. Browse to the site where you want to use the workflow, click Site Actions, and then click Site Settings.

8. Under Site Actions, click Manage Site Features.

9. Click the Activate button to the right of the workflow template.

Working with Workflows and Visual Studio

Earlier in this chapter, you used the standard Three-State workflow template, and then you used Visio 2010 Premium and SharePoint Designer 2010 to create custom workflows. You should use SharePoint Designer, with or without Visio, whenever you can to create custom workflows. However, there might be some scenarios for which you need more than the out-of-the-box conditions and actions that SharePoint Designer provides. This is when you should consider using Visual Studio 2010.

For more information about using Visual Studio to create SharePoint Foundation solutions and how to set up your development environment, see Chapter 16, "Developing SharePoint Solutions by Using Visual Studio 2010."

Visio Studio can help your organization to use workflows with SharePoint Foundation in two ways:

- By developing custom actions that can be used in SharePoint Designer

- By developing custom workflow templates.

You can find information about developing workflows in SharePoint Foundation at *http://msdn.microsoft.com/en-us/library/ms416312.aspx.*

Visual Studio provides several pieces of functionality that aide in the creation of workflows for SharePoint Foundation. One of these components is the SharePoint Customization Wizard. With the SharePoint Configuration Wizard, you can specify settings about the workflow that you are creating. You can specify the following for workflows in the customization wizard:

- The site and security level that the workflow will use

- The workflow association with a list or a site

- The list that you will use when debugging the workflow

- The conditions for how your workflow is started

One of the key differences in the workflows that are created in SharePoint Foundation when compared to previous versions of SharePoint is the ability to create workflows that run against a site, not against a list item or document. However, as stated earlier in this chapter, site workflows in most cases must be started manually. In that case, it can be started through the SharePoint applications programming interface (API). Figure 10-6 shows an example of the new SharePoint Customization Wizard setting with which you can specify if the Workflow is associated with a site or a list.

Chapter 10

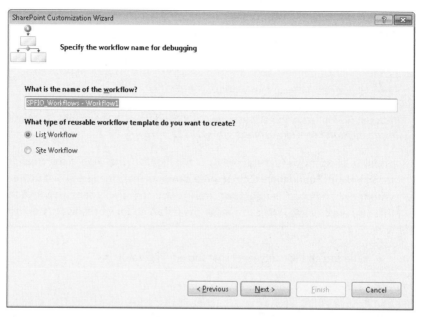

Figure 10-6 Specifying if a workflow will be associated with a site or a list in the SharePoint Customization Wizard.

Once you select the desired settings for the workflow that is being defined, the SharePoint Configuration Wizard generates a project in Solution Explorer. This project contains the base files and references that are used to create a custom SharePoint workflow in Visual Studio.

Developing Custom Actions

Visual Studio provides two methods for creating custom actions:

- **Sandboxed actions**   These custom actions are loaded with partial trust and can be executed in a sandboxed environment, hence the name. Microsoft Office 365—where SharePoint 2010 is hosted online in the cloud, and therefore, you do not have access to the server—is an example of where you would use sandboxed actions. With such actions, cross Site Collection queries are not possible; therefore, you cannot, for example, retrieve a list value if the list is in a different Site Collection than the site or list with which the workflow is associated.

- **Full trust actions**   These actions are created by using custom activity classes and are deployed on the server; however, they require more knowledge of the Windows Workflow Foundation (WF) and SharePoint Designer workflow architecture. Such actions are therefore more powerful but harder to develop.

To view Hands-On Labs and videos for building workflow solutions for SharePoint Online and in sandboxed environments, go to *http://msdn.microsoft.com/en-us/Office365TrainingCourse*.

INSIDE OUT   Where are the SharePoint Designer actions and conditions stored?

When you create a workflow by using SharePoint Designer, it connects to the SharePoint Foundation server and retrieves a list of available actions. You can find these actions in the SharePoint 2010 root folder in the Template\<LCID>\Workflow subfolder. Here, you will find a number of XML .actions files that define the actions that are available and how they should be configured.

Creating a SharePoint Workflow Project in Visual Studio

Visual Studio provides several methods for creating workflows for SharePoint Foundation. With these workflows, users can programmatically control the life cycle of documents and list items in a SharePoint site.

When deciding to create workflows in SharePoint Foundation, you must decide what type of workflow to create. There are two basic types of workflows that are created in Visual Studio for SharePoint Foundation:

- **Sequential workflows**   These are considered predictable workflows. This is because the execution of the workflow must follow the activities, conditions, and rules that have been defined to move forward in the workflow. So in this case, the defined workflow is in control of the path that the process must take. This also means that any steps that occur in the workflow must be done one after another until the last activity is completed. This is the type of workflow you create when using SharePoint Designer.

- **State Machine workflows**   These do not have a defined path that it must follow. A State Machine Workflow is driven by events that take place during the lifecycle of the workflow. The workflow is given a state based on a set of states, transitions, and actions. The workflow always remains in some state until an event occurs that causes it to move to another state. So the path that a workflow takes is not predefined, and the steps in the workflow execute asynchronously. The state machine workflow has a final state that determines the end of the workflow.

Once you have determined the required type of workflow, you need to actually create it in Visual Studio. Perform the following steps to create a workflow:

1. Open Visual Studio with administrative privileges. On the Start Page tab, click New, Project, or on the toolbar, click File, select New, and then click Project to open the New Project dialog box.

2. Under Installed Templates, under the appropriate language (such as Visual C#), expand SharePoint, if not already expanded, and then click 2010.

3. In the middle pane, select Sequential Workflow.

4. In the Name textbox, type **SPFIO_SequentialWorkflow**, and then click OK.

5. Specify the site on which you want to deploy and test the application page, select Deploy As A Farm Solution for the trust level, and then click Next.

6. Leave the default value for the Name Of The Project and leave List Workflow for the type of workflow template to create, and then click Next.

7. Select the library or list that you want to use for debugging your workflow. Leave all the other default values for this page, and then click Next.

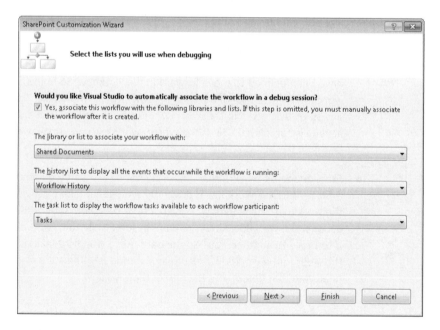

8. Leave the default values for this page to be able to start the workflow manually or start the workflow any time an item is created.

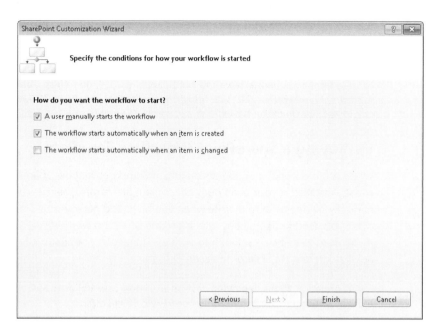

9. Click Finish. The Project is created with a single project item, Workflow1, and the workflow designer is displayed.

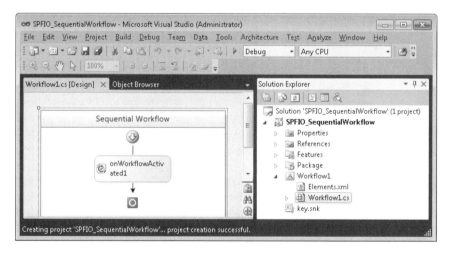

10. Open the Toolbox on the left (Ctrl+Alt+X), and then under SharePoint Workflow, drag a LogToHistoryListActivity on the screen after the onWorkflowActivated1.

11. Open the Properties box for LogToHistoryListActivity.

12. Type **SPFIO Workflow** in for the HistoryDescription and HistoryOutcome.

13. Save, Build, and deploy the Project.

To see a sample sequential workflow for SharePoint 2010, go to *http://archive.msdn.micro-soft.com/SharePointDev2010*, and *http://channel9.msdn.com/Learn/Courses/Office2010/ClientWorkflowUnit/ClientWorkflowLab/Exercise-3-Building-a-Workflow-in-Visual-Studio-2010*.

Deploying a SharePoint Workflow Template

When you are working on the development computer that has SharePoint Foundation already installed, if your build does not contain any errors, your new workflow will auto-matically be deployed to the site when you build and deploy your solution. This only works when you need to deploy this solution to the server on which Visual Studio 2010 is running. If you need to deploy a solution to another SharePoint Foundation installation, you will need a different set of steps to accomplish this.

For information about deploying custom workflow assemblies to SharePoint Foundation, go to *http://msdn.microsoft.com/en-us/library/ee538248.aspx*.

You can use SharePoint Foundation to easily package and deploy Workflows via the Pack-aging Designer in Visual Studio and PowerShell. The packaging and deployment of a work-flow template in Visual Studio is no different from deploying any other solution, because the process has been standardized in Visual Studio 2010. However, SharePoint Foundation provides a new method for deploying SharePoint Designer workflows into SharePoint Foun-dation by utilizing Visual Studio 2010.

In previous versions of SharePoint, out of the box, it was not possible to take a workflow developed in SharePoint Designer and use it on other sites. Also, there was no way to take a workflow in SharePoint Designer and automatically create a workflow in Visual Studio. With SharePoint Designer 2010, you can now take a workflow developed in SharePoint Designer and import it into Visual Studio. This is accomplished by using the Visual Studio Import Reusable Workflow project template.

To import a workflow into Visual Studio 2010, using SharePoint Designer, create a .wsp file based on a reusable workflow, as described earlier in this chapter. You can also create a .wsp file when you save the whole site as a template, which saves the .wsp file in the Site Collec-tion's solutions gallery. To import the reusable workflow from a .wsp file in Visual Studio, perform the following steps:

1. Open Visual Studio 2010. In the middle pane, select the Import Reusable Workflow.

2. In the Name text box, type **SPFIO_WorkflowImportProject**, and then click OK.

3. Enter the Site to use for debugging, and then select Next.

4. Click Browse to open the Open dialog box.

5. Navigate to and select the .wsp file you saved by using SharePoint Designer, click Open, and then click Next to display the Select Items To Import page of the SharePoint Customization Wizard.

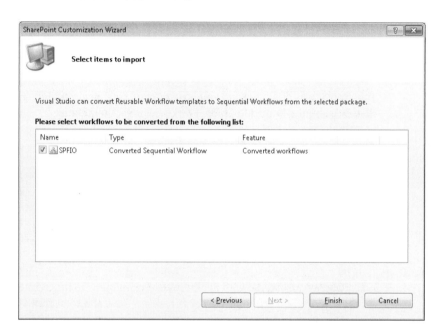

6. Select the workflow to be converted from the list, and then click Finish.

The Import Completed dialog box opens, stating that the SharePoint solution import completed successfully. Click OK. Visual Studio has converted the reusable workflow from the .wsp file into a workflow project.

7. In Solution Explorer, expand the Workflows and double-click the imported workflow folder to display the workflow in designer.

8. Select WorkflowImportProject1, and then set the Startup Item property to the Imported Workflow.

At this point, the workflow has been imported into Visual Studio, but there are still a few items that might need to be set up. The imported reusable workflow does not import association properties for the workflow, so for each workflow listed you will need to:

1. Select the workflow project Item in Solution Explorer.

Chapter 10

2. Open the Properties task pane, if not already open, and then to the right of Target List, select the Ellipse button to open the SharePoint Customization Wizard.

3. Enter the appropriate information in the SharePoint Customization Wizard for the workflow.

4. When the Customization Wizard is complete, repeat the previous two steps for any other properties that need values.

5. Build and deploy your project.

The Workflow is deployed and you have now successfully imported and deployed a workflow by using the Import Reusable Workflow project template.

Create a Custom Site Workflow Activity

Earlier in this section, we talked about the different types of workflows that can be created for SharePoint Foundation in Visual Studio. Using one of the newest workflow types, you can create a site workflow activity that allows you to apply a workflow for an entire site. The following procedure illustrates how to set up a site workflow activity. To test this sample code you need an announcements list created in the top-level site of your Site Collection on your development computer.

1. Open Visual Studio with administrative privileges. On the Start Page tab, click New, Project, or on the toolbar, click File, select New, and then click Project to open the New Project dialog box.

2. In the middle pane, select the Sequential Workflow.

3. In the Name textbox, type **SPFIO_SiteLevelActivity1**, and then select OK.

4. Enter the Site to use for debugging, and then select Next.

5. Leave the default value for the name of the project, select Site Workflow for the type of workflow template to create, and then click Next.

6. On the Select The Lists You Will Use When Debugging page, you are unable to select a list or library. Leave all the default values for this page, and then click Next.

7. On the Specify The Conditions For How Your Workflow Is Started, only the option to start the workflow manually is available and is selected by default. Leave the option selected, and then click Finish.

8. Once the project is created, right-click the project SPFIO_SiteLevelActivity1, click Add, and then click New Item.

9. In the Add New Item dialog box, under Installed Templates, click Code, and then in the middle pane, click Class.

10. In the Name text box, type **CustomActivity1**, and then click Add.

The CustomActivity1.cs file opens.

11. Replace the code in the CustomActivity1.cs file with the following code. Use your Site Collection URL in place of wideworldimporters:

```
using System;
using System.Collections.Generic;
using System.Linq;
using System.Text;
using Microsoft.SharePoint;
namespace SPFIO_SiteLevelActivity1
{
    class CustomActivity1 : System.Workflow.ComponentModel.Activity
    {
        public CustomActivity1()
        {
        }
         // Triggers when the activity is executed.
        protected override System.Workflow.ComponentModel.ActivityExecutionStatus
            Execute(System.Workflow.ComponentModel.ActivityExecutionContext
executionContext)
        {
            try
            {
                // Referencing the Site
                SPSite site = new SPSite("http://wideworldimporters");
                SPWeb web = site.OpenWeb("/");
                // Getting the Announcements list
                SPList TaskList = web.GetList("Lists/Announcements");
                // Adding an Announcement
                SPItem SiteAnnouncement = TaskList.AddItem();
                SiteAnnouncement["Title"] = "SPFIO";
                SiteAnnouncement["Body"] = "SPFIO Announcement Body";
                // Saving the changes
                SiteAnnouncement.Update();

            }
            catch (Exception ex)
            {
                System.Diagnostics.Debug.WriteLine("Error: " + ex.ToString());
            }
            return base.Execute(executionContext);
        }
    }
}
```

Chapter 10

12. Build the solution.

13. Open the Workflow1.cs in Design mode.

14. In the Toolbox task pane, under SPFIO_SiteLevelActivity1 Components, drag the CustomActivity1 below onWorkflowActivated1.

15. Build and deploy the solution.

Now that you have built and deployed the workflow, you should test it. You can do this as follows:

1. Go to the top-level site of your Site Collection that you selected for debug purposes.

2. On the Quick Launch, click All Site Content, and then to the right of Create, click Site Workflows.

3. Under Start A New Workflow, click SPFIO_SiteLevelActivity1 - Workflow1. The home page of the site is displayed.

4. On the Quick Launch, click All Site Content, and then under Lists, click Announcements. A new announcements list item should appear.

Summary

SharePoint Foundation provides the Three-State workflow template that can be used to meet many customer requirements with no further effort. If it doesn't meet your specific requirements, you can design your own workflows by using Microsoft Visio Premium 2010, which can then be imported into Microsoft SharePoint Designer 2010, where the configuration of the workflows can be completed. SharePoint Designer also gives you an expanded capability to design workflows and reusable workflows within a site and to promote those workflows to globally reusable workflows so that they can be used by any site in a Site Collection. In addition, you have the ultimate flexibility to design your own workflow components and SharePoint Designer activities within Windows Workflow Foundation by using Visual Studio 2010.

CHAPTER 11

Integrating SharePoint with Microsoft Office 2010

The Microsoft SharePoint 2010 platform has many strengths; one of the greatest is its integration with the Microsoft Office desktop client. Not only do Office applications installed on the client desktop interface directly with SharePoint sites and workspaces, but they also interface with the entities within these sites, such as document libraries, content, and workflows.

Throughout this chapter, we will cover the differences in Office 2010 versions as they relate to SharePoint Foundation 2010. We will also make reference to other, non-Windows Office versions which provide a measure of interaction with the SharePoint 2010 platform; it should be noted that these are not the core focus of this chapter and are not covered in detail.

Also, there are several books dedicated to the unique features and functionality present in each individual Office product as well as books written to cover the entire suite. This chapter is not intended to cover each Office product in detail; instead, it is intended to focus on functionality specifically related to SharePoint Foundation.

Office Client Versions

As you might imagine, it is rare for an organization to upgrade all of its desktop client software at once. Installations are generally accomplished a section at a time by department or business unit, for instance. At the same time, others within the organization continue to use the older products.

SharePoint 2010 does not abandon users of the older products; to the contrary, it accommodates backward-compatible functionality. The level of this backward compatibility depends greatly on what version of the client software you have installed.

Table 11-1 presents the versions of Microsoft Office for Windows that SharePoint 2010 supports.

Table 11-1 **Microsoft Office vs. SharePoint 2010 Compatibility Matrix**

Office version	Compatibility level
Microsoft Office 2000 or XP	Fair
Microsoft Office 2003	Good
Microsoft Office 2007	Better
Microsoft Office 2010	Best

INSIDE OUT   Comparing Office functionality within SharePoint

Microsoft offers a white paper that details the levels of interoperability and other SharePoint 2010 client information. The document is named *Business Productivity at Its Best—Office 2010 and SharePoint 2010*, and you can download it at *http://go.microsoft. com/FWLink/?Linkid=209803*.

Exceptions

There are always exceptions to any rule. Over the course of ten years and several versions (plus Service Packs) of the Office platform, products such as Microsoft OneNote, Microsoft InfoPath, and Microsoft Visio have been added into the mix. Some of these items, for example, InfoPath and OneNote, have version or format requirements that you need to keep in mind when planning interaction with your SharePoint farm.

Microsoft InfoPath

InfoPath was initially released as a component of the Office 2003 Professional product. It is used for developing forms to capture data. The forms themselves are stored as XML Form Template (XSN) files, and the data that fills each form is stored as eXtensible Markup Language (XML) files. This product has always had a strong connection to the SharePoint platform, and you can use it for building forms in a SharePoint form library.

One of the major requirements for InfoPath has been that the version of the InfoPath tool must at least match that of the server. For example, it is not possible to use InfoPath 2007 to generate forms for SharePoint 2010; however, InfoPath Designer 2010 can be used to generate forms for both 2007 and 2010 versions of the SharePoint Platform.

Thus, if you are designing forms for use with SharePoint 2010, you must use InfoPath Designer 2010—no other version will work.

Microsoft OneNote

OneNote was introduced in late 2003 as a free-form information gathering tool. Initially built as a single-user tool, OneNote has quickly become a tool for interaction within business teams. OneNote 2007 expanded this functionality by giving a user the ability to store "Notebooks" in SharePoint 2007 document libraries. OneNote 2010 expands this sharing of notebooks even further; users can now take advantage of even more detailed collaboration in a notebook as well as the ability to store and synchronize information between a local computer, mobile platforms, SharePoint, and Windows Live.

When planning for different versions of OneNote in your organization, you should be mindful of a change in the file formats between OneNote 2007 and 2010. Both OneNote 2007 and 2010 formats use the same file extension, and 2007 OneNote files can be opened in OneNote 2010; however, for a OneNote Notebook to fully utilize all of the 2010 features, it must be converted from the 2007 to the 2010 version. Of course, by converting the format to 2010, the file can no longer be used by OneNote 2007. Should you need to, a file can be converted back to the OneNote 2007 format, but some loss of functionality will likely occur.

Microsoft Visio

Visio is a professional diagramming tool. Just about anything that you would normally place on a whiteboard (organizational charts, workflows, and other diagrams) you can draw in Visio. Visio provides additional functionality by which diagrams can become functional constructs in other Line-of-Business (LoB) systems; a great example of this is how workflows can be visualized in Visio 2010 and then exported as true business process workflows into SharePoint Designer 2010 (this requires the Visio Premium edition—we will discuss editions in the next section).

Although Visio officially became a Microsoft product in 2000, it did not officially join the Office family of products until 2003, at which point, it was branded as Office Visio 2003. As time and versions have progressed, Visio has become better integrated into both the Office products and the SharePoint platform.

Microsoft Visio is offered in three editions: Visio Standard, Visio Professional, and Visio Premium. Each of these editions offers a different level of interaction with SharePoint 2010; however, only the Visio Premium edition gives you the ability to create and manipulate SharePoint Designer workflows from a Visio diagram.

> **Note**
> Visio 2010 is not provided as a basic component of any Office license. You must always purchase it separately, regardless of edition.

Chapter 11

Microsoft Project

SharePoint Foundation 2010 also provides a level of integration with the Microsoft Project client that was unavailable in the previous versions. A SharePoint site can now host a Project Tasks list, and this list will integrate with the Project Professional 2010 client.

> **Note**
>
> Project 2010 is not provided as a basic component of any Office license. You must always purchase it separately, regardless of edition.

> # INSIDE OUT   Extending SharePoint Server 2010 with Project Server 2010
>
> The Microsoft Project client fully integrates with a product called Project Server 2010. This product installs on top of a Microsoft SharePoint Server 2010 server (required) and provides a robust project management ecosystem with full PMO capabilities. Project Professional 2007 SP2 (and greater) or Project Professional 2010 is required in order to access Project Server 2010. You can find more information about Project Server 2010 at *www.microsoft.com/project/en/us/project-server-2010.aspx*.

Editions

Microsoft provides many different editions of the Office 2010 client platform; this is important to the context of this book because Office integration with SharePoint varies based on the edition you choose to install. For instance, users who want to utilize the SharePoint Workspace (renamed from "Groove") functionality must purchase the Professional Plus edition of Office 2010.

In most editions, SharePoint is tightly integrated with the Office 2010 platform. What this means to you or your business is that in most of the Office client editions, you will be able to work with SharePoint directly, editing and saving documents to your site without the need to first save a copy of the documents to your computer.

There are notable exceptions to this rule: Office Starter 2010, and Office Home and Student 2010. Both of these editions provide the ability to generate standard Office documents, but the documents will need to be uploaded and downloaded via the SharePoint web interface.

The following sections discuss the products available in each of the Office 2010 suites. Each one is also categorized by availability, as distinguished between OEM, Retail, Academic, and Volume Licensing:

- **OEM**   This stands for Original Equipment Manufacturer, which means that the product is only available on a new computer.

- **Retail**   The product can be purchased from a computer hardware or software retailer.

- **Academic**   The product is available to students through a college or university.

- **Volume Licensing**   The product is for businesses that require more than five Office 2010 client licenses, either directly from Microsoft or a software reseller.

INSIDE OUT   Choosing an Office client platform

The Windows Office clients are available in 64-bit (x64) and 32-bit (x86) editions. Both versions will work with SharePoint, and both will install on a 64-bit computer; however, there are a significant amount of controls used by SharePoint that are 32-bit–compatible only (such as the Grid view component, used when viewing a list). Many organizations choose to use the 32-bit Office client specifically to avoid difficulties with Office add-in availability; if you choose instead to deploy the 64-bit Office client, you should first determine whether necessary 64-bit add-ins are available for your users.

Office Starter 2010 (OEM)

This edition of Microsoft Office includes reduced functionality versions of Microsoft Word and Microsoft Excel and is a direct replacement for the older Microsoft Works product line. Office Starter 2010 is only provided on an OEM installation. It comes preinstalled on a computer that you purchase; it also provides a quick and easy upgrade path to other versions of Office.

Files generated from this edition of Office 2010 can be used in SharePoint via its web interface; SharePoint 2010 functionality is not directly integrated into Office Starter 2010. For example, you cannot save your document directly to a SharePoint site.

Office Home and Student 2010 (Retail)

This edition of Office includes full versions of Word, Excel, Microsoft PowerPoint, and One-Note. Office Home and Student 2010 is intended for non-commercial use and does not directly integrate with the SharePoint platform.

It is licensed either of two ways:

- As a single license (key card)

- For installation on up to three machines within the same household

Office Home and Business 2010 (Retail)

This edition of Office includes Word, Excel, PowerPoint, OneNote, and Microsoft Outlook 2010. The retail version of Office 2010 Home and Business 2010 is geared toward home and small business use.

It is licensed either of two ways:

- As a single license (key card)

- For installation on up to two machines (one home, one portable)

Office Professional 2010 (Retail)

This edition of Office includes Word, Excel, PowerPoint, OneNote, Outlook, Microsoft Access, and Microsoft Publisher. Office Professional 2010 is intended for professional use, providing most of the functionality available in the complete Office 2010 platform.

Office Professional 2010 (Academic)

This edition of Office includes Word, Excel, PowerPoint, OneNote, Outlook, Access, and Publisher, but is offered at a reduced price for students at an educational institution in the United States (your email address must end in .edu).

The academic version of Office Professional 2010 is otherwise identical to its retail counterpart, providing most of the functionality available in the complete Office 2010 platform.

Office Standard 2010 (Volume Licensing)

This edition of Office includes Word, Excel, PowerPoint, OneNote, Outlook 2010 (with Business Contact Manager), and Publisher 2010. It is targeted toward organizations that need most of the functionality of the Office platform but do not require advanced functionality such as Access, InfoPath, SharePoint Workspace, or Microsoft Lync (renamed from Microsoft Office Communicator).

Office Professional Plus (Volume Licensing)

This edition of Microsoft Office includes all functionality available in the core Office platform (except Visio 2010 and Project 2010, which are licensed separately). Office Professional Plus 2010 includes Word, Excel, PowerPoint, OneNote, Outlook (with Business Contact Manager), Publisher, Access, InfoPath, SharePoint Workspace, and Lync.

INSIDE OUT   Office 2010 comparison grid

The six Windows-based versions of Office 2010 are compared in the Office 2010 suites section of the Office 2010 Resource Kit. You can view the version comparison grid at *http://technet.microsoft.com/en-us/library/ee523662.aspx.*

Other Office Clients

Microsoft offers other ways to interact with Office documents and SharePoint 2010 besides the traditional Windows-based Office client. In addition to Office Mac 2011, Office Web Apps and Office Mobile 2010 platforms provide a seamless online/offline experience and contribute to the notion of a "Use Office anywhere" user experience.

As integration with the following platforms is a relatively new occurrence, each provides a level of SharePoint 2010/Office 2010 compatibility, although not all functionality may be the same as in an Office 2010 (for Windows) client. This chapter focuses primarily on the Office 2010 Windows platform.

Office for Mac Home and Student 2011 (Retail)

This edition of Office includes Word, Excel, and PowerPoint for Apple's Mac platform; it is designed for non-commercial home and student use. Files generated from this edition of Office 2011 are fully compatible with Office 2010 for Windows and can also be used in SharePoint via its web interface.

It is licensed either of two ways:

- As a single license

- For installation on up to three machines within the same household

Office for Mac Home and Business 2011 (Retail)

This edition of Office includes Word, Excel, PowerPoint, and Outlook for the Mac platform; it is geared toward home and small business use. Files generated from this edition of Office 2011 are fully compatible with Office 2010 for Windows and can also be used in SharePoint via its web interface.

It is licensed either of two ways:

- As a single license

- For installation on up to two machines (one home, one portable)

Office for Mac Academic 2011 (Academic)

This edition of Office includes Word, Excel, PowerPoint, and Outlook for the Mac platform, but it is offered at a reduced price for students at an educational institution in the United States (your email address must to end in .edu).

Files generated from this edition of Office 2011 are fully compatible with Office 2010 for Windows and can also be used in SharePoint via its web interface.

Office for Mac Standard 2011 (Volume Licensing)

This edition of Office includes Word, Excel, PowerPoint, and Outlook for the Mac platform. It is licensed for larger organizations; files generated from this edition of Office 2011 are fully compatible with Office 2010 for Windows.

INSIDE OUT Planning Office for Mac 2011 client integration

Office Mac 2011 client integration with SharePoint is detailed in the "Planning to Use Office for Mac 2011 with SharePoint" section of the Office:mac site, which is on the "Office for Mac 2011 and SharePoint integration features" page at *http://mac2.microsoft.com/help/office/14/en-us/admin*.

Office Web Apps

This edition of Office is either provided online (for consumer use) or provided in your organization as part of SharePoint 2010 (for business use). With Office Web Apps, you can generate Word, Excel, PowerPoint, and OneNote documents without having the Office 2010 client loaded directly on your personal computer. This functionality can be combined with Microsoft's free SkyDrive and Live Mesh offerings, which means that the documents you generate are portable and accessible anywhere there is an Internet connection.

Office Mobile 2010

This edition of Office is available for download to your Windows Mobile 6.5 or 7.0 device. With it, you can interact with Word, Excel, PowerPoint, OneNote, and Outlook information. SharePoint Workspace Mobile is also included in this version, so you can take SharePoint documents offline and work on them when a network is not available.

Using the Office Backstage View with SharePoint

Microsoft introduced the ribbon menu in Office 2007. This menu system is adaptive, meaning that it changes its appearance and the items that it presents based on the context of the actions that you are performing within the document (for instance, changing a font).

In the 2010 version of Microsoft Office, the ribbon was joined by another new concept called the Backstage view. The purpose of this view is to give the author of a document the ability to work with items that affect the document rather than the content of the document itself; these items include:

- Opening/Closing/Saving a document

- Adding/Changing/Removing metadata (descriptive data) about a document

- Converting a document from an editable version to Adobe System's Portable Document Format (PDF) or Microsoft's XML Paper Specification (XPS) version

Revealing Office Backstage

Office Backstage is revealed simply by selecting the File tab on the ribbon, at the top left of any Office 2010 program. Because the various Office programs (Word, Excel, and so on) offer differing functionality, the items shown in Backstage view will also differ, based on the program that you are using. For this section's examples, we will be using Word, which is one of the core Office programs, and which offers a high level of integration with SharePoint.

To begin working with Backstage view, select the File tab. Immediately located beneath the tabs are four actions: Save, Save As, Open, and Close. We will work with these shortly. Following the actions are six sections: Info, Recent, New, Print, Save & Send, and Help. We are going to be concentrating on the integration capabilities of Office with respect to SharePoint, so we will focus on the Info and Save & Send tabs.

Saving Documents to a SharePoint Foundation Site

Most new SharePoint users begin working with a Team Site by simply uploading documents to it. Creating documents in this fashion is perfectly acceptable, but it overlooks the true level of integration between Office and SharePoint. What happens if all of your documents are not contained in a single site, and you need to quickly interact with multiple SharePoint document libraries?

There are (at least) three basic ways to connect SharePoint sites with an Office 2010 product: you can click File | Save As, File | Recent, or File | Save & Send.

File | Save As

With the document open in Word, click the File menu, and then select Save As. Place your cursor in the File Name text box and enter the URL (the web address) of the SharePoint site, then click Save, as shown in Figure 11-1.

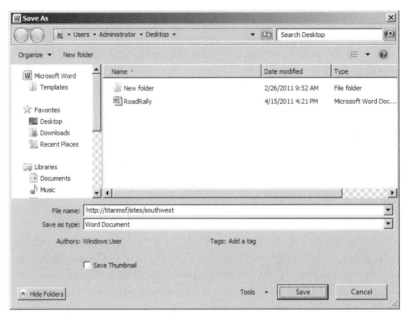

Figure 11-1 Saving a file from Word to a SharePoint site by clicking File | Save As.

Clicking Save this first time does not actually save the document; instead, it instructs Word 2010 to open the Team Site, showing the document libraries (notice that the original file name has reappeared in Figure 11-2).

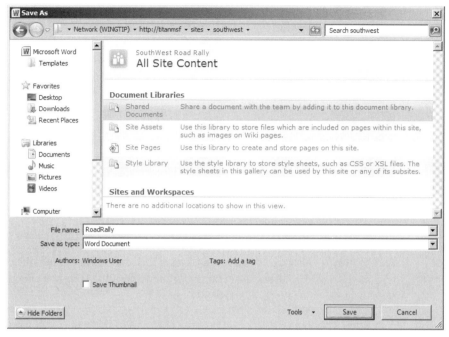

Figure 11-2 After clicking Save, the file name reappears in Save As dialog box.

Next, double-click the library name (in this case, the Shared Documents library), and then click Save to store the document in SharePoint.

File | Recent

Continuing from the previous section, at this point, the document has been stored in your SharePoint Document Library; now comes the fun part. Click the File menu, and then select Recent, which shows two columns: Recent Documents and Recent Places.

Figure 11-3 demonstrates that as you interact with Word documents, both of these columns will begin to fill with information about the documents and places (including Share-Point sites) with which you have interacted.

Chapter 11

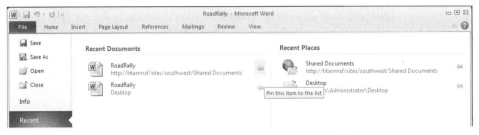

Figure 11-3 The Recent Documents and Recent Places menu in the Office Backstage view.

You can *pin* both documents and document libraries to the Recent menu, which gives you quick access these items. To pin a document or document library, simply click the pushpin image to the right of the desired item.

File | Save & Send

Another way to quickly switch between Sites is to use the Save & Send menu selection. This is located below the Recent selection, and it shows both the current working location and other SharePoint locations, as shown in Figure 11-4.

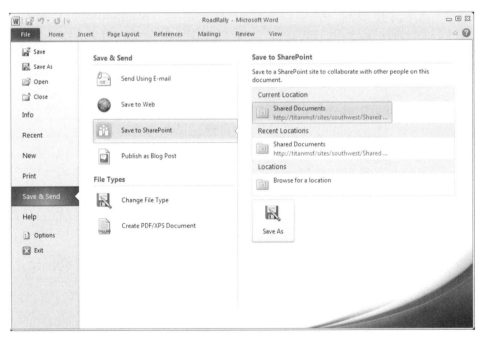

Figure 11-4 The Save & Send Menu in the Office Backstage view.

Metadata Management

SharePoint brings the concept of metadata management to documents in the enterprise. Metadata is a useful and practical way to classify documents without the need to resort to folders. Metadata is simply external data that describes a document or its purpose.

Documents can be assigned descriptive text (stored in columns) to help categorize and classify them within a SharePoint document library. Additionally, if these columns have been assigned via a Content Type, documents generated in this manner can be aggregated from multiple document libraries into a single view contained within a Web Part.

When creating the document library, the owner of the library can choose which columns are required and which are optional. Figure 11-5 illustrates a sample document library in which several fields have been added, including Track, Driver Name, and Event Type.

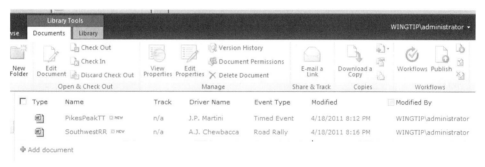

Figure 11-5 New fields added in document library.

When a new document is created in this library, the Office client (Word in this case) prompts the user for field values (metadata) that will be associated with the new document. The fields appear in a section above the document called the Document Information Panel (DIP), as shown in Figure 11-6.

Figure 11-6 The Document Information Panel.

Chapter 11

When you save the document to the library, one of two scenarios will come into play:

● No fields are mandatory (required), and the document is uploaded successfully.

● One or more fields are required, and the document cannot be saved to the library until these fields are populated.

If the document is rejected due to missing metadata, then two things will happen. Initially, a message will appear, prompting the user to open the DIP (Figure 11-7).

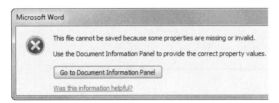

Figure 11-7 The dialog box that you see if metadata properties are missing when you save a document to the library.

If you press the Go to Document Information Panel button, the DIP appears, as shown in Figure 11-8.

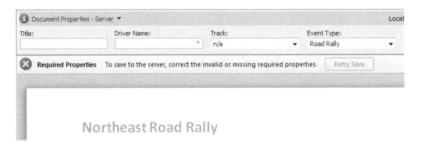

Figure 11-8 The DIP shows which properties are required (indicated by the * [asterisk] character).

Once the DIP reappears, you are prompted to fill in the required fields; when these are completed, the document can successfully be saved to the document library.

Interacting with Lists by Using Excel and Access

Lists are a concept that was very familiar to information workers long before SharePoint existed. List information is entered in a tabular format, which displays column header information to prompt the user for corresponding field values. Both worksheet (Excel) and database (Access) users employ lists; the difference primarily being that Excel captures list information in worksheets within a workbook, whereas Access captures this information in tables for use inside a relational database.

Within SharePoint, lists are maintained within a site. These lists are interactive and capable of having their content displayed in one or more Web Parts. OK, so there's nothing fancy there—people have been showing key performance indicators (KPIs) from within Excel sheets for a long time now. SharePoint, however, takes the notion of lists to the next level by making them extensible via a concept known as *web services*.

SharePoint provides web services to allow other programs and websites to display and interact with list content. SharePoint list content can be displayed in a Web Part, subscribed to as a Really Simple Syndication (RSS) feed, or displayed in a client program (such as Excel or Access).

Using Excel to Display SharePoint List Content

An Excel workbook can be used to display the content of a SharePoint list; by default, this is a one-way, read-only connection. This list information can be refreshed in the Excel client so that the user can get an "at a glance" view of content as it changes on the SharePoint site.

In earlier versions of SharePoint, Excel was used as a two-way connection to a SharePoint list, allowing information to be both read from and written to the list. This behavior was deprecated (removed and no longer supported by Microsoft) beginning with Windows SharePoint Services 3.0 and Microsoft Office SharePoint Server 2007.

INSIDE OUT   Moving away from Excel integration with SharePoint lists

While it is technically possible to use the Excel 2007 add-in for synchronizing tables with SharePoint lists, it would be a good idea to avoid this and move toward using Microsoft Access as quickly as you can become accustomed to it. Using the 2007 add-in has its own set of issues, not the least of which is the requirement that you save the file in .xls (Office 97-2003) format instead of the XML-based .xlsx (Office 2007 and 2010) version.

SharePoint list information that has been brought into an Excel workbook can be manipulated in the same way as any other Excel content. Pie charts, graphs, conditional analysis, and other functionality works exactly the same as it would with standard Excel data.

Connecting a SharePoint List to Microsoft Excel

Figure 11-9 depicts a SharePoint list that contains books and short stories. This list also happens to include the number of books that are on hand for sale. We will be taking the information from this list and analyzing it in Excel.

☐	⬙	Title	Author	Genre	Recommended For	Price	In Stock	On Hand
		Cujo	Stephen King	Fiction	M. Lanphier	$19.99	Yes	23
		Something Wicked This Way Comes	Ray Bradbury	Fiction	S. Lanphier	$15.99	Yes	46
		2001: A Space Odyssey	Arthur C. Clarke	Science Fiction	T. Burton	$12.99	Yes	3
		The Devil In The White City	Erik Larson	History	T. Lanphier	$16.99	Yes	6
		Do Androids Dream Of Electric Sheep?	Philip K. Dick	Science Fiction	M. Lanphier	$17.99	No	0
		Founding Brothers: The Revolutionary Generation	Joseph Ellis	History	T. Lanphier	$20.99	Yes	9
		The Cobra in the Barn: Great Stories of Automotive Archaeology	Tom Cotter	History	T. Lanphier	$22.95	Yes	14
		The Healey Story: A dynamic father and son partnership and their world-beating cars	Geoffrey Healey	Biography	S. Lanphier	$19.95	Yes	57

⊕ Add new item

Figure 11-9 A "Favorite Reads" list in SharePoint.

To begin analyzing the data, we must first establish the connection between SharePoint and Excel by performing the following procedure:

On the ribbon, on the List Tools tab, select the List tab. In the Connect & Export group, click the Export To Excel button (see Figure 11-10).

Figure 11-10 Exporting a list to Excel.

A File Download window appears on your desktop (see Figure 11-11). The file being down-loaded always displays as OWSSVR.IQY; this is the name that will always appear when you make this type of connection. When the connection has been established between Share-Point and Excel, the resulting Excel Workbook can be saved with whatever name you prefer.

Figure 11-11 Downloading the Excel Web Query File.

A security notice appears. This setting is used to prevent Excel from running untrusted workbooks when downloaded from a web browser and gives you a chance to verify the file before opening it. Click the Enable button to allow the data connection between Excel and your SharePoint list (Figure 11-12).

Figure 11-12 Enabling the data connection.

The data connection between SharePoint and Excel is now in place. Figure 11-13 shows that all of the columns from the SharePoint list are represented in your Excel worksheet, along with a couple of new additions, Item Type and Path.

	A	B	C	D	E	F	G	H	I
1	Title	Author	Genre	Recommended For	Price	In Stock	On Hand	Item Type	Path
2	Cujo	Stephen King	Fiction	M. Lanphier	$19.99	TRUE	23	Item	Lists/FavoriteReads
3	Something Wicked This Way Comes	Ray Bradbury	Fiction	S. Lanphier	$15.99	TRUE	46	Item	Lists/FavoriteReads
4	2001: A Space Odyssey	Arthur C. Clarke	Science Fiction	T. Burton	$12.99	TRUE	3	Item	Lists/FavoriteReads
5	The Devil In The White City	Erik Larson	History	T. Lanphier	$16.99	TRUE	6	Item	Lists/FavoriteReads
6	Do Androids Dream Of Electric Sheep?	Philip K. Dick	Science Fiction	M. Lanphier	$17.99	FALSE	0	Item	Lists/FavoriteReads
7	Founding Brothers: The Revolutionary Generation	Joseph Ellis	History	T. Lanphier	$20.99	TRUE	9	Item	Lists/FavoriteReads
8	The Cobra in the Barn: Great Stories of Automotive Archaeology	Tom Cotter	History	T. Lanphier	$22.95	TRUE	14	Item	Lists/FavoriteReads
9	The Healey Story: A dynamic father and son partnership and their world-beating cars	Geoffrey Healey	Biography	S. Lanphier	$19.95	TRUE	57	Item	Lists/FavoriteReads

Figure 11-13 SharePoint list Information displayed in an Excel Worksheet.

Chapter 11

Two extra columns appear in your Excel workbook that were not apparent in your Share-Point list (see Figure 11-14). Item Type is a field that indicates whether the row item is a particular item or a folder within the list. Path displays the folder path of the item within the list.

Item Type	Path
Item	Lists/FavoriteReads
Item	Lists/FavoriteReads
Item	Lists/FavoriteReads
Item	Lists/FavoriteReads
Item	Lists/FavoriteReads
Item	Lists/FavoriteReads
Item	Lists/FavoriteReads
Item	Lists/FavoriteReads

Figure 11-14 The Item Type and Path fields.

If these columns are not required for analysis within your Excel worksheet, you can delete them without adverse effect.

Excel has evolved over time to become a key player in Business Intelligence. Data retrieved from SharePoint can be easily analyzed like any other Excel data. In the sample presented in Figure 11-15, the total amount of books on hand is calculated, and a 3-D pie chart shows the distribution of books on hand by title.

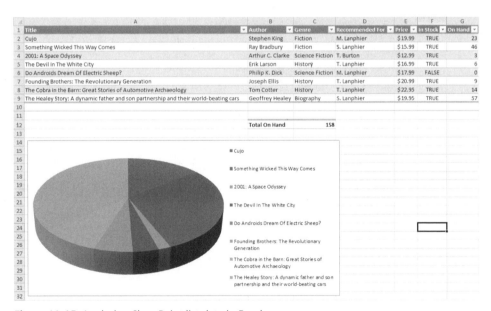

Figure 11-15 Analyzing SharePoint list data in Excel.

As the quantity of books changes, the distribution also changes. Items can be changed in the SharePoint list and these changes can be reflected in the Excel workbook. The book quantities in the SharePoint list have been changed from their previous values, as shown in Figure 11-16.

Libraries		Title	Author	Genre	Recommended For	Price	In Stock	On Hand
Site Pages		Cujo	Stephen King	Fiction	M. Lanphier	$19.99	Yes	16
Shared Documents		Something Wicked This Way Comes	Ray Bradbury	Fiction	S. Lanphier	$15.99	Yes	13
Lists		2001: A Space Odyssey	Arthur C. Clarke	Science Fiction	T. Burton	$12.99	Yes	20
Calendar								
Tasks		The Devil In The White City	Erik Larson	History	T. Lanphier	$16.99	Yes	9
Project Tasks		Do Androids Dream Of Electric Sheep?	Philip K. Dick	Science Fiction	M. Lanphier	$17.99	No	2
Favorite Reads		Founding Brothers: The Revolutionary Generation	Joseph Ellis	History	T. Lanphier	$20.99	Yes	6
Discussions		The Cobra in the Barn: Great Stories of Automotive Archaeology	Tom Cotter	History	T. Lanphier	$22.95	Yes	12
Team Discussion		The Healey Story: A dynamic father and son partnership and their world-beating cars	Geoffrey Healey	Biography	S. Lanphier	$19.95	Yes	27
Recycle Bin								
All Site Content	⊕ Add new item							

Figure 11-16 New item changes in the SharePoint list.

For these book quantity changes to reflect in the Excel worksheet, it must be manually updated to include the new values from the SharePoint list. On the ribbon in Excel, on the Data tab, click the Refresh button to update the values in the worksheet, as illustrated in Figure 11-17.

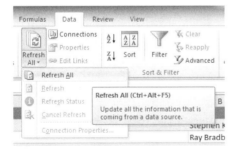

Figure 11-17 Refreshing the Excel Worksheet.

The updated values from the SharePoint list are presented in the Excel workbook; Figure 11-18 shows that the book total and 3-D pie chart are also updated.

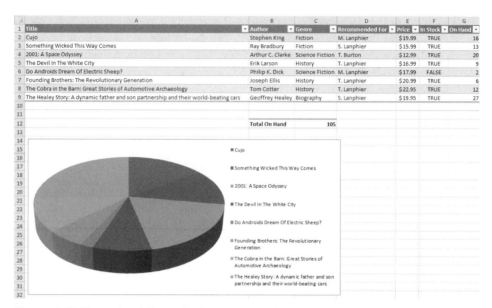

	A	B	C	D	E	F	G
1	Title	Author	Genre	Recommended For	Price	In Stock	On Hand
2	Cujo	Stephen King	Fiction	M. Lanphier	$19.99	TRUE	16
3	Something Wicked This Way Comes	Ray Bradbury	Fiction	S. Lanphier	$15.99	TRUE	13
4	2001: A Space Odyssey	Arthur C. Clarke	Science Fiction	T. Burton	$12.99	TRUE	20
5	The Devil In The White City	Erik Larson	History	T. Lanphier	$16.99	TRUE	9
6	Do Androids Dream Of Electric Sheep?	Philip K. Dick	Science Fiction	M. Lanphier	$17.99	FALSE	2
7	Founding Brothers: The Revolutionary Generation	Joseph Ellis	History	T. Lanphier	$20.99	TRUE	6
8	The Cobra in the Barn: Great Stories of Automotive Archaeology	Tom Cotter	History	T. Lanphier	$22.95	TRUE	12
9	The Healey Story: A dynamic father and son partnership and their world-beating cars	Geoffrey Healey	Biography	S. Lanphier	$19.95	TRUE	27
10							
11							
12			Total On Hand	105			

Figure 11-18 The updated SharePoint list content displayed in the Excel workbook.

Using Access to Display and Update SharePoint List Content

As with Excel, Microsoft Access can be used to display the content of a SharePoint list; the key difference between the two concerns two-way synchronization. Excel is the more appropriate tool for retrieving KPI-style information from a SharePoint list (such as graphs and charts), whereas Access is well suited for interacting and reporting on SharePoint list content.

In addition to altering content in a SharePoint list (such as adding a new row/item to the list), Access can do more detailed tasks such as modifying the structure of the list itself and generating reports. In this section, we will not only interact with SharePoint list content, but also generate SharePoint lists directly from within Access.

As in the previous example, we will use the SharePoint list called "Favorite Reads," shown in Figure 11-19. We begin this section by showing how this list can be modified and presented in reports. We then progress to building a new SharePoint list from within the Access client.

		Title	Author	Genre	Recommended For	Price	In Stock	On Hand
☐		Cujo	Stephen King	Fiction	M. Lanphier	$19.99	Yes	14
		Something Wicked This Way Comes	Ray Bradbury	Fiction	S. Lanphier	$15.99	Yes	13
		2001: A Space Odyssey	Arthur C. Clarke	Science Fiction	T. Burton	$12.99	Yes	20
		The Devil In The White City	Erik Larson	History	T. Lanphier	$16.99	Yes	9
		Do Androids Dream Of Electric Sheep?	Philip K. Dick	Science Fiction	M. Lanphier	$17.99	No	2
		Founding Brothers: The Revolutionary Generation	Joseph Ellis	History	T. Lanphier	$20.99	Yes	6
		The Cobra in the Barn: Great Stories of Automotive Archaeology	Tom Cotter	History	T. Lanphier	$22.95	Yes	12
		The Healey Story: A dynamic father and son partnership and their world-beating cars	Geoffrey Healey	Biography	S. Lanphier	$19.95	Yes	27

✚ Add new item

Figure 11-19 Our stalwart "Favorite Reads" SharePoint list.

Linking Access to a SharePoint List

There are three distinct ways by which Access can be connected to a SharePoint list:

- The Open With Access command from within SharePoint

- The SharePoint List command from within Access

- The Track This List command from within SharePoint

Using the Open With Access Command

The Open With Access command establishes a connection between a list in SharePoint and a corresponding table within an Access database (known as an *Access Linked Table*). As the connection is created, Access gives you the opportunity to carry out one of the following tasks:

- Link to data on the SharePoint site via:

  — A new table within a new database.

  — A new table within an existing database.

- Export a copy of the data:

  — This action simply makes a copy of the SharePoint list data in an Access table.

  — No permanent link is maintained.

Open the SharePoint site in your web browser and navigate to the list. On the ribbon, on the List Tools tab, select the List Tab. In the Connect & Export group, click the Access logo button, as shown in Figure 11-20.

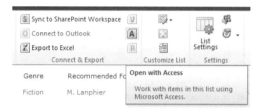

Figure 11-20 Using the Open With Access command.

You have the option of opening up a new or existing database and choosing whether the new table is linked to the SharePoint list. In this example, we will leave the link intact, creating a linked table within an Access database, as illustrated in Figure 11-21.

Figure 11-21 Leave the option to Link To Data On The SharePoint Site selected.

Because the link is being requested from a web browser, your security settings in Access might display a Security Warning (see Figure 11-22) prompting you to verify that you want to open active content. Because this information is being requested from a trusted source (in this case, our intranet), click the Enable Content button.

Figure 11-22 Enabling content in the Security Warning pop-up.

The linked table appears within Access. If the contents of the table do not immediately appear on your screen, simply double-click the icon of the table that you want to view (in this example, Favorite Reads).

A yellow alert bar labeled Save Changes (see Figure 11-23) appears, giving you the opportunity to save your Access database to a SharePoint site; if this is encouraged by your IT staff, go ahead and do so; otherwise, you can also choose to save this database to your client computer. Either way, it wouldn't hurt to save this database before you begin making changes.

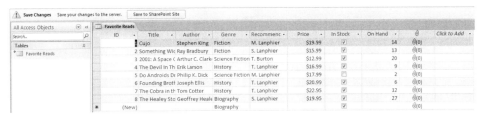

Figure 11-23 A linked table (Favorite Reads).

Using the SharePoint List Command

Unlike the Open With Access command, the SharePoint List command is executed from within Access. To begin the process, an Access database must first be created (unless you already have an existing one to which you want to add a table).

Open Access on your computer and display the Backstage view. On the New tab, select Blank Database. In the right panel, toward the bottom, fill in the File Name (**Books**, in this example), and then select Create (see Figure 11-24).

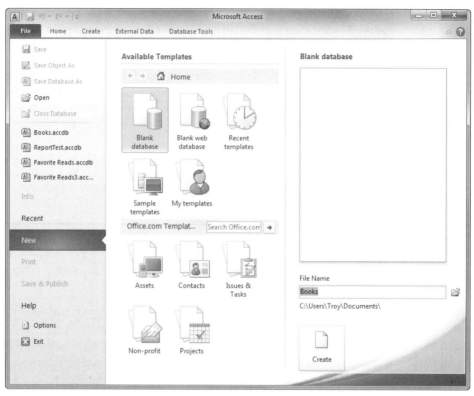

Figure 11-24 Creating a blank Access database.

The newly created database appears in Access 2010. Note that the title bar indicates that the database is compatible with Access 2007.

INSIDE OUT   A note about Access file formats

If you are not familiar with Access, you should know that both Access 2007 and 2010 use the same format for their databases, which is known as *Access 2007*. This is not an error, nor is it a special exception caused by linking the table to a SharePoint list.

When a new database is created, a corresponding default table named Table1 is also created (see Figure 11-25). Let's leave this table in for now; we'll compare it to our SharePoint linked table later, before removing it altogether.

Figure 11-25 The new table (Table1) created by default.

Now that a database exists, we can build a linked table (see Figure 11-26) which connects to a SharePoint list. On the ribbon, select the External Data tab. In the Import & Link group, select the More drop-down menu, and then click the SharePoint List menu item; this will begin the linking process.

Figure 11-26 Importing a SharePoint list.

In the Get External Data window, enter the URL of the site (not the list itself) to which you want to connect. You also need to decide how and where you want to store data in the current database. You have two choices:

- Import a copy of the source data. To do so, choose Import The Source Data Into A New Table In The Current Database.

- Create a linked table. To do so, choose Link To The Data Source By Creating A Linked Table.

Chapter 11

In our example, we want to link to the data source by creating a linked table. Click the Next button to proceed, as depicted in Figure 11-27.

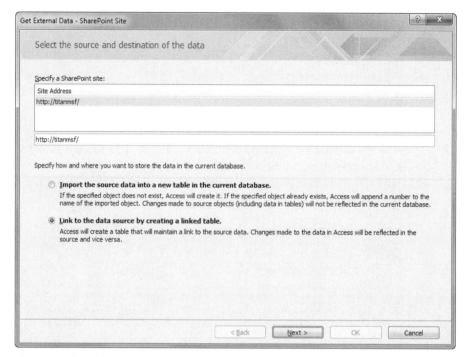

Figure 11-27 Linking to the data source.

Access allows you to choose from a list on the SharePoint site. For this example, choose the Favorite Reads list (see Figure 11-28), and then select OK.

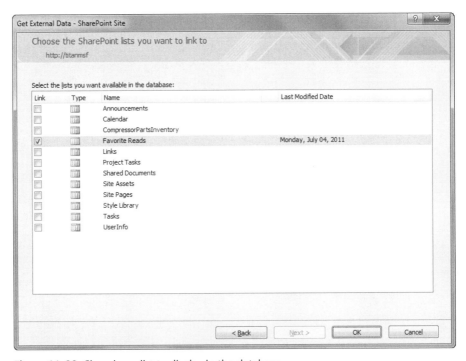

Figure 11-28 Choosing a list to display in the database.

You might see the message shown in Figure 11-29 appear briefly, indicating that the linking process is underway.

Figure 11-29 Linking to "Favorite Reads."

Figure 11-30 demonstrates that the linked table appears in Access as it did in the previous section.

Figure 11-30 The linked table in Access.

Take note of the two different Table types in this database (see Figure 11-31). Currently, there is a standard Access table called Table1; there is also a linked table that we just created, called Favorite Reads. These tables can co-exist within the same database.

Figure 11-31 Two table types: one standard, and one linked.

If you want, you can remove default Table1 table, leaving just the SharePoint linked table, as illustrated in Figure 11-32.

Figure 11-32 You can remove the default Table1 table, to display the linked table only.

At this point, you can add other tables to the database (linked or otherwise).

Using the Track This List Command

Similar to the Open With Access command, you execute the Track This List command from within your SharePoint site. This command has three options:

- Track This List In Access

- Export To Access

- Report With Access

The first two options should be familiar to you if you've looked over the last two sections. You use Track This List In Access to create a linked table that connects to your SharePoint List. Export To Access copies your list to an Access Table without retaining a link.

The third option, Report With Access, is something new altogether; it creates the ability to report interactively against a SharePoint list. Because we've covered the creation of linked (and nonlinked) tables already, this section focuses on this third option.

When you first open the list, the Browse tab on the ribbon is selected by default, as shown in Figure 11-33. Select the List Tools tab, and then select List.

Figure 11-33 The contents of List tab.

The Track This List command is not present in the Standard View. To access it, in the View Format group, select Datasheet View, as shown in Figure 11-34.

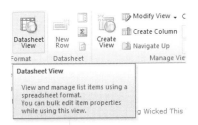

Figure 11-34 To access the Track This List command, you need to change to Datasheet View.

The Datasheet View of the list appears (see Figure 11-35); if you've never used this view in SharePoint, just know that it is a grid view, very similar to how data appears in an Excel workbook.

Chapter 11

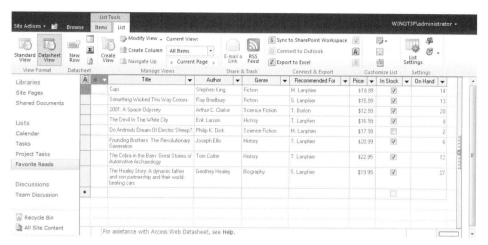

Figure 11-35 The Datasheet view of the SharePoint list.

On the far right side of the screen, locate the Task Pane slider bar. The menu you're looking for is hiding in this section of the screen. Hover your cursor over the bar until it turns blue, and then click the bar or arrow to expand the Task Pane, as demonstrated in Figure 11-36.

Figure 11-36 Click Show Task Pane (click the arrow) to reveal the Office links.

When the Task Pane opens, it shows the Office links menu (see Figure 11-37). Note the Track This List In Access and Export To Access links. Click the Report With Access link.

Figure 11-37 The Office Links menu.

Creating a report involves the creation of a linked table, which must be contained within a database (either an existing or a new one). For this example, choose New Database, and then click the OK button, as illustrated in Figure 11-38.

Figure 11-38 Choosing a database in which to create a table.

Similar to the previous examples, call this database **Books** (see Figure 11-39), and again note that Access 2010 builds databases in the Access 2007 Databases format (compatible with Access 2007 and 2010). Click the Create button.

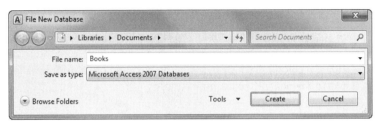

Figure 11-39 Creating the Books database.

The new report appears (Figure 11-40). Note that both a linked table and a report were created in the past few steps.

Figure 11-40 The linked table and report from the SharePoint List.

At this point, you can continue to modify this report to your requirements. Remember that this report is related to the linked table, and the linked table is updated when the Share-Point site is updated. We will examine how this interaction works in the next section.

Chapter 11

INSIDE OUT   Additional SharePoint information in Access

An extra bonus provided by Access and SharePoint is the inclusion of the UserInfo table in your database (not shown above in the tables section). Although we won't go into detail about this table, it is added to any database that is linked to SharePoint, and in it, you can find site information like user names, email addresses, phone numbers, and so on.

Adding Content to SharePoint from Access

Have a look at the Favorite Reads table (see Figure 11-41); this table is identical to those we generated previously. It shows columns that have been linked from the SharePoint list. We will start adding a column from this view in the next section, but for now, let's add a couple of new books to the SharePoint list from Access.

ID	Title	Author	Genre	Recommend	Price	In Stock	On Hand		Click to Add
1	Cujo	Stephen King	Fiction	M. Lanphier	$19.99	✓	14	(0)	
2	Something Wicked This Way Comes	Ray Bradbury	Fiction	S. Lanphier	$15.99	✓	13	(0)	
3	2001: A Space Odyssey	Arthur C. Clark	Science Fiction	T. Burton	$12.99	✓	20	(0)	
4	The Devil In The White City	Erik Larson	History	T. Lanphier	$16.99	✓	9	(0)	
5	Do Androids Dream Of Electric Sheep?	Philip K. Dick	Science Fiction	M. Lanphier	$17.99	☐	2	(0)	
6	Founding Brothers: The Revolutionary Generation	Joseph Ellis	History	T. Lanphier	$20.99	✓	6	(0)	
7	The Cobra in the Barn: Great Stories of Automotive	Tom Cotter	History	T. Lanphier	$22.95	✓	12	(0)	
8	The Healey Story: A dynamic father and son partner	Geoffrey Heale	Biography	S. Lanphier	$19.95	✓	27	(0)	
11	Gracie: A Love Story	George Burns	Biography	M. Lanphier	$14.95	✓	4	(0)	
12	The Old Man and The Sea	Ernest Heming	Biography	S. Lanphier	$9.95	✓	23	(0)	
(New)			Biography			✓		(0)	

Figure 11-41 The Favorite Reads linked table.

Any items added to this database are updated automatically on the SharePoint site. Click the row with the * (asterisk) character, and then begin adding a few items.

Also note the items that have previously been added and deleted from this SharePoint list. This is indicated by the gap between items 8 and 11. At one point, there must have been books #9 and #10 (this ID number is issued automatically by SharePoint), but these items were deleted before we opened this linked table. The new items and the gap are shown in Figure 11-42.

ID	Title	Author	Genre	Recommend	Price	In Stock	On Hand		Click to Add
1	Cujo	Stephen King	Fiction	M. Lanphier	$19.99	✓	14	(0)	
2	Something Wicked This Way Comes	Ray Bradbury	Fiction	S. Lanphier	$15.99	✓	13	(0)	
3	2001: A Space Odyssey	Arthur C. Clark	Science Fiction	T. Burton	$12.99	✓	20	(0)	
4	The Devil In The White City	Erik Larson	History	T. Lanphier	$16.99	✓	9	(0)	
5	Do Androids Dream Of Electric Sheep?	Philip K. Dick	Science Fiction	M. Lanphier	$17.99	☐	2	(0)	
6	Founding Brothers: The Revolutionary Generation	Joseph Ellis	History	T. Lanphier	$20.99	✓	6	(0)	
7	The Cobra in the Barn: Great Stories of Automotive	Tom Cotter	History	T. Lanphier	$22.95	✓	12	(0)	
8	The Healey Story: A dynamic father and son partner	Geoffrey Heale	Biography	S. Lanphier	$19.95	✓	27	(0)	
11	Gracie: A Love Story	George Burns	Biography	M. Lanphier	$14.95	✓	4	(0)	
12	The Old Man and The Sea	Ernest Heming	Fiction	S. Lanphier	$9.95	✓	23	(0)	
13	The Grapes of Wrath	John Steinbeck	Fiction	M. Lanphier	$13.98	✓	2	(0)	
14	Pride and Prejudice and Zombies	Jane Austen ar	Fiction	S. Lanphier	$21.98	✓	56	(0)	
(New)			Biography			✓		(0)	

Figure 11-42 New books displayed in the linked table.

Books added to the linked table are also updated automatically in the corresponding SharePoint list. Refreshing the web browser, you can see the new books in the list, as demonstrated in Figure 11-43.

Figure 11-43 New books now appear in the SharePoint list, as well.

Of course, we had built a report for this linked table/SharePoint list, so let's have a look at the changes in the report. Switch back to Access, and then click the Favorite Reads tab with the icon just to its left (which indicates that this is a report). Figure 11-44 shows that nothing has changed and that the person editing the report has added a total to the On Hand column.

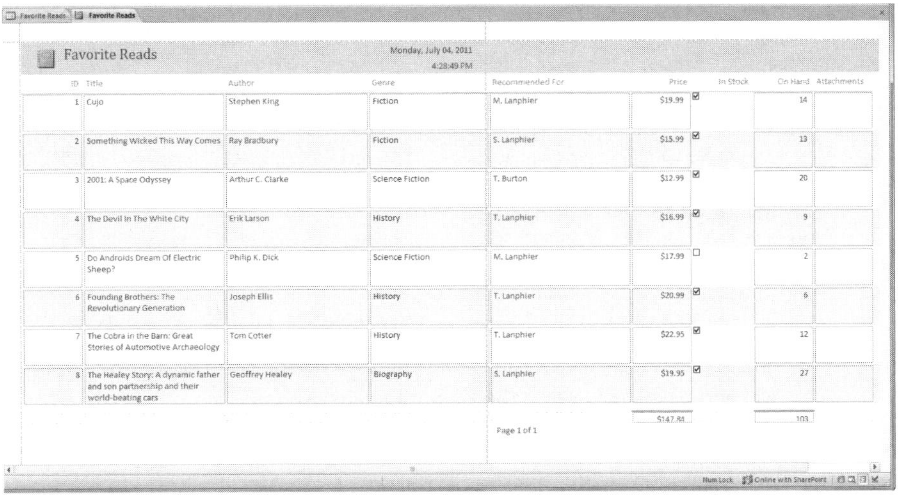

Figure 11-44 An unchanged report in Access.

For the changes to appear in the Access report, you need to refresh the data being pulled from the SharePoint list. This is always the case with the Access client—although SharePoint is automatically updated from Access, Access must be manually refreshed to pull data that is changed from within SharePoint.

Refreshing the content within Access is as simple as clicking the Refresh All button (see Figure 11-45) on the Access ribbon.

Figure 11-45 Refreshing the linked table and report.

The resulting data refresh updates data in both the linked table and the report, as illustrated in Figure 11-46.

7	The Cobra in the Barn: Great Stories of Automotive Archaeology	Tom Cotter	History	T. Lanphier	$22.95 ☑	12
8	The Healey Story: A dynamic father and son partnership and their world-beating cars	Geoffrey Healey	Biography	S. Lanphier	$19.95 ☑	27
11	Gracie: A Love Story	George Burns	Biography	M. Lanphier	$14.95 ☑	4
12	The Old Man and The Sea	Ernest Hemingway	Fiction	S. Lanphier	$9.95 ☑	23
13	The Grapes of Wrath	John Steinbeck	Fiction	M. Lanphier	$13.98 ☑	2
14	Pride and Prejudice and Zombies	Jane Austen and Seth Grahame-Smith	Fiction	S. Lanphier	$21.98 ☑	56
					$208.70	188

Page 1 of 1

Figure 11-46 The refreshed report.

Adding a Column to a SharePoint List from Access

Access provides an easy way to add columns to a SharePoint list. The column, its field type, and its values can all be added without ever opening a web browser. In this exercise, you will add a new column to the Favorite Reads list.

Clicking the Table tab for Favorite Reads displays the current information in the list. Notice the column on the far right called Click To Add (see Figure 11-47); that's where you will start.

▾	On Hand ▾	📎	Click to Add ▾
	14	📎(0)	
	13	📎(0)	
	20	📎(0)	
	9	📎(0)	
	2	📎(0)	
	6	📎(0)	
	12	📎(0)	
	27	📎(0)	
	4	📎(0)	
	23	📎(0)	
		📎(0)	

Figure 11-47 The Click To Add column.

To add a new column, select the Click To Add header at the top of the column. A menu appears that presents a selection of field types (see Figure 11-48), which are identical to those provided for any SharePoint list. For this example, click the Yes/No field.

Figure 11-48 Adding a Yes/No Column.

The newly added field appears as Field1, as shown in Figure 11-49. Note that it does not as yet have a name.

▾	On Hand ▾	📎	Field1
	14	📎(0)	☐
	13	📎(0)	☐
	20	📎(0)	☐
	9	📎(0)	☐
	2	📎(0)	☐
	6	📎(0)	☐

Figure 11-49 The new, blank field, waiting for a name.

Type the name **Hardcover?**, and then select which books in the table are hardcover versions, as demonstrated Figure 11-50.

On Hand		Hardcover?	
14	(0)	✓	
13	(0)	☐	
20	(0)	✓	
9	(0)	✓	
2	(0)	☐	
6	(0)	☐	
12	(0)	✓	
27	(0)	☐	

Figure 11-50 The new field name and values.

If you refresh the SharePoint list in your web browser, it's likely that it has already been updated with the new column and values, as illustrated in Figure 11-51.

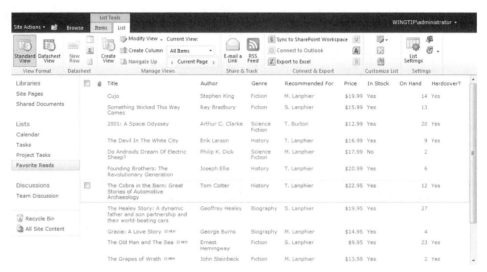

Figure 11-51 The updated SharePoint list.

Adding a New SharePoint List from Access

Let's take a moment to review—we've displayed, modified, and updated the contents of a SharePoint list from a linked table within Access 2010. The one thing we haven't (yet) done is create and populate an entire SharePoint list from within Access.

Fortunately, Access provides this functionality. Let's try it out. Begin by building a new data-base as you did for the example of the SharePoint list command. Your new database should look like the one shown in Figure 11-52.

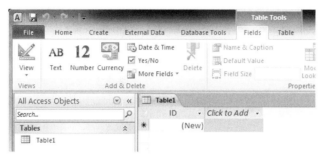

Figure 11-52 A newly created database.

On the ribbon, select the Create tab, and then click the SharePoint Lists button to display its drop-down menu (see Figure 11-53). Click the Contacts item.

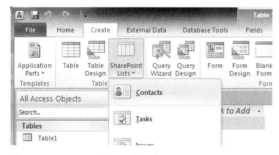

Figure 11-53 Creating a list of contacts.

Next, you are prompted to enter the URL of a SharePoint site, (for this example, use **http://titanmsf**). You also need to enter the name for the new list, and optionally, enter a descrip-tion, as well (see Figure 11-54). Note that although DriverContacts is two distinct words, there is no space between them—you'll see why in the next few steps.

Chapter 11

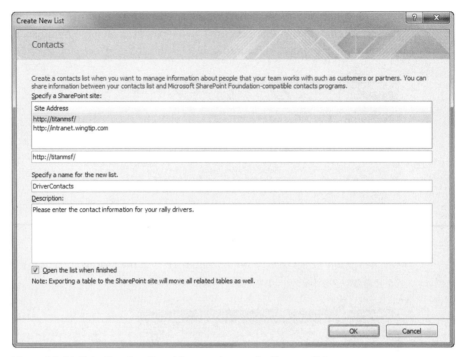

Figure 11-54 Selecting the site address and name for the new list.

The new SharePoint list is created and the linked table is built and added to your database. Notice that because you chose to use the Contact List template, the appropriate list columns were selected and added to the table/list, as shown in Figure 11-55.

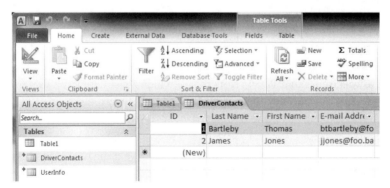

Figure 11-55 The new table values.

Let's have a look at what this linked table looks like in SharePoint. Upon opening the site, you see...well, nothing.

That's right; the newly created list does *not* appear in the Quick Launch on the left side of the screen. The new list would appear under the Lists heading, but instead, it's conveniently hidden so that we might configure its permissions, appearance, and so on.

Click the Lists heading (highlighted by the box in Figure 11-56) to configure the appearance of the library.

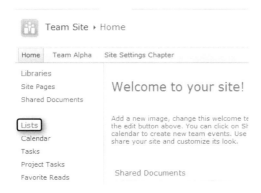

Figure 11-56 Your new list doesn't appear in the Quick Launch. Why?

When the Lists page appears, so too does the newly created list, DriverContacts (see Figure 11-57). Click its link to begin editing the list.

Figure 11-57 The DriverContacts list on the Lists page.

When the list appears in the browser, open the List tab within the List Tools tab group on the ribbon. Note that all of the values that you populated earlier in Access have already made their way to the SharePoint list (see Figure 11-58).

Chapter 11

Figure 11-58 The contents of the DriverContacts list.

In the Settings group, select the List Settings button to begin changing the appearance of this list. The List Settings page opens, as shown in Figure 11-59.

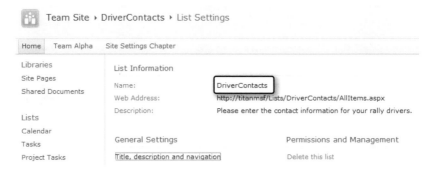

Figure 11-59 The List Settings page.

Here's where you find out why we left the space out of "DriverContacts." Notice that the Name and Web Address fields make use of the name from the list:

- Name: DriverContacts

- Web Address: *http://titanmsf/Lists/DriverContacts/AllItems.aspx*

If we had left the space in the list name when creating the list, the name would have been correct, but the web address would be kind of strange, as demonstrated in the following (notice the "%20" characters between Driver and Contacts):

- Name: Driver Contacts

- Web Address: *http://titanmsf/Lists/Driver%20Contacts/AllItems.aspx*

INSIDE OUT   Avoiding escaped characters in SharePoint URLs

See anything different in the web address? The space character has been replaced by its "escaped value" equivalent. Special characters (a space in this particular case) are not allowed in a web address, so SharePoint replaces them with something web browsers can understand. This is not a SharePoint-specific phenomenon, but rather an Internet standard that SharePoint observes.

In the General Settings section, select the Title, Description And Navigation link. On the General Settings page (see Figure 11-60), in the Name field, add a space between "Driver" and "Contacts." This only changes the Name field, not the Web Address.

While you're here, you should choose to have the list show on the Quick Launch. Notice that the navigation breadcrumb currently reads "Team Site > DriverContacts > List Settings > General Settings." Select the Yes option, and then click the Save button to save these changes.

Figure 11-60 The General Settings page, showing the Name And Description and Navigation fields.

Notice that the breadcrumb now reads "Team Site > Driver Contacts > List Settings." Also notice that this list appears under the Lists section of the Quick Launch, as shown in Figure 11-61.

Chapter 11

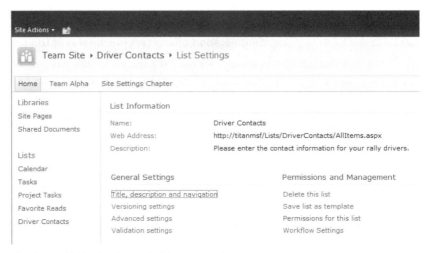

Figure 11-61 Navigation and Title corrected.

Selecting the Driver Contacts link in the breadcrumb shows the completed list, as shown in Figure 11-62.

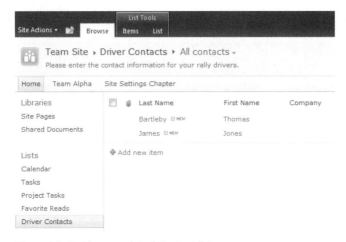

Figure 11-62 The completed Contact list.

Summary

SharePoint Foundation 2010 has functionality that is truly woven into the heart of the Microsoft Office 2010 Suite. These client applications possess the ability to not only interact with content from the SharePoint site, but also (in some cases) to modify the structure of the site.

There are many versions of the Office 2010 suite, ranging in scope from the very limited Office Starter product through the complete Office Professional Plus Suite. There are also additional products, such as Visio 2010 and Project 2010 that, while not part of any Office edition, add value to a SharePoint site.

While we have touched on the core integration of certain components from the Office 2010 Suite (in this case Word, Excel, and Access), Outlook 2010 provides a detailed level of integration, which is covered extensively in Chapter 12, "Taking Lists and Libraries Offline."

Chapter 11

Taking Lists and Libraries Offline

I n the not too distant past, going to work literally meant just that—getting in your car, driving to the office, and working in front of a desktop computer all day. Sure, there were a few intrepid souls (mostly consultants and salespeople) whose jobs required them to travel, but for most of us, the concept of having all of our important work available offline was just that—a concept.

Then we began to collaborate via email. Documents went back and forth over the Internet, which got the job done, but this process often resulted in confusion about which documents were the current revision. For some, this was an inconvenience; for others, this was unacceptable.

When Microsoft SharePoint was first introduced, it fostered a very real sense of team collaboration. Document and list libraries could be configured such that, although there were multiple versions of a document available, there was only one definitive version at any given time. This model held up well until the notion of offline availability was discussed. Suddenly, we were back to square one, emailing copies of documents to people who were on the road and then trying to re-integrate any changes or revisions that those individuals contributed to the information.

SharePoint 2007 had similar issues with offline availability, although the story was made somewhat better by the ability of Microsoft Outlook 2007 to store SharePoint document and list data on the local drive of a computer. This functionality was enhanced when paired with the Microsoft Groove platform, which allowed offline and remote collaboration functionality.

In SharePoint 2010, there are several ways to take content offline:

- Synchronize content using Outlook 2010

- Use the Local Drafts folder

- Use a SharePoint Workspace

- Use a Shared folder

The reason for having several choices is simple: some people only need to take a document or two offline while others need to interact with an entire list, folder, or library.

INSIDE OUT   Office versions required for offline content

The Professional Plus edition of Microsoft Office 2010 is required to utilize the Share-Point workspace and shared folder functionality; if you do not have this program available to you, then only the first two options shown in the previous list would be of interest to you.

There are also tools available (from Microsoft and other vendors) that take the "offlining" process a bit further, allowing either single-direction or bi-directional synchronization with one or more sites within your farm. A good example of such a technology is Groove Work-space. These add-on tools are beyond the scope of what is covered in this chapter because they are not included in the SharePoint Foundation 2010 platform.

Taking Content Offline by Using Outlook 2010

Some SharePoint 2010 lists and libraries can easily be synchronized and taken offline by using the Microsoft Outlook 2010 client. This client can be found in most versions of the Office 2010 client (see Chapter 11, "Integrating SharePoint with Microsoft Office 2010," for details).

SharePoint content that can be synchronized by using Outlook 2010 includes:

- Calendars

- Contact lists

- Task lists

- Document libraries

- Other lists

INSIDE OUT   **Reference information for using Outlook 2010 with SharePoint 2010**

You can find detailed information about using Outlook 2010 with SharePoint 2010 at *http://office.microsoft.com/en-us/sharepoint-foundation-help/synchronize-sharepoint-2010-content-with-outlook-2010-HA101881295.aspx#_Toc262734698.*

Synchronizing Calendars by Using Outlook 2010

SharePoint sites often include calendars to track events, which are important to a team. These calendars can be synchronized with an Outlook 2010 client; this information is stored in a calendar alongside a user's Microsoft Exchange calendar. Calendar information synchronized between SharePoint and Outlook is bi-directional, which means that changes made in Outlook appear in SharePoint (and vice versa).

To take a Team calendar offline, browse to the SharePoint site that contains the calendar, and then open the SharePoint calendar in your browser window. On the ribbon, select the icon labeled Connect To Outlook, as shown in Figure 12-1.

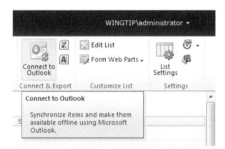

Figure 12-1 The Connect To Outlook icon.

Your browser might prompt you to allow the SharePoint website to initiate a connection to your computer. If this appears, select the Allow button. Optionally, you can choose to have the browser never show you this prompt again for SharePoint content by simply clearing the Always Ask Before Opening This Type Of Address check box before clicking Allow, as shown in Figure 12-2.

Figure 12-2 Allowing SharePoint to connect to Outlook.

Outlook also prompts you for verification (see Figure 12-3) before connecting to your SharePoint calendar.

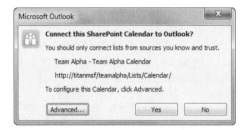

Figure 12-3 Connecting the calendar to Outlook.

You can simply choose Yes to complete the connection, or optionally, you can click the Advanced button to view and configure additional information about the connection (shown in Figure 12-4). Click OK when you are through with the advanced settings.

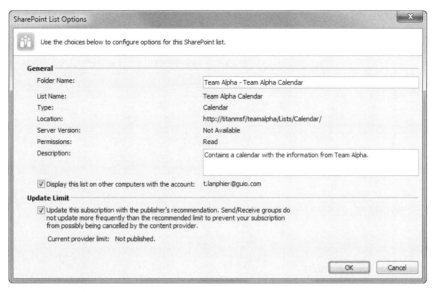

Figure 12-4 You can set the advanced settings for the connection.

Select the Yes button to complete the connection to Outlook, as shown in Figure 12-5.

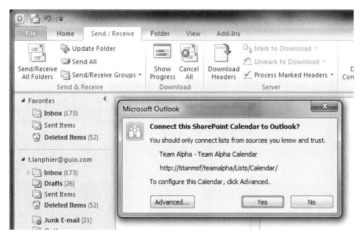

Figure 12-5 Completing the connection to Outlook.

Once your Outlook client has been connected to SharePoint, both Exchange and SharePoint Team calendars are displayed side by side, as shown in Figure 12-6.

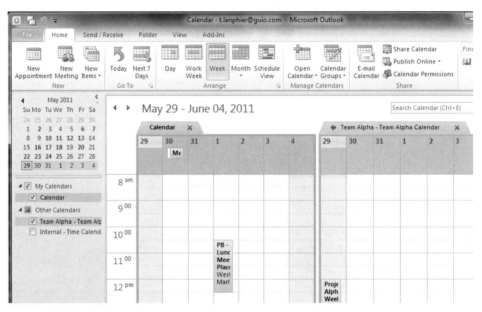

Figure 12-6 Both calendars displayed in Outlook.

As with any other calendar in Outlook, the overall color can be modified to help distinguish your SharePoint calendar from other calendars. To change the color of a calendar, right-click it to display the context menu, select the Color menu item, and then choose a color (Figure 12-7).

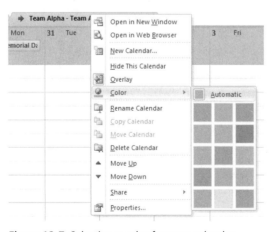

Figure 12-7 Selecting a color for your calendar.

You might occasionally have the need to see a combined view of your calendars. To see multiple calendars in one view, click the arrow in the Calendar tab (Figure 12-8).

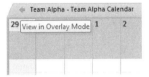

Figure 12-8 You can combine two calendars by clicking the View In Overlay arrow.

The calendars now appear on top of one another. To add an item to a particular calendar, select its tab by clicking once, and then add your calendar items. The next time your computer connects to the network, the calendars will update automatically as part of the Send/Receive process, as illustrated in Figure 12-9.

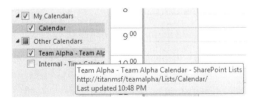

Figure 12-9 Viewing both calendars in Overlay Mode.

If you have limited space available on your computer's screen, you can choose to display or not to display each calendar at a time by selecting or clearing its check box, as shown in Figure 12-10.

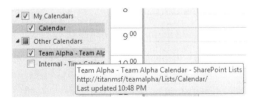

Figure 12-10 You can choose which calendars are shown in Outlook.

Chapter 12

Synchronizing Contact Lists by Using Outlook 2010

As with calendars, contact lists in SharePoint can be directly synchronized with the Outlook 2010 client. Contact list information synchronized between SharePoint and Outlook is bi-directional, which means that changes made in Outlook appear in SharePoint (and vice versa).

To take a contact list offline, browse to the Contact list that you wish to synchronize. Then, on the ribbon, click Connect To Outlook, as shown in Figure 12-11.

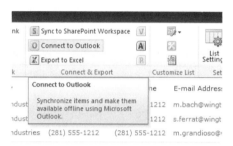

Figure 12-11 The Connect To Outlook icon.

Your browser might prompt you to allow the SharePoint website to initiate a connection to your computer. If this appears, select the Allow button. Optionally, you can choose to have the browser never show you this prompt again for SharePoint content by clearing the Always Ask Before Opening This Type Of Address check box before clicking Allow, as shown in Figure 12-12.

Figure 12-12 Allowing SharePoint to connect to Outlook.

Outlook also prompts you before connecting to your SharePoint contact list, as illustrated in Figure 12-13.

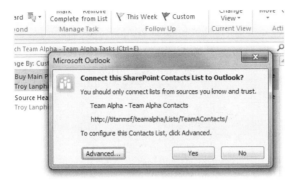

Figure 12-13 Connecting the contacts list to Outlook.

You can choose Yes to complete the connection, or optionally, you can select the Advanced to view and configure additional information about the connection (shown in Figure 12-14). Click OK when you are through with the advanced settings.

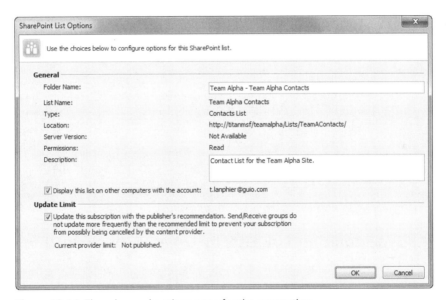

Figure 12-14 The advanced settings page for the connection.

Select the Yes button to complete the connection to Outlook (see Figure 12-15).

Figure 12-15 Completing the connection to Outlook.

Figure 12-16 shows that SharePoint contact lists are presented in the Other Contacts group alongside the My Contacts list in Outlook 2010.

Figure 12-16 Two sets of contacts (Other Contacts).

Synchronizing Task Lists by Using Outlook 2010

As with SharePoint calendars, Task lists in SharePoint can be directly synchronized with the Outlook 2010 client. These tasks are stored in a separate task list within Outlook. Task list information synchronized between SharePoint and Outlook is bi-directional, meaning that changes made in Outlook appear in SharePoint (and vice versa).

To take a Task list offline, browse to the SharePoint site that contains the list, and then open the SharePoint Task list in your browser window. On the ribbon, click Connect To Outlook, as shown in Figure 12-17.

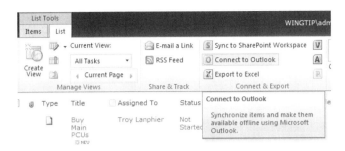

Figure 12-17 The Connect To Outlook icon.

Your browser might prompt you to allow the SharePoint website to initiate a connection to your computer. If this appears, click the Allow button. Optionally, you can choose to have the browser never show you this prompt again for SharePoint content by clearing the Always Ask Before Opening This Type Of Address check box before clicking Allow, as shown in Figure 12-18.

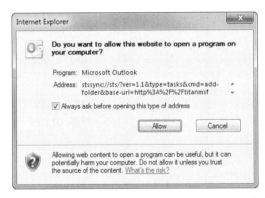

Figure 12-18 Allowing SharePoint to connect to Outlook.

Outlook also prompts you before connecting to your SharePoint Task list, as shown in Figure 12-19.

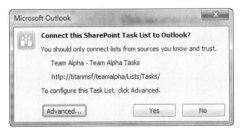

Figure 12-19 Connecting the Task list to Outlook.

Chapter 12

You can choose Yes to complete the connection, or optionally, you can select the Advanced button to view and configure additional information about the connection (shown in Figure 12-20). Click OK when you are through with the advanced settings.

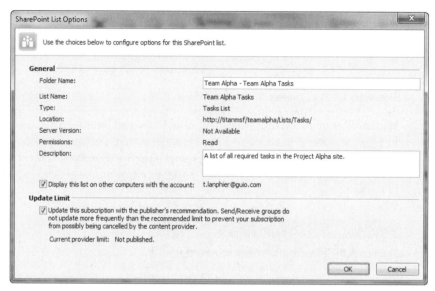

Figure 12-20 The advanced settings page for the connection.

Select the Yes button to complete the connection to Outlook (Figure 12-21).

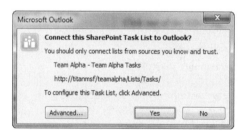

Figure 12-21 Completing the connection to Outlook.

Figure 12-22 shows that SharePoint task lists are presented in the Other Tasks group alongside the My Tasks list in Outlook 2010.

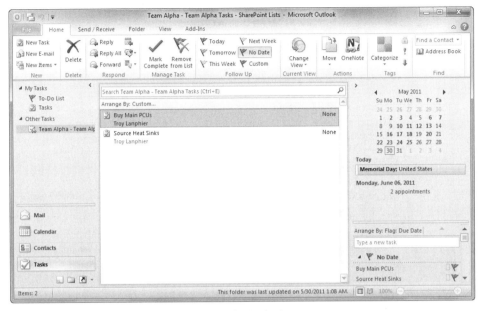

Figure 12-22 The SharePoint Task list appears in Outlook.

Synchronizing Document Libraries Using Outlook 2010

Like calendars, Contact lists, and Task lists, SharePoint document libraries can be synchronized with Outlook. Unlike them, however, SharePoint document libraries can only synchronize
in one direction—from SharePoint to Outlook 2010.

At first, this process sounds only marginally useful—after all, Outlook 2010 can only read
from, but not write to a SharePoint document library. When this functionality is combined
with the SharePoint drafts folder, documents that are downloaded can be edited offline and
uploaded to the SharePoint site.

To take a document library offline, browse to the SharePoint site that contains the list, and
then open the SharePoint document library in your browser window. On the ribbon, click
Connect To Outlook, as shown in Figure 12-23.

Figure 12-23 The Connect To Outlook icon.

Your browser might prompt you to allow the SharePoint website to initiate a connection to your computer. If this appears, select the Allow button. Optionally, you can choose to have the browser never show you this prompt again for SharePoint content by clearing the Always Ask Before Opening This Type Of Address check box before clicking Allow, as shown in Figure 12-24.

Figure 12-24 Allowing SharePoint to connect to Outlook.

Outlook prompts you before connecting to your SharePoint Document Library, as shown in Figure 12-25.

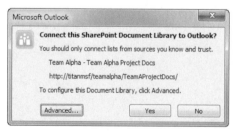

Figure 12-25 Connecting the Document Library to Outlook.

You can choose Yes to complete the connection, or optionally, you can select the Advanced button to view and configure additional information about the connection (shown in Figure 12-26). Click OK when you are through with the advanced settings.

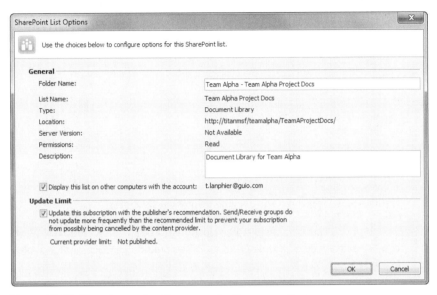

Figure 12-26 The advanced settings page for the connection.

Select the Yes button to complete the connection to Outlook, as shown in Figure 12-27.

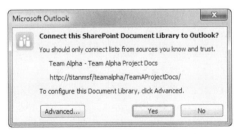

Figure 12-27 Completing the connection to Outlook.

The synchronized document library appears in the left pane of Outlook 2010. When this library is selected, the items within it are displayed in the Downloaded Documents section in the center pane. When you select a document from the library, a preview of it appears in the right pane, as shown in Figure 12-28.

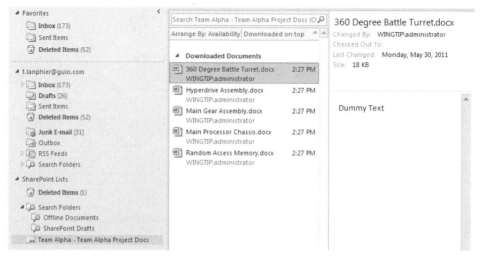

Figure 12-28 A synchronized document library in Outlook.

Although you cannot directly edit a document from within Outlook 2010, you can edit the copy that has been downloaded to it. To begin editing a document, double-click the downloaded copy.

INSIDE OUT   When is the content synchronized?

Once a document library has been synchronized and its content appears in Outlook, you can disconnect your computer from the network and still have access to your local copy of the document library.

When the document appears, a message is displayed, indicating the document is in read-only mode, along with an Edit Offline button (see Figure 12-29). Select this button to begin editing by using the SharePoint Drafts folder.

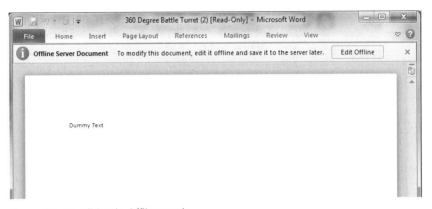

Figure 12-29 Editing in Offline mode.

To edit the document, it must be transferred into the SharePoint Drafts folder on your local computer. Once transferred, the document can be edited and uploaded to the Share-Point site. Select the OK button to begin offline edits of the document, as illustrated in Figure 12-30.

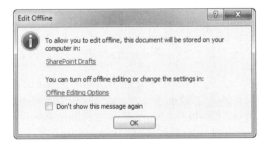

Figure 12-30 Verifying Offline Edit mode.

We will cover the use of the SharePoint Drafts folder in the upcoming section "Taking Content Offline by Using the Local Drafts Folder."

Synchronizing Other Lists by Using Outlook 2010

There are other lists within SharePoint that fully synchronize with Outlook 2010, including standard SharePoint lists (such as Discussion Boards) and custom lists that you can create. The process for adding lists to Outlook 2010 is identical to how other lists (such as Con-tacts, for example) are added.

Additionally, SharePoint Foundation 2010 includes the ability to connect SharePoint lists to external, Line-of-Business (LoB) systems (such as non-SharePoint databases). The information retrieved from these systems can be used to populate list content in a SharePoint site, including the descriptive metadata associated with the database. When External lists are configured correctly, information can be both read from and written to the database.

INSIDE OUT   Licensing requirements

The ability to connect SharePoint to these external systems is included in both SharePoint Foundation 2010 and SharePoint Server 2010 Standard; however, the SharePoint Server 2010 Enterprise license is required if you want to take this information offline by using Microsoft Outlook 2010.

Taking Content Offline by Using the Local Drafts Folder

As stated previously, there are several ways to take SharePoint content offline; the simplest mechanism is to use the local drafts folder (also referred to in some menus as the *Share-Point Drafts* folder. The process is easy and only requires that you 1) check out a document for editing from a document library, and 2) select the Use My Local Drafts Folder check box.

When you use this process to check out a document from its library, the original document is locked to prevent modification by any other user. A copy of the document is downloaded to the local file system where it can be altered. When the necessary alterations are complete, the document can again be uploaded to your SharePoint site and checked in for others to use.

Taking a Document Offline via Check Out

The next few steps detail the process of taking a document offline by using the Check Out functionality. We begin by locating the document library that contains the document you want to edit. Hover your mouse over the file name to display the list item menu, and then select the Check Out menu item, as shown in Figure 12-31.

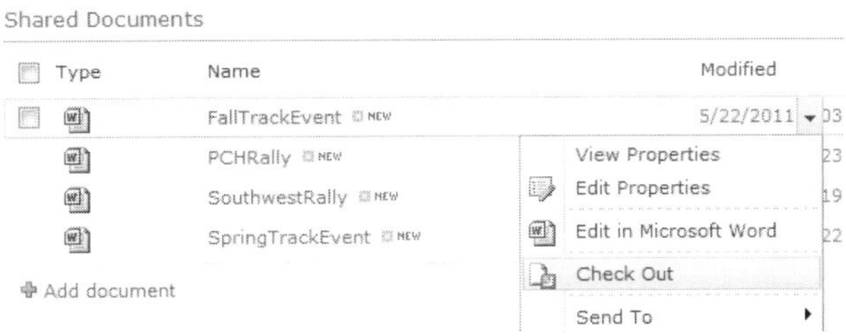

Figure 12-31 Checking out a document.

A dialog box appears, indicating the name and location of the document that you are checking out. Ensure that the Use My Local Drafts Folder check box is selected, and then click the OK button, as depicted in Figure 12-32.

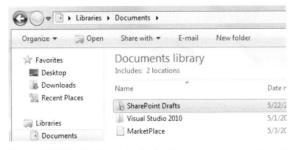

Figure 12-32 Be sure to select the Use My Local Drafts Folder check box when checking out a document.

At this point, the original document is locked for editing (exclusively to you) and a copy is downloaded to your computer. If you have never checked out a file using this process, a new folder called SharePoint Drafts is created on your computer in your default Documents folder, as demonstrated in Figure 12-33.

Figure 12-33 The local drafts folder on your computer (SharePoint Drafts).

> **Note**
> Unless this location has been changed by your Administrator, the default location of this folder is C:\Users\yourusername\Documents\SharePoint Drafts.

Figure 12-34 shows that opening the SharePoint Drafts folder in Windows Explorer displays all of the documents that are currently checked out to you.

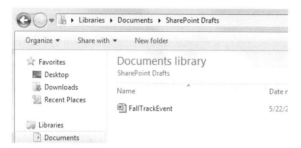

Figure 12-34 A document in the SharePoint Drafts folder.

INSIDE OUT   Check-out required

Checking out a document in this manner is a very deliberate action; if a document library is not configured to require check-out for edits, you will not get a copy of the document in your local drafts folder when editing the document. The ability to use the local drafts folder is specifically dependent on the check-out mechanism found in SharePoint 2010.

Taking a Document Offline via Document Edit

When building a new document library, it is recommended that document check out be required for edits. This setting change is useful because people might want to be able to take versions of their files offline without having to explicitly choose Check Out first. If this setting is changed when the library is created, then a user can easily choose to store a copy of the document in their local drafts folder as part of the document edit process.

INSIDE OUT   Enforcing check-out in a document library

If you happen to be the administrator of a document library, you can enforce check-out in a couple of steps. Open the document library, and then on the ribbon, on the Library tab, choose Library Settings | Versioning Settings. Under Require Check Out, select the Yes option, and then click OK.

To begin editing a document, open the document library. Hover your mouse over the item that you want to edit, and then select Edit In Microsoft Word in the list item menu that appears, as shown in Figure 12-35.

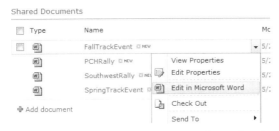

Figure 12-35 Choose the Edit In Microsoft Word option.

A dialog box appears (as shown in Figure 12-36), indicating the name and location of the document that you are checking out. Ensure that you select the Use My Local Drafts Folder check box, and then click the OK button.

Figure 12-36 Checking out a document to the local drafts folder.

At this point, the original document is locked for editing (exclusively to you) and a copy of it is downloaded to your computer. Anyone visiting the site while you have the file in a Checked Out status will see a green arrow on the icon for the file, as illustrated in Figure 12-37.

 FallTrackEvent ☐ NEW

Figure 12-37 A green arrow (shown here in the lower-right corner of the Word icon) indicates that the document is checked out.

Interacting with an Offline Document

Now that you know how to obtain an offline copy of a document, let's have a look at how SharePoint and Office 2010 keep track of the relationship between documents in a Share-Point Document Library and their counterparts on the local computer.

Document Information

If Office 2010 has a document open that originated from a SharePoint site (whether your local computer is online or offline), the document knows what its relationship is to the server and what its status is.

Let's see this functionality in action. When a local computer is connected to an intranet, an Office file has an active record of where it came from and its status. Select File, and then in the Backstage view, click the Info tab to view active information about the document. Particularly important are the following items (shown in Figure 12-38):

- The Check In/Check Out status of the file

- The Version status of the file

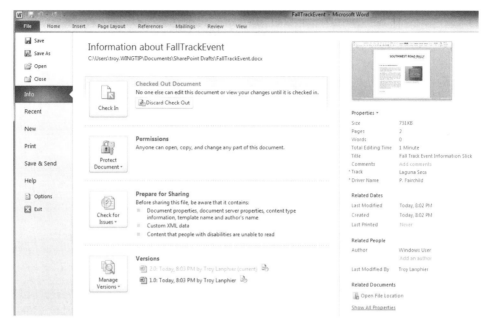

Figure 12-38 Viewing file information—Online.

When the same computer goes offline (no connection to the network), the document status changes; specifically, as shown in Figure 12-39, the file's Check In/Out button is gone, and its version status no longer matches the information presented when the computer is online.

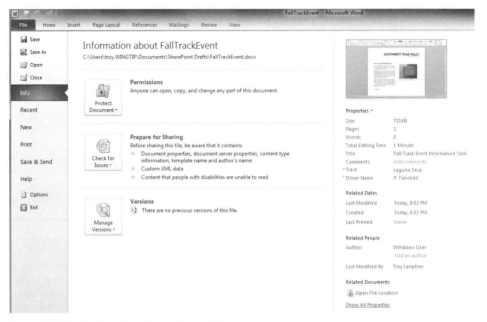

Figure 12-39 Viewing file information—Offline.

Reconnecting an Offline Document to SharePoint 2010

The next order of business is to make your changes to the document and then reconnect it to the farm. You begin by opening the file, just as you would any other. Open your Office application, and then select File | Open. Browse to the SharePoint Drafts folder in your My Documents folder (see Figure 12-40).

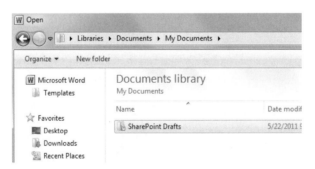

Figure 12-40 The SharePoint Drafts folder.

Open the SharePoint Drafts folder, and then open the document that you want to edit by selecting it and choosing the Open button or by simply double-clicking it, as illustrated in Figure 12-41.

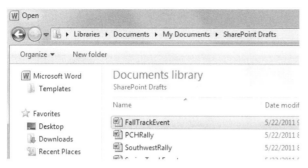

Figure 12-41 A document in the SharePoint Drafts folder.

Make and save your edits to the document. Note that all changes are saved to the document in the SharePoint Drafts folder (Local Drafts).

When you reconnect to the network, you will see that the document Check In/Out status and Version status reappears in File Information. Now the document must be checked back in to the library so that others can see your edits. Be sure that you are connected to your network before proceeding to the next step.

Open the document as you did previously, and then select the File menu item. The Info tab should appear automatically, as shown in Figure 12-42.

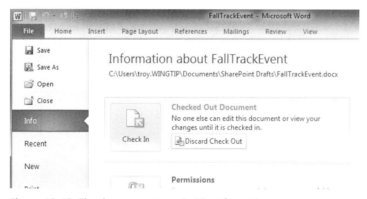

Figure 12-42 The document status in File Information.

Next, SharePoint gives you the opportunity to add comments to your new document version. In this example, you will not be leaving the document in a Checked Out state, so click the OK button to complete this step, as shown in Figure 12-43.

Chapter 12

Figure 12-43 Check In with comments.

The document reappears on your screen (see Figure 12-44), indicating that it will require Check Out before being modified again.

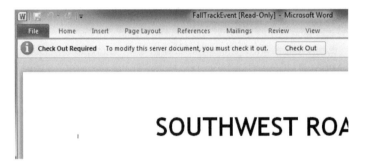

Figure 12-44 The checked-in document.

Now, there is no longer a copy of this document being held in your local drafts folder, and it is safe to close your Office application. If you would like, you can also verify the document's status by opening the document library and viewing the document's status, as shown in Figure 12-45.

Figure 12-45 The document checked in to SharePoint.

Using SharePoint Workspace 2010

While local drafts are a reasonable way to work offline with SharePoint, it can become a bit unwieldy and cumbersome when you have to take a series of lists or libraries offline. But what if you do not know in advance what documents you will need to work with or for how long? It's likely that neither your site owners nor co-workers will be pleased to find a series of libraries with all of the documents in Check Out mode. To avoid these scenarios, you might want to consider using SharePoint Workspace 2010.

Configuring SharePoint Workspace 2010 on Your Computer

SharePoint Workspace will need to be configured for your account—you should check with your farm administrator in advance to see if there is a defined set of instructions for how to connect within your organization.

We will configure an account by using the out-of-the-box settings. To begin, from the Windows Start button, click All Programs | Microsoft Office | Microsoft SharePoint Workspace 2010. A dialog box appears (see Figure 12-46), prompting you to either create a new account or restore an existing account.

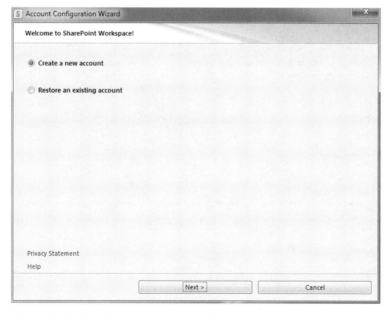

Figure 12-46 Creating a new SharePoint Workspace account.

INSIDE OUT SharePoint Workspace availability

If you do not see Microsoft SharePoint Workspace 2010 as an option in your Office menu, you might want to check with your Help Desk/farm administrator to see if you have this license available—not all versions of Office have this functionality included. For details, see Chapter 11.

If you are in a larger organization, you might have been issued an Account Configuration Code and an Account Configuration Server, which will configure your SharePoint Workspace (see Figure 12-47) with all necessary information.

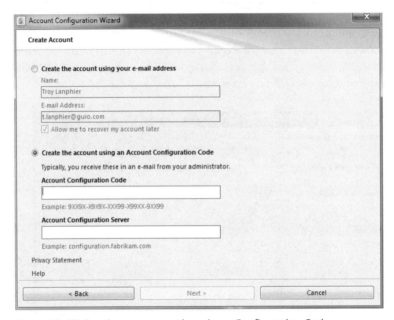

Figure 12-47 Creating an account by using a Configuration Code.

If you have this information:

1. Select the Create The Account Using An Account Configuration Code option.

2. Fill in the Account Configuration Code and Account Configuration Server fields.

3. Click Next to end the configuration steps, and then click Finish.

If you do not have an Account Configuration Code or Account Configuration Server information, then you will need to configure the SharePoint Workspace 2010 client manually (see Figure 12-48), by performing the following procedure:

1. Select the Create The Account Using Your E-Mail Address radio button.

2. Fill in the Name and E-Mail Address fields.

3. Optional, (but highly recommended) select the Allow Me To Recover My Account Later.

4. Click Finish

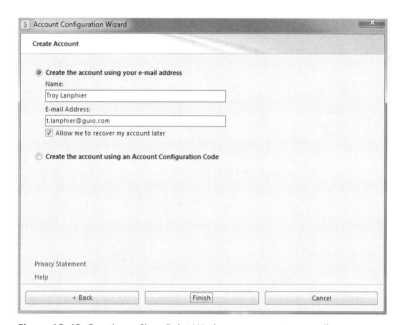

Figure 12-48 Creating a SharePoint Workspace account manually.

SharePoint Workspace 2010 opens on your computer, showing the default configuration, as appears in Figure 12-49.

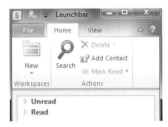

Figure 12-49 The default view of the SharePoint Workspace.

Before you begin using SharePoint Workspace 2010, it is recommended that you do the following:

- Enable Account Recovery

- Save your SharePoint Workspace account as a file

Enable Account Recovery

Account Recovery has two core functions: you can restore a backup file when you have forgotten your password, and you can reconnect when your Windows logon has changed such that your SharePoint Workspace account no longer works correctly.

If you need to restore your SharePoint Workspace account backup file but have forgotten the password, enabling Account Recovery will allow you to use the Forgot Your Password option. Using this functionality, you can have an account reset code sent to your email address.

Save Account as File

Having your account saved as a file is useful in the event that something happens to your Groove client installation and you are using a single computer. If you have multiple computers that you use to interact with your Groove account, the need for the account to be saved as a file is diminished.

SharePoint Workspace Options

Both of the preceding preferences are set from the same menu. To make these changes, select the File tab, and then in the Backstage view, click Options (see Figure 12-50).

Figure 12-50 Click Options in the Backstage view to make changes to the SharePoint Workspace preferences.

Next, click the Preferences button shown in Figure 12-51.

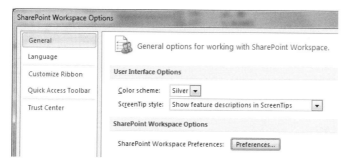

Figure 12-51 Click the Preferences button to access SharePoint Workspace options.

Select the Account tab (see Figure 12-52). At this point, you can choose whether to enable account recovery by selecting a check box. To save your account as a file, you must select the Save button under the label Save Account As File.

Figure 12-52 Save Account As File.

Next, provide a file name for your account, as shown in Figure 12-53, and then save it to a safe place.

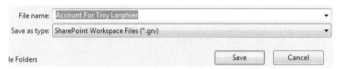

Figure 12-53 Save the account as a file (*.grv).

INSIDE OUT   What is a .grv file?

You might have noticed that the SharePoint Workspace account uses a .grv extension. This is because SharePoint Workspace shares some core functionality with Groove Server 2010. Groove Server 2010 is an add-on enterprise-level server product, which is capable of enhancing and centralizing functionality found in SharePoint Workspace. Go to *http://office.microsoft.com/en-us/servers/groove-server-2010-features-and-benefits-HA101810271.aspx* for detailed information about Groove Server 2010.

Taking Content Offline with SharePoint Workspace 2010

Now that your configuration is safe, it's time to put your new SharePoint Workspace to work. With SharePoint Workspace 2010, mobile users can stay up to date with content located on a SharePoint farm by replicating SharePoint information and storing it offline on a local computer.

There are three distinct types of entities that you can create in SharePoint Workspace:

- SharePoint Workspaces

- Shared Folder Workspaces

- Groove Workspaces

For the purposes of this chapter, we will be discussing the first two items, SharePoint Workspaces and Shared Folder Workspaces. Groove Workspace is not covered because it is an additional product that extends SharePoint Workspace functionality, in much the same way that SharePoint Server and Project Server extend SharePoint Foundation functionality.

Limitations in SharePoint Workspace

There are certain items that cannot be synchronized in a SharePoint Workspace. These include:

- Calendar/Events lists

- Wikis

- Blog sites

- Form libraries

- Slide libraries

- Surveys

- Site directories

- OneNote notebooks stored in document libraries

- IRM-protected document libraries

INSIDE OUT   How information is stored on your computer

SharePoint Workspace actually uses three distinct storage mechanisms to store Share-Point information on a computer. You can find a complete discussion of these technologies and how they are utilized within SharePoint at *http://blogs.msdn.com/b/sharepoint_work-space_development_team/archive/2010/03/12/sharepoint-workspace-and-the-office-document-cache.aspx*.

Synchronizing a SharePoint Workspace

Configuring synchronization between a SharePoint site and SharePoint Workspace is a fairly straightforward process. Begin by opening the site to be synchronized in your web browser. On your SharePoint Site, select Site Actions | Sync To SharePoint Workspace, as shown in Figure 12-54.

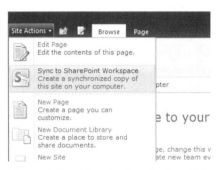

Figure 12-54 Select the Sync To SharePoint Workspace option in the Site Actions menu.

A prompt appears, asking you to trust the SharePoint Site (see Figure 12-55). Click the OK button to continue.

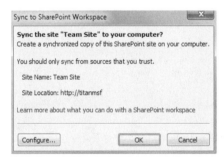

Figure 12-55 Synchronizing the site to your computer.

To see the newly synchronized site, start SharePoint Workspace 2010, as shown in Figure 12-56.

Figure 12-56 Starting SharePoint Workspace 2010.

The Launchbar for SharePoint Workspace appears, as illustrated in Figure 12-57. Click the Team Site icon to open it.

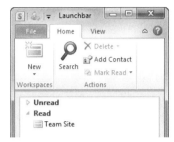

Figure 12-57 Opening the Team Site.

The Team Site opens in SharePoint; two major panes appear, which are shown in Figure 12-58.

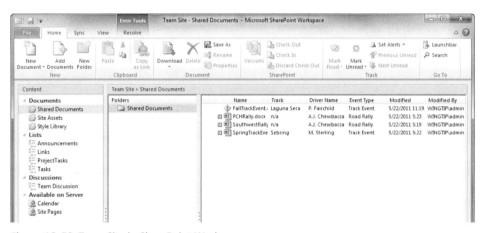

Figure 12-58 Team Site in SharePoint Workspace.

The Content pane on the left (presented in Figure 12-59), displays the items available from the SharePoint Workspace as well as links to items that are not available locally. From this menu, you can choose which library or list with which you want to interact.

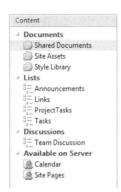

Figure 12-59 Available items on the Team Site.

The contents of the SharePoint list or library are shown in the right pane. In this example (see Figure 12-60), you can see that the top document is experiencing a synchronization issue, while the other three documents are in a checked out state.

Name	Track	Driver Name	Event Type	Modified	Modified By
FallTrackEvent.	Laguna Seca	P. Fairchild	Track Event	5/22/2011 11:19	WINGTIP\admin
PCHRally.docx	n/a	A.J. Chewbacca	Road Rally	5/22/2011 5:23	WINGTIP\admin
SouthwestRally	n/a	A.J. Chewbacca	Road Rally	5/22/2011 5:19	WINGTIP\admin
SpringTrackEve	Sebring	M. Sterling	Track Event	5/22/2011 5:22	WINGTIP\admin

Figure 12-60 The right pane presents list or library contents.

Because the computer is currently online, you can select the Sync button and choose Sync Workspace (shown in Figure 12-61). Let's see if this resolves the issue.

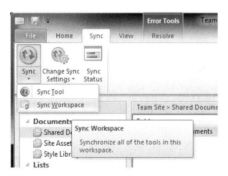

Figure 12-61 Synchronizing the SharePoint Workspace.

Verify the current status by selecting the Sync Status button shown in Figure 12-62.

Figure 12-62 To verify the synchronization status, click the Sync Status button.

All of the libraries in the SharePoint Workspace are showing as synchronized (see Figure 12-63)—so far, so good. Now click the Close button.

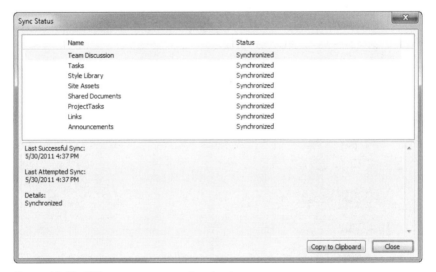

Figure 12-63 All items are now synchronized.

Looking at the Content pane in Figure 12-64, it is apparent that the topmost document is continuing to have a synchronization issue. Let's see what the issue is.

Name	Track	Driver Name	Event Type	Modified	Modified By
FallTrackEvent..	Laguna Seca	P. Fairchild	Track Event	5/22/2011 11:19	WINGTIP\admin
PCHRally.docx	n/a	A.J. Chewbacca	Road Rally	5/22/2011 5:23	WINGTIP\admin
SouthwestRally	n/a	A.J. Chewbacca	Road Rally	5/22/2011 5:19	WINGTIP\admin
SpringTrackEve	Sebring	M. Sterling	Track Event	5/22/2011 5:22	WINGTIP\admin

Figure 12-64 One file is still experiencing a synchronization problem.

Chapter 12

Double-click the item to open the Upload Center. Figure 12-65 shows that problem is the result of the document not being checked out in our SharePoint Team Site; therefore, it cannot be overwritten with the copy contained in SharePoint Workspace.

Figure 12-65 The Upload Center reveals why the upload failed.

To begin resolving the issue, select the Resolve button from the menu. In this example, you need to open the website and check the document out. Select the Open Web Site menu item, as depicted in Figure 12-66.

Figure 12-66 To begin resolving the conflict, open the website.

When the Team Site appears, click the list item menu next to the document, and then select Check Out, as illustrated in Figure 12-67.

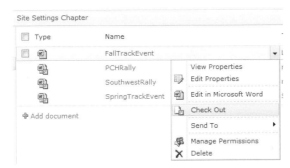

Figure 12-67 Check out the document.

Return to the Upload Center and select Resolve, this time choosing to upload the document, as shown in Figure 12-68.

Figure 12-68 Click Resolve, and then choose Upload.

The document is shown pending upload in Figure 12-69.

Figure 12-69 The document is now pending upload.

Finally, the document uploads (Figure 12-70).

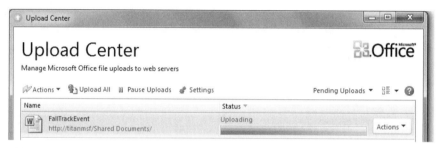

Figure 12-70 Uploading.

The status of Upload Center changes, indicating that all files are uploaded (see Figure 12-71). Close the Upload Center.

Figure 12-71 Complete—no files are pending upload.

The SharePoint Workspace updates (see Figure 12-72), indicating that the document has been uploaded but still in a checked-out state.

Name	Track	Driver Name	Event Type	Modified	Modified By
FallTrackEvent	Laguna Seca	P. Fairchild	Track Event	6/4/2011 10:48	WINGTIP\admin
PCHRally.docx	n/a	A.J. Chewbacca	Road Rally	5/22/2011 5:23	WINGTIP\admin
SouthwestRally	n/a	A.J. Chewbacca	Road Rally	5/22/2011 5:19	WINGTIP\admin
SpringTrackEve	Sebring	M. Sterling	Track Event	5/22/2011 5:22	WINGTIP\admin

Figure 12-72 The updated SharePoint Workspace.

Right-click the document, and then select Check In, as shown in Figure 12-73.

Check Out	
Check In	
Discard Check Out	
Mark Read	Ctrl+F4

Figure 12-73 Checking in the Document.

Add Version Comments for the document (shown in Figure 12-74), and then select OK.

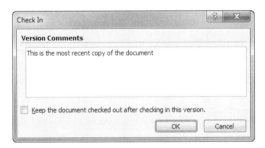

Figure 12-74 In the Version Comments text field, you can enter document version notes.

The updated document status is shown in SharePoint Workspace. Notice in Figure 12-75 that the document is no longer in a checked-out state.

Name	Track	Driver Name	Event Type	Modified	Modified By
FallTrackEvent	Laguna Seca	P. Fairchild	Track Event	6/4/2011 10:55	WINGTIP\admin
PCHRally.docx	n/a	A.J. Chewbacca	Road Rally	5/22/2011 5:23	WINGTIP\admin
SouthwestRally	n/a	A.J. Chewbacca	Road Rally	5/22/2011 5:19	WINGTIP\admin
SpringTrackEve	Sebring	M. Sterling	Track Event	5/22/2011 5:22	WINGTIP\admin

Figure 12-75 The document is now checked in.

Using Shared Folders in SharePoint Workspace 2010

Shared Folders is another concept that was originally introduced in Groove Workspace 2007. This technology provides an easy way to share documents in a folder that can be synchronized between different business users.

There are two different ways to build a Shared Folder: the first method is to build it from within SharePoint Workspace, the second is to build a folder on your computer and then choose to share it by using SharePoint Workspace.

Chapter 12

Although you are not creating a SharePoint Workspace *per se*, Shared Folder relies on SharePoint Workspace 2010 to provide its core functionality. SharePoint Workspace 2010 is not available in every version of Office 2010; it is only installed as part of the Office Professional Plus 2010 edition (see Chapter 11 for details).

In the following examples, you will begin by building a Shared Folder, both from within SharePoint Workspace 2010 and in Windows Explorer itself. After that, you will see how to utilize the Shared Folder.

Building a Shared Folder by Using SharePoint Workspace 2010

To begin sharing a folder in SharePoint Workspace 2010, select File | New | Shared Folder, as illustrated in Figure 12-76.

Figure 12-76 Creating a new Shared Folder.

Give the new folder the name **Rally Metrics**, and then click Create (see Figure 12-77).

Figure 12-77 Creating a folder named Rally Metrics.

You are presented with three options:

- Create a new folder on the desktop,

- Create a new folder in a location that you designate

- Select an existing folder to share

In this example, you will create a new folder on the desktop (see Figure 12-78). Click the OK button.

Figure 12-78 Selecting a folder for synchronization.

The new folder appears on the desktop and is ready for use.

Build a Shared Folder by Using Windows Explorer

This process is very similar to building a Shared Folder from within SharePoint Workspace 2010. Again, find a folder that you want to share on your system (see Figure 12-79). Note that this folder is not currently shared (there is no SharePoint Workspace icon on it).

Figure 12-79 Select the folder to be shared.

Right-click the folder to open the shortcut menu (see Figure 12-80), select Shared Folder Synchronization, and then click Start Synchronizing.

Figure 12-80 Start the synchronization process.

SharePoint Workspace prompts you to verify that you want to share the folder, as shown in Figure 12-81. Click Yes to continue.

Figure 12-81 Verify that you want to share the folder.

As in the previous section, the new folder appears on the desktop and is ready for use (Figure 12-82). Compare the folder's appearance with its original state in Figure 12-79.

Figure 12-82 The icon indicates that this is now a shared folder.

Using Shared Folders

No matter which method you used, you now have a folder with which multiple users can share and store information on multiple client machines.

When you double-click the folder you shared, what appears to be a standard Windows Explorer session opens, as shown in Figure 12-83.

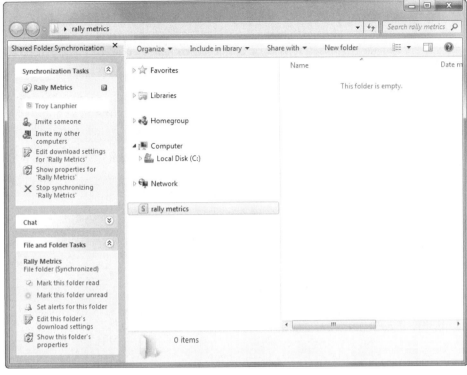

Figure 12-83 Opening the folder to show synchronization menus.

A new panel appears to the left of the Explorer window, containing three major sections: Synchronization Tasks, Chat, and File Folder Tasks, which are described here:

- **Synchronization Tasks**   This section provides you with mechanisms to administer your Shared Folder; inviting users, inviting other computers, and controlling properties and settings for your folder are under this menu.

- **Chat**   This provides you with the ability to send instant messages to others working on your folder.

- **File And Folder Tasks**   Use this section to carry out core administrative tasks such as marking a folder Read/Unread and viewing Download Settings and Properties.

Chat and File And Folder Tasks are fairly self-explanatory; once you understand the Synchronization Tasks, you should understand the Download Settings and Folder Properties items under File And Folder Tasks—so, let's have a look at the Synchronization Tasks in detail.

Chapter 12

Invite Someone

Let's walk through the process of administering this Shared Folder. To begin, you need to invite other users to share it. Select the Invite Someone link in the Synchronization Tasks section.

A dialog box appears, prompting you to select one or more users to invite to use the Shared Folder. Next, select the Role drop-down menu (the down arrow adjacent to Participant).

Notice that there are three roles available to select from. These roles (see Figure 12-84) do not control permissions within the folder—everyone sharing the folder has full rights to the folder. Roles simply govern the ability to make configuration changes for the Shared Folder.

Figure 12-84 Assigning folder roles.

Unless permissions have been changed in your Shared Folder for these roles, the rights of each role are as follows:

- **Manager**   This role can Invite/Uninvite users. It can also cancel all outstanding invitations.

- **Participant**   This role can only Invite users to the Shared Folder.

- **Guest**   This role has no ability to make any configuration changes to the Shared Folder.

Next, write an invitation message (shown in Figure 12-85) that will be displayed in the email to your new invitee.

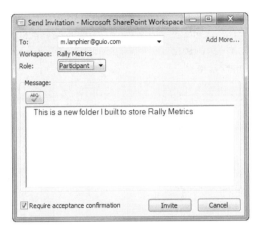

Figure 12-85 The invitation that's sent to other users.

Notice the check box in the lower-left of the screen labeled Require Acceptance Confirmation. This setting means that when the person receiving this invitation accepts it, SharePoint Workspace will ask you to confirm that this person should have access to the Shared Folder.

Ironically, the invitation confirmation takes place whether you choose to select the option or not, as is demonstrated in Figure 12-86. Click OK to close the tip.

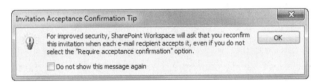

Figure 6-86 The invitation confirmation.

When you have completed the invitation, click the Invite button to send the invitation on its way.

Invite My Other Computers

Next, consider the following scenario: you have both a desktop computer for office use and a laptop for travel. Both of which have SharePoint Workspace 2010 installed, so you can choose to use the Shared Folder functionality. Only your desktop has the correct SharePoint Workspace 2010 account configured, but you need to get the laptop configured, as well.

The good news is that you do not necessarily need to get your corporate Help Desk involved to configure your laptop; SharePoint Workspace 2010 has a mechanism that allows you to export your account settings to another computer and connect that computer to your Workspace or Shared Folder.

To begin the configuration process, select the Invite My Other Computers link. Figure 12-87 presents the configuration steps and shows how to use your account information on another computer. Select a location to store the file by using Browse, select Save, and then OK.

Figure 12-87 Setting up an account on another computer.

The saved file (.grv) can be copied to your other computer; if you double-click it, Share-Point Workspace will automatically configure the new computer using the settings provided in the file. Click Save to store the file in the location selected (see Figure 12-88) to store it for this use.

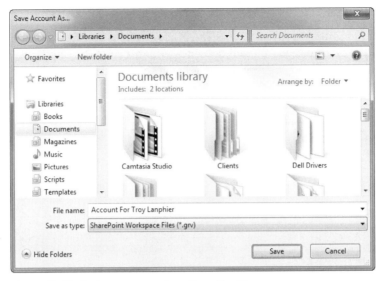

Figure 12-88 Saving an account configuration file.

For security purposes, SharePoint Workspace requires that you generate a password for this backed up account. Adding a password, as shown in Figure 12-89, means that no one can get a copy of your backup file and automatically have access to the files that you have stored in the Shared Folder or SharePoint Workspace.

Enter a Password, and then select OK.

Figure 12-89 Enter a password to protect the SharePoint Workspace account.

Download Settings

Download Settings (shown in Figure 12-90) allows you to specify what sort of changes should be synchronized. You can choose to perform a Full Automatic Download, a Limited Automatic Download (specifying the maximum size for downloaded changes), or a Manual (on-demand) Download.

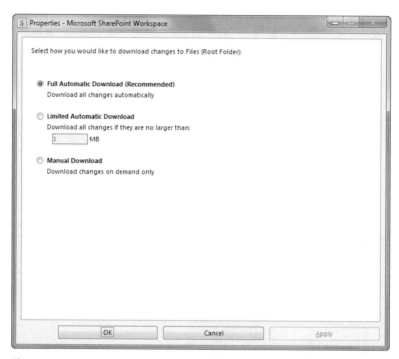

Figure 12-90 You can choose your download settings.

Show Properties

Show Properties is a fairly detailed menu setting. From here, you can choose one of five tabs:

- **General**   (Figure 12-91) This displays folder creation information and the description as well as providing a choice as to whether the folder is downloaded automatically onto all computers for this user.

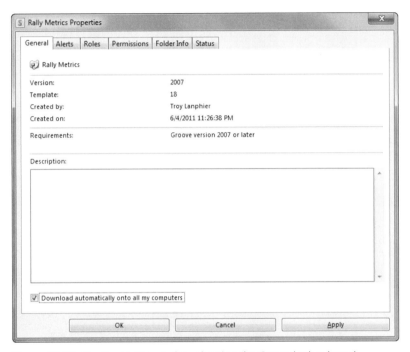

Figure 12-91 The Properties window, showing the General tab selected.

- **Alerts** (Figure 12-92) You can specify the alert level for the folder (Auto, High, Medium, Off). You can also specify which notification sound is used for the alert.

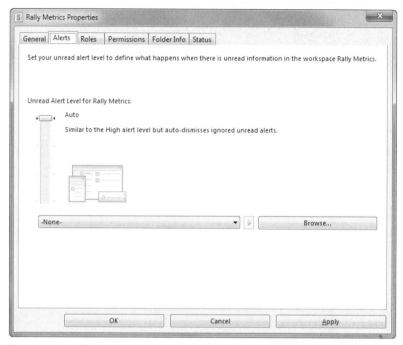

Figure 12-92 The Properties window, showing the Alerts tab selected.

- **Roles**   (Figure 12-93) This tab lists all users for the Shared Folder and allows a manager to change the role held by each.

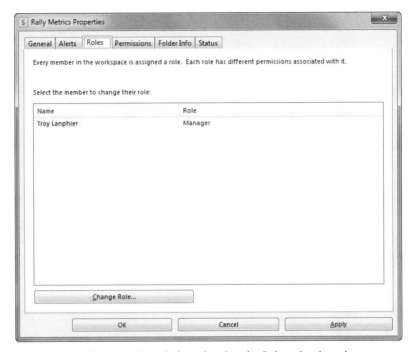

Figure 12-93 The Properties window, showing the Roles tab selected.

- **Permissions**   (Figure 12-94) Sets the Permission level (Invite, Uninvite, Cancel All Outstanding Invitations) that is available for each role level (Manager, Participant, Guest).

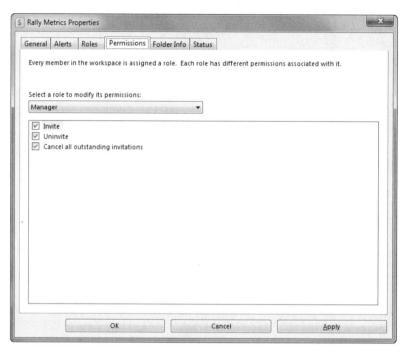

Figure 12-94 The Properties window, showing the Permissions tab selected.

- **Folder Info**   (Figure 12-95) This tab details information about the folder itself such as which files are and are not synchronized as well as which are excluded from synchronization.

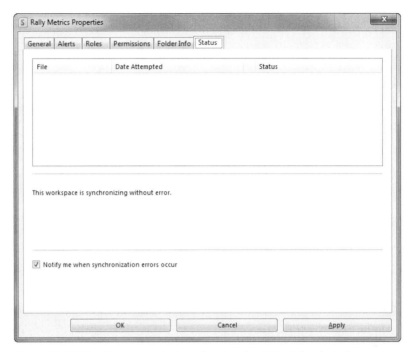

Figure 12-95 The Properties window, showing the Status tab selected.

Stop Synchronizing

Using the last menu item under Synchronization Tasks, Stop Synchronizing (shown in Figure 12-96), you can discontinue the synchronization of items in your Shared Folder with those currently contained on your computer. Note that selecting to stop synchronization does not affect any other users or computers currently using the Shared Folder.

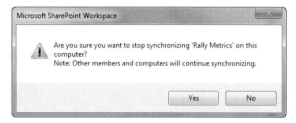

Figure 12-96 Halting Shared Folder synchronization.

Summary

In this chapter, you learned about the four major ways that files can be taken offline in SharePoint Foundation 2010. The differences in functionality were detailed between using Outlook 2010, local drafts, and SharePoint Workspace 2010 to provide offline access to files.

You also learned which two of the four offline methods require SharePoint Workspace 2010 in order to function, and that the use of this technology is provided with the Office Professional Plus edition of Microsoft Office 2010.

Finally, you saw the major steps necessary to configure, utilize, and troubleshoot each of the offline technologies, evaluating why each might be useful in a given scenario. You also learned about the interdependencies between Outlook 2010 and the local drafts folder as well as those between SharePoint Workspace 2010 and Shared Folders.

Managing Site Settings

So you've spent some time becoming familiar with Microsoft SharePoint, and before you know it, your team considers you the go-to SharePoint person. You've learned how to add items to a library, build new documents and list items, change existing items, and even administer the document and item libraries on your Team Site. What's next?

Perhaps it's time to take your SharePoint skills to the next level. You've been asked by your management team to build a team collaboration site. You send in a Help Desk ticket to build the site, and IT responds by making *you* the site owner—perhaps even the Site Collection administrator.

But wait... is this going to be a problem? Not for you—you're going to learn about being both site owner and Site Collection administrator in this section. Specifically, you are going to learn about site settings within a SharePoint Foundation 2010 site/Site Collection.

Sites vs. Site Collections

Chapter 3, "End-User Features and Experience," presents a fairly detailed discussion of sites versus Site Collections. If you came directly to this chapter, don't worry, we'll briefly discuss this again before diving into the site settings menus.

Simply put, a Site Collection is a grouping of sites. These sites are grouped hierarchically, with the first site in the Site Collection being called a top-level site. The top-level site is identical to all other sites, with the exception of additional menu items to control Site Collection–specific settings. Sites other than the top-level site are referred to as Subsites.

Site Settings (Subsite)

Let's begin with the site settings menu items of a Subsite. Why? Because this is probably the first set of items that you'll be administering for your team.

Site settings define all of the different behaviors within a SharePoint site. The effects of most site settings changes are scoped to the site itself. Items such as theme changes, permissions, creation/deletion of content, and more are all controlled from a single menu.

Let's begin by opening the site in your browser. Notice the Site Actions menu in the upper-left corner of the screen (Figure 13-1); this menu exists for any authenticated user of the site, regardless of that user's permissions on the site.

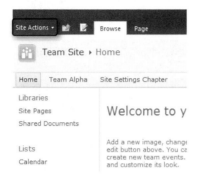

Figure 13-1 The Site Actions menu.

The content of the Site Actions menu itself changes based on the user's permissions. For instance, if you only have Viewer permissions on the site (you'd be a member of the Visitors group), your Site Actions menu will show only the Sync To SharePoint Workspace and View All Site Content links, as shown in Figure 13-2.

Figure 13-2 The Site Actions menu at Viewer permission level.

The next permissions level on a site is Full Control; members of the owners site group have this permissions level. Owners can control every aspect of a SharePoint site; thus, they see the following additional items on the Site Actions menu:

- New Document Library

- New Site

- More Options

- Edit In SharePoint Designer

- Site Permissions

- Site Settings

This chapter concentrates heavily on the last menu item, Site Settings (see Figure 13-3).

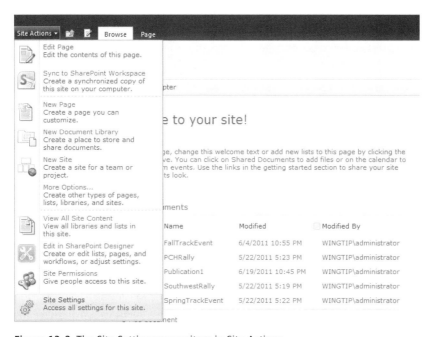

Figure 13-3 The Site Settings menu item in Site Actions.

Assuming that you have been assigned Site Owner permissions, clicking the Site Settings link shows that there are six menus on the Site Settings administrative page (see Figure 13-4) of a SharePoint Foundation 2010 site:

- Users And Permissions

- Galleries

- Site Administration

- Look And Feel

- Site Actions

- Site Collection Administration

Figure 13-4 The Site Settings administrative page.

You will learn about each of these menus later in the chapter, with a special emphasis on the items each of these menus control within your SharePoint site. Note that Figure 13-4 depicts the Site Settings page for a Subsite; compare this with the Site Settings page for a top-level site illustrated in Figure 13-13, later in the chapter.

INSIDE OUT   Additional Site Settings menu items

Do you see more than six sections on your Site Settings page? If so, this is because the Site Settings menu is extensible; items, functionality, and whole sections can be added to the existing menu system. A good example of this behavior is when installing Microsoft SQL Reporting Services, which adds the aptly-titled section, Reporting Services.

Users and Permissions

This section provides two major components of security administration within your SharePoint site: People And Groups and Site Permissions, which you can see in Figure 13-5.

Figure 13-5 The Users And Permissions menu.

People And Groups

From this menu, you can:

- Add and remove users from a group

- Communicate with selected users via email or phone (Voice over IP [VoIP])

- Control group settings (such as the group name or membership permissions)

- View group permissions (provides a summary of items this group can access and at what level)

- Define a default group (chooses the default group to which users are added)

When a new Team Site is created, there are three default groups created: Visitors, Members, and Owners. Each group is assigned a permission level within the site.

Users in the Visitors group have the lowest possible privilege level within the site (Read), and are usually only able to view content within the site. Members (Contribute) have a higher privilege level than Visitors and are able to read, write, create, and delete content within the existing lists and libraries. The Owners group is just that—these users can fully administer all content and users within the site, and they have the ability to administer all content and the site itself (including deleting it).

This can be a bit confusing at first, but here's the easy way to remember how security is applied within a SharePoint Site:

Users → Groups → Permissions

Permissions levels are created first; groups are then assigned permissions; and users are assigned to groups.

Can you assign a user a permission level without assigning that person to a group? Yes, you can. Is it a good idea? No, not really. You see, if you assign permissions on a per-user basis, you might have a difficult time determining which users have which permission; worse yet, there is no easy way to change permissions levels for the user, once assigned.

But what if none of these existing permission levels are suitable for your particular site? Perhaps you have a requirement to assign users the ability to read, write, create, but *not* delete files—what then? That's where the Site Permissions Level menu can help you.

Site Permissions

SharePoint provides the ability to create new permissions levels via the Site Permissions menu. This menu makes use of the ribbon. When you use it, the Permissions Tools tab appears.

INSIDE OUT   **Don't alter the built-in groups, create new ones**

It is recommended that you *not* alter the permissions granted to the default groups (Visitor: Read, Contributor: Change, Owner: Full Control). Instead, create a new group and assign your users and new security level to that group. This is covered in great detail in the TechNet Article "Determine permission levels and groups (SharePoint Foundation 2010)," which is available at *http://technet.microsoft.com/en-us/library/cc287625.aspx*.

A site can inherit its permission levels and groups from its parent site (see Figure 13-6); this makes administration of a series of Team Sites easier because they all retain the same permissions structure. If a site is inheriting its permissions structure, the Permission Tools tab will have five main actions, controlling Inheritance, Grant, and Check functions:

- Manage Parent (Inheritance)

- Stop Inheriting Permissions (Inheritance)

- Grant Permissions (Grant)

- Create Group (Grant)

- Check Permissions (Check)

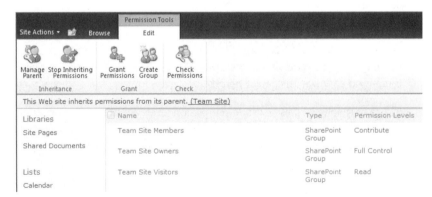

Figure 13-6 The Permission Tools tab (shown here with the site inheriting permissions from its parent site).

INSIDE OUT   Verifying user permissions in a site

One of the last items in the Site Permissions menu is Check Permissions. With this functionality, which is new to SharePoint 2010, you can select users and instantly see what items they can access on your site. This is a very powerful tool, especially in larger sites with multiple document libraries and lists.

A site can also be configured to *not* inherit its permission levels and groups from its parent site (see Figure 13-7). When set up this way, a site can maintain its own security and can even prevent access to some users from a higher level (more general audience) site. If a site is not inheriting its permissions structure, the Permissions Tools tab will have the following seven main actions that control inheritance, grant, modify, check, and manage functions:

- Inheriting Permissions (Inheritance)

- Grant Permissions (Grant)

- Create Group (Grant)

- Edit User Permissions (Modify)

- Remove User Permissions (Modify)

- Check Permissions (Check)

- Permissions Level (Manage)

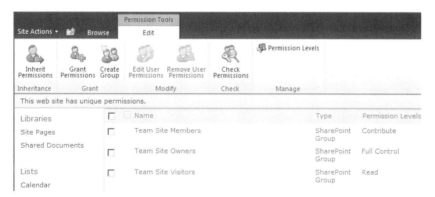

Figure 13-7 The Permission Tools tab when the site does not inherit permissions from its parent site.

INSIDE OUT Caveats associated with altering permissions inheritance

Choosing to stop permissions inheritance does not remove these permissions from your site. It's likely that you will create new groups and users if you choose to break permissions inheritance from a parent site, increasing the amount of administration that you must do. Be sure that you consider if you really are looking for different permissions before choosing to break inheritance.

Galleries

With galleries, you can reuse different content and functionality throughout a Site Collection. There are three main galleries offered in SharePoint Foundation 2010 (also shown in Figure 13-8):

- Site Columns

- Site Content Types

- Master Pages

Galleries
Site columns
Site content types
Master pages

Figure 13-8 The Galleries menu.

Site Columns

In any document library or list, you will find the underlying principle of metadata at work. We use metadata constantly in our day-to-day lives:

- How cold/warm is the weather (Number)?

- What should I have for lunch today (Choice)?

- Should I buy an item or not (*Boolean*)?

Basically, any item stored in a library can have metadata stored that describes it—by default, this is the type of document, its name, when it was modified, and who modified it. These are referred to as site columns.

SharePoint Foundation ships with literally hundreds of out-of-the-box site columns. You can choose to use these columns in your library to allow you to classify your documents or perhaps store them in a view (for example, Red Jelly Beans, Blue Jelly Beans, or All Jelly Beans). Site column design is covered in Chapter 5, "Designing Lists and Libraries."

Content Types

Suppose now that you want to choose multiple site columns at once to create a document describing an item, such as a car:

- How many doors does it have (Choice)?

- What color is it? (Choice)?

- How expensive is it (Currency)?

- When did you buy it (Date)?

With SharePoint, you can wrap all of this metadata up at once, assigning it a content type (such as a brochure or purchase contract). This content type can be used over and over again (as can the site columns) in different sites.

Additionally, document management functionality, such as what type of document template is used for the content type, can be specified, adding more and more features to your document libraries.

As time goes on, and your use of SharePoint becomes more advanced, you will find that you can "roll up" information from child sites to the parent, accumulating information by content type. Content type design is covered in Chapter 5.

Master Pages

A master page is a type of web document that specifies the look and feel of a webpage and how it behaves. Often associated with "branding" a site, this functionality (the master page library) is stored in a SharePoint Foundation 2010 site for use by advanced web designers.

This functionality can be made more accessible by site owners; when you purchase and install SharePoint Server 2010, you can select the master page from the web interface, which is something that is not possible (without programming code) in SharePoint Foundation 2010. Master page design is covered in Chapter 14, "Creating, Managing, and Designing Sites by using SharePoint Designer 2010."

Site Administration

The Site Administration menu (shown in Figure 13-9) brings configuration settings (such as regional settings) and informational settings (such as site libraries and lists) together into one easy-to-use group. This menu includes the following items:

- Regional Settings

- Site Libraries And Lists

- User Alerts

- RSS

- Search And Offline Availability

- Sites And Workspaces

- Workflow Settings

Site Administration
Regional settings
Site libraries and lists
User alerts
RSS
Search and offline availability
Sites and workspaces
Workflow settings

Figure 13-9 The Site Administration menu.

Regional Settings

Because SharePoint sites can be deployed in many different locations and languages, it becomes important to have Team Sites that can represent information in a format specific to a country, culture, or locale:

- **Locale**   Specifies the way numeric and date-related items are displayed within a site. For instance, some countries display dates by using a DD/MM/YYYY format, whereas others might display it by using MM/DD/YYYY.

- **Sort Order**   Controls the order in which items are sorted in lists and document libraries.

- **Time Zone**   Specifies the default time zone used by the particular site. Default time zones for a SharePoint web application can be specified by SharePoint administrators, but the time zone setting for a site overrides the default.

- **Set Your Calendar**   With this setting, a site owner can specify the default type of calendar used in the SharePoint site. This also offers the option to show week numbers in the Date Navigator.

- **Enable An Alternate Calendar**   This is useful to display alternate calendar information, such as displaying Hebrew calendar information alongside that of a Gregorian calendar.

- **Define Your Work Week**   This setting is similar to that found in Microsoft Outlook—you can choose what days are displayed as active in the calendar, along with specifying the first day of the week, first week of the year, and start/end times for the workday.

- **Time Format**   You use this to specify whether times are displayed by default in 12 or 24-hour format.

Site Libraries And Lists

This menu provides three functions:

- Display all lists and libraries in the site

- Provide links to the list settings menu for each list or library

- Provide a link to create new content in a site (lists, libraries, or child sites/workspaces)

User Alerts

User Alerts can be administered in two distinct places: first, within the Files | Manage Rules And Alerts menu of Outlook, and second, within the site itself. You can display a user and delete Alerts that have been subscribed to by the user as well as those that have been assigned by others.

RSS

Really Simple Syndication (RSS) is a technology that allows a user to subscribe to information and have the information show in an RSS reader. SharePoint offers the ability to securely syndicate information from a list or library, allowing users to see these changes as they appear; the "securely" portion of this statement is important—as a rule, an RSS reader must be able to authenticate to SharePoint as a user in order to view syndicated material.

Using this setting, the site owner can specify whether this functionality is available in the SharePoint site; it also allows the site owner to specify the copyright, managing editor, and webmaster for a site. A Time-To-Live setting can be specified to determine how long information is current (in minutes).

Search And Offline Availability

A SharePoint site owner can choose whether the content of a site can appear in search results. For more detailed control, site pages and webpages can also be excluded from search (if desired).

A SharePoint user can use SharePoint and Outlook to take a copy of information from document libraries and lists offline. This is useful for people who travel or who might not be able to consistently connect to the corporate network; document and list information can be stored on a user's laptop and then synchronized to the network when a network connection is made.

By simply changing the status of the Offline Client Availability setting, a site owner can choose whether or not information found in the site can be taken offline.

For more information about working with document and list information offline and synchronization, see Chapter 12, "Taking Lists and Libraries Offline."

INSIDE OUT   Excluding a site from being indexed

Removing a site from SharePoint indexing is a very deliberate decision; a site that has been removed has no chance of being searched. There is often a business requirement to secure sensitive information from search. You should work with your IT department to find other means of securing your information—segregation of search information in SharePoint is quite possible and can provide great benefit to your legal staff, particularly to speed along legal inquiries.

Sites And Workspaces

Site owners can use this menu to view all child sites, document workspaces, and meeting workspaces to which you have access. You can also see when the site was last modified (useful to find unused sites) or delete a site. Additionally, a Create menu item is provided, with which you can quickly create any one of these site types.

Chapter 13

INSIDE OUT   Deleting sites is a permanent action

Because there is a site Recycle Bin (for users) and a site Collection Recycle Bin (for Site Collection administrators), new SharePoint users often are under the impression that a deleted site can be retrieved from the Recycle Bin. This is distinctly *not true*. A site that is deleted is truly gone for good (unless IT can restore the site from backups). Be sure that you want to remove a site permanently before deleting it. SharePoint Foundation 2010 Service Pack 1 adds recycling for sites and site collections. For more details, read the TechNet article "Restore a deleted site collection" at *http://technet.microsoft.com/ en-us/library/hh272537.aspx*.

Workflow Settings

A site owner can use this menu to create and administer workflows for use on a site; this menu also displays the workflows currently in progress. Changes that are applied to a workflow are not applied to workflows that are already in progress.

The Look And Feel Menu

The Look And Feel menu (shown in Figure 13-10) manages how a site appears in the browser; items such as navigation and branding fall under the control of this menu. This menu includes the following items:

- Title, Description, And Icon

- Quick Launch

- Top Link Bar

- Tree View

- Site Theme

Look and Feel
Title, description, and icon
Quick launch
Top link bar
Tree view
Site theme

Figure 13-10 The Look And Feel menu.

Title, Description, And Icon

Using Title, you can specify a friendly name for the site—perhaps Project Management Central would be easier for users to understand than PrjMgmtCtrl (found in the URL).

The description of the site is nearly as important, for two primary reasons: the first is Search; the more information that exists about a site, the better its ranking in search. The second reason is to accommodate vision impaired users who need assistance to navigate a website.

By default, a SharePoint site has a small orange icon that is displayed on each site. This icon can be replaced with an icon of your choosing. Simply upload the icon and provide the link.

Quick Launch

There are two navigation zones used on a SharePoint Site: the Top Link bar (across the top of the page), and the Quick Launch (most often located down the leftmost side of the page).

Use the Quick Launch menu to specify navigation links, group these links under headings, and change the order in which the items appear in Quick Launch.

Top Link Bar

The second of the two navigational zones, the Top Link bar, appears across the top of a SharePoint Site. You use the Top Link bar menu to create new navigational links and change the order of links across the bar.

INSIDE OUT   Navigation changes in SharePoint Server 2010

If you've upgraded from SharePoint Foundation 2010 to SharePoint Server 2010, you might be wondering where the Quick Launch and Top Link Bar went. These two navigational zones are replaced in SharePoint Server 2010 by Current Navigation (replaces Quick Launch) and Global Navigation (replaces Top Link Bar).

Site Actions

The Site Actions menu (see Figure 13-11) controls activities that have to do with altering the functionality available in the site, viewing metrics regarding its use, the templating of sites, and other functions. This menu includes the following items:

- Manage Site Features

- Save Site As Template

- Site Collection Web Analytics Reports

- Site Web Analytics Reports

- Reset To Site Definition

- Delete This Site

Site Actions
Manage site features
Save site as template
Site Collection Web Analytics
reports
Site Web Analytics reports
Reset to site definition
Delete this site

Figure 13-11 The Site Actions menu.

Manage Site Features

A SharePoint site is modular in design. You can think of this concept along the lines of a car being manufactured. The car itself provides a basic function, but packages can be added for climate control, entertainment, interior trim, and others options; in a SharePoint site, these are referred to as *Features*.

Features are a grouping of one or more sets of functionality that can be added to a Share-Point site. An example of this functionality is the Team Collaboration Lists Feature, which creates the document libraries and issues lists on your Team Site. These Features can be activated or deactivated from the Manage Site Features menu.

> ### TROUBLESHOOTING
>
> **I deactivated my Team Collaboration Lists Feature, but one of these lists still exists. Why?**
> If you look inside the list itself, it's likely that you'll find a document or list item has been inserted into the library; SharePoint Features being deactivated purposely will not remove a list that is in use.

Save Site as Template

So you spent 5 hours configuring a new Team Site, getting it exactly the way you want it. You show the site to your boss, and she loves it—so much, in fact, that she asks you to build 30 more just like it.

Fortunately for you, a configured site can be saved as a template. In fact, a list or document library can be saved as a template, too, but that's not in this chapter. This template is stored at the top of the Site Collection in a gallery of templates. We will examine this functionality further in the next section.

TROUBLESHOOTING

I recently upgraded to SharePoint Server 2010 and activated the Publishing Features for my site. Now I cannot save a template of my site, is this normal? Actually, this is a normal behavior for Publishing-enabled sites. Here's why: publishing pages track changes between versions, have workflow and approvals, along with other functionality. Disabling the feature will break or remove these items, so the Save Site As Template menu item is removed when Publishing is enabled.

Site Web Analytics Reports

SharePoint Foundation 2010 provides built-in web analytics about sites. Analyzing web analytics reports helps tune the searchability, browsability, performance, and overall impression that the site offers to your user base.

Although this is not critical to Team Sites, these metrics provide insight into how users arrive at the site, what pages they visit, what browser(s) they use to visit the site, and other metrics. The official list is:

- Number Of Page Views

- Number Of Unique Visitors

- Number Of Referrers

- Top Pages

- Top Visitors

- Top Referrers

- Top Browsers

The Reset To Site Definition Menu

It is possible to make customizations to the page or pages in a SharePoint site that render the site unusable; what is odd is that the actual document and list information contained in the site is unharmed, and the pages themselves can be restored back to a precustomization state.

Using the Reset To Site Definition menu, you can reset a single page or all pages in a site to the version of the page included in the original site definition. This is particularly useful if modifications you have performed damage a page in a SharePoint site and you need a quick way to get it operational again.

INSIDE OUT   Resetting to the site definition is a dramatic change

Resetting a page to its site definition removes customizations to a page by reverting it to its out-of-the-box state; this can have undesired effects, particularly if you have a heavily customized page. Be sure that you want to take this action and that you have communicated its effects to your team before executing this change.

The Delete This Site Menu

The last menu item is perhaps the most powerful—after all, what can affect a site more than deleting it? This menu is quite straightforward: select it and you get one (and only one) chance to change your mind.

Once you select the Delete button, the site is gone forever—it is not retained in the either site or Site Collection recycle bins.

One More Thing—Site Information

OK, so it's not a technically a site setting menu like the others, but site information provides two URLs:

- **Site URL**   The URL for the site itself

- **Mobile Site URL**   The URL for the site as it is represented on mobile devices

Site Collection Administration

So now you've got the hang of administering a site. It's time to up the ante and make you a Site Collection administrator.

There is only one item in this menu: click the Go To Top Level Site Settings item, and then move on to the next set of menu items: Site Settings (Top Level Site, Figure 13-12).

Figure 13-12 The Site Collection Administration menu.

Site Settings (Top-Level Site)

Clicking the Go To Top Level Site Settings automatically takes you to the top-level site of the Site Collection you are in. It is important to note that you might have several Site Collections in the farm, so yours might not be the first in the web address. A good example of this would be a Portal Site Collection with departmental Site Collections beneath it, such as the following:

http://portal/department

There could be one set of Site Collection administrators for *http://portal* and another for *http://portal/department*, provided that each of these addresses is created specifically as a Site Collection.

Assuming that you have been assigned Site Collection administrator permissions, there will be six sections on the site settings administrative page of a SharePoint Foundation 2010 top-level site (Figure 13-13); these will appear familiar to site owners:

- Users And Permissions

- Galleries

- Site Administration

- Look And Feel

- Site Actions

- Site Collection Administration

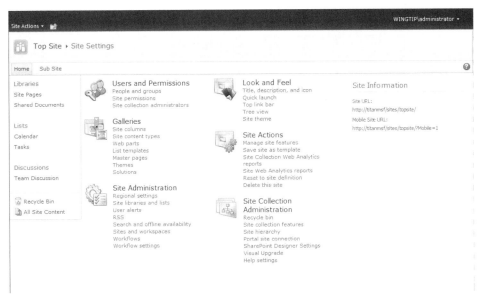

Figure 13-13 The Site Settings menu for the top-level site.

It looks the same, doesn't it? In fact, the site settings menu for the top-level site is nothing more than a superset of the items present in a normal site settings menu. This is the *only* site in the Site Collection that has these extra menu items.

We will cover the settings menus again, but this time, only focusing on the specialized items.

The Users And Permissions Menu

There is only one new item in the Users And Permissions menu: Site Collection Administrators (see Figure 13-14). You use this menu to select people who will ultimately have the ability to control each and every site in this Site Collection.

Figure 13-14 The Users And Permissions menu (top-level site).

Galleries

There are four new items in Galleries (Figure 13-15):

- Web Parts

- List Templates

- Themes

- Solutions

Figure 13-15 The Galleries (top-level site).

Web Parts

This menu item lists all of the Web Parts available to sites within this Site Collection. You can add Web Parts to this library to make them available to users in the Site Collection.

INSIDE OUT   Not all Web Parts are created equal

Some Web Parts are simply ones that have been created by users from existing Web Parts, but others have code and other components on which they are dependent. If you need such an item available in your Site Collection, you will need to work with your SharePoint farm administrator to have these added to the farm.

List Templates

Earlier, we discussed the notion of making an entire site into a template. Perhaps this is overkill for your needs. A list in any site (in this Site Collection) can be saved as a template. When the list is "templatized," it is automatically uploaded into the List Template gallery for use within this Site Collection.

It is also possible to download a List Template and then upload that to a different Site Collection, should you prefer.

Themes

You can apply a Theme to any SharePoint site. A theme is a set of colors and other styling elements that are used to lightly brand a site. Themes can be created and uploaded to this library for use by sites in this Site Collection.

Solutions

Earlier in this chapter, we discussed the concept of features. A Solution takes this concept one step further by wrapping one or more features into a larger package (called a Solution) which can be used in a Site Collection. Once the Solution has been deployed and activated within the Site Collection, it can be used by any site.

The Solutions menu specifically shows Solutions that are applied to the Site Collection. A site or a workflow can be saved as a template; these templates are stored as a Solution in this menu.

Other Solution packages can be obtained, uploaded, and activated to add functionality to your Site Collection; these Solutions consume resources on your SharePoint farm. To indicate how many resources are consumed and what your available resource quota is, the Solutions menu also shows a resource quota bar. When you reach the available resource quota limit (it resets daily), the Solution ceases to function for the rest of the day—or, the SharePoint farm administrator raises your quota.

Site Administration

There is only one change in the Site Administration menu, and that is Workflows. While the Workflow Settings menu is available in any site within the Site Collection, workflows themselves are controlled and stored in the top-level site of the Site Collection, as shown in Figure 13-16.

Figure 13-16 The Site Administration menus for a top-level site.

From this menu, you can see what workflows are in use as well as their status and associations. Although you can see the associations and progress of all workflows in the Site Collection, this page does not show you which workflows are associated with what sites or lists and does not show you the specific status of those workflows.

The Look And Feel Menu

No additional functionality was introduced to the Look And Feel menu in a top-level site (Figure 13-17).

Figure 13-17 The Look And Feel menu for a top-level site.

Site Actions

Site Collection Web Analytics Reports are added to the Site Settings menu of a top-level site (see Figure 13-18). Unlike the standard site web analytics reports, the Site Collection reports are specifically used to report high-level usage in your Site Collection. The information captured in this report is as follows:

- **Storage**   The Current Storage in megabytes, how much is used by Web Discussions, and the maximum storage allocated to your Site Collection Quota.

- **Users**   The number of users that have been added to the Site Collection.

- **Activity**   The total number of hits and bandwidth use on a per-day basis for the Site Collection.

Figure 13-18 The Site Actions menu for a top-level site.

The Site Collection Administration Menu

All of the items in Site Collection Administration affect the Site Collection as a whole (see Figure 13-19). These settings include the following items:

- Recycle Bin

- Site Collection Features

- Site Hierarchy

- Portal Site Connection

- SharePoint Designer Settings

- Visual Upgrade

- Help Settings

Site Collection
Administration
Recycle bin
Site collection features
Site hierarchy
Portal site connection
SharePoint Designer Settings
Visual Upgrade
Help settings

Figure 13-19 The Site Collection Administration menu.

Recycle Bin

Users often delete list and library items from a Site; in an effort to clean up a site, a site owner might choose to empty a Site Recycle Bin before a user realizes that he did not mean to delete an item. Fortunately, there is a Site Collection Recycle Bin also provided. This bin contains items that are deleted from a site and retains items (by default) up to 30 days after they were originally deleted. This value for the length of time a site is retained is configurable in Central Administration.

Items can be restored from this Recycle Bin directly to the affected site. Additionally, you can choose to see End User Recycle Bin items or items that were deleted from an end user (Site) Recycle Bin.

Items can also be deleted from this Recycle Bin—the Site Collection Recycle Bin is the last stop before an item is gone for good. Items deleted from here will require the help of a SharePoint farm or system administrator's to restore.

The Site Collection Features Menu

Features can be scoped (applied) to a Site Collection, just as they can to sites. Scoping a Feature to a site simply means that the Feature is only available for that site. Similarly, scoping a Feature to a Site Collection means that the Feature is available for all of the sites in a Site Collection (whether top-level or Subsites).

From this menu, you can activate or deactivate a Feature within the Site Collection.

The Site Hierarchy Menu

This menu has two functions: the first shows you the parent-child relationship structure between sites in the Site Collection, and the second provides you with links to directly manage the sites in the Site Collection.

Portal Site Connection

Site collections are truly independent structures within a SharePoint farm. Relationships between sites can be implied by the URL (web address) of a site. Once you are in the Site Collection, you might want to manually build a connection back to a portal (perhaps the first site in the URL).

To create a connection back to a portal site, you can select Connect To Portal Site and enter the Portal Web Address and Portal Name (which is the friendly name that will show up on the upper-left of your Site Collection.

SharePoint Designer Settings

These settings specifically deal with how SharePoint Designer can affect sites in your Site Collection. Allowing your site owners or designers to have access to SharePoint Designer can be very beneficial; however, great care should be taken to avoid allowing this functionality to be available to inexperienced or untrained personnel.

Site collection administrators can use SharePoint Designer unless prohibited by the SharePoint farm administrators. There are four selections available in this menu, none of which apply to Site Collection administrators:

- Allow Site Owners And Designers To Use SharePoint Designer In This Site Collection

- Allow Site Owners And Designers To Detach Pages From The Site Definition

- Allow Site Owners And Designers To Customize Master Pages And Page Layouts

- Allow Site Owners And Designers To See The Hidden URL Structure Of Their Web Site

INSIDE OUT   Improvements in restricting SharePoint Designer access

In the last version of SharePoint, removing the ability to use SharePoint Designer was something that applied to everyone in a SharePoint web application. In SharePoint 2010, this choice is more granular—both SharePoint farm administrators and Site Collection administrators have the ability to allow/disallow SharePoint functionality. SharePoint farm administrators can change these settings for Site Collection administrators by using Central Administration. Additionally, the four previously described selections can be allowed or disallowed to enable/disable different SharePoint Designer functionality.

Enabling/Disabling SharePoint Designer

SharePoint Designer is enabled by default. This means that site owners and designers can use SharePoint Designer 2010 to customize any site in this Site Collection. Clearing the Allow Site Owners And Designers To Use SharePoint Designer In This Site Collection check box prevents these two groups of users from making modifications by using this tool.

Detaching Pages from the Site Definition

SharePoint pages can exist in one of two states; either they are attached to the site definition (meaning that they are stored on the local file system of the web servers) or they are detached from the site definition (meaning that they are stored in the content database).

Pages stored in the content database have a mildly negative impact on performance; moreover, they also do not inherit modifications made to the site definition.

Some organizations choose to prohibit pages from being detached from the site definition, instead opting to produce new page layouts for users to choose from.

Customizing Master Pages and Page Layouts

A master page is used to make visual and functional changes that can apply to multiple pages in a site. A page layout is used to provide the template for pages created in a site. If either of these items is incorrectly configured, the site will not render correctly.

Hidden URL Structures

SharePoint Designer can display the underlying URL structure of a SharePoint site. Items in this structure are shown in a series of folders, such as _cts, _catalogs, _private, and so on. Altering items in these structures can be a key component of customization; however, incorrectly altering items in these structures can render an entire site or Site Collection unusable. You can use this menu selection to hide/show these structures to site owners and designers running SharePoint Designer 2010.

Visual Upgrade

If your company upgraded your SharePoint to 2010 from SharePoint 2007, it's likely that you did not initially notice any changes on your site. The SharePoint site structure literally looks unchanged from its 2007 counterpart; this is intentional, and intended to provide continuity of service and functionality to users, without the need to immediately retrain them.

Choosing to visually upgrade SharePoint is pretty much a one-way street; although it is possible to revert a SharePoint site back to its 2007 look and feel, it is not possible to do so unless you involve a SharePoint farm administrator. As Site Collection administrator, therefore, you might choose to hold off on allowing a visual upgrade until your user base has been trained to use the new interface.

If you want to hide the Visual Upgrade options, you can choose to do so by going into this section and selecting the Hide Visual Upgrade option. If on the other hand, you have already prepared your users for the change in appearance, you can click the Update All Sites button, and the interface will change to adopt the SharePoint 2010 look and feel.

Help Settings

Help subjects available for SharePoint can be available or not available for users in your SharePoint environment. Going into this menu item and selecting the check box for a SharePoint subject allows help information to be made available to your users. In a SharePoint Foundation 2010 environment, the subjects available are:

- SharePoint Foundation 2010

- SharePoint Foundation 2010 Central Administration

Summary

You began reading this chapter as a SharePoint user; you finished the chapter with an understanding of what it is to be a site owner, designer, or Site Collection administrator. You now have an idea of the items and functionality available to your SharePoint staff as well as an understanding of the functionality available to each of these roles in your organization.

Mᴵᶜᴿᴼˢᴼᶠᵀ SharePoint is not just another web development platform that IT uses to develop applications, which are then handed over to the users. SharePoint changes the game. SharePoint empowers users to do whatever they need to do for themselves. Users no longer need to send content in an email to someone else for them to add it to a website. When solutions are built on top of SharePoint, the aim is to remove IT staff from the day-to-day tasks, make users self-sufficient, and even to let users build solutions for themselves.

Using the browser and other what-you-see-is-what-you-get (WYSIWYG) tools such as, SharePoint Designer 2010, Microsoft InfoPath 2010 and Microsoft Visio Premium 2010, users can create successful SharePoint non-code solutions because they know what they want to achieve, they understand the business needs, and with a bit of SharePoint knowledge, they can wire together the business processes or sets of tasks. Such users have been termed by Gartner[1] as *citizen developers*.

SharePoint Designer 2010 is not just another HTML editing tool; it is a tool for business users. And because business users rarely have access to any environment other than the production environment, Microsoft expects users to use SharePoint Designer in the production environment. However, new with SharePoint Designer 2010 is that you can now develop solutions in non-production environments and transfer them to the production environment.

SharePoint Designer's focus is not on adding static images and text to webpages, rather; it is an alternative tool for Site Collection and site owners to administer and manage sites and go beyond what the browser provides.

This chapter details a number of techniques that are useful when working with SharePoint Designer 2010 and SharePoint Foundation 2010 sites. SharePoint Designer adheres to the security settings of the site; therefore, to use SharePoint Designer you need to be a Site Collection owner, site owner, or someone who has the Add and Customize Pages, Remote Interfaces, and Browse Directory site permissions. To create and delete lists, add or remove

---

[1]   *www.gartner.com/it/page.jsp?id=1212813*

columns in a list, add or remove public views of a list in SharePoint Designer, you also need the Manage Lists permission. These permissions are automatically selected in the Full Control and Design permission levels.

This is not the first chapter to use SharePoint Designer. Chapter 6, "Creating and Formatting Webpages," details how to use SharePoint Designer for creating and customizing webpages, and Chapter 9, "Working with External Content, details how to use SharePoint Designer to connect with content that is not stored within SharePoint and how to use SharePoint Foundation to present that data.

This chapter along with the next two chapters will give you the tools and techniques you need to build solutions with SharePoint Foundation to meet your organization's custom business and functional requirements. In this chapter, we go into more detail on how to use SharePoint Designer to create, design, and manage sites.

INSIDE OUT   When to use the 64-bit version of SharePoint Designer

Similar to its predecessor, Microsoft Office SharePoint Designer 2007, SharePoint Designer 2010 is available as a free download in both 32-bit and 64-bit versions from Microsoft's download site at *www.microsoft.com/downloads*. The 32-bit version is strongly recommended for most users.

SharePoint Designer 2010 can only be used with SharePoint 2010 sites. To connect to SharePoint 2007 and earlier sites, you must continue to use SharePoint Designer 2007, which can be installed side-by-side with the 32-bit version of SharePoint Designer 2010. Install SharePoint Designer 2007 first before installing SharePoint Designer 2010.

Install the 64-bit version of SharePoint Designer when all of the following points are true:

- You have a 64-bit supported operating system on your computer.

- You have not installed any 32-bit Office applications, including SharePoint Designer 2007 or Microsoft Expression Web. All these applications share common components with SharePoint Designer 2010. If 32-bit Office applications are installed on your computer, a 64-bit SharePoint Designer 2010 installation is blocked by default.

- You do not maintain SharePoint sites built on Windows SharePoint Services 3.0 or Microsoft Office SharePoint Server 2007 or earlier versions of SharePoint.

- You intend to use the 64-bit version of Microsoft Office 2010 applications.

- All applications, ActiveX controls, or third-party add-ins can communicate with the 64-bit version of Office 2010.

To learn more about which version of Office 2010 to install, go to *http://technet. microsoft.com/en-us/library/ee681792.aspx* and *http://blogs.technet.com/b/ office2010/archive/2010/02/23/understanding-64-bit-office.aspx*.

Introducing SharePoint Designer

Microsoft SharePoint Designer 2010 has been the beneficiary of major improvements over its predecessor, Microsoft Office SharePoint Designer 2007. It is now the preferred tool for site owners and citizen developers (users operating outside the scope of IT who create new business applications for use by others).

Opening Sites

You can open a site in SharePoint Designer from the browser or by opening SharePoint Designer first and then opening a site from within SharePoint Designer. You cannot open Microsoft Office SharePoint Server 2007 or Windows SharePoint Services 3.0 sites with SharePoint Designer 2010. You can open a file in SharePoint Designer, such as an HTML file, that does not reside in a SharePoint site; however, to do so a SharePoint site must already be open in SharePoint Designer.

> **Tip**
> If you are using a different authentication authority for your SharePoint sites than the one you use when you sign on to your computer—for example, when your SharePoint site is hosted by a third party—then it is easier to open the SharePoint site in the browser and then use one of the methods detailed below to open SharePoint Designer from the browser.

To open a site from within SharePoint Designer, use the following steps:

1. On the Windows Start menu, point to All Programs, click SharePoint, and then click Microsoft SharePoint Designer 2010.

Chapter 14

The SharePoint Designer window opens, displaying Backstage view with the Sites tab highlighted. If you previously opened a SharePoint site, these will be listed under Recent Sites.

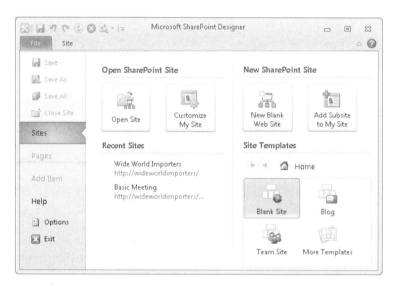

2.   To open a site not listed under Recent Sites, under Open SharePoint Site, click Open Site to display the Open Site dialog box.

3.   In the Site Name text box, type the URL of your SharePoint site, and then click Open. You might be prompted for your user name and password.

When you have a site already open in SharePoint Designer, you can open subsequent sites by clicking the File tab to display the Backstage view, and then click Sites in the left pane. Then under Open SharePoint Site, click Open Site. Alternatively, on the Subsites tab (which can be displayed by clicking Subsite in the Navigation pane), you can use the Open Site command in the Edit group. If you have a SharePoint site already open in SharePoint Designer, when you open additional sites, a new SharePoint Designer window opens.

> **Tip**
>
> SharePoint Designer's focus is still on an individual site in a Site Collection; that is, when you customize a site, your customizations are applied to the site that you have open. Therefore, if you want to customize more than one site, SharePoint Designer opens a separate window for each site. As you drill down sites in a Site Collection, you can open a massive number of instances of SharePoint Designer. Because sites can look very similar in SharePoint Designer, to ensure that you do not customize the wrong site, only open one site at a time.

To open a site in SharePoint Designer from the browser, use one of the following methods:

- Click Site Actions, and then click Edit in SharePoint Designer.

- On a wiki page, on the Page tab, click the Edit command down arrow, and then click Edit in SharePoint Designer, as shown in Figure 14-1.

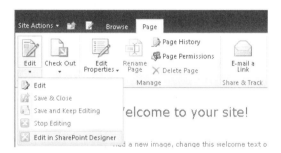

Figure 14-1 Opening SharePoint Designer from the Page tab in the browser.

- When viewing a list or a library, in the Library Tools tab set, click the Library tab, and then in the Customize Library group, click Edit Library as illustrated in Figure 14-2.

Figure 14-2 Opening SharePoint Designer from the Library tab in the browser.

When you use any of the browser commands to open SharePoint Designer but you do not have SharePoint Designer installed on your computer, and if you have an Internet connection, you will be presented with a dialog, (see Figure 14-3) from which you can download and install SharePoint 2010.

Figure 14-3 Installing SharePoint Designer 2010.

When you click Free Download, a File Download dialog box opens, with which you can install SharePoint Designer or save SharePointDesigner.exe to a location on your computer and install it at a later time. You can prevent the installation of SharePoint Designer, as you can any product, by using software restriction policies.

To read about software restriction policies, go to *http://technet.microsoft.com/en-us/library/dd348653(WS.10).aspx*.

INSIDE OUT   Site Pages and the Site Assets libraries

No matter which site you open, in the Navigation pane you will always see references to the Site Pages and Site Assets libraries. These libraries are created by default on a Team Site. The Site Pages library contains the home page for the Team Site and any other wiki pages that you create. The Site Assets library should be used for files that are referenced within a page, such as images. It should not be used to store files that are used by the members of the team as part of their day-to-day tasks. Instead, use the Shared Documents library or create new libraries for those tasks. Cascading Style Sheet (CSS) or XSL files should be stored in the Style Library, which is created when any site is first created.

On sites that do not contain the Site Pages or Site Assets libraries, such as blogs, meeting workspaces, group work sites, or document workspaces, if you click one of these two libraries in SharePoint Designer's Navigation pane, they will be created.

Exploring SharePoint Designer

Don't be put off by its name; SharePoint Designer is not aimed at just web designers. With SharePoint Designer, you can carry out similar tasks to the browser; however, you can now complete more tasks natively, without the need to jump back and forth between SharePoint Designer and the browser. For example, when you first open a site with SharePoint Designer, within the SharePoint Designer workspace, you are presented with a site's summary page, as shown in Figure 14-4. This page provides you with key site information organized in five areas: Site Information, Customization, Settings, Permissions, and Subsites. You can use this page to change many site settings, manage permissions, and create new Subsites. You will see settings pages for other site artifacts, such as, for a list, library, master page, and workflow.

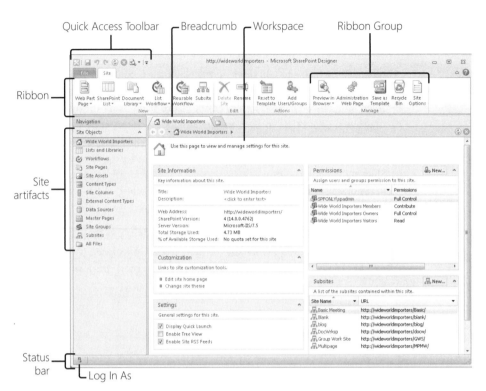

Figure 14-4 Site summary page and SharePoint Designer components.

Notice also in Figure 14-4 that SharePoint Designer has a redesigned user interface (UI) that uses the Microsoft Office Fluent UI. The ribbon contains one or more tabs, and it works in a similar manner to the server ribbon when a SharePoint site is displayed in the browser—that is, the tabs are dynamic and context sensitive. The commands are organized into groups, and if there is not sufficient space on the ribbon, then the commands are displayed as an icon or options in a drop-down menu.

Similar to other Microsoft applications, SharePoint Designer has a Quick Access Toolbar that contains a set of commands that are independent of the currently active ribbon tab. You can add commands to the toolbar, which is very useful when you find that you frequently use a SharePoint Designer command. For example, if you often create a Web Part page or create a list or library, you can add these commands to the Quick Access Toolbar. To add commands to the Quick Access Tool bar, complete one of the following steps:

- On the ribbon, click the appropriate tab to display the command that you want to add to the Quick Access Toolbar. Right-click the command to open the shortcut menu, and then click Add To Quick Access Toolbar, as shown in Figure 14-5.

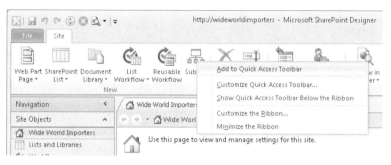

Figure 14-5 Adding a command to the Quick Access Toolbar via the ribbon.

- On the Quick Access Toolbar, click the last icon, and then click More Commands, as shown in Figure 14-6.

Figure 14-6 Adding a command to the Quick Access Toolbar via the Quick Access Toolbar.

- Click the File tab to display the Backstage view. Click Options to display the Share-Point Options dialog box, and then click Add and OK.

> **Tip**
> The Quick Access Toolbar can be located either in the upper-left corner or below the ribbon.

In Figure 14-4, in the Navigation pane, selecting the first site object provides a summary of the SharePoint site, and makes the Site tab in the ribbon available. When you click the icon to the left of a Subsite in the Subsites area, the Site tab set appears, which contains one tab, the Subsites tab. If you then select the Lists And Libraries site object in the Navigation pane, a gallery page displays a list of site artifacts, which in this case is lists and libraries, and in the ribbon, the Site tab and the Site tab set are replaced with the List And Libraries tab, as shown in Figure 14-7.

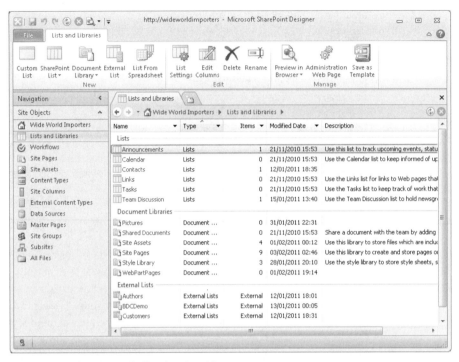

Figure 14-7 The Lists And Libraries site object.

The workspace breadcrumb can be compared to Windows Explorer in as much as you can drill down and step upward, as shown in Figure 14-8. Use the back and forward arrows in the breadcrumb as you would use then in the browser to display previous or following content.

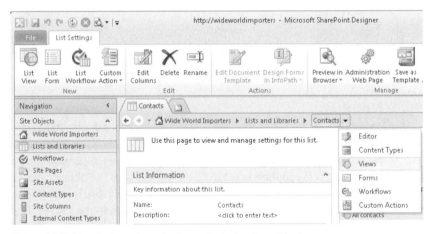

Figure 14-8 Use the breadcrumbs to navigate to site artifacts.

The status bar is context sensitive and provides you with additional tools and information, depending on what is displayed in the workspace. It also contains a Log In command with which you can log in as a different user, similar to the Sign In As Different User command that appears when you click the down-arrow to the right of your name in the upper-right corner of a SharePoint site in the browser.

You might have also noticed that when you open a site in SharePoint Designer 2010, you are no longer presented with the file and folder structure of the site, known as the *Web Site URL Structure*. Although the URL structure in a SharePoint site does not exist—it is created from a combination of files from the SharePoint server and content in the SQL content database—it is what web developers expect to see in a web editing tool for non-SharePoint sites.

The URL structure, which was the default view in SharePoint Designer 2007, did not make it easy for business users to find SharePoint objects—you had to know where each of the site objects lived within that URL structure; for example, master pages can be found in the _catalog/masterpage folder. Now in SharePoint Designer 2010, the Navigation pane allows Site Collection and site owners to browse easily between the site objects that they wish to create and manage. You can now easily create a custom application by creating a Subsite, lists and libraries on that Subsite, associate site columns, content types and work-flows with those lists and libraries, as well as manage the security groups, without leaving SharePoint Designer.

You can use SharePoint Designer to add static content, such as text or images to your web-pages; however, its strength is to help present and manipulate content to develop no-code solutions and customizations that meet business needs. These solutions and customizations can then be exported from SharePoint Designer and handed over to the IT department, where they can be imported into Visual Studio, making SharePoint Designer a rapid appli-cation, prototyping, no-code tool. When you have developed as far as you can by using the browser and SharePoint Designer, the developer can take your modifications as a starting point.

For more information on editing pages with SharePoint Designer, see Chapter 6.

> **Note**
>
> **Although you can upload files into libraries by using SharePoint Designer, you cannot associate metadata with those files or create, modify, or delete list items with Share-Point Designer. You must use the browser to complete those tasks.**

The URL structure of a site is still available by clicking All Files in the Navigation pane, as shown in Figure 14-9.

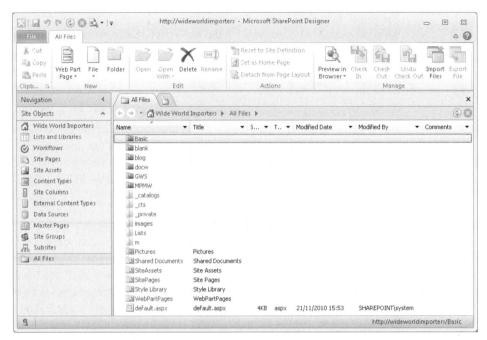

Figure 14-9 Click the All Files in the Navigation pane to view the URL structure of a SharePoint site.

Controlling the Use of SharePoint Designer

SharePoint Designer has historically been a very powerful and useful tool for customizing SharePoint sites and creating solutions. However, the long lasting implications of using SharePoint Designer 2007 and its predecessor, Microsoft Office FrontPage 2003, on SharePoint sites, caused organizations to prohibit the installation of SharePoint Designer or to limit its use to all but a few trained users.

When the save command was clicked in SharePoint Designer 2007 or FrontPage 2003, SharePoint would unnecessarily break the link between a page and its site definition file stored on the SharePoint Server, resulting in what is known as a *customized* or *unghosted* page. A copy of the page from the SharePoint server would be stored in the SQL server content database. The customizing or unghosting of a page was not always made obvious to the untrained user. SharePoint Designer 2007 and FrontPage 2003 also did not provide an easy method for controlling the level of modifications that users could carry out with SharePoint Designer.

Customizing pages by using SharePoint Designer 2010, as with SharePoint Designer 2007, in most cases does not adversely affect the performance of a page—it is more of a maintenance issue, which is most often experienced when upgrading from one version of SharePoint to another, or when an organization implements a major change to the look and feel of their installation.

For more information on customized and unghosted pages, read the section "Site Template Pages," in Chapter 6.

SharePoint Designer 2010 contains many improvements and implements a "safe by default" approach that places reasonable limits around its usage so that citizen developers do not accidently create solutions that have a negative effect. You can still customize a page in SharePoint Designer; however, first you need to be allowed to customize a page, and second, you must explicitly change your edit mode to advanced mode before you can customize a page.

SharePoint 2010 implements a new set of settings at the web application and Site Collection levels that can be used to prevent or restrict the usage of SharePoint Designer. These are SharePoint Designer usage settings and not security settings. When configured at the web application level, these settings affect all users, including Site Collection administrators for all Site Collections and sites within the web application. When they are configured at the Site Collection level, they apply only to site owners and designers for sites within that Site Collection.

> ## Note
> SharePoint Designer 2007 employed contributor settings to control the use of SharePoint Designer, which were configured on a site-by-site basis by the site owner. This feature is removed in SharePoint Designer 2010.

SharePoint Designer Usage Settings

At both web application and Site Collection levels, there are now four settings that allow or disallow the following SharePoint Designer usages (when a web application is created, by default all four security settings are selected):

- **Enable SharePoint Designer**   If a user has SharePoint Designer open and you clear this check box, then it will not close SharePoint Designer for that user. However, the next time that user tries to open the site in SharePoint Designer, the Web Site Editing Is Disabled message box opens, stating that the website has been configured to disallow editing with SharePoint Designer, as shown in Figure 14-10.

Figure 14-10 Clearing the Enable SharePoint Designer check box or amending attributes in the ONET.XML file can affect the editing of a website using SharePoint Designer.

- **Detach pages from site definitions**   Use this option to prevent any pages associated with a site definition file from being customized (unghosted), including master pages and publishing page layouts. Content within Web Parts or within the *Embedded FormField* can still be modified. This option does not affect pages that are created in the content database and have never been associated with site definition files.

- **Customize master pages and page layouts**   This is similar to the previous option; however, by selecting this option, you will only prevent the customization of master pages and publishing page layouts that are associated with site definition files. These are often the types of pages that cause organizations major maintenance problems if they are customized, because it is often to these page types that organizations want to apply global changes across all sites. If this option is not selected, then the Master Page object will not be available on the Navigation pane in SharePoint Designer. If you are using SharePoint Server 2010 and displaying a publishing site in SharePoint Designer, then the Page Layout option will also not be available in the Navigation pane.

- **See the URL structure of the web site**   Within SharePoint Designer, users will not see the All Files option on the Navigation pane, the All Files gallery page in the workspace, or All Files in the mini-gallery. If this option is enabled but the Customize Master Pages And Page Layouts option is selected, then site owners and designers can see the master pages and page layouts, but they are not allowed to modify them.

You cannot use these options to control the usage of SharePoint Designer for different groups of people or to apply different usage rules on a per-site basis within the same Site Collection.

When any of the out-of-the-box site templates are used to create the root site of a Site Collection, site owners and designers can use SharePoint Designer; however, they cannot detach pages from site definitions, customize master pages or page layouts, or see the URL structure of their websites. Site collection owners are only restricted by the settings at the web application level and are not affected by the selection of check boxes on the SharePoint Designer Settings page at the Site Collection level.

If you are using SharePoint Server 2010 and the root site of a Site Collection was created by using a publishing site, then all four check boxes on the SharePoint Designer settings page at the Site Collection level are selected.

INSIDE OUT   Other methods of controlling the use of SharePoint Designer

SharePoint Designer 2010 can use all but the contributor settings methods for controlling the use of SharePoint Designer 2007 and FrontPage 2003; that is:

- Disabling the Add And Customize Pages permission.

- Disabling the Manage List permission.

- Disabling the Browse Directories permission.

- Disabling the Use Remote Interfaces permission.

- At the server level, preventing any user, including SharePoint server administrators, from opening sites created from specific site definition by modifying the Project element to include the attribute `DisableWebDesignFeatures="wdfo pensite"` in the ONET.XML file for that site definition. You need to make this change on all SharePoint servers in your farm, and it affects all sites created from the site definition across all web applications created on the farm. You can change the *DisableWebDesignFeatures* attribute retroactively after a site is created and SharePoint will not allow the site to be opened with SharePoint Designer.

  As the site definition files are cached, to make this attribute change take effect, you need to do an IISREST. The *DisableWebDesignFeatures* attribute can be set to other values, most of which are no longer applicable to SharePoint Designer 2010, for example, *sdfbackup* and *wdfrestore* were used to disable SharePoint site backup and restore, but because SharePoint Designer 2010 cannot be used to backup or restore SharePoint sites, they have no effect.

  However, the attribute *wdfnewsubsite* can be used to prevent the creation of new Subsites using SharePoint Designer. No user feedback is provided when you set the *wdfnewsubsite* attribute and the user clicks the Subsite command in the New group on the Sites tab. However, when you set the *wdfopensite* attribute, the Web Site Editing Is Disabled dialog box opens stating that the website has been configured to disallow editing with SharePoint Designer, as shown in Figure 14-10.

- Per user or per computer, using group policies.

Permissions can be disabled at the web application level and excluded from permission levels at sites or Site Collections.

You can find information on locking down SharePoint Designer 2007 at *http://blogs.msdn. com/b/sharepointdesigner/archive/2008/11/25/locking-down-sharepoint-designer.aspx*.

Chapter 14

Implementing SharePoint Designer Settings for a Web Application

To apply restrictions at the web application level, complete the following steps. Note that you must be a SharePoint Server administrator to complete these steps:

1. In SharePoint Server, on the Windows taskbar, click Start, point to All Programs, click Microsoft SharePoint 2010 Products, and then click SharePoint 2010 Central Administration.

2. In the Application Management section, click Manage Web Applications to display the Web Applications page.

3. Click the web application for which you want to restrict the use of SharePoint Designer.

4. On the Web Applications tab, in the Manage group, click General Settings, and then click SharePoint Designer.

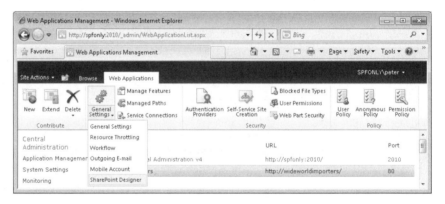

The SharePoint Designer Settings dialog is displayed.

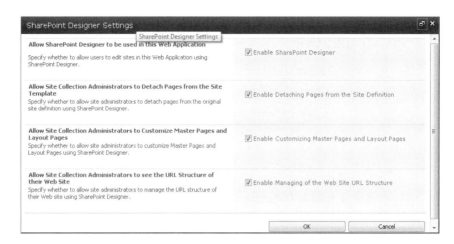

5. Clear or select the check boxes, as needed, and then click OK.

Alternatively, in the SharePoint 2010 Central Administration website, you can configure SharePoint Designer usage settings at the web application level by going to the General Application Settings page. Click Configure SharePoint Designer settings to display the SharePoint Designer Settings page, and then select the appropriate web application in the Web Application section.

Implementing SharePoint Designer Settings for a Site Collection

To configure SharePoint Designer settings at the Site Collection level, complete the following steps. Note that you must be a Site Collection administrator to complete these steps:

1. Open the root site of your Site Collection in the browser. Click Site Actions, and then click Site Settings to display the site settings page.

2. Under Site Collection Administration, if you see only Go To The Top Level Site Settings, you have opened a Subsite in the browser. Click the link to go to the root site's Site Settings page. If you do not see the Site Collection Administration section on the Site Settings page, you are not a Site Collection owner and cannot complete the rest of the steps.

3. Under Site Collection Administration, click SharePoint Designer Settings.

The SharePoint Designer Settings page is displayed. When any of the four check boxes is not selected at the web application level, then the corresponding check boxes at the Site Collection level are unavailable and a red text message that the option was disabled by your server administrator is displayed.

4. On the SharePoint Designer Settings page, select the check boxes, as needed, and then click OK.

Using Windows PowerShell to Set SharePoint Designer Settings

SharePoint Foundation now contains native support for Windows PowerShell with the SharePoint Management Shell, which can be opened on the Windows Taskbar in SharePoint Server by clicking Start, pointing to All Programs, clicking Microsoft Share-Point 2010 Products, and then clicking SharePoint 2010 Management Shell. You can then enable or disable any of the SharePoint usage settings by using PowerShell; for example, to prevent the customization of pages and to disable the view of the URL folder structure at the web application level, type the following command, using the name of your web application in place of `wideworldimporters`:

```
Set-SPDesignerSettings -WebApplication http://wideworldimporters '
    -AllowRevertFromTemplate $False -ShowURLStructure $False
```

To display the SharePoint Designer usage settings for a web application, type the following command:

```
Get-SPDesignerSettings -WebApplication http://wideworldimporters
```

There is no equivalent specific *SPDesignerSettings* command for Site Collections. You will need to use the *Get-SPSite* command, to display the SharePoint Designer usage settings for a Site Collection. By default, this command only displays the URL property of the Site Collection. To display all of the properties associated with the Site Collection, you need to pipe the results of the *Get-SPSite* command into the *Select* command, as shown in the following example. Use the name of your Site Collection in place of `wideworldimporters/sites/hr`:

```
Get-SPSite http://wideworldimporters/sites/hr | select *
```

The properties concerning the SharePoint Designer usage settings are: *AllowDesigner*, *AllowRevertFromTemplate*, *AllowMastPageEditing,* and *ShowURLStructure*. To prevent site owners and designers from using SharePoint Designer on a Site Collection, type the following command:

```
Get-SPSite http://wideworldimporters/sites/basic).AllowDesigner=$False
```

With PowerShell, you can batch together and automate repetitive tasks, or you can use it to ensure that a set of tasks are completed again exactly as they were the last time they were executed. Therefore, if you have a large number of Site Collections for which you want to configure the SharePoint Designer usage settings, create a text file—sitecollection.txt—that contains a list of those Site Collections, such as the following:

```
http://wideworldimporters/sites/hr
http://wideworldimporters/sites/marketing
http://widworldimporters/sites/sales
```

Place the text file in your %USERPROFILE% directory, which is the directory that the SharePoint 2010 Management Shell uses, and then type the following:

```
$content = Get-Content sitecollection.txt
$content | ForEach-Object {
   (Get-SPSite $_).AllowDesigner = $False}
```

The contents of the sitecollection.txt file is stored in the variable *$content* and the *ForEach-Object* command acts like a loop, reading a line from the text file, one at a time. The variable *$_* represents one line from the text file, which in this example is the name of one Site Collection. To display the *AllowDesigner* property for each Site Collection together with its server-relative URL and using the *ForEach* alias %, type the following:

```
$content | % {
  Get-SPSite $_ |
  select ServerRelativeUrl, AllowDesigner }
```

More examples of using PowerShell with SharePoint 2010 (such as the example of using PowerShell to create a SharePoint 2010 site structure) are available on Gary Lapointe's blog site at *http://blog.falchionconsulting.com/index.php/2009/12/ creating-a-sharepoint-2010-site-structure-using-powershell/*.

Creating Sites

In Chapter 4, "Creating Sites and Workspaces by Using the Browser," you learned that the first portion of a SharePoint site's URL—for example, *http://wideworldimporters* or *http:// intranet.wideworldimporters.com*—is known as the web application, and a web application can consist of one or more Site Collections; each Site Collection always has one top-level site and, optionally, one or more Subsites, also called child sites. If you are a SharePoint Server administrator, then by using the browser and the SharePoint 2010 Central Administration website, you can create web applications and Site Collections. Users with the Create Sites permissions can use the browser to create Subsites from the Site Actions menu. Such users can also use SharePoint Designer to create Subsites. You cannot create web applications or Site Collections by using SharePoint Designer.

To create a Subsite by using SharePoint Designer, choose one of the following options:

- From the Backstage view, on the Sites tab, under New SharePoint Site, click New Blank Web Site, or under Site Templates, click Blank Site, Blog, or Team Site.

   This will create Subsites beneath the current site. The Add Subsite To My Site option is only applicable if you are using SharePoint Server 2010.

- From the Backstage view, on the Sites tab, under Site Templates, click More Templates to open the Site To Load Templates From dialog box. Here, you can specify a different site than the one currently open. The site templates from that site are then retrieved and displayed in the Backstage view, as shown in Figure 14-11.

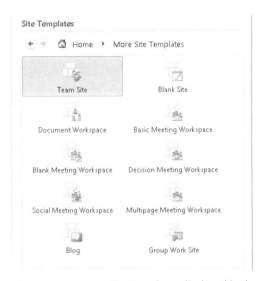

Figure 14-11 More Site Templates displayed in the Backstage view.

- Display the Site Settings page in the workspace, and then click New in the Subsites area title bar.

- In the Navigation pane, click Subsites to display the Subsites gallery in the workspace, and then on the Subsites tab, click Subsite in the New group.

When using the last two options, the New dialog box opens and displays the site templates in the middle pane, as shown in Figure 14-12. The right pane displays a description of the site template selected from the middle pane. If the middle pane does not include any site templates, then in the Specify The location Of The New Web Site text box, type the URL of the Subsite, and then click in the middle pane. SharePoint Designer will communicate with the SharePoint server hosting your SharePoint site and then populate the middle pane from the information retrieved from it.

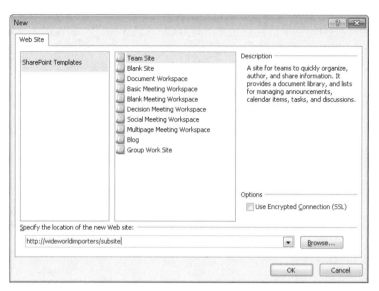

Figure 14-12 The New dialog box displays the available site templates.

If you have a site open already in SharePoint Designer, then the new site will open in a new SharePoint Designer window.

Note

Whenever you create a site in SharePoint Designer, it only asks you for the URL of the site and the site template to use. It does not prompt you for any other site properties such as the title of the site or the permissions to use. The title of the site will be the name of the site template that was used to create the site. The site will inherit its permissions from its parent site, and the site will not appear as a link in the top navigation bar. Therefore, the first task you should complete once you create a site is to use the site settings page in SharePoint Designer to modify the title of the site and, if appropriate, its permissions. If you do not change the title immediately, then you could have many sites with the same name. This can be very confusing for users because it is the title of the site that is displayed in the browser's UI. Also, if you plan to use the new site as a basis to create a solution or customization, which you will then use as a template for new or existing sites, then it is best practice to change the permissions of the site so that only you and other users who are helping develop the solution have access to the site.

Managing Sites

SharePoint Designer is not a tool for general use by all those who visit or have access to a SharePoint site; instead, it is a tool targeted to site owners, business analysts, project managers, developers, and IT professionals.

There are a few tasks that still cannot be completed within SharePoint Designer. For those tasks, click the site object in the Navigation pane to display the site settings page, and then on the Site tab, in the Manage group, click Administration Web Page. A browser window opens and displays the Site Settings page.

When you first open a site in SharePoint Designer, the site settings page is displayed in the workspace, as shown in Figure 14-4. The page is divided into five sections:

- **Site Information**   Use this section to change the site's title and description, which are important properties, because they appear on each page within a site and communicate to users the purpose and function of the site. They are also important because the words in the title and description fields are used to rank content items that are returned in a search result set.

- **Customization**   Use this section to open a new workspace tab when the home page is displayed in Edit mode. The Change Site Theme link in this section opens the browser and displays the Site Theme page. Themes are discussed later in this chapter.

- **Settings**   Use this section to select the options to display the Quick Launch, enable tree view, and enable site Really Simple Syndication (RSS) feeds. The Quick Launch and tree view options are the same as you would find in the browser when on the Site Settings page; under Look And Feel you click Tree View. To select the RSS feeds option, in the browser on the Site Settings page, under Site Administration, click RSS.

- **Permissions**   Use this section to assign users and groups permission to this site. When you click the icon to the left of a user or group, the Site tab set becomes active and displays the Permissions tab (see Figure 14-13), which you can use to add new users and groups, edit permissions, inherit permissions from the site's parent site if the site is using unique permissions, and manage anonymous access, permission levels, access requests, and Site Collection administrators.

Figure 14-13 On the Permissions tab, you can manage permissions for the site.

Chapter 14

- **Subsites** Use this section to list all the Subsites created below the site. When you click in the area below Site Name, the Site tab set becomes active and displays the Subsites tab, as shown in Figure 14-14, which you can use to create a new Subsite, open, delete, or rename a site, view the Subsite in the browser, view the Site Settings page in the browser for the Subsite, or save the Subsite as a template.

Figure 14-14 Use the Subsite tab to manage sites created below this site.

INSIDE OUT Using the Grow Size and Shrink Size commands

You will see the Grow Size and Shrink Size command in the List View group on many ribbon tabs, especially when a settings page is displayed in the workspace. Settings pages contain many sections, and you can use these two commands to reduce the space taken on the workspace for each section. Alternatively you can collapse a section, leaving only the section title visible—by clicking the section title or the up arrow in the title bar.

You can use the SharePoint artifacts listed in the Navigation pane to manage other components of the SharePoint Site, for example:

- **Lists And Libraries** You can use the List And Libraries gallery (see Figure 14-7) to create new lists and libraries, manage list settings, edit columns, delete or rename a list or library, preview the list or library in the browser, open a browser window, and display the list settings page and save the list as a template. If you click a list in the workspace, the list settings page is displayed in the workspace, as shown in Figure 14-15. An alternative method of navigating to this page is to click the icon to the left of the list in the List and Library gallery, and then on the Lists And Libraries tab, in the Edit group, click List Settings.

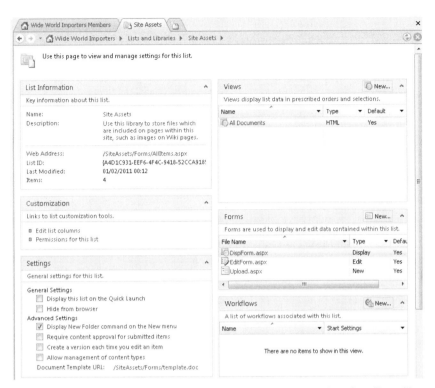

Figure 14-15 Use the List Settings page to view and manage settings for a list or library.

The List Settings page contains eight sections in which you can view list information, edit list columns and the permissions for the list; manage general settings for the list, such as hiding the list from the browser so that is does not display on the View All Sites Content page; manage the content types and workflows associated with the list; create and manage list views and forms; as well as create custom actions.

- **Site Groups** When you click this option in the Navigation pane, the Site Groups gallery opens in the workspace and the Site Groups tab is displayed in the ribbon, on which you can add users to an existing group, create new groups, edit and delete a group, make a group the default members group, or view the group permissions. When you click one of the groups, the settings page for that group is displayed in the workspace, as shown in Figure 14-16.

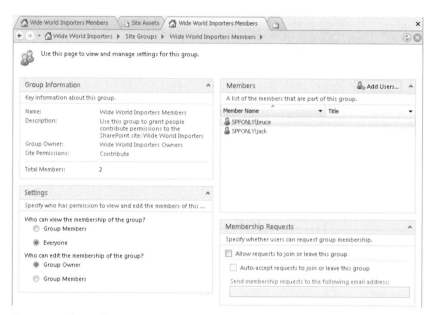

Figure 14-16 Use the group settings page to manage settings for a SharePoint group.

Designing Sites

The first step to designing your site is to understand your content. Too often, people start designing their sites by creating wireframes without understanding the content. Content is King, and as such, you should try to find the answers to the following questions:

- How often is it going to be updated?

- Who is going to update it?

- How often are they going to update it?

- Where is the content coming from?

- What is the main message of the site, of the page, or parts of the page?

- When you design a page, if users to your site could walk away with just one thing from your site, what would it be? What is going to make users come back to our site?

These questions will help you to decide the site template to use, the content types, site columns, workflows, lists, libraries, and types of pages to create, as well as which Web Parts to place on those pages. For example:

- When users have a great deal of static content and images to add to a page, if you design your site so that this content is stored, for example, in a Content Editor Web Part (CEWP), then not only will you have to train users on how to use that Web Part, but users might find this too hard and time consuming to update at the frequency they require. Therefore, the information on the page will become dated and other employees will not visit the site because it is not a representation of the business process. You should perhaps use a wiki page.

- When content is not going to change frequently, such as company policies, but information on company polices must be readily available to all employees. There might also be associated information that you want to be displayed on the page, such as when the policy is to be reviewed; plus your company's human resources (HR) department might own the production of the policy pages and they might also require that part of the page is used to tell visitors to the page of the HR department's plans, and an RSS feed of the directors' blog sites as well as what they are twittering about. So the page you design needs to contain both static content that needs to go through an approval process and dynamic content. This affects the page layout and how you layout the content onto your pages. Is there any special branding consideration that the HR department requires for their site? Are they using any custom Web Parts that do not follow the same CSS style as the other Web Parts?

- You need to understand the navigation requirements. You do not want to use a different navigation standard that is used elsewhere on your site. This will confuse visitors of your site. The larger the organization, the more complex the navigation is. If the navigation does not follow a consistent pattern, the users will not know what they are doing and how to get back to where they were originally, or how to get back to a specific step in a business process.

You must also consider the user experience—UX. Although computers have been around for over half a century there are still many users in organizations who have an aversion to computers, and therefore, it is important to gather requirements and understand the skill level of the users who will make use of your solution. Most users of SharePoint are not developers or administrators—they do not understand the technology behind the pages, lists, and libraries that they need to use and maintain. Many users have experienced myriad system changes, and to a large number of them, your solution is just one more in a very long line of systems that they are going to use. They don't have the time to sit down and learn your new system—they've got their day job to get on with.

So when you design your site, there are many aspects to consider, which not only affect your page layout, content types, site columns, lists, and libraries that you should use, but also how you want your sites to look. Do you want to move some of the UI objects and do you want your sites to represent your company's branding? Do you want to brand all sites—Team Sites, Group Work Sites, Document Workspaces, Meeting Workspaces—or only some of them? Do you want the site owners to be able to choose and apply their own branding? This will also help you identify if you need any custom development or whether you can meet your design requirements by using the browser and SharePoint Designer.

Using Themes

When you modify the look and feel of your site, you can change the colors and the fonts by using themes. SharePoint Foundation offers a choice of 20 themes, and you can also create your own custom themes. This is the easiest method of changing the branding of your site, and it requires the least amount of effort and no knowledge of web technology.

In Windows SharePoint Services 3.0, a theme was a CSS file and images. Custom themes were files stored on the SharePoint server, and therefore, you needed administrative access to the server to deploy them. Not so with SharePoint Foundation 2010, where the theme engine has been completely redesigned. Now when we talk about themes, we are talking only about colors, fonts and effects. There are two distinct fonts: one for the heading and the other for the body text; and the color palate can be anything.

Themes consist of combinations of colors, fonts and effects. You can choose from an existing combination, known as Quick Styles, or you can build your theme by choosing each component individually.

You can choose from among twelve colors: four text and background colors, six accent colors, and two hyperlink colors, as shown in Figure 14-17. All of these colors have variations: Lightest, Lighter, Medium, Darker and Darkest. The twelve theme colors are associated with CSS attributes and rules in the SharePoint 2010 CSS files. When you apply a theme, those CSS attributes are overridden by the colors in the theme. When you develop your own CSS files and you do not associate the theme tags with CSS attributes, then the theme will take no affect.

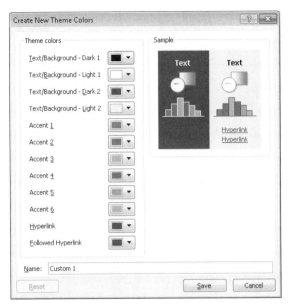

Figure 14-17 Office theme colors.

The four text and background colors are labeled Dark 1, Light 1, Dark 2, and Light 2. Text that is created with the light colors are legible over dark colors, and text that is created with dark colors are legible over the light colors. Light 1 is a base white color, and Light 2 is a slightly darker color than Light 1, for example, beige. The dark and light colors are not used just for text or backgrounds, they can be intermixed. However, if you are working with an out-of-the-box template from Microsoft, then Light 1 is the text color on the Dark 2 background and Dark 1 is the text color used on the Light 2 background color.

The other colors you might want to modify are the Hyperlink and Followed Hyperlink colors. You can also change the Accent colors. You will typically need to experiment with changing the colors to get the theme you require.

If you prefer, you can also create a theme by using one of the Microsoft Office 2010 client applications, such as Microsoft PowerPoint 2010 or Microsoft Word 2010. You then save your theme and upload it via the browser. It's that simple! To create your custom theme, find a color scheme that is similar to what you want to create and then perform the following steps:

1.   Open PowerPoint 2010.

2.   On the Design tab, in the Themes group, click Colors, and then click Create New Theme Colors.

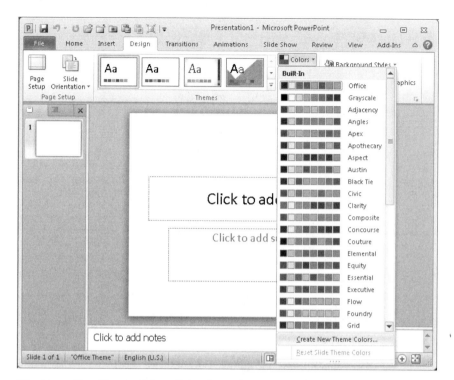

The Create New Theme Colors dialog box opens, in which you can make your color selections.

3. Select the colors as required for each theme color, and then type the name of your custom theme in the Name text box. Click Save to close the Create New Theme Colors dialog box.

4. On the Design tab, in the Themes group, click Fonts, and then click Create New Theme Font.

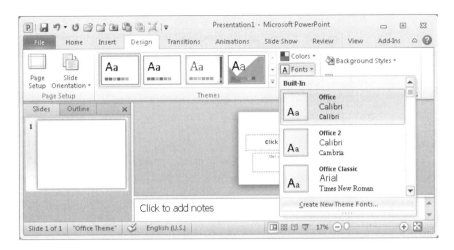

5. In the Create New Theme Fonts dialog box, select the fonts for the text that appears in the heading and body areas of your page, and then click Save.

6. On the Design tab, click Effects, and then choose the effect that you want to use in your theme.

7. On the Design tab, to the right of the Quick Styles gallery, click the More button, and then click Save Current Theme.

8. In the Save Current Theme dialog box, browse to where you want to save your theme, such as your desktop, and then, in the File Name text box, type the name of your custom theme. Click Save.

Once you have created your custom theme, you need to upload it to the Theme library for your SharePoint site. You can use the browser or SharePoint Designer to upload your custom theme. To upload your custom theme by using the browser, perform the following steps:

1. Open the SharePoint Site Collection that contains the sites for which you want to use the theme, click Site Actions, and then click Site Settings.

2. Under Galleries, click Themes, and then on the Documents tab, click Upload Document.

3. In the Theme Gallery – Upload Document dialog box, browse to where you saved your theme file. The default location for saving theme files is %UserProfile%/AppData/Roaming/Microsoft/Templates/Document Themes/. Click OK.

4. In the Theme Gallery dialog box, type a description, and then click Save.

To upload your theme by using SharePoint Designer, complete the following steps. You will need permissions to see the URL structure of your site, as explained in the section, "Controlling the Use of SharePoint Designer," earlier in this chapter:

1. Open the SharePoint Site Collection that contains the sites on which you want to use the theme, and then in the Navigation pane, click All Files.

   This displays the All Files gallery in the workspace.

2. Click _catalogs, and then click theme.

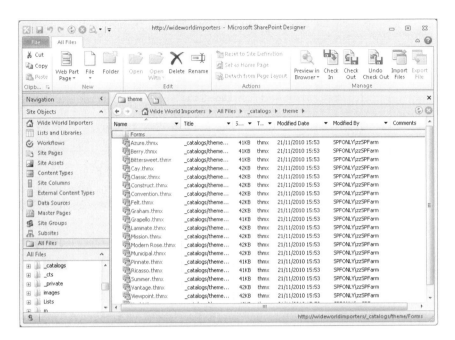

3. On the All Files tab, in the Manage group, click Import Files to display the Import dialog box.

4. Click Add File. In the Add File To Import List that appears, browse to where you stored your custom theme file, and then click Open.

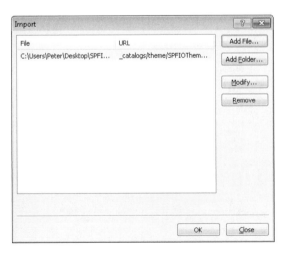

5. Click OK to close the Import dialog box and upload the theme file.

To apply the theme to your site, by using the browser, execute the following steps:

1. Browse to the site on which you want to apply the theme, click Site Actions, and then click Site Settings.

2. Under Look And Feel, click Site Theme to display the Site Theme page.

3. Click your custom theme, and then click Apply.

> **Note**
>
> Using SharePoint Designer to display the site settings page in the workspace, you can use the Change Site Theme link in the Customization section to display the Site Theme page in the browser.

When a theme is applied to a site, SharePoint opens the .thmx file and creates a number of CSS files and images. A _themes folder and a subfolder is created in the root of the Share-Point site where these files are stored. The first time a theme is applied, the subfolder is named 0 (see Figure 14-18). Each time you apply a new theme, the subfolder name is incremented by 1. You can change the files in this folder; however, your changes will be deleted if another theme is applied, including changing the theme to the default (no theme).

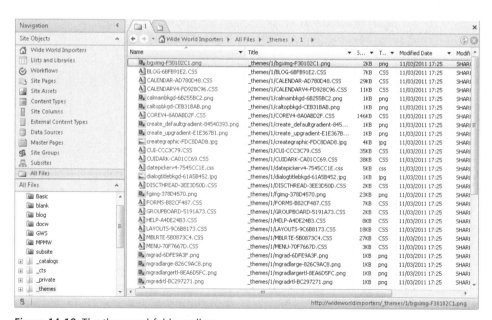

Figure 14-18 The theme subfolder gallery.

INSIDE OUT   Applying a theme to more than one site

On a SharePoint Server 2010 site where the publishing feature has been activated, you can modify theme colors and fonts by using the browser. You can also apply the theme to all Subsites by using the browser. However, in SharePoint Foundation, there is no browser page with which you can do this. You can use PowerShell to apply a theme to a number of sites in a similar fashion to the method used earlier in this chapter for Share-Point Designer usage settings. You can also apply a theme to all sites in a Site Collection by using PowerShell, similar to that used in the following example:

```
$themeName = "SPFIOTheme";

Start-SPAssignment -Global;

$sc = Get_SPSite http://wideworldimporters;
$theme = [Microsoft.SharePoint.Utilities.ThmxTheme]::GetManagedThemes($sc) |
    where { $_.Name -eq $themeName };
$sc.AllWebs | foreach { $theme.ApplyTo ($_, $true) };

Stop-SPAssignment;
```

This example uses the SharePoint 2010 *SPAssignment* cmdlet to dispose of the memory used to store the object that contains Site Collection information for *http://wideworldimporters*. To restore the default setting, that is no theme applied, use the following commands:

```
Start-SPAssignment -Global;

$sc = Get_SPSite http://wideworldimporters;
$sc.AllWebs |
    foreach {
      [Microsoft.SharePoint.Utilities.ThmxTheme]::SetThemeUrlForWeb( $_, $null)
    };

Stop-SPAssignment;
```

Working with Master Pages

If themes do not meet your needs, you will probably need to create your own master pages and CSS files. Both of these processes take some time, especially if you are new to branding and have never tried to change the look and feel of a SharePoint site before, and you have no previous web design or development knowledge. Using a theme can be likened to painting your house; CSS is analogous to moving or hanging new pictures in your house; and you use master pages to add an extension to your house.

Chapter 14

> **Note**
>
> Although you could create your company's Internet website by using SharePoint Foundation to create your master page and CSS files, most companies will use SharePoint Server to create such a site. SharePoint Server contains many web content management features that are required by an Internet site. If you are asked to create an Internet presence for a company based on SharePoint 2010, you should investigate the two editions: SharePoint Server 2010 for Internet Sites, Standard Edition and Enterprise Edition. You can find more information on these two editions at *http://sharepoint. microsoft.com/en-us/internetsites/products/Pages/SharePoint.aspx?Product=SharePoint*, and a trial version can be downloaded from the Microsoft download site at *www. microsoft.com/downloads/en/details.aspx?displaylang=en&FamilyID=895a1 dba-0c3f-47a0-8d6d-163b50364335*.

When you want to change the structure of the pages and apply those changes to all pages within a site or across a number of sites, that is when you need to create a new master page. Master pages were introduced in Chapter 6.

For more information about master pages, go to *http://msdn.microsoft.com/en-us/library/ ms443795.aspx*.

When you use a browser to request a page from a site, it combines two Microsoft ASP.NET pages: a master page and a content page. In Chapter 6, you discovered that when you open a content page in SharePoint Designer, the Design view displays the merged page (not only the content page). In Code view, only the source code from the content page is displayed. A master page is a special ASP.NET 2.0 page that is used to provide a consistent appearance and navigation for each page within one or more sites. Components that are usually placed on master pages are your company's branding images and logo, navigation tabs and links such as a breadcrumb component and the Site Actions button; footer links, such as contact us, accessibility, and copyright statements; and links to CSS files and JavaScript files that contain common functions. A master page cannot be viewed in a browser, but you can view and customize a master page by using SharePoint Designer.

SharePoint 2010 makes heavy use of master pages to control the general layout of pages within a SharePoint site. When you install SharePoint 2010, the default master page and other master pages are located on the web server. SharePoint Foundation contains a number of master pages:

- **v4.master**   This is the master page that is applied when you first create a site.

- **default.master**   This provides the look and feel and controls for Windows Share-Point Services and SharePoint Server 2007 but does not include the ribbon. If you have upgraded to SharePoint Foundation 2010 from Windows SharePoint Services 3.0, and you have not upgraded the user interface, the default master page used by your sites will be default.master.

- **mwsdefaultv4.master** and **mwsdefault.master**   These are the default master pages for meeting workspaces.

- **Minimal.master**   This can be used on pages where you want the minimum amount of controls and branding. None of the out-of-the-box site definitions in SharePoint Foundation use this master page, however, in SharePoint Server 2010; it is used with the Search Center site definitions.

- **simple.master**   This is a slimmed down master page used for logon and error pages. It is stored in the layouts folder on the servers and cannot be modified by using SharePoint Designer.

Each page in a site is initially configured to use the site's default master page. The *@Page* directive at the top of the content page specifies the master page to be used. When you first create a SharePoint Foundation site, all pages but a select few use the site's default master page. The *MasterPageFile* attribute of the *@Page* directive is set to token, *~masterurl/default.master*. To set a master page as the site's default master page, perform the following steps:

1. In the Navigation pane, click Master Pages, and then click the icon to the left of the master page that you want to use as the site's default master page.

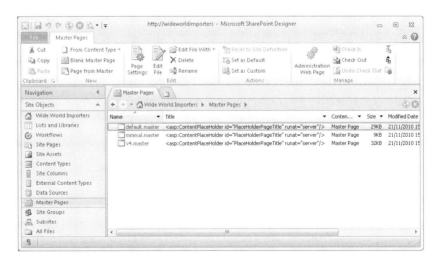

2. On the Master Pages tab, in the Actions group, click Set As Default.

INSIDE OUT   When is the Custom command available?

The Set As Custom command in the Action group of the Master Pages tab is for use with SharePoint Server and publishing pages.

You can modify which master page a content page uses. For example, you can specify whether you want to use the default master page or a different master page. Theoretically, each page within a Site Collection can use a different master page. Such a scenario would defeat the purpose of using master pages, however, because as stated earlier, master pages were introduced to support a common look and feel across entire sites. However, making a content page use a specific master page can be very useful when you are developing a new master page, because you can test your modification on one page without affecting all pages within a site. To attach a master page other than the site's default master page to a content page, perform the following steps:

1. In SharePoint Designer, browse to the content page; for example, in the Navigation pane, click Site Pages.

2. Click the icon to the left of the content page. On the Pages tab, click the down-arrow on the Edit File command, and then in Advanced Mode, click Edit File.

    For more information about the Advanced Edit mode, see Chapter 6.

3. On the Style tab, in the Master Page group, click Attach, and then click the master page that you want to attach to the content page.

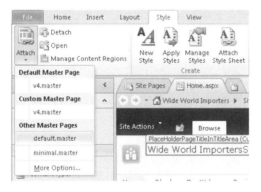

If you now switch to Code view, you will see that the @*Page* directive at the top of the content page, no longer uses the *~masterurl/default.master* token, but points to a specific master page, for example:

```
<%@ Page Language="C#" Inherits=Microsoft.SharePoint.WebPartPages.WikiEditPage"
    MasterPageFile="../_catalogs/masterpage/SPFIIO.master"
    meta:webpartpageexpansion="full"
    meta:progid="SharePoint.WebPartPage.Documet" %>
```

4. Save the content page, and if the content page is a site definition page, you will need to click Yes to the Site Definition Page Warning dialog box that is displayed. View the page in the browser.

INSIDE OUT   Migrating pages from a non-SharePoint site

You can also use these steps if you have an .aspx page that is not associated with any master page. This can be very useful if you are migrating pages from a non-SharePoint site and you want the pages to look like all other pages within your site.

You can also create new content pages from a master page, and then add the necessary controls to the content page by using the following steps. However, users will not be able to edit the page in the browser if you do not include Web Part zones or the SharePoint control, *EmbeddedFormField*. Therefore, it is easier to create these by using the browser, especially if you do want to create a wiki page:

1. In the Navigation pane, click Master Pages, and then on the Master Pages tab, click Page From Master to open the Select A Master Page dialog box.

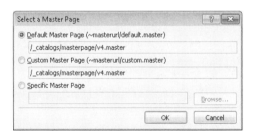

2. Select the Default Master Page if you want to create the page from the site's default master page, or select Specific Master Page, if you want to create a page from a specific master page.

3. Click Browse to choose the specific master page.

Master Pages Anatomy

Unlike content pages, master pages contain the tags <HTML>, <HEAD>, <BODY> and <FORM>. Master page file names have the extension .master, whereas content pages have an extension of .aspx. Master pages can also contain most of the content and functionality of content pages, including JavaScript, Web Parts (including Data Views and XLV Web Parts), and components such as the Search box and the component that displays the Quick Launch headings and links. Master pages cannot contain Web Part zones, however.

Each master page contains multiple core controls, which can be divided into four types:

- Controls for links, menus, icons, and navigation components such as the *SiteMapPath* control that populates the global navigation breadcrumb.

- Content placeholders, such as the *PlaceHolderMain* control, that match areas on the content page where you can enter information.

- Delegate controls, which define a region on the page in which content can be substituted by another control driven by feature activation.

- Controls for scripts. These manage the communication of the page and assist with the ribbon, toolbars, and other controls.

You can include style information in a master page, but it's good practice to use a CSS file linked to the master page. The key benefit of using a master page is that any global design changes to your site can be made in one place. By using a master page, you can design your site efficiently and quickly and avoid the need to make changes on every page in the site. To locate and edit a master page, perform the following steps:

1. Open your SharePoint site in SharePoint Designer, and then in the Navigation pane, click Master Pages.

2. Click the icon to the left of the master page that you want to edit, and then on the Master Pages tab, click Edit File.

    The master page opens in the workspace, and on the breadcrumb, the text Advanced Editor indicates that the page is open in Advanced Edit mode.

3. In the mini-gallery below the Navigation pane, right-click the master page that you want to edit, and then click Check Out. A green check mark appears to the left of the master page.

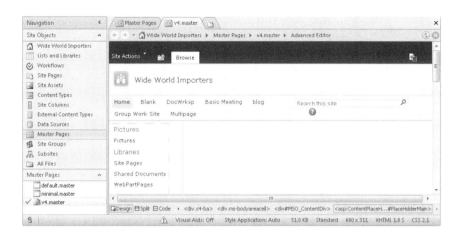

If you want to make a simple customization to v4.master, make a copy of the file or create a blank master page and paste the contents from v4.master into the blank master page. Make your changes to the copy and test those changes by attaching your copied file to a single page. Then when you have tested your changes, make your copied file the default master page, as described earlier in this chapter. It is good practice to never modify the files provided by Microsoft.

INSIDE OUT   The Master Page gallery

Master pages are stored in the master page gallery which is a hidden library. Each site has its own master page gallery. In the browser, you can browse to the Master Page Gallery at the top level of the Site Collection by using the Site Settings page. Using SharePoint Designer, you can navigate to each site's Master Page Gallery by using the Navigation pane and clicking Master Pages or using All Files and navigating to _catalogs/masterpage. The master page gallery has major versioning enabled; therefore, you can restore a previous version of a master page. In SharePoint Server, in a Site Collection where the SharePoint Server Publishing Infrastructure feature is enabled, this library is also used for page layouts and is also configured with content approval and major and minor versions.

The key component of a master page is the content placeholder control. It is placed on the master page where content will eventually appear. The content page specifies which content placeholder the components should be placed in, such as:

```
<asp:Content ContentPlaceHolderID="PlaceHolderMain" runat="server">

</asp:Content>
```

On the master page, the following code defines the content placeholder and specifies where on the page the content placeholder is located:

```
<asp:ContentPlaceHolder id="PlaceHolderMain" runat="server">

</asp:ContentPlaceHolder>
```

A master page typically has a number of content placeholders, the most important of them being *PlaceHolderMain*, which usually maps to the region on the master page where the elements from the content page should be placed.

For a list on SharePoint Foundation content placeholders and how to upgrade a Windows SharePoint Services 3.0 master page, go to *http://msdn.microsoft.com/en-us/library/ ee539981(office.14).aspx.*

To locate content placeholders on a master page, complete the following steps:

1. Open the master page in edit mode and look in the SharePoint Designer status bar. If Visual Aids is Off, click Visual Aids on the View tab, and then select Show.

   The controls on the page are displayed surrounded by a purple line.

2. Click the content placeholder, if you know where it is positioned on the page; for example, click Search This Site.

   The label, PlaceHolderSearchArea, appears above a purple box. In the workspace status bar, <asp:PlaceHolderSearchArea> is highlighted in orange to identify it as the active tag.

3. When you are unsure where the placeholder is positioned on the page, you can search for the control in Code view or in Design view on the Style tab, click Manage Content Regions in the Master Page group.

   The Manage Content Regions dialog box opens, which lists all the regions on the page. Using this dialog box, you can rename, delete, or go to the placeholder.

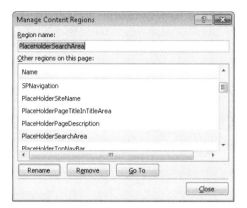

> **Note**
>
> You can only use the above steps to navigate to content placeholders when you are working with a master page. On content pages, when you want to find a reference to a content placeholder, and it is not obvious in Design view where that reference is, you need to use the Code view of the page and the find functionality in SharePoint Designer.

Other placeholders contain components that you can decide not to incorporate in the page, on a content page-by-content page basis. That is, the components stored within a content placeholder in a master page can be viewed as optional. For example, the components that display the Quick Launch, are stored in the master page in the *PlaceHolderLeftNavBar* content placeholder. When you create a Web Part page, the template used modifies the contents of the *PlaceHolderLeftNavBar* so that the Quick Launch does not appear. On a content page, those content placeholders that inherit their components from the master page are appended with (Master), and those content placeholders that do not inherit the components within the content placeholders from the master page are appended with (Custom). To modify the contents of a content placeholder on a content page, perform the following procedure:

1. In SharePoint Designer, browse to the content page, and then open it in Advanced Edit mode.

2. Click the content placeholder; for example, click the name of the site so that the *PlaceHolderSiteName* content placeholder is the active control.

3. Click the On Object User Interface (OOUI), which is represented by a small floating arrow to the far right of the content placeholder, and then click Create Custom Content.

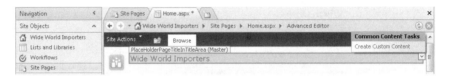

The placeholder and its content are copied from the master page, which you can now edit. The text (Custom) is appended to the name of the content placeholder.

On a content page that has modified the contents of a content placeholder, you can restore the content in the content placeholder back to the content that was defined on the master page by using the following steps:

1. In SharePoint Designer, browse to the content page, and then open it in Advanced Edit mode.

2. Click the content placeholder that you want to revert back to the master page. Click the OOUI, and then click Default To Master's Content.

A Confirm dialog box opens, warning you that everything in the content placeholder (region) will be removed from the page. Click Yes to confirm that you want to continue. The code for the content placeholder is removed from the page.

INSIDE OUT   Do not start with a blank master page

If you want to create your own master page, then do not start with a blank master page and add the controls yourself. It is likely that you will not include all the controls that are needed, and any content page associated with that master page will not display, as shown in Figure 14-19.

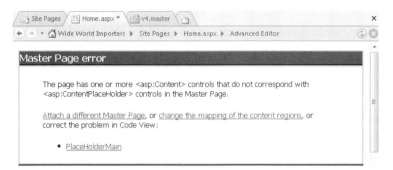

Figure 14-19 Content page displayed in SharePoint Designer, where the master page does not contain all the necessary content placeholders.

Use the master pages at the following locations as starting points for your master page:

- *http://archive.msdn.microsoft.com/odcSP14StarterMaster*

- *http://startermasterpages.codeplex.com*

These two master pages contain comments and the required content placeholders and SharePoint controls on the page. They will be placed in a hidden section on the page. You can move these controls into other locations, based on your design.

Working with CSS

Like most industry-standard sites, SharePoint sites use CSS, and SharePoint Designer contains style sheet editors that make it easy to identify and edit the CSS rules and attributes. SharePoint Designer uses a set of configuration options to decide how it should add the CSS tags to your page. You can change these default settings from within the Page Editor Options dialog box, which you can open on the File tab by clicking Options.

CSS separates the look and feel from the content in your webpages. It is a declarative language that browsers use to format fonts, the color within the page, as well as the size and position of elements on the page. All modern browsers support CSS, and CSS functions exactly the same for SharePoint Foundation sites as it does with any other website.

The main CSS file in SharePoint Foundation is corev4.css, which contains over 7,000 lines of code and defines most of the styles you need to customize your site. Corev4.css is stored on the server in the root directory, %ProgramFiles%\Common Files\Microsoft Shared\Web Server Extensions\14\Template\Layouts\<LCID>\Styles, where <LCID> is the locale for the language packs you have installed. You should not modify this file, but instead create your own style files, which contains only those styles from corev4.css that you need to modify. All of the CSS files provided by Microsoft are linked into the master page using the SharePoint control:

```
<SharePoint:CssLink runat="server" Version="4" />
```

When the master page is merged with your content page, and the *CssLink* control is run on the server, the following code is generated on a wiki page and sent to the browser, together with the CSS files:

```
<link rel="stylesheet" type="text/css"
 href="/_layouts/1033/styles/Themable/wiki.css?rev=9pXM9jgtUVYAHk21JOAbIw%3D%3D"
/>

<link rel="stylesheet" type="text/css"
  href="/_layouts/1033/styles/Themable/corev4.css?rev=iIikGkMuXBs8CWzKDAyjsQ%3D%3D"
/>
```

On a Web Part page, only a link to the corev4.css file is generated.

If you want to change the CSS styles for your site or a number of sites and if you do not have a development environment, create your own Site Collection, or if that is not possible, a test site. On your test site, create a new .css file in your site's Style Library, add the required CSS styles to your .css file, and then edit your master page and add the following code after the *CssLink* SharePoint control:

```
<SharePoint:CSSRegistration Name="/Style Library/SPFIO.css"
   After="corev4.css" runat="server" />
```

In the preceding example, *SFPIO.css* is the name the custom .css file. If your site is not the root site of a Site Collection, you will need to change the URL specified in the *Name* attribute. The *CSSLink* control reads the information from the *CSSResgistration* SharePoint control and inserts a link tag into the page sent to the browser after the link tag for corev4.css, thereby ensuring that your CSS styles are applied after the styles in corev4.css. If you create multiple custom CSS files, you can also use the *CSSRegistration* control to ensure that your custom CSS files are applied in the correct order by using the *After* attribute.

You might need to reference image files from your CSS files. Upload these into the Style Library in a subfolder named images.

INSIDE OUT Creating themeable CSS rules

If you look inside the corev4.css file, you will notice that some of the CSS attributes are prefixed by CSS comments, such as in the following example:

```
.ms-gb {
 padding-bottom:1px
 /* [ReplaceColor(themeColor:"Light2-Medium")] */ border-bottom-color:#b5bdc7;
 }
```

When a theme is applied to your site, the *CSSLink* control recompiles the CSS files, and for the above CSS code, it substitues the color code *#b5bdc7* with the one specified in the theme by *Light2-Medium*. This recompilation will only occur when the Theme SharePoint control is included with the *CSSLink* control. If you wish to create CSS rules that can be themed, you need to create a Themeable folder in your site's style library.

Deploying Your Design

Earlier in this chapter, we discussed how to customize a master page and CSS files by using SharePoint Designer. You might now want other sites to use a master page, CSS files, and associated files. If you want other site owners in your Site Collection to use your design, you could export the master page from your site's Master Page gallery and the associated files from your site's style library, and upload them to the Site Collections Master Page gallery and style library. You might need to change the URL reference specified in the Name attribute in the *CSSRegistration* control and references to images in your custom CSS file. Using relative URL references to files might overcome this problem.

The best option is to deploy the master page plus its associated files as a Feature. You will need Visual Studio 2010 to create a Feature. Visual Studio does not provide a master page designer; however, when teamed with SharePoint Designer, each tool can compensate for the other tool's shortcoming. For example, SharePoint Designer stores any changes to the content database and provides no source code control. Visual Studio supports source control and can deploy files to the SharePoint server's file system, as you will see in the following steps.

To export the customized master page, perform the following steps. In the steps, the customized page is called SPFIIO.master, and the module is named *SPFIOMaster*. Replace these names when you complete the steps with the name of your customized master page and any naming standards that you might use in your organization:

1. Using SharePoint Designer, open the site for which you customized the master page.

2. On the Navigation pane, click Master Pages, and then click the icon to the left of the appropriate master page, such as SPFIO.master.

3. On the Master Pages tab, in the Manage group, click Export File to display the Export Selected As dialog box and save the master page, say, on your desktop, and then click Save.

4. At this point you might consider deleting the customized master page from the Master Page gallery by clicking Delete in the Edit group.

Use Visual Studio to create a package to deploy the master page as a Feature. As Visual Studio does not provide any built-in support to deploy SharePoint artifacts such as master pages, you will need to use the SharePoint 2010 Module project template. The following steps outline the process:

For more information on using Visual Studio to create SharePoint Foundation solutions, and how to set up your development environment, see Chapter 16, "Developing SharePoint Solutions by Using Visual Studio 2010."

1. Open Visual Studio with administrative privileges. On the Start Page tab, click New, Project, or on the toolbar, click File | New, and then click Project to open the New Project dialog box.

2. Under Installed Templates, under the appropriate language (such as Visual C#), expand SharePoint, if it is not already expanded, and then click 2010.

3. In the middle pane, select Empty SharePoint Project.

   This is the most basic SharePoint project type. If you want to add this project to source control, select Add To Source Control.

4. In the Name text box, type **SPFIOBranding** for the Project Name, and then click OK.

   The SharePoint Customization Wizard is displayed.

5. Specify the site where you want to deploy and test the master page, and then select Deploy As A Farm Solution for the trust level.

If you are using a hosted solution such as Office365, you could select the sandbox option. Click Finish to close the SharePoint Configuration Wizard.

6. In Solution Explorer, under Features, right-click Feature1, click Rename, and then type **Main**.

7. In Solution Explorer, under Main, double-click Main.feature to display the Feature designer, and then on the Main.feature tab, in the Scope drop-down list, select Site.

8. Add a module to the project by right-clicking the project name, click Add, and then click New Item. In the Add New Item window, click Module, type **SPFIOMaster** in the Name text box, and then click Add.

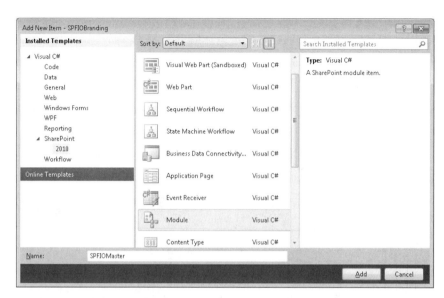

In Solution Explorer, the _catalogs module is added with an Elements.xml file and a Sample.txt file. The Elements.xml file is opened.

9. In Solution Explorer, right click _SPFIOMaster, click Add, and then click Existing Item. Browse to where you exported your custom master page, and then click Add.

10. Under the _SPFIOMaster module, right click Sample.txt, and then click Delete.

11. Modify the Elements.xml so that it deploys the master page into the master page gallery by changing the *Url* attribute on the *Modules* tag. Remove SPFIOMaster/ from the *Url* attribute of the *File* tag so that the feature does not create a subfolder, named SPFIOMaster in the master page gallery, and then add a *Type* attribute with a value of GhostableInLibrary so that the master page is visible in the master page gallery.

12. Add two property tags to the module to set the necessary column values in the master page gallery. The Elements file should match the following code:

```xml
<?xml version="1.0" encoding="utf-8"?>
<Elements xmlns="http://schemas.microsoft.com/sharepoint/">
  <Module Name="SPFIOMaster" Url="_catalogs/masterpage">
    <File Path="SPFIOMaster\SPFIO.master" Url="SPFIO.master"
      IgnoreIfAlreadyExists="True" Type="GhostableInLibrary">
        <Property Name="ContentType" Value="Master Page" />
        <Property Name="UI Version" Value="4" />
    </File>
  </Module>
</Elements>
```

13. Deploy the project. Browse to the site settings page for the site you chose as the target when you created the project, and check that your custom master page is in the master page gallery and the SPFIOMasterPage feature is activated at the Site Collection level.

To add your CSS files and images to your solution, perform the following steps:

1. Repeat the previous sets of steps to add a second module to the project, named **SPFIOCSS**.

2. Remove Sample.txt from the modules, and then in the new Elements.xml, change the *Url* attribute on the *Module* tags to Style Library.

3. Right-click SPFIOCSS, click Add, and then click New Folder. Name the folder *Images*.

4. Right-click, SPFIOCSS, click Add, and then click Existing Item. Remove SPFIOMaster/ from the *Url* attribute of the *File* tag, and then add a *Type* attribute with a value of *GhostableInLibrary*. Repeat this step for each CSS and image file.

5. Move any image files into the Images folder.

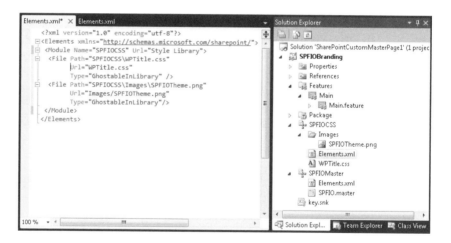

6. Deploy the project. Browse to the Style library for the site you chose as the target when you created the project and check that your files are visible.

You have only added the master page and associated files to one site where Visual Studio has deployed the solution in this exercise. You could use PowerShell to set each site's master page property, *MasterURL*, to the new master page, or you could create an event receivers on the Visual Studio project and write code in that event receiver so that when the feature is deployed and activated, all sites within the Site Collection have the *MasterURL* propery set to the new master page.

Chapter 14

You can find information on deploying branding solutions for SharePoint 2010 sites by using sandboxed solutions and an example of the code to write in the event receiver at *http:// msdn.microsoft.com/en-us/library/gg447066.aspx.*

INSIDE OUT   Using the *AlternateCSSURL* site property

If you only create one custom CSS file and you need to make no other changes to the master page, then do not use the *CSSRegistration* control; instead, modify the *AlternateCssUrl* site property to point to the custom CSS file that you have uploaded into the Style Library.

Summary

SharePoint Designer is more than an HTML editing tool. This chapter demonstrated techniques that you can use when designing SharePoint sites and solutions and explained that the focus of SharePoint Designer is now on how a site or Site Collection owners can use it to manage their sites. For those organizations that implement development, test, and production environments, SharePoint Designer can be used in the pre-production environments and amendments can be transferred to the production environment in a controlled manner. These improvements and SharePoint Designer's emphasis on safe-by-default editing, together with its security settings at the web application and Site Collection level should persuade organizations to no longer say no to using SharePoint Designer.

The next chapter will go into more depth on how to customize the user interface such as the addition of commands on the server ribbon and notification messages. This will provide a more holistic result to the solutions you created in this chapter.

CHAPTER 15

Customizing the User Interface

So far, this book has detailed how to install and manage Microsoft SharePoint 2010 sites as well as how to add unique content to pages. Using previous chapters, specifically Chapter 6, "Creating and Formatting Webpages," Chapter 10, "Using and Creating Workflows," and Chapter 14, "Creating, Managing, and Designing Sites by Using SharePoint Designer 2010," you should now be able to see how you can create and customize SharePoint 2010 solutions to meet your business needs.

However, when you build a SharePoint 2010 solution, it should be more than a collection of lists, libraries, pages, and workflows. Each of these components should be combined to provide users with a holistic solution, in which the components work together and not as discrete entities. Using Web Part connections and customizing the Data Form Web Part (DFWP) Form Action button to initiate workflows are just two examples of how you can achieve this. But SharePoint 2010 provides other components that you can use to improve user experience (UX).

SharePoint 2010 User Experience Improvements

Microsoft did considerable refactoring of the user interface (UI), introducing the Office 2007 client application ribbon to SharePoint Foundation, targeting standard tasks that users need to complete and reduce the use of tables. In addition to Microsoft Internet Explorer, SharePoint Foundation now supports Mozilla Firefox and Apple Safari. Browser support extends even further with SharePoint 2010 Service Pack 1. In addition, when migrating from Windows SharePoint Services 3.0, the UI can be upgraded separately from content database upgrade; thus, you can keep the Windows SharePoint 3.0 UI, yet take advantage of much of the SharePoint Foundation 2010 functionality. Microsoft split Cascading Style Sheet (CSS) files into multiple files that are only downloaded when necessary, thereby reducing the time needed to render pages. Similarly, Microsoft introduced *script on demand*, which allows delaying JavaScript downloads until they're needed.

These improvements all help to improve UX, and your solutions can extend many of these improvements, specifically by displaying links, relevant text, and commands on the following interface elements:

- **Server ribbon**   SharePoint 2010 contains its own version of the Microsoft Office Fluent UI, as shown in Figure 15-1, which was designed to make it easier for users to find and manipulate features within a product. The new ribbon interface is fully extensible by using SharePoint Designer and Microsoft Visual Studio 2010.

Figure 15-1 The Server ribbon and Status bar.

- **Status bar**   Figure 15-1 Demonstrates that this element is similar to the status bar that you see in the client Office application. It is used to display persistent information. It uses four predefined background colors to identify the importance of the text displayed in the status bar. You can post the status of multiple items in the status bar such that, the most important ones are displayed at the top. The format of the status bar message is HTML. The predefined background colors and meaning are described by Microsoft as:

  - Red—Very Important

  - Yellow—Important

  - Green—Success

  - Blue—Information

  The status bar can contain multiple messages, but it will only reflect the color that equates to the highest level of importance or priority.

- **Notification area**   This displays on the right side of the page and shows transitory messages (see Figure 15-2). By default it is only visible for five seconds; however, you can make it a *sticky* parameter.

Figure 15-2 The Notification area.

- **List item menu (LIM)**   Also known as the Edit Control Block (ECB), this is a contextual menu that is associated with all list items or files and is displayed in list views and list view Web Parts, as shown in Figure 15-3. The LIM is available in a list view on the Title column of an item, when Title (linked to an item via the edit menu) is displayed, and in a library view (on the name of the document), and when the Name (linked to the document via the edit menu) is displayed.

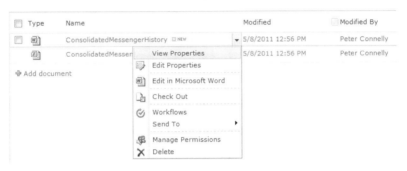

Figure 15-3 The list item menu (LIM).

On an announcements list, the LIM contains controls with which you can complete the following tasks: View Item, Edit Item, Manage Permissions and Delete Items. On a document library, the LIM contains the commands View Properties, Edit Properties, Check Out, Send To, Manage Permissions and Delete. Depending on the document type, the LIM might also contain a command so that you can edit the file. Other commands might appear depending on the configuration of the list or library; for example, if a workflow is attached to the list or library and versioning is enabled, you will see the Workflows and Version History commands.

- **Modal dialogs**   To help users stay within the context of a page, yet display new information, SharePoint Foundation introduces a new Ajax-based dialog framework. The new information is displayed in modal dialogs, without the need to navigate away from the page, thereby reducing the need for the page to refresh. The content of the original page is grayed-out, as shown in Figure 15-4.

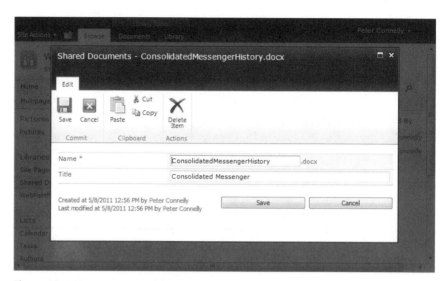

Figure 15-4 You can use modal dialogs to complete tasks such as adding or editing list items, without leaving the page.

It is the modification of these components that is detailed in this chapter.

Server Ribbon Terminology

Microsoft expended considerable effort on the commands that are placed on the server ribbon; that is, the ribbon you see when you open a SharePoint site in the browser. However, this is its first attempt at creating a ribbon for SharePoint and it might not meet the needs of all users, all of the time, for all solutions. When you consider the business needs of your users, the commands and the grouping of those commands plus the tabs displayed on the ribbon, it might be different than what you require. However, before you can create one of your own or modify the existing server ribbon to meet your business needs, you first need to understand the ribbon terminology.

The SharePoint 2010 server ribbon is an extension of the Office ribbon that was first introduced with some of the Office 2007 client applications and later added to all Office 2010 client applications, including Microsoft Access 2010, Microsoft InfoPath 2010, Microsoft SharePoint Designer 2010, and Microsoft Visio 2010. The commands themselves have changed very little, and if you're familiar with Windows SharePoint Services 3.0, you will recognize the same functionality—it's just presented in a very different way.

Ribbon references for SharePoint and Office 2010 applications are available on the Microsoft Office site at *http://office.microsoft.com*, and you can find them by typing the keywords *2010 ribbon*. On the results page, under All Results, click Templates to view the interactive ribbon references. If you have upgraded sites from Windows SharePoint Services 3.0, then you might like to point your users toward the How-To Training course, "Make the switch to the SharePoint 2010 user interface," which is available at *http://office.microsoft.com/en-us/sharepoint-server-help/make-the-switch-to-the-sharepoint-2010-user-interface-RZ101806469.aspx.*

The SharePoint Server ribbon mimics the behavior and functionality that you would expect from the ribbon in an Office client application; however, it is implemented in SharePoint as a number of server controls, grouped into tabs across the top. You navigate through the tabs to complete SharePoint-related tasks. Some tabs are contextual, which means that they appear or hide depending on where you are and the SharePoint object that is selected in the main portion of the webpage.

These contextual tabs can be grouped together into contextual tab sets that are color coded for quick identification (see Figure 15-5). For example, the Editing Tools tab set and its associated contextual tabs (Format Text and Insert) are orange; the Library Tools tab set is blue; Web Part Tools tab set, purple; and the Picture Tools tab set is violet.

Figure 15-5 New ribbon tabs require fewer clicks to carry out a task, and you can take advantage of color coding to assist in the quick identification of commands.

Within each tab, there are groups. Groups contain controls with similar functionality. For example, in the Edit group, you can complete tasks associated with editing a file, such as the Save & Close and the Check Out buttons. The controls in a group are arranged based on a ribbon template that also describes how the controls are to be scaled when the width of the browser window is changed. Therefore, when the width of the browser window is reduced, some controls will continue to show as a large icon (32x32 pixels) with text, others as small icons (16x16 pixels) with text, or just a small icon with no text. Yet others might be displayed as text on a menu item on a drop-down menu, as shown in Figure 15-6.

Figure 15-6 Controls within groups on tabs are reduced when the browser window is reduced in size.

The Server ribbon contains many types of controls. These can include simple controls, such as buttons, toggle buttons, and combo boxes, or they can be more advanced, such as a split button or color picker control (see Figure 15-7). The split button is used as both a button and a menu. Each control is associated with a command that executes when you click the control.

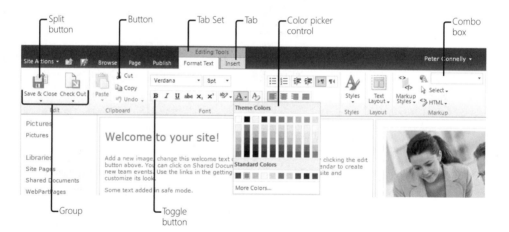

Figure 15-7 The architecture of the Server ribbon: components, tab sets, tabs, groups and controls.

For a list of control types that you can use on the ribbon, go to *http://msdn.microsoft.com/ en-us/library/ee537017(office.14).aspx*.

INSIDE OUT   Ribbon controls that can be modified by using CSS

Some of the ribbon controls can be extended by making modifications to the CSS classes. For example, you can modify the styles that are presented in the split button drop-down menu for the following controls:

- Styles on the Format Text tab in the Editing Tools tab set. This control uses the CSS classes that match the naming standard .ms-rteStyle-SSSS, where SSSS is the style name in the drop-down list.

- Markup Styles on the Format Text tab in the Editing Tools tab set. This control uses the CSS classes that match the naming standard .ms-rteElement-SS, where SS is the style name in the drop-down list.

- Styles on the Design tab in the Table Tools tab set. This control uses the CSS classes that match the naming standard .ms-rteTableXXX–NNN, where XXX is the table section, and NNN is the name to identify the table styling.

- Image Styles on the Design tab in the Picture Tools tab set. This control uses the CSS classes that match the naming standard .ms-rteImage-x, where x is a number.

- Position on the Design tab in the Picture Tools tab set. This control uses the CSS classes that match the naming standard .ms-rtePosition-x, where x is a number.

For more information about each of these controls, read Chapter 6.

Unlike tabs, which can appear or hide, controls on a tab are never hidden; they are either enabled (active) or disabled (inactive). Therefore, all commands on a tab might not be enabled. Commands might be disabled for the following reasons:

- The user might not have permissions to a complete task; for example, on the Page tab, if the user does not have contribute rights, then all the controls that require that level of permissions will be inactive (grayed-out), as shown in Figure 15-8.

Figure 15-8 The ribbon commands on the Library Tools tab set are disabled if you are only a member of the Visitors SharePoint group for a list or library.

- An object is not selected in the main portion of the page; for example, when working in a list, you must first select a list item before the commands become active.

- The computer on which a user is working does not have the appropriate Office 2010 client application installed; for example, the Connect To Outlook command will be active if Microsoft Outlook 2007 or 2010 is installed, and the Sync To SharePoint Workspace will be active if SharePoint Workspace is installed.

- A page or list setting might not be configured or enabled; for example, on the Documents tab, the Version History control in the Manage group will only be active if the list or library has enabled versioning.

- An ActiveX control might need to be installed; for example, when the view displays the content of a library, code in the file OWS.js determines whether Office applications are installed and, if they are, instantiates an ActiveX control—*SharePoint.OpenDocuments.3*. This control allows users to create documents based on the libraries or content types document template. This control also allows users to edit documents by using their associated application.

> **Note**
>
> Groups that contain no controls are not displayed. For example, by default, the Quick Steps group on the Documents or Items tab contains no controls. This is so you can use SharePoint Designer to add controls to this group, which will then become visible.

Each of the ribbon components are related to each other in a hierarchical structure, as illustrated in Figure 15-9. This hierarchical structure is also true for other elements such as the Site Actions menu, which is another type of ribbon, except it is a drop-down menu.

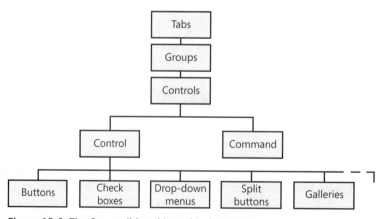

Figure 15-9 The Server ribbon hierarchical structure.

The location of each control is represented by dot-separated notation, as demonstrated here:

Ribbon.[tab].[Group].Controls

For example, ribbon.Documents.New.AddDocument is the split button control in the New group on the Documents tab with which you can upload documents into a document library; Ribbon.List.Actions.ExportToSpreadsheet is the button control in the Actions group on the List tab that you use to export list items to a Microsoft Excel spreadsheet.

INSIDE OUT   Where are the core ribbon components defined?

Most of the core SharePoint Foundation ribbon components are defined as XML in the file CMDUI.XML, which you can find in the TEMPLATE\GLOBAL\XML\ subfolder in the SharePoint root %Program Files%\Common Files\Microsoft Shared\Web Server Extensions\14\. The ribbon XML is then translated into the ribbon by two JavaScript files: GUI.js and SP.Ribbon.js. SharePoint features might also implement changes and additions to the ribbon. You should not modify the CMDUI.XML file directly.

Using the Browser to Add Custom Actions

The creation of new controls to the ribbon together with the commands that should execute when the control is clicked is often referred to as custom actions. Using the browser, custom actions can be added to the ribbon on the Documents or Items tab of List View pages. They are added to the Quick Steps group, as shown in Figure 15-10.

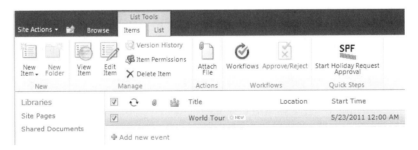

Figure 15-10 Use commands in the Quick Steps group to start a workflow instance on a list item or document.

The ribbon command that allows you to add the custom action to these tabs is displayed on the Library or List tab in the Customize Library or Customize List groups. To make it more confusing, the command you use is called, New Quick Step, as highlighted in Figure 15-11.

Figure 15-11 Use the New Quick Step command to create custom actions that you can access on the Items or Documents tab.

When you use the New Quick Step command to add a control, the browser opens Share-Point Designer; it's SharePoint Designer together with the SharePoint server that actually adds the custom action to the Quick Steps group. That means that you can only use the New Quick Step command if you have SharePoint Designer installed on your computer. In addition, you can only use the New Quick Step command to start workflows.

INSIDE OUT   Custom Actions and SharePoint Designer

If you first open a site in SharePoint Designer and then browse to a list or library, you can create a Custom Action that can do more than start workflows. To change a quick step, you need to use SharePoint Designer. Both of these tasks are described in the next section.

To create a Quick Step, perform the following steps:

1. Using the browser, navigate to the list or library to which you want to add the Quick Step, and then in the List or Library tab.

2. On the List or Library tab, in the Customize Library group, click New Quick Step. In a list, this group is named Customize List.

   Your site opens in SharePoint Designer and the Add A Button dialog box appears.

3. In the Choose What Your Button Will Do section, select the option to either create a new workflow, or work with an existing workflow.

   For a workflow to appear in the Start An Existing Workflow drop-down list, you must have previously added a workflow to your list or library.

4. In the Define The Label And Image For Your Button section, in the Button Label text box, type the name that will appear below your button on the ribbon.

5. In the Button Image text box, enter the address for an image for your button, and then click OK.

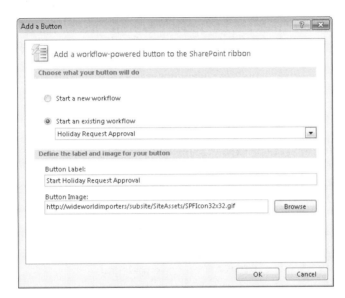

TROUBLESHOOTING

If the New Quick Step command is not displayed in the Customize Library or Customize List groups, then the current view might not allow you to add custom actions to the ribbon or display a Quick Step control. For example, a Calendar view will not allow you to create a new Quick Step or start a workflow instance on a calendar item; however, if you display the calendar list by using the All Events view, you can create a new Quick Step and start a workflow instance.

To modify a quick step, edit the list in SharePoint Designer by clicking Edit List in the Customize List group on the List, Library, or Calendar tab, and then use the details described in the following section.

Working with the Ribbon and LIM in SharePoint Designer

SharePoint Designer can be used to add server controls without the need for a developer or the involvement of the IT department. In SharePoint Designer, the addition of ribbon server controls is known as adding custom actions. These custom actions can only be added to the ribbon of list views, list forms; and to the LIM. List forms are pages that display and edit a single list item, whereas views are pages that display a number of list items. In lists, the list and form pages are stored in the root of the list; for libraries they are stored in the Forms folder, which by default is hidden when a library is displayed in the browser, but is visible in Explorer view and in SharePoint Designer. There are three types of list forms:

- **Display**   This is used to display the properties (also known as the metadata) of a single list item. When a list or library is first created this form is named DispForm.aspx.

- **Edit**   You use this to edit the metadata of a single list item. When a list or library is first created this form is named EditFrom.aspx.

- **New**   This is used to create a new list item. When a list is first created, this form is named NewForm.aspx, whereas in libraries, the name is Upload.aspx.

INSIDE OUT   Custom Actions: two meanings

The term "Custom Actions" is used twice within SharePoint Designer: first to add new actions on the LIM and the server ribbon and second, to describe the ability to extend SharePoint Designer workflows. To read more about creating workflow custom actions, refer to Chapter 10.

You can use SharePoint Designer to add custom actions to:

- Show an existing page that displays a list form.

- Run a workflow.

- Browse to another page, including form pages for other lists and libraries.

For each custom action you can specify:

- **An image**   For a custom action on the LIM, you can only specify a 16x16-pixel image, whereas for a custom action on the server ribbon, you can provide two images: 16x16 or 32x32 pixels. The smaller image is used when the browser window is reduced in size and the amount of space for the custom action is limited. A good place to upload your images for custom actions is in the Site Assets library. If you plan to create a site template from your site, then do not use absolute URL addresses for your images, but make use of the *~sitecollection* or *~site* token to point to libraries within your Site Collection or site. For example, replace *http://wideworldimporters/ subsite/SiteAssets/SPFIcon16x16* with *~site/SiteAssets/SPFIcon16x16.gif*.

- **A sequence order**   This is the order in which the custom action appears on the ribbon or LIM.

- **A Rights Mask**   This specifies which users can see the custom action. When you want the custom action to appear for any user of the list, leave the Rights Mask empty or type **EmptyMask**.

The Rights Mask uses *SPBasePermission* member names, which you can find at *http://msdn.microsoft.com/en-us/library/microsoft.sharepoint.spbasepermissions.aspx*

SharePoint Designer cannot be used to:

- Add tabs or tab sets.

- Add groups.

- Add controls, such as check boxes, drop-down menus, text boxes, fly-out anchors or the color picker.

- Add controls to groups that do not exist.

- Remove the actions/controls that were not added by SharePoint Designer.

Also, you cannot take a copy of your custom actions from one list to another. To duplicate a custom action that you created on a previous list, you need to add a new custom action and then configure it the same as the previous action.

Adding a Custom Action

Custom actions, including Quick Steps, are displayed in the Custom Actions area, which is the last area displayed in the right column of the List Settings page within SharePoint Designer. There are two methods for adding custom actions within SharePoint Designer: use the Custom Action command in the New group on the List Settings tab, or use the New button in the title of the Custom Actions area within the List Settings page.

To add a custom action to the Server ribbon for a list view, form, or LIM, perform the following steps:

1. Using the Navigation pane in SharePoint Designer, click Lists And Libraries, and then in the workspace, click the list or library to which you want to add the custom action.

    The List Settings page opens in the workspace.

2. On the List Settings tab, in the New group, click Custom Action, and then select where you would like the custom action to appear.

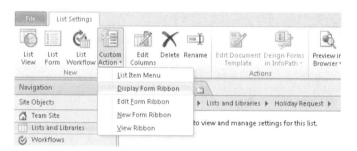

The Create Custom Action dialog box opens.

3. In the Create Custom Action dialog box, in the Name text box, type the name of the action and in the Description text box, type a description, and then select and enter details of the action you wish to create.

Exploring the Create Custom Action Dialog Box

The Create Custom Action dialog box is very similar to the Add A Button dialog box, which opens when you add a Quick Step to the ribbon (described in the previous section). However, the Create Custom Action dialog box allows you to select the type of action to navigate to a form or a URL as well as initiate a workflow, plus when you scroll down you can specify a 16x16-pixel icon; the Rights Mask and sequence number, as shown in Figure 15-12.

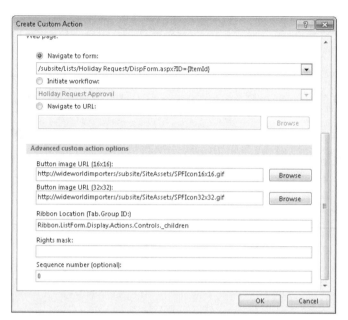

Figure 15-12 Use the Create Custom Action dialog box to add custom actions to the Server ribbon.

The Create Custom Action dialog box for a LIM custom action restricts you to entering a URL for a 16x16 button image only. You also cannot specify the ribbon location of the custom action. By default, the ribbon location for each custom action type is:

- **Display Form ribbon**   Ribbon.ListForm.Display.Actions.Controls._children.

- **Edit Form ribbon**   Ribbon.ListForm.Edit.Actions.Controls._children for lists, and Ribbon.DocLibListForm.Edit.Actions.Controls._children for libraries.

- **New Form ribbon**   Ribbon.ListForm.Edit.Actions.Controls._children for lists, and Ribbon.DocLibListForm.New.Actions.Controls._children for libraries.

- **View ribbon**   Ribbon.ListItem.Actions.Controls._children for lists, and Ribbon.Documents.Manage.Controls._children for libraries.

If you add a custom action as a quick step, then the ribbon location is set as Ribbon.ListItem. QuickSteps.Controls._children. The Controls._children tells SharePoint to add a new button to the Control collection for the group.

You do not have to place your custom action at the default ribbon locations. You can place them in any group that is currently defined for the tab that is active when the form or view is displayed. For example, you can add custom actions to any of the following groups of a library view: New, EditCheckout (which on the Documents tab is labeled Save & Check Out), Manage, Share (which is labeled Share & Track), Copies, Workflow and QuickSteps. Share-Point Designer will display error messages if you misspell or specify a nonexistent ribbon location.

INSIDE OUT   Custom actions on the document library's New forms

When adding a custom action for a New form for document libraries, the custom action is added to the Upload.aspx page. This page does not contain a tab and there-fore does not display a ribbon when you create a new document or upload a docu-ment, but it does contain a tab when you create a new folder; therefore, the default location for this custom action is incorrect. You should change it to one of the groups on the edit tab, for example, Ribbon.DocLibListForm.Edit.Actions.Controls._children. When you want a custom action to appear when a document is uploaded into a library, you need to add the custom action to the Edit form. The valid groups for DocLibListForm.Edit tab are Commit, Clipboard, or Action. You can add your custom action to any of these groups.

By default, all custom actions have a sequence number of 0, which means that your custom actions are the first control in the group. You can place your custom action elsewhere in the group. The out-of-the-box controls in a group have a sequence order that increments by 10, as presented in Table 15-1. Therefore, by changing the sequence order of your custom action to, for instance 15, you can place your custom action between two of the existing controls.

Table 15-1 **Out-of-the-Box Controls and Their Sequence Number for the Default Ribbon Locations for Custom Actions**

Ribbon location	Action control	Sequence order
ListFormDisplay	CheckIn	10
	CheckOut	20
	Alert	30
	ApproveReject	40
	ManageCopies	50
	Workflows	60
	EnterFolder	70
	ClaimReleaseTask	80
	DistributionListsApproval	90
	DeleteItemVersion	100
	RestoreItemVersion	110
ListForm.Edit	DeleteItem	10
	EditSeries	20
	ClaimReleaseTask	30
	AttachFile	40
	DistributionListsApproval	50
DocLibListForm.Edit	DeleteItem	10
	CheckIn	20
	CheckOut	30
	VersionHistory	40
	ExportWebPart	50
	ViewWePartXML	60
	ManagePermissions	70
ListItem	AttachFile	10
	ChangeItemOrder	20
Documents.Manage	ViewProperties	10
	EditProperties	20
	ViewVersions	30
	ManagePermissions	40
	Delete	50

To find the core out-of-the-box groups, their relevant ribbon location URL, together with the defined controls for each group and sequence numbers, review the contents of the XML file CMDUI.XML, which you can find in the TEMPLATE\GLOBAL\XML\ subfolder in the SharePoint root %Program Files%\Common Files\Microsoft Shared\Web Server Extensions\14\.

Extending the LIM

Using SharePoint Designer, you can extend the LIM by adding custom actions and by placing the LIM on a column other than the Title column of a list.

Adding Custom Actions to the LIM

You can add a custom action to the LIM by using the method described previously; in addition, there is an alternative method of adding a custom action to the LIM by using the New
button in the Custom Action. To do so, perform the following steps:

1. Using the Navigation pane in SharePoint Designer, click Lists And Libraries, and then
   in the workspace, click the list or library to which you want to add the custom action.

   The List Settings page opens in the workspace.

2. Click New in the title of the Custom Actions area. (You might need to scroll down to
   see this area.)

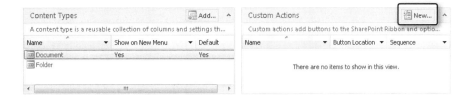

Showing the LIM on a Column in a List

Using the browser, you can configure a view to display the LIM on the Title column of a
list. Views are pages that contain the XSLT List View (XLV) Web Part; therefore, you can also
configure whether to display the LIM on other pages that contain the XLV Web Part. Using
SharePoint Designer, you can place the LIM on another column in a list. This could prove
very useful if you create a view for which you do not want to display the Title column for
lists or the Name column for documents. However, if you do change the location of the
LIM from the default location, you need to inform the users of the page, for example, on a
Web Part page, by placing a Content Editor Web Part above the XLV Web Part and entering
appropriate text, or in the case of a wiki page, by adding appropriate static text above the
XLV Web Part.

CAUTION

As of the writing of this chapter, when you create the LIM on another column, by using SharePoint Designer, not all links continue to work. You must test your solution to ensure that the links work as required.

Use the following instructions to show the LIM on a column of a list or library:

1. Browse to the page that contains the XLV Web Part, for example, AllItems.aspx, and then place the page in Edit mode.

2. In a list item row, click the cell in the column where you want the LIM to appear.

3. Click the On Object User Interface (OOUI) icon (a chevron icon) that appears, to display the Common xsl:value-of dialog.

4. On the Common xsl:value-of dialog, select Show List Item Menu, and then save the page.

5. Preview the page in the browser to verify that the LIM is displayed for a list item on the column that you selected, and that all the links on the LIM work as expected.

Modifying a Custom Action or Quick Step

To modify a custom action, including Quick Steps, perform the following steps:

1. Browse to the List Settings page for the list that contains the custom action that you want to modify.

2. Scroll down to the Custom Actions area and either double-click the icon to the left of the custom action or click the name of the custom action, which is a hyperlink.

   The Create Custom Action dialog box opens.

Deleting a Custom Action or Quick Step

To delete a custom action or Quick Step, perform the following steps:

1. Browse to the List Settings page for the list that contains the custom action that you want to modify.

2. Scroll down to the Custom Actions area, and then click the icon to the left of the custom action.

   This activates the Custom Actions tab. In the Edit group, click Delete.

Extending the Ribbon by Using Visual Studio

You can use Visual Studio to extend the ribbon further than can be achieved with the browser or SharePoint Designer. For example, you can extend the ribbon on pages other than the view and form pages. You can create new tab sets, tabs, groups, and add other types of buttons, such as check boxes, drop-down menus or text boxes. Or, you can remove existing controls. Your extensions with Visual Studio can target specific types of pages or all pages and is not limited to just the ribbon but to other elements, such as the Site Action menu.

So far in this chapter, the contents of the XML file CMDUI.XML have been used to obtain information on how the core Server ribbon has been defined. Like other XML files that Microsoft provides and SharePoint Foundation uses for configuration, you should not modify the CMDUI.XML file to extend the ribbon with you own tab sets, tabs, groups, and controls.

The development process for other XML files allows you to create your own XML file with similar content to the Microsoft-provided files that SharePoint uses, as long as the files follow a specific naming convention. For example:

● The out-of-the-box site definitions that are shown on the Create page are defined in the WEBTEMP.XML file on the server in the TEMPLATE\[*LCID*]\XML subfolder of the SharePoint root, where [*LCID*] represents the locale of the SharePoint installation and any language packs that are installed. For site definitions that you create to appear on the Create page, you should not modify WEBTEMP.XML, but create your own XML file, using a naming convention, WEBTEMP*.XML, where * can be any number of characters such as WEBTEMP_SPFIO.XML or WebTempWideworldimpoorters.xml. The name of the file is case-insensitive.

- When you create a workflow by using SharePoint Designer, the out-of-the-box, SharePoint Designer conditions and actions that you can use are based on information found on the server in the WSS.ACTIONS XML file stored in the TEMPLATE\[LCID]\ Workflow subfolder. Using Visual Studio, you can publish your own custom actions; however, users of SharePoint Designer will not have access to them until the relevant XML is placed in an ACTIONS file. Again, you should not modify the Microsoft-provided file, but create your own. Any file found in the workflow folder with an ACTIONS extension will be pulled down to the computer running SharePoint Designer, when the user tries to create a workflow.

However, the way to develop extensions to the ribbon is not to create new XML files in a SharePoint root subfolder or modify CMDUI.XML; instead, you should use Visual Studio to develop a package that contains a Feature, in which an XML file is an element, and the ribbon components are declared in the XML file.

Understanding the Custom Actions Ribbon Schema

The ribbon XML element file consists of an outer <Elements> tag, which contains one or more <CustomAction> tags that can be used to define a ribbon control, a link on a Site Settings page, a script block, or a link to a file that contains a script to be executed. When defining a ribbon control, the <CustomAction> tag contains a <UrlAction> tag or a <CommandUIExtension> tag, which also contains a number of other tags.

The <CustomAction> Tag

Each elements file can contain one or more <CustomAction> tag; therefore, if your solution requires a set of controls on a list view, and another set of controls on the Site Action menu, and yet another set of controls on the LIM, these can all be included in one elements file.

A <CustomAction> tag can define where one or more ribbon controls should be located. This is a high-level location such as a list or one of the standard menus. If the location is the ribbon and not a menu, then the specific information as to which tab and group each ribbon control is to be placed in is defined in the <CommandUIDefinition> tag, which is a child tag of the <CommandUIDefinitions> tag.

The code that follows defines the content of an element file that contains one <CustomAction> tag, which can contain ribbon controls that only appear on pages where the list view Web Part is used to display the contents of announcement lists:

```
<?xml version="1.0" encoding="utf-8"?>
<Elements xmlns="http://schemas.microsoft.com/sharepoint/">
   <CustomAction Id="SPFIO.Ribbon.AnnList"
      Location="CommandUI.Ribbon">
      RegistrationType="List"
      RegistrationId="104"
      Title="SPFIO Announcement Ribbon Button">
         <CommandUIExtension> …. <CommandUIExtension>
   </CustomAction>
</Elements>
```

The <CustomAction> tag consists of a number of attributes, such as the following:

- **Location**   When the <CustomAction> defines ribbon controls, it must contain a <CommandUIExtension> tag, and the *Location* attribute must start with CommandUI. Ribbon. When the location is CommandUI.Ribbon and not one of its descendants and the RegistrationType equals *List*, then the pages on which the ribbon controls will be placed are list views, and the edit, new, and display forms of a list or library. If you only want the commands to effect views of a list or library, the location attribute should be set to CommandUI.Ribbon.ListView. If the *RegistrationType* attribute is not included, then all page types could be targeted.

- **Id**   This is used to specify a unique identifier for the custom action. It can also be used to document the purpose of the custom action.

- **RegistrationType**   This is an option attribute that is used to define a per-item action.

- **RegistrationID**   This is an option attribute that can be used to target a specific *RegistrationType*; for example, if the *RegistrationType* equals *List*, then the *Id* attribute can be used to target a specific list or library type.

- **Text**   This is a required attribute that defines the end-user description for the custom action.

To learn more about the attributes for the <CustomAction> tag, go to *http://msdn.microsoft. com/en-us/library/ms460194.* **For more information about the list and library Id numbers, go to** *http://msdn.microsoft.com/en-us/library/microsoft.sharepoint.splisttemplatetype.aspx.*

The code that follows is an example of a <CustomAction> tag that adds a link to the Site Actions menu. In this example, the link is to the StorMan.aspx page that was introduced with SharePoint 2010 Service Pack 1. This page displays information with which a user can understand the quota, if one is applied, and make decisions regarding the removal of content to reduce the size of their sites:

```
<CustomAction Id="SPFIO.SiteActionsMenu"
    Location="Microsoft.SharePoint.StandardMenu"
    GroupId="SiteActions"
    ImageUrl="/_layouts/images/Settings.gif"
    Sequence="500"
    Title="SPFIO Navigate to Storage Management page">
    <UrlAction Url="/_layouts/StorMan.aspx" />
</CustomAction>
```

In the next example, a <CustomAction> tag adds a custom action to the LIM, similar to the one added previously in this chapter by using SharePoint Designer. Note that the ribbon schema uses the acronym, ECB, whereas SharePoint Designer refers to it as the LIM:

```
<CustomAction Id="SPFIO.ECB.LIM"
    Location="EditControlBlock"
    RegistrationType="List"
    RegistrationId="104"
    Rights="ManageLists"
    ImageUrl="~site/SiteAssets/SPFIO16x16.gif"
    Sequence="205"
    Title="SPFIO Navigate to site owners edit form for this item">
    <UrlAction Url="~site/Lists/Tasks/SOEditForm={ItemID}" />
</CustomAction>
```

In both the preceding examples, the <UrlAction> tag is used to identify the page to be displayed when the control is clicked.

The previous example also uses the *Rights* attribute, which specifies the set of rights that a user must have for the link to be visible. This is a common requirement for when you create a list form that allows contributors to modify a subset of the values for a list item, and another form that allows list and site owners to modify other values for a list item. Therefore, in this example, this link will only be available to users who have the Manage Lists right.

The *Rights* attribute uses the values of the *SPBasePermissions* enumeration, the details of which you can find at *http://msdn.microsoft.com/en-us/library/microsoft.sharepoint.spbase permissions.aspx.*

The <CommandUIExtension> Tag

When defining a ribbon control, the <CustomAction> tag has a location starting with CommandUI.Ribbon, and contains a <CommandUIExtension> tag that contains <CommandUIDefinitions> and <CommandUIHandlers> tags. The first of these tags defines the visual presentation of one or more controls, whereas the second tag defines the actions to be performed by the ribbon controls. The *Command* attribute of the control tag must match with one of the *Command* attributes of the <CommandUIHandler> tags.

The <CommandUIDefinitions> Tag

The <CommandUIDefinitions> tag can contain one or more <CommandUIDefinition> tags. Each <CommandUIDefinition> tag defines one ribbon control. Some of values of the attributes of the <CommandUIDefinition> tag are similar to those used to define a custom action in SharePoint Designer. For example, the *Location* attribute specifies the tab and group of the control in dot-separated notation, as used in the Ribbon Location text box of the Create A Custom Action dialog box. The value of the *Id* attribute can be anything; however, the convention is to mimic the dot-separated notation of the *Location* attribute.

In the code that follows, a new button control is defined on the display form of a list. Referring to Table 15-1, using a sequence number of 25 instructs SharePoint to place the control between the Check Out and Alert Me controls:

```
<CommandUIDefinition Location="Ribbon.ListForm.Display.Controls._children">
  <Button Id="Ribbon.List.Display.SPFIONewControl"
      Sequence="25"
      Command="SPFIONewCommand"
      Description="SPFIO New Control"
      LabelText="New SPFIO Control"
      Image32by32="~sitecollection/SiteAssets/SPFIO32x32.gif"
      Image16by16="~sitecollection/SiteAssets/SPFIO16x16.gif"
      TemplateAlias="o1"
      ToolTipTitle="SPFIO New Control Tool Tip"
      ToolTipDescription="SPFIO Tool Tip Description"
      ToolTipShortcutKey="Ctr-T,E"
      ToolTipImage32by32="~sitecollection/SiteAssets/SPFIO32x32.gif"
      ToolTipHelpKeyWord="SPFIO"
  />
</CommandUIDefinition>
```

The *TemplateAlias* attribute instructs SharePoint where in the group template to place the image for this control. A number of templates are predefined in the CMDUI.XML file. Microsoft recommends that you create your own, especially when creating your own tabs, because the templates from the CMDUI.XML file might not be loaded when your tab is displayed. To define a new template, use the <CommandUIDefinition> tag with a location of Ribbon.Templates._children and a child tag of <GroupTemplate>.

To replace a ribbon control, use the <CommandUIDefinition> tag, and on the *Location* attribute, specify the name of the control. In the code example that follows, the *New Folder* control in the New group on the Documents tab is replaced with a different icon and calls the *SPFIOExScriptBlock* command defined in the <CommandUIHandler> tag. For SharePoint to overwrite the existing *New Folder* control, the sequence number must be lower than the out-of-the-box sequence number for that control. You can find this number by referring to the CMDUI.XML file. If you and other developers have created many custom actions for the same control, then the lowest sequence number will win:

```
<CommandUIDefinition Location="Ribbon.Documents.New.NewFolder">
    <Button Id="Ribbon.Documents.New.NewFolder.SPFIOFolderButton"
        Alt="SPF New Folder control"
        Sequence="5"
        Command="SPFIOExScriptBlock"
        LabelText="SPFIO New Folder"
        Image32by32="~site/SiteAssets/SPFIO32x32.gif"
        TemplateAlias="o1" />
</CommandUIDefinition>
```

The following code is an example of a custom action that adds a group and a button to the
ribbon of Web Part pages:

```
<CustomAction Id="SPFIO.WebPage" Location="CommandUI.Ribbon">
    <CommandUIExtension>
        <CommandUIDefinitions>
            <CommandUIDefinition Location="Ribbon.WebPartPage.Groups._children">
                <Group Id="Ribbon.WebPartPage.SPFUI.WebPart"
                    Sequence="20"   Description="SPFIO Ribbon group"
                    Title="SEF Group" Template="Ribbon.Templates.Flexible2">
                    <Controls Id="Ribbon.WebPartPage.SPFIO.WebPart.Controls">
                        <Button Id="Ribbon.WebPartPage.SPFIO.WebPart.Command"
                            Command= "SPFIOExScriptBlock"
                            Description="SEF Custom action"
                            Image16by16="~sitecollection/SiteAssets/SPFIO16x16.gif"
                            Image32by32="~sitecollection/SiteAssets/SPFIO32x32.gif"
                            LabelText="SEF Action"
                            TemplateAlias="o2"
                            Sequence="35" />
                    </Controls>
                </Group>
            </CommandUIDefinition>
        </CommandUIDefinitions>
        <CommandUIHandlers>
            <!-see next section ->
        </CommandUIHandlers>
    </CommandUIExtension>
</CustomAction>
```

When this control is clicked, the command that is defined in the <CommandUIHandler>
tag, which has a command named *SPFIONewCommand*, is executed.

To learn more about customizing the ribbon, read Chris O'Brien's series on Ribbon Customization, which is available at *www.sharepointnutsandbolts.com/2010/01/customizing-ribbon-
part-1-creating-tabs.html*. You can also read Wictor Wilen's series on Creating a SharePoint
2010 Ribbon extension at *www.wictorwilen.se/Post/Creating-a-SharePoint-2010-Ribbon-
extension-part-1.aspx*.

INSIDE OUT   Using the out-of-the-box images with your custom actions

For consistency, when your control executes an action, similar to an existing control, you might want to use the same icon to represent your new custom action. Many of these images are in the SharePoint root folder in the TEMPLATE\IMAGES subfolder. To quickly find the image file that's used, in Microsoft Internet Explorer (IE), open the page on which the icon is displayed, and then press F12 to open the IE developer tools. On the HTML tab, click the pointer, and then on the page, select the relevant image.

Not all out-of-the-box ribbon images are stored in their own file, and therefore, you might see code similar to the following:

```
<img style="left: -80px; top: -176px; " alt=""
  src="/_layouts/1033/format16x16.png" unselectable="on" />
```

SharePoint 2010 uses special image files—formatmap32x32.png and format16x16.png—which contain a collection of images, as shown in Figure 15-13. These files are stored in the SharePoint root, in the subfolder TEMPLATE\LAYOUTS\[LCID]\IMAGES.

Figure 15-13 Use images from the format32x32.png or format16x16.png for your controls.

You can refer to images from these two files in your action controls by using the *Image32by32Top* and *Image32by32Left* attributes when you use the *Image32by32* attribute or the equivalent attributes for a 16×16-pixel image.

The top and left attributes identify the upper-left corner of an image in the image map and are used to set the CSS top and left attributes for the inline style of an HTML <IMG> tag. To calculate the upper-left corner of an image, open the image in Microsoft Paint, display the status bar, and then place the cursor on the upper-left corner of the desired image. In the format32x32.png file, the upper-left coordinate is a multiple of 32, and in the format16x16.png file, the upper-left coordinate is a multiple of 16. This number represents the offset from the upper-left corner of the image map and is a negative number.

For example, the image used for the New Quick Step command can be found in the second column and eleventh row of the format32x32.png file, and whose coordinates would be −32, −320. In a custom action this image would be referred as:

```
Image32by32="_layouts/1033/images/formatmap32x32.png"
        Image32by32Top="-32" Image32by32Left="-320"
```

The <CommandUIHandlers> Tag

The <CommandUIHandlers> tag can contain one or more <CommandUIHandler> tags. The value of the *Command* attribute of the <CommandUIHandler> tag has the same name as the value of the *Command* attribute in the <CommandUIDefinition> tag.

Each <CommandUIHandler> tag defines one command, written by using ECMAScript, which is the scripting language (such as JavaScript and Jscript) that is commonly used for client-side scripting; that is, code that is parsed and executed by the browser. There are two types of commands that you can use:

- **UI handlers**   These are a mixture of declarative markup and ECMAScript. All of the code for this type of command is contained in the same file as the definition for the control that calls them. This type of command, although easy to write, can be hard to troubleshoot and debug.

- **Page components**   These are ECMAScript objects that are defined in an external file, which can be targeted by the *ScriptSrc* attribute of a <CustomAction> tag or added to the script from managed code. This type of command might be harder to code; however, you can utilize Visual Studio for troubleshooting and debugging, and because the code is independent of the features file, page components can be modified separately and used by a number of independent features.

Both types of commands are targeted by using the <CommandUIHandler> tag. The code that follows contains three examples of UI handlers. The first contains the JavaScript within the <CommandUIHandler> tag, the second calls a script block defined in a <CustomAction> tag, and the third displays a page when a control is clicked:

```
<CommandUIHandler Command="SPFIONewCommand"
    CommandAction="javascript:alert('SPFIO New Display Form Control Clicked!');"
/>

<CommandUIHandler Command="SPFIOExScriptBlock"
    CommandAction="javascript:SPFIOCode();"
/>

<CommandUIHandler Command="SPFIONavSiteSettings"
    CommandAction="/_layouts/settings.aspx"
/>
```

The <CustomAction> section that defines the script block inline would look similar to the following code:

```
<CustomAction Id="Ribbon.ListForm.Display.NewButton.Script"
    Location="ScriptLink"
    ScriptBlock="
       function SPFIOCode()
       {
          alert('SPFIO Ribbon Script Block');
       }"
/>
```

Use the *ScriptBlock* method to quickly insert short amounts of code, which will be merged into the page with other JavaScript that is included by using the <link> tag. If your code is large or needs to be referenced by a number of custom action solutions, you should place your JavaScript code in one file, and then use a custom action to reference the file, as shown in the following code:

```
<CustomAction Id="Ribbon.ListForm.Display.Script"
    Location="ScriptLink"
    Scrptsrc="~site/SiteAssets/SPFIO_RibbonControls.js" />
```

An MSDN white paper, "Customizing and Extending the SharePoint 2010 Server Ribbon," by Andrew Connell, contains two complete examples that use both UI handlers and page components. You can view this white paper at *http://msdn.microsoft.com/en-us/library/gg552606. aspx*, together with the source code.

Creating a Ribbon Feature File by Using Visual Studio 2010

Visual Studio 2010 provides out-of-the-box templates with which developers can quickly create an application page in Visual Studio. However, there is no template that is specific to custom actions. Therefore, you need to use an Empty SharePoint project template.

The following steps outline how to remove the Edit HTML Source control in the Markup group on the Format Text tab in the Editing Tools tab set. This tab set appears when you have a wiki page open in Edit mode or when you are editing the contents of a Content Editor Web Part:

For more information about using Visual Studio to create SharePoint Foundation solutions, and how set up your development environment, see Chapter 16," Developing SharePoint Solutions by Using Visual Studio 2010."

1. Open Visual Studio with administrative privileges. On the Start Page tab, click New, Project, or on the toolbar, click File | New, and then click Project to open the New Project dialog box.

2. Under Installed Templates, under the appropriate language (such as Visual C#), expand SharePoint, if not already expanded, and then click 2010.

3. In the middle pane, select Empty SharePoint Project.

4. In the Name text box, type **SPFIO_RibbonActions** for the Project Name, and then click OK.

    The SharePoint Customization Wizard opens.

5. Specify the site on which you want to deploy and test the extension to your ribbon.

    You can select either to deploy the solution as a sandboxed solution or as a farm solution. Click Finish to close the SharePoint Configuration Wizard.

6. In Solution Explorer, right-click the SPFIO.RibbonActions project node. Click Add a new item, and then select Empty Element and type a name for the elements file, such as, **SPFIO_RibbonElementsFile**.

    The Elements.xml file opens. Note in Solution Explorer that Feature1 was added under the Features node.

7. Type the code that follows; place it between the opening and closing <Elements> tags.

Notice that Visual Studio understands the ribbon schema and provides IntelliSense to your coding experience:

```
<CustomAction Id="SPFIO_RemoveControl" Location="CommandUI.Ribbon" >
    <CommandUIExtension>
        <CommandUIDefinitions>
          <CommandUIDefinition
          Location="Ribbon.EditingTools.CPEditTab.Markup.Html.Menu.Html.EditSource"
          />
        </CommandUIDefinitions>
    </CommandUIExtension>
</CustomAction>
```

8. Press F5 to build and deploy your project. In the browser, navigate to a Team Site's wiki page, and then place the page in Edit mode.

On the Format Text tab, the HTML control in the Manage group should only have one drop-down menu option: Convert To HTML.

Microsoft has provided a Visual Studio add-in that can be used as a learning tool toward customizing the ribbon. You can find this add-in at *http://code.msdn.microsoft.com/vsix-forsp*. This site also contains a hands-on lab and a walkthrough video. You can read A blog post by Paul Stubbs that introduces the add-in at *http://blogs.msdn.com/b/pstubbs/archive/2010/04/26/sharepoint-2010-extensibility-projects-server-ribbon.aspx*.

The ribbon is aggressively cached; therefore, while you are developing your custom actions, to test your modifications you will need to clear your browser cache. If you are using the IE developer tools, you can use the keystroke Ctrl+R. To avoid the need to repeatedly purge your cache, a better option might be to use *InPrivate Browsing*, which does not use caching.

The Internet contains many examples if you wish to learn more about extending the ribbon. Here are just some of the websites that you might find useful:

- User Interface Enhancements: Channel 9 Videos: *http://channel9.msdn.com/learn/courses/SharePoint2010Developer/UiEnhancements/*

- Microsoft SharePoint Team Blog: Enabling a Button on the Ribbon Based on Selection: *http://sharepoint.microsoft.com/blog/Pages/BlogPost.aspx?pID=436*

- How to Create a Web Part with a Contextual Tab: *http://blogs.msdn.com/b/ sharepointdeveloperdocs/archive/2010/01/28/how-to-create-a-web-part- with-a-contextual-tab.aspx*

- How to Add a Tab to the Ribbon in SharePoint Foundation: *http://blogs.msdn. com/b/sharepointdeveloperdocs/archive/2009/12/07/sharepointfoundationhow- toaddtabtoribbon.aspx*

- SharePoint 2010 Ribbon Customization series: *http://makarandrkulkarni.blogspot. com/2010/01/architecture-of-sharepoint-2010-ribbon.html*

- Code to Hide the Ribbon and Site Actions Menu for Anonymous Users: *www.elumenotion.com/Blog/Lists/Posts/Post.aspx?ID=106*

Using Modal Dialogs

A problem with Windows SharePoint Services 3.0 was that every time a user clicked some-thing, they were redirected to another page. Many users found this confusing; especially when they didn't know what to do on the new page—should they click the browser's back button or the Cancel button on the new page?

Microsoft has rewritten the interface to display information in a modal window by using Ajax so that the user never really leaves the page to complete most tasks. This reduces the number of page refreshes and round trips to the server. Now, much of the information that was displayed on page redirects and dialog boxes is displayed in the modal window, called modal dialogs. These are created by using the modal dialog framework that creates an overlay with a grayed background and provides the code that is needed for the different browsers that SharePoint supports.

You can find information about the browsers that SharePoint 2010 supports in Chapter 2, "Administration for Business Users," and Chapter 4, "Creating Sites and Workspaces by Using the Browser."

The modal dialog is really a <DIV> tag that is embedded in the SharePoint page, and the technology involved in creating modal dialog is part of the SharePoint 2010 Client Object Model (COM).

INSIDE OUT   The three SharePoint 2010 COMs

You can use the SharePoint 2010 COM to create client applications for SharePoint. There are three COMs, JavaScript, Silverlight and ASP.NET CLR. If you use JavaScript and JQuery, use the JavaScript object model; for Silverlight, use the Silverlight object model; and if you are creating PowerShell, command prompt, and Windows Presentation Foundation (WPF) applications, use the ASP.NET CLR object model. More information about COM is available in Part Three: Client Models of the Patterns and Practices of "Developing Applications for SharePoint 2010," which you can find at *http://msdn. microsoft.com/en-us/library/ff770300.aspx*. You can also obtain this in print and eBook from Microsoft Press at *http://oreilly.com/catalog/9780735656086*.

You can pass parameters to the modal dialogs as you would to a real browser window, and as far as users are concerned, it can be thought of as another page. You can create modal windows by using Visual Studio's design window. You can also create them dynamically from your own code by using JavaScript and HTML tags.

The namespace in the object model that is used to create modal dialogs is *SP.UI.ModalDialog*, which takes one parameter, an options dialog object. There are many ways of using the modal dialog, some of which are described next.

Note

You can prevent the use of modal dialogs for forms on a list-by-list or library-by-library basis. On the List Settings page, under General Settings, click Advanced Settings. On the Advanced Settings page, scroll to the bottom of the page, and then in the Dialogs section, select No. The New, Edit, and Display forms will no longer be displayed in a dialog. The user will be redirected to the full page view for these forms.

Chapter 15

Displaying the Content Within a <DIV> Tag as a Modal Dialog

The modal dialog can be defined inline by creating a <DIV> tag within your webpage and then placing the content that you want to see in the modal dialog within the <DIV> tags. Configure the <DIV> tag so that when the page is displayed the contents within the <DIV> tag are not displayed, similar to the following code:

```
<div id="SPFIO_div" style="display:none; padding:5px">
   Modal dialog content

   Click button to close dialog
   <input type="button" value="Close" onclick="closeSPFIO_Dialog()" />
</div>
```

Next, create two JavaScript functions, one to display the contents within the <DIV> tags in a modal dialog, and then a function to close the model dialog:

```
<script language="ecmascript" type="text\ecmascript" >
   var vSPFIO_dialog;
   function showSPFIO_Dialog(){
      var vSPFIO_div = document.getElementById("SPFIO_div");
      SPFIO_div.style.display = "block";
      var vOptions = { html:vSPFIO_div, width: 150, height: 150};
      vSPFIO_dialog = SP.UI.ModalDialog.showModalDialog(vOptions);
   }
   function closeSPFIO_Dialog() {
      SPFIO_dialog.close();
   }
</script>
```

To call the JavaScript *showSPFIO_dialog* function, place code elsewhere on the page or as a command on the ribbon. You can also dynamically create the HTML that you want to display in the modal dialog by assigning it to the *html* attribute in the options parameter, for example:

```
html: '<html><body>dynamic content</body></html>'
```

Displaying an Image File or Webpage as a Model Dialog

You can display an image or a webpage by replacing the code within the *showSPFIO_Dialog* function with the following code:

```
var vOptions = {
   url: 'http://wideworldimporters/SitePages/NewPage.aspx',
   title: 'SPFIO New Page',
   allowMaximize: true,
   showClose: true,
   width:200,
   height:200
};
vSPFIO_dialog = SP.UI.ModalDialog.showModalDialog(vOptions);
```

The dialog options object has a number of properties such as the *allowMaximize* property that specifies whether to display the Maximize icon in the upper-right corner. The *showClose* property specifies whether to display the close icon in the upper-right corner, and if you want the dialog to fill all the space in the window, set the *showMaximized* property to *true*. If you do not specify the width and or height property, the dialog is automatically sized to fit the browser window.

Returning Values to the Calling Page

On the dialog options object you can register a function, known as a callback function, that is called when the modal dialog is closed. Thereby, you can perform any actions that are needed, including retrieving the result of the dialog. You register the callback function by using the *dialogReturnValueCallback* options property, as shown in the following code:

```
<script language="ecmascript" type="text\ecmascript" >
   function showSPFIO_Dialog() {
      var vOptions = SP.UI.$create_DialogOptions();
      vOptions.url = "http://wideworldimporters/SitePages/NewPage.aspx";
      vOptions.width = 150;
      vOptions.height = 400;
      vOptions.dialogReturnValueCallback =
         Function.createDelegate(null, SPFIO_callback);
      SP.UI.ModalDialog.showModalDialog(vOptions);
   }
   function SPFIO_callback(result, target) {
      if(result === SP.UI.DialogResult.OK)
      {
         alert("OK clicked");
      }
   }
}
</script>
```

The callback function consists of two parameters, *result* and *target*. The *result* parameter is a number that contains one of the *SP.UI.DialogResult* enumerations. You use the *target* parameter to pass values from the page displayed in the modal dialog and the callback function. For example, the NewPage.aspx could contain a text box, and when the user clicks the OK button on the NewPage.aspx, then the following code would be called, returning the result and target parameters:

```
SP.UI.ModalDialog.commonModalDialogClose(SP.UI.DialogResult.OK, textBoxValue);
```

MSDN offers a How-To topic called "How to: Display a Page as a Modal Dialog box" which you can read at *http://msdn.microsoft.com/en-us/library/ff798390.aspx*.

Chapter 15

Using the Status Bar

To display, change, append a message on the Status Bar, and close the Status Bar, use the JavaScript SharePoint COM namespace *SP.UI.Status*. To display and then remove the Status Bar, use JavaScript functions similar to the following code:

```
<script language="ecmascript" type="text\ecmascript">
    var statusId = '';
    function displayStatusBar() {
        statusId = SP.UI.Status.addStatus("SPFIO Status Bar Title",
         "SPFIO message text", true)
        SP.UI.Status.setStatusPriColor(statusId, 'red');
    }
    function removeStatusBar() {
        SP.UI.Status.removeStatus(statusId);
        statusId = '';
    }
</script>
```

The *addStatus* method takes three parameters, the status message title, the content of the status message, and whether the status message appears at the beginning of the list. The content of the Status Bar is in HTML message format and therefore can be more than just text; for example, it can consist of links and visual elements. The *addStatus* method returns the ID of the status message that can then be used by other status bar methods. The other status bar methods are:

- *SP.UI.Status.updateStatus(statusId,strHtml)*

- *SP.UI.Status.appendStatus(statusId, strTitle, strHtml)*

- *SP.UI.Status.removeStatus (statusId)*

- *SP.UI.Status.removeAllStatus(hide)*—can be used to remove status messages produced by other applications. It is not best practice to use this method.

INSIDE OUT   Where can you find the source code for the Microsoft-provided JavaScript COM?

The signatures for all the versions of the JavaScript COM application programming interfaces (APIs) can be found in the SP*.debug.js files in the SharePoint root in the Template\LAYOUTS subfolder. These are the equivalent of the minified SP*.js files. Therefore, you can look at the source code for all the client-side code provided by Microsoft.

Managing Notifications

To display a notification message, use the JavaScript SharePoint COM namespace *SP.UI.Notify*. Similar to the Status Bar, the content of the notify message is in HTML format; however, there is no method to modify the background color. By default, the notify message is visible for five seconds, but you can configure it to permanently display. Place the following code in the HTML Form or Content Editor Web Part on a Web Part or wiki page to display the Add Notification and Remove Notification buttons:

```
<script language="ecmascript" type="text\ecmascript">
   var notifyId = '';
   function displayNotification() {
      notifyId = SP.UI.Notify.addNotification(
       "<span style=\'background-color: yellow\'>SPFIO notify message</span>",
       true);
   }
   function removeNotification() {
      SP.UI.Notify.removeNotification(notifyId);
      notifiyId = '';
   }
</script>

<p>Click to display Notification message</p>
<p><input id=bAddNotify onclick="displayNotification()"
   type="button" value="Add Notification" /></p>
<p>Click to remove Notification message</p>
<p><input id=bRemoveNotify onclick="removeNotification()"
   type="button" value="Remove Notification" /></p>
```

Summary

SharePoint 2010 is a platform, and therefore, the components that are available out of the box with SharePoint Foundation 2010 are only a subset of the components that can be developed. You can almost guarantee that for anything you see within SharePoint Foundation, there is a SharePoint 2010 API, web service, data structure, and framework that you can use to mix and match components into your own solution.

With SharePoint 2010, Microsoft has tried to present users with the tools to complete a task as quickly as they can within the context of the page, with a simple interface and reusable controls.

In this chapter, you explored extending the UI by using the browser, SharePoint Designer, and Visual Studio. Use SharePoint Designer for unique business solutions, prototypes, and custom actions where you want to extend the server ribbon on views, forms, and list item menus (also known as edit control blocks) for a specific list or library. Use Visual Studio for everything else.

Chapter 15

CHAPTER 16

Developing SharePoint Solutions by Using Visual Studio 2010

W ITH the flexibility of powerful prewritten Web Parts, Web Part pages, browser-based editing, Microsoft SharePoint Designer–based editing, and connectivity to Microsoft Office applications, it's amazing how much you can do in SharePoint Foundation 2010 without programming.

Inevitably, however, no tool or set of tools can do everything an organization might want to accomplish right out of the box. For those situations in which a custom set of business or functional requirements must be met, that's the time to think about writing your own code. In a SharePoint environment, writing your own code usually means writing solutions such as Web Parts, custom workflows, and master pages. These items integrate smoothly with the rest of your SharePoint site, taking advantage of its existing appearance, organization, security, and data management. What's more, these solutions are reusable. You can write them once and use them for as many pages as you would like or even setup your organization's own *codeplex*-type site to share the solutions for SharePoint that you and others have developed.

The purpose of this chapter is to introduce you to the development of SharePoint artifacts and solution development programming. This chapter assumes that you already have some experience with Microsoft .NET programming and with web-based programming in general. Once you learn the added skill set of developing solutions for SharePoint, you will become a valuable asset to your organization.

Configuring Your Development Environment

Configuring a good development environment and using the right tools are essential factors for a pleasant (and more important, productive) SharePoint Foundation 2010 development experience. When you are developing solutions for SharePoint Foundation, it is best to do the development on a computer that is running SharePoint Foundation. This way, you can take full advantage of the development and debugging improvements provided by Microsoft Visual Studio 2010.

The development environment should be installed on a computer that has an x64-capable CPU and at least 4 gigabytes of RAM. The operating system of the computer can be Windows Vista x64 SP1 or SP2, Windows 7 x64, or Windows Server 2008 SP2, or Windows Server 2008 R2. However, it is recommended that the operating system is Windows Server 2008 SP2 or Windows Server 2008 R2. Because the basic requirements for a SharePoint Foundation development environment are not the same as a production environment, it is highly recommended that you do not use the requirements listed in this development section as the requirements when creating in a production environment.

Setting Up Your Development Infrastructure

You can use several different configurations for your SharePoint Foundation development environment. If your organizational budget allows, it is recommended that you use more than one computer—one with SharePoint Foundation, and the other running Microsoft SQL Server 2005 SP2 or Microsoft SQL Server 2008 x64 or SQL Server 2008 R2.

INSIDE OUT   Testing your code

Even though your development environment might only consist of one or two computers. If your code is to be deployed on a SharePoint farm that consists of more than one web front-end, then your company will need to invest in an environment that mimics such a configuration in order to accurately test your code.

Additional computers add extra cost to the development process, so in many cases, using virtual machines is preferred. Use virtual machine tools such as Microsoft Hyper-V, VMware Workstation, or Sun Microsystem's VirtualBox to virtualize your SharePoint environment.

You should also think seriously about your hard disk choices, especially if you are going to use virtualization, and therefore, you might consider using solid-state technology, but definitely 7,200 rpm disk drives and multiple disks.

For more information about setting up a development environment, go to *http://msdn.micro-soft.com/en-us/library/ee554869(office.14).aspx*.

Post-Installation Configurations

Once the development environment has been set up with one of the recommended versions of Windows Server 2008 and SharePoint Foundation, create a web application to host a Site Collection, based on a site template of your choice. Next, install the development tools.

You will need to install Visual Studio 2010 on the development computer, together with the latest Service Packs. When you first start Visual Studio, you will need to choose your environment settings. This is usually a personal preference. If you are new to Visual Studio, then the General Developer Settings is as good a choice as any.

To use the SharePoint features within Visual Studio, Visual Studio must be run with administrative privileges. You can either choose to right-click the Microsoft Visual Studio 2010 shortcut each time you want to start it and then click Run As Administrator, or you could modify the properties of the shortcut, and then on the Compatibility tab, click Run The Program As An Administrator, as shown in Figure 16-1.

Figure 16-1 Configure the Visual Studio 2010 shortcut to run as administrator.

Depending on the solutions that you plan to create, you might need to install Microsoft Office 2010 client applications, including Microsoft SharePoint Designer 2010 and possibly Microsoft Visio Premium 2010. Office 2010 applications are provided in both 32-bit and 64-bit versions. Ensure that you install the version that your company uses, which in most cases is the 32-bit version.

SharePoint Designer is a free product that can be downloaded from *http://office.microsoft. com/en-us/sharepoint-designer-help/*.

Chapter 16

Next, install and configure all browsers with which you need to test your solutions. Set the browser's home page to the web application you created earlier and configure it to automatically authenticate you when the browser opens by adding your web application to the Local intranet zone. To configure this in Microsoft Internet Explorer (IE), in the Tools menu, click Internet Options. In Internet Explorer 9, open the Tools menu by clicking the cog icon located to the far right of the address box, as shown in Figure 16-2.

Figure 16-2 Use Internet Options to configure your browser development environment.

Depending on your company's source code strategy, you might need the Team Foundation client installed on your development environment. Otherwise, you will also need to decide on your source code methodology.

Development environments can be large and time consuming to build; companies usually invest time to automate the creation of these environments and virtualize them, thereby enabling their developers to use stable configurations, create restore points prior to testing code changes, and to reliably capture the environment when a problem occurs. Other tools that you should consider for your development environment are listed in the sidebar that follows.

You can download scripts to automate the installation of SharePoint from the AutoSPInstaller codeplex project at *http://autospinstaller.codeplex.com*, and on the Microsoft script repository, which you can find at *http://gallery.technet.microsoft.com/scriptcenter/site/search?f%5B0%5D. Type=RootCategory&f%5B0%5D.Value=sharepoint&f%5B0%5D.Text=SharePoint&f%5B1%5D. Type=SubCategory&f%5B1%5D.Value=deploymentandupgrade&f%5B1%5D.Text=Deployment% 20and%20Upgrade.*

Tools SharePoint Developers Should Use

As you develop your SharePoint solutions, you will need a number of tools, including:

- **CAML Builder**   Collaborative Application Markup Language (CAML) is an XML-based markup language that is used in SharePoint to query lists and other SharePoint artifacts. There are a number of free tools to help you create CAML queries. Use v4.0 of the U2U CAM Query Builder, which you can find at *http://u2u.be/ res/Tools/CamlQueryBuilder.aspx*, or the Stramit SharePoint 2007 CAML Viewer, which is available at *http://spcamlviewer.codeplex.com*.

- **CAML.NET IntelliSense for SharePoint 2010**   This free tool extends the default schema files with detailed annotations, adds a custom Windows Presentation Foundation (WPF) IntelliSense Presenter to the Visual Studio environment, automatically downloads schema updates, and links directly to the online Software Development Kit (SDK) documentation. You can find more information about this tool at *http://sharepointarchitects.us/johnholliday/post/category/caml-net*.

- **Fiddler 2**   A free web debugging proxy that logs all http and https traffic between the computer requesting web-based information and the server that is responding to those requests. You can download this tool at *http://fiddler2.com/ fiddler2*, and the MSDN site, Channel 9, which hosts a large number of webcasts has several shows on tools, one of which you can find at *http://channel9.msdn. com/shows/toolshed/Tool-Shed-Tooltip-4-Fiddler-from-Episode-1*. YSlow is a similar tool, which you can get at *http://developer.yahoo.com/yslow*.

- **PowerGUI**   This is a graphical user interface and script editor for Microsoft Windows PowerShell, which can be found at *http://powergui.org*.

- **.NET Reflector**   An assembly browser for the .NET platform, which helps developers understand how assemblies work and how they interact with other parts of a .NET application. You can purchase this once-free utility at *reflec- tor.net*. For alternatives, see *http://mlichtenberg.wordpress.com/2011/02/23/ alternatives-to-net-reflector*.

- **SPDisposeCheck**   This tool checks custom SharePoint solutions that use the SharePoint server-side Object Model and draws your attention to the parts of code that potentially do not conform to Microsoft's best practices regarding disposal of SharePoint objects. It might not show all memory leaks and therefore does not negate the review of the code. You should also regularly review the ULS logs for Dispose() related leaks that have occurred during runtime. You can obtain the tool at *http://archive.msdn.microsoft.com/SPDisposeCheck*, and for details on the best practices for SharePoint disposable objects, see *http://msdn. microsoft.com/en-us/library/aa973248.aspx*.

- **Microsoft SDKs**   These include SharePoint Visio, other Office 2010 applications, OpenXML, Windows Identity Framework (WIF), PowerShell, and any other SDKs that you might need for your solutions. You can download them from *http:// microsoft.com/downloads.*

- **ULSView**   This is a log viewer that displays events in real time. This tool can be found at *http://code.msdn.microsoft.com/ULSViewer.*

- **Visual Studio 2010 Community Kit for SharePoint (CKS) Development Tools**   Use this tool to extend Visual Studio 2010 with SharePoint 2010 advanced templates and tools. It includes a quick deploy feature, the introduction of keyboard shortcuts, attach and restart process menus, and new SharePoint project items (SPI), such as for branding, visual Web Part and PowerShell cmdlets. You can get this codeplex project at *http://cksdev.codeplex.com.*

- **Visual Studio 2010 Productivity Power Tools**   A tool created by the Microsoft Visual Studio platform team that you can download from *http://visualstudiogallery.msdn.microsoft.com/d0d33361-18e2-46c0-8ff2-4adea1e34fef.*

- **Visual Studio 2010 SharePoint Power Tools**   This is a set of templates and extensions, including an SPI to create a sandbox-compatible visual Web Part and an extension that displays sandbox compilation errors. You can be find this at *http:// visualstudiogallery.msdn.microsoft.com/8e602a8c-6714-4549-9e95-f3700344b0d9.*

- **Content Generator 2011**   This is a free tool that allows you to automatically create content and lists to stress test your solutions. You can find it at *http:// andreasglaser.net/page/downloads.aspx.*

- **Microsoft SQL Server Profiler**   A graphical user interface tool available when you install SQL server, which can be used to monitor how SQL Server resolves queries. More information on this tool can be found at *http://msdn.microsoft. com/en-us/library/ms181091.aspx.*

By using these tools, developers can optimize and develop SharePoint sites for performance. Successful completion of such a task depends on the developers' knowledge and the interpretation of the data provided by these tools. You can find information about optimizing SharePoint sites at *http://sharepointnutsandbolts.com* and at *http:// zimmergren.net/archive/2010/12/18/sp-2010-developing-for-performance-part-1- developer-dashboard.aspx.*

Overview of Visual Studio 2010 Features

In the past, SharePoint development caused considerable confusion among developers regarding the right set of tools to use when creating and deploying a custom solution for SharePoint. Developers used so many documented methods and tools that there ended up being no true standards for SharePoint development. This has changed with the release of Visual Studio 2010 and SharePoint Foundation. Visual Studio provides many tools out of the box that allow easy and efficient integration with your SharePoint Foundation environment.

SharePoint Project Type and SharePoint Project Item Templates

To create a SharePoint solution by using Visual Studio, open Visual Studio with administrative privileges. On the Start Page tab, click New | Project, or on the toolbar, click File | New, and then click Project to open the New Project dialog box (see Figure 16-3). Under Installed Templates, under the appropriate language (such as Visual C#), expand SharePoint, if not already expanded, and then click 2010. In the middle pane, select the appropriate project template for the new project.

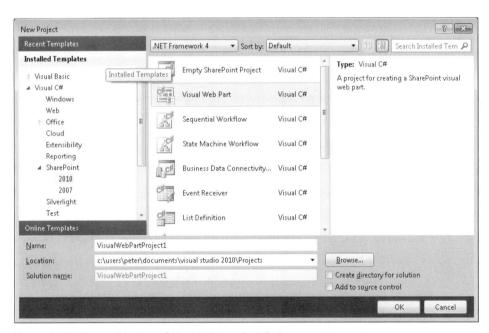

Figure 16-3 Choose the type of SharePoint project that you want to create.

Visual Studio offers several templates for creating SharePoint solutions. This not only includes project templates, but also project item templates that are used to create different types of features and solutions for your SharePoint environment. Visual Studio includes the following 12 project templates for SharePoint 2010:

- Empty SharePoint Project

- Visual Web Part Project

- Sequential Workflow

- State Machine Workflow

- Business Data Connectivity Model

- Event Receiver

- List Definition

- Content Type

- Module

- Site Definition

- Import Reusable Workflow

- Import SharePoint Solution Package

The Empty SharePoint Project template is a basic template in which you can add any project items including any SPIs. The other project templates are similar to the empty project template, but they include one SPI; for example, the Sequential Workflow template includes a Workflow SPI. Similar to the empty project, you can add other project items including SPIs to the other SharePoint projects. A number of these project templates have been used in other chapters of this book. The Sequential Workflow template was used in Chapter 10, "Using and Creating Workflows."

INSIDE OUT   SharePoint 2010 workflows use .NET Framework 3.5

Once you have created a SharePoint project, if you right-click the project name in Solution Explorer and then click properties, you will notice that the target framework for the project is .NET Framework 3.5. This is because SharePoint 2010 is built on the .NET Framework 3.5 and not .NET Framework 4.0.

Visual Studio includes the following SPI templates, which you can access by right-clicking the project title in Solution Explorer, clicking Add, and then clicking New Item:

- Visual Web Part

- Visual Web Part (Sandboxed)

- Web Part

- Sequential Workflow

- State Machine Workflow

- Business Data Connectivity Model

- Application Page

- Event Receiver

- Module

- Content Type

- List Definition From Content Type

- List Definition

- List Instance

- Empty Element

- User Control

Depending on the SPI you select, if you then select to add a new item, the following additional four SPI templates are available:

- Workflow Association Form

- Workflow Initiation Form

- Business Data Connectivity Resource Item

- Global Resource File

An Overview of the SharePoint Customization Wizard

Once you have chosen your project type, typed your project name, and selected whether to add your project to source control, the SharePoint Customization Wizard opens. This is one of the most useful tools included with Visual Studio 2010, and it helps you to specify Share-Point settings that determine how the solution should be configured and deployed in your environment. It also helps to provide the necessary components to debug your solution.

One of the new configurations offered by the SharePoint Customization Wizard is the ability to set is the trust level of the solution that you are deploying, as shown in Figure 16-4.

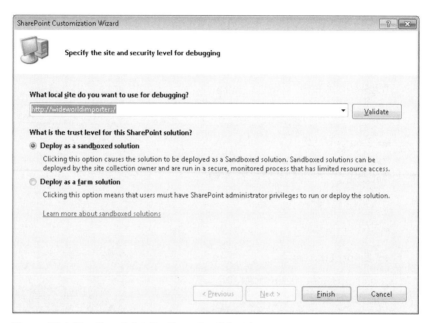

Figure 16-4 The SharePoint Configuration Wizard.

In the previous versions of SharePoint, deploying a solution with the appropriate trust level that would not damage or impair the SharePoint farm was a challenge. SharePoint 2010 introduced a new concept of a sandboxed solution that provides Site Collection owners with a new way to deploy a solution such that the solution is developed in a secure, monitored process that has limited resource access. This stability is achieved through the use of code access security (CAS) policies and by restricting access to portions of the SharePoint server-side object model. Solutions can still be deployed as farm solutions, however SharePoint farm solutions require you to be a SharePoint administrator in order to run or deploy the solution. In general, you should try to develop your solution as a sandboxed solution, and then if you run into limitations, develop it as a full-trust farm solution.

For more information, read the MSDN magazine article "Developing, Deploying, and Monitoring Sandboxed Solutions in SharePoint 2010," which is available at *http://msdn.microsoft. com/en-us/magazine/ee335711.aspx*.

INSIDE OUT   Creating sandboxed solutions

If you are creating sandboxed solutions, you must ensure that the Microsoft SharePoint Foundation Sandboxed Code Service is started. You can use either the SharePoint 2010 Central Administration website to do this (click Manage Services On Server) or by using the following PowerShell command:

```
Get-SPServiceInstance | where { $_.TypeName -match "sandbox" } |
Start-SPServiceInstance
```

Depending on the chosen project type, you can use the SharePoint Customization Wizard to set other configurations, as well. For example, Figure 16-5 demonstrates that you can specify the settings for event receivers deployed in SharePoint Foundation 2010.

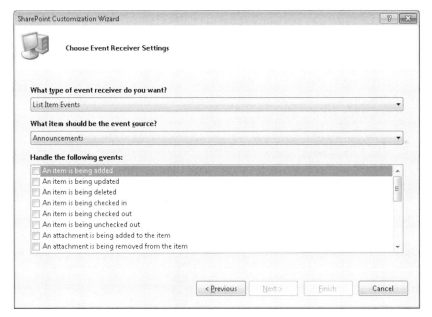

Figure 16-5 You can use the SharePoint Configuration Wizard to specify the settings for event receivers deployed in SharePoint Foundation 2010.

INSIDE OUT Personalizing your Visual Studio environment

The Visual Studio environment remembers some settings from project to project. When you first open Visual Studio, you should configure these one-off settings; for example, using the Server Explorer, you should connect to the site that you are using for your development work. If the Server Explorer window is not open, on the menu, click View, and then click Server Explorer. Right-click SharePoint Connections to open the Add SharePoint Connection dialog box, as shown in Figure 16-6, type the URL of your web application, and then click OK.

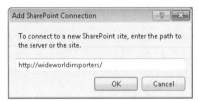

Figure 16-6 Use the Add SharePoint Connection dialog box to add your development web application to the Server Explorer window.

You can now explore the structure of your development site and the sites below it from within Visual Studio. When you click on a SharePoint artifact in Server Explorer, the Properties window (if open) displays more information concerning that artifact, as shown in Figure 16-7.

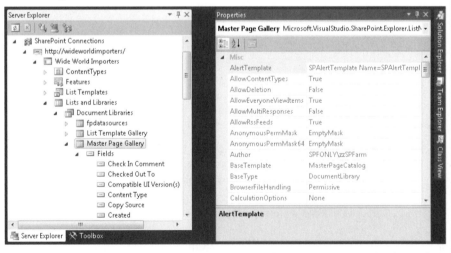

Figure 16-7 Use Server Explorer and the Properties window to explore your development site and Subsites.

Elements of a SharePoint Project

In previous versions of Visual Studio, custom tools, extensions, and custom scripts had to be used to create SharePoint Projects and the required file structures. Several of the files used for SharePoint Projects, such as the manifest.xml, feature.xml, and the elements.xml you had to create manually or through custom extensions for Visual Studio. Having to validate the creation of these files created more overhead in the development of SharePoint solutions, both simple and complex. With a new set of tools and project templates, Visual Studio 2010 provides a great starting block for creating projects to deploy solutions for SharePoint Foundation 2010. Visual Studio also creates the appropriate files and structure needed to create a SharePoint Project to build a deployable solution.

After you create a project, Visual Studio creates a number of default files and nodes that can be viewed in Solution Explorer (see Figure 16-8). These make up the sequential work-flow of the project and the new structure that was automatically created for the SharePoint 2010 project.

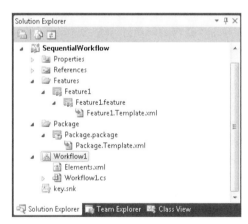

Figure 16-8 A sequential workflow project that illustrates the structure of a newly created project.

The SPI consists of two components: an elements XML file and a code file. The elements XML file, also known as the elements manifest file, refers to the code file. The elements manifest file is targeted by the Features file, which in turn is targeted by the package. When Visual Studio deploys a SharePoint project, it deploys the package to the SharePoint server. Share-Point reads each Feature file contained in the package, and then from each Feature file, reads the elements file, which in turn points to the assembly. An assembly can contain the code for one or more Features. When you want to create more than one assembly for your solution, you should divide your solution into multiple projects.

Visual Studio 2001 SP1 and SharePoint 2010

In early 2011, the first Service Pack for Visual Studio 2010 was released. Like many other Service Packs, it contained an accumulation of hotfixes that improved the stability and performance of the product, plus it contained some new features. This Service Pack enabled IntelliTrace debugging technology for 64-bit and SharePoint solutions.

You can read a description of Visual Studio 2010 Service Pack 1 at *http://support.microsoft. com/kb/983509* and *http://msdn.microsoft.com/en-us/vstudio/aa718359.aspx*. For information on how to use IntelliTrace, go to *http://msdn.microsoft.com/en-us/vstudio/gg542173*, *http://msdn.microsoft.com/en-gb/magazine/ee336126.aspx*, and *http://channel9.msdn.com/ shows/10-4/10-4-Episode-28-An-Introduction-to-the-Historical-Debugger*.

Developing SharePoint Features

SharePoint uses the concept of a Feature to deploy a set of components and functionalities into the SharePoint environment. Features can be activated and applied at the website, web application, or the farm Level. A Feature in previous versions of SharePoint typically contained a Feature.xml and Elements.xml file that were used to determine what elements to include in the Feature or solution.

Figure 16-8 illustrates a new node in Solution Explorer called Features. This is a new structural component that is automatically created for SharePoint solutions in Visual Studio when a project is created. This Features node is also updated automatically as certain items are added to the project that are required to be deployed through the use of a Feature. This structure also allows multiple Features to be applied under this Features directory and multiple Features to be packaged into one solution package.

Visual Studio also provides additional interfaces with which you can add, update, or remove existing items in a solution or project that are part of a Feature. To access this interface, double-click the Feature file in your solution. A dialog box similar to that depicted in Figure 16-9 opens.

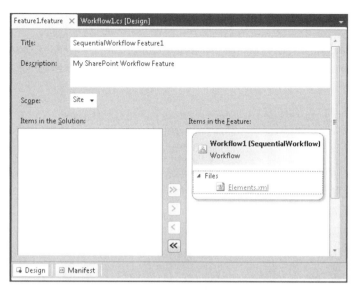

Figure 16-9 Visual Studio provides additional interfaces that allow existing items in a solution or project to be added, updated, or removed from the feature.

Notice that you have the option to edit the title, description, and the scope of the Feature from this interface. Also notice that the Feature contains a directory called Files. This contains all the Elements.xml files that are needed for this solution.

The contents of an elements file will be different depending on the SPI type. An example of the Elements.xml file for a sequential workflow is listed in the following example:

```xml
<?xml version="1.0" encoding="utf-8"?>
<Elements xmlns="http://schemas.microsoft.com/sharepoint/">
  <Workflow Name="SequentialWorkflow - Workflow1"
    Description="My SharePoint Workflow" Id="8b4529c1-d057-4e9a-4c36f9f8111"
    CodeBesideClass="SequentialWorkflow.Workflow1.Workflow1"
    CodeBesideAssembly="$assemblyname$">
    <Categories/>
    <MetaData>
      <AssoicationCategories>List</AssociationCategories>
      <StatusPageUrl>_layouts/WrkStat.aspx</StatusPageUrl>
    </Metadata>
  </Workflow>
</Elements>
```

You also have the ability to preview or edit the manifest.xml file from this location by clicking the Manifest button at the bottom of the Feature1.feature window. Figure 16-10 shows an example features.xml manifest file. The preview area is read-only; however, you can edit the file if you expand Edit Options. Any modifications you make here are merged with the generated XML by the Feature designer.

Figure 16-10 A preview of a Feature manifest file.

Using Packages

Visual Studio also has another new node that's automatically included when you create a SharePoint 2010 project. This new node is called the Package. The Package contains Features and other components that are used when building and deploying a SharePoint 2010 solution. One of the other important components that the Package contains is the assembly deployment information. This is used to determine where the assemblies for the solution are to be deployed.

To make the process standard for managing and viewing Packages, Visual Studio 2010 now includes a Packaging Designer. The designer makes it's easier for you to add or remove Features to the Deployment Package for your SharePoint solution. To access the Package Designer, double-click the .package node in Solution Explorer. Figure 16-11 shows an example of the SharePoint Packaging Designer.

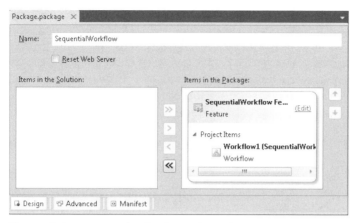

Figure 16-11 An example of a SharePoint Packing Designer.

To automatically restart IIS once a Package is deployed, select the Reset Web Server option.

At the bottom of the Package Designer window are three buttons: Design, Advanced, and Manifest. Click the Design button to display a view of the packaging information (see Figure 16-11); click Advanced to perform advanced tasks such as adding additional assemblies to the deployment; click Manifest to display the Package manifest file. As with the Feature manifest file, you can preview the contents or use the Edit Options button to type additional packaging information.

The Package Designer also has one additional window called the Packaging Explorer (see Figure 16-12) with which you can view the hierarchy of the configuration files and items included in your package. The Packaging Explorer opens automatically when you have the Package Designer window open.

Figure 16-12 The Packaging Explorer.

The Packaging Explorer behaves similar to Windows Explorer in as much as you can drag and drop components. It shows all Packages and Features in a solution as well as the associated SPIs, such as Workflow1 and its associated project items (for example, Elements.xml).

Using Event Receivers

When you create a Feature, you will commonly need to create code to either set up the SharePoint environment when a Feature is installed or activated, or clean up the environment when the Feature is deactivated or uninstalled. This is when you would use Feature event receivers, which can respond to the following events:

- *FeatureActivated*

- *FeatureDeactivated*

- *FeatureInstalled*

- *FeatureUninstalling*

- *FeatureUpgrading*

There are also a number of other events raised by SharePoint that in certain scenarios will be more applicable to use than the Feature event receivers. For example, in Chapter 14, "Creating, Managing, and Designing Sites by Using SharePoint Designer 2010," you created a Visual Studio project that deployed a custom master page and custom Cascading Style Sheets (CSS) files. This was developed as a Site Collection Feature. Therefore, when new Subsites are created in the Site Collection, where the Feature is activated, you need to associate the master page and CSS files to the newly provisioned child sites. In this scenario, the event *WebProvisioned*, which is a new event introduced with SharePoint 2010 and is called each time a new child site is created, should be used.

Using the project developed in Chapter 14, perform the following steps:

1. Open the SPFIOBranding project in Visual Studio.

2. Right-click SPFIOBranding, select Add, and then click New Item.

3. In the Add New Item dialog box, click Event Receiver and in the Name text box, type SiteProvision. Click Add. The SharePoint Customization Wizard opens.

4. In this section What Type Of Event Receiver Do You Want, select Web Events, and then under Handle The Following Events, select A Site Was Provisioned.

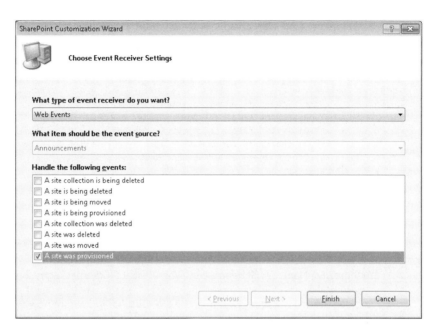

5. Click Finish. The SiteProvision.cs file opens in the workspace and a new SPI named SiteProvision is presented in Solution Explorer that contains an Elements.xml file together with the SiteProvision.cs code file.

6. Replace the code of SiteProvison.cs with the following code:

```
using System;
using Microsoft.SharePoint;

namespace SharePointCustomMasterPage1.SiteProvision
{
  public class SiteProvision : SPWebEventReceiver
  {
    public override void WebProvisioned(SPWebEventProperties properties)
    {
      SPWeb spWeb = properties.Web;
      SPWeb topSite = spWeb.Site.RootWeb;
      spWeb.MasterUrl = topSite.MasterUrl;
      spWeb.AlternateCssUrl = topSite.AlternateCssUrl;
      spWeb.Update();
    }
  }
}
```

Chapter 16

The content of the elements file is shown in the following code:

```xml
<?xml version="1.0" encoding="utf-8"?>
<Elements xmlns="http://schemas.microsoft.com/sharepoint/">
  <Receivers >
     <Receiver>
       <Name>SiteProvisionWebProvisioned</Name>
       <Type>WebProvisioned</Type>
       <Assembly>$SharePoint.Project.AssemblyFullName$</Assembly>
       <Class>SharePointCustomMasterPage1.SiteProvision.SiteProvision</Class>
       <SequenceNumber>10000</SequenceNumber>
     </Receiver>
  </Receivers>
</Elements>
```

The value of the <Sequence Number> tag is used if there is more than one event receiver for the same event, where the event receiver associated with the smaller number is executed first. The replaceable token in the <Assembly> tag, $SharePoint.Project. AssemblyFullName$, will be resolved when Visual Studio packages the solution.

Looking at the Packaging Designer, the SPFIOBranding Feature now references three SPIs: two modules, *SPFIOMaster* and *SPFIOCSS*, and the event receiver *SiteProvision*.

Developing SharePoint Solutions

Developing SharePoint Solutions for SharePoint Foundation provides developers with many opportunities to build powerful and dynamic solutions. It also helps lower costs to the organization because of the ability to quickly develop solutions. In the past, some organizations were hesitant when considering implementing custom SharePoint Solutions, because they felt that it would be a long and costly process to develop a solution. This fear has been greatly reduced with SharePoint Foundation because of the improved development process, new features, and tools.

These new tools help developers to:

- Streamline the design of workflows to build automated business processes.

- Develop SharePoint solutions faster, based on SharePoint project templates.

- Integrate with external systems more efficiently by utilizing the Business Data Connectivity services.

- Create powerful custom application pages for SharePoint.

- Create and validate solution packages faster.

- Debug SharePoint solutions faster.

- Import and modify solution packages faster.

Getting solutions packaged and deployed to other SharePoint Foundation environments is another critical component of development. In earlier versions of SharePoint, tools such as the WSP Builder and the *stsadm* command line were used to create a .wsp file and deploy custom workflows to the server. In Visual Studio 2010, packaging and deploying custom workflows to a SharePoint Foundation environment has been made simple and more efficient through the use of the Package Designer, Packaging Explorer, and PowerShell scripts.

Microsoft has released a number of developer resources including the SharePoint Guidance 2010 Hands-On Labs, which you can view at *http://spg.codeplex.com/releases/view/60343*; and the SharePoint 2010 Developer Resource Centers at *http://msdn.microsoft.com/en-us/sharepoint/bb964529.aspx*.

Importing WSP Solution Packages

Once you have modified your site via the browser and SharePoint Designer, you can package it as a .wsp file and hand it over to the central SharePoint support team so that they can make it available to other users or use your work as a basis for further customizations. In previous versions of SharePoint, when you saved a site as a template, a .stp file was created which contained the differences between the site created from the site definition and the customizations that were created by using the browser or SharePoint Designer. Now a .wsp file is used when you create a site template. It contains the ONET.XML file from the original site definition and details of features, elements, and optionally, the content from the site.

> **Note**
> You can create a site template by using Visual Studio.

You can use one of the new features in Visual Studio, Import SharePoint Solution Package, to import the .wsp file to create reusable artifacts, such as list definitions, content types, and fields. This greatly improves the development process—developers now have the ability to quickly create a list or site template by using out-of-the-box functionality in the browser. You can take the templates and automatically generate the schema and configuration for the definitions in Visual Studio. You can then manipulate the files to fit your specific need. Once you're done, you can easily deploy this solution to your farm where it can be used across multiple sites. Currently this is restricted to items created in SharePoint Foundation 2010 and SharePoint Server 2010. In the following, you will find an example of how to import a solution.

To import the components into Visual Studio for this example, you will need to create a Site called *Import Demo* by using the browser or SharePoint Designer in your SharePoint Foundation environment. Once this site is created, start a new document library called *Test*

Template. Save the site as a template called **ImportDemoTemplate**. Once the template is created, save the ImportDemoTemplate.wsp file to a location on your computer.

Now that you have a customized site set up, you can work on creating a solution based on the list definition by completing the following procedure:

1. Open Visual Studio, click New | Project, and then in the New Project dialog box, under Installed Templates, in the language of your choice, select SharePoint and click 2010.

2. Click Import SharePoint Solution Package.

3. Type **SPFINWspImportProject1** for the Project Name, and then click OK.

4. Specify the site and security level for debugging, and then click Next to display the Specify The New Project Source page of the SharePoint Customization Wizard.

5. Click Browse, navigate to the location where you saved the .wsp file, click Open, and then click Next.

6. On the Select Items To Import wizard page, clear all of the items in the list, by pressing Ctrl+A and then pressing the Space bar.

7. Select Test Template List Instance from the list, and then click Finish.

8. A Selection Dependency Warning dialog box opens, asking whether you want Visual Studio to automatically include all the required dependencies detected in the .wsp file. Click Yes, and then click OK to the Import Completed dialog box.

A new project named SPFINWspImportProject1 is created.

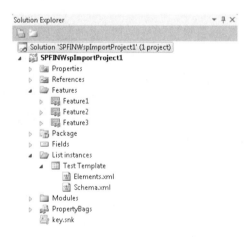

Notice that the wizard has automatically created the Features and Packages needed to build and deploy the solution. It has also created a List Instances folder that contains the Elements.xml and Schema.xml files.

You can now build and deploy the solution to your SharePoint environment.

Deploying Solutions

Up to this point in this chapter, the customizations and solutions you've built can be used *in situ*; that is, they have been developed on the site where they are to be used. However, there might be occasions where you build the solution on one site and need to recreate it on one or more other sites. This is particularly true in large organizations, where you build your solution in a development environment, and then it must go through a release management process before being deployed to the production environment.

There are many ways to deploy customizations and solutions in the SharePoint environment. In a small organization, the ability to re-create customizations and solutions quickly relies on fast installation and deployment methods. In larger organization, there might be a need for a more complex method.

Once you have completed your testing, you need to build a release version of your solution. As with any other Visual Studio project, the finished files are created in the *<project name>/bin/Release* folder. It is in this folder that you will find the .wsp file that you will hand over to the build managers of the other environments or to the server administrators of your production environment.

SharePoint solutions are often created by non-IT users—citizen developers—who have a day job and do not have the time or business sign-off authority to maintain and enhance the solutions. Therefore, once customizations and solutions are developed, with the recognition that these need to be deployed again, the responsibility for these customizations and solutions might need to be handed over to a central department. No matter which packaging and deployment method is used, customizations and solutions must always be documented and tested, and depending on the solution, there must be plans for installation, upgrade, patching, and removal.

Debugging SharePoint Applications

Debugging applications developed for SharePoint Foundation 2010 has been greatly simplified in Visual Studio 2010. When a project is started based on one of the SharePoint 2010 templates, the SharePoint Customization Wizard assists you in specifying the different components that you will need to debug your solution. For example, when a workflow is created, the Customization Wizard prompts the user to enter the site and lists the components that the solution is to use for debugging. Once the user has added the necessary code to the solution, the user need only press the run button (F5) to deploy the solution and start the debugging process. The default deployment configuration performs the following steps:

- Run predeployment command

- Recycles the Internet Information Services (IIS) application pool.

- Retracts the solution, if it was previously deployed

- Adds the solution

- Activates the Feature(s)

- Runs the post-deployment command

At this point, the user can place breakpoints in the code and step through the process, just as you can with any other .NET application.

INSIDE OUT Modifying the default Visual Studio deployment configuration

To create, modify, delete, or to change the default Visual Studio deployment configuration, open the SharePoint property page by right-clicking the project name in Solution Explorer. Click Properties, and then click the SharePoint tab.

Developing SharePoint Web Parts

SharePoint Foundation comes packed with many Web Parts that can be used with little configuration. They should meet most of your business requirements, but inevitably, at some point you will want to create your own.

For more information about the out-of-the-box Web Parts that are available with SharePoint Foundation, read Chapter 7, "Adding, Editing, Connecting, and Managing Web Parts on the Page."

One of the big differences for Web Parts in SharePoint 2010 is the manner in which they are added to pages. In SharePoint 2007, Web Parts could only be added by using the browser in Web Part Zones. In SharePoint Foundation 2010, using the browser and wiki pages, Web Parts can be added outside of a Web Part zone into a content zone on the page along with text and images.

For more information about adding content to Web Part and wiki pages, read Chapter 6, "Creating and Formatting Webpages."

Pages that can contain SharePoint Web Parts work differently from ordinary Microsoft ASP.NET pages and much differently from legacy ASP pages. As a result, developing and deploying a Web Part requires a different mindset and a somewhat different tool set than does developing other kinds of server-based web components.

In Visual Studio 2010, the Web Part development process has been radically improved. Visual Studio now ships with project and item templates that do not require extra extension or tools to develop and deploy Web Parts. SharePoint 2010 and Visual Studio now provide the ability for developers to create two types of Web Parts:

- **Standard Web Part**   Essentially the same type of Web Part that existed in Share-Point Server 2007 and Windows SharePoint Services 3.0. Visual Studio 2010 now ships with a new Web Part called the Visual Web Part. Visual Studio provides no design experience for standard Web Parts; you need to manually create the controls that make your user interface. Standard Web Parts can only be added to a project as SPIs; that is, there is no standard Web Part project template.

- **Visual Web Part**   A type of Web Part, that allows developers to visually design a Web Part in Visual Studio and can be deployed to a SharePoint 2010 environment. This Web Part essentially contains .NET. This is a great improvement to previous versions of Visual Studio because no out-of-the-box solution existed for creating Web Parts visually. In previous versions this could only be accomplished by using custom tools and workarounds. Visual Web Parts can be added to projects as SPIs or you can create a project with a Visual Web Part SPI already added by using the Visual Web Part project template.

How Web Parts Work

One of the core components of SharePoint that makes it attractive to organizations is the use of Web Parts. The Web Parts used in SharePoint Foundation are designed and built to lie on top of the Microsoft ASP.NET Web Part Infrastructure. You can build your Web Parts by inheriting them from either of the following two Web Parts:

- **The ASP.NET Web Part**   *System.Web.UI.WebControls.WebParts.WebPart* can be used in most cases to create a Web Part. Web Parts that utilize this class can be deployed in ASP.Net applications as well as SharePoint applications.

- **The SharePoint Foundation Web Part**   *Microsoft.SharePoint.WebPartPages.WebPart* provides additional functionality for connecting Web Parts, client-side connections, cross page connections, and data-caching infrastructure. The Web Parts developed from this class can only be utilized in a SharePoint environment.

Creating a Visual Web Part

Creating a Web Part in Visual Studio is pretty simple. In the following example, you will see how to create a sample "Hello World" Visual Web Part:

1. Create a new project named **SPFINVWP** that is based on the Visual Web Part template, and then click Ok.

2. Enter the site to use for debugging, and then click Finish.

    The file VisualWebPart1UserControl.ascx opens in the workspace, with the buttons, Design, Split, and Source displayed at the bottom of the window.

3. Open the Toolbox window (if it's not already open), and then drag a Label component from the Standard section.

4. Open the Properties window (press F4 if it is not open), and then change the Text Attribute to **Hello World**.

5. Select Deploy Solution from the Build menu.

6. Once the deployment process has succeeded with no errors, browse to a SharePoint Page and add the VisualWebPart1 to the page. You should find it under the Custom category.

Building Connected Web Parts

Building Web Parts in SharePoint Foundation 2010 is a common development task. However, sometimes it is necessary to create a Web Part that connects to other Web Parts. SharePoint provides a set of connection interfaces with which Web Parts can send and receive information at runtime. This would allow a user to enter information on a webpage, and it would automatically update information contained in other Web Parts on the page that had connections to that Web Part. This is a solution that can deliver long term return on investment (ROI) within an organization because the owners of sites do not need to repeatedly modify a page as the data changes.

Connection Interfaces

There are multiple types of data that can be passed between connected Web Parts. The movement of data is performed by using different types of connection interfaces. Each connection interface has an interface that consumes information and an interface that provides information; therefore, each connection interface is a paired set of events, as listed here:

- ***ICellProvider*, *ICellConsumer***   Provides or consumes a single value item such as a cell or field.

- ***IRowProvider***, ***IRowConsumer***   Provides or consumes a single or multiple rows of values.

- ***IListProvider***, ***IListConsumer***   Provides or consumes an entire list.

- ***IFilterProvider***, ***IFilterConsumer***   Provides or consumes a filter value. This allows one list to filter another connected list.

- ***IParametersInProvider***, ***IParametersInConsumer***   Provides or consumes a set of parameters between Web Parts. This is used when a consumer Web Part owns the parameter list and needs to connect with another Web Part.

- ***IParametersOutProvider***, ***IParametersOutConsumer***   Provides or consumes a set of parameters between Web Parts. This is used when a provider Web Part owns the parameter list and needs to connect with another Web Part.

Not all Web Parts can connect to other Web Parts; for example, a Web Part can only connect to other Web Parts if the connection interfaces are using a matching connection interface. As such, an *ICellProvider* connection interface can always connect to an *ICellConsumer* connection interface because they are a pair.

In the event that a connection interface from one Web Part is not a pair to the second Web Part connection interface, a transformer might be available for the interface. A transformer gives two Web Parts, with mismatched interfaces, the ability to communicate. Four transformers are provided out of the box:

- *IRowProvider* to *ICellConsumer*

- *IRowProvider* to *IFilterConsumer*

- *IParametersOutProvider* to *IParametersInConsumer*

- *IRowProvider* to *IParametersInConsumer*

For a Web Part to connect to Web Parts on other pages, there are five out-of-the-box interfaces that provide cross-page communication. These interfaces are for a source page to a target page interface connection:

- *RowProvider* to *IFilterConsumer*

- *IRowProvider* to *IParametersInConsumer*

- *IFilterProvider* to *IFilterConsumer*

- *IParametersOutProvider* to *IParametersInConsumer*

- *IParametersInProvider* to *IParametersInConsumer*

Creating Web Part Connections

To create a custom Web Part that can connect to other Web Parts, perform the steps that follow. This example builds on the Visual Web Part project (SPFINVWP) that you created earlier in this chapter. To test the functionality of this example, you need a Tasks list with a number of task items on the site with which you associated the SPFINVWP project:

1. Open the SPFINVWP project in Visual Studio, if it is not already open.

2. Right-click the SPFINVWP project name, click Add, and then click New Item.

3. Under Installed Templates, select Visual C#, and then click Interface.

4. In the Name text box, type **TaskInterface.cs**, and then click Add.

5. Replace the code in TaskInterface.cs with the following code:

```
using System;
using System.Collections.Generic;
using System.Linq;
using System.Text;

namespace SPFINVWP
{
  public interface TaskInterface
  {
    int Id { get; }
    string Name { get; }
  }
}
```

You have created a connection interface file, next you will create a provider Web Part by using the following procedure:

1. Right-click the SPFINVWP project name, click Add, and then click New Item.

2. Under SharePoint 2010, click Web Part. In the Name text box, type **ProviderWebPart1**, and then click Add.

3. Replace the code in ProviderWebPart1.cs with the following code:

```
using System;
using System.ComponentModel;
using System.Web;
using System.Web.UI;
using System.Web.UI.WebControls;
using System.Web.UI.WebControls.WebParts;
using Microsoft.SharePoint;
using Microsoft.SharePoint.WebControls;
```

```
namespace SPFINVWP.ProviderWebPart1
{
  [ToolboxItemAttribute(false)]
  public class ProviderWebPart1 : Microsoft.SharePoint.WebPartPages.WebPart,
    TaskInterface
  {
    DropDownList _TaskPicker = null;
    int TaskInterface.Id
    {
      get { return int.Parse(_TaskPicker.SelectedValue); }
    }

    string TaskInterface.Name
    {
      get { return _TaskPicker.SelectedItem.ToString(); }
    }

    protected override void CreateChildControls()
    {
      try
      {
        _TaskPicker = new DropDownList();
        using (SPSite spSite = new SPSite(SPContext.Current.Web.Url))
        using (SPWeb spWeb = spSite.OpenWeb())
        {

          SPList TaskList = spWeb.Lists["Tasks"];

          foreach (SPListItem Task in TaskList.Items)
          {
            _TaskPicker.Items.Add(new ListItem(Task.Name, Task.ID.ToString()));
          }
        }
        _TaskPicker.AutoPostBack = true;

        this.Controls.Add(_TaskPicker);
      }
      catch (Exception ex)
      {
        this.Controls.Clear();
        this.Controls.Add(new LiteralControl(ex.Message));
      }

    }

    [ConnectionProvider("Task Name and ID")]
    public TaskInterface ReturnThis()
    {
      return this;
    }
  }
}
```

Chapter 16

Next you will create the consumer Web Part by using the following procedure:

1. Right-click the SPFINVWP project name, click Add, and then click New Item.

2. Under SharePoint 2010, click Web Part. In the Name text box, type **ConsumerWebPart1**, and then click Add.

3. Replace the code in ConsumerWebPart1.cs with the following:

```
using System;
using System.ComponentModel;
using System.Web;
using System.Web.UI;
using System.Web.UI.WebControls;
using System.Web.UI.WebControls.WebParts;
using Microsoft.SharePoint;
using Microsoft.SharePoint.WebControls;

namespace SPFINVWP.ConsumerWebPart1
{
    [ToolboxItemAttribute(false)]
    public class ConsumerWebPart1 : WebPart
    {
        TaskInterface _provider = null;
        Label _lbl = null;

        protected override void CreateChildControls()
        {
            try
            {
                _lbl = new Label();

                if (_provider != null)
                {
                    if (_provider.Id > 0)
                    {
                        _lbl.Text = _provider.Name + " was selected.";
                    }
                    else
                    {
                        _lbl.Text = "Nothing was selected.";
                    }
                }
                else
                {
                    _lbl.Text = "No Provider Web Part Connected.";
                }
                this.Controls.Add(_lbl);
            }
```

```
            catch (Exception ex)
            {
                this.Controls.Clear();
                this.Controls.Add(new LiteralControl(ex.Message));
            }
        }

        [ConnectionConsumer("Task Name and ID")]
        public void ReturnProvider(TaskInterface providerInterface)
        {
            _provider = providerInterface;
        }

    }
}
```

You have now created both the consumer and provider Web Parts. To deploy and test the solution, perform the following steps:

1. From the Build menu, click Deploy Solution. Correct any errors you might have.

2. When the deployment has succeeded with no errors, browse to the site you selected for debugging.

3. Click Site Actions, and then select More Options.

4. Under Filter By, click Page. Select Web Part Page, and then click Create.

5. On the New Web Part Page, in the Name text box, type **ConnectionWebPartPage**, and then click Create.

6. Add the ConsumerWebPart1 to one of the zones, and then add the ProviderWebPart1 to a different zone.

7. Click the down-arrow on the ConsumerWebPart1 Web Part title. Click Connections, click Get Task Name And ID From, and then Click ProviderWebPart1.

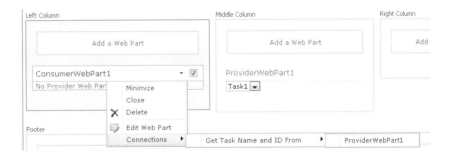

You have now successfully created a Consumer and Provider Web Part Connection.

Developing SharePoint Site Definitions

One of the advantages of using SharePoint for hosting websites is the ability to create additional sites based on templates. A site template contains a customization of a base site, and it has a .wsp extension. If the solution you want to implement consists of only a set of customizations (such as adding some libraries, lists, and so on), you could use a site template. However, the use of site templates might not always be the optimal solution when the need arises to create sites with similar or identical functionality. Site templates cannot contain custom Web Parts, workflows, events, or master pages; that is, SharePoint components that are based on custom files stored on the servers, and the site templates need to be used on a SharePoint installation where these files will not be distributed. This is where developing custom site definitions provide more benefits. A site definition includes the look and feel of the needed site as well as the core functionality of a SharePoint Foundation site.

Using site definitions also provides performance benefits over using site templates. Site definitions have the ability to be cached on the web server when first accessed at runtime. Each time a site is accessed that uses a site definition, the core information for this site is pulled from the cache for each request.

SharePoint Foundation comes with pre-installed site definitions, which are located on the web server in a subdirectory in the SharePoint root \Program Files\Common Files\Microsoft Shared\Web Server Extensions\14\TEMPLATE\SiteTemplates. Each site definition contains its own subdirectory under this folder. By default, this is the location for all of the out-of-the-box site definitions. This includes Team Sites, Blank Sites, Group Work Sites, and many of the other default site definitions.

One site definition is STS, which provides site templates for common sites, such as Team Sites, Blank Sites, and Document Workspaces. The other site definitions you'll find in that folder provide templates for blogs, group work sites and meeting sites.

A site definition consists of a WEBTEMP.XML and the ONET.XML.

Exploring WEBTEMP.XML

When you first install SharePoint Foundation, a file named WEBTEMP.XML identifies each site definition, where *Temp* in this context means template, not temporary. It contains information pertaining to the site definitions and configurations for the site definition. It also determines how the site appears to users who are creating new sites. You can find this file at \Program Files\Common Files\Microsoft Shared\web server extensions\14\ TEMPLATE\1033\XML, where 1033 is the current locale ID. A shortened version of this file is as follows:

```
<?xml version="1.0" encoding="utf-8"?>
<!-- _lcid="1033" _version="14.0.4762" _dal="1" -->
<!-- _LocalBinding -->
<Templates xmlns:ows="Microsoft SharePoint">
  <Template Name="GLOBAL" SetupPath="global" ID="0">
    <Configuration ID="0" Title="Global template" Hidden="TRUE" ImageUrl=""
      Description="This template is used for initializing a new site." >
    </Configuration>
   </Template>
  <Template Name="STS" ID="1">
    <Configuration ID="0" Title="Team Site" Hidden="FALSE"
      ImageUrl="/_layouts/images/stts.png"
      Description="A site for teams to quickly organize, author, and share
        information. It provides a document library, and lists for managing
        announcements, calendar items, tasks, and discussions."
      DisplayCategory="Collaboration" >
    </Configuration>
    <Configuration ID="1" Title="Blank Site" Hidden="FALSE"
      ImageUrl="/_layouts/images/stbs.png"
      Description="A blank site for you to customize based on your requirements."
      DisplayCategory="Collaboration" AllowGlobalFeatureAssociations="False" >
    </Configuration>
    <Configuration ID="2" Title="Document Workspace" Hidden="FALSE"
      ImageUrl="/_layouts/images/stdw.png"
      Description="A site for colleagues to work together on a document. It
        provides a document library for storing the primary document and supporting
        files, a tasks list for assigning to-do items, and a links list for resources
        related to the document."
      DisplayCategory="Collaboration" >
    </Configuration>
  </Template>
. . .
</Templates>
```

Each <Template></Template> block identifies a set of similar site definitions. Each <Template> tag contains:

- The Name attribute, which supplies a mnemonic name

- The ID attribute, which supplies a unique identifier

Within each <Template></Template> block, there's one <configuration> tag for each site definition, which contains:

- The ID attributes, which provide a unique identity within each <Template> node.

- The Title and Description fields, which specify values that the Template Selection page displays when a team member creates a site.

- The Display category, which is the tab on which you want the name of the site to appear when you create a new site. You can specify one of the existing names (Collaboration or Meetings) or specify a new one.

- Hidden, which determines whether the site should be shown to the users.

- ImageURL, which is an image that will be shown when the configuration is selected.

Working with ONET.XML Files

Further information about each site definition appears in a file named ONET.XML. Because the WEBTEMP.XML file specified several template names (STS, MPS, Blog, Wiki, Central Administration), there are more than one ONET.XML files. To find these files, first browse to \Program Files\Common Files\Microsoft Shared\Web server extensions\14\TEMPLATE\ SiteTemplates\, and then go to the following locations:

- \Blog\XML\ONET.XML

- \CENTRALADMIN\XML\ONET.XML

- \MPS\XML\ONET.XML

- \sgs\XML\ONET.XML

- \sts\XML\ONET.XML

- \TenantAdmin\XML\ONET.XML

- \Wiki\XML\ONET.XML

Each ONET.XML file defines a series of common elements for individual sites to use. These include the following:

- Navigation bars such as the Top Link Bar and the Quick Launch

- Web-scoped and Site Collection–scoped features that are built into sites

- Built-in Web Parts and pages

- List templates

- Document templates

- Configurations

- Modules

- Footer sections used in server emails

Several types of tasks can be performed in ONET.XML to customize a site definition:

- Specify an alternate CSS file, JavaScript file, or ASPX header file for a site definition.

- Modify navigation areas for the home page and list pages.

- Add a list definition as an option to the Create page.

- Define a configuration for a site definition.

- Specify the lists, modules, files, and Web Parts to be included when a site is instantiated.

SharePoint Foundation includes the global site definition file, which you can find at \Program Files\Common Files\Microsoft Shared\web server extensions\14\TEMPLATE\ GLOBAL\XML\ONET.XML. This file contains provisioning information that can be used by every site definition such as base types, base master page, and so on. This file alleviates redundant data from being inserted into each ONET.XML file for each site definition. The following code snippet shows the base structure and elements that are included in the ONET.XML file:

```xml
<?xml version="1.0" encoding="utf-8"?>
<Project Title="Site Definition" Revision="1" ListDir=""
      xmlns:ows="Microsoft SharePoint">
  <NavBars/>
  <ListTemplates/>
  <DocumentTemplates/>
  <BaseTypes/>
  <Configurations>
...
    <Configuration ID="0" Name="Default">
      <Lists/>
      <Modules>
        <Module Name="Default" />
      </Modules>
      <SiteFeatures>
        <!-- BasicWebParts Feature -->
        <Feature ID="00BFEA71-1C5E-4A24-B310-BA51C3EB7A57" />
...
      </SiteFeatures>
      <WebFeatures>
        <!-TeamCollab Feature -->
        <Feature ID="00BFEA71-4EA5-48D4-A4AD-7EA5C011ABE5" />
...
      </WebFeatures>
    </Configuration>
```

Chapter 16

```
...
    </Configurations>
    <Modules>
        <Module Name="Default" Url="" Path="">
            <File Url="default.aspx" NavBarHome="True" />
        </Module>
...
    </Modules>
    <Components>
        <FileDialogPostProcessor ID="BDEADEE4-C265-11d0-BCED-00A0C90AB50F" />
    </Components>
    <ServerEmailFooter>$Resources:ServerEmailFooter;</ServerEmailFooter>
</Project>
```

NavBars defines the top and side navigation bar. This node can contain additional *NavBar* elements, and the links can be added by using *NavBarLink* elements.

The *ListTemplates* section specifies the list definitions that are part of a site definition. The *ListTemplate* element also specifies a display name for the list definition and whether the option to add a link on the Quick Launch appears selected by default on the new page.

In addition, this element specifies the description of the list definition and the path to the image representing the list definition, which are both displayed on the Create page. This element is supported in SharePoint Foundation 2010 only for backward compatibility. If a list type needs to be defined, it needs to be defined as a Feature.

The *DocumentTemplates* elements describe what document templates will be used in document libraries.

The *BaseTypes* element of the global ONET.XML file is used during site or list creation to define the basic list types on which all list definitions in SharePoint Foundation are based. Each list template that is specified in the list templates section is identified with one of the base types: Generic List, Document Library, Discussion Forum, Vote or Survey, or Issues List. It is important to note that the *BaseTypes* section can only be implemented in the Global. XML file.

The *Configurations* element contains one or more configuration elements that contain the lists, modules, and Features that are created when the site definition is used to create a site.

The *Components* element specifies components to include in sites created through the definition.

The *ServerEmailFooter* element is used to determine the footer used in email sent from the server.

Creating a New Site Definition

Making changes to the default WEBTEMP.XML and ONET.XML files that come with Share-Point Foundation is not a best practice. The two main reasons are:

- Microsoft considers these to be system files. As a result, any reinstallation, repair, or upgrade to SharePoint Foundation might replace them and overlay any changes you have made.

- Any site created from a site definition continues to use the WEBTEMP.XML, ONET. XML, and schema.xml files indefinitely.

Therefore, an incorrect change, even if it works for new sites, could break hundreds or thousands of existing sites. Thus, the correct approach is to create new site definitions rather than change existing ones.

You can utilize Visual Studio to create a new site definition and package the site definition, which you can then deliver to a client. To create a site definition, use Visual Studio to create a Site Definition project, which automatically generates an ONET.XML, WEBTEMP*.XML, and default.aspx files. These files can be modified to include the configuration needed for your custom site definition. You can deploy the Site Definition project to your debug site and test your solution.

If there is a site definition that already exists from the out-of-the-box site definitions that closely resembles your needed solution, you can use a copy of those files as a template from which to create your custom site definition. This will save time as you will not need to create the entire solution from scratch.

Feature Stapling

When working with site definitions, you might want to add an additional Feature to a site definition, but don't want to modify the site definition files themselves. This is sometimes the case when you want to extend the functionality of an out-of-the-box site definition in SharePoint. This can be accomplished by utilizing a concept called *Feature Stapling*.

Feature stapling is accomplished by creating a new Feature that references one or more existing site definitions by utilizing a *FeatureSiteTemplateAssociation* element. This element defines the association between the new feature and existing site definitions so that the associated Features will be automatically activated.

One of the new improvements to SharePoint 2010 that makes the stapling process easier is the implementation of new out-of-the-box event receivers. The event receivers that are beneficial to Feature Stapling are the web events that capture when a site is being provisioned and when a site has been provisioned.

A good example of how these events can be used is when you need to manipulate a list that is associated with a site definition after a site is provisioned. Previously, developers would use the *FeatureActivated* event and place some type of custom check and delay the activation process to make sure that any changes to the list occurred once the entire site was provisioned. This was required because by default the *FeatureActivated* event would fire before the list you needed to manipulate was created. If you did not provide the custom check, in many instances a *System.Argument* exception occurred, letting you know that list did not exist. Now with SharePoint 2010, you can accurately capture events after a site has been provisioned and then make the needed changes to the list without delaying the activation process.

Choosing Between Site Templates, Site Definitions, and Features

With the release of Windows SharePoint Services 3.0, the discussion between site templates and site definitions has broadened to include Features. Consider the following issues when deciding which method is best:

- **Ease of Use**   Site templates are easy to create and deploy. You can find or create a site with the features you want, save it as a template, deploy the template, and start creating new sites—all without leaving the browser interface or SharePoint Designer. Generating a site definition requires working with XML code in a text editor. Then, when you deploy it, you must do so on each front-end web server in the same farm. Without a doubt, site definitions are harder to create and deploy. Site templates can be deployed as sandboxed solutions or as farm solutions. Additional functionally can be added to sites created from site templates by using Features.

- **Who Performs the Work?**   Any SharePoint web designer can create a sample site and save it as a template. Then, any Site Collection administrator can deploy it. Because site definitions require access to the web server's file system, development requires administrative access to test web servers, and deployment requires the cooperation of production server administrators. Features allow you to add new functionality and can be scoped to the farm, web application, site, or web.

- **Extent Modifications**   Modifications cannot be made to the files installed as part of the SharePoint Foundation installation, or of subsequent hotfixes or Service Packs. However, by using Feature Stapling, you can extend the out-of-the-box site definitions. Site templates can be extended by importing and modifying them by using Visual Studio, but any modifications do not affect sites already created from them.

- **Maintainability** Once you create a site from a template, modifying the template has no effect on that site. This gives you the freedom to change a template and thereby add, remove, or modify Features in future sites. Because templates reside in the configuration database or in a Site Template gallery, a single command deploys them for an entire server farm. Once you've deployed a site definition, there's no safe way to delete or change its Features. This is because sites created from the site definition refer to it on an ongoing and active basis, and they depend on it remaining constant. If a site definition is no longer adequate, you can only add Features or create a new site definition. Features can be used by existing sites and stapled to site definitions.

Performance Web pages "ghosted" from a site definition run faster than pages that reside in a content database. This is because:

- The web server's file system is faster than a SQL Server database. Caching files from the web server's file system is more efficient than caching them from a content database.

- The fewer cache hits, the more often ASP.NET must compile any ASPX pages.

- Each compilation incurs a performance penalty.

Using PowerShell with SharePoint Foundation 2010

In previous versions of SharePoint, many administrative tasks were completed through the command-line tool, *stsadm*. This tool was not only used by administrators, it was used by developers who needed to add, deploy, upgrade, or delete solutions in the environment.

However, *stsadmn* has been replaced in SharePoint Foundation by PowerShell as the preferred command-line tool. *stsadm* has not totally been removed; it remains as a part of SharePoint to support compatibility with previous versions of SharePoint. Several *stsadm* commands have been added, and some have been removed. Even though *stsadm* still exists, it is recommended that any command-line operations be handled with PowerShell.

PowerShell Basics

PowerShell is a command-line scripting tool that provides administrators and developers full access to applications programming interfaces (API). This is very powerful for SharePoint 2010 because it allows you to create scripts that interact with lists, sites, Site Collections, and many other components of a SharePoint environment. PowerShell can be used to create complex or simple automated processes.

One interesting thing to note is that PowerShell is written on top of the .Net Framework. However, it still does take advantage of some of the functionality related to cmd.exe, which allows it to have more flexibility over traditional command line tools.

Windows PowerShell utilizes the concept of a cmdlet for its scripts. A cmdlet consists of at least two components, a command and an object, and has the ability to accept as well as return .NET objects. Another thing to note is because a cmdlet can return objects, it also provides the ability for one cmdlet to pass an object to another cmdlet. This allows for complex cmdlets to be created.

PowerShell is a prerequisite for SharePoint Foundation 2010 and will by default, be installed on your development computer. Also, once the SharePoint Installation is complete, a custom PowerShell console is created called the SharePoint 2010 Management Shell, which executes commands from a PowerShell profile file, sharepoint.ps1 before presenting you with a command prompt. The main aim of the SharePoint profile file is to load the PowerShell for SharePoint snap-in so that you can then use the new cmdlets specific to SharePoint. The SharePoint profile file contains the following code, plus a signature:

```
$ver = $host | select version
if ($ver.Version.Major -gt 1) {$Host.Runspace.ThreadOptions = "ReuseThread"}
Add-PsSnapin Microsoft.SharePoint.PowerShell
Set-location $home
```

This code obtains the version of PowerShell, checks that it is greater than 1, and then if that is true, it sets the threading model so that the first thread will be reused, loads the SharePoint PowerShell snap-in, and then changes directory to the home folder, such as C:\ users\<userid>, where userid is the person who is currently logged on.

INSIDE OUT   Managing the disposal of SharePoint objects when using PowerShell

Running each command, function, or script in the first thread mitigates many of the memory leaks that occur. However, the care you undertake when writing SharePoint code that implements the *IDisposable* interface, you must also take when calling such objects with PowerShell. These are the objects that represent sites, Site Collections, and the site administration object. Hence, the two SharePoint cmdlets that you should learn to use are the *Start-SPAssignment* and the *Stop-SPAssignment*. These relate to the *–SPAssignmentCollection* parameter that you might see used with a number of Share-Point cmdlets to return a "disposable object."

You can see an example of how to use the *Start-SPAssignment* and *Stop-SPAssignment* cmdlets in Chapter 14. In that example, they were used in a script that applies a Theme to all sites in a Site Collection.

You can also dispose of the objects as you would in code by using the *Dispose()* method, as shown in the following example, that alters the *MasterURL* property of all sites in a Site Collection:

```
$scURL = "http://wideworldimporters";
$sc = Get-SPSite $scURL;
$sc.AllWebs | foreach {
  $spWeb = $_.
  $spWeb.MasterUrl = "/_catalogs/masterpage/SPFIO.master";
  $spWeb.Update();
  $spWeb.Dispose();
}
$sc.Dispose();
```

PowerShell contains an extensive built-in Help system, and you can access it quickly by typing **help** at the command-line interface. This is an alias for the cmdlet *Get-Help*. To find more information on the *SPAssignment* cmdlets, type **Get-Help Start-SPAssignment** in the SharePoint 2010 Management Shell.

Creating Cmdlets for SharePoint Foundation 2010

SharePoint Foundation 2010 contains over 240 SharePoint-related cmdlets. The exact number can be found by typing the following command:

```
@(Get-Command -PSSnapin "Microsoft.SharePoint.PowerShell").count
```

These cmdlets provide functionality in the following areas:

- Backup and recovery

- Databases

- Features and solutions

- General

- Import and export

- Logging and events

- Performance

- Security

- Service application

Chapter 16

- SharePoint Foundation 2010 Search

- Site management

- Timer jobs

- Upgrade and migration

- Workflow management

PowerShell cmdlets will be the standard command-line tool for administrative operations going forward in SharePoint. They are very beneficial to developers, as well, because developers can use them to deploy and remove solution packages in their development environments. In particular, the following commands are some that developers will find useful:

- ***Add-SPSolution***   Uploads a SharePoint solution package to the farm

- ***Install-SPSolution***   Deploys an installed SharePoint solution in the farm

- ***Update-SPSolution***   Upgrades a deployed SharePoint solution

- ***Uninstall-SPSolution***   Retracts a deployed SharePoint solution

- ***Remove-SPSolution***   Removes a SharePoint solution from a farm

To get the complete list of SharePoint cmdlets installed on your environment, you can run the following command from your SharePoint 2010 Management Shell:

```
gcm -pssnapin microsoft.sharepoint.powershell |
  select Name, Definition | fl > .\filename.txt
```

In general, cmdlets use a verb-noun pair. The noun specifies the object about which you want information or that you want to manipulate, and the verb states what you want to do with that object. The verbs and nouns are always separated by a hyphen with no spaces, and SharePoint cmdlet verbs have a prefix of SP. When you design SharePoint-specific cmdlets, always do the following:

- Maintain a consistent naming standard for your cmdlets. For example, prefix your cmdlet verbs or nouns with two or three characters that represent your organization.

- Define cmdlet nouns.

- Define cmdlet noun properties.

- Define cmdlet verbs and parameters.

- Define your cmdlet errors, progress, and pipeline.

- Implement the *IDisposable* interface for objects that are not disposed.

- Provide help functionality.

When you follow this process, the set of cmdlets that you are developing will be meaningful and comprehensive.

Define Cmdlet Nouns

To define cmdlet nouns, perform the following:

- When you define a cmdlet noun, be very clear about the artifact it will manipulate. Think of nouns used SharePoint Foundation cmdlets and the names of SharePoint objects that the system administrator manages, such as the out-of-the-box objects: SPSite or SPWeb or SPFeature. Try not to create a new name for a noun if one already exists for that object, because this can be confusing to administrators, and just as with any development, do not develop a cmdlet for functionality that already exists. Also if administrators are heavy users of the *Get-Help* cmdlet to search for SharePoint cmdlets that manage SharePoint objects, such as using the command, `Get-Help *SPSite*`, then ensure that you use the commonly used filter characters as part of your nouns. To list all SharePoint related nouns, type the following:

  ```
  gcm -PSSnapin "Microsoft.SharePoint.PowerShell" |
    sort noun | group noun | more
  ```

  As a general rule, it is better to have a greater number of nouns that have fewer properties than to have a small number of nouns that have a great many properties. Any noun that has more than 15 properties is overburdened.

- Identify the nonpersisted runtime state information that you want to expose to system administrators. Also, identify state information that may not be persisted but must nevertheless be returned to system administrators, for example, the running state of a service.

- Evaluate whether a newly defined noun should be split into two or more different nouns. Create separate nouns for items that are semantically distinct. Use Feature or component specifications to identify whether a noun spans multiple concepts or features.

- If a noun spans multiple data sources, either physical or logical, split the noun along data-source boundaries. Identify a logically independent subset of properties that is persisted in a single database or SharePoint object only. In most cases this subset should become a separate noun, but only if the resulting nouns are logically independent and only if they can be clearly understood as distinct entities (that is, easily separated) without confusing system administrators.

Chapter 16

- For every persisted data source object that is used by more than one noun, unify these nouns into a single noun. Also, unify nouns whose primary difference is that they have different lifetimes, because their creation and deletion can be managed separately.

Define Cmdlet Noun Properties

To define cmdlet noun properties, perform the following:

- Define an *Identity* property. All nouns must have an *Identity* property whose value is unique and immutable, such as a GUID, and make this identity property the default property.

- Create a pipebind for the noun. The pipebind should combine all properties that can uniquely identify the object.

- Define the complete set of public properties for the noun. Treat the noun definition as though it were a public API. All related public properties are exposed in the command line when an instance of the noun is returned.

- Define a data type for each property. Properties should be strongly typed so that format validation code can be attached to the property type rather than to the noun. For example, a property that represents an email address should be of type *email address* rather than of type *String*.

- Identify atypically large properties. Ensure that unusually large properties (larger than 10 KB) are split into two or more properties.

- Identify collections of properties that have a large number of elements (for example, a collection with more than 100 elements). Remove such large property collections and split the elements into separate nouns. Then, define the *New*, *Remove*, *Get*, and *Set* verbs for the new nouns.

  For example, consider a scenario in which *Users* is a property of a *SPWeb* object, which can have a large number of elements. To avoid problems, a separate noun called *SPUser* exists, that represents one element in the list, then associated with the *SPUser* noun is the *New*, *Remove*, *Get*, and *Set* verbs. Also because it makes sense with this object, there is another verb associated with the *SPUser* object: *Move*.

Define Cmdlet Verbs and Parameters

Determine which of the base verbs (*Get*, *Set*, *New*, *Remove*) apply to your noun. At a minimum, system administrators must be able to get settings and to change (or *Set*) them. Additionally, administrators might also need to create new instances (*New*) and delete existing ones (*Remove*):

INSIDE OUT   Verbs used by SharePoint cmdlets

To find all the verbs that the out-of-the-box SharePoint cmdlets use, type the following command:

```
Get-Command -PSSnapin "Microsoft.SharePoint.PowerShell" | sort verb |
group verb | sort count -descending
```

- Define the behavior of your *Get* cmdlet.

  The *Get* verb must retrieve all instances if no parameters are specified, and it must do so by writing the instances to the PowerShell pipeline. However, any operation that can potentially return a very large result set should include a *Limit* parameter for which a default limit is specified. Of course, when limiting a result set in this way, you must alert users that additional results might be excluded from the limited result set.

  The *Get* verb must have an *Identity* parameter. When specified, the corresponding cmdlet must return only the instance associated with that identity. If the identity that is specified is not unique, the cmdlet should return all instances that have the specified identity value.

  The *Get* verb can have additional optional filtering parameters. For example, the cmdlet *Get-SPSite* has a *ContentDatabase* parameter that restricts the result set to the Site Collections that are located in a specified content database. Furthermore, the *Get* verb must have a *Server* parameter if the cmdlet returns local (that is, computer-specific) configuration information.

- Define the behavior of the *Set* cmdlet.

  The *Set* verb must have an *Identity* parameter to identify the instance that is being changed. The parameter must be able to take either an identity (for example, a GUID) or a name. If a name is specified and this name matches more than one instance, the cmdlet must return an error.

  The *Identity* parameter of the *Set* cmdlet must accept pipeline input.

  The *Set* verb must expose all writable properties of the noun that are received using the corresponding *Get* cmdlet, except those that cause negative effects when set.

  The *Set* verb must have an optional *Instance* parameter that represents an entire instance of this noun type. The *Instance* parameter must accept pipeline input (by value).

Chapter 16

- Define the behavior of the *New* cmdlet.

  The *New* verb must take a limited subset of the writable properties of the noun as parameters. The remaining properties should be set to default values. Furthermore, the *New* cmdlet must return the newly created instance object to the pipeline so that further cmdlets in the pipeline can act on the new instance.

- Define the behavior of the *Remove* cmdlet.

  Your *Remove* cmdlet must have an *Identity* parameter that can take either an identity value or a name. If a name is specified and it matches more than one instance, the cmdlet must return an error.

  The *Identity* parameter must accept pipeline input. Furthermore, any destructive operation must support *Confirm* and *WhatIf* parameters. This requires little effort, as PowerShell and base classes of SharePoint Foundation 2010 provide the means for supporting these parameters.

- Identify and define additional verbs for the noun.

  For example, a *SPContentDatabase* noun might need a *Mount* verb to support mounting the specified database. Use well-tested administrative scenarios and use cases to support selecting appropriate verbs.

  Remember that all additional cmdlets must have an *Identity* parameter that accepts pipeline input. The *Identity* parameter must accept the identity (*PipeBind*) of the object. Furthermore, any destructive operation must support *Confirm* and *WhatIf* parameters.

- Identify properties that have potential negative side effects.

  Properties that have potential negative side effects might require additional operations to mitigate the negative effects. These additional mitigating cmdlets must have an *Identity* parameter that accepts pipeline input.

- For each cmdlet that you define, perform the following:

  — Identify the list of prerequisites for the cmdlet. For example, in a case where a cmdlet can be executed only in a certain system state, the cmdlet must verify that all state prerequisites are met before executing.

  — Identify the list of operations. Specify the complete list of operations that the cmdlet is able to perform. The cmdlet must perform and then validate these operations. This operation list comprises the functional breakdown of the cmdlet.

Define Cmdlet Errors, Progress, and Pipeline

To define cmdlet errors, progress, and pipeline, perform the following:

1. Identify all error conditions and error-state behaviors. That is, list all conditions in which a cmdlet can error out. Then, for each condition, describe the expected behavior. Your cmdlets must provide basic error management.

   Your cmdlets must clean up partial changes when an error occurs, and they must return a meaningful (and localized, if appropriate) error message. Furthermore, cmdlets must determine and reveal how a system administrator can recover from any error condition.

2. Differentiate between terminating and non-terminating errors.

3. Identify long-running operations. If a cmdlet is expected to take longer than about twenty seconds, on average, to complete an operation, the cmdlet must provide progress information to avoid the appearance of a suspended operation.

4. Ensure that cmdlets write their return objects directly to the pipeline. Avoid buffering retrieved objects to an internal array. Writing to the pipeline allows the downstream cmdlets to act upon preceding objects in the pipeline without delay.

5. Group similar parameters. Limit cmdlets to sixteen parameters (not including the *Identity* and *Name* parameters). In cases where object methods are rarely called, and where an object model method exists, no cmdlet parameter is needed. In cases where a large number of parameters can be grouped, write a single parameter that accepts the group object.

For more information about cmdlet development and guidelines, go to *http://msdn.microsoft. com/en-us/library/ms714657(v=VS.85).aspx.*

Summary

This chapter explained advanced techniques that you can use when designing your Share-Point sites and solutions. The techniques will assist your organization in developing Share-Point solutions in a best-practices manner that makes them more stable, more robust, and more easily governed.

The process of developing SharePoint solutions in Visual Studio 2010 has been greatly improved when compared to previous versions. This includes enhanced debugging, IntelliSense, statement completion, new built-in tools, and new project templates. Share-Point projects can also be written in Visual Basic or Visual C#.

This chapter explained also the basics of how Web Parts work and what tools you need to create Web Parts of your own as well as some of the best practices. In addition, it explained the basic programming techniques you need to successfully create and deploy custom Web Parts.

Index

About the Authors

Errin O'Connor is the Founder and Chief Executive Officer for EPC Group. Errin focuses his efforts on implementing Microsoft Technologies in organizations throughout the country. Errin manages EPC Group's corporate strategy as well as architects the proven methodologies around collaboration, enterprise content management/records management, and custom application development that have set EPC Group apart from its competitors.

Errin is one of the most respected Enterprise Content Management (ECM)/Enterprise Records Management (ERM) architects in the country having designed solutions for the United States Navy, the Federal Reserve Bank, CSL Behring, Stewart Title, Chevron, NASA, Northrop Grumman, the National Institute of Health, Schlumberger, Continental Airlines (United Airlines merger), Thomson Reuters, PepsiCo, Department of Defense related initiatives, and many other organizations.

Errin is also the author of *Windows SharePoint Services 3.0 Inside Out* by Microsoft Press. He has completed more than 165 highly successful individual SharePoint implementations and has worked with some of the largest organizations in the United States. Errin is an "Expert SharePoint Blogger" on AIIM.ORG and Focus.com. Errin is also the founder of WebPartGallery.com an online solutions provider of SharePoint Web Parts and custom solutions and is a frequent speaker at Microsoft SharePoint events throughout the United States and Canada. Errin has spoken at more than 150 SharePoint-related events in the past 2 years. He has a passion for working with Department of Defense–related clients to ensure technology can continue to improve the mission of our nation's Armed Services.

Penelope Coventry is a Microsoft Most Valuable Professional (MVP) for Microsoft SharePoint Server and an independent consultant, based in the United Kingdom. She has more than 30 years of industry experience. Penelope focuses on the design, implementation, and development of SharePoint technology–based solutions. She has worked with SharePoint since 2001. Most recently, Penelope has worked for the international financial services group Aviva PLC. She has also provided consultancy services to Microsoft Gold partners ICS Solutions and Combined Knowledge.

Penny has authored and co-authored a number of books. They include both editions of *Microsoft Office SharePoint Designer Step by Step*, *Microsoft SharePoint 2010 Administrator's Companion*, *Microsoft Office SharePoint Server 2007 Administrator's Companion*, *Microsoft SharePoint Products and Technologies Resources Kit*, *Microsoft SharePoint Foundation 2010 Step by Step*, and both editions of *Microsoft Windows SharePoint Services Step by Step*.

Penny is frequently seen at TechEd, either as a technical learning guide or on the SharePoint Ask-the-Experts panels. She also speaks at the SharePoint Best Practices conferences, the Swedish SharePoint and Exchange Forum, SharePoint User Group U.K. meetings, and U.K. SharePoint Saturdays.

Penny lives in Hinckley, Leicestershire, England, with her husband, Peter, and dog, Poppy.

Troy Lanphier is a Senior SharePoint Solutions Designer with GUIO, LLC. As a long-standing member of the computer geek community, he has been hooked on computers since 1980, when his dad surprised him with a TRS-80 Model I Level II (16 kb of RAM). He has been involved in enterprise server infrastructure design since the mid-1990s, training and writing about Windows technologies since the early 2000s, and implementing SharePoint solutions since the 2003 beta. When not working on or writing about SharePoint, he enjoys spending time restoring vintage cars, playing videogames with his daughters Sam and Kate, browsing antiques with his wife, Marlene, taking his mom, Linda and Marlene's mom, Eleanor to dinner, collecting Red Line Hot Wheels, and building LEGOS.

Johnathan Lightfoot is the principal SharePoint architect with General Physics Corporation. He has been involved with IT for more than 20 years. He has worked in various roles including Help Desk, Level II and III Desktop Support, Windows, and AS-400 Server Administration and Development. Companies he is fortunate to have worked for in the past include Electronic Data Systems, Hawaiian Telcom, and Norwegian Cruise Line (yes, he actually worked on the ships). However, the best experiences he says he has had were his 9 years serving in the United States Navy. Johnathan is a Microsoft Certified Trainer (MCT) who specializes in SharePoint 2010, MOSS 2007, WSS 3.0 and Office 2007 and 2010 technologies along with providing Soft Skills training for organizations.

Johnathan has also authored *Microsoft SharePoint 2010 Plain & Simple*. He also speaks at SharePoint conferences and SharePoint user groups throughout the year.

Johnathan is from Miami, Florida (originally) but grew up in Mesquite, Texas; he has lived and worked literally around the world. Currently, he lives in Columbia, Maryland with his wife, Genevievette, daughter, Giavrielle, and dog, Mocha-Chip.

Thomas Resing is a Microsoft Certified Master (MCM) – SharePoint and a Principal Software Engineer for Applied Information Sciences (*http://appliedis.com*). With more than 14 years as an information technology professional and consultant, Tom is happy to have been helping people and organizations succeed with SharePoint most recently. He has been focusing his work on SharePoint development, architecture and implementation for the last 5 years. Tom has spoken at the Best Practices Conference, many SharePoint Saturdays and a few user groups. He leads the San Antonio SharePoint User Group (*www.sasug.net*) and writes regularly about SharePoint on his website, *www.tomresing.com*. As the owner of two successful children's businesses, Tom also brings a manger's experience to his technical clients.

Tom lives in San Antonio, Texas with his wife, Kerri; daughter, Elise; and a miniature dachshund named Toulouse.

Michael Doyle started his IT career nearly twenty years ago as a programmer for Federal Express Corporation (now FedEx). Since then, he has had the opportunity to work for corporate icons, such as Intel, HCA, Deloitte, as well as the United States Navy. For the last eight years, he has worked almost exclusively with Microsoft SharePoint in a various capacities. He can be found speaking at SharePoint conferences around the world and throughout the United States or blogging and tweeting under the SharePoint Ninja name. The SharePoint Ninja name rose from the early days of SharePoint when it was much harder to find information about the product and many of the solutions required esoteric knowledge. (Luckily, knowledge is more freely available thanks to the ever widening SharePoint community.) When he isn't working with SharePoint he can found spending time outdoors, kayaking, hiking, diving, or any excuse he can find to enjoy nature.